p. 269
S 80

URBAN RIVALRIES IN THE FRENCH REVOLUTION

URBAN RIVALRIES
IN THE
FRENCH REVOLUTION

TED W. MARGADANT

PRINCETON UNIVERSITY PRESS

PRINCETON, NEW JERSEY

Library of Congress Cataloging-in-Publication Data

Margadant, Ted W., 1941–
Urban rivalries in the French Revolution / Ted W. Margadant.
p.   cm.
Includes bibliographical references and index.
ISBN 0-691-05687-0 (cloth) — ISBN 0-691-00891-4 (pbk.)
1. France—Administrative and political divisions. 2. Central-
local government relations—France—History. 3. Cities and
towns—France—History. 4. Political culture—France—History.
5. France—History—Revolution, 1789–1799—Influence. I. Title.

JS4903.M37   1992
306.2'0944'09033—dc20   92-9563   CIP

This book has been composed in Linotron Galliard

Princeton University Press books are printed
on acid-free paper and meet the guidelines for
permanence and durability of the Committee on
Production Guidelines for Book Longevity
of the Council on Library Resources

Printed in the United States of America

10   9   8   7   6   5   4   3   2   1

To Joby, Ashley, and Thad

WITH MY LOVE

CONTENTS

MAPS

TABLES

ACKNOWLEDGMENTS

I N ONE OF THOSE bookstalls along the river Seine, where books are rarely worth as much as they cost, I found, one summer day in 1974, a thick volume of what appeared to be an old book, bound in black leather. It was Adolphe Joanne's *Dictionnaire des communes de la France*, published in Paris in 1864. The bookseller must have calculated that few buyers would be interested in a volume that contained much tedious information, without any illustrations, about the population, administrative institutions, transport facilities, and economic specialties of every commune in France during the 1860s, listed in alphabetical order from Aaron (Saint-) to Zuytpeene. He sold the book to me for only thirty-five francs. It was the best buy of my career as a historian, although I must admit that the binding turned out to be cardboard rather than leather. Joanne's dictionary became the starting point for a computerized data base about French towns and bourgs that has expanded over the years to provide me with the systematic evidence for this book. It is now marked up and falling apart, but I still consult it whenever I need to verify information about a particular community in nineteenth-century France.

The path from Joanne's dictionary to the present book has been long and arduous. It has taken me back to the old regime and forward to the end of the nineteenth century, and it has led from census data and geographical dictionaries to thousands of pamphlets and petitions written during the French Revolution. Along the way, I have been encouraged and assisted by many people. I would like to begin by acknowledging the funding that I have received from the University of California at Davis, whose generous sabbatical leave policy enabled me to undertake a year of archival research in France in 1981–82. Annual faculty research grants from UC Davis, and special grants for computer programming, gave indispensable support to my computer data base and mapping project that underlie the quantitative and cartographical aspects of this book. From the National Endowment for the Humanities, I received a fellowship during the academic year 1985–86 that enabled me to draft several chapters. An additional sabbatical leave from UC Davis during the fall quarter of 1988 brought the book closer to completion.

Several people have been especially helpful to me in preparing the computer maps for this book. In France, Jacques Mallet, formerly the director of the Centre d'études et de réalisations cartographiques géographiques at the Institut de Géographie in Paris, provided me with copies of an unpublished map produced in his laboratory that displayed all the towns and other communes in France that had a nucleated population of at least

1,000 inhabitants in 1806. This map, divided into four large quadrants, also traced the course of all the major rivers and many smaller ones. I used it to digitize the boundaries of France, the location of towns and bourgs, and the river system. I am also very grateful to Mr. Mallet for giving me a beautiful set of color maps on the administrative boundaries of France on the eve of the Revolution, produced in his laboratory and published in 1986.

At UC Davis, Peter Hunter, the director of the computational facility of the Department of Environmental Studies, wrote the programs and gave me the indispensable technical advice I needed for generating computer maps from an SPSS data base. I especially appreciate his patience in showing me how to run the mapping program on my desktop computer and how to plot the maps on the HP plotter. Hal Grady, formerly a consultant for the Social Science Data Service (SSDS), and Susan Wilcox, the programmer for SDSS, taught me how to construct a system file and analyze data in SPSS, a statistical package for the social sciences. Caroline Smadja, a former graduate student in the history department at UC Davis, coded much of the data that I collected in France about towns during the Revolution.

One of the greatest pleasures related to my research for this book has been the opportunity to develop friendships with French historians who are interested in urban history. I remember many stimulating conversations with Marie-Vic Ozouf-Marignier, a young historian and geographer who was working through the same archival series that I was examining at the National Archives in 1980–81 and who has since published several articles and an important book on the formation of departments. Bernard Lepetit, another young historian whom I met at that time, has shared with me on numerous occasions his extensive knowledge of French urban development. Without the example of his sophisticated methodology for analyzing the impact of institutional change on urban growth rates, which he showed me in manuscript form. I would not have been able to write the last chapter of this book. André Burguière, a good friend and esteemed colleague in French history, invited me to apply for an associate directorship at the Ecole des Hautes Etudes in the fall of 1986, and he asked me to prepare a talk for his graduate seminar after I received this appointment. Jacques Revel, equally well known among French historians and also a director of research at the Ecole, invited me to give a talk at his graduate seminar, too. In these seminars, and in a talk to a faculty research seminar at the Ecole attended by geographers as well as historians, I had the opportunity of presenting concise versions of two chapters of this book and to reflect on methodological issues involving my computer mapping project.

Among my colleagues in the United States, I would like to offer special thanks to the members of the French history group who have been meeting for a number of years in Berkeley. Lynn Hunt, who led the group until she moved to the University of Pennsylvania, set an example for me of interpreting French revolutionary politics from a cultural as well as a social perspective. Susanna Barrows, who agreed to take over the task of organizing and hosting the group after Lynn's departure, has been one of my closest friends and most inspiring colleagues for many years. Peter Sahlins, Carla Hesse, Gene Irschik, Roger Hahn, and Richard Herr, from UC Berkeley; Mark Traugott, Jonathan Beecher, and Tyler Stovall, from UC Santa Cruz; and Keith Baker and Karen Offen, from Stanford, have been frequent participants in the group, and most of them read several chapters of my work and offered me useful criticism as well as much encouragement when I presented a draft of the manuscript to the group last year. Later I asked Peter to read the entire manuscript, and I benefited greatly from his suggestions for revisions.

I have been fortunate for many years in having colleagues at UC Davis who have given me unwavering support throughout my career. Senior colleagues such as Roy Willis, Dick Schwab, Bill Bowsky, Rollie Poppino, K. C. Liu, David Brody, and Paul Goodman have always trusted me to bring this long work to fruition. Colleagues closer to me in age or length of service to the university, such as Arnold Bauer, Bill Hagen, Dan Brower, Roland Marchand, Don Price, Norma Landau, and Barbara Metcalf have been equally enthusiastic about my work. I would like to thank Arnie and Bill, in particular, for friendships that date back over twenty years and that I value more now than ever before. Among more recent colleagues at UC Davis, I owe a special debt of gratitude to G. William Skinner, who shared with me his own unpublished work on cities and regional systems in nineteenth-century France and then helped me refine my analysis and presentation of data about institutional hierarchies of towns on the eve of the Revolution. I would also like to thank graduate students at UC Davis and UC Berkeley who have studied French history with me over the years, including Rosemary Wakeman and Claire Zeni, whose research stimulated my own work; and the staff of the history department at UC Davis, including Charlotte Honeywell, Karen Hairfield, Debbie Lyon, and Eteica Spencer, who assisted me in preparing this manuscript.

Among colleagues elsewhere in the United States, I would like to single out Eugen Weber, who invited me to give a public lecture on my research to the Clark Library at UCLA and who wrote on my behalf for fellowship applications; David Pinkney and Patrice Higonnet, who also supported my requests for fellowships; Donald Sutherland, one of the two reviewers for Princeton University Press, who gave me useful advice on how to improve the manuscript; Charles Tilly, who has inspired my work in French history ever since I was a graduate student and who wrote letters for me, read this manuscript, and offered valuable advice in the midst of a dozen other academic commitments; and John Merriman, one of my oldest and best friends among French historians, whose enthusiasm for research in French archives is matched only by his enjoyment of French food.

My wife, Joby, has been my closest friend and my most sympathetic critic. She has stood with me through the inner turmoil that so often accompanies a project of this scope, and she has given me unlimited love and support. Frequently, she helped me launch a new chapter or refine a rough passage of the text, and she made our home a place of beauty even when I was too deeply absorbed in my work to admire the flowers in the garden or the plants in the hallway. I would also like to thank her for bringing Ashley and Thad into my life. They were both too young when we married to remember our early delight in sharing our knowledge of French history, but both of them have developed a love of France that makes them my favorite audience for this book. To Joby, who has already read it in myriad drafts, and to Ashley and Thad, who have waited patiently for me to finish it, I dedicate this book.

URBAN RIVALRIES IN THE FRENCH REVOLUTION

INTRODUCTION

THIS BOOK is about urban rivalries in the French Revolution. It focuses attention on an event of fundamental importance in the history of French towns: the division of the provinces of the old regime into a modern hierarchy of administrative regions. This spatial reorganization generated an unparalleled competition among towns of every size and description. At its height, the struggle for urban rank and power involved over fifteen hundred towns and bourgs, over two thousand deputies and special deputies, and tens of thousands of petitioners. Some rivalries persisted for years afterward, and the entire movement to shape the new urban hierarchy expressed enduring features of the relationship between towns and the state in modern France. The history of this movement offers a unique vantage point for studying the regional context of town life, the social perceptions of urban elites, and the political dynamics of bourgeois leadership during the French Revolution.

As an event that involved hundreds of towns in revolutionary change, the division of France has a special significance for historians of urban development. A majority of the urban population in eighteenth-century France lived in small towns, which served as microregional centers of marketing, justice, and administration for the peasantry. These communities, ranging in size from several hundred to several thousand inhabitants, mediated between the wider urban world of cities, increasingly dominated by Paris, and the narrow circumference of rural life, bounded for many country dwellers by poverty and slow means of transport. Small towns were in the forefront of the movement for departments and districts, partly in order to defend their existing role as central places, partly in the hope of expanding their regional influence. Urban historians rarely have an opportunity to study dynamic aspects of urban hierarchies and networks, which usually appear as structures that change only slowly over long periods of time, especially in preindustrial societies. Yet France transformed its central place system in a single year, and it did so under political conditions that permitted the spokesmen for hundreds of towns to bargain for a share of the new regional institutions. Behind the contrast between the overlapping hierarchies of central places in the old regime and the radically simplified system invented at the beginning of the Revolution, historians can study townspeople as well as towns, change as well as structure.

The clash of opinion between rival towns also provides a wealth of insights for social and cultural historians, who have extended their scope of inquiry in recent years from elites to the broad mass of the population. Landlords, lawyers, and merchants in small towns were marginal members of the governing elite in eighteenth-century France, prominent in their own communities and nearby villages, but much less wealthy and socially distinguished than the nobles of the sword and nobles of the robe, bankers, and businessmen who dominated society in Paris and other large cities. Living in close association with agriculture and retail trade, the leaders of small towns were often as parochial in their concerns as villagers. They knew which roads to avoid in the winter months and which markets to frequent for the best provisions. Above all, they knew that the prestige of a small town in eighteenth-century France depended primarily on law-courts and other public establishments. Many townspeople also believed with good reason that lawcourts and administrative agencies, like bishop-rics and colleges, attracted wealth from the countryside and stimulated lo-cal markets and retail trade. Their world, so different from our own, seemed suddenly to collapse when the National Assembly abolished the institutions of the old regime in 1789. The history of local responses to this moment of crisis reveals a pride in place, an attachment to community, and a resolve to defend local interests that have too often been overlooked or dismissed by historians of the French nation. Through the claims and counterclaims of townspeople for new establishments, it is possible to write a social history of the parochial, which for most of the time, and in most places, was the only history that counted deeply for the vast majority of the population in early modern France.

Yet during the French Revolution, parochial concerns became translated into national issues. At the heart of the political history of modern France is the growth of centralized institutions and national solidarities. How and why did ordinary people, far from the halls of power, become engaged in national political struggles? When did they become fully integrated into national life? Some historians of peasant politics in the nineteenth century, myself among them, have argued that townspeople played a crucial role in the diffusion of political ideology into the countryside. This book asks re-lated questions about the origins of political modernity among small-town elites themselves. Why did the magistrates and lawyers who dominated most provincial towns on the eve of the Revolution become so rapidly engaged in national politics? How did they proceed to mobilize support for their political goals at both the local and the national level? The move-ment to divide France into departments and districts is a good example of the process of politicization. Townspeople who sent petitions to the Na-tional Assembly not only boasted of their own communities and deni-grated rival towns; they also appealed to abstract principles, adopted rev-olutionary slogans, organized petitioning campaigns, and traveled to Paris as special deputies to the National Assembly. While other issues such as the price of grain and the abolition of seigneurial rights aroused more pop-ular passion during the Revolution, the division of France raised vital issues for the provincial bourgeoisie. To an important degree, the leaders of towns embraced new political ideals and practices in the struggle to capture national institutions for local communities.

The history of France during the Revolution has generated an enormous literature, and my work builds in important respects on earlier generations of scholars. In the early decades of the Third Republic, local historians began to analyze how the Revolution changed the territorial framework of administration. A series of books and articles on the formation of particular departments contrasted the extraordinary complexity of jurisdictions in the old regime with the clear and precise administrative boundaries drawn by the Constituent Assembly in 1790. Using national and local archives, some of these local studies documented in rich detail the kinds of arguments that townspeople used in their petitions to the National Assembly for new administrative institutions and lawcourts. The best of them also used the private correspondence of deputies to analyze how urban interests shaped the decisions of the Assembly about the location of departmental capitals such as Chaumont, in the Haute-Marne; Clermont-Ferrand, in the Puy-de-Dôme; and Laon, in the Aisne. In like manner, they followed the political intrigues of deputies concerning the location of district seats and tribunals within such departments.[1]

As local studies, however, these works were filled with many details that seemed irrelevant to the general history of the Revolution. A few works of synthesis did ask broad questions about the significance of the formation of departments for the administrative geography of modern France. For Charles Berlet, the revolutionary assault on provincial institutions explains why large provinces were subdivided into relatively small departments. Inspired by a regionalist current of geographical theory and administrative reform in the years before World War I, Berlet's *Les provinces au XVIIIe siècle et leur division en départements* criticized the Constituent Assembly for creating artificial administrative divisions that lacked any historical unity or geographical coherence.[2] By contrast, Berlet's contemporary, Georges

---

[1] Henri Mettrier, *La formation du département de la Haute-Marne en 1790* (Chaumont, 1911); Francisque Mège, *Formation et organisation du département du Puy-de-Dôme, 1789–1801* (Paris, 1874); René Hennequin, *La formation du département de l'Aisne en 1790* (Soissons, 1911). More recent local studies that emphasize urban rivalries include Jean Louis Masson, *Histoire administrative de la Lorraine: Des provinces au départements et à la région* (Paris, 1982); and Jean Bourdon, "La formation des départements de l'Est en 1790," *Annales de l'Est* (1951): 187–217. See also the essay of synthesis by Jean Soulas, "Rivalités urbaines en France, 1789–1790," *L'information historique* 18 (1956): 138–43.

[2] (Paris, 1913). See also the critical analysis of the departments by Patrice Amans, "Les départements français, étude de géographie administrative," *Revue de géographie* 24 (Jan.–June 1889): 401–11; 25 (July–Dec. 1889): 35–43, 108–16. For a critique of the work of the Constituent Assembly by one of its architects, see Jean Bourdon, "Pinteville de Cernon,

Mage, argued that the departments founded in 1790 were a great improvement over the complex and overlapping jurisdictions of the old regime. Mage's survey of the formation of departments, published in 1924, emphasized the modernity of the revolutionary project to transform the administrative geography of eighteenth-century France.[3]

Recently, Marie-Vic Ozouf-Marignier has reexamined this debate from the perspective of the history of geographical ideas. In a remarkably original book, *La formation des départements*, which is subtitled *La représentation du territoire français à la fin du 18e siècle*, she compares the spatial preconceptions and ideological goals that influenced the plan of division adopted by the National Assembly with more traditional beliefs about territorial organization, derived from historical experience, observations about local geography, and the economic interests of townspeople.[4] Ozouf-Marignier also demonstrates that many theories and concepts developed by professional geographers in the Third Republic were prefigured in the detailed arguments that townspeople made about natural boundaries, economic regions, and central places in their petitions requesting departments or districts. The second part of her book is based on a comprehensive analysis of the geographical ideas expressed in these petitions. Chapter 4, on "representations of towns," presents a particularly useful analysis of the rhetorical themes that townspeople deployed against the claims of rival towns. Although Ozouf-Marignier does not attempt to explain why some towns succeeded and others failed to become capitals of the new departments and districts, her book highlights the variety and complexity of arguments about space that characterized urban rivalries at the beginning of the Revolution.[5]

Bernard Lepetit, the author of a fundamental book in French urban history entitled *Les villes dans la France moderne, 1740–1840*, has also situated

---

ses chiffres de population, et sa critique des départements," *Annales historiques de la Révolution française* (1954): 345–56.

[3] *La division de la France en départements* (Toulouse, 1924). See also the favorable analysis by Alphonse Aulard, "Départements et régionalisme," in *Etudes et leçons sur la Révolution française*, 7th ser. (Paris, 1913).

[4] (Paris, 1989). Ozouf-Marignier has also published three important articles on the formation of the departments: "Politique et géographie lors de la création des départements français, 1789–1790," *Hérodote* 40 (1986): 140–60; "Territoire géometrique et centralité urbaine: Le découpage de la France en départements, 1789–1790," *Les annales de la recherche urbaine* 22 (1984): 58–70; and "De l'universalisme constituant aux intérêts locaux: Le débat sur la formation des départements en France, 1789–1790," *Annales: Economies, Sociétés, Civilisations* (hereafter E.S.C.) 41 (1986): 1193–1213.

[5] On geographical thought in eighteenth-century France, see also Numa Broc, *La géographie des philosophes: Géographes et voyageurs français au XVIIIe siècle* (Paris, 1975). For a summary of recent research on the formation of departments that situates this process in a broad historical context, see Daniel Nordman and Jacques Revel, "La formation de l'espace français," in *L'espace français*, ed. Jacques Revel (Paris, 1989), pp. 116–51.

the subject of territorial reorganization during the Revolution in a larger historical perspective.[6] Using sophisticated statistical techniques for analyzing structural continuity and change in the rank-order and institutional hierarchies of towns, Lepetit proves that the formation of departments had a significant impact on both of these features of spatial organization in modern France. He also finds that major shifts in the institutional rank of towns were correlated with variations in urban growth rates during the early decades of the nineteenth century. Furthermore, Lepetit relates urban history to theoretical ideas about the spatial environment and economic functions of towns. In successive chapters, he contrasts traditional images of towns as privileged communities, surrounded by walls, with new ideas that emerged during the Enlightenment about the growth of towns as centers of administrative power and economic exchange.[7] In this manner, Lepetit draws suggestive parallels between intellectual history and urban history. He also shows how the "departmentalization" of France and improvements in transport networks encouraged government statisticians and social theorists in early nineteenth-century France to analyze spatial relationships from the perspective of administrative jurisdictions, economic regions, and urban networks rather than from the vantage point of particular towns. The originality of Lepetit's own work derives from his theoretical ambition to redefine urban history as a systematic enterprise, grounded in spatial analysis of relationships between towns and regional systems.

Like Lepetit, I am interested in the institutional hierarchies of towns before and after the Revolution. This was the central political issue at stake in the division of the kingdom into departments and districts in 1789, and it continued to influence the attitudes of townspeople toward the state long after the Revolution had ended. I also use quantitative techniques to analyze the distribution of towns by population size, economic importance, and institutional rank, and to measure the long-term impact of territorial reorganization on urban growth rates in the nineteenth century. While Lepetit restricted his study to towns that had at least 5,000 inhabitants in 1806, I have included hundreds of smaller towns that also competed for districts and lawcourts during the Revolution. In addition, my data base includes nearly a thousand other communities that had lawcourts, administrative jurisdictions, bishoprics, abbeys, convents, colleges, military garrisons, and/or markets that gave them a role as central places before or after the Revolution. Finally, I have gathered demographic evidence about all the cantonal seats in nineteenth-century France, numbering

[6] (Paris, 1988).

[7] On new conceptions of space during the Enlightenment, see also Paul Alliès, *L'invention du territoire* (Grenoble, 1980); and Pierre Dockès, *L'espace dans la pensée économique du XVIe au XVIIIe siècle* (Paris, 1969).

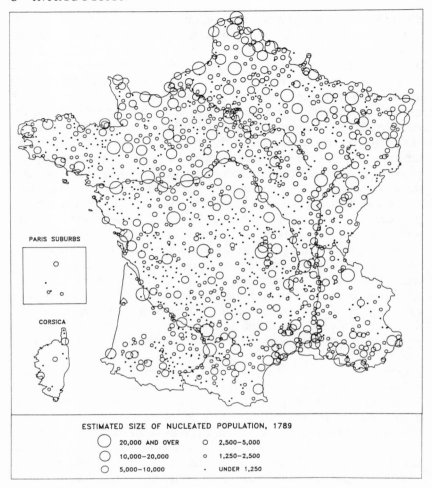

PARIS SUBURBS

CORSICA

ESTIMATED SIZE OF NUCLEATED POPULATION, 1789

◯ 20,000 AND OVER   ○ 2,500–5,000

◯ 10,000–20,000   ○ 1,250–2,500

◯ 5,000–10,000   · UNDER 1,250

Map A.1. Contenders for Districts or Lawcourts, 1789–1790

around 2,800 towns and bourgs. This data base has been linked to a computer program that can plot the location of towns on a map of France. Map A.1 shows how this program works. Each circle on the map signifies one of the 1,508 towns and bourgs that requested departmental seats, districts, or lawcourts during the Revolution. The size of the circles varies in accordance with the size of the towns, as indicated by the legend on the map. In the lower left-hand corner, the island of Corsica is brought into view, and so are several small towns near Paris, in the department of the Seine (inside the rectangle). This particular map dramatizes the fact that many small towns, located throughout the kingdom, were competing for districts and lawcourts. Closer inspection reveals particularly dense arrays of contending towns in a few areas, but nearly everywhere, urban rivalries involved small as well as large towns.

Within the systematic framework of analysis provided by this data base, I devote considerable attention in this book to the kinds of documents that Ozouf-Marignier used in her study of ideas about space.[8] In studying these texts, however, I have been influenced less by geographers than by political and cultural historians of the French Revolution. My central purpose in this book is to study the relationship between national and local politics in the context of the collapse and reconstruction of the French state. In its ideological dimension, the formation of departments represented a radical break with the past. The revolutionary politics of space expressed a will to unify the nation in a "mythic present," as Lynn Hunt has aptly described the belief that a new community could be founded on the ruins of the old regime.[9] Yet the debate over the project to regenerate the state by redrawing the map of the kingdom quickly revealed the strength of earlier beliefs and traditions. The National Assembly could abolish the fiscal privileges of towns, but it could not abolish the towns themselves, unlike all the corporate institutions that it destroyed in 1789. Towns survived as particular communities within the larger nation, and townspeople continued to share local interests, rooted in historical experience. In their struggles to defend these interests, deputies and lobbyists from towns exercised considerable influence over the manner in which the National Assembly reconstructed the state on new territorial foundations. The politics of parochialism had much more important consequences for the institutional history of the Revolution than most general histories of the period have recognized.

In making this argument about the impact of urban rivalries on the Revolution, I am taking issue with historians who interpret the rhetoric of revolutionary leaders in Paris as evidence for a fundamental break with the political culture of the old regime.[10] By following the efforts of townspeople to defend local interests throughout the Revolution and into the post-

---

[8] All translations of primary sources are my own, unless otherwise indicated.

[9] *Politics, Culture, and Class in the French Revolution* (Berkeley, 1984), p. 27. On the cultural dynamics of the Revolution, see also Patrice Higonnet, "Cultural Upheaval and Class Formation during the French Revolution," in *The French Revolution and the Birth of Modernity*, ed. Ferenc Fehér (Berkeley, 1990), pp. 69–102; and the essays in *The French Revolution and the Creation of Modern Political Culture*, vol. 1, *The Political Culture of the Old Regime*, ed. Keith Baker (New York, 1987); vol. 2, *The Political Culture of the French Revolution*, ed. Colin Lucas (New York, 1988); and vol. 3, *The Transformation of Political Culture, 1789–1848*, ed. François Furet and Mona Ozouf (New York, 1989).

[10] See the influential essays by François Furet, *Interpreting the French Revolution*, trans. Elborg Forster (Cambridge, 1981). For a more balanced analysis of ideological continuity and discontinuity between the old regime and the Revolution, see the essays by Keith Baker, *Inventing the French Revolution: Essays on French Political Culture in the Eighteenth Century* (New York, 1990).

revolutionary years of the Consulate, the Empire, and the early Restoration, I show instead that beneath the changing political rhetoric of the period, underlying beliefs about the relationship between towns and the institutions of the state persisted from the old regime. Although arguments for cultural continuity are often traced to Alexis de Tocqueville, my interpretation of this continuity bears little resemblance to Tocqueville's harsh criticism of administrative centralization and its cultural consequences in the old regime.[11] Instead of dividing towns from the countryside and undermining the solidarity of towns themselves, as Tocqueville argued, royal institutions strengthened the influence of urban elites over rural populations and created common interests among townspeople. This was particularly true of the royal lawcourts that existed in hundreds of towns.[12] Civil litigation provided services to landowning peasants, employment for substantial numbers of townspeople, and rural clients for urban tradesmen and artisans, or so many townspeople believed. Just as rivalries over lawcourts were rooted in beliefs about the interests of urban populations, so institutional conflicts between towns during the Revolution often had an economic dimension. Precisely because territorial jurisdictions seemed to foster urban prosperity, townspeople had a powerful incentive to stay abreast of the latest ideological fashions in Paris.

An affinity did exist between the spokesmen for small towns and the revolutionary ideal of equality. This affinity helps explain the success of politicians in the Constituent Assembly who attacked the institutional power of provincial capitals. Here, too, the deployment of egalitarian ideology against large towns can be construed less as a radical break with the past than as an expression of long-standing resentments on the part of small-town notables who were at the bottom of the hierarchies of institutional wealth and social prestige in the old regime. By adopting a strategy of institutional egalitarianism, deputies in the Assembly, who often came from this milieu themselves, tried to consolidate support for the Revolution in a large number of provincial towns. Their strategy succeeded with respect to the subdivision of provinces into departments, which established a territorial equilibrium among large and medium-sized towns as well as an administrative framework for the state that have survived in essential respects down to the present day.[13] At the level of districts and lawcourts,

[11] Alexis de Tocqueville, *The Old Regime and the French Revolution*, trans. Stuart Gilbert (New York, 1955). On Tocqueville's interpretation of the Revolution, see Furet, *Interpreting the French Revolution*, pp. 132–63.

[12] Drawing on Marxist social theory, Alliès develops a similar argument about the relationship between the institutional density of lawcourts, the social interests of officeholders, and territorial conceptions of state power in early modern France. *L'invention du territoire*, pp. 99–145.

[13] On this achievement of the Constituent Assembly, see Mona Ozouf, "Département," in

however, institutional egalitarianism jeopardized the stability of the new regime. Deputies in the National Assembly debated whether to suppress many of the districts in the fall of 1790, and Girondins and Montagnards disputed the relative power of districts and departments in 1793. Finally, in 1795, the Thermidorians abolished all of the district directories and law-courts, a policy directed in part against officials in the small towns who had supported the Jacobin dicatorship. Not until Napoleon reorganized the administrative and judicial system in 1800 did the political controversy over institutional egalitarianism cease. That it flared up again at the beginning of the Restoration Monarchy only seemed to prove how little the fundamental attitudes of urban elites toward the state had changed since the beginning of the Revolution.

The tripartite organization of this book is designed to emphasize the interplay of institutional structures, urban interests, and revolutionary politics. The first part situates the crisis and reconstruction of the French state in the context of urban geography during the old regime and urban rivalries at the beginning of the Revolution. In an opening chapter, I argue that the institutional heritage of the old regime, like the development of commerce and industry in early modern France, varied dramatically through regional space, with corresponding variations in the functional hierarchies that linked cities, towns, and rural communities. The complex and overlapping jurisdictions of administrative, judicial, and religious institutions, as well as regional contrasts in the density of commercial and industrial towns, help explain why any effort to replace the old regime with a new territorial organization of the state would generate considerable controversy among townspeople. This sets the stage for a discussion, in chapter 2, of the debate in the National Assembly over the audacious plan of division into departments, districts, and cantons, designed by the abbé Sièyes and the Norman lawyer Thouret. Unlike Marignier-Ozouf, who characterizes the deputies as hostile to the interests of towns, I emphasize the favorable implications of this plan for small and medium-sized towns, whose deputies rallied to its support against spokesmen for the old provincial capitals. The final chapter in this section describes how townspeople responded to the decisions of the National Assembly, on November 11–12, 1789, to form between seventy-five and eighty-five departments and to subdivide each of the departments into at least three and no more than nine districts. While a mood of crisis gripped the leaders of some provincial towns, others welcomed the opportunity to expand their territorial jurisdictions. These divergent reactions can be related in many cases to the rel-

---

François Furet and Mona Ozouf, eds., *A Critical Dictionary of the French Revolution*, trans. Arthur Goldhammer (Cambridge, Mass., 1989).

ative position of towns within the institutional hierarchies and commercial networks of the old regime.

The second part of the book analyzes the rhetorical strategies and political activities of townspeople who tried with varying degrees of success to obtain departmental seats, district directories, and lawcourts. It begins with chapter 4, which traces the relationship between the institutional rhetoric of the old regime and new ideological themes that shaped public debate during the Revolution, such as egalitarianism and patriotism. By invoking revolutionary principles, the spokesmen for hundreds of small towns tried to convince the National Assembly to grant their demands. The proliferation of such rhetoric had the paradoxical effect, however, of limiting the power of words alone to guarantee success. Townspeople needed lobbyists in the National Assembly to help them achieve their objectives. The role of deputies and special deputies in translating local ambitions into public policy is the central theme of chapter 5, on the politics of parochialism. Chapters 6, 7, and 8 then examine the political decisions that shaped the formation of departments, the location of departmental capitals, and the subdivision of departments into districts. The geographical context of these decisions is described in sufficient detail to illustrate the importance of urban rivalries in shaping the institutional reconstruction of the state.

The third section of the book focuses attention on the struggle of small towns to preserve an important position within the institutional hierarchy of the state after the formation of departments and districts in 1790. The first chapter of this section develops the theme of rivalries between large and small towns over lawcourts in order to explain why the National Assembly decided in July 1790 not to create appellate lawcourts above the district tribunals, and why many deputies then became convinced that too many districts had been formed back in January and February. This chapter shows that disputes over small districts, headed by small towns, continued during the Terror, when urban rivalries became deeply politicized. It concludes with an analysis of the Thermidorian reaction against institutional egalitarianism, which relegated many small towns permanently to the rank of cantonal seats. Chapter 10 completes the history of urban rivalries during the revolutionary epoch by analyzing local responses to the institutional reforms of the Consulate and the Empire. It confirms an underlying continuity in urban political culture by showing how townspeople adopted Bonapartist rhetoric in the hope of obtaining subprefectures and tribunals, and how they revived the language of royalism as soon as Louis XVIII replaced Napoleon as the patron, in principle if not in practice, of loyal towns.

Chapter 11 returns to the structural issues raised in chapter 1. It asks to what extent the institutional changes of the revolutionary epoch confirmed the hopes and fears of townspeople by stimulating the growth of administrative towns at the expense of less fortunate rivals. Using statistical methods such as analysis of variance and multiple regression, it demonstrates that in the early decades of the nineteenth century, small towns that gained larger jurisdictions between 1789 and 1815 did grow more rapidly than small towns that lost institutional influence over the countryside. Later in the century, nearly all the seats of prefectures benefited from their favored position within the institutional hierarchies of the French state. By contrast, lawcourts had no independent effect on urban growth rates in the later nineteenth century, nor did subprefectures do more than forestall the population decline of small administrative towns after the transport revolution of the railroads. It was the strategic position of departmental seats within railroad and banking networks, not their lawcourts, that gave them a competitive edge in the industrializing world of modern France. Following this quantitative analysis of urban growth rates, a brief conclusion discusses the implications of the book for general interpretations of the French Revolution.

PART ONE

THE INSTITUTIONAL CRISIS OF THE

OLD REGIME

O N SEPTEMBER 29, 1789, Jacques-Guillaume Thouret, speaking on behalf of the Constitutional Committee (Comité de Constitution, or C.C.) of the National Assembly, submitted a plan for a territorial reorganization of the kingdom into 81 departments, 720 *grandes communes*, and 6,480 cantons. With the exception of a small department for Paris and its suburbs, each department would encompass an area of approximately 324 leagues that would be subdivided into 9 *grandes communes*, each 36 square leagues in area, and 81 cantons, each 4 square leagues in area. This startling plan, with its geometrical rigor, was designed to establish a uniform hierarchy of electoral constituencies and administrative institutions. Despite offering assurances to deputies from historic provinces such as Brittany and Languedoc that the boundaries of the new divisions would respect as much as possible "the old limits," Thouret emphasized that none of the institutional hierarchies of the old regime provided a suitable framework for establishing a constitutional order based on the principle of territorial equality. The kingdom was divided into as many different divisions as there were diverse kinds of regimes and powers: into dioceses as concerned ecclesiastical affairs; into *gouvernements* as concerned the military; into *généralités* as concerned administrative matters; and into *bailliages* as concerned the judiciary. The accumulation of historical traditions rather than the expression of any rational plan, these overlapping divisions varied greatly in size and were so defective in many respects that habit alone had made them tolerable. The National Assembly needed to seize the opportunity of creating a new division of the kingdom instead of slavishly preserving old imperfections.[1]

Such sudden and drastic changes in the territorial organization of a large state had not been undertaken in Europe since the conquests of the Romans. As Thouret implied, the French state had grown since the Middle Ages through a slow process of territorial accretion, aided by dynastic alliances as well as military power. Each stage of expansion had involved patient negotiations with local authorities, particularly in the towns where medieval duchies, bishoprics, and other territorial jurisdictions had been centered. Royal guarantees of provincial traditions were embodied in the sovereign law-

---

[1] "Rapport sur les bases de la représentation proportionnelle," AP 9:202–3.

courts and provincial estates that survived in some peripheral areas of the kingdom until the end of the old regime. In much of northern and central France, however, provincial institutions had been replaced by royal jurisdictions that increased the authority of the king, albeit through concessions to magistrates who gained property rights to the offices that they purchased from the Crown. Even in the *pays d'état*, royal *bailliages* or *sénéchaussées* had been introduced, along with the custom of buying and selling offices. Only one province, Alsace, still retained a judicial system based nearly entirely on local traditions of municipal self-government and seigneurial authority. Furthermore, administrative and fiscal institutions, more subservient to centralized control than were the royal lawcourts, had proliferated throughout the Kingdom since the sixteenth century. The intendants, numbering thirty-two at the end of the old regime, symbolized this new "fiscal state" that overlapped with the older "judicial state." As for ecclesiastical institutions, they, too, supported the authority of the Most Catholic King of France, who appointed the bishops and received sizable "free donations" from the clergy to supplement his regular sources of revenue.[2]

This complicated institutional heritage, which revolutionaries like Thouret were determined to replace, had generated vested interests in hundreds of towns that served as central places for the lawcourts, fiscal agencies, bishoprics, and other jurisdictions of the old regime. Indeed, all the institutional hierarchies of the old regime can best be understood as expressions of urban social power, despite their formal subordination to the monarchy. Consequently, the spatial distribution, economic functions, and institutional characteristics of towns in eighteenth-century France need to be analyzed in order to understand the social impact of the territorial reorganization of France. In like manner, the implications of a new division of the kingdom for the existing hierarchy of judicial and administrative capitals became an important aspect of the political debate within the National Assembly over the number of lawcourts and administrative assemblies that should be created. Many townspeople has-

---

[2] On the emergence of a "fiscal state" in sixteenth-century France, see Pierre Chaunu's chapter in *Histoire économique et sociale de la France*, ed. Fernand Braudel and Ernest Labrousse, tome 1, vol. 1, *De 1450 à 1660* (Paris, 1970), 121–91. On the importance of negotiated settlements between centralizing rulers and local elites in early modern Europe, see Charles Tilly, *Coercion, Capital, and European States, A.D. 990–1990* (Cambridge, Mass., 1990), pp. 99–103.

tened to urge the Assembly to preserve or expand their existing ju-risdictions over the countryside. The institutional crisis of the old regime became an urban crisis that stimulated bourgeois fears and ambitions. This is the overarching theme of the following three chapters.

Chapter 1

TOWNS AND THE OLD REGIME

T WO IMAGES of towns have influenced interpretations of French social and political development in the old regime: the town as an instrument of royal power and the town as an agent of capitalist development. Some historians have emphasized the subordination of French towns to a centralizing monarchy whose juridical pretensions and fiscal demands transformed autonomous communities of merchants and craftsmen into a hierarchical order of magistrates and other officeholders. Thus, Bernard Chevalier has pondered the fate of the *bonnes villes* that allied themselves with the Crown in the late Middle Ages. Tempted by the proliferation of royal offices and by the profits of litigation, the bourgeois elites of these towns abandoned the pursuit of commerce in order to purchase offices, obtain law degrees, and acquire the trappings of nobility. Like other forms of property, offices became inheritable, and a closed milieu of officeholders, led by the magistrates of the *parlements*, undermined the social cohesion of French towns. The compartmentalization of urban society into mutually exclusive corporations of officeholders brought an end to the circulation of elites that had previously characterized the *bonnes villes*. Whether these institutional changes also harmed the economic development of towns is more doubtful, although royal magistrates were prohibited by law and custom from engaging in commerce. According to Chevalier, the profits of trade were modest in many provincial towns, due to the small demand for imported goods, the low productivity of agriculture, and the high cost of transport. It was the political liberties of towns that officeholders betrayed in their eagerness to serve the king and to join the nobility.[1]

A second image of the town in eighteenth-century France dramatizes the role of commerce in urban development. According to Fernand Braudel, who follows Max Weber in attributing the economic dynamism of European civilization to the "unparalleled freedom" of its towns, "capitalism and towns were basically the same thing in the West."[2] Braudel questions whether the centers of territorial states such as Paris and Madrid generated productive investments, but he praises the European merchants and ship-

---

[1] Bernard Chevalier, *Les bonnes villes de France du XIVe au XVIe siècle* (Paris, 1982), pp. 129–50.

[2] Fernand Braudel, *Civilization and Capitalism, Fifteenth–Eighteenth Century*, vol. 1, *The Structures of Everyday Life* (London, 1981), pp. 509–14.

pers who drove the "wheels of commerce" in an emerging "world economy."[3] Such a conception of capitalism highlights the role of port cities such as Bordeaux and Nantes in accumulating profits from overseas trade. The eighteenth-century became the golden age of such gateways to the Atlantic world, whose merchants created fortunes for themselves and wealth for their cities by outfitting ships for the Spanish empire, the African coast, and the West Indies. Powered by maritime commerce, Bordeaux increased in population from 45,000 to 111,000, and Nantes from 42,500 to over 70,000 by the eve of the French Revolution. Lesser ports of the Atlantic, such as Le Havre, Dunkerque, and Lorient, also expanded dramatically. So did the naval ports of Brest, Cherbourg, and Rochefort. Despite the relative stagnation of Mediterannean trade, the free port of Marseille, devastated by the plague of 1720, recovered rapidly and improved its own position as a outlet for trade with the Turkish empire. By 1789, Marseille had 110,000 habitants, making it the fourth largest city in the kingdom, after Paris, Lyon, and Bordeaux. Altogether, the population of French's major seaports increased by 50 percent during the eighteenth century.[4]

The dynamism of port cities at the end of the old regime has inspired the geographer Edward Fox to develop a general theory of the relationship between towns, capitalism, and the state in early modern France. He argues that seaports belonged to an international network of cities whose access to cheap modes of transport encouraged the invention of a "linear" or "circular" economic system, capable of indefinite rationalization and expansion. By contrast, townspeople in the interior of the kingdom, where transport costs remained high throughout the old regime, had to rely on local trade and political influence to accumulate resources. These towns transformed the agricultural surpluses of the countryside into goods, services, and cash with which to finance their own elites and the royal bureaucracy. Urban development in this landlocked world depended ultimately on military coercion, which enforced the demands of landlords and tax collectors for a share of the harvest. By articulating a bureaucratic system that linked these towns together through commands rather than markets, the French monarchy fostered a political solution to the problem of urban

[3] Braudel, *Civilization and Capitalism*, vol. 2, *The Wheels of Commerce* (New York, 1982), pp. 374–432.

[4] Tabulation is based on population estimates compiled by Philip Benedict for Bayonne, Bordeaux, Boulogne, Brest, Cherbourg, Dunkerque, Honfleur, La Rochelle, Le Havre, Lorient, Marseille, Nantes, Rochefort, Rouen, Saint-Malo, Sète, and Toulon in 1700 and 1790. Benedict, ed., *Cities and Social Change in Early Modern France* (London, 1990), pp. 24–25, and unpublished data that Professor Benedict kindly sent to me. I have adjusted some of the estimates for 1789, as described in appendix 1. On the expansion of foreign trade and port cities, see Georges Duby, ed., *Histoire de la France urbaine*, vol. 3, *La ville classique: De la Renaissance aux Révolutions* (Paris, 1981), pp. 367–70.

growth. Towns of the interior became large and powerful only if they shared in the wealth that servants of the Crown commanded: the seigneuries of noblemen and benefices of churchmen, the property of magistrates, and the tax revenues of financiers. From this perspective, absolutism served the interests of towns as well as the king, bourgeois proprietors as well as nobles and prelates. Towns dominated the countryside, just as the territorial state dominated towns.[5]

Fox's model of port cities and administrative towns makes an important distinction between commerce and trade, and it recognizes the power of the state to mobilize resources in a predominantly landed society. According to Fox, all towns participate in trade, which involves simple transactions between buyers and sellers in a local market, but only towns with access to distant markets engage in commerce, which requires the shipment of goods over long distances. It follows that if the transport network is inadequate to sustain commerce, towns must either remain small and unimportant or rely on other methods of mobilizing wealth. The monarchy, with its appetite for taxes and its rewards to loyal subordinates, became a natural ally of towns that had emerged in the Middle Ages as central places for rural populations. The larger the territory over which a town exercised jurisdiction, the greater the potential for urban growth. No natural tendency inherent in a capitalist economy elevated Paris to a population of over 500,000 by the beginning of the eighteenth century. Thousands of magistrates, lawyers, financiers, and rich noblemen gravitated to the capital of the kingdom, as royal institutions multiplied their personnel and intensified their territorial control. The conspicuous consumption of the rich on servants and carriages, town houses and fancy clothing, fine wines and luxury crafts gave employment to tens of thousands more Parisians, whose expenditures in turn supported a great mass of petty shopkeepers, poor artisans, and common laborers. On a lesser scale, the *parlements* and other provincial institutions of towns such as Aix-en-Provence, Besançon, Dijon, and Rennes attracted a host of families that would otherwise have remained in the countryside or small towns. These provincial capitals ranged in size from 22,000 to 35,000 inhabitants at the end of the old regime, smaller than the great ports of the Atlantic but far larger than most towns in the interior of the kingdom.[6]

---

[5] Edward Fox, *History in Geographic Perspective: The Other France* (New York, 1971), pp. 33–53.

[6] For an excellent survey of urban development in early modern France, see Philip Benedict, "French Cities from the Sixteenth Century to the Revolution: An Overview," in his edited volume *Cities and Social Change*, pp. 7–64. Concerning the relationship between proprietary elites and political capitals, see Braudel, *Civilization and Capitalism* 1:411–16; Duby, *Histoire de la France urbaine*, 3:391–408; and Daniel Roche, *Le siècle des lumières en province: Académies et acadaméciens provinciaux, 1680–1789* (Paris, 1978), 1:75–96. For case studies of the

The relative importance of commerce and the state in fostering urban growth is greatly complicated, however, by the existence of an internal system of transportation along rivers, canals, and roads in early modern France. Fox mistakenly assumes that unless towns were located on the seacoast, they had no access to international markets.[7] As Fernand Braudel has pointed out, the economic history of eastern France is difficult to reconcile with Fox's model of "two Frances," one capitalist and maritime, and the other bureaucratic and continental.[8] Braudel, like Fox, contrasts the dynamism of cities along the periphery of France with the stagnation of cities in the interior of the kingdom, but he argues that eastern France constituted a second periphery, no less important than the Atlantic facade in linking France to international trade routes. Lyon is the great example of such a city along the eastern periphery of the kingdom. Straddling two navigable rivers and several highways connecting northern France to Italy and the Mediterannean, Lyon attracted hundreds of foreign merchants to its annual fairs in the sixteenth century. Many foreigners settled in this capital of international finance, whose bankers corresponded with all the major cities of Europe. From commerce, the merchants of Lyon entered the silk industry, importing weavers from Italy and expanding production as the Lyonnais themselves mastered the art of making fine silks. In the course of the eighteenth century, Lyon became the greatest textile town on the European continent, with 14,000 looms, around 30,000 silk workers, and nearly 150,000 inhabitants.[9]

From the 1750s onward, the merchants of Lyon also began to finance and coordinate industrial production in nearby provinces, as new and improved roads brought the populations of the Forez, Beaujolais, and Dauphiné into contact with the city.[10] Merchants at Saint-Etienne, a flourishing town of 28,000 inhabitants to the west of Lyon, served as intermediaries for much of this industrial development, which involved the

wealth and influence of parlementary magistrates, see Maurice Gresset, *Gens de justice à Besançon de la conquête par Louis XIV à la Révolution française, 1674–1789* (Paris, 1978); William Doyle, *The Parlement of Bordeaux and the End of the Old Regime, 1771–1790* (New York, 1974); and Albert Colombet, *Les parlementaires bourguignons à la fin du XVIIIe siècle,* 2d ed. (Dijon, 1937). For a general view of towns with parlements, see Jean Meyer, *Etudes sur les villes en Europe occidentale,* vol. 1, *Généralités: France* (Paris, 1983), pp. 117–18.

[7] On the importance of towns that organized "commercial space" in the interior of France, see Louis Bergeron and Marcel Roncayola, "De la ville pré-industrielle à la ville industrielle: Essai sur l'historiographie française," *Quaderni storici* 24 (1974): 844–45.

[8] Braudel, *Civilization and Capitalism,* vol. 3, *The Perspective of the World* (New York, 1984), pp. 339–44.

[9] Richard Gascon, *Grand commerce et vie urbaine au XVIe siècle: Lyon et ses marchands, environs de 1520–environs de 1580,* 2 vols. (Paris, 1971); and Maurice Garden, *Lyon et les lyonnais au XVIIIe siècle* (Paris, 1975).

[10] Pierre Léon, "La région lyonnaise dans l'histoire économique et sociale de la France, une esquisse, XVIe–XXe siècles," *Revue historique* 237 (1967): 31.

distribution of silk thread to thousands of ribbon weavers in the mountains of the Forez.[11] The extension of industry from towns to the surrounding countryside became an increasingly important phenomenon in many regions of eighteenth-century France.[12] Sometimes urban and rural workers competed in the same markets, but more often they specialized in different fabrics or different phases of production. Generally speaking, weavers in the towns produced the higher grades of cloth, while those in the countryside, with cheaper materials and less skill, wove cruder fabrics. Spinning tended to be a rural occupation, while the bleaching and dyeing of cloth took place in towns. This complementarity helps explain why merchants in long-established textile towns such as Amiens, Beauvais, and Reims rarely opposed the expansion of rural industry: they were the main beneficiaries of "protoindustrialization," which turned entire villages into outposts of industry.[13] Equally important, however, were the lower costs of production that a regional system of production permitted. At Troyes, for example, where merchants imported raw cotton from the West Indies and exported finished cloth to southern France, Italy, and Spain, piece rates remained low because the rapid expansion of the putting-out system into the nearby countryside undercut the regulations of the clothiers' guild.[14] It was this combination of urban commerce and rural proletarianization that fostered the development of industrial regions in eighteenth-century France.

Towns with an advantageous location on internal waterways also stimulated trade in agricultural commodities, which involved interregional and even international commerce. The fertile lands of the Ile-de-France and Beauce could meet only a portion of the enormous demand of Paris for foodstuffs, and the city drew much of its grain from an elaborate network of river ports, which reached westward to Normandy, northward into Picardy, eastward to Champagne, and southward toward Burgundy and the Loire River valley.[15] In southwestern France, a comparable system of wa-

[11] Max Perrin, *Saint-Etienne et sa région économique: Un type de la vie industrielle en France* (Tours, 1937).

[12] Duby, *Histoire de la France urbaine* 4:375–80; Pierre Jeannin, "La protoindustrialisation: Développement ou impasse?" *Annales: E.S.C.* 35 (1980): 52–65.

[13] On the process of protoindustrialization, see the special issue of *Revue du Nord* 63 (1981), ed. Pierre Deyon and Franklin Mendels. For case studies of textile towns, see Pierre Deyon, *Amiens, capital provinciale: Étude sur la société urbaine au 17e siècle* (Paris, 1967), pp. 205–16; and Pierre Goubert, *Beauvais et le Beauvaisis de 1600 à 1730* (Paris, 1960), pp. 304–17.

[14] Lynn Hunt, *Revolution and Urban Politics in Provincial France: Troyes and Reims, 1786–1790* (Stanford, 1978), pp. 11–13.

[15] On the organization of the Paris grain trade, see Jean Meuvret, *Etudes d'histoire économique: Recueil d'articles* (Paris, 1971), pp. 199–229; and Steven L. Kaplan, *Provisioning Paris:*

terways funneled grain toward the Mediterannean and the Atlantic. Marseille imported grain from Toulouse and other ports along the Canal du Midi, while Bordeaux purchased flour from millers at Montauban and other ports along the Tarn and the Garonne rivers. With its location at the juncture of the Garonne and the Canal du Midi, the town of Toulouse might have shipped grain in either direction, but price differentials and transport costs favored exports to the Mediterannean. Grain dealers at Toulouse bypassed local markets and purchased grain directly from farmers in the region for shipment down the canal to the seaport of Agde. With canal fees for this transit absorbing only 9 percent of the value of the grain in the late-eighteenth century, exports rose to an average of 450,000 hectoliters a year, which equaled the flow of grain from the port of Soissons to Paris along the Aisne, Oise, and Seine rivers.[16] Toulouse maintained its reputation for lawcourts rather than commerce, but this was not because of its isolation from distant markets. The dealers who purchased grain for shipment down the canal lacked the cash to finance such large-scale operations, so they worked on commission for merchants at Marseille, who extended them credit and enjoyed a monopoly of knowledge about prices in Mediterannean markets. Toulouse basked in the prosperity of its nobles, who extracted rents from the farmers, while Marseille enjoyed most of the profits from the grain trade between upper Languedoc, Provence, and Italy.[17]

From the perspective of such commercial networks, capitalism fashioned its own hierarchy of dominant and subordinate towns, which extended from ocean and river ports to smaller centers of industrial production and agricultural marketing in each major river basin of the kingdom. As the anthropologist William Skinner has shown for nineteenth-century China, France, and Japan, the watersheds of such river basins constituted the outer limits of macroregional systems, centered on cities in the lowlands, where navigable waterways and higher agricultural productivity stimulated high population densities and urban growth.[18] My own research confirms the fundamental importance of navigable waterways in the regional sys-

Merchants and Millers in the Grain and Flour Trade during the Eighteenth Century (Ithaca, 1984).

[16] Georges Frêche, Toulouse et la région Midi-Pyrénées au siècle des lumières, vers 1670–1789 (Toulouse, 1974), pp. 596–97, 780.

[17] Ibid., 785–96; and Georges Frêche, "Etudes statistiques sur le commerce céréalier de la France méridionale au XVIIIe siècle," Revue d'histoire économique et sociale 49, no. 2 (1971): 185–92.

[18] Skinner has kindly shown me his unpublished paper "The Population Geography of Agrarian Societies: Regional Systems in Eurasia" (May 1988), which includes a detailed map of the core-periphery structure of macroregional systems in nineteenth-century France. See also his classic analysis of Chinese regional systems, in G. William Skinner, ed., The City in Late Imperial China (Stanford, Calif., 1977), pp. 275–352.

tems of preindustrial France. Among the ninety-one cities with 10,000 or more inhabitants at the beginning of the Revolution, thirty-four had river ports, another ten combined river trade with maritime commerce, twelve had ocean ports, and five had canals.[19] Eleven of the thirteen largest cities, numbering at least 40,000 inhabitants, had water transport, and so did seventeen of the twenty-six cities that had from 20,000 to 40,000 inhabitants.[20] Map 1.1 illustrates this relationship between navigable waterways and the location of cities. Paris commands a hierarchy of towns along the river system of northern France, with Rouen downstream on the Seine, Amiens on the Somme, Châlons on the Marne, Sens and Auxerre on the Yonne, and Orléans, linked to the Seine River by canal, on the Loire. Other important cities in this region, such as Reims and Troyes, are near the navigable waterways leading to Paris. Farther north, the large town of Lille, with around 62,500 inhabitants, heads a cluster of towns along the rivers and canals of Flanders, Artois, and Hainaut, while to the east, Nancy, Metz, and Strasbourg, ranging in size from 30,000 and 50,000, straddle the rivers leading northward into Germany. A series of towns along the Loire River valley and its tributaries, reaching from the port of Nantes deep into the Massif Central, shows the importance of that river basin for the urban development of early modern France. A comparable pattern of linear communication links Lyon to towns in the Saône and Doubs river valleys of east-central France. Similarly, large towns in southwestern France follow the Garonne River valley and the Canal du Midi from Bordeaux to the Mediterannean.

Rivers alone do not explain, however, why large towns developed in the interior of France. Only roads could link towns to the surrounding plains or establish direct communications between separate river valleys. River ports doubled as river crossings, and their roads improved substantially in the eighteenth century. The royal corps of road engineers implemented a coherent plan for a network of well-paved highways that radiated outward from Paris to administrative capitals, seaports, and other commercial towns in the provinces. The speed of stagecoach travel on these roads doubled in the course of the century, and a trip overland from Paris to Bor-

[19] For a map of the system of navigable waterways on the eve of the Revolution, see Serge Bonin and Claude Langlois, eds., *Atlas de la Révolution française*, vol. 1, *Routes et communications*, ed. Guy Arbellot and Bernard Lepetit (Paris, 1986), p. 25. For a list of these ninety-one cities (plus Avignon, which was annexed after the Revolution), with estimates of their population size, see appendix 2.

[20] Nîmes and Versailles, each with around 50,000 inhabitants, were the largest towns that did not have ports, but Versailles was near the Seine and Nîmes was close to the Rhône River valley. The river town of Arles is not included in the category of towns with 20,000–40,000 inhabitants, despite a total population of around 22,000, because nearly one-quarter of its inhabitants resided on farms outside the town itself.

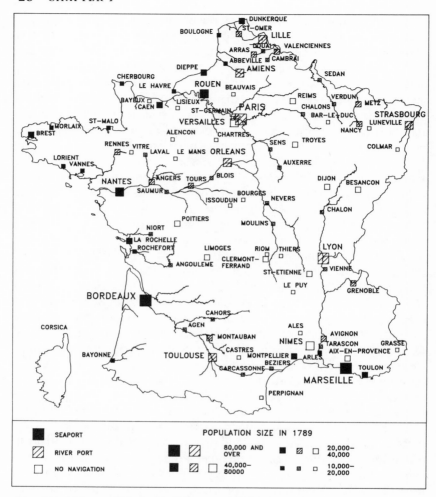

Map 1.1. Cities and Navigable Waterways, 1789

deaux that took two weeks in 1765 could be completed in under six days by 1780. Using peasant labor conscripted by the intendants, engineers also built new roads to connect provincial capitals with each other and with smaller towns. The plains of the northeast attracted the most attention, but relatively isolated regions of the Massif Central also became more accessible. A few towns developed important wholesaling functions exclusively on the basis of roads. For example, Clermont-Ferrand and Limoges both became entrepôts for goods transported across the Massif Central. More generally, however, roads reinforced the commerce of river towns and strengthened the influence of their merchants over the cores of regional systems.[21]

The relationship between capitalism and urbanization can be examined more systematically on the basis of a commercial directory published in Paris just before the Revolution. Compiled by a Parisian lawyer named Gournay, this directory lists bankers, shippers, wholesale merchants, and manufacturers in 334 French towns.[22] Despite excessive coverage of small towns near Paris, as compared with larger towns in eastern and southern France, Gournay's survey confirms a strong relationship between the size of towns and the number of firms and individuals engaged in commerce and industry. Table 1.1 ranks towns on two scales, population and listings in Gournay. Among the ninety-one towns with at least 10,000 inhabitants, all but three had merchants listed in Gournay's dictionary.[23] Of the largest towns, 85 percent (11/13) had more than 80 listings; 73 percent (19/26) of the towns with 20,000–39,999 inhabitants had over 20 listings; and 69 percent (36/52) of the towns with 10,000–19,999 inhabitants had over 10 listings, as compared with only 42 percent (54/126) of the towns with 5,000–9,999 inhabitants.[24] As for smaller market towns, the vast majority of them were not listed at all in Gournay's directory. Map 1.2, which displays the geographical distribution of the towns that had listings in Gournay, can be compared with map 1.1. Rectangles symbolize the most important commercial towns (over 80 listings), followed by circles for towns of intermediate importance (21–80 listings), and crosses for the least important commercial and industrial towns (1–20 listings). The symbols are

[21] Guy Arbellot, "La grande mutation des routes de France au XVIIIe siècle," *Annales: E.S.C.* 28 (1973): 765–91; Louis Trénard, "De la route royale à l'age d'or des diligences," in *Les routes de France depuis les origines jusqu'à nos jours* (Paris, 1959), pp. 101–13; Bernard Lepetit, *Chemins de terre et voies d'eau: Réseaux de transports, organisation de l'espace* (Paris, 1984). For maps of the road network on the eve of the Revolution, see Bonin and Langlois, *Atlas de la Révolution française* 1:14–24.

[22] M. Gournay, *Tableau général du commerce des marchands, négociants, armateurs, etc., de la France, de l'Europe, et des autres parties du monde, années 1789 et 1790* (Paris, 1789). In order to facilitate comparisons with other market towns, I have excluded from my tabulation 172 bourgs and villages listed in Gournay that did not have weekly markets. Only 13 of these communities had a nucleated population of at least 1,000 inhabitants in 1809, and only 11 of these, headed by the bourg of Darnétal (population 5,163, eleven listings), had five or more listings. Here as elsewhere in this chapter, the table excludes towns that were annexed by France during the Revolution, but map 1.2, like the other maps, includes such towns where appropriate in order to give an accurate representation of urban geography in the regions where they were located.

[23] Gournay did not list any of the grain merchants at Arles or Vannes, and he overlooked the important textile industry of Lisieux.

[24] Among towns with at least 10,000 inhabitants, the statistical correlation between population size and the number of listings in Gournay is very high ($R = +.92$, R square $= .85$).

TABLE 1.1
Wholesale Merchants, Shippers, and Manufacturers, by Population of Towns

Listings in Gournay	Population Size of Town in 1789					
	40,000 and over	20,000–39,999	10,000–19,999	5,000–9,999	Under 5,000	Total
Over 80	11	5	3	0	0	19
41–80	1	4	6	4	3	18
21–40	1	10	20	18	12	61
11–20	0	7	7	20	22	56
6–10	0	0	9	15	39	63
1–5	0	0	4	17	96	117
None	0	0	3	55	1,899	1,957
TOTAL	13	26	52	129	2,071	2,291

Sources: M. Gournay, *Tableau général du commerce des marchands, négociants, armateurs, etc., de la France, de l'Europe, et des autres parties du monde, années 1789 et 1790* (Paris, 1789). The classification of towns by population size is based on the sources discussed in appendix 1.

Notes: For comparative purposes, I have included most towns and bourgs that had a weekly market, as described in appendix 1. All the tables in this chapter include only towns located within the kingdom of France on the eve of the Revolution, although a few other towns that were annexed by France after the Revolution, such as Avignon and Mulhouse, are represented, where appropriate, on the maps.

magnified in turn by the size of towns, with ranges of 20,000 or more inhabitants, 10,000–19,999, 5,000–9,999, 2,500–4,999, and fewer than 2,500. In this manner, the regional distribution of the largest and most important commercial towns can be compared with that of smaller towns engaged in commerce and industry. The map reveals a thickening of the urban networks around Rouen, Lille, and Lyon, all important industrial towns; a concentration of commercial and industrial towns in the plains north of the Loire and near the Mediterannean coast; and a scarcity of such towns in the uplands of Burgundy, the Massif Central, the Pyrenees, the Alps, and Brittany. This contrast between the pattern of urbanization in the lowland cores and highland peripheries of macroregions corresponds to variations in the extent of navigable waterways and access to international markets.

If the administrative, judicial, military, ecclesiastical, and educational functions of large and commercially active towns are examined systematically, it becomes clear that the institutions of the French state overlapped

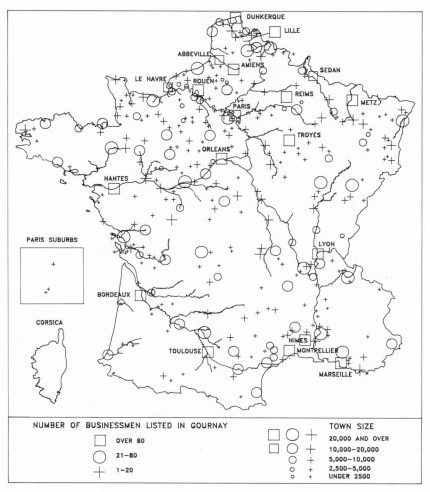

Map 1.2. Towns in Commercial Directory of Gournay, 1789

to a considerable extent with the commercial networks of merchants.[25] On the eve of the Revolution, the intendants who supervised the collection of taxes and the expenditure of public funds resided in thirty-two towns, of which twenty-two had direct access to navigable waterways. All but three of these administrative centers had at least 10,000 inhabitants, and three-

---

[25] Using the statistical procedure of factor analysis, Bernard Lepetit has reached similar conclusions about the convergence of commercial and administrative functions at the highest

quarters of them had at least 20,000 inhabitants.[26] With few exceptions, the most important lawcourts of the realm were also concentrated in towns that had commercial facilities: Paris set the example of a river town that combined commerce with a *parlement*, followed by Douai, Grenoble, Metz, Nancy, Rennes, and Toulouse, along with the seaports of Bordeaux and Rouen. Other towns with navigable waterways and sovereign courts included Arras and Bastia (*conseils souverains*), Montauban (a *cour des aides*), and Montpellier and Nantes (*chambres des comptes*). All but two of the twenty-two seats of sovereign courts in 1789 had at least 10,000 inhabitants, and sixteen of them had at least 20,000 inhabitants. As for the old seats of the most important military governors, known as *gouvernements-généraux*, here a new group of eleven seaports and river towns appears, alongside twenty-six seats of intendancies or sovereign courts and two small towns of the interior. Even archbishoprics and universities, which had a less direct connection to the monarchy, tended to be well endowed with transport facilities. Eleven of the eighteen archbishoprics and fourteen of the twenty-two faculties of law or medicine were located in towns that had ports, most of them along inland waterways rather than near the sea.

Of course, not all commercial towns had an important role to play in the institutional life of the monarchy, nor did provincial capitals attract merchants in direct proportion to their political influence. For example, Gournay's directory lists 289 bankers, shippers, merchants, and manufacturers at Marseille, and only 35 at Aix-en-Provence, yet nearly all the regional institutions of Provence were located at Aix instead of Marseille. In the province of Brittany, the seaport of Nantes, with a listing of 218 commercial firms, did have a *gouvernement-général* and a medical faculty, but the intendancy and the *parlement* were located at Rennes, a river town that counted only 39 merchants in Gournay's directory. Similarly, in the province of Champagne, the intendant resided at the town of Châlons-sur-Marne, where only 26 merchants were listed, while the archbishopric and university were at Reims, with 130 listings, and the *gouvernement-général* was at Troyes, with 102 listings.

These cases are exceptions, however, to the general rule that the largest

---

level of the French urban hierarchy on the eve of the Revolution. See *Les villes dans la France moderne*, pp. 123–71. For an older view that commercial networks only partially coincided with judicial, administrative, ecclesiastical, and military networks, see Jean Meyer, *Etudes sur les villes* 1:112–34. Data on the location of intendants, sovereign courts, *gouvernements-généraux*, archbishoprics, and universities can be found in Léon Mirot, *Manuel de géographie historique de la France*, 2d ed. vol. 2, *Les divisions réligieuses et administratives de la France* (Paris, 1950).

[26] See appendix 2 for details about the population size of particular towns that had higher-level institutional functions at the end of the old regime.

town of an administrative region, or *généralité*, served as the seat of the intendant.[27] Here financiers could purchase the right to collect taxes, and merchants could cash money orders from Paris drawn on the treasuries of these tax collectors. The fiscal system of the monarchy, with its private tax farmers and its receivers of public funds, played an important role in settling commercial accounts. For example, a merchant at Bordeaux who exported wine to a London merchant needed a means of collecting his debt in cash, so he could purchase more wine from vintners in the Bordelais. By selling the letter of change that he received from the London merchant to a Paris banker, he could purchase a money order known as a *rescription*, drawn on a tax receiver's account in Bordeaux. The merchant obtained his coin from the coffers of this receiver, who obtained reimbursement from the banker in the form of a remittance to the treasury in Paris. In effect, the funds for these payments came from foreign merchants, which enabled merchants and tax collectors in Bordeaux to avoid the cost of transferring specie to and from Paris. Tax receivers in industrial towns of the interior, such as Reims and Laval, also accepted promissory notes from merchants who had dealings with clients elsewhere in France. By making short-term loans of the cash "on deposit" in their treasuries, these fiscal agents of the Crown functioned as local bankers. In this manner, taxation sustained commerce, just as commerce generated revenues for the state.[28]

Large towns not only commanded more fiscal resources and attracted more fiscal agents of the Crown than did small towns; they were also more likely to concentrate other public establishments within their walls. The twenty-two towns that possessed at least three important institutions—intendancies, sovereign courts, *gouvernements-généraux*, archbishoprics, and universities—had a median population of 30,500, and the fourteen towns with two high-ranking establishments had a median of 26,000, as compared with a median of 10,500 inhabitants for the twenty-five towns that had only one such establishment. The most important provincial capitals in eighteenth-century France had merchants engaged in commerce and industry, as well as administrators, magistrates, military officers, churchmen, and educators. They were complete towns, subordinated to

[27] The only other exceptions are the *généralités* of Auch and Soissons, but no large towns existed in these *généralités* (Auch had 7,000, as compared with 9,700 at Pau, and Soissons had 8,000, as compared with 9,000 at Saint-Quentin).

[28] Paul Butel, "Contribution à l'étude de la circulation de l'argent en Aquitaine au XVIIIe siècle: Le commerce des rescriptions sur les recettes des finances," *Revue d'histoire économique et sociale* 52 (1974): 83–109; Mettrier, *La formation de la Haute-Marne*, p. 139; dossiers for Reims and Laval, AN DIV bis 10:234. Concerning the private loans that tax receivers made with the funds in their *caisses*, see J. F. Bosher, *French Finances, 1770–1795: From Business to Bureaucracy* (Cambridge, 1970).

wider networks of capitalism and the state, while coordinating the activities of smaller communities within their respective regions.

It is useful to describe such towns as "cities" and to analyze their interactions from the perspective of contemporary theories of urbanization. According to historians such as Jan de Vries, Paul Hohenberg, and Lynn Lees, cities formed an urban system in early modern Europe, based on international trade and state centralization. Seaports and political capitals were the most dynamic elements of this system, but urban growth also involved smaller cities in the most densely populated and commercially active regions of Europe. De Vries presents systematic evidence that cities in preindustrial Europe, like their modern successors, formed a "rank hierarchy" based on population size. The mathematical properties of this hierarchy can be investigated systematically by postulating a lower threshold of membership in the urban system. The theoretical presupposition of such analysis is that cities form a functional hierarchy, in which size varies in accordance with spatial influence.[29] The wider the geographical scope of a city's activities, the greater the potential for urban growth. According to Hohenberg and Lees, two principles of spatial organization operate within the urbanization process: a principle of networking, whereby cities interact with each other directly over long distances, and a principle of centrality, whereby they exchange goods and services with a surrounding hinterland. These principles have different implications for the spatial configuration of urban systems: networks vary in their density, depending on whether cities are spaced closely together or form a loose pattern of "gateways" between adjacent or more distant regions. By contrast, a uniform density of cities exists within a "central-place" system, as regions and subregions are organized into a precise hierarchy of markets and administrative institutions. Although large cities usually participate in both urban systems, the role of small cities varies, depending on whether they function as nodal points in commercial networks or as central places in regional hierarchies. The spatial configuration of an urban system depends on the array of small cities that belong to it.[30]

This rather abstract discussion takes for granted, of course, that French towns—the *villes* of the old regime—can be equated with cities and easily distinguished from rural communities. In the absence of systematic data about the occupational distribution of early modern cities, historians have tried to infer urban rank from population data. Large and densely popu-

---

[29] De Vries, *European Urbanization, 1500–1800* (Cambridge, Mass., 1984), pp. 81–120. For an ingenious application of this theory to subtle changes in the demographic hierarchy of French towns during the revolutionary era, see Lepetit, *Les villes dans la France moderne*, pp. 177–99.

[30] Paul M. Hohenberg and Lynn Hollen Lees, *The Making of Urban Europe, 1000–1950* (Cambridge, Mass., 1985), pp. 47–73.

lated settlements are more likely to share the functional characteristics of a city, such as interregional activities and a nonagricultural labor force, than are small and thinly populated settlements. De Vries suggests that a threshold of 3,000 inhabitants "would embrace very nearly all the functionally urban population" in early modern Europe.[31] Of course, this threshold refers to the nucleated population of a community. A large parish consisting of several dozen villages and hamlets would be classified as a rural community even if its combined population exceeded 3,000–4,000 inhabitants. Government officials in nineteenth-century France recognized this when they defined *villes* as communes that had a central "agglomeration," or nucleus, of over 2,000 inhabitants. Such a threshold includes large agricultural settlements in some parts of France, so historians and urban geographers have generally adopted a higher limit of 3,000 or 5,000 inhabitants for studying urbanization in the nineteenth century.[32]

How meaningful are such demographic criteria for analyzing urban hierarchies in the old regime? Table 1.2 presents the distribution by population size of nucleated settlements that became the seats of basic administrative units, or communes, during the Revolution. The far-right column of the table distinguishes between all settlements that had the reputation of being *villes* and those described in contemporary sources as bourgs or villages. By tabulating the proportion of *villes* in various size intervals, we can see that only 14 percent of them had over 5,000 inhabitants, and only 11 percent had between 3,000 and 5,000 inhabitants. Population size is a particularly unreliable predictor of urban status in nucleated settlements that ranged in size from 1,000 to 1,999 inhabitants. While 538 *villes* were in this range, so were 936 other communities. As table 1.2 shows, population size needs to be combined with a functional analysis of communities as central places in order to distinguish between towns and other communes. Over nine-tenths of the localities that had a market and an institution such as a royal lawcourt, a branch of a national administrative hierarchy, a bishopric, a college, or a military garrison, were described as *villes*. Most of these towns also numbered over 1,000 inhabitants. By contrast, only 140 smaller market towns and bourgs had any significant institutions besides markets. Below this demographic threshold, *villes* usually resembled bourgs in holding weekly markets for surrounding rural populations, but only a minority of them also had royal jurisdictions or other significant institutions.

Alongside these functional characteristics of towns, cultural and geo-

---

[31] De Vries, *European Urbanization*, p. 22.

[32] Georges Dupeux, "La croissance urbaine en France au XIXe siècle," *Revue d'histoire économique et sociale* 52 (1974): 173–89; Bernard Lepetit and Jean-François Royer, "Croissance et taille des villes: Contribution à l'étude de l'urbanisation de la France au début du XIXe siècle," *Annales: E.S.C.* 35 (Sept.–Oct. 1980): 987–1010.

TABLE 1.2
Villes and Other Communities, by Functions and Population Size

Nucleated Population Size	Urban Functions									
	Market and Other Institutions		Market Only		Other Institution Only		None		Total	
	Ville	Other	Ville	Other	Ville	Other	Ville	Other	Ville	Other
5,000 and over	218	1	4	1	—	—	1	—	223	2
4,000–4,999	55	1	2	—	—	1	—	1	57	3
3,000–3,999	102	4	18	3	1	—	5	2	126	9
2,000–2,999	153	7	50	24	1	1	9	32	213	64
1,000–1,999	256	25	239	199	10	10	33	702	538	936
Under 1,000	94	46	228	536	17	19	54	35,909	393	36,510
TOTAL	878	84	541	763	29	31	102	36,646	1,550	37,524

Sources: The tabulation of *villes* includes communities described as *villes* in petitions from townspeople to the National Assembly in 1789–90 (AN ser. C, DIV bis, and AD XVI); or in prefectoral reports in the *Enquête dite 1,000*, in 1809–12 (AN F 20 428–29). On the nucleated population of towns, see appendix 1 for this and subsequent tables. I have inferred the total number of rural communes with fewer than 1,000 nucleated inhabitants from an "Etat concernant le nombre des communes de la République," which gives a total of 39,074 communes throughout France, AN F20:396, cited by Bernard Lepetit, *Les villes dans la France moderne, 1740–1840* (Paris, 1988), p. 197.

Note: Other institutions include royal lawcourts; subdelegations; *recettes* for direct taxation; *recettes de la régie générale; receveurs des fermes*; bishoprics; universities and colleges; and military garrisons with at least one regiment or *escadron* of troops in 1789. Markets are periodic markets held at least once a week, as discussed in appendix 1.

graphical criteria also influenced the classification of communities in early modern France. Some *villes* that did not even have weekly markets still claimed, nonetheless, an urban rank on the basis of juridical rights inherited from the past. From a legal point of view, a *ville* was a title or a dignity that distinguished a privileged community from an ordinary village. During the late Middle Ages, the foremost of these privileges had been the right to build walls in order to defend the lives and property of residents against marauding bands of soldiers.[33] Long after these walls ceased to play an important military role, they remained a symbol of urban identity. Thus, the dictionary of the Académie française defined a *ville* as "an assemblage of houses inside an enclosure of walls and moats," and Diderot's famous encyclopedia agreed that a *ville* was "an enclosure formed by walls."[34] In fact, fortifications were neither the exclusive prerogative of *villes* in early modern France nor the sole legal criterion of urban rank. Royal charters for markets and lawcourts, municipal institutions such as mayors and aldermen, voting rights in provincial estates, and regulations for the levying of sales taxes all served to distinguish *villes* from other communities, regardless of population size.[35] Legal traditions, which varied from province to province, encouraged a cultural definition of urban rank in the old regime.

Regional variations in the density of large settlements also influenced the distribution of *villes*, as compared with bourgs and villages. Map 1.3 shows that communes with a nucleated population of 2,000–5,000 were relatively common in the northeast and the southeast and relatively rare in central and western France. A more detailed map of all settlements with over 1,000 inhabitants would accentuate this geographical contrast.[36] Among the regions that had a high density of such agglomerations, two distinct patterns of urbanization existed, depending on whether peasants as well as artisans and textile workers resided in large settlements. Mediterannean France had many "urbanized villages" of 1,000–2,000 inhabitants that consisted mainly of wine growers and agricultural laborers, while

[33] Duby, *Histoire de la France urbaine*, vol. 2, *La ville médievale* (Paris, 1980), pp. 190–219.

[34] Bernard Lepetit, "L'évolution de la notion de ville d'après les tableaux et descriptions géographiques de la France, 1650–1850," *Urbi* 2 (1979): 102; and *L'Encyclopédie* 35: 447, cited by Frêche, *Toulouse et la région midi-Pyrénées*, p. 59.

[35] Jacques Dupaquier, "Le réseau urbain du bassin Parisien au XVIIIe et au début du XIXe siècle: Essai de statistique," in *Actes du 100e Congrès National des Sociétés Savantes: Le développement urbain de 1610 à nos jours, questions diverses* (Paris, 1977), p. 125.

[36] Settlements with a population of 1,000–1,999 were disproportionately concentrated in the Ile-de-France (140 cases), Picardy (126), Alsace (118), Flanders, Artois, and Hainaut (114), Provence (105), and lower Languedoc (97), as compared with Limousin (18), Poitou (23), Aunis, Saintonge, and Angoumois (24), Brittany (32), Bourbonnais, Berry, and Nivernais (32), Touraine (38), and Aquitaine (55). Tabulation based on departmental data, regrouped to approximate the provinces of the old regime.

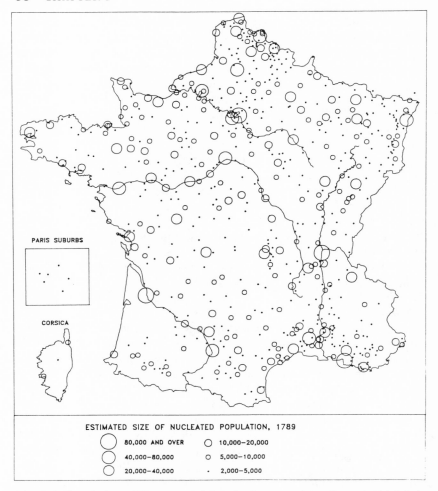

Map 1.3. Population of Towns and Other Settlements with at Least 2,000 Inhabitants

Flanders and Picardy had substantial numbers of textile workers residing in protoindustrial villages.[37] Neither type of community was closely associated with the cultural conception of a *ville* in the old regime. A large majority of the settlements that contained between 1,000 and 2,000 inhabitants in Flanders, Alsace, Provence, and lower Languedoc remained

---

[37] Maurice Agulhon, "La notion de ville en Basse-Provence vers la fin de l'ancien régime," in *Actes du 90e Congrès National des Sociétés Savantes (Nice, 1965)* (Paris, 1966), 1:277–301. On the regional contrast between Mediterannean France and Flanders, see Bergeron and Roncayola, "De la ville pré-industrielle à la ville industrielle," p. 843.

bourgs or villages in the eyes of contemporaries. By contrast, many settlements of this size in central and western France possessed an urban status. Apart from the fertile plains of lower Auvergne, the provinces in the Massif Central had very few large settlements, and their market centers, which ranged upward in size from several hundred to a few thousand inhabitants, contrasted sharply with the hamlets and farmsteads where the bulk of the peasantry resided. Extreme dispersal also characterized rural settlement patterns in the Atlantic plains and hill country of western France. Here the bourg tended to replace the *ville* as a term to designate a market center, but many settlements of fewer than 2,000 inhabitants bore the title of *villes*. Thus, Brittany had 70 *villes* below this demographic threshold, Aquitaine had 56, and even Normandy had 36, despite a strong legal distinction in this province between a relatively small number of *villes* and a much larger number of market bourgs.

Despite these cultural and geographical variations, it makes sense to combine market bourgs and small *villes* into a single analytical category of market towns, based on the functions that such communities exercised as central places. Townspeople themselves in eighteenth-century France became increasingly aware of the importance of economic exchange in differentiating urban and rural communities. Their cultural conception of a town acquired a functional dimension in keeping with the expansion of trade, improvements in communication, and new social attitudes toward the accumulation of wealth.[38] Regardless of their size, market towns served as points of concentration for activities of exchange within rural society. They held periodic markets for peasants in nearby villages, offered a place of residence to specialized craftsmen, provided legal services to proprietors, and collected taxes for the state. Frequent interactions with residents of the countryside distinguished such communities from cities in an urban system, while linkages to regional markets and centralized institutions differentiated them from villages. This mediation between rural society and the wider world of commerce and the state is the most salient characteristic of a *town* in early modern Europe.[39] Thousands of little market towns emerged in England, France, and Germany during the Middle Ages, and they survived as vital centers of marketing and justice as long as the bulk of the population continued to reside in the countryside, far from port cities

---

[38] For an excellent analysis of this changing image of towns, with its implications for the economic and social theory of the French Enlightenment, see Lepetit, *Les villes dans la France moderne*, pp. 52–122. On the relationship between commercial expansion and the growth of small towns in an inland region, see René Favier, "Economic Change, Demographic Growth, and the Fate of Dauphiné's Small Towns, 1698–1790," in Benedict, *Cities and Social Change*, pp. 221–41.

[39] Georges Duby, "L'urbanisation dans l'histoire," *Etudes rurales* 49–50 (1973): 10–13.

and provincial capitals.[40] In the case of France, some market towns were called *villes*, others bourgs, but all of these communities derived their social unity and their political significance from the concentration of activities in central places. Depending on the scale of exchange and the territorial jurisdiction of lawcourts and other institutions, small towns varied in their capacity for growth and power. Some thrived on market activity within a small region or *pays*, others exported goods to larger towns, and still others relied on lawcourts, fiscal jurisdictions, or religious institutions to attract clients and consumers. The relationship of market towns to the commercial networks and institutional hierarchies of the old regime needs to be studied from a variety of perspectives.

Weekly markets typically supplied residents of the market centers with grain and other foodstuffs, but many of them also provisioned nearby rural communities, especially in areas where a significant number of peasant households were engaged in the production of wine or handicrafts. Such markets were especially common along the borders of ecologically distinct microregions, or *pays*, where grain flowed on a regular basis from areas of surplus to areas of shortage. Markets that attracted a considerable surplus of grain also functioned as entrepôts for shipments to larger towns.[41] Generally speaking, small towns in the plains and river valleys had better access to large towns and seaports than their counterparts in the highlands did. The concept of a nodal region, structured around a hierarchy of central places, applies best to the core areas of each major river basin. In the far periphery of the Massif Central, the Pyrenees, and the Alps, where goods had to be transported on pack animals, local grain markets were not as well integrated into large-scale circuits of exchange.[42]

A further distinction needs to be made between trade in foodstuffs and trade in other commodities, such as livestock or textile goods. While consumers needed to purchase food frequently in local markets, dealers in livestock, cloth, ironware, and other merchandise followed a more seasonal rhythm of exchange, centered on regional as well as local fairs. Most large and medium-sized towns of the interior held a major fair each year that attracted merchants from a considerable distance. Such fairs functioned as

---

[40] Hohenberg and Lees, *Making of Urban Europe*, p. 51.

[41] For an analysis of these different types of markets, see Dominique Margairaz, *Foires et marchés dans la France préindustrielle* (Paris, 1988), pp. 169–88.

[42] Concerning the fragmentation of economic regions in areas that had poor transportation, see Jean-Claude Claverie, "Les cadres spatiaux de la vie de relation dans le sud-oeust de la France durant la première moitié du XIXe siècle," *Revue géographique de l'Est* 13 (July–Sept. 1973): 335–51. For an analysis of a regional system centered on the river and maritime port of Bordeaux, see Jean-Pierre Poussou, *Bordeaux et le sud-oeust au XVIIIe siècle: Croissance économique et attraction urbaine* (Paris, 1982), pp. 227–74, 343–85. For a subregional system in Normandy, centered on the large town of Caen, see Jean-Claude Perrot, *Genèse d'une ville moderne: Caen au XVIIIe siècle* (Paris, 1975), 1:177–234.

wholesaling centers for the redistribution of goods to retail merchants from smaller towns. As for local fairs, they became increasingly numerous in eighteenth-century France and they proliferated during the Revolution, when fairs ceased to be privileged institutions regulated by the monarchy. By 1794, when systematic evidence about the location of markets and fairs was compiled nationally for the first time, 4,624 towns, bourgs, and villages reported holding a total of 16,535 annual fairs. Most of these fairs involved the livestock trade, whose complex spatial configuration differed sharply from the hierarchical organization of the grain trade, especially in western and southwestern France.[43]

Some of the complexity of marketing networks can be inferred from maps 1.4, 1.5, and 1.6, which examine the distribution of towns and bourgs that played a significant role in the grain trade, the textile industry, and wine production.[44] Map 1.4 distinguishes between four levels of grain markets, depending on the volume of urban demand for grain and the importance of grain exports from lower-ranking to higher-ranking market centers. The other two maps distinguish between three types of towns, depending on the importance of the textile industry, in map 1.5, and on the scale of wine commerce, in map 1.6. The concentration of grain markets in the cores of each of the major river basins suggests a hierachical model of central places, although the most important river ports gave a linear shape to the flow of grain within each regional system. This principle of linearity dominated the structure of the wine trade along navigable waterways as far north as the Marne, Moselle, and Meuse rivers, down the main trunk and tributaries of the Loire and Garonne rivers, and throughout the corridor formed by the Saône and the Rhône rivers. A quite different geographical pattern characterized the textile industry, which reached deeply into the interior between the Loire and Seine river basins and, again, to the south, between the Garonne and Rhône river basins. Here the greater value in proportion to bulk of thread and cloth enabled merchants in the major textile towns of the lowlands to bring market towns that were far from any navigable waterways into extensive circuits of trade. Map 1.5 also indicates the absence of textile towns in a wide belt of territory that stretched from the southwest through the northern Massif Cen-

[43] Margairaz, *Foires*, pp. 31–72, 101–68. See also Serge Chassagne, "Essai d'analyse d'un marché: L'exemple des foires de Poitou au XVIIIe siècle," in *Actes du 97e Congrès National des Sociétés Savantes*, vol. 2, *Les pays de la Loire* (Paris, 1977), pp. 137–51.

[44] These maps are based on the numbers of specialized merchants listed in Gournay, *Tableau*; a tabulation of the most important grain markets and centers of wine commerce in P. E. Herbin et al., *Statistique générale et particulière de la France* (Paris, an XII [1803]); monographs on the grain trade by Abbott Payson Usher, *The History of the Grain Trade in France, 1400–1710* (Cambridge, Mass., 1913); Kaplan, *Provisioning Paris*; Frêche, "Etudes statistiques sur le commerce céréalier"; Joseph Letaconnoux, *Les subsistances et le commerce des grains en Bretagne au XVIIIe siècle* (Rennes, 1909); and petitions from townspeople in AN DIV bis.

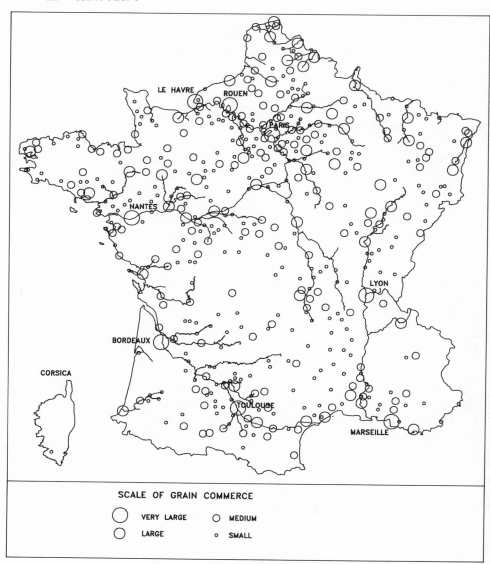

Map 1.4. Towns and Bourgs with Grain Commerce, 1789

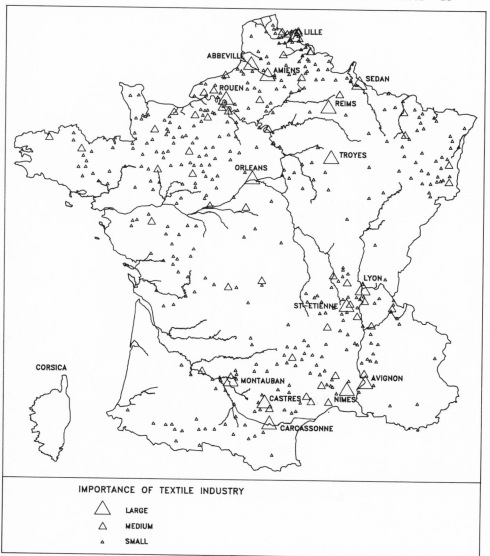

IMPORTANCE OF TEXTILE INDUSTRY

△ LARGE

△ MEDIUM

▵ SMALL

Map 1.5. Towns and Bourgs with Textile Industry, 1789

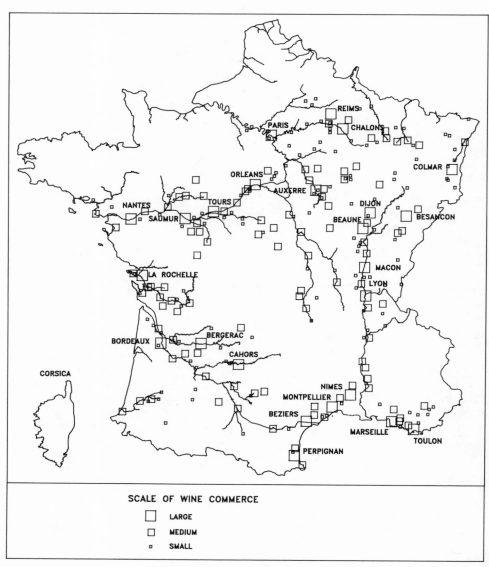

Map 1.6. Towns and Bourgs with Wine Commerce, 1789

tral and into Burgundy and the mountains of the Jura to the east. Viewed side by side, the three maps show contrasting patterns of regional economic integration, all of which involved small towns and bourgs ranging downward in size from 10,000 to fewer than 2,000 inhabitants. Such market towns formed the building blocks for specialized regional economies in eighteenth-century France.

The workings of particular markets can illustrate the role of small towns in linking rural communities to commercial networks. For example, the markets of Sommières, a textile town in lower Languedoc, supplied grain from the nearby plains to peasants in the mountains of the Cévennes, who sold cloth in turn to wholesale merchants from the cities of Montpellier and Nîmes. If local grain harvests were inadequate, merchants from ports along the Mediterannean also provisioned these markets, which reportedly sold as many as 440,000 livres worth of grain in a single year.[45] Peasants in the mountains of upper Auvergne engaged in comparable transactions at the small town of Murat, whose merchants supplied them with grain during the summer months in exchange for deliveries of cheese in the autumn. Traders from Languedoc and Provence, bringing wine, soap, and oil to the markets and fairs of Murat, purchased the cheese in turn for export to the lowlands.[46] Along the edge of the Pyrenees the markets of Mirepoix provisioned larger towns in Languedoc as well as villages in the mountains. Dealers from Limoux, Carcassonne, Narbonne, and Castelnaudary came to purchase grains, fowl, vegetables, and fruits; merchants from Agde, Pézénas, and Montpellier imported wheat; carters brought wine and olive oil overland from the plains; peasants from the mountains sold oats and bought cheap grains such as millet; and cattle merchants from all over upper Languedoc and the Pyrenees attended four annual fairs at Mirepoix.[47]

Small towns in northern France were even more involved in regional circuits of trade. The markets of Montereau, a river port on the Seine, offered "everything that can be imagined" to dealers from nearby towns such as Fontainebleau, Moret, Rozoy, Pont-sur-Yonne, and Bray-sur-Seine: all kinds of grains; cattle and other livestock; cloth, small wares, stockings. Merchants at Montereau also shipped wood to Paris and exported terra-cotta pottery throughout the Paris basin. In Normandy, small towns such as Orbec had equally extensive commercial relations. Orbec served as a warehouse for merchants in larger towns who supplied as many as 40,000 workers in the nearby countryside with raw materials for the production of woolen cloth and linen ribbons. Each market day brought

[45] Ivan Gaussen, *Considérations sur les foires et les marchés de Sommières en Languedoc depuis leurs origines jusqu'à la Révolution* (Nîmes, 1921), pp. 65–72.

[46] Printed *réclamation* for Murat (Paris, 1790), in AN DIV bis 21:332 (Cantal).

[47] AN DIV bis 20:318 (Ariège).

hundreds of weavers and grain farmers, livestock dealers and wool merchants, butchers, fishmongers, and peddlers into town, where they filled several public squares and adjacent streets. Even in Brittany, where country roads were notoriously bad, small towns of the interior channeled goods between rural parishes and coastal ports. Peasant weavers frequented markets at Quintin on Tuesdays and Fridays, at Uzel on Wednesdays, and at Loudéac on Saturdays, where they sold linen cloth to merchants who prepared it for shipment to the ports of Saint-Malo, Nantes, and Morlaix. Uzel was the smallest of these towns, with a nucleated population of only 1,200, but its markets not only accumulated cloth for export but supplied raw materials, small wares, and foodstuffs to all the parishes within a radius of four leagues. During the Revolution, the townspeople of Uzel boasted that indirect taxes levied on these market transactions amounted to 38,800 livres per year, which ranked them just below "towns of the first order." In fact, Quintin was the main center of the textile trade in the region, but market centers such as Uzel played a vital role in an industry that exported six or seven million livres worth of linen cloth to Spain, the Caribbean, and the south of France.[48]

The periodicity of markets and fairs generated complex rhythms of concentration and dispersal in the lives of townspeople and peasants. Texts from eighteenth-century France confirm Fernand Braudel's description of preindustrial towns that "welcomed movement, recreated it, scattered people and goods in order to gather new goods and new people."[49] From Lignières, a little town in Berry, came word that eight large fairs each year attracted "nearly incredible crowds of strangers"; townspeople at Aubenas, in the Vivarais, boasted that their weekly markets drew "a prodigious number of strangers"; and petitioners from Billom, a market center in the Auvergne, wrote of "astonishing numbers" of buyers and sellers at their Monday markets.[50] Of course, markets also drew a familiar clientele from nearby villages, who frequented town not only to sell crops but to obtain specialized goods and services. Among the 980 inhabitants of Anizy-le-Chateau, a market bourg in Picardy, were "butchers, bakers, masons, carpenters, weavers, surveyors, bailiffs, notaries, surgeons and shopkeepers to help feed, lodge and clothe the nearby rural populations, to handle their legal affairs, and even to treat their illnesses."[51] Such a division of labor between town and countryside should not be exaggerated. Peasant households catered to many of their own needs in eighteenth-century France, and poor cultivators often had to contract debts simply to purchase grain

---

[48] AN DIV bis 31:435 (Seine-et-Marne), 6:183 (Côtes-du-Nord); AF III 33 (Orbec); Gournay, *Tableau*, pp. 656–57.

[49] Braudel, *Civilization and Capitalism* 1:389.

[50] Dossiers in AN DIV bis 21:335 (Cher), 34:496 (Puy-de-Dôme); DXVII 1 (Aubenas).

[51] Dossier Anizy, AN DIV bis 81:2.

in local markets.[52] Nonetheless, even towns in relatively impoverished regions attracted clients from the countryside. Thus, townspeople at Saux-illanges, in the mountains of the Auvergne, offered the residents of nearby parishes "legal advice, notaries, a registrar's office, and treatment for their illnesses. Here they have craftsmen to make their furniture, household linen, cloth, kitchen utensils, and farm tools; and here they can supply themselves with salt, iron, bread, meat, and everything their households need."[53] Each market center provided services to rural populations, as well as connections to larger towns.

If markets fostered movement in eighteenth-century France, lawcourts symbolized the institutional stability of towns. Nearly all the royal *bail-liages* and *sénéchaussées* that exercised rights of appeal over seigneurial juris-dictions were located in towns, and so were the more important seigneurial courts. Even in provinces where hundreds of judgeships still existed in the countryside, most magistrates and lawyers preferred to reside in towns and market bourgs.[54] Here they made up a bourgeois elite of officeholders and law graduates whose display of wealth and public authority attracted lesser men of property from the countryside. By encouraging landlords to pur-chase offices, acquire law degrees, and settle in towns, lawcourts fostered a distinctive pattern of social mobility and urban growth. In the *bonnes villes* that possessed royal courts, and in hundreds of seigneurial towns and bourgs, magistrates and law graduates, or *avocats*, dominated local soci-ety.[55] Around them gravitated a clientele of solicitors (*procureurs*), notaries, bailiffs, clerks, and legal apprentices (*praticiens*). Disputes over fiefs and seigneurial rights, tithes, debts and annuities, marriage contracts and tes-taments, property boundaries and common lands, social rank and personal honor brought a host of litigants to town. Here plaintiffs and defendants alike could consult barristers schooled in the intricacies of jurisprudence and solicitors trained in the complexities of legal procedure. Litigants might patronize shopkeepers and artisans in the course of their visits, and they were often able to combine appearances in court with marketing. Courts typically held their sessions on the same day of the week that traders gathered in the marketplace. The business of the courts seemed to create business for the town as a whole.[56]

---

[52] For an analysis of how rents, tithes, and taxes reduced the purchasing power of the peas-antry in early modern France, see Meuvret, *Etudes d'histoire économique*, pp. 139–50.

[53] AN DXVII 2.

[54] Royal policy encouraged this trend in some provinces, such as the Vivarais, where an edict of 1767 combined many seigneurial courts in market centers. See Dossier Saint-Agrève, AN DIV bis 4:156 (Ardèche).

[55] For the social role of lawyers even in small bourgs, see P. M. Jones, "The Rural Bour-geoisie of the Southern Massif Central: A Contribution to the Study of the Social Structure of Ancien Regime France," *Social History* 4 (Jan. 1979): 65–83. Jones emphasizes that land-ownership rather than professional titles gave this elite its social unity.

[56] Among many examples, see the petition of magistrates from Lyons-la-Forêt, in upper

Many townspeople agreed that lawcourts were vital institutions of the urban economy. This view derived from historical experience. As Bernard Guénée has shown in a detailed study of the *bailliage* of Senlis, the development of a hierarchy of lawcourts during the late Middle Ages imparted new prosperity to the towns that became seats of large jurisdictions, thereby attracting talented lawyers and wealthy clients.[57] By the seventeenth century, *parlements* had replaced the *bailliages* as symbols of regional power, but smaller lawcourts continued to receive credit for stimulating urban growth. In 1699, the mayor of Issoire urged his fellow townspeople to support the establishment of a royal *prévoté*: "Beyond the punishment of crimes, this institution would bring very great advantages to our town. A number of officeholders and their families would settle here, commerce and the marketing of foodstuffs would increase, and the town would acquire more prestige."[58] In the province of Lorraine, the "wretched hamlet" of Bouzonville acquired several lawcourts in the mid-eighteenth century, including a royal *bailliage*. Landowners from elsewhere sold their inherited properties and settled in Bouzonville, where they purchased offices in the new lawcourts and contracted marriage alliances with local families. They also built private houses and public edifices "on an impressive scale," and a new town emerged in the midst of an impoverished countryside.[59] Just as this story, narrated by townspeople at the beginning of the Revolution, resembles a myth of origins, so others told a tale of ruin. The trade of Machecoul, in Brittany, supposedly declined by over three-quarters when its "splendid jurisdiction" was dismembered a decade before the beginning of the Revolution; the markets of Pierrefonds-en-Valois collapsed, and local consumers had to purchase food elsewhere at greater expense after this bourg lost its royal *prévoté* in 1767; and trade "suffered greatly" at La Ferté-Alais after its royal *bailliage* disappeared in 1769, forcing most of the legal specialists to move elsewhere and ending the visits of litigants.[60] The

---

Normandy, who boasted that their ducal court met on Tuesdays and Thursdays, both market days, AN DIV bis 17:283 (Eure). On the increasing tendency of rural communities and individual peasants to seek legal redress in royal lawcourts during the eighteenth century, see Hilton Root, *Peasants and King in Burgundy: Agrarian Foundations of French Absolutism* (Berkeley, 1987), pp. 155–204; and Steven G. Reinhardt, "Crime and Royal Justice in Ancien Régime France: Modes of Analysis," *Journal of Interdisciplinary History* 13 (Winter 1983): 437–60. For a more nuanced view of regional and social variations in the extent of rural litigation, see Olwen Hufton, "Le paysan et la loi en France au XVIIIe siècle," *Annales: E.S.C.* 38 (1983): 679–701.

[57] Bernard Guénée, *Tribunaux et gens de justice dans le bailliage de Senlis à la fin du Moyen Age, vers 1380–vers 1550* (Paris, 1963), pp. 334–42; see also Chevalier, *Les bonnes villes*, pp. 56–63.

[58] Albert Longy, *Histoire de la ville d'Issoire* (Clermont-Ferrand, 1890), p. 385.

[59] Dossiers AN DIV bis 28:404 and 11:242 (Moselle).

[60] Dossiers AN DIV bis 26:383 (Loire-Inférieure); DXVII 1.

smaller the town, and the weaker its commerce and industry, the greater the threat posed by the loss of its lawcourts.

The vested interest of magistrates in their offices, lawyers in their clients, and shopkeepers in their customers ensured that changes in the jurisdictions and prerogatives of lawcourts would arouse public controversy. Disputes among rival lawcourts easily became conflicts between entire towns in early modern France. Royal policy exacerbated these rivalries by manipulating the composition and appellate rights of lawcourts in order to extract money from the sale of offices. The number of *bailliages* tripled during the last three centuries of the old regime, and appellate jurisdictions known as *présidiaux* increased from 58 in 1552 to 103 by the eve of the Revolution.[61] While *parlements* resisted the creation of *présidiaux*, the magistrates in these intermediate courts tried to expand their appellate jurisdiction over *bailliages*, whose panels of judges competed in turn with seigneurial courts for legal business.[62] The Crown sometimes practiced extortion on a massive scale before resolving such disputes in favor of one lawcourt rather than another. Thus, magistrates at Montbrison paid over 100,000 livres in 1645 to preserve the jurisdiction of their *bailliage* over rival courts established by the king in the towns of Roanne and Saint-Etienne; and the municipality of Riom paid 10,000 livres to Francis I in 1531, 20,000 livres to Henry II in 1575, and 66,000 livres to Louis XIII in 1638 in the vain hope of preserving the superior rank of their royal court over the rival town of Clermont-Ferrand.[63] Townspeople at Riom became so discontented after Clermont acquired a *sénéchaussée* and the title of provincial capital in the mid-sixteenth century that they backed the Catholic League during the religious wars.[64] Kings might retaliate for such disloyalty by transferring lawcourts to rival towns. Thus, Henry III ordered the *bailliage* and *présidial* of Chaumont moved to Langres after Chaumont joined the revolt of the League, although Henry IV restored these establishments to Chaumont in his amnesty of 1594.[65] Lawcourts became proofs of royal favors that townspeople had to earn. As petitioners for Meulan, a small town near Paris, wrote proudly in 1790, their ancestors had acquired the right to a royal lawcourt "by their love of our kings, through the sacrifice of their blood, at the expense of their properties, and in accordance with solemn

[61] Philip Dawson, *Provincial Magistrates and Revolutionary Politics in France, 1789–1795* (Cambridge, Mass., 1972), pp. 34–35.

[62] On such rivalries, see Ernest Laurain, *Essai sur les Présidiaux* (Paris, 1896); and John A. Dickinson, "L'activité judiciare d'après la procédure civile: Le bailliage de Falaise, 1668–1790," *Revue d'histoire économique et sociale* 54 (1976): 145–68.

[63] Laurain, *Essai*, pp. 60–61; E. Everat, *La sénéchaussée d'Auvergne et siège présidial de Riom au XVIII siècle* (Paris, 1886), p. 96.

[64] On this long-standing rivalry between Clermont and Riom, see Mège, *Formation du Puy-de-Dôme*, pp. 30–77.

[65] Mettrier, *La formation de la Haute-Marne*, pp. 143–44.

conventions."[66] In this manner, towns and the monarchy cemented an alliance founded on lawcourts and officeholders.

The survival of seigneurial jurisdictions complicated the hierarchy of lawcourts that emerged in early modern France. Royal judges in provinces where the seigneurial system remained deeply entrenched, such as Normandy and Brittany, were often hard-pressed to attract rural clients. Seigneurial courts were more widespread than royal courts, and they provided valuable services for the peasantry by adjudicating disputes over inheritances, wardships, property transactions, and debts.[67] Royal *bailliages* and *sénéchaussées* had appellate authority over all these matters, but their legal procedures were more costly and time-consuming than seigneurial courts. Criticism of these courts came less from the peasantry than from royal magistrates who feared competition. In the town of Falaise, for example, officeholders complained that a variety of *hautes justices*, created by the Crown itself for fiscal purposes at the end of the seventeenth century, were reducing the volume of civil litigation at their *bailliage*.[68] Alienations of portions of the royal domain compounded the confusion between royal and seigneurial jurisdictions, as entire lawcourts passed in and out of private hands. When the Prince de Conty leased the royal *châtellenie* of Cessenon from the king in 1747, he sold new offices in the court, whose judges, clerks and solicitors again became royal officers after the king reintegrated this seigneury into his domain in 1784.[69] Not only courts of first instance but appellate *bailliages* existed outside the royal domain. Some of these "seigneurial *bailliages*" had larger panels of judges, employed more men of law, and received appeals from more extensive jurisdictions than did many royal *bailliages*. Thus, the ducal *sénéchaussée* at the town of Ussel, in the Limousin, had five magistrates, twelve barristers, and ten solicitors, who received appeals from nearly five hundred other seigneurial courts.[70] By contrast, royal *bailliages* in Brittany typically had only two judges, who had to compete with impressive ducal and baronial lawcourts for jurisdiction over civil suits.[71] As for criminal justice, here the *bailliages* of the king did increase their jurisdiction during the eighteenth century, due to the reluctance of seigneurs to pay the costs of investigating crimes

[66] AN DIV bis 30:431 (Seine-et-Oise).

[67] Roland Mousnier, *The Institutions of France under the Absolute Monarchy, 1598–1789, vol. 1, Society and the State*, trans. Brian Pearce (Chicago, 1979), pp. 521–28; Donald Sutherland, *The Chouans: The Social Origins of Popular Counter-Revolution in Upper Brittany, 1770–1796* (New York, 1982), pp. 182–84.

[68] Dickinson, "L'activité judiciare," pp. 159–66.

[69] Dossier Cessenon-en-Languedoc, AN DXVII 1.

[70] AN DXVII 2; and Nicole Lemaitre, *Un horizon bloqué: Ussel et la montagne limousine aux XVIIe et XVIIIe siècles* (Ussel, 1978), pp. 168–69.

[71] Dawson, *Provincial Magistrates*, pp. 365–66; and André Giffard, *Les justices seigneuriales en Bretagne au XVIIe et XVIIIe siècles* (Paris, 1902), pp. 47–55, 134–42.

and imprisoning suspects. Criminal suits might be initiated by private parties over affairs of honor, and *bailliage* courts in some provinces benefited from an increase in such litigation. On balance, however, civil procedure was a more lucrative branch of justice than criminal prosecution, and royal *bailliages* often had less direct authority over such cases than did seigneurial courts, except when nobles or priests were involved.[72]

As a result of royal policy, the ambitions of magistrates, and the heritage of feudalism, substantial regional variations existed in the distribution of royal courts on the eve of the Revolution. Map 1.7 classifies by population size the towns possessing *parlements*, *présidiaux*, and royal *bailliages* and *sénéchaussées*.[73] It reveals a concentration of small towns with *bailliages* in the Paris region, where the domain of the Capetians originated, and in Lorraine, where a royal edict of 1751 more than doubled the number of *bailliages* in order to sell more offices.[74] By contrast, small towns in the northwest and the center rarely had any royal courts of appeal, while those in the southwest were more likely to have *présidiaux* than *bailliages*. The *parlements* of Aix and Grenoble prevented such a proliferation of *présidiaux* in the southeast, where *bailliage* courts were evenly distributed among relatively small towns.[75] Only in a few areas such as the Loire River valley does the judicial hierarchy of *présidiaux* and *bailliages* seem to reflect the population rank of towns.

Table 1.3 shows that in the aggregate, however, towns with *présidiaux* were substantially larger than towns with simple *bailliages* and *sénéchaussées*. Seventy-one percent of the *présidiaux* were located in towns with at least 5,000 inhabitants, as compared with only 23 percent of the royal *bailliages* and *sénéchaussées*. An even smaller proportion of the towns with seigneurial *bailliages* and lower-ranking royal and seigneurial courts were above this population threshold. Furthermore, *présidiaux* exercised *bailliage*-level jurisdiction over considerably more territory, on average, than did simple *bailliage* courts.[76] Table 1.4, which is based on an estimate of the number

---

[72] For the direct *ressort* of *bailliage* courts in civil cases, see Mousnier, *The Institutions of France under the Absolute Monarchy*, vol. 2, *The Organs of State and Society* (Chicago, 1984), pp. 266–74. For an example of where a seigneurial court had a larger *ressort* than a *bailliage* had, see Goubert, *Beauvais et le Beauvaisis*, pp. 11–17.

[73] Towns with sovereign courts other than *parlements* are classified separately on this map, and all the lawcourts treated as royal *bailliages* in 1789 are also included. See Armand Brette, *Les limites et les divisions territoriales de la France en 1789* (Paris, 1907), appendix.

[74] On this edict, see Pierre Paquin, *Essai sur la profession d'avocat dans les duchés de Lorraine et de Bar au dix-huitième siècle* (Verdun, 1967), pp. 37–46.

[75] Concerning the impact of provincial *parlements* on the distribution of *présidial* and *bailliage* courts, see Dawson, *Provincial Magistrates*, pp. 36–39.

[76] This analysis focuses on the *bailliage* jurisdictions of *présidiaux-bailliages*, which have been mapped by Armand Brette, along with the jurisdictions of simple *bailliages* and *sénéchaussées*, in *Atlas des bailliages ou juridictions assimilées ayant formé unité électorale en 1789*

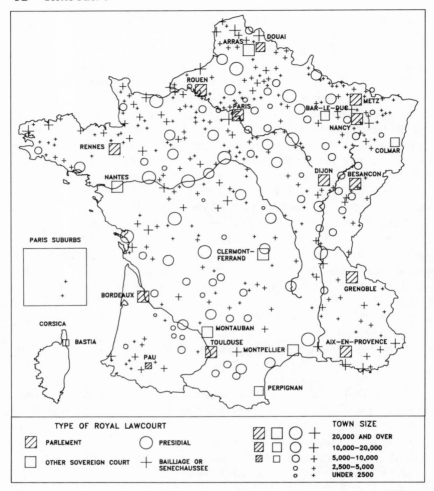

Map 1.7. Sovereign Courts, *Présidials*, Royal *Bailliages*, and *Sénéchaussées*, 1789

of cantons formed during the First Empire within the former jurisdictions of *présidiaux-bailliages* and simple *bailliages*, reveals this contrast, which existed at all levels of the population hierarchy of towns. Equally noteworthy is the tendency for the territorial jurisdiction of both ranks of royal law-

(Paris, 1904). As for the specifically *appellate* jurisdiction of *présidiaux* over other *bailliages*, it seems to have been relatively unimportant, to judge from the complaints of *présidial* court magistrates in eighteenth-century France. See Laurain, *Essai sur les Présidiaux*, whose discussion of the supposed "decline" of *présidiaux* overlooks the continuing importance of their relatively large *bailliage* jurisdictions.

TABLE 1.3
Judicial Rank by Town Size, 1789

	Size of Nucleated Population of Towns						
	20,000 and Over	10,000– 19,999	5,000– 9,999	2,500– 4,999	1,250– 2,499	Under 1,250	Total
Royal lawcourt							
Sovereign Court	16	4	2	0	0	0	22
Présidial	12	22	37	16	3	0	90
Royal bailliage, sénéchaussée	7	15	42	81	82	61	288
Other royal court	3	7	18	50	74	126	278
All Royal Courts	38	48	99	147	159	187	678
Seigneurial court only							
Seigneurial bailliage	1	1	12	27	36	44	121
Other seigneurial court	0	3	16	70	178	310	577
None known	0	0	6	48	226	789	1,069
No Royal Courts	1	4	34	145	440	1,143	1,767

Sources: For présidiaux, bailliages, and sénéchaussées, I have used the lists in Philip Dawson, Provincial Magistrates and Revolutionary Politics in France, 1789–1795 (Cambridge, Mass., 1972), appendix. For seigneurial bailliages, lesser royal courts, and other seigneurial courts located in market towns, I have relied primarily on petitions from nearly 1,300 towns seeking royal lawcourts in 1789–90 (archival series listed in the bibliography). Towns with admiralty courts (amirautés) or commercial courts (juridictions consulaires) are classified as seats of lesser royal courts if they did not have royal bailliages or sénéchaussés. The residual category of "none known" refers to other market towns and/or seats of administrative, religious, educational, or military institutions analyzed in this chapter. Seigneurial judges may have resided in some of these little towns and bourgs, but they were not mentioned in petitions for lawcourts in 1789–90.

TABLE 1.4

Average Size of Jurisdiction of Royal *Bailliages* and *Sénéchaussées*, by Town Size

Rank of Royal Lawcourt	Size of Nucleated Population of Towns						
	20,000 and Over	*10,000– 19,999*	*5,000– 9,999*	*2,500– 4,999*	*1,250– 2,499*	*Under 1,250*	*Total*
Présidial	18 cantons	16 cantons	10 cantons	6 cantons	6 cantons	—	12 cantons
Number of cases	25	22	37	16	3	0	103
Bailliage or *sénéchaussée* only	8 cantons	6 cantons	5 cantons	4 cantons	3 cantons	2 cantons	4 cantons
Number of cases	9	17	43	81	82	61	293

Sources: These averages are based on estimates of the number of cantonal seats located within the jurisdiction of each royal *bailliage* or *sénéchaussée*, which have been mapped in great detail by Armand Brette, *Recueil de documents relatif à la convocation des Etats Généraux de 1789*, vol. 5, *Atlas des bailliages ou juridictions assimilées ayant formé unité électorale en 1789* (Paris, 1904). In the absence of systematic evidence about the size of *présidial* jurisdictions, the *bailliage* jurisdictions of lawcourts that also exercised *présidial* functions are compared with the jurisdictions of ordinary *bailliages* and *sénéchaussées*. The number of cases refers to the number of towns whose average jurisdictions have been estimated.

courts to increase with the size of towns. While the typical *bailliage* located in a small town of fewer than 2,500 inhabitants had jurisdiction over only two or three cantons, *bailliages* in towns with at least 5,000 inhabitants exercised jurisdiction over upward of five cantons. The same trend existed among *présidiaux*. Those located in towns with fewer than 5,000 inhabitants had *bailliage* jurisdiction over an average of around six cantons, as compared with upward of fifteen cantons for towns with 10,000 or more inhabitants. The volume of litigation and the number of practicing lawyers within a town depended less on a lawcourt's rank per se than on the extent of its territorial jurisdiction. Little royal *bailliages* could have only a modest effect on urban growth, which helps explain why they were so often located in the smallest towns.

In addition to the regular lawcourts that enforced justice, a series of extraordinary lawcourts and administrative agencies imposed the fiscal demands of the monarchy on towns and rural communities. This fiscal apparatus emerged gradually as new officials were superimposed on older magistrates, and as new territories were incorporated into the kingdom. The power of taxation had originally been granted to French kings by representative assemblies known as estates, whose own officials raised the taxes, authorized local expenditures, and verified accounts.[77] A few provinces on the periphery of the kingdom, called *pays d'etats*, still retained such estates during the eighteenth century, whose periodic meetings stimulated retail trade in the towns where they were held. As the English traveler Smollett noted in his journal, "The estates of Languedoc assemble in January, so that Montpellier will be extremely gay and brilliant."[78] Such traditional gatherings, which involved nobles and high clergy as well as deputies from urban communities, were restricted to a handful of towns at the end of the old regime.[79] A few towns also hosted meetings attended exclusively by members of the Third Estate, but most of the former provincial capitals became centers instead of royal tax collectors and officeholders.[80]

All the old provinces that lost their estates were divided for tax purposes into *élections* and became known as *pays d'élection*. These territorial divisions possessed extraordinary lawcourts, whose magistrates, known as *élus*, were authorized to apportion the *taille* among rural communities and to settle

[77] For the history of such assemblies, see J. Russell Major, *Representative Government in Early Modern France* (New Haven, Conn., 1980).

[78] Tobias Smollett, *Travels through France and Italy*, ed. Frank Felsenstein (New York, 1979), p. 88.

[79] Gatherings of over one hundred dignitaries from all three estates continued to be held at Montpellier, Rennes, Dijon, Arras, Pau, Tarbes, and Foix.

[80] Meetings of the Third Estate were still held at Lille and Cambrai in the north; Mâcon, Bourg, and Belley along the southern edge of Burgundy; and Saint-Gaudens, Saint-Jean-Pied-du-Port, Ustaritz, and Villeneuve-de-Marsan, in the Pyrénées. See Maurice Bordes, *L'administration provinciale et municipale en France au XVIIIe siècle* (Paris, 1972), pp. 67–96.

disputes over tax assessments. Grouped together into *généralités*, whose higher-level lawcourts, called *bureaux des finances*, were supposed to supervise them, the *élections* also served as jurisdictions for tax collectors, or *receveurs*. While these taxmen played an important role in the financial system of the old regime, the *élus* were increasingly displaced by the intendants as administrators of direct taxes, and so were the *trésoriers* in the *bureaux de finances*, whose offices became largely honorific.[81] The intendants received new powers when additional taxes, known as *capitations* and *vingtièmes*, were introduced by Louis XIV and Louis XV. Appointed by the Crown and therefore liable to dismissal, intendants were more detached from local communities than were the *élus* and thus more likely to apportion taxes in an impartial manner. To assist them in their duties, the intendants delegated authority to "subdelegates," who acquired their own territorial jurisdictions, or subdelegations.[82]

In this manner, subdelegations replaced *élections* as the basic units of royal administration during the eighteenth century. Subdelegates lacked the clienteles of more traditional lawcourts, and their fiscal powers did not increase their popularity among townspeople. Nonetheless, these loyal agents of the intendants proliferated throughout the realm, until they numbered over 700 on the eve of the Revolution.[83] By contrast, only a few *élections* were added to the 177 that existed in 1648, and none were introduced into the provinces conquered by Louis XIV, which became known as *pays d'imposition* to distinguish them from the old *pays d'états* and *pays d'élections*.[84] As table 1.5 indicates, *élections* were generally found in larger towns than were many of the subdelegations. So were *recettes* for the collection of taxes outside the *pays d'élection*. While 64 percent of the seats of *recettes* numbered over 2,500 inhabitants, 65 percent of the seats of subdelegations that lacked either *élections* or *recettes* had fewer than 2,500 inhabitants.

Substantial regional variations existed in the number of subdelegations, depending on the policies of particular intendants. Map 1.8 illustrates the complexity of the administrative structure of France on the eve of the Rev-

[81] Mousnier, *Institutions*, 2:277–83, 206; Bosher, *French Finances*.

[82] Julien Ricommard, "Les subdélégués des intendants aux XVIIe et XVIIIe siècles," *L'information historique* 24 (1962): 139–48.

[83] A total of 705 subdelegations existed on the eve of the Revolution, but five towns had two of them, making a total of 700 seats of subdelegations. They are listed and mapped in Guy Arbellot, Jean-Pierre Goubert, Jacques Mallet, and Yvette Palazot, *Carte des généralités, subdélégations, et élections en France à la veille de la Révolution de 1789* (Paris, 1986). See also Guy Arbellot and Jean-Pierre Goubert, "De la cartographie historique à l'histoire de l'espace administratif: Les subdélégations française à la fin du XVIIIe siècle," *Francia: Beiheft* 9 (1980): 405–21.

[84] Mousnier, *Institutions* 2:283, who mentions 5 permanent suppressions and 7 permanent creations between 1633 and 1691; 179 *élections* existed in 1789.

TABLE 1.5
Administrative Rank by Town Size, 1789

Administrative Rank	Size of Nucleated Population of Towns						
	20,000 and Over	10,000– 19,999	5,000– 9,999	2,500– 4,999	1,250– 2,499	Under 1,250	Total
Intendancy	24	5	3	0	0	0	32
Other *election* or *recette*	5	18	51	57	23	5	159
	7	20	40	43	27	28	165
Subdelegation only	3	9	21	95	135	98	361
None	0	0	18	97	414	1,199	1,728
TOTAL	39	52	133	292	599	1,330	2,445

Sources: Intendancies, *élections*, and subdelegations on the eve of the Revolution are listed and mapped in Guy Arbellot, et al, *Carte des généralités, subdélégations, et élections en France à la veille de la Révolution de 1789* (Paris, 1986). *Recettes*, or subordinate administrative jurisdictions for tax collection in intendancies that did not have *élections*, are listed in Léon Mirot, *Manuel de géographie historique de la France* 2d ed., 2 vols. (Paris, 1947). Most of these *recettes* are also listed in Expilly's *Dictionnaire géographique, historique, et politique des Gaules et de France* under entries for particular provinces or intendancies (Paris, 1766; reprint, Nendeln, 1978). The category of "none" refers to other towns and bourgs that had weekly markets and/or other institutions analyzed in this chapter.

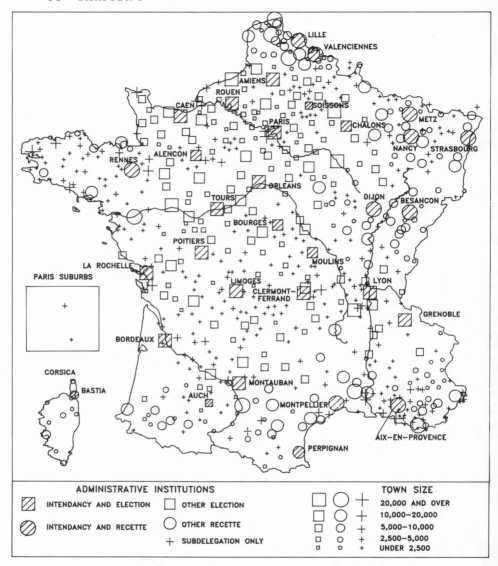

Map 1.8. Intendancies, *Elections*, *Recettes*, and Subdelegations, 1789

olution. It distinguishes between the seats of intendancies in the *pays d'élection* (rectangles with crosshatching); the seats of intendancies located in provinces that did not have *élections* (circles with crosshatching); subordinate towns that had *élections* (empty rectangles); subordinate towns that had other *recettes* for tax collection (empty circles); and subordinate towns that only had subdelegations. The map reveals the density of subdelegations, as compared with the seats of *élections* or *recettes*, in areas such as Brittany (intendancy of Rennes), parts of central France (intendancies of Limoges and Bourges), and Provence (intendancy of Aix). In these same areas, many of the subdelegations were located in small towns, as symbolized by the smallest triangles on the map. By contrast, in *généralités* such as Caen (northwest Normandy) and Montpellier (Languedoc), subdelegates usually resided in towns of over 5,000 inhabitants where *élections* or *recettes* were also located.[85]

Like the jurisdictions of *bailliages*, the territorial range of administrative institutions varied with the size of towns. Table 1.6 compares the average number of cantonal seats established during the Empire within the jurisdictions of the former intendancies, *élections*, *recettes*, and subdelegations. The column to the far right of the table indicates the hierarchical organization of space around large intendancies, and it shows the tendency for fiscal institutions to cover a larger area than did subdelegations. The other columns indicate whether the average size of jurisdictions within each level of the administrative system varied in accordance with the population of the towns where officials resided. With the exception of the intendancies, where the relatively small towns of Auch and Soissons had larger jurisdictions than did several medium-sized capitals, these columns reveal a systematic tendency for the jurisdiction of administrative institutions to increase with town size. For example, the *élus* who resided in small towns of fewer than 2,500 inhabitants had jurisdiction over only four or five cantons, on average, as compared with twice as large an area for the *élus* in towns that ranged in size from 10,000 and 20,000 inhabitants, and three times as large an area for the *élus* in towns with more than 20,000 inhabitants. In like manner, the average territorial jurisdiction of subdelegates encompassed fewer than four cantons in the smallest towns (under 2,500 inhabitants) and upward of seven cantons in the largest towns (20,000 or more inhabitants).

To complicate further the administrative geography of the kingdom, extraordinary lawcourts existed in some provinces to supervise other fiscal operations, involving the sale of salt, the exploitation of forests, and the

---

[85] All but seventeen of the higher-level administrative towns also had subdelegations. The exceptions were the intendancy of Paris, the *élection* of Montivilliers (subdelegation at Le Havre), and fifteen seats of *recettes*.

TABLE 1.6
Average Size of Administrative Jurisdictions, by Town Size

Type of Jurisdiction	Size of Nucleated Population of Towns						
	20,000 and Over	10,000–19,999	5,000–9,999	2,500–4,999	1,250–2,499	Under 1,250	Total
All intendancies	89 cantons	58 cantons	70 cantons	—	—	—	82
Number of cases	24	5	3	0	0	0	32
All *elections*	16 cantons	10 cantons	9 cantons	7 cantons	5 cantons	4 cantons	8 cantons
Number of cases	19	22	53	57	23	5	179
All *recettes*	10 cantons	8 cantons	7 cantons	5 cantons	5 cantons	3 cantons	6 cantons
Number of cases	16	21	40	41	26	21	165
All subdelegations	7 cantons	5 cantons	5 cantons	4 cantons	3 cantons	2 cantons	4 cantons
Number of cases	38	52	114	193	181	122	70

Sources: For intendancies, *élections*, and subdelegations estimates of jurisdictional size are based on the number of cantonal seats located on the detailed map of these jurisdictions in Guy Arbellot, et al., *Carte des généralités*. For other *recettes*, estimates are based on the number of parishes, as listed in Expilly's entries for intendancies or *pays d'état* in *Dictionnaire géographique*. For the computational procedures used to create a standardized scale of "cantonal units," see appendix 1. The number of cases refers to the number of towns whose average jurisdictions have been estimated.

control of international commerce. Salt was a government monopoly in the *pays de grande gabelle* of northern France, where lawcourts known as *greniers à sel* compelled nonprivileged households to purchase allotments of salt at greatly inflated prices. Around 250 towns, many of them quite small, served as the seats of these peculiar lawcourts, whose jurisdictions were often based on customary marketing areas.[86] Wood was another vital resource that the government attempted to control through a system of extraordinary courts, known as *maîtrises des eaux et forêts*. Following Colbert's reform of forest administration, these magistrates took their orders from an *intendant des finances* in Paris, and they handled important business for the Crown by leasing forest rights to merchants. In their role as judges, they imposed heavy fines on peasants who tried to exercise traditional rights of usage in the forests. The water and forest courts were organized into two levels, with 20 *grandes maîtrises* in major towns and 154 *maîtrises particuliers* in smaller towns that were located near important forests, mainly in northern and central France.[87] A third set of extraordinary lawcourts known as *amirautés*, located exclusively in around fifty seaports, had a specialized role to play in the regulation of maritime affairs. Their magistrates inspected ships to prevent smuggling, enforced order in the ports, and judged lawsuits involving merchants and shipowners.[88] Taken together, the *greniers à sel*, *maîtrises des eaux et forêts*, and *amirautés*, like the *élections*, were corporations of proprietary officeholders whose fiscal responsibilities were as important as their judicial functions.[89] Their proliferation in ecologically distinct regions of the kingdom—*greniers* in the interior, *amirautés* along the seacoasts, *maîtrises* near forests—helps explain why royal magistrates, or *officiers*, were so common in small and medium-sized towns during the old regime.

The salt warehouses belonged to yet another series of fiscal institutions that administered government monopolies, customs, indirect taxes, and

---

[86] Mousnier cites a total of 253 salt courts (*Institutions* 2:283–84), but I have found only 248 mentioned in various sources: Jacques Dupaquier, *La population du bassin Parisien à l'époque de Louis XIV* (Paris, 1979); J. J. de Expilly, *Dictionnaire géographique, historique, et politique des Gaules et de France*, 6 vols. (Paris, 1766); and petitions in AN DIV bis.

[87] Mousnier, *Institutions* 2:284–92. For a list of all the seats of these lawcourts, see Patricia Rodriguez Ochoa, "Les rapports entre l'évolution de la structure administrative et le réseau urbain de la France (1789–1856)," *mémoire*, Ecole des Hautes Etudes en Sciences Sociales (Paris, 1976), pp. 72–74.

[88] Mousnier, *Institutions* 2:292–295.

[89] The only extraordinary courts of civilians that did not follow this model of old regime institutions were the *juridictions consulaires* that settled disputes among merchants in important commercial towns. The judges on these courts were merchants elected by their peers, and they followed simple legal procedures that guaranteed cheap and rapid justice. For an example of this institution, which existed in around seventy-five towns on the eve of the Revolution, see Gresset, *Gens de justice*, pp. 78–79.

the royal domain. Several private companies, unified in the General Farms in 1726, employed tens of thousands of accountants, supervisors, clerks, and armed guards to collect tax revenues throughout the kingdom. A separate company of tax farmers operated the postal system and supplied horses for travel on postal roads. After Necker's fiscal reforms in 1780, government officials took over management of indirect taxes and of the royal domain, but the company of General Farms continued to lease the right to monopolize the sale of salt and tobacco and to levy duties, or *traites*, at toll barriers within the kingdom as well as at ports of entry from foreign countries. Just as it provisioned the *greniers à sel* and received the funds collected by local agents of this monopoly, so this powerful company supplied several hundred tobacco warehouses and as many as ten thousand *bureaux*, or official shops, for the sale of tobacco. Along the borders of the provinces subjected to internal customs, known as the Cinq grosses fermes, this private company employed a veritable army of customs agents who had the right to arrest smugglers, including the *faux sauniers* who dealt in contraband salt. Bourgs and even villages housed a dense line of customs posts between provinces such as Champagne and Lorraine, or Burgundy and Franche-Comté.[90]

Comparable agents operated throughout the *généralités* where Necker's Régie Générale collected *aides*, or taxes on wine and other beverages, along with a host of other indirect taxes. In order to enforce strict controls on the transport and consumption of goods subjected to these taxes, the Regie Générale deployed armed *contrôleurs* and clerks in thousands of towns, market bourgs, and villages. An elaborate administrative hierarchy linked these agents to supervisors in larger towns. For example, the province of Champagne was divided into 5 *recettes générales*, 15 *recettes principales*, 86 *départements*, and 1,480 *bureaux*. At the higher levels of this hierarchy, elaborate staffs of directors, receivers, controllers, and clerks were employed.[91] A comparable organization known as the Administration Générale des Domaines collected all the fiscal rights that the king claimed as lord of his domain and as the sovereign guarantor of written contracts. In this latter capacity, the company operated an extensive network of offices for the registration of notarized documents, whose controllers and clerks resided in

---

[90] On the General Farms, see George T. Matthews, *The Royal General Farms in Eighteenth-Century France* (New York, 1958); Mousnier, *Institutions* 2:410–50; Bosher, *French Finances*; and Mettrier, *La formation de la Haute-Marne*, pp. 54–63. For the location of the main branches of this organization, see *L'Almanach royal* (Paris, 1789), pp. 571–86.

[91] Mousnier, *Institutions* 2:420–21; Mettrier, *La formation de la Haute-Marne*, pp. 51–53. For the location of the main branches of this organization, see *L'Almanach Royale* (Paris, 1789), pp. 593–96; and Vida Azimi, *Un modèle administratif de l'ancien régime: Les commis de la ferme générale et de la régie générale des aides* (Paris, 1987), pp. 23–27.

hundreds of towns and bourgs.[92] Finally, the tax farmers who ran the postal service employed 12,000 agents in 1,284 post offices and 3,000 relay stations. Their postal system encompassed a great many small towns and bourgs, particularly in northern France, where the network of postal roads was especially dense.[93]

From the original heartland of the French kingdom, centered in Paris, extraordinary lawcourts and administrative agencies for the collection of indirect taxes had spread outward since the sixteenth century to incorporate many small towns in the Seine and Loire river basins. By contrast, these institutions rarely existed outside the larger towns in peripheral areas of the kingdom, whether in Brittany, Gascogny, Languedoc, Provence, Franche-Comté, or Alsace. Map 1.9 illustrates this pattern of geographical differentiation in the density of several fiscal institutions: the *directeurs* and *receveurs* of the General Farms; the *receveurs-généraux* and *receveurs particuliers* of the Régie Générale; the *greniers à sel*; and the *maîtrises des eaux et forêts*. Based on a ranking that measures the concentration or dispersal of these institutions in particular towns of each *généralité*, the map shows the deeper penetration of such fiscal agencies into the countryside of northern France.[94] Descriptive evidence about minor branches of such agencies confirms the exceptional density of fiscal institutions in small towns of the Seine and Loire river basins. In the Orléanais, for example, the little town of Boiscommun, numbering 1,100 inhabitants, had a subdelegation, a *grenier à sel*, a *département des aides*, a *bureau de contrôle*, a *greffe des insinuations*, an *entrepôt de tabac*, and a *direction des postes et lettres* in 1789. Similarly, petitioners from La Ferté-Macé, a town of 1,700 inhabitants in Normandy, boasted that they had "absolutely the same establishments" as larger towns: a subdelegation, a *bureau de contrôle des actes*, a *greffe des présentation*, a *recette domaniale*, a *recette de la régie, des commis à pied et à cheval*,

[92] Mousnier, *Institutions* 2:425–29; and Mettrier, *La formation de la Haute-Marne*, pp. 50–63.

[93] Guy Cabourdin and Georges Viard, *Lexique historique de la France d'ancien régime* (Paris, 1978), p. 261. For a listing of all post offices on the eve of the Revolution, see M. Guyot, *Dictionnaire des postes et du commerce* (Paris, 1787). For maps of the postal network, see Bonin and Langlois, *Atlas de la Révolution française* 1:38–54.

[94] Towns are ranked if they were the seats for any of the 46 *directeurs* or 135 *receveurs des fermes* who supervised the administration of the General Farms; the 90 *receveurs-généraux* or 134 *recettes particulier* who managed the Régie Générale; the 248 *greniers à sel*; or the 174 *maîtrises particuliers des eaux et forêts*. The ranks are based on the total area covered by these jurisdictions, as estimated by the number of higher-level agencies and lower-level branches located within each *généralité*, in the case of the General Farms and the Régie Générale; the number of *maîtrises* within each arrondissement, which generally served as the framework for branches of the water and forest administration after the Revolution; and the number of parishes obliged to purchase salt at each *grenier à sel*. These estimates are then converted into cantonal scales and aggregated to rank the towns. For more details on computational procedures, see appendix 1.

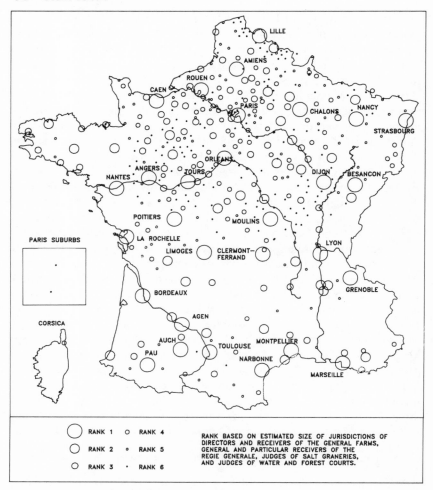

Map 1.9. Rank of Indirect Tax Jurisdictions, 1789

a *brigade de gabelle*, and *des bureaux de marques et poids du Roy*. Such market centers served as outposts for a baffling variety of tax collectors, customs officials, inspectors, clerks, and armed guards.[95]

Among the public institutions that towns valued in early modern France were the bishoprics, abbeys, chapters, and religious congregations of the Catholic church. During the Middle Ages, the Church had been a more powerful force in the life of many towns than the monarchy. Bishops

[95] AN C 96:110 (Boiscommun); DIV bis 29:413 (Orne).

wielded civil as well as religious authority over dioceses that often corresponded to the territories of Gallic tribes and roman *civitates*. Although French kings and urban "communes" reduced the political authority of bishops in the later Middle Ages, new religious orders of mendicant monks, implanted primarily in towns, became important agencies of urban culture.[96] With the challenge of the Reformation, bishops joined royal officials in defense of Catholic piety, discipline, and good works. A new wave of religious congregations swept over French towns, purchasing property, recruiting men and women from local elites, and ministering to the needs of the poor. Schools, hospitals, and charity workshops, staffed by secular institutes as well as by religious orders, increased the public visibility of the Church.[97] So did the landed wealth that older congregations and the secular clergy possessed. Bishops, abbots, and canons drew revenues from a variety of proprietary rights, including farms, tithes, seigneuries, and houses. For example, the cathedral chapter of Chartres received an annual revenue of 200,000–300,000 livres from nearly 7,000 hectares of land, 113 houses, and tithes and seigneurial dues in 124 villages; while that of Langres received 100,000–150,000 livres from 4,200 hectares of land, 46 seigneuries, and tithes in 88 localities.[98] In transferring wealth from the countryside to towns, such religious institutions played an important role in the urban economy. They employed craftsmen, consumed luxury goods, and dispensed charity to the poor. The resources of the Catholic church, like the landed wealth of nobles and bourgeois, enabled towns to become centers of conspicuous consumption within a predominantly rural society.

The distribution of bishoprics varied in accordance with historical traditions. These centers of clerical power were relatively common in the south of France, where a network of Roman towns had shaped ecclesiastical geography in the late Roman empire, and where the popes of Avignon had created additional bishoprics at the end of the Middle Ages.[99] Some of the southern bishoprics were located in towns that had fewer than 2,500 inhabitants, such as Glandève and Senez, in Provence; Vabres and Viviers in Languedoc; and Saint-Bertrand and Saint-Lizier, in the Pyrenees. By contrast, in northern and central France, bishoprics were usually located in towns of over 5,000 inhabitants. Map 1.10 shows this regional contrast in the size of towns that served as the seats of archbishoprics and bishoprics.

Just as most of the small towns that had bishoprics were located in southern France, so these dioceses were considerably smaller, on average, than their counterparts in the north. Table 1.7 shows that four thresholds

[96] Jacques Le Goff, "Ordres mendiants et urbanisation dans la France médiévale," *Annales: E.S.C.* 25 (1970): 924–46.

[97] Duby, ed., *Histoire de la France urbaine* 3:94–100.

[98] Cabourdin and Viard, *Lexique historique*, p. 59.

[99] Mirot, *Géographie historique* 2:309–24.

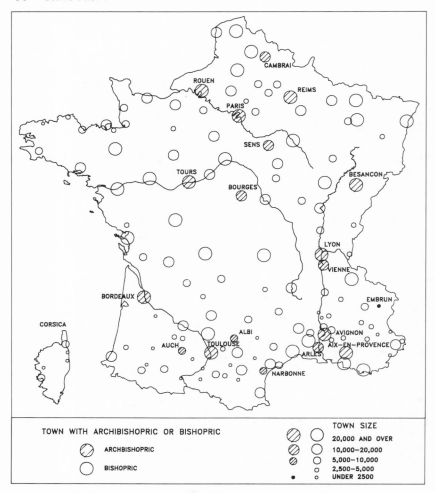

Map 1.10. Archbishoprics and Bishoprics, 1789

existed in the size of bishoprics, depending on whether their sees had fewer than 1,250 inhabitants, 1,250–5,000 inhabitants, 5,000–20,000 inhabitants, or over 20,000 inhabitants. The table also indicates that the chief dioceses of archbishoprics were larger than the dioceses of bishoprics only if their sees had over 10,000 inhabitants. The few archbishoprics located in smaller towns resembled bishoprics in the size of their chief dioceses. The evidence about bishoprics, like that concerning royal lawcourts and administrative institutions, confirms that the smaller the town, the smaller the territory covered by its jurisdiction.

TABLE 1.7
Average Size of Dioceses, by Ecclesiastical Jurisdiction and Town Size

Ecclesiastical Rank	Size of Nucleated Population of Towns						
	20,000 and Over	10,000–19,999	5,000–9,999	2,500–4,999	1,250–2,499	Under 1,250	Total
Diocese headed by an archbishop	38 cantons	38 cantons	20 cantons	—	7 cantons	—	33 cantons
Number of cases	9	5	3	0	1	0	18
Diocese headed by a bishop only	25 cantons	20 cantons	20 cantons	11 cantons	11 cantons	7 cantons	17 cantons
Number of cases	11	9	21	29	26	22	118

Souces: Estimates based on the number of parishes in each diocese, as published in Robert de Hesseln, *Dictionnaire universel de la France* (Paris, 1771), pp. 180–88. Proportions of parishes per diocese in each intendancy or group of contiguous intendancies have been multiplied by the number of cantonal seats in these intendancies to create a standardized scale for comparison with the scales of administrative and judicial circumscriptions. The number of cases refers to the number of towns whose average jurisdictions have been estimated.

Table 1.8 looks at a broader measure of the relationship between religious institutions and the population of towns. Here towns within various size intervals are compared with respect to the number of convents and monasteries located in them. The table shows that large towns tended to contain considerably more regular orders of the clergy than did small towns, just as towns had attracted mendicant orders during the Middle Ages in proportion to their population.[100] Equally striking, however, is the fact that hundreds of little towns crossed this threshold of religious activity *after* the Middle Ages. While only 226 towns had any convents of the mendicant orders in 1330, 673 had institutions of the regular clergy on the eve of the Revolution. Map 1.11 shows the regional distribution of monasteries and nunneries. Towns with the largest concentrations of the regular clergy tended to be located along the major rivers and in the cores of the major river basins, but convents and monasteries were widely dispersed throughout the interior of the kingdom, with a few exceptions, such as inner Brittany and the southern highlands of the Massif Central.[101] In early modern France, the Church, like the state, drew increasing numbers of market centers into institutional networks that reached outward from large towns into the countryside.

Education in the old regime was closely associated with religion, but towns formed a distinct educational hierarchy, based on the distribution of universities and colleges. Universities were rare institutions that existed primarily in large towns. The most important faculties of law, theology, and medicine were located in Paris, and most of the other universities were located in provincial capitals that had *parlements* or intendancies. These faculties served as professional schools rather than as centers of general education or scholarly research.[102] Some of the law schools played an important role in provincial life by attracting men from smaller towns who wanted to acquire legal titles that they could display for professional and social purposes back home.[103] However, the faculties of the universities

---

[100] Le Goff, "Ordres mendiants," pp. 939–40.

[101] It is noteworthy that in these areas, most of the parish clergy refused to take the oath of allegiance to the civil constitution of the clergy during the Revolution, and counterrevolutionary opposition became widespread. Compare the maps and analysis in Timothy Tackett, *Religion, Revolution, and Regional Culture in Eighteenth-Century France: The Ecclesiastical Oath of 1791* (Princeton, 1986); and P. M. Jones, *The Peasantry in the French Revolution* (Cambridge, 1988).

[102] Jean de Viguerie, "Quelques remarques sur les universités françaises au dix-huitième siècle," *Revue historique* 262 (1979): 29–49. For the distribution and relative importance of these faculties, see Bonin and Langlois, *Atlas de la Révolution française*, vol. 2, *L'enseignement, 1760–1815*, ed. Dominique Julia (Paris, 1987), pp. 70–77.

[103] Richard L. Kagan, "Law Students and Legal Careers in Eighteenth-Century France," *Past and Present* 68 (Aug. 1975): 38–72; Lenard R. Berlanstein, *The Barristers of Toulouse in the Eighteenth Century, 1740–1793* (Baltimore, 1975).

TABLE 1.8
Number of Convents and Monasteries in Towns and Bourgs, by Town Size

Number of Convents and Monasteries	Size of Nucleated Population of Towns						
	20,000 and Over	10,000– 19,999	5,000– 9,999	2,500– 4,999	1,250– 2,499	Under 1,250	Total
16 or more	19	4	1	0	0	0	24
8–15	9	23	19	7	0	0	58
4–7	6	11	50	64	21	4	156
2–3	2	7	28	64	79	32	212
1	1	2	12	43	79	86	223
None	2	5	23	114	420	1,208	1,772
TOTAL	39	52	133	292	599	1,330	2,445

Sources: The number of monasteries and convents in towns and bourgs that had a post office is given in Guyot, *Dictionnaire des postes et du commerce* (Paris, 1787); all abbeys are listed in Hesseln, *Dictionnaire universel de la France*, pp. 4–27; petitions from many towns and bourgs also mention the number of religious orders in 1789, in AN DIV bis. The category of "none" refers to other towns and bourgs that had weekly markets and/or other institutions analyzed in this chapter.

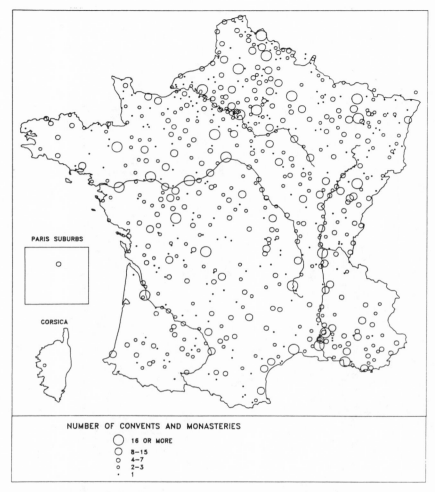

Map 1.11. Convents and Monasteries in Towns and Bourgs, 1789

had no administrative role to play in the many colleges that inherited the task of teaching students the classical curriculum of letters and arts. Removed from the universities in the sixteenth century, these colleges became the most important establishments of higher learning in early modern France. Nearly 50,000 students were enrolled in several hundred colleges on the eve of the Revolution, as compared with at most 15,000 university students in twenty-two universities.[104] Most of these colleges were subsi-

[104] Dominique Julia and Paul Pressly, "La population scolaire en 1789: Les extravagances statistiques du ministre Villemain," *Annales: E.S.C.* 30 (1975): 1545.

dized by municipal governments and operated by Catholic teaching orders. Widely dispersed in the provinces, they formed a network of educational institutions whose curriculum provided a standard course of instruction in Latin. Many colleges recruited students from the countryside, although they were usually located in towns. In their combination of classical learning and religious training, colleges transmitted the urban culture of the Renaissance and the Counter-Reformation to regional and local elites.[105]

Not all colleges were equally important. Their enrollment varied from several dozen to several hundred students, and their course of instruction was more or less comprehensive, depending on the number of teachers on their staff. The largest and most prestigious colleges offered a course in philosophy as well as in Latin grammar and rhetoric. These *collèges de plein exercice* generally had five or six professors, as compared with three or four in *collèges d'humanités*, two in *petites collèges*, and only one *régent*, or Latin instructor, in the most basic secondary schools. At the end of the old regime, 161 towns had colleges that offered the complete classical curriculum, 127 had *collèges d'humanities*, and 338 towns had colleges with one or two *régents*.[106] Table 1.9 shows a strong relationship between the size of towns and this hierarchy of educational institutions. While towns with over 5,000 inhabitants had all the universities and 69 percent (97/140) of the other colleges that offered a course in philosophy, smaller towns had 63 percent (80/127) of the *collèges d'humanités*, 82 percent (70/85) of the *petites collèges*, and 94 percent (238/253) of the colleges that had only one *régent*. Schools offering instruction in Latin and the classics were not nearly as common in very small towns, however, as markets, lawcourts, or fiscal institutions. They existed in only 7 percent (95/1,235) of the market towns and other central places that had fewer than 1,250 inhabitants, and in only 26 percent (158/599) of those with 1,250–2,500 inhabitants, as compared with 60 percent (178/292) of those with 2,500–5,000 inhabitants, and 94 percent (86/91) of those with at least 5,000 inhabitants. Seaports and industrial towns were also less likely to have colleges than were administrative and judicial centers, whose proprietary elites wanted their children to receive a classical education. Thus, Brest, Lorient, Rochefort, and Saint-Etienne lacked colleges, although they all numbered over 10,000 inhabitants. The network of colleges reflects the importance of middling administrative towns, ranging in size from 2,500 to 10,000 inhabitants, in the cultural life of eighteenth-century France.[107]

---

[105] Duby, *Histoire de la France urbaine* 3:243–59.

[106] Tabulation based on the sources listed in table 1.10. Twenty-one of the towns with universities also had *collèges de plein exercice*, and one (Valence) had a *collège d'humanités*. These tabulations exclude Avignon and other towns annexed to France during the revolutionary era.

[107] Julia and Pressly, "La population scolaire en 1789," pp. 1531–39.

TABLE 1.9
Universities and Colleges in 1789, by Town Size

Educational Institution	Size of Nucleated Population of Towns						
	20,000 and Over	10,000–19,999	5,000–9,999	2,500–4,999	1,250–2,499	Under 1,250	Total
University	16	3	3	0	0	0	22
Collège de plein exercise	15	28	54	26	12	5	140
Collège d'humanités	6	12	29	49	21	10	127
Petite collège	0	3	12	34	20	16	85
One régent only	0	3	12	69	105	64	253
None	2	3	23	114	441	1,235	1,818
TOTAL	39	52	133	292	599	1,330	2,445

Sources: The classification of colleges is based on Marie-Madeleine Compère and Dominique Julia, *Les collèges français, 16e–18e siècles*, vol. 1, *Répertoire, France du Midi*; vol. 2, *Répertoire, France du Nord et de l'Ouest* (Paris, 1984, 1988). For the location of *collèges de plein exercise* in towns of eastern France not covered in these volumes, see Dominique Julia and Paul Pressly, "La population scolaire en 1789: Les extravagances statistiques du ministre Villemain," *Annales: E.S.C.* 30 (1975): 1548–55. Other colleges in this area have been classified on the basis of the number of *régents* listed in the table in the appendix to the Serge Bonin and Claude Langlois, eds., *Atlas de la Révolution française*, vol. 2, *L'enseignement, 1760–1815*, ed. Dominique Julia (Paris, 1987), pp. 97–102. The category of "none" refers to other towns and bourgs that had weekly markets and/or other institutions analyzed in this chapter.

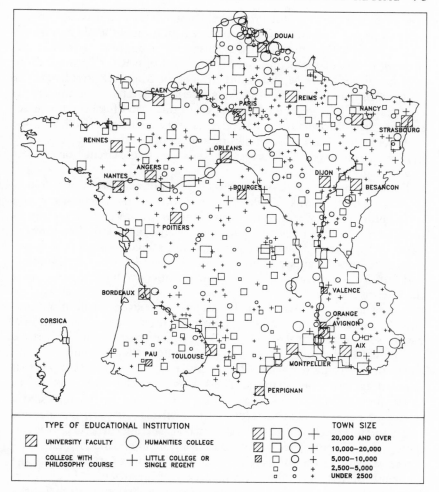

Map 1.12. Universities and Colleges, 1789

Map 1.12 shows the regional distribution of universities, *collèges de plein exercise*, *collèges d'humanities*, and smaller colleges. In the plains and river valleys of northern France, the colleges that offered a full classical curriculum were usually located in towns of over 10,000 inhabitants, but in the uplands of Burgundy, the highlands of the Massif Central, the Garonne River basin, and parts of southeastern France, smaller towns, sometimes with fewer than 5,000 inhabitants, also had such colleges. *Collèges d'humanités* were especially common in the commercial and industrial towns of Flanders and in provinces of eastern and southeastern France such as Lorraine, Franche-Comté, and Provence. These contrasts reflect the importance of provincial traditions of secondary education in the old regime. As for the *petites collèges*, they formed a dense array of educational institutions in small towns of the Seine River basin, the Loire River basin, and the Garonne River basin. Mountainous areas of the Massif Central had fewer *petites collèges*, and the Breton-speaking interior of western Brittany had no colleges at all. The general configuration of this map of college towns resembles that of towns that had convents and monasteries. Colleges, like religious orders, expressed the cultural ambitions of urban elites, especially in relatively commercialized areas that were open to the circulation of ideas as well as goods.[108]

The royal army and navy constituted yet another institutional framework for French towns. Unlike the *bonnes villes* of the fifteenth century, towns no longer maintained their own walls or mustered their own military forces. The monarchy guaranteed the defense of the kingdom through a national system of military recruitment, supply, and command. This system concentrated manpower and munitions in naval ports along the coasts and fortified towns along the continental frontiers. While many towns in the interior became demilitarized, those in frontier provinces such as Flanders, Lorraine, and Alsace acquired highly specialized fortifications and large garrisons of troops. Military engineers constructed a few entirely new towns, such as the naval arsenals of Brest and Rochefort and the fortress towns of Sarrelouis and Rocroi.[109] More often, they modified existing towns in the frontier provinces by constructing citadels and bastions that guarded against artillery attack. The towns themselves were obliged to house the soldiers, a considerable burden on municipal finances and a source of conflict between soldiers and civilians. As garrisons became larger and more permanent, towns began constructing barracks for the soldiers, aided in some cases by subsidies from the intendants. Military personnel sometimes outnumbered civilians in the fortress towns along the German frontier, with a dramatic impact on urban society. While soldiers frequented the taverns, military officers graced local salons with their titles and their gallantry. Even a town as large as Metz, which had a *parlement* and an intendancy as well as a garrison, was deeply influenced by the army, whose officers and men made up nearly one-quarter of the entire population. As for small fortress towns such as Sarrelouis, where over half of the population were soldiers, here the royal army became the dominant institution of urban life.[110]

[108] Of the towns that had at least one monastery or convent, 62 percent also had a college, and so did 76 percent of the towns that had two or more religious orders.

[109] Concerning the planned seaports of Brest and Rochefort, see Josef W. Konvitz, *Cities and the Sea: Port City Planning in Early Modern Europe* (Baltimore, 1978), pp. 73–147.

[110] Meyer, *Etudes sur les villes* 2:321–29.

In addition to this concentration of military power near foreign borders and along the seacoasts, troops were also deployed in the interior of the kingdom for the purpose of internal security. A special military institution known as the *maréchaussée* had responsibility for arresting and punishing deserters, vagabonds, brigands, and rioters. Organized into companies at the level of intendancies, the ranks of the *maréchaussée* included 117 *lieutenances* in the larger towns, 105 *sous-lieutenances* in smaller towns, and a total of 800 brigades that patrolled the market bourgs.[111] These five-man brigades were too small, however, to repress large-scale revolts. Following the revocation of the Edict of Nantes, troops were used to crush Protestant uprisings in the Cévennes, and throughout the eighteenth century, troops were stationed in important towns where grain shortages might lead to bread riots. Map 1.13 shows all of these factors at work in the stationing of troop regiments on the eve of the Revolution. The map distinguishes between towns that had at least two regiments of troops (rectangles with narrow crosshatching); those with a single regiment (rectangles with a single diagonal line); and towns that had only *lieutenances* or *sous-lieutenances* of the *maréchaussée* (circles). Many of the largest garrisons were concentrated along the northeastern frontier, in small fortified towns as well as in cities such as Lille, Sedan, Metz, Nancy, and Strasbourg. A second line of defense, stretching between the Seine River and the eastern frontiers, consisted of large and medium-sized towns that had a single regiment of troops. Nearly all the Atlantic and Mediterannean ports of any consequence also had troop garrisons. In the interior of the kingdom, regiments were deployed along the Loire, Garonne, Saône, and Rhône rivers, and they continued to ring the Protestant communities of the southern Massif Central. They were largely absent, however, from the Massif Central and from the plains between the Seine and the Loire rivers. Here commanders of the *maréchaussée* were responsible for maintaining internal order.[112]

Many garrison towns also had military governors, who received substantial pensions from the king without commanding any troops. The institution of *gouvernements*, which encompassed over 300 towns and fortresses at the beginning of the eighteenth century, served to reward court nobles rather than to guard the kingdom.[113] Some of the 39 *gouvernements-généraux* and 240 *gouvernements-particuliers* that still existed in 1789 were important military centers, but others retained only token numbers of

[111] De Roussel, *Etat militaire de France pour l'année 1788* (Paris, 1788), pp. 409–26; Cabourdin and Viard, *Lexique historique*, p. 205.

[112] For the location of regiments of infantry, cavalry, or artillery in 1788, see De Roussel, *Etat militaire*, pp. 121–416, *passim*.

[113] Saugrain's *Dictionnaire universel de la France* (Paris, 1726) mentions *gouvernements-particuliers* in 147 towns that lost this institution when it was reorganized in March 1776.

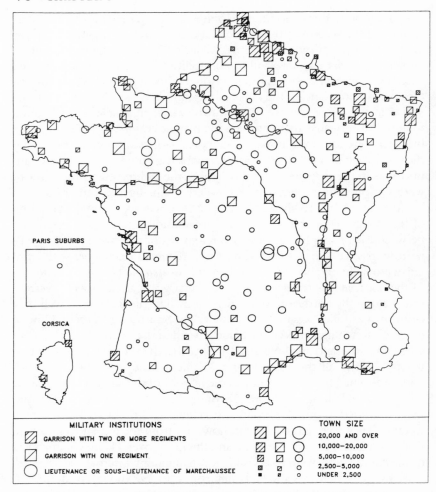

Map 1.13. Military Garrisons and Command Posts of the *Maréchaussée*, 1789

troops.[114] As relics of an earlier military system, governorships in small towns rarely had regiments of troops unless they were located near the northeastern frontier.[115] The larger garrison towns also served as centers of military administration, whose paymasters used the *généralités* rather than

[114] Only 161 of the *gouvernements-particuliers* listed in Roussel's *Etat militaire*, pp. 12–58, were located in towns; the rest were isolated forts along the seacoasts and frontiers of the interior.

[115] Among towns with fewer than 5,000 inhabitants, 86 had governors, but only 37 had troop regiments in 1789. By contrast, 95 larger towns had governors, and 93 had regiments.

the *gouvernements* as territorial divisions. The intendants in these *généralités* were responsible for drafting soldiers into the militia. Most of the 105 recruitment centers that they designated were located in administrative and marketing towns of the interior. Finally, military reformers created a new structure of command on the eve of the Revolution. Based on the consolidation of infantry, cavalry, and artillery units into 21 military divisions, this new structure called for 17 *commandements*, located mainly in provincial capitals near the frontiers and coastal areas. Henceforth, military commanders could ignore altogether the anachronistic institution of the *gouvernements* and base their deployment of soldiers on strategic considerations. As a result of such reforms in recruitment and command, a minority of towns were acquiring more specialized functions within a national system of military administration.[116]

Despite the complexity of institutional hierarchies in the old regime, we have seen that the importance of towns as central places for the countryside tended to vary in accordance with proximity or distance from navigable waterways and in relation to the size of the urban population. Apart from the army, whose strategic requirements favored towns near the continental and maritime frontiers of the kingdom, institutional densities were usually greater near the cores of the major river basins. These densities also depended, however, on historical traditions. Consequently, towns in some provinces depended to a greater extent on institutions such as royal *bailliages* or bishoprics than did towns of a comparable size that were located in other provinces. Just as the commercial and industrial functions of towns varied through regional space, so did institutional functions. These variations can be examined systematically by comparing the rank of towns as commercial centers with their rank on an institutional scale that takes into account the size of judicial and administrative jurisdictions and the importance of religious and educational institutions. Of course, such a scale is a statistical artifact that does not measure directly the contribution of lawcourts, administrative agencies, bishoprics, religious orders, and colleges to the economic life of towns. Nonetheless, by adopting a rigorous procedure for weighting these institutional hierarchies, each of which can be scaled with considerable precision, an aggregate measure of the institutional importance of towns can be constructed. The bottom row of table 1.10 shows the numbers of towns at each level of an eightfold scale of institutional rank, based on an equal weighting of (1) administrative institutions; (2) judicial institutions; and (3) religious and educational institutions. As the capital of the monarchy, Paris is the only city in rank I; 15

---

[116] André Corvisier, "Les circonscriptions militaires de la France: Facteurs humains et facteurs techniques," in *Actes du 101e Congrès National des Sociétés Savantes*, vol. 1, *Frontières et limites* (Paris, 1978), pp. 207–23.

TABLE 1.10
Average Nucleated Population of Towns, by Economic Rank and Institutional Rank in 1789

Economic Rank	Institutional Rank								Average Population
	I	II	III	IV	V	VI	VII	VIII	
I. Average population	660,000	—	—	—	—	—	—	—	660,000
Number of towns	1	—	—	—	—	—	—	—	1
II. Average population	—	72,000	44,400	66,100	—	—	—	—	62,000
Number of towns	—	8	5	2	—	—	—	—	15
III. Average population	—	24,800	20,400	17,500	23,800	24,200	—	—	21,900
Number of towns	—	7	13	4	6	3	—	—	33
IV. Average population	—	—	9,700	10,400	9,100	9,100	10,700	9,000	9,800
Number of towns	—	—	16	39	17	12	2	1	87
V. Average population	—	—	—	5,100	4,500	4,200	4,100	3,200	4,500
Number of towns	—	—	—	44	115	63	10	4	236
VI. Average population	—	—	—	2,700	2,300	2,200	2,000	1,800	2,100
Number of towns	—	—	—	4	79	214	121	51	469
VII. Average population	—	—	—	—	1,300	1,200	1,000	900	900
Number of towns	—	—	—	—	10	187	523	708	1,428
VIII. Average population	—	—	—	—	700	36	900	*	900
Number of towns	—	—	—	—	5	36	86	*	126
Average population	660,000	50,000	18,900	9,100	4,300	2,300	1,200	900	900
Total number of towns	1	15	34	93	231	515	742	746	—

Sources: The classification by economic rank is based on the importance of towns as centers for commerce, industry, retail trade, and periodic marketing, as indicated in Gournay's *Tableau général du Commerce*; P. E. Herbin, et al., *Statistique générale et particulière de la France* (Paris, an XII [1803]); and petitions for commercial tribunals and administrative and judicial institutions during the Revolution, in AN DIV bis and other series listed in the bibliography. The classification by institutional rank is based on five scales, for field administration (intendancies, *élections* and fiscal *recettes*, and subdelegations); indirect taxation (*régie générale, ferme générale, greniers à sel*, and *maîtrises des eaux et forêts*); sovereign lawcourts, royal *bailliages*, and lesser courts that adjudicated property disputes; bishoprics and religious orders; and universities and colleges. These scales have been combined in a manner that assigns equal weights of one-third to administrative institutions, one-third to judicial institutions, and one-third to religious and educational institutions. The average size of towns in each category is based on the nucleated population, as estimated by multiplying the total population of towns in 1789–90 by the proportion of nucleated to total population in the *Enquête dite 1,000* (AN F 20:428–29). Where population size in 1789–90 is unknown, I have used either the census of the year II, which often gives the nucleated population; the *enquête dite 1,000*, which includes many communes that had fewer than 1,000 inhabitants; or, in rare cases, the census of 1861, extrapolated back to 1809 on the basis of the average growth rate of other small towns within the same department between 1809 and 1861.

* Refers to the tens of thousands of rural communities that ranked at the bottom of both hierarchies. They did not have periodic markets or any institutions that have been included in the institutional scale.

provincial capitals, all of them the seats of large intendancies or sovereign lawcourts as well as of bishoprics and colleges, are in rank II; and 34 other seats of intendancies or important lawcourts, bishoprics or numerous religious orders, and colleges are in rank III. Lesser institutional centers are classified in ranks IV through VII, depending on the size of their jurisdictions and/or the importance of their religious institutions and colleges. Market bourgs that did not have any of the institutions in question are assigned to rank VIII.[117]

Table 1.10 also shows the distribution of towns on a separate scale that measures the importance of commerce, industry, and markets. Again, Paris is in the highest rank, followed by 15 large cities that had the highest number of listings in Gournay; 33 medium-sized cities that had substantial numbers of listings in Gournay or other evidence of important commercial activity; and 87 small cities, averaging around 10,000 inhabitants, that had some wholesale merchants or industrial exports. Ranks V to VII classify smaller towns into three levels, depending on the importance of their markets. Rank VIII consists in theory of all the communities that did not have any weekly markets, but only the few localities of this sort that had an institutional rank of VII or higher are included in the table.

The diagonal cells of the tables, from upper left to lower right, give the number of towns that had an equal rank on the institutional and the economic scales. As central places, the 913 towns along this diagonal formed a hierarchy with regular population thresholds, as we can see by moving up the diagonal from the smallest towns, at rank VII, to the much larger towns in rank III. At each step of this progression, the average population size of towns doubles. However, if we look at the cells that do not fall on the diagonal, which give the average population size of towns that ranked higher on the economic scale (above the diagonal) or higher on the institutional scale (below the diagonal), we find a consistent pattern only with respect to the economic rank of towns. Within every column of the table,

---

[117] One scale was constructed for lawcourts, based on the numbers of cantonal seats within the jurisdictions of sovereign lawcourts and *présidials* or *bailliages*, with lesser royal lawcourts and seigneurial lawcourts ranked below all the *bailliage* courts; a scale for administrative institutions, based on the number of cantonal seats within the jurisdictions of intendancies, *élections* or *recettes*, and subdelegation, was cross-tabulated with the scale of fiscal institutions used in map 1.9; cells along each diagonal of this table, from lower left to upper right, were combined to form a single administrative scale that gave equal weight to administrative and fiscal jurisdictions; the judicial and administrative scales were then cross-tabulated and merged in the same manner; separate scales for religious institutions, based on the size of dioceses and the numbers of monasteries and convents, and educational institutions, based on the numbers of *régents*, were cross-tabulated and merged with equal weightings; and, finally, the scale of administrative and judicial institutions was cross-tabulated with the scale of cultural institutions, and the two scales were merged in a manner that gave double weighting to the administrative and judicial institutions.

the largest towns, with the highest economic rank, are at the top, and the smallest towns, with the lowest economic rank, are at the bottom. Looking across the top four rows of the table (economic ranks I, II, III, and IV), we see, by contrast, that the institutional rank of towns is not correlated with population size. Yet if we examine the next three rows (economic ranks V, VI, and VII), we find a consistent trend across institutional ranks: the higher the institutional rank, the larger the population. This trend does not have a very steep gradient, unlike the trend across the economic ranks, but it suggests that variations in the institutional importance of market towns did have an independent effect on population size. On the basis of this evidence, we can see why the leaders of many small towns would insist during the Revolution that their prosperity depended on institutions such as lawcourts.

Such beliefs would also characterize many of the spokesmen for larger towns that ranked higher on the institutional than the economic scale. Yet our two-dimensional analysis of the central place hierarchy has also called attention to the fact that many towns had commercial rather than institutional advantages. If we compare the geographical distribution of the towns above and below the diagonal in table 1.10, we can see to what extent towns favored by commerce or by judicial, administrative, and cultural institutions were located in different areas of the kingdom. Map 1.14 plots this distribution for the 689 towns off the diagonal that had a rank of VI or higher on either scale: circles with crosshatches represent the 388 towns that had a higher institutional rank, and empty circles represent the 301 towns that had a higher economic rank. The map shows that throughout the realm, discrepancies existed between the economic and the institutional rank of many small towns. Towns favored by commerce and industry were especially common in provinces such as Alsace, Flanders, and Languedoc, where local privileges had restricted the spread of royal institutions and where commerce was well developed. At the other extreme, little towns whose institutions were more important than their commerce were widespread in provinces such as Brittany, Burgundy, Lorraine, and Provence, as well as in the Paris basin, where the monarchy had encountered the least resistance to its institutional development. In these outlying provinces, subdelegations and either fiscal *recettes* or royal *bailliages* distinguished many towns from other market centers, especially in upland areas where commerce and industry were relatively unimportant. Yet if such towns were overinstitutionalized, other towns and bourgs in most areas, including the Massif Central, thrived on their markets, as a close inspection of the map reveals. In the southwest, for example, functionally differentiated towns, some specializing in lawcourts or bishoprics, others in the marketing of agricultural commodities, were often located near each other.

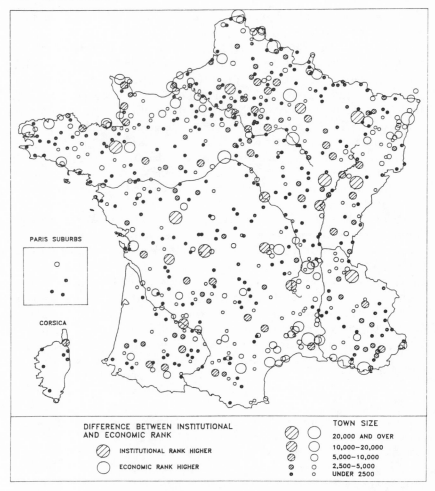

Map 1.14. Towns with Different Rankings on Economic and Institutional Scales, 1789

Similar contrasts between nearby towns existed in provinces of the northwest, including Brittany, and even in the Paris basin.

As we move up the hierarchy of central places to larger towns, the map reveals two characteristic features of urban geography in the old regime: provincial capitals that were not located on the major navigable waterways often ranked higher on the institutional than the economic scale; and seaports often ranked higher on the economic scale. Here is the geographical differentiation between commercial and administrative towns that Edward

Fox has emphasized, although Bordeaux, Nantes, and Rouen, all major seaports, do not appear on the map because they shared many of the same institutions as provincial capitals of the interior. These cities were located near the mouths of major rivers that were deep enough for oceangoing ships to reach them. It was seaports without access to an extensive hinterland through a navigable river, such as Brest, Cherbourg, and Toulon, that would conform best to Fox's model—if so many of them were not dependent on the royal navy or, like Dunkerque, Lorient, and Marseille, favored in their trade by royal privileges.

Discrepancies in the ranking of towns as commercial and institutional centers were so widespread that any effort to rationalize the institutions of the kingdom in accordance with the principle of territorial equality would generate considerable conflict between towns. Indeed, such a revolutionary change in the organization of space would call into question the very meaning of central places. Would the new jurisdictions favor large towns or small ones, towns engaged in long-distance commerce or those dependent on institutions that stimulated local trade? Would the seats of *généralités* and sovereign courts preserve their institutional superiority or would other towns, either more commercial in orientation or smaller and more determined to overcome their institutional inferiority, carve up the large jurisdictions of the intendants and the *parlements* into smaller and more equal ones? What would happen to the seats of little bishoprics, small *bailliages*, minor subdelegations? In a society where hundreds of small towns played a role in only one of the institutional hierarchies of the old regime, and where thousands of market centers existed, how many intermediate jurisdictions would survive between important administrative towns and rural communities? If the new division of the kingdom promised to increase the territorial influence of some towns, it would in all likelihood reduce others to the level of bourgs or even villages. Such were the uncertainties that confronted townspeople when the French Revolution sounded the death knell of the old regime.

Chapter 2

THE NEW DIVISION OF THE KINGDOM

THE FRENCH REVOLUTION undermined the authority of nearly all the public institutions of the old regime. Intendants and subdelegates were swept aside, venal offices suppressed, seigneurial lawcourts abolished, tax farms suspended, monasteries dissolved, bishoprics displaced. The entire infrastructure of the state seemed to collapse as the National Assembly launched its famous assault on privilege in the summer of 1789. This frenzy of destructive energy was supposed to prepare the way for national regeneration. In the words of Rabaut Saint-Etienne, an advocate of total revolution instead of gradual reform, the French people "must be renewed, rejuvenated, changed in their institutions to change their ideas, changed in their laws to change their morals. Everything must be destroyed, yes destroyed, since everything must be re-created."[1] Foremost among the tasks of revolutionaries was the creation of a new territorial division of the kingdom. The old territorial framework of *généralités*, *bailliages*, bishoprics, and *gouvernements* was "a monstrous and contradictory pile of inequalities, that time, hazard, abuse, privilege, and the favor of despotism have composed out of chaos."[2] Boundaries inherited from the past symbolized privilege and particularism. A new division, founded on the principle of territorial equality, would consolidate the rights of all French citizens within a unified system of electoral constituencies, administrative assemblies, and lawcourts. In redrawing the map of France, revolutionaries hoped to liberate civic energies from the despotic authority of royal bureaucrats and the stultifying influence of privileged corporations. Through a new organization of space, they would perfect the state, revive the economy, and rejuvenate society.

Precedents for territorial reform existed in the ideas of the French Enlightenment and the practice of royal administrators. Two schools of thought existed among critics of the old regime, who either attacked the intendants for being too strong or complained that the central government was too weak. Admirers of the traditional social order, such as Fénélon, Saint-Simon, and Montesquiou, defended provincial estates against royal bureaucracy, while theorists of a more rational administrative system, such

---

[1] Pamphlet titled *Reflexions sur la nouvelle division du royaume et sur les privilèges et les assemblées des provinces d'etats* (Paris, 1789), reprinted in M. J. Madival, ed., *Archives parlementaires*, 1st ser. (Paris, 1878), 10:37–38, henceforth cited AP 10:37–38.

[2] Ibid., p. 37.

as the marquis d'Argenson, Le Trosne, and Turgot, decried corporate institutions and proposed measures to strengthen the monarchy. The former thinkers exalted provincial liberties; the latter praised national unity; all agreed that the existing system of bureaucratic authority conflicted with the social order in the provinces. Either the intendants should be replaced by a resurgent aristocracy, governing the provinces through traditional estates, or they should be assisted by an enlightened elite of landowners, mobilizing public opinion through new administrative assemblies. Whether provincial estates were revived or assemblies of landowners were introduced, territorial reforms would also be necessary. The intendants administered *généralités* that varied greatly in size and population. Some of the *pays d'élection* contained several historic provinces that could acquire separate estates, and the larger *généralités* needed to be subdivided if a hierarchy of representative assemblies was introduced. Historical traditions and more abstract conceptions of space provided alternative justifications for revising territorial boundaries within the kingdom.[3]

Critics of the traditional estates developed the most novel ideas about administrative regions. The marquis d'Argenson, who feared the power of *pays d'état* such as Brittany and Languedoc, proposed that the *généralités* be partitioned into areas large enough to permit administrative initiative but small enough to eliminate the danger of resistance to the central government. His goal was a uniform system of obedient assemblies, subdivided into districts that enjoyed "perfect equality." In creating "departments" instead of *généralités* for the intendants, the government should take into account local customs, habits, geography, and commerce.[4] Le Trosne, a disciple of the physiocrats, invoked the rational criteria of "proximity and convenience" against the accidents of history when he recommended that large *généralités* be subdivided into smaller ones, and that square arrondissements, each 3,000 *toises*, or one league wide, become the basic units of administration.[5] As for Turgot, this luminary of administrative reform calculated that in a rational hierarchy of provinces and districts, no province should have a radius of over ten leagues, and no district should contain any villages over 8,000–12,000 *toises*, or three to four leagues, from its *chef-lieu*.[6] Turgot had discovered the geographical principle that

[3] Ozouf-Marignier, *La formation des départements*, pp. 19–33; Berlet, *Les provinces*, pp. 21–44.

[4] D'Argenson, *Considerations sur le gouvernement ancien et présent de la France* (Amsterdam, 1764), pp. 30–31, 203–34.

[5] Le Trosne, *De l'administration provinciale et de la réforme de l'impôt* (Basle, 1779), pp. 331–44.

[6] Letter from Dupont de Nemours to the *Journal de Paris*, July 2, 1787, cited by Ernest Lebègue, *La vie et l'oeuvre d'un Constituant: Thouret, 1746–1794* (Paris, 1910), pp. 171–72. As Turgot's secretary, Dupont drafted a *mémoire* that developed Turgot's plan for administra-

centrality depends on time as well as distance. Under the road conditions that prevailed in eighteenth-century France, travelers would need one day to reach a provincial capital ten leagues away, and another day to return home. Similarly, they would need a day to travel to and from a district capital three or four leagues away. Unless provinces and districts remained within these parameters of time and space, the trouble and expense of administrative business would become unreasonable.[7]

Ministers of the king who tried to change the administrative system were less interested in such abstract principles than in practical measures to mobilize public support for their policies. Even Turgot was careful not to propose any changes in the boundaries of *généralités* and *élections* when he advised the king in 1775 to introduce a hierarchy of assemblies for the *pays d'élections*. The most important issues that he raised concerned the selection and composition of these assemblies. Turgot wanted deputies to be elected by constituencies of landowners rather than appointed by the king, and he emphasized that property rather than social rank should determine eligibility for office and voting rights.[8] After Turgot fell from power, a new controller-general, Necker, attempted to experiment with provincial assemblies, but he preserved separate representation for the clergy and the nobility in accordance with the traditional division of society into three orders. Furthermore, the initial deputies from each order, or estate, were chosen by the government. Subsequently, deputies were co-opted by the two provincial assemblies that actually began operations, one for Berry, and the other for Haute-Guyenne. Public opinion remained indifferent to these new institutions, especially after their biennial assemblies and permanent bureaus were firmly subordinated to the intendants in all financial matters. Only the townspeople of Villefranche-de-Rouergue, which displaced Montauban as the capital of Haute-Guyenne, benefited tangibly from this institution.[9]

In 1786, Calonne, who had succeeded Necker as controller-general of finance, returned to Turgot's plan for elected assemblies of proprietors. His motive for this reform was entirely fiscal. The government faced a budget-

---

tive assemblies: *Des administrations provinciales: Mémoire présenté au Roi, par feu M. Turgot* (Lausanne, 1788).

[7] Turgot's friend, the marquis de Condorcet, used this transport principle in his "Essai sur la Constitution de la fonction des Assemblées provinciales," written in 1788. See *Oeuvres de Condorcet*, ed. A. Condorcet O'Connor and M. F. Arago (Paris, 1847), 12:273–74; and Keith Michael Baker, *Condorcet: From Natural Philosophy to Social Mathematics* (Chicago, 1975), pp. 252–60.

[8] Dupont de Nemours, *Des administrations provinciales*; Baker, *Condorcet*, pp. 202–14.

[9] Mousnier, *Institutions* 1:630–32; Léonce de Lavergne, *Les assemblées provinciales sous Louis XVI* (Paris, 1864); for a more sympathetic account of Necker's administrative reforms, see Robert D. Harris, *Necker: Reform Statesman of the Ancien Regime* (Berkeley, 1980), pp. 176–91.

ary crisis, and "the only way to bring real order into the finances is to revitalize the entire state by reforming all that is defective in its constitution."[10] Overlooking the corruption and inefficiency of the financial apparatus that supplied cash to the government, Calonne blamed the tax exemptions of wealthy landowners for the deficit. By equalizing the fiscal burden among all regions and social groups, he hoped to restore public confidence, float new loans, and amortize the enormous debt. The purpose of provincial assemblies, elected by municipal and district assemblies of landowners, would be to apportion the new land tax that Calonne wanted to impose on all proprietors without exception. If nobles and clergy had special rights of representation in these assemblies, they would try to preserve their fiscal privileges. Thus, Calonne opposed the traditional organization of provincial estates. Not surprisingly, the Assembly of Notables, convoked in 1787 to approve this reform, balked at the idea of a proportional tax on land and insisted that administrative assemblies must preserve the distinction between nobles, clergy, and the Third Estate. When Calonne issued a public appeal for support against the Notables, the king abandoned him. This was the first act in the aristocratic revolution that preceded the triumph of the Third Estate in 1789.[11]

Calonne's successor, Loménie de Brienne, agreed to organize provincial assemblies in accordance with the traditional social order. Brienne even conceded that the nobles and clergy should be allowed half the votes in these assemblies instead of only one-third, as he first proposed.[12] His edict of June 1787, ratified without protest by the *parlement* of Paris, established the guidelines for a hybrid institution. The assemblies that he introduced into twenty-three *généralités* combined the social features of traditional estates with relatively modern administrative practices. Praised by some historians as the beginning of a veritable revolution in French administration, and condemned by others as a maneuver designed to strengthen royal authority, Brienne's provincial assemblies were a technical success and a political failure.[13] They began the task of creating a more rational hierarchy of administration, starting with municipal assemblies and proceeding upward through intermediate districts or departments to the level of *généralités*. Significant territorial changes accompanied Brienne's reform. Sub-

[10] Jean Egret, *The French Prerevolution, 1787–1788*, trans. Wesley D. Camp (Chicago, 1977), p. 2.

[11] Ibid., pp. 1–24. For a critical appraisal of Calonne's program, see Bosher, *French Finances*, pp. 166–96.

[12] Egret, *Prerevolution*, p. 64.

[13] Tocqueville emphasized the revolutionary impact of the assemblies in his classic, *The Old Regime and the French Revolution*, pp. 193–203; for a detailed history of this reform, see Pierre Renouvin, *Les assemblées provinciales de 1787: Origines, développement, résultats* (Paris, 1921). Among recent works of synthesis, compare Egret's sympathetic analysis, *Prerevolution*, p. 68, with Mousnier's derogatory remarks, *Institutions* 1:636.

ordinate provinces within the *généralités* of Bordeaux, Tours, and Moulins obtained their own provincial assemblies; *élections* in some of the *pays d'élection* were regrouped into departmental assemblies; and *bailliages* in Lorraine and Alsace were consolidated into districts.[14] Yet plans for elections to the provincial assemblies were postponed, and members were nominated by the government and co-opted by each other. The intendants designated many of the nominees and preserved authority over most financial matters, which persuaded critics of royal centralization that the assemblies were a sham. After Brienne tried without much success to manipulate the sessions of November 1787 into approving higher taxes, the government itself began to lose interest in the new administrative system. Confronted with a sudden financial crisis in August 1788, Brienne announced the convocation of the Estates-General for May 1, 1789, and urged the restoration of provincial estates. The intermediate commissions of the provincial assemblies continued to meet, but, henceforth, public debate centered on the composition and powers of the estates.[15]

Spokesmen for the Third Estate of Dauphiné set the tone of this debate by demanding an equal share of power for their estate in the assembly of this province, whose freely elected deputies would deliberate as a single body instead of forming separate orders.[16] The slogans of "doubling the Third" and "voting by head" quickly captured the enthusiasm of patriots throughout France, who applied the Dauphiné model to the organization of the Estates-General. Led by the Paris *parlement*, some nobles tried to preserve their power as a separate order, but their voices were overwhelmed by hundreds of petitions from provinces, towns, communities, and corporations that demanded equality for the Third Estate.[17] Having granted the reform of the estates of Dauphiné on October 22, 1788, the Royal Council agreed on December 27 to double the representation of the Third Estate to the Estates-General, which would organize particular estates in all the provinces. This concession to the patriot party convinced the public that the example of Dauphiné would be followed elsewhere. When voters gathered in *bailliage* assemblies to elect their deputies to the Estates-General, they frequently included a demand for provincial estates in their *cahiers de doléances*, or statements of grievances. Nearly half of the general *cahiers* endorsed this idea, with those of the Third Estate taking the lead (53 percent), followed by the nobility (47 percent) and the clergy (39 percent).[18] Throughout the nation, spokesmen for the Third Estate in-

[14] On these territorial changes, see Berlet, *Les provinces*, pp. 69–83.

[15] Mousnier, *Institutions* 1:636–38.

[16] On the reform movement in Dauphiné, see Jean Egret, *Le Parlement de Dauphiné et les affaires publiques dans la deuxième moitié du 18e siècle* (Grenoble, 1942), 2:241–318.

[17] Egret, *Prerevolution*, pp. 205–10.

[18] Tabulation based on the general cahiers published in *Archives parlementaires*, vols. 1–7,

voked their rights to equal representation in provincial estates, which would be reorganized in the *pays d'état* and introduced elsewhere in imitation of Dauphiné. As the *cahier* of the Third Estate from the *bailliage* of Etampes explained, "Because the members of the provincial assemblies were nominated by the king, we ask that they be suppressed and replaced by provincial estates, organized uniformly thoroughout the kingdom; each will consist of a single chamber whose deputies are freely elected by the three orders, half from the nobility and clergy together, and the other half from the Third Estate."[19] The *cahiers* of the nobility and the clergy rarely challenged this plan of reform, but neither did they endorse it. They might approve vaguely of provincial estates, but the Third Estate had seized the initiative for constitutional reform.

In their enthusiasm for equality and uniformity in provincial administration, spokesmen for the Third Estate overlooked the enormous discrepancies that existed in the size of historic provinces. Languedoc and Brittany were the largest *pays d'état*, with nearly 2,200 and 1,800 square leagues of territory, respectively; Normandy, a former *pays d'état* that had been subdivided into three *généralités*, contained around 1,600 square leagues; and the *pays d'état* of Burgundy, Dauphiné, and Provence ranged in size from 1,000 to 1,200 square leagues. By contrast, the entire *généralité* of Lille, which included the provinces of French Flanders, maritime Flanders, and Artois, had only 414 square leagues; and the *généralité* of Valenciennes, with the provinces of Hainaut and Cambrécis, had only 257 square leagues.[20] The *pays* of the Pyrénées that had preserved traditional estates, such as Béarn, Bigorre, and Foix, were even smaller. In the *pays d'élection* that did not have estates, similar discrepancies existed between large provinces such as Champagne and Auvergne, and small ones such as Beaujolais and Saumurois. While the idea of a *pays* often implied a natural unity based on geography as well as history, the concept of a "province" might refer to a feudal duchy or county, a jurisdiction governed by a single customary law, a diocese, a *gouvernement*, a *généralité*, or a *pays*, all with different boundaries. Some provinces contained subprovinces based on well-defined geographical characteristics, such as the mountains of upper Auvergne and the plains of lower Auvergne; others grouped together separate provinces or *pays*, such as Agenais, Angoumois, Bordelais, and Périgord, all of which were in the province of Guyenne. No geographical term appeared more frequently in the *cahiers de doléances* than "province," and none had more varied implications for the organization of space.[21]

---

and inventoried in Beatrice Fry Hyslop, *French Nationalism in 1789 According to the General Cahiers* (New York, 1968), 313–28.

[19] AP 3:283.

[20] Necker's estimates of the size of *généralités*, published by Paul Boiteau, *Etat de la France en 1789* (Paris, 1861), p. 72.

[21] On the multiple meanings of the term *province* in the old regime, see Gustave Dupont-

Behind many of the demands for provincial estates were rivalries between towns or regions. Only *pays d'état* that coincided with intendancies,
such as Brittany, Dauphiné, Languedoc, and Provence, had well-defined
boundaries that the *cahiers* simply took for granted. In the *pays d'élection*
and the *pays d'imposition*, the intendants usually administered a composite
territory, whose several provinces or *pays* each had different historic capitals. For example, the *généralité* of Moulins contained the duchy of Bourbonnais, with its capital at Moulins, the *gouvernement* of the Marche, at
Guéret, and the duchy of Nivernais, at Nevers; the *généralité* of La Rochelle combined the *gouvernements* of Aunis and Saintonge, whose separate
capitals of La Rochelle and Saintes had long disputed administrative primacy; and the *généralité* of Nancy included the duchy of Bar as well as the
duchy of Lorraine. From the *cahiers* of voters who gathered at Guéret,
Nevers, Saintes, and Bar-le-Duc came demands for separate provincial estates, which *cahiers* in the *bailliages* of La Rochelle and Nancy opposed.
Cahiers from Orléans and Chartres, Riom and Saint-Flour, Lyon and
Villefranche, Poitiers and Fontenay-le-Comte expressed similar conflicts
between existing *généralités* and subordinate provinces or *pays*. In the
southwest, where the nobility of Bordeaux had proposed the restoration
of estates for the entire province of Guyenne, *cahiers* at Angoulême, Limoges, Périgueux, Dax, and Nérac called instead for particular estates in
their respective areas. Although the nobles and clergy usually neglected to
mention which towns deserved to become the capitals of estates, this issue
naturally concerned townspeople in the Third Estate. Through their dominance of the *bailliage* assemblies that drafted general *cahiers*, deputies from
Périgueux, Bergerac, and Sarlat formed an alliance to rotate the seat of the
estates of Périgord among themselves; deputies from Dax insisted on the
primacy of this old bishopric in the *pays* of *Lannes*; and spokesmen for Dôle
invoked the historic rights of their town over Besançon as the capital of
Franche-Comté. Old claims and new pretensions came from *cahiers* of the
Third Estate at Cahors, Rodez, and Meaux, whose dioceses encompassed
the provinces known as Quercy, Rouergue, and Brie, respectively. Even
spokesmen for small towns such as Bellême, in Perche, and Trévoux, in
Dombes, entered the competition for provincial estates. The prospect of
dividing the *généralités* into smaller provinces awakened the ambitions of
townspeople throughout the kingdom.[22]

Mounting discontent with the judicial system of the old regime compounded pressures for territorial reorganization. Here, too, the government itself sparked much of the agitation by attempting to transform the

---

Ferrier, "Sur l'emploi du mot 'province,' notamment dans le language administratif de l'ancienne France," *Revue historique* 160 (1929): 241–67; 161 (1929): 278–303; and Armand
Brette, *Les limites et les divisions territoriales de la France en 1789* (Paris, 1907), pp. 57–84.

[22] Analysis based on the general *cahiers* from these *bailliages*, in AP, vols. 1–7.

hierarchy of lawcourts. Obstructed at every turn by the *parlements*, which refused to register edicts for new taxes or loans, the ministers resolved in May 1788 to take drastic action. Lamoignon, the keeper of the seals, issued a series of ordinances that stripped the *parlements* of their political rights and eliminated most of their jurisdiction over civil and criminal litigation. Forty-seven new courts known as *grands bailliages* would become appellate courts of last resort in all cases involving less than twenty thousand livres worth of property. This reform elevated forty of the existing *présidiaux* courts to the rank of *grands bailliages*, while promoting most of the *bailliages* and *sénéchaussées* to the rank of *présidiaux*. The rest of the ordinary royal courts, including *prévôtés* and *châtellenies*, would lose the right to judge civil suits, while the extraordinary lawcourts would either be suppressed or confined to purely administrative functions. As for seigneurial courts, they would survive as patrimonial rights, but their cases could be transferred immediately to a royal court at the request of either party in a civil suit. Thus, Lamoignon's reforms combined the decentralization of appellate justice with the consolidation of civil litigation in a smaller number of royal courts. Torture would also be abolished and criminal suspects protected from hasty or ill-founded judgments. Critics of old-regime justice had long advocated most of the measures that Lamoignon introduced. The government had reason to expect support from an enlightened public for its "coup d'état" against the *parlements*.[23]

Yet Lamoignon's edicts seemed to be motivated by political expediency, and they provoked a storm of controversy in the provinces. Defenders of the *parlements* denounced the minister for his "sinister project of bringing everything into a unitary system . . . , leaving the whole of France, instead of a beloved king, only a feared master, and miserable slaves instead of faithful subjects." Riots broke out in several towns that had *parlements*, as the nobles of the robe issued fiery remonstrances against Lamoignon's edicts and refused to suspend their sessions.[24] Patriots leapt into the fray. "Let everybody unite," wrote the *avocat* Barnave in Dauphiné. "Rally to the party of the magistracy, and speak out in your turn because they can no longer express their will. Let all municipalities, provincial orders, classes and corps join their supplications." The ministry retaliated with numerous pamphlets that accused the *parlementaires* of false patriotism. Why did

[23] Marcel Marion, *La Garde des Sceaux Lamoignon et la réforme judiciare de 1788* (Paris, 1905); and Egret, *Prerevolution*, pp. 71–77, 154–78. On the background of the debate over the administration of justice, see John A. Carey, *Judicial Reform in France before the Revolution of 1789* (Cambridge, Mass., 1981).

[24] Nobles of the robe were magistrates whose titles of nobility derived from the ownership of offices in *parlements* and other sovereign courts. They were distinguished from the nobles of the sword, who generally inherited their titles from distant ancestors and followed a family tradition of military service to the king.

these bodies oppose the land tax and judicial reform? "Because once the land tax is approved, they see themselves, the richest proprietors in the realm, carrying the major share of the burden they never minded, up to now, imposing on your misery; because the judicial reform with its more numerous courts, although to your benefit, must humble their pride and shackle their greed."[25]

Such ideological disputes overlapped with rivalries between towns that calculated their gains or losses from the reforms. Towns with *parlements* would suffer from the declining business of their lawcourts. Spokesmen for such provincial capitals decried the location of appellate courts in small and undistinguished towns, where "people see each other all the time; a thousand emotions unite or divide them. The sanctuary of justice would be frequently tainted with prejudice, hatred or vengeance."[26] Towns promoted in rank by Lamoignon's reforms took a different view of matters. "You no doubt knew . . . of the folly that gripped all Valence against the *parlement* [of Grenoble]," confided Madame de la Rollière to Mademoiselle de Franquières. "They have gleefully predicted and hoped that the *grand bailliage* established at Valence would bring them a fortune based on the ruins of Grenoble."[27] In Champagne, the merchants and shopkeepers of Châlons-sur-Marne urged the judges on the *présidial* to accept their promotion to a *grand bailliage*, which would serve "the general interest of the town" by attracting rich and opulent magistrates and numerous litigants. Several officeholders on the *bureau des finances* and the *élection*, both destined for suppression, also agreed to serve on the new lawcourt.[28] At Troyes, however, the officers of the *présidial*, which was passed over by the ministry, greeted with contempt news that their opportunistic colleagues at Châlons had registered the edicts.[29] Several dozen other *présidiaux* that failed to achieve promotion to *grand bailliages* also denounced the reforms, motivated less by sympathy for the *parlements* than by envy for more fortunate rivals.[30]

After so much tumult and intrigue, Lamoignon's edicts were withdrawn in September 1788 as abruptly as they had been introduced in May. Henceforth, only the Estates-General would possess the authority to reform the judicial system. Men of law filled many of the *cahiers de doléances*

---

[25] Pamphlets cited in Egret, *Prerevolution*, pp. 158–62.

[26] Pamphlet cited in ibid., pp. 156–57.

[27] Letter cited in Anatole de Gallier, *La vie de province au 18e siècle* (Paris, 1877), pp. 117–18.

[28] Pamphlet in AN ADXVI 49.

[29] Albert Babeau, *Histoire de Troyes pendant la Revolution* (Paris, 1873), 1:55.

[30] Egret cites 17 out of the 27 *présidiaux* not promoted to *grands bailliages* within the jurisdiction of the Paris *parlement*, all 10 of those subordinated to the *parlement* of Toulouse, and all 3 of those subordinated to the *parlement* of Dijon, in *Prerevolution*, p. 167.

with proposals for improving the administration of justice. They often agreed with the underlying principles of Lamoignon's edicts: *rapprochement*, or bringing justice closer to the people; simplification; and uniformity. Although very few *cahiers* attacked the *parlements* directly, many wanted to reduce the hierarchy of appeals and abolish the venality of office.[31] All three estates joined in the criticism of extraordinary lawcourts, which were obviously destined for suppression. A vocal minority of the Third Estate also wanted to eliminate all the seigneurial courts, which might be replaced by justices of the peace or transferred to the jurisdiction of royal courts.[32] Many *cahiers* also protested the government's reliance on the *bailliages* as a territorial framework for elections to the Estates-General. No population census of the *bailliages* had ever been undertaken, but these circumscriptions obviously varied enormously in size, just like their chief towns. Efforts to distinguish between primary and secondary *bailliages* only compounded inequities in the representation of regions and communities. While 174 primary *bailliages* elected deputies directly, another 243 *bailliages* had to choose delegations to general assemblies in other towns, whose deputies often stood a better chance of being elected to the Estates-General.[33] The *cahier* of the Third Estate of Vitry-le-François reported that "the greater number of citizens" were complaining about the "astonishing medley in the composition of the *bailliages*." Future elections should be based on "districts equal either in population or in taxation."[34] Whether critics wanted to reorganize the lawcourts or redraw the boundaries of electoral constituencies, they advocated changes in the territorial hierarchy of jurisdictions.

Dramatic events in the summer of 1789 provided further impetus for a new division of the kingdom. The Estates-General, transformed into a National Assembly of all three orders and empowered to regenerate the state by writing a constitution, found itself confronted by uprisings in the provinces. As reports reached the Assembly that crowds of peasants were burning seigneurial registers and assaulting tax collectors, deputies met on the night of August 4 and agreed to destroy privilege in all its forms. Serfdom

---

[31] The general *cahier* of the Third Estate in the *bailliage* of Quimper wanted to suppress all the *parlements*, and those in the *bailliages* of Amiens and Poitiers wanted new sovereign courts for their own towns: AP 5:420, 515; AP 6:108. By contrast, 223 general *cahiers* denounced the venality of office, according to Hyslop, *French Nationalism*, p. 72.

[32] Hyslop counted 63 general *cahiers* that wanted seigneurial courts abolished, *French Nationalism*, p. 115. Concerning the ideological background of this demand, see John Mackrell, "Criticism of Seigniorial Justice in Eighteenth-Century France," in *French Government and Society, 1500–1850: Essays in Memory of Alfred Cobban*, ed. J. F. Bosher (London, 1973), pp. 123–44.

[33] Tabulation based on Armand Brette, *Les Constituants: Liste des députés et des suppléants élus à l'Assemblée Constituante de 1789* (Paris, 1897).

[34] Cited by Hyslop, *French Nationalism*, p. 75.

would be abolished, seigneurial lawcourts and venal offices suppressed, taxes levied equally on all citizens, tithes replaced, and the privileges of particular provinces and towns abandoned. In a single blow, the Assembly leveled the entire superstructure of rights and exemptions that had distinguished nobles from bourgeois, clerics from laymen, royal officials from ordinary townspeople, *pays d'état* from *pays d'élection*, and *bonnes villes* from bourgs and villages. Henceforth, the kingdom resembled a tabula rasa, awaiting the creation of a new judicial system, a new fiscal administration, a new electoral procedure, and even a new religious hierarchy.[35]

A series of proposals for territorial reform accompanied this critical assault on the old regime. Abbé Sièyes, Duport, Bergasse, Mounier, and Dupont de Nemours all agreed that a new organization of space needed to be introduced, but each of these influential deputies approached the problem from a different point of view. Sièyes wanted to "melt the various peoples of France into a single people, and the various provinces into a single Empire."[36] As he wrote in defending a geometrical plan of division into 80 departments and 720 districts, "I have sensed for a long time the necessity of submitting the area of France to a new division. If we miss this occasion, it will not return again, and the provinces will guard eternally their esprit de corps, their privileges, their pretensions, their jealousies."[37] Duport agreed that large provinces would endanger the authority of the National Assembly, but he developed a different rationale for a division into around 70 smaller provinces, shaped like squares and subdivided into districts and municipalities. Only the prompt organization of provincial and district assemblies could prevent anarchy from spreading in the countryside. At a moment of general collapse in public authority, existing bonds of solidarity needed to be reinforced, so Duport wanted to subdivide the large provinces rather than ignore traditional boundaries altogether. Bergasse had yet another concern, the establishment of a uniform system of justice. His report on judicial reform, delivered in the name of the Comité de Constitution, or C.C., on August 17, proposed that each province acquire a supreme court, and each district a second-order tribunal. To achieve uniformity, Bergasse wanted the provinces to be approximately equal in area, which would also facilitate provincial administration. As for Mounier, his constitutional plan, submitted on August 31, focused attention on elections to the national legislature and proposed a division of the kingdom into districts equal in population rather than area. Each district would con-

---

[35] Measures voted on the night of Aug. 4, 1789, AP 8:350, and ratified in a general decree on Aug. 11, AP 8:397–98.

[36] Sièyes, *Vues sur les moyens d'éxecution*, cited by Lebègue, *Thouret*, 178–79.

[37] [Emmanuel Joseph Sièyes], *Observations sur le rapport du Comité de Constitution concernant la nouvelle organisation de la France, par un député à l'Assemblée Nationale, au 2 octobre 1789* [Paris, 1789], pp. 1–2.

tain around 150,000 people and would elect three deputies to the national legislature. Finally, on September 24, Dupont de Nemours followed Turgot and Condorcet in describing a plan to divide the kingdom into seventy circles, each with a radius of ten, twelve, or at most fifteen leagues. These circles would increase administrative efficiency while reducing the distance that citizens had to travel in order to pay taxes or seek justice. They could also serve as dioceses for a state-funded church, and each of them could be subdivided into four or five districts or *bailliages* for the purposes of justice and administration.[38]

Only Dupont de Nemours and Abbé Sièyes suggested how the map of France might be redrawn in accordance with their ideas. Dupont alluded to a mysterious plan of division that has left no other trace in the historical record: a map with seventy circles, each drawn around one of the seventy largest towns, and each following the natural limits of rivers and mountains.[39] If anyone did draw such a map, its territorial imbalances would quickly have become apparent. As noted in chapter 1, large towns were concentrated along the seacoast and in densely populated river valleys, so that circles drawn around them would vary dramatically in area. Furthermore, circles with equal radiuses might encompass areas that had quite different population densities, resulting in substantial deviations from the average population size of all circles, which Dupont calculated as 360,000 souls. Finally, any administrative system would need to cover the entire kingdom, but Dupont's plan would leave gaps between the circumference of each circle. Modern geographers have shown that hexagons provide the most rational modeling of space within a hierarchical system of central places, but for eighteenth-century thinkers, squares offered a simple model for dividing a map into uniform areas.[40] Convinced that territorial equality was a more important principle than centrality, Abbé Sièyes became the leading advocate of a division into squares. At one point, Sièyes had proposed to designate on a map of France, at roughly equal distances, eighty-one towns to serve as departmental seats. Municipalities in the provinces would then be free to choose whatever central place they preferred. He discovered, however, that "the execution of this idea seemed to involve too many disadvantages," so he abandoned it in favor of dividing the kingdom into squares first, and then choosing the central places afterward.[41] The interests of towns, which would often conflict with each other, should be subordinated to a preliminary map of departmental boundaries.

[38] The texts by Duport, Bergasse, Mounier, and Dupont de Nemours are in AP 8:306, and 9:224–26, 48–82; AP 8:440–50, 523; and AP 9:149, n. 1.

[39] AP 9:149.

[40] The first geographer to develop a hexagonal model of space was Walter Christaller, *Central Places in Southern Germany*, trans. C. W. Baskin (Englewood Cliffs, N.J., 1966).

[41] [Sièyes], *Observations*, pp. 6–7.

Sièyes's ingenious plan of division combined an algebraic calculus of electoral representation with a geometrical analysis of space. As a deputy from Paris, he began his reasoning with the premise that the nation's capital should have a unique position within the constitution of the kingdom. Its population and wealth merited a larger representation in the National Assembly than that of any other electoral constituency, and its municipality needed to exercise the same powers as provincial administrations. To define the territory of Paris as both a "municipality" and a "province," he reasoned as follows: "Let us begin by supposing that all the territory of France can be divided into 720 parts, or Communes, each around 36 square leagues in area, approaching as much as possible a square of 6 by 6 leagues. Paris will be the central city."[42] This mathematical supposition was consistent with the fact that the territory of the kingdom measured around 26,000 square leagues, a number very close to the product of 36 square leagues by 720 districts (25,920). Each district would possess a municipal administration, but it would also need a higher-order constitution "in order to make all the parts of France a great totality, governed by the same legislation and the same national administration."[43] Squares can be combined in accordance with many numerical factors that yield a total of 720, ranging from 2 to 360, but Sièyes wanted an intermediate number divisible by three, which would simplify calculations of the number of deputies that each circumscription would be entitled to elect. As Sièyes wrote about his calculus of proportional representation, "I exhausted a thousand combinations before settling on the one that I am presenting."[44] The number 9 suited his calculus perfectly. With 9 communes per department, and 80 departments in the kingdom, he could attach an invariable representation of 3 deputies to each department, for a total of 240 deputies, while distributing an additional 480 deputies to departments in proportion to their population and taxable wealth. Sièyes argued that in this scheme of representation, Paris should have a unique position as both a commune *and* a department, with all its deputies based on population and wealth, and none based on territory. Thus, the commune of Paris would form an 81st department, whose existence would not affect the territorial calculus that Sièyes had devised for the 80 other departments.

Sièyes's simple geometry of squares could easily be represented on a map, whose 80 departments would each have 18 leagues to a side, or 324 square leagues. The cartographic procedure that Sièyes recommended involved several steps. First of all, an ideal map of squares would be traced

---

[42] Sièyes, *Quelques idées de constitution applicable à la ville de Paris en juillet 1789* (Versailles, 1789), p. 3. Sièyes wrote this document in July for the new municipality of Paris, but he did not publish it until Sept. 24.

[43] Ibid., p. 4.

[44] Ibid., p. 15.

on the standard map of the kingdom that the famous cartographer Cassini had made in the eighteenth century. As Sièyes explained:

> Taking Paris as the center, I would form a perfect square with radiuses of 9 leagues, or sides of 18 by 18 leagues, giving an area of 324 square leagues. On each side of this map, I would form another square with the same size, and so on until I reached the most distant frontiers. It is clear that in approaching the frontiers, I would no longer have my perfect square, but I would always circumscribe, as much as possible, spaces encompassing around 324 square leagues. . . . It is more than likely that this method will result in 80 departments, because 80 divisions of 324 square leagues in area just about exhausts the 26,000 leagues that the entire territory of France is supposed to have.[45]

Like the mathematical model of an experimental scientist, this map would then be used to circumscribe equal areas within the existing boundaries of *généralités*, provinces, *bailliages*, and so forth, as indicated by a series of overlay maps. Sièyes insisted on the practicality of this operation. The ideal squares would become irregular forms as they were modified in accordance with historical and geographical circumstances, but each department would still approximate a standard area of 324 square leagues. This done, Sièyes would hold a preliminary conference with deputies from the various provinces, show them his work, and ask for their advice. After determining the departmental boundaries, he would divide each department into 9 communes each with an area of 36 square leagues, using the same procedure of moving from an ideal type to a practical application. Only at this point would he indicate the towns that might have pretensions to become the seats of departments or communes. The deputies themselves could assemble by *généralité* to choose these chief towns, after which a finished copy of the map would be made. All this work would then be submitted to communal and departmental assemblies, whose proposals for appropriate changes would be granted by the National Assembly.[46]

A royal cartographer by the name of Robert de Hesseln had already developed a technique for measuring distances from Paris by imposing a rectangular grid on Cassini's map. De Hesseln used a double system of straight lines, parallel to the meridian of Paris and perpendicular to it. First he traced a tripartite grid to create 9 large "regions," and then he followed the same procedure to subdivide each region into 9 "countries" and each country into 9 "districts." This yielded a total of 81 countries and 729 districts, which resembled Sièyes's model of 80 departments and 720 communes. However, de Hesseln's countries were nearly twice as large as Sièyes's departments, which implies that Sièyes arrived independently at

[45] [Sièyes], *Observations*, p. 3.
[46] Ibid., pp. 4–6.

the idea of subdividing the kingdom into 80 squares, each with an area of 324 leagues. De Hesseln published his *Nouvelle topographie de la France* in 1780 and died shortly before the outbreak of the Revolution. The successor to his establishment, L. Hennequin, became a professional consultant for the C.C. in September 1789. Hennequin used the same grid map that de Hesseln had invented in order to apply Sièyes's ideas. In a preliminary sketch, he inscribed a checkerboard of perfect squares on Hesseln's map by combining Hesseln's "districts," two by two, into squares four-ninths as large as de Hesseln's "countries." This checkerboard consisted of 84 squares located entirely within the kingdom and another 30 squares that contained portions of territory near the frontiers. Hennequin noted that this "first sketch" would be accompanied as soon as possible by a more realistic map of departmental boundaries that deviated as little as possible from "the old boundaries and those formed naturally by rivers, mountains, etc., for ease of communications." Indeed, he prepared this second map from another copy of de Hesseln's rectangular grid. It traced the irregular shapes of exactly 80 departments, some rectangular and others oblong, and in doing so it preserved the external boundaries of large *pays d'état* such as Brittany and Languedoc. Hennequin made no effort to place large towns in the center of their respective departments. His realistic map of departments, like Sièyes's plan, represented a division of the kingdom into equal territories, not an array of central places.[47]

In addition to Sièyes, seven other deputies served on the reorganized Comité de Constitution that drafted legislation in September for a territorial reorganization of the state. The coauthor of this committee's plan was a lawyer from Normandy, Jacques-Guillaume Thouret, who had considerable administrative experience. Thouret had served on the intermediate commission of the provincial assembly of Rouen, where he had corresponded with departmental assemblies and municipalities. Convinced by Sièyes that the existing provinces should be divided into 80 departments, he designed a plan for a second tier of administrative and electoral assemblies in the 720 communes that Sièyes had mentioned only with respect to Paris. Thouret's master idea was to base the double edifice of national representation and provincial administration on a common foundation. He worked out the details of this system, which used the territorial divisions that Sièyes proposed in order to form electoral colleges, administrative as-

[47] On de Hesseln and L. Hennequin, see René Hennequin, *La formation de l'Aisne*, pp. 54–59. For the differences between Sièyes's plan and Hesseln's rectangular grid, see Bourdon, "La formation des départements de l'Est," 189–91. Both of Hennequin's maps, which refer to the plan of division submitted to the National Assembly by the Constitutional Committee on Sept. 29, 1789, have been reproduced by Josef Konvitz, *Cartography in France, 1660–1848* (Chicago, 1987), pp. 45–46, on the basis of originals in AN NN 50:6–7. Map 6.1 is based on another copy of Hennequin's second map, preserved in the Bibliothèque Nationale.

semblies, and executive directories in the departments and communal districts. Beneath these new circumscriptions, an additional level of primary assemblies would be established for electoral purposes in small territories known as cantons, each four leagues square. Only "active citizens," who paid taxes worth three days of labor, would vote in these primary assemblies. They would choose delegates to electoral assemblies in the communal districts, who would vote in turn for delegates to departmental assemblies, where deputies to the National Assembly would finally be chosen. Electors delegated to the communes and departments would also vote for the representatives who would form the administrative assemblies and choose the directories in these respective territories. Thus, a hierarchy of electoral colleges would generate the hierarchy of administrative institutions.[48]

Speaking in the name of the C.C., Thouret presented this system in a report to the National Assembly on September 29. The first section of his report, "On the Bases of Proportional Representation," emphasized that none of the ancient divisions of the kingdom—dioceses, *gouvernements*, *généralités*, and *bailliages*—could be applied to an electoral system based on territorial equality. "Since the order that the Constitution is going to establish is something new, why subjugate ourselves to old imperfections that violate its spirit and obstruct its operation, when reason and public utility command us to avoid both of these dangers?"[49] In order to guarantee proportional representation and increase administrative efficiency, Thouret disregarded local communities as well as provinces. Primary assemblies within the cantons would subdivide the voters of towns and aggregate those of villages in accordance with an abstract rule of one assembly per nine hundred voters. As Thouret emphasized in the second part of his report, towns and villages would also be reorganized into nine communal municipalities in each department. Separate administrative institutions in each village were too often at the mercy of seigneurs or priests, and those in small towns were easily dominated by a few notables. He reasoned that "the only means of emancipating municipal authority is to distribute it in larger masses, and to bestow more enlightenment and power on its agents by reducing their numbers."[50] The communities in which townspeople and villagers lived and worked should have only mayors and small municipal bureaus to handle routine business. All serious matters, including taxation, public order, and the deployment of the milita, should be under the authority of administrators in the communal districts.

[48] Concerning Thouret's role in the division of France, see Lebègue, *Thouret*, pp. 170–206.
[49] AP 9:202. For excellent maps that show the discrepancies in the territorial boundaries of the *gouvernements*, *généralités*, *parlements*, *bailliages*, and subdelegations in 1789, see Nordman and Revel, "La division de l'espace français," pp. 124–26, 131.
[50] AP 9:208.

Like the intendants of the old regime, Thouret and his colleagues on the C.C. opposed local autonomy, which they equated with inefficiency and corruption. Their goal was an authoritarian system of administration, tempered by elections, that would unify the nation and strengthen the National Assembly.[51]

Debate on the committee's plan did not begin until November 3, mainly because the political crisis known as the October Days interrupted the deliberations of the National Assembly and forced the deputies as well as the royal court to move from Versailles to Paris. This delay also permitted members of the Assembly to consult with their constituents back home, and to discuss among themselves the advantages and disadvantages of the committee's abstract approach to the division of the kingdom. Thouret initiated the debate by challenging deputies who raised objections to the plan on the basis of local and provincial interests:

> If we viewed ourselves less as the representatives of the nation than as spokesmen for the town, the *bailliage*, or the province that sent us; if, misled by this false opinion of our duties, speaking much of our *pays* and very little of the kingdom, we placed provincial loyalties on an equal level with the national interest; I dare to ask, would we be worthy to have been chosen as the regenerators of the state?[52]

Provincial loyalty, which some deputies from the *pays d'état* were trying to defend, is "nothing in the state but an individual ethos, enemy of the true national ethos." Yet Thouret himself appealed to the interest of towns that would benefit from the creation of several administrative bodies in large provinces: "This is the means of sharing among several towns the advantage of becoming administrative centers, which otherwise would be enjoyed, with all the corresponding influence, exclusively by the former capitals."[53] Indeed, the debate over the division of the kingdom quickly revealed that urban fears and ambitions influenced the views of many deputies. Having begun as a territorial division that ignored towns, the C.C.'s plan became the focal point of a controversy over the role of urban communities in the organization of the state.

Mirabeau, one of the most prominent orators in the National Assembly, followed Thouret to the podium with a different plan of division that favored large towns in densely populated areas of the nation. As a deputy elected from both Aix and Marseille, which were in the same area of lower Provence, Mirabeau must have known that a division into 80 departments of equal area would probably place these two towns, one an old provincial

---

[51] For an excellent analysis of the ideological goals of this project, see Ozouf-Marignier, *La formation des départements*, pp. 35–43, 69–107.

[52] AP 9:655.

[53] Ibid., pp. 656–57.

capital and the other a great seaport, in the same department.[54] He proposed instead that population rather than territory be used as the main criterion for dividing provinces, and that 120 instead of 80 departments be established. A division based on equal areas would result in monstrous inequalities: "The same extent of territory can be covered by forests or by cities; either sterile wastelands or fertile fields; here uninhabited mountains, and there an excessively dense population."[55] Departments should be formed for men and not for the soil. In his speech of November 3, Mirabeau pointed out that by multiplying departments, a greater number of towns would be accorded the advantage of becoming administrative centers and a larger number of citizens would have access to a career in public affairs. A week later, he linked his plan more explicitly to the interests of large towns. By varying the territory of 120 departments while equalizing their populations, at least 25 of these divisions would consist primarily of a single town, such as Marseille, Lyon, Bordeaux, Rouen, Rennes, Nantes, and Toulouse. Departments containing a large town would need only a small number of villages in order to complete their populations, which would average 200,000 inhabitants per department.[56] The little agglomerations in such departments would not need to form communal districts either. Indeed, Mirabeau argued that every town and village should possess its own municipal administration and send delegates directly to the departmental electoral assembly. Intermediate constituencies and agencies of administration would only create chaos and confusion. In his plan, the 720 communes and 6,480 cantons that the C.C. proposed would be eliminated.

A large number of deputies agreed with Mirabeau that municipal institutions in the towns and villages should be strengthened, but not many supported his plan to multiply the departments. Deputies from several provincial capitals tried instead to defend medium-sized provinces against any subdivision at all. They raised fears of Parisian domination over the rest of the nation. In the words of Pison du Galand, a lawyer from Grenoble, the system of the committee would "break the balance or equilibrium between each province." Paris would have a department of 600,000–700,000 inhabitants, as compared with an average population of only 300,000 in the other departments. "Right now, the provinces are on an equal level with Paris, because of their population. . . . Why break up this happy harmony? You fear the spirit of the provinces. But is the spirit of great cities no less dangerous?"[57] Contrasting the luxury of moneyed men in Paris with the

[54] Mirabeau opted for Aix, but unlike the other deputies from this town, he supported the partition of Provence into departments.

[55] Speech on Nov. 3, AP 9:660.

[56] Speech on Nov. 10, AP 9:735.

[57] Speech on Nov. 10, AP 9:737.

frugality of agricultural populations in the provinces, Pison du Galand proposed a third plan of division that would counterbalance Parisian influence by creating only 36 large departments, each with an average population of 700,000 inhabitants. Such a system would preserve the administrative and judicial unity of provinces such as Dauphiné, where it would parallel the existing division into *généralités*. Pison did not submit his plan until November 10, but it inspired prompt support from deputies who represented the historic capitals of Franche-Comté and Auvergne, both medium-sized provinces that resembled Dauphiné in territory and population. As François Martin, a lawyer from Besançon, argued, "Paris already has a population larger than my province. Well, in the plan of the Comité de Constitution, Paris will remain Paris . . . but my province will be cut up into three pieces."[58] Whichever department of Franche-Comté included Besançon would be crushed by the costs of military administration in this town, while the other two departments would refuse to contribute to the improvement of navigation or the construction of roads in the center of the province. Martin was willing to support the partition of large provinces such as Brittany and Languedoc, but he feared that Besançon would suffer from a division of Franche-Comté that reduced the scale of administration, undermined public works, multiplied administrative costs, and encouraged the proliferation of appellate lawcourts.[59]

Supporters of a division into eighty departments countered such arguments with appeals to the interests of small towns and the countryside. Duquesnoy, a deputy from the little town of Briey, in Lorraine, assured the National Assembly that "if the operation which the Comité de Constitution has proposed encounters any obstacles, these will come uniquely from the large towns that want to perpetuate the terrible aristocracy that they have been exercising over the countryside and small towns. The small towns, in particular, will greet with joy the project of your committee, because, above all, their inhabitants want administration to be closer to them."[60] Duquesnoy singled out for praise the plan to subdivide departments into communal districts, which would "bring life to small towns and villages" and would spare rural dwellers "the enormous cost of frequent trips to provincial capitals." Otherwise, all administration would be concentrated in large towns, killing agriculture and increasing "the awful and terrifying immensity of towns that, like polyps, are exhausting the king-

[58] "Opinion" delivered on Nov. 11, AP 9:752.

[59] Ibid., 752–55. See also the speech of Malouet, a deputy from Riom, Nov. 12, AP 10:4–5. Riom claimed to be the capital of Auvergne, a province with a population of around 700,000, and Malouet called for 40 provinces, ranging in population from 600,000 to 800,000.

[60] Speech on Nov. 4, reported in *Le point du jour*, vol. 4, issue 125 (henceforth cited as 4:125), p. 48.

dom."[61] Gossin, a deputy from Bar-le-Duc, agreed that the plan of the Committee would decentralize administrative activity so that a few large towns would no longer monopolize all the advantages of the government: "The old provincial administrations were truly useful only to large towns; their intermediate commissions were nearly always composed of deputies from the capital. . . . Everything always moves toward the center of interests or the theater of honor, so the dominant town monopolized wealth, resources, and incentives for growth."[62]

Just as a small number of departments would restrict the advantages of administration to the old provincial capitals, so an excessive number of departments would enable large towns to dominate the feeble rural areas attached to them. In countering Mirabeau's plan, Thouret argued that a division into eighty departments, "by extending administrative areas, gives the countryside greater strength against the towns."[63] Another member of the C.C., the Parisian lawyer Target, added that departments based on population would be excessively large in areas of the nation that had low population densities. Yet the National Assembly hoped to stimulate the economic development of such backward areas. "I insist, above all, that the greater the poverty of a *pays*, the more means of assistance should be provided for it."[64] Furthermore, poor citizens should not be obligated to travel long distances in order to speak to administrators. A division into eighty rectangular departments, each with a half-diagonal of eleven to twelve leagues, would permit travelers from any point to reach the administrative center in a day's journey. In like manner, subdivisions of the departments into communal districts would reduce travel costs and bring together townspeople and villagers in "schools of patriotism." A deputy from the province of Berry, Bengy de Puyvallée, had argued that the Committee's plan of local administration would consolidate a "municipal aristocracy" of towns, but Target replied that urban commerce and rural property have common interests, based on a market economy. "Far from separating the agents of commerce from the agents of production, let us unite them in the same patriotic assemblies."[65]

A substantial majority of deputies supported these arguments in favor of dividing the provinces into departments, and the departments into communal districts. Many viewed themselves as the representatives of towns that had not possessed any provincial institutions during the old regime. Indeed, deputies from more than four hundred towns sat in the National Assembly, and only one-tenth of them came from provincial capitals that

[61] Different version of the same speech, in AP 9:672.
[62] "Opinion" published in AP 10:703–4.
[63] Speech on Nov. 11, AP 9:758.
[64] Speech on Nov. 11, AP 9:744.
[65] Ibid., AP 9:748, replying to Bengy de Puyvallée's speech on Nov. 5, AP 9:683.

might lose territorial influence if eighty departments were created.[66] The parochial ambitions of townspeople reinforced arguments based on political ideology and administrative rationality. Why preserve the existing *généralités* when they benefited so few towns? Why run the risk of fostering federalism by organizing representative assemblies in the large *pays d'état*, which had always resisted the authority of the monarchy? Just as the National Assembly was about to open its debate on territorial reform, word arrived that nobles were gathering in Brittany and Languedoc to protest the abolition of provincial rights and freedoms. Those from Toulouse declared "the most formal opposition to the geometrical division of the kingdom in general, and the province of Languedoc in particular."[67] Such aristocratic pretensions only strengthened the determination of patriots in the National Assembly to destroy the old provinces. Defenders of the *pays d'état* argued in vain that large provinces such as Languedoc offered great financial resources for public works.[68] Henceforth, all towns and regions would benefit equally from the revenues of a united empire. Territorial uniformity and political equality went hand in hand. Even some deputies from Languedoc followed Rabaut Saint-Etienne, a member of the C.C. from Nîmes, who argued that "in the distribution of power and the means of action, equality is perfection."[69]

To achieve this goal of equality, the National Assembly might adopt a plan based on a division into equal areas or equal populations. Here the technical virtues of Thouret's plan appealed to many deputies. It combined a variable measure of voting strength, based on population and taxable wealth, with a permanent framework of administration. As one Parisian newspaper reported, the system of representation, election, and administration that Thouret presented seemed "well integrated in all its parts; it was very much applauded."[70] Mirabeau's critique aroused initial enthusiasm, too, but Thouret pointed out that the boundaries of departments based on equal populations would be much more difficult to determine than those based on equal areas. A division into departments with 500,000–600,000 inhabitants, such as Gaultier de Biauzat, a deputy from Clermont-Ferrand, proposed, would require amalgamating all kinds of lo-

---

[66] I have calculated that only 71 of the 616 deputies from the Third Estate, 22 of the 255 nobles from the Second Estate, and 34 of the 296 deputies from the First Estate who sat in the Assembly between Nov. 1789 and Feb. 1790 came from provincial seats of *généralités* that were subdivided into smaller departments. A further 25 deputies from the Third Estate, at least 79 from the Second Estate, and 12 from the First Estate resided in Paris. Data based on Brette, *Les Constituants*; and Brette, *Recueil de documents*, vol. 2. For further details on the geographical and social origins of the deputies, see chapter 5.

[67] Declaration on Oct. 16, reported by *Le point du jour* 4:121, pp. 2–3.

[68] Speech of Ramel-Nogaret, a lawyer from Carcassonne, Nov. 11, AP 9:751.

[69] *Nouvelles Réflexions*, reprinted in AP 9:667.

[70] *Le point du jour*, 4:94, p. 154.

calities and *pays* that had never been associated before. Existing limits would be violated, ranging from the natural barriers of mountains and rivers to provincial boundaries involving custom and language. How could the population of the kingdom be subdivided so accurately? While the departmental plan of the C.C. had already been traced on a map, Thouret asked Biauzat whether he had done the same. "How many months will he need before showing it to us?"[71] The same technical problem would confront Mirabeau, who wanted an even more complicated division based on taxable wealth as well as population. Furthermore, the boundaries that Mirabeau and other critics proposed would have to be changed in accordance with the growth or decline of population in the future. Such changes would be an "intolerable vice" in the administrative order, which must be based on fixed and permanent boundaries. Redistricting for electoral purposes would also be difficult to undertake in a timely fashion.[72] Far from being "useless, impractical and dangerous," as a lawyer from the small province of Bugey had claimed, the map drawn up by the C.C. served as a realistic guide to a territorial division that would be stable and enduring.[73]

Critics of the Committee's plan did succeed, however, in persuading Thouret and his colleagues to adopt a flexible procedure for creating the departments. "Your committee has cut France into eighty pieces, like scraps of cloth," complained Bengy de Puyvallée.[74] In reply, the Committee agreed to modify its plan in accordance with the views of deputies from the various provinces, meeting in committees. These modifications would take into account the existing boundaries of provinces and natural relations of proximity, communications, and commerce.[75] Furthermore, the total number of departments would not be specified in advance of this committee work. When the National Assembly voted on November 11, 1789, to begin a new process of division, it adopted an amendment that "the number of departments will be from 75 to 85" instead of "around 80."[76] Thus, the average size of departments could vary appreciably from the norm of 324 square leagues, depending on local circumstances. By consulting with deputies from the various provinces before submitting decrees for the formation of particular departments, the C.C. tried to conciliate public opinion. Its summary report on the new division of the kingdom, delivered by Bureaux de Pusy on January 8, 1790, emphasized the importance of these consultations: "It was essential not to break too abruptly the moral and

[71] Speech on Nov. 9, AP 9:724. In fact, none of the advocates of a division based on population tried to illustrate his plan on a map.

[72] Speech on Nov. 11, AP 9:755–56.

[73] Speech by Brillat-Savarin, Oct. 19, AP 9:460.

[74] Speech on Nov. 5, AP 9:683.

[75] Speech by Target, Nov. 11, AP 9:748.

[76] AP 9:759.

political relations that exist among the various parts of the empire."[77] Deputies in the committees first agreed on the respective limits of their provinces and then recommended how many departments and lesser administrative divisions should be established. The C.C. tried to mediate disputes among the members of each provincial committee, and it referred all decisions to a final vote in the National Assembly.[78]

These consultations were all the more necessary because the deputies rejected the Committee's plan to divide every department into precisely nine "communes." A very large majority agreed that variations in population and wealth should be taken into account at this intermediate level of the administrative system.[79] Several deputies invoked the example of provinces that were already subdivided into a smaller number of dioceses, *élections*, or districts; others calculated that nine communes per department would increase administrative costs excessively and would employ too many people; and some probably anticipated that lawcourts for their hometowns would have a larger jurisdiction if they reduced the number of communes. Although Mirabeau received little support for his plan to eliminate them altogether, other critics proposed three, four, or six communes per department, and a few argued persuasively that the number should vary according to local circumstances.[80] Deputies also insisted that intermediate assemblies should not absorb the municipalities in the towns and villages, as the Committee had proposed. To preserve social order and reduce conflicts between town and countryside, the existing municipalities should be reformed rather than replaced by only 720 "communes." As Ramel-Nogaret, a lawyer from Carcassonne argued, "The French are not like Tartars, dispersed over the surface of the land; they are united in towns, in bourgs, in villages. Give these separate towns, bourgs and villages their own particular and separate administrations."[81] If every community obtained a municipality, fewer intermediate assemblies would be needed. Thus, a majority of deputies voted on November 12 to establish municipalities, or communes, in every town, bourg, and rural community; to describe intermediate institutions as "districts" rather than "communes"; and to permit

---

[77] AP 11:119.

[78] On these procedures, see Berlet, *Les provinces*, pp. 233–37.

[79] *Journal des Etats-Généraux*, Nov. 12, 5:472, reporting the vote against a decree for 9 districts per department.

[80] Pison du Galand was the only deputy who agreed publicly with Mirabeau; Adrien Duport wanted 240 districts in the entire kingdom; Malouet proposed 320; M. Reubell, a lawyer from Colmar, wanted 6 per department; Barnave, a lawyer from Grenoble, wanted 3 or 4 per department; Pellerin, a lawyer from Nantes, argued that the number should depend on the area, population, and wealth of each province; and Pétion de Villeneuve thought it should vary according to local circumstances such as the size of towns, bourgs, and villages. AP 9:482, 660, 673, 686, 722, 738; and 10:5–6.

[81] Speech on Nov. 11, AP 9:752.

as few as three districts in each department. The National Assembly itself would decide precisely how many districts to establish, after deputies reorganized themselves into committees based on the new departments.[82]

Provincial and departmental committees also had the task of recommending which towns would become administrative seats. This question exercised profound influence over the manner in which deputies divided the provinces and the departments. The new boundaries would determine the geographical location of towns at the center or periphery of administrative regions. Deputies who defended the interests of particular towns were quick to recognize that the argument for *rapprochement*, or bringing justice and administration closer to the people, hinged on the centrality of towns. As one lawyer from Angoulême wrote to his constituents, "In all the proposed divisions, our town always forms a central point that will necessarily obtain the seat of an administration."[83] Many deputies were not so sanguine about the location of their hometowns on the map that the C.C. had prepared. They would need to redraw the boundaries of departments in order to improve their chances of obtaining a departmental seat for their constituents. Townspeople in the provinces forwarded their own petitions for departments to the National Assembly, and many municipalities sent special deputies to lobby on their behalf. On December 9, Rabaut Saint-Etienne reported that the C.C. was receiving requests for departmental seats "from the four corners of France." If all these petitions were accepted, it would be necessary to establish over one hundred departments. Urban rivalries were threatening to paralyze the work of the C.C., which had already been obliged to add four commissioners to its eight regular members in order to negotiate with deputies and special deputies.[84]

Rabaut Saint-Etienne proposed two kinds of compromises between the claims of rival towns: *partage*, or the sharing of various kinds of establishments; and *alternats*, or the rotation of administrative seats. The idea of *partage* implied that whichever town became a departmental seat would be excluded from receiving the other establishments that the National Assembly intended to create in each department, such as bishoprics and appellate lawcourts. The C.C. believed that it would be especially appropriate to share such institutions in departments that did not contain any large

---

[82] The initial decree of Nov. 12, 1789, stipulated a ternary division of each department into three, six, or nine districts, which would permit a three-stage electoral process. After the deputies eliminated the second stage of elections to the National Assembly, a decree was passed on Dec. 14 permitting a minimum of three and a maximum of nine districts per department. AP 10:7, 564.

[83] Pierre Du Chambon, *La formation du département de la Charente* (Ruffec, 1934), p. 64, citing a letter from Antoine-Joseph Roy, Nov. 11, 1789.

[84] Report published in *Journal des Etats-Généraux*, 6:359. The four deputies who served as *commissaires-adjoints* on the C.C. were Gossin, Dupont de Nemours, Aubry Du Bochet, and Bureaux de Pusy.

towns. As for *alternats*, they could be introduced even in departments where a single town was so large that it would necessarily concentrate the major religious and judicial establishments. Here Rabaut Saint-Etienne appealed to the egalitarian sentiments of deputies from small towns and the countryside: "The capitals, in attracting a large number of citizens, acquire corresponding influence, which results in privileges and a sort of despotism over the countryside. Just as you have favored rural populations by bringing them closer to the various parts of administration, so the rotation of departmental administration among several towns would achieve the same goal."[85] In the debate over these proposals, a few deputies from small towns argued that establishments should always be dispersed rather than concentrated in a single capital, but a majority agreed simply to permit *partages* and *alternats*.[86] The C.C. would recommend such arrangements to the National Assembly, following negotiations with deputies from the various provinces.[87]

The announcement that lawcourts might be located in towns different from administrative seats brought into public view an issue that preoccupied hundreds of towns. How would the new administrative division of the kingdom influence the distribution of lawcourts? In its plan of division, the C.C. had adopted the strategy of focusing attention exclusively on administrative and electoral institutions. According to Sièyes—who did not hide the fact that "sooner or later the new departments will lead us to dispense with all the other divisions"—a gradual approach, beginning with electoral representation, would minimize the clash of opposing interests and passions.[88] Only one advocate of the Committee's plan suggested in November that the empire could also be divided into 80 tribunals, 80 bishoprics, 80 national schools, 720 tax bureaus, and 720 first-order lawcourts.[89] It was critics such as Pison du Galand and Malouet who linked together administrative and judicial jurisdictions in their defense of large departments with appellate lawcourts.[90] Yet the suppression of seigneurial

---

[85] Report on Dec. 9, *Le point du jour* 156:58.

[86] Mougin de Rouquefort, the mayor of Grasse, and Malouet, from Riom, spoke strongly in favor of departmental alternates, and Delay d'Agier, the mayor of Romans, proposed that no town that obtained a bishopric could also become a departmental seat. Session of Dec. 9, AP 10:453; and *Le point du jour* 156:59. Grasse was competing with Toulon, Riom with Clermont-Ferrand, and Romans with Valence (a bishopric) for a departmental seat.

[87] Decree of Dec. 9, AP 10:453.

[88] [Sièyes], *Observations*, pp. 9–10.

[89] Speech of Duquesnoy, Nov. 4, AP 9:672.

[90] Speeches on Nov. 10 and 12, AP 9:739; 10:4–5. See also Aubry du Bochet's plan for 25 provinces, each with a superior lawcourt, and 110 departments, each with one or several *présidiaux*, in AP 9:698; Châteauneuf-Randon's defense of 120 departments, each with a diocese and a *cour supérieur*, in AP 9:675; and Bengy Puyvallée's critique of that same plan for creating too many dioceses and appellate courts, in AP 9:683.

lawcourts and venal offices back in August had already provoked a veritable flood of petitions and supplications from towns and bourgs that wanted new or more important royal courts.[91] Once word spread that departments and districts would be created, many towns sent new petitions that included requests for lawcourts as well as administrative institutions. By early December, several petitions for new establishments were being read at the bar of the National Assembly every day.[92] On December 22, Thouret confirmed that the C.C. intended to use the departments and districts as a territorial framework for lawcourts. In a preliminary report on judicial reform, he proposed a hierarchical system, with justices of the peace in each canton, civil lawcourts in each district, appellate tribunals in each department, superior courts with jurisdiction over three or four departments, and a supreme court of appeal in Paris.[93] This plan would be greatly modified before the National Assembly approved a new judicial system in August 1790, based primarily on the districts, but it convinced many townspeople who wanted lawcourts that they should also enter the competition for departments and districts.

In a prescient observation on the division of the kingdom, petitioners from the town of Béziers wrote to the National Assembly on November 19, 1789:

> Now is the moment when the nation is really going to organize itself. . . . The largest cities, like the smallest towns, are eager to cooperate in order to share as best they can in the French government. Each town would like to increase its rank in relation to rival towns. This prodigious competition, this great shock of opposing interests, must necessarily plunge the representatives of the nation into embarrassment and difficulty.[94]

Indeed, it was so. The more the C.C. tried to accomodate the demands of rival towns, the more petitions and special deputies arrived to complicate its decisions. If towns were denied departments, they insisted on large districts; if they failed to obtain districts, they demanded tribunals. Dupont de Nemours reported at the end of January 1790 that 1,824 special deputies were besieging the C.C. and new ones were arriving every day.[95] As Rabaut Saint-Etienne acknowledged, if the National Assembly granted all

---

[91] Many of the petitions for lawcourts never reached the Constitutional Committee. They were filed with other petitions in the archives of the National Assembly, AN C 90–123.

[92] Listed at the beginning of each session, in AP 10.

[93] For an analysis of Thouret's report, see Lebègue, *Thouret*, 207–34; the text is in AP 10:725–34.

[94] AN DIV bis 25:366 (Hérault).

[95] *Observations sur les principes qui doivent déterminer le nombre des districts et celui des tribunaux dans les départements* (Paris, 1789), pamphlet reprinted in AP 11:606. See also Dupont's influential speech to the National Assembly on this subject on Jan. 27, 1790, AP 11:350–51.

of the requests for establishments, "There would be no proportion left in the distribution, no more equality in the various parts: departments and districts would be multiplied to infinity, without rule and without proportion."[96] The hope of *partage* among district seats and tribunals stimulated a new wave of petitions in the spring and summer. Over fifteen hundred towns and bourgs joined the struggle for lawcourts, submitting a total of six thousand petitions by September 1790.[97] The division of the kingdom began as an assault on the old regime. It risked turning into a battle among towns of every size and description for the institutions of the new state.

[96] *Nouvelles Réflexions*, AP 10:38.
[97] Tabulation based on dossiers in AN DIV bis; and report by Gossin, Sept. 23, 1790, AP 19:173.

Chapter 3

URBAN CRISIS AND BOURGEOIS AMBITION

W ILL THE EPOCH of regeneration for France also be the epoch of destruction for this unhappy town?" With such foreboding did the mayor of Villeneuve-le-Roy, a little town in the province of Champagne, plead for a new royal court in the first year of the French Revolution.[1] Spokesmen for hundreds of provincial towns agreed that the territorial reorganization of the kingdom created unprecedented dangers and opportunities for urban communities. Their rhetoric reveals the paradox of a bourgeois revolution that threatened to subvert the social order of towns. Public establishments such as royal and seigneurial lawcourts symbolized the fusion of political authority and social prestige in the hands of urban magistrates. What would happen to townspeople if these institutions simply disappeared without a trace? Would the bourgeoisie of officeholders and men of law, which dominated many towns, be compelled to migrate elsewhere? Would peasants continue to frequent the markets of towns that no longer housed lawcourts and administrative agencies? In changing the map of central places, the National Assembly prefigured a new administrative and judicial hierarchy that would expand the regional influence of some towns while it would reduce that of others. Depending on whether townspeople anticipated losses or gains from the new division of the kingdom, they adopted a rhetorical style that projected anxiety or ambition. In either case, their petitions to the National Assembly shared an underlying assumption that the prosperity of towns and the reform of the state were closely interrelated.

All in all, nearly 600 towns and bourgs sought reparations from the new regime. Lawcourts aroused by far the greatest concern, with 257 towns bemoaning the loss of their seigneurial courts and another 202 towns pleading for the survival of their royal courts. Next in importance were the religious establishments that the Revolution intended to abolish. A total of 155 towns, many of whom were also losing lawcourts, complained that urban prosperity depended to a significant degree on the wealth and charitable donations of bishops, canons, monks, and nuns. A miscellaneous category of 95 towns and bourgs deplored their general poverty, loss of privileges, or heavy taxes. Most of these communities, along with several dozen others, lamented their decline from an earlier period of prosperity. By contrast, only 38 towns emphasized the importance of fiscal institu-

[1] *Mémoire*, AN DIV bis 32:448 (Yonne).

tions, whose tax agents were among the least popular residents of most urban communities. Taken at face value, the petitions from all these towns and bourgs create an overwhelming impression of economic crisis and social discontent. Yet nearly 400 other localities in contention for new establishments did not ask for compensation at all. Instead, they boasted of their commerce and industry, described the vitality of their markets, or vaunted their potential for urban growth and prosperity. These enthusiastic towns and bourgs, joined by even a few villages, looked to the Revolution for improvement in their rank and status. In trying to boost their political fortunes, the spokesmen for such communities adopted a self-confident rhetoric of growth and progress. They reveal the ambition beneath the anxiety of so many townspeople who looked to the National Assembly for the determination of their fate in the new political order.[2]

In a mode of tragic irony, petitioners from a small town in upper Provence judged the impact of the division on their own community: "By what fatality does the town of Moustiers, seat of a royal jurisdiction, lose everything in this new order of things, instead of gaining the advantages that it had reason to expect? What horrible destiny prevents it from participating in the universal joy, robs it of its share of public felicity, and condemns it forever to tears and despair?"[3] For the leading citizens of many towns, such a cruel destiny spelled economic collapse, demographic decline, and cultural ruin. The spokesmen for medium-sized and small towns alike complained of imminent destruction unless they received new establishments from the National Assembly.[4] At one extreme were provincial capitals such as Moulins, whose special deputies claimed that its many lawcourts and tax offices "support and give a livelihood to a large portion" of its inhabitants. Unless Moulins received a sovereign court as well as a department in compensation for its losses, "a large number of the judges, left without any functions, will abandon the town; they will soon be followed by other rich people. . . . The workers, the craftsmen of all kinds will be unemployed; and the town of Moulins, deserted, abandoned, will present only the spectacle of distress and misery."[5] At the other extreme were small

---

[2] These estimates of the numbers of towns that sought compensation or emphasized their economic vigor are based on a systematic analysis of the documents sent to the National Assembly from provincial towns, in C 90–123; DIV bis 1–34, 56–76, 81–91, 93–110; DXVII 1–4; ADXVI 18–81; and ADXIX 23–29. All my discussion of these petitions relies on the same collection of sources.

[3] Printed *Mémoire . . . par la ville de Moustiers*, AN DIV bis 3:155, p. 4 (Basses-Alpes).

[4] In comparison with petitions that expressed optimism about the future, no correlation existed between these expressions of fear and the size of towns: 83 percent (355/425) of the towns and bourgs that supposedly faced ruin had fewer than 5,000 nucleated inhabitants in 1809–11, but so did 83 percent (286/341) of the towns and bourgs that boasted of their economic dynamism.

[5] Letter, AN DIV bis 19:306 (Allier). For examples of fearful rhetoric on the part of other

towns with seigneurial courts, such as Varzy, in Nivernais, whose special
deputies decried a similar fate unless their town obtained a district tribunal:

> The rich citizens will take up residence elsewhere, where they can find lawcourts
> and administrative agencies; the men of law who comprise the remainder of the
> wealthy and bourgeois class in this town will necessarily be forced to settle in the
> place where the tribunal is located; plaintiffs will no longer come to Varzy, so
> retail trade will decline, and the inhabitants of the countryside will no longer
> come to sell their crops or buy what they need. Merchants and craftsmen will
> have to leave, too.[6]

From top to bottom of the social order, the displacement of political institutions would lead to ruin. In the words of officials at Château-du-Loir, a
small town in Anjou, "To destroy the establishments of a town is to paralyze it."[7]

This trickle-down theory of the urban economy, whereby shopkeepers,
artisans, and laborers depended on magistrates, lawyers, and litigants, implied a cultural as well as an economic process of deurbanization. Without
officeholders, towns would lose their "polite society" and suffer a humili-
ating decline in rank and prestige. Montauban would "fall into a state of
dependency and degradation," and Saumur would enter "an inferior class
of towns"; Tarascon would become "an object of mockery for its neighbors" and "return to nothingness and oblivion"; Noyers would become
"nothing but a cipher in the French Empire"; Sainte-Ménéhould would be
"erased from the list of French towns"; and Langres would be reduced to
the status of "a simple bourg or even a village."[8] Petitions from several
dozen towns adopted this trope of metamorphosis into a village, and a few
imagined an even worse fate: Seignelay would be worth less than "the most
wretched settlements in the surrounding countryside"; Lixheim would become a "hamlet"; Montier-en-Der a "lair of brigands"; Richelieu "a collection of hovels"; and La Roche-Derrien a "pile of stones."[9] Of course, these
images were rhetorical devices rather than sociological predictions, and a
special deputy from Meulan revealed the calculation behind such meta-
phors by modifying a petition that read "the desertion of magistrates, notaries, solicitors, and wealthy bourgeois is going to reduce this unhappy

---

provincial capitals, see the dossiers of Montpellier, Bourges, and Poitiers, in AN DXVII:1;
DIV bis 21:336 (Cher); and DIV bis 32:444 (Vienne).

   [6] *Mémoire*, AN DIV bis 28:405 (Nièvre).

   [7] Letter, AN DIV bis 16:279 (Sarthe).

   [8] AN DIV bis 10:224 (Lot); DIV bis 10:228 (Maine-et-Loire); DIV bis 5:168 (Bouches-
du-Rhône); DIV bis 32:450 (Yonne); DIV bis 27:395 (Marne); DIV bis 10 (Haute-Marne).

   [9] AN DIV bis 32:450 (Yonne); DIV bis 11:235 (Meurthe); DXVII 1; DIV bis 9:219
(Indre-et-Loire, but mistakenly filed in Loiret); DIV bis 22:340 (Côtes-du-Nord).

town to the state of a simple village." He crossed out the last five words of
this sentence and wrote instead "to the saddest condition."[10] Yet all the
images of decline that townspeople used were expressions of a common
belief that urban status, like retail trade, depended on the establishments
that made towns centers of public authority rather than mere sites of production. As special deputies from Issoudun complained, if their town
failed to obtain a lawcourt, it would be "nothing more than a settlement
of wine growers, cultivators, and workers."[11]

In interpreting the abolition of lawcourts as the destruction of urban
elites, petitioners were equating the wealth of bourgeois proprietors with
the professional activities of magistrates and lawyers. Although the social
order of the old regime did encourage this conflation of property, office,
and law degrees, not all proprietors who purchased offices or attended law
school were preparing to engage in a liberal profession. Many royal offices
involved little work, and the young men who registered at a *parlement* after
completing law school were acquiring a title—*avocat en parlement*—as well
as a professional qualification. They might display this title in a small royal
or seigneurial town where they lived "nobly" from their rents instead of
engaging in any legal practice.[12] Yet nearly all the *bailliages* did have lawyers who represented clients in civil litigation, and lesser courts offered
some employment for men educated in the law, whether as judges, prose-
cutors, or juriconsultists. Furthermore, written procedures of litigation
called for the assistance of solicitors, notaries, clerks, and bailiffs, who had
lower social origins and less property than most of the *avocats*. Members of
these occupational groups practiced a craft rather than a liberal profession,
and like master craftsmen, they purchased offices in order to obtain security
of employment. Still other practitioners of the law offered their services to
a clientele that could not afford the fees of solicitors or the honorariums of
barristers. Thus, the world of litigation provided employment for many
people who were neither magistrates nor professional lawyers. Lawcourts
signified not only the social authority of rich and well-educated proprietors
but the employment of modest officeholders, who were ancestors in some
respects of white-collar workers.

It was by no means uncommon for 5 or 10 percent of all the families in
provincial towns to be directly connected to lawcourts.[13] By enumerating

[10] AN DIV bis 30:431 (Seine-et-Oise).

[11] *Mémoire*, AN DIV bis 25:371 (Indre).

[12] Jones, "Rural bourgeoisie," 81–82.

[13] For example, the proportion of magistrates, barristers, solicitors, clerks, and bailiffs exceeded 2 percent of the entire population of Dijon, Pau, Janville, Le Dorat, and Bouzonville,
and reached 1 percent of the population of Toulouse, Chartres, Vendôme, Montargis, Pithiviers, and Dourdan. Legal personnel listed in *Almanach historique de la province de Languedoc
pour l'année 1788* (Toulouse, 1788), pp. 181–315; *Almanach de la province de Bourgogne* . . . ,

these men of law, petitioners tried to impress the National Assembly with the magnitude of the losses that they faced. Riom counted two hundred heads of families who would be "absolutely ruined" unless the lawcourts that employed them were replaced by a sovereign court; Guingamp described eighty families that faced unemployment and poverty because their fathers were attached to an important seigneurial court; Montélimar tabulated over sixty families whose fortunes would be ruined if its royal *sénéchaussée* and seigneurial courts were not replaced; and Montmorillon argued that the abolition of its *sénéchaussée* would compel forty families to desert the town in order to avoid starvation.[14] Itemizing the professions that would be deeply affected by the abolition of a lawcourt, petitioners from Beaufort, a small town in Anjou, asked, "What would happen to the eight magistrates who hold offices in the court? Or the seven barristers and solicitors, six notaries, and a large number of other officeholders and practitioners? After serving their fatherland, will they be precipitated into the chaos of reform and buried under the debris of aristocracy?"[15] Even the magistrates and barristers were not wealthy enough to remain at Beaufort with nothing to do. They would have to go elsewhere in search of establishments, and no one would remain in the town but petty shopkeepers and poor artisans, who would be reduced to the most lamentable misery.

Thus, the loss of lawcourts brought into question the fate of many families. Although royal judges expected financial compensation for their offices, they had reason to fear the transfer of lawcourts to other towns. As two judges at the *sénéchaussée* of Concarneau complained, "We will lose the hope of transmitting these offices to our children as a sacred property, the most inviolable of all laws."[16] Furthermore, the precise valuation of such offices would be difficult to determine, and magistrates who wanted to continue their professional activities would have to compete for the new judgeships in the district courts.[17] The lieutenant-general of the *bailliage* of Ardres protested that his personal position would become "very disagreeable" if the lawcourts of Boulogne and Calais incorporated his *bailliage* into their jurisdictions. The youthful magistrates who headed both of these rival courts would probably obtain preference over this old judge, who had

---

pour l'année 1786 (Dijon, 1786), pp. 1–113; *Calendrier historique de l'Orléanais* (Orléans, 1788); *procès-verbal* from the *bailliage* of Bouzonville, AN DIV bis 28:404 (Moselle); *observations* from Le Dorat, AN DIV bis 32:445 (Haute-Vienne).

[14] AN DIV bis 29:416 (Puy-de-Dôme); DXVII 1; DIV bis 6:189 (Drôme); DIV bis 32:444 (Vienne).

[15] *Mémoire*, AN DIV bis 26:389 (Maine-et-Loire).

[16] Letter, AN DIV bis 23:352 (Finistère).

[17] Many failed to continue their careers. For example, only 27 out of 118 *bailliage* court magistrates in Burgundy were elected to the 80 judgeships created in the district courts of this province. A majority of the new judges were small-town attorneys. See Dawson, *Provincial Magistrates*, pp. 254–55.

served in his post for forty years.[18] As for solicitors in the royal courts, they feared unemployment. In the words of petitioners from the *sénéchaussée* of Gourin, "Several notaries and solicitors have numerous families, and they have sacrificed everything to advance themselves by purchasing their offices and by exercising their responsibilities with probity and every sentiment of honor. What is going to happen to these officeholders if their posts are suppressed?"[19] From Roye, in Picardy, came even more alarming news. A local solicitor, M. Bourlon, had thrown himself from the heights of the town ramparts in despair at the loss of his place in the royal *bailliage*, also destined for suppression. Petitioners from this town had already complained that magistrates would be despoiled, juriconsultists left without a profession, notaries and solicitors stripped of their resources. Now the scandal of suicide compounded their fears of poverty.[20]

As for officeholders at the seigneurial courts, they would bear the full brunt of legal reform. The National Assembly neglected to provide any financial compensation for the judges and solicitors who had purchased their offices from seigneurs, who were supposed to reimburse such officeholders privately. "Have pity on the solicitors in the countryside who have been commissioned by seigneurs," wrote a *procureur* at the principality of Carvin, a bourg in Artois. "If we cannot work anymore at our lawcourt, or purchase another little office, we are going to become poor and miserable, eating up what little property we possess." In the Breton duchy of Retz, which used to have three important seigneurial courts, petitioners argued that consolidation into a single district court would "reduce to starvation a crowd of judicial officers, fathers of families who are burdened with children." A special deputy from Paimpol made a similar plea for "a crowd of men of law" who had fixed the business of seventeen lawcourts in this little Breton port. These seigneurial agents would remain without bread unless a local district or lawcourt provided them with new means of subsistence. On a more personal note, a clerk of the seigneurial court at Chemillé, a small town in Anjou, begged the National Assembly to take pity on his fate. Thrown into extreme misery when his office was abolished, he requested a post in a new lawcourt for the town. "Without your benevolence, Messieurs, Chemillé is a town entirely ruined and reduced to nothing, as am I myself."[21]

Of course, ambitious men of law had the option of migrating from towns which lost establishments to those which consolidated or improved their position in the new administrative and judicial system. Yet strong ties

---

[18] Letter, AN DIV bis 29:415 (Pas-de-Calais).

[19] *Adresse*, AN C 113:277.

[20] Anonymous letter and *adresse*, AN DIV bis 31:439 (Somme).

[21] AN DIV bis 29:415 (Pas-de-Calais); DXVII 2; DIV bis 22:340 (Côtes-du-Nord); DIV bis 26:389 (Maine-et-Loire).

of property and affection bound many legal specialists to the little towns that feared decline in 1789. The leaders of these towns viewed geographical mobility less as a promise than as a threat. In the words of a *procureur* who represented the interests of a small town in Burgundy, "If the town of Noyers is reduced to the rank of a poor village, several of its wealthiest and best-educated citizens are resolved to desert it, to leave with chagrin, even with despair, the place where they were born and to transport far away their talents and their activities."[22] Married men were especially reluctant to seek employment elsewhere; they would have to leave their families behind or uproot their wives and children at considerable expense. Many magistrates in eighteenth-century France were strongly attached to the town where they administered justice. As Thouret pointed out in a debate over the English system of assize courts that rotated among several towns,

> This ambulatory function, which obliges judges never to live at home, to wander from town to town, to suffer, after the inconvenience of travel, all the discomforts of incommodious and often barely decent lodgings, cannot suit a large number of judges. We would be deprived of the services of many worthy subjects, whose tastes, ingrained habits, or domestic circumstances would absolutely prevent them from following this style of life.[23]

In addition to family ties, landed property restricted the mobility of married judges and lawyers in small towns. For example, the magistrates and other officeholders at Châtillon-sur-Marne owned local vineyards that required their constant attention, as well as houses in town that they would have difficulty selling or leasing. Similarly, a petition from Le Buis reported that all the men of law in this *bailliage* resided in town, where "their fortunes do not permit them to become expatriates, without being ruined." At Villeneuve-de-Berg, where prominent legal families also owned property in the town and surrounding countryside, the mayor concluded that they would be unlikely to move elsewhere "because of the quite natural repugnance of all landowners to abandon their properties, their homes, their families, and their social relations."[24]

Age as well as marital status helps explain the sedentary habits of men who had devoted a lifetime to legal practice. Municipal leaders at Mirepoix, a small town in Languedoc, reported that most of the judges and lawyers were "too old and too burdened with family cares to seek their livelihood elsewhere and to take up another profession." Such older men faced a loss of prestige as well as income. "Without any profession, lacking

---

[22] Printed *mémoire*, AN DIV bis 23:350 (Yonne).

[23] Speech on Apr. 16, 1790, AP 12:557.

[24] AN DIV bis 10 (Marne); DIV bis 6:190 (Drôme); DIV bis 19:313 (Ardèche).

social respect, no longer distinguished from their former litigants, they would drag out their useless and idle days in obscurity and perhaps in misery. Who knows if they would not even be exposed to insults from litigants who might complain about their former verdicts." From the Breton town of Jugon came similar anxiety about the "cruel choice" that faced magistrates and lawyers who were "advanced in age." Transfer of the local court to another town would "force them to leave the places of their birth and their properties, or to abandon a profession that brings them wealth." If legal reformers in the National Assembly had their way, one man of law in each canton might become a justice of the peace, but these jurisdictions would follow such simple procedures that litigants would no longer need to employ barristers or solicitors. For the great majority of older magistrates and lawyers, opportunities for employment would be confined to district directories and lawcourts, whose location became a matter of personal interest and family honor.[25]

Geographical mobility had different implications for young men who wanted to enter the legal profession. They were accustomed to studying the law in Paris or provincial capitals such as Dijon or Toulouse, where *parlements* as well as universities attracted men of ambition from smaller towns. Some migrants launched successful careers far from home, but others felt the pull of family obligations. Thus, Félix Faulcon, a young law student in Paris before he became a *présidial* magistrate in his hometown of Poitiers, wrote to his father in 1780, "My homeland has always been uniquely dear to me, and beyond it, nothing else interests me. . . . In accordance with all the cherished ties that blood, nature, and friendship have fashioned into duty and rendered the sweetest of my pleasures, only overpowering reasons could have persuaded me to make myself unhappy by leaving the country that contains everything dearest to my heart."[26] Such local patriotism informed a memorial from Villeneuve-le-Roy, which boasted that many young men, having acquired legal knowledge in the tribunals of Paris, "await nothing but the establishment of a district to return and settle in their hometown [*patrie*]." From Varzy came similar word that "young men, through assiduous work in the law offices of royal *bailliages* in the province, the *châtelet* of Paris, and the *parlement*, are in a position to display their talents to the satisfaction of the public." These aspiring lawyers already faced an overcrowded profession, and if their hometowns ceased to possess lawcourts, they would be compelled to idleness or permanent exile. Special deputies from Mamers probably described a common attitude when they wrote, "We have a large number of law grad-

---

[25] AN DIV bis 20:318 (Ariège); DIV bis 22:340 (Côtes-du-Nord). Concerning the effort of the National Assembly to discourage adversary litigation, and the great decline in the number of professional judges, see Dawson, *Provincial Magistrates*, pp. 243–46.

[26] Letter of Sept. 11, 1780, in G. Debien, ed. *Correspondance de Félix Faulcon*, 2 vols. (Poitiers, 1955), 1:71–72.

uates who are waiting for positions, but they do not want to move elsewhere." Parents were equally reluctant to "expatriate" their children, for whom they developed "great expectations" of professional success in local communities, as several townspeople from Ernée explained. Families with a tradition of employment in the courts wanted hometown careers for fathers and sons alike.[27]

The crisis in the legal profession had larger social repercussions in many towns, although petitioners often exaggerated the economic resources that shopkeepers and artisans derived from lawcourts. In identifying the professional interests of magistrates with the welfare of urban communities, notables drew on a rhetorical tradition that equated any reduction in the jurisdiction of a lawcourt with a decline in retail trade. As a memorial for the *présidial* court of Riom had stated back in 1731, "The interest of all the inhabitants of the city is so closely intertwined with that of their tribunal, that the preservation of their town depends absolutely on that of the court's jurisdiction."[28] This argument implied that no commercial relations existed beyond such a jurisdiction, and that even local trade depended entirely on the clientele that lawcourts attracted. Some townspeople denied that they had *any* resources except a lawcourt. High in the mountains of Auvergne, the seat of the *bailliage* of Salers had neither land nor commerce to sustain its inhabitants; and the *duché-pairie* of Ussel, also in the Massif Central, was "the only thing that compensated the town and its surroundings for the aridity of the land, the rigor of the climate, and the absence of any commerce or major road."[29] Other petitioners complained that local produce could not be marketed unless litigants frequented the town. The town of Coucy, lacking roads, industry, or grainlands, produced nothing but cheap wine that visitors to the *bailliage* court consumed; and Château-meillant, a little town in Berry, relied on a seigneurial court to attract "large gatherings of people from surrounding localities," who purchased local crops and a "prodigious quantity of wine."[30] The spokesmen for dozens of small towns argued that lawcourts sustained their exchange with the countryside. As an assembly of townspeople from the barony of Mirebeau reported, markets in this town flourished "only because the inhabitants of the countryside, in coming here to seek legal advice, handle their affairs, or plead in court, also come to sell their crops."[31] Unless such towns acquired district courts, their markets would supposedly decline or even disappear.[32]

Spokesmen for larger towns shifted their emphasis from weekly markets

---

[27] AN DIV bis 18:301 (Yonne); DIV bis 28:405 (Nièvre); DIV bis 30:429 (Sarthe); DIV bis 10:234.

[28] *Mémoire* cited by Everat, *La sénéchaussée d'Auvergne*, pp. 91–92.

[29] AN DIV bis 5:174 (Cantal); DXVII 2.

[30] AN DIV bis 3:144 (Aisne); DIV bis 21:335 bis (Cher).

[31] AN DIV bis 32:444 (Vienne).

[32] Petitions from 80 towns voiced fear that their markets would decline or collapse.

to permanent shops in explaining why the urban economy depended on lawcourts. Special deputies from Valognes reported panic among the shop-keepers at news that the town's *bailliage* would lose much of its jurisdiction: "Valognes exists essentially because of the money that litigants spend here. A considerable number of inhabitants who earn a living entirely from the resale of goods are frightened that they will lose the only resource that sustains them." Tradesmen in provincial capitals that lacked navigable waterways, such as Poitiers and Pau, faced the future with equal anxiety. Corporations of artisans at Poitiers opposed the division of the province of Poitou, whose large jurisdiction brought many clients to their shops; and the leaders of Pau presented the National Assembly with a telling analogy to the "tremendous blow" that the abolition of their *parlement* was inflicting on tradesmen as well as lawyers: "Imagine that Bordeaux, Nantes or Marseille had seen their ports closed, or that an unnatural event had removed industry from Lyon, Rouen or Abbeville. This is the state to which the town of Pau has been reduced by losing its high rank in the distribution of judicial power." Craftsmen as well as shopkeepers would suffer from the dwindling purchasing power of towns that no longer presided over extensive jurisdictions. In the words of municipal leaders at Douai, the loss of their sovereign court would "reduce the workers to beg for alms or oblige them to take their industry and their energy to neighboring towns."[33]

If the wealth of a town declined, so would the value of its real estate. Urban growth in eighteenth-century France had stimulated land speculation, especially in residential centers for *parlementaires* and tax officials. For example, the *parlement* of Douai, acquired in 1713 at the cost to the municipality of two hundred thousand livres, had encouraged proprietors to construct new buildings for the wealthy magistrates. A building boom, probably aided in the second half of the century by rising rents from grain farms in the agricultural hinterland of Douai, culminated in the decade before the Revolution. According to deputies from Douai, "A crowd of proprietors have exhausted their capital recently in the construction of new houses. They did so in the firm confidence that the price of houses could only go up in the future, and they have succeeded in making Douai one of the best-built towns in the kingdom." Now these investors feared a collapse in the housing market if Douai failed to obtain a department as compensation for the loss of its sovereign court. Spokesmen for Bastia reported a similar trend in the land market. As the capital of the island of Corsica, Bastia concentrated all the employees of civil and military administration: "Consequently, the wealthiest landowners used their fortunes to build houses there, so that rents are the principle and nearly the only revenues of

---

[33] AN DIV bis 10:231 (Manche); DIV bis 18:295 (Vienne); DIV bis 21:335 (Côte-d'Or); DIV bis 14:258 (Basses-Pyrénées); DIV bis 12:244 (Nord).

a majority of inhabitants." Bastia requested a department to preserve the value of its real estate, and so did Versailles, whose proprietors could no longer rent their buildings to courtiers and government officials, now that the king and his ministers had moved to Paris. In smaller towns such as Charmes, where over one hundred houses had been sold or subdivided in the past fifteen years, the loss of a *bailliage* court provoked similar anxiety among proprietors. Houses would become vacant, rents would collapse, and the new owners would suffer immense losses unless Charmes obtained a district court.[34]

Many commercial and industrial towns also derived economic benefits from public establishments that attracted a regional clientele. Special deputies from Maubeuge, a manufacturing town near the Belgian border, emphasized that the residents of nearly eighty villages visited town frequently for business at the royal *prévôté* or the subdelegation.

> None of them came to town without spending some money, without taking home some foodstuffs, some groceries, some cloth for their families or some furnishings for their households. They spread cash in abundance throughout the town, bringing a constant circulation that was all the more precious because it did not require credit. Six furnished hotels, thirty inns, cafes, or cabarets, and at least two hundred shops thrived as a result.

Previously, another spokesman for Maubeuge had boasted of the town's weapons factory, hardware manufacture, and textile industry, but these deputies argued instead that nine-tenths of the inhabitants depended on retail trade for a livelihood.[35] In like manner, municipal leaders at Guingamp, a port that served as a gateway between the linen industry of northern Brittany and the Atlantic world, pretended that their town had only local trade.[36]

While some townspeople concealed their commerce and industry, others argued that their exports depended on administrative institutions that financed roads and lawcourts that stimulated trade. Thus, special deputies from Rethel, a river town in upper Champagne, admitted that they had a textile industry, but they claimed that it would languish and collapse in the absence of public works that only a department seat could command, leaving over two thousand individuals without any means of subsistence. Townspeople at Montélimar, on the banks of the Rhône River, also conceded that they had commerce and industry, whose sales financed the im-

---

[34] AN DIV bis 36:581 (Nord); DIV bis 6:181 (Corse); DIV bis 17:280 (Seine-et-Oise); DIV bis 18:298 (Vosges).

[35] AN DIV bis 29:410 and 12:244 (Nord).

[36] AN DIV bis 22:340 (Côtes-du-Nord). But spokesmen for Guingamp emphasized their commercial role in Brittany when they requested an *ecole centrale* in the year VII. See the printed *opinion* by the deputy Bachelot, AN ADXVI 32.

port of grain from Burgundy to feed the local population for eight months a year. Yet they emphasized that without a departmental seat, commercial relations with the nearby countryside would decline, grain imports would cease, and the "precious class of worker-citizens would be reduced to despair."[37]

Even townspeople who took pride in their industry were determined to defend their existing jurisdictions over the countryside. The duchy of Harcourt, in Normandy, had "all kinds of commerce, and especially cotton spinning, which employs over 3,000 women and children in the area." Yet if Harcourt did not obtain a royal court to replace its seigneurial *bailliage*, which encompassed fifty parishes, "good-bye to order, the perpetual concourse of people, the mutual relations of the area, and its industry, commerce, and agriculture."[38] Merchants at Elbeuf complained in similar language that weavers in the nearby countryside were being assigned to the department of Evreux, while Elbeuf itself was being incorporated into the department and district of Rouen: "We join hands to ask you not to tarnish our luster, and not to ruin our commerce and our properties by removing these parishes from their correspondance with a town that spreads abundance in the countryside and makes industry flourish."[39] In fact, justices of the peace would be authorized to settle small disputes between merchants and workers, but many townspeople imagined that commerce depended on prestigious lawcourts that obliged peasants to undertake all their transactions in the same central place. This widespread belief helps explain why a total of 193 towns sent contradictory information to the National Assembly about their economy, alternately stressing its dynamism and its vulnerability. Not until towns began competing for commercial tribunals in the fall of 1790 would such equivocation cease, as merchants revealed the full scale of their commerce with other towns and regions.[40]

Like the transformation of the judicial system, the reorganization of the Catholic church had a dramatic impact on many towns. Even before the National Assembly voted to divide the kingdom into departments and districts, it had taken the first steps to abolish the tithe, nationalize Church lands, and suppress religious congregations. In April 1790, an ecclesiastical committee issued draft legislation for a civil constitution of the clergy, whose new dioceses would be modeled on the departments. The committee did not announce its recommendations for the location of bishoprics until July 6, 1790, but townspeople began anticipating their chances of preserving ecclesiastical establishments back in December 1789, when the

[37] AN DIV bis 4:157 (Ardennes); DIV bis 6:189 (Drôme).

[38] AN DIV bis 23:350 (Eure).

[39] AN DIV bis 5:173 (Seine-Inférieure, misclassified in dossier for Calvados).

[40] Some of these petitions for commercial tribunals, which are filed in AN DIV bis 33–34, directly contradict statements in earlier petitions for districts and district lawcourts. See, for example, the cases of Châtillon-sur-Marne and Montdidier.

departments were being formed. A total of sixty-one bishoprics would have to be abolished in thirty-three departments that used to contain at least two diocesan capitals. Furthermore, all the benefices of cathedral chapters and other colleges of canons would be suppressed and their lands sold at public auction, along with the properties of the regular orders of monks and nuns. Although a decree of February 13, 1790, permitted educational and charitable institutions to remain "for the present," it forbade anyone from taking religious vows, opened the gates of monasteries to inmates who chose their freedom, and abolished all contemplative and mendicant orders. The expropriation of Church lands and the drastic reduction in the size of the clergy would affect the urban economy wherever ecclesiastical establishments had been transferring tithes and rents from villages to towns. Of course, much of this property would end up in the hands of townspeople, and urban as well as rural proprietors would benefit from the abolition of the tithe. Nonetheless, petitioners from some towns feared that the upheaval in the Church would undermine their living standards. Whether these prophets of doom were trying to preserve their religious establishments or seeking a new role in the secular organization of the state, they adopted a familiar rhetoric of demanding compensation for their losses.[41]

The most anxious voices came from townspeople who feared the suppression of their bishoprics, along with all the ecclesiastical institutions that surrounded these offices. Typically, such petitioners claimed that their cathedral towns had no commerce. "Our stability depends on the possession of an episcopal see," wrote the municipality of Alet, a town of only eight hundred inhabitants in Languedoc. Bereft of agricultural land or industry, Alet depended on the revenues that its bishop, chapter, seminary, girls' school, and diocesan administration brought to town every year and spread among its families. The bishopric of Saint-Pol-de-Léon, though serving as a market center along the coast of Brittany, drew much of its wealth, too, from the Church. Municipal officials expressed "astonishment and consternation" at news that they would lose both their lawcourt and their bishopric. This would drive away "a large number of respectable families and rich individuals, whose consumption maintained the industry of artisans and encouraged agriculture."[42] Deputies from the more important cathedral town of Laon, in Picardy, had larger ambitions, as well as grimmer words of warning:

> The just hope of becoming a departmental seat is for the town of Laon the plank in the shipwreck. This town has no commerce. It is threatened with the loss of all that used to sustain it: its cathedral chapter, with eighty canons, and another

[41] John McManners, *The French Revolution and the Church* (New York, 1970), pp. 24–31; and legislative reports and debates in AP 11:591–92; 13:166–75; 16:714–46.
[42] AN ADXVI:22 (Alet); DIV bis 23:353 (Finistère).

chapter with thirty canons; its three large abbeys for men; several other religious communities for women; the superb jurisdiction of its *bailliage*. Unless it obtains some compensation, it will be annihilated. Surely it is not the intention of the National Assembly to destroy cities thoughtlessly. Is there any right more sacred than the right to existence?[43]

As for cathedral towns that did have commercial advantages, they also competed for departments and bishoprics, but they usually placed less emphasis on their religious institutions. Exceptions include Lisieux, a textile town in Normandy whose workers expressed alarm at news that they might lose their bishopric, and Luçon, a market town in lower Poitou whose spokesmen attributed the prosperity of agriculture and trade to the resources of the Church. According to the guild of lace trimmers at Lisieux, workers would be "driven to despair" if they lost the support of the lord bishop and his clergy, whose charity alone permitted them to survive whenever they were sick or unemployed. The joiners' guild also worried that abolition of the bishopric would reduce the purchasing power of the town so much that farmers in the area would receive less money for their crops. This in turn would diminish rural demand for the goods of artisans and shopkeepers at Lisieux. As for the guild of bakers, it hoped that the town would not only preserve its bishopric but acquire new establishments, which would "increase the population, and consequently, the consumption in the town."[44] The revolutionary committee of Lisieux agreed to ask for a department, less to expand the town than to salvage the bishopric.

> We cannot exaggerate how much the town of Lisieux has owed to the benevolence of its bishops for the past several centuries. All the most useful establishments of this town—hospitals, seminaries, colleges, charity schools, shelters for the homeless, and similar charitable institutions—are so many monuments to their benevolence and their piety. It is their alms, as well as those of the cathedral chapter and other religious houses, that provide subsistence for a prodigious crowd of poor people, whose numbers are increasing every day. What would become of the town if she lost all this support simultaneously?[45]

Reduced instead to a district in the department of Calvados, Lisieux found itself in competition with the smaller town of Orbec for a tribunal. Now its spokesmen abandoned their talk of the Church and boasted of their excellent roads, their large population, and the "immensity of business that the industry and commerce of Lisieux generate every day." The rhetoric of ruin continued, but the Church disappeared from view: citizens would be

---

[43] AN DIV bis 3:144 (Aisne).
[44] *Délibérations* of guilds, AN DIV bis 5:173 (Calvados).
[45] AN DIV bis 5:172 (Calvados).

obliged to abandon their industry in order to seek justice five leagues away if Orbec triumphed over Lisieux.[46]

Petitioners from Luçon were more consistent in their defense of a bishopric, which symbolized the historical development of their town. Since the founding of a bishopric at Luçon in the fourteenth century, "canals have been dug, dikes have been raised, barriers have been opposed to the tides of the sea, and a town has emerged in the midst of the salt marshes." All this growth flowed from the wealth of the Church: "Take away from Luçon its bishopric, its chapter, its seminary, and its college, and soon, through a retrograde movement, wealthy citizens, merchants, workers, cultivators, and artisans will leave successively, and the town will return to its primary state of nothingness." Rural parishes also benefited from the clergy, who not only purchased many goods but attracted "a crowd of consumers" from elsewhere. As the most important outlet for agricultural produce within fifteen leagues in any direction, the market at Luçon brought "the sweetness of life" to surrounding *bourgades* and provided the means of paying taxes to the government.[47] Here was a dynamic analysis of growth in agriculture, markets, and population, all linked to the wealth of the Church. However, few cathedral towns that decried the fate of their bishoprics placed as much emphasis as Luçon did on agricultural trade. Instead, they tabulated the annual revenues that the clergy extracted from the countryside and spent inside their walls: 100,000 livres at Alet, 200,000 at Lombez, 300,000 at Saint-Paul-de-Léon, 400,000 at Mâcon, 500,000 at Bayeux, 600,000 at Poitiers. As petitioners from Toul explained, religious chapters, monasteries, and convents owned large farms whose revenues they consumed by employing workers inside the town.[48]

More than the general wealth of the Church, it was the *local* influence of religious establishments that petitioners emphasized, not only in cathedral towns, but elsewhere. Each collegiate church had a specified number of canons who resided in town, which helps explain the popularity of this institution. Municipal officials at Tours made a special effort to preserve the rich and famous chapter of Saint-Martin, whose revenues, coming from distant possessions, helped provide subsistence for several thousand inhabitants. By contrast, members of a revolutionary committee at one of those possessions, the little town of Léré, denounced this chapter for siphoning off the revenues from their best lands. Instead, Léré praised its own collegiate church, whose canons consumed their revenues locally. Petitioners from Flavigny pointed out that the canons of their collegiate

---

[46] AN DIV bis 20:328 (Calvados).

[47] AN DIV bis 18:294 (Vendée).

[48] AN ADXVI 22 (Alet); DIV bis 24:361 (Gers); DIV bis 23:353 (Finistère); DIV bis 16:275 (Saône-et-Loire); DIV bis 60:3 (Calvados); DIV bis 18:295 (Vienne); ADXVI 51 (Toul).

church had to be born and baptized in town. Modestly endowed with 10,000 livres in annual revenues, this chapter increased the majesty of religious services, received confessions, provided moral education and instruction for young people, assisted the poor, and served as "a resource for the placement of children who have a vocation for the priesthood." Notables at the small town of Levroux had equal praise for their chapter, with its sixteen canons, nine vicars, organist, and four choirboys: "This chapter brings life to the town, by the concourse of inhabitants from surrounding parishes that it attracts on Sundays and feast days; by the workers of all kinds that it employs; by the abundant charity that it spreads; and by its revenues which turn entirely to the benefit of the inhabitants." If the chapter were destroyed, "the town would be no more than a vile bourg, deserted and absolutely ruined." Even Saint-Quentin, an important textile town in Picardy, would suffer "an immense loss" from the suppression of its royal chapter, whose "very considerable revenues helped provide the means of subsistence for a large number of workers." Yet towns were powerless to prevent the destruction of such institutions, whose defense they generally coupled with requests for new establishments, such as districts at Léré, Flavigny, and Levroux, and a department at Saint-Quentin.[49]

Townspeople greeted the suppression of monasteries and convents with less concern. Some did add religious orders to the list of resources that they were losing: a Benedictine abbey at Saint-Florent with local expenditures of 18,000–20,000 livres a year, one at Pont-Saint-Esprit with annual revenues of 50,000 livres; church lands worth 4 million livres at Saint-Gilles; a total of four abbeys at Sens, three religious congregations at Saint-Emilion, four at Salon, five at Saint-Rémy, nine at Provins, twenty-four at Limoges.[50] Just as commonly, however, petitioners suggested that the buildings of regular orders would provide excellent facilities for new establishments. Rethel pointed to a priory, a convent of Minimes, and a large Capuchin monastery, with only three inmates left, as suitable premises for a departmental administration; Fumay hoped to transform its convent of Carmelite nuns, "nearly all aged and decrepit," into a royal courthouse or a college; and Bernay offered properties of the Church as "premises for all the establishments that the National Assembly judges this town worthy of acquiring": a Benedectine abbey whose five or six residents enjoyed a "vast and superb" site; a monastery of Cordeliers, large and well built, occupied by only two or three monks; a monastery of Pénitents,

---

[49] AN ADXVI 42 (Tours); DIV bis 6:179 (Cher); DXIX 23:366 (Flavigny); DIV bis 25:371 (Indre); DIV bis 3:145 (Aisne).

[50] AN DIV bis 26:388 (Maine-et-Loire); DIV bis 7:195 (Gard); DIV bis 7:195 (Saint-Gilles); DIV bis 32:448 (Yonne); DIV bis 24:364 (Gironde); DIV bis 20:325 (Bouches-du-Rhône); DIV bis 5:169 (Bouches-du-Rhône); DIV bis 17:287 (Seine-et-Marne); DIV bis 32:445 (Haute-Vienne).

agreeably and solidly built around a vast courtyard, with gardens and a beautiful orchard, also occupied by only two or three monks; a convent of Cordelier nuns; and a convent of the congregation of Notre Dame. Monasteries that combined great wealth with nearly deserted premises offered convenient targets for ambitious townspeople who embraced the rhetoric of the Enlightenment. As townspeople from Meulan reasoned, if their three abbeys were replaced by a district and a tribunal, "the nation would see industry reborn, commerce maintained, and patriotism elevated on the ruins of laziness and inactivity."[51]

Religious reform also threatened the educational system of the old regime, but only a few towns recognized this danger at the beginning of the Revolution. Municipal officials at Poitiers did point out that the suppression of lawcourts and religious establishments would reduce career opportunities for students of law and theology, so enrollments at their university would noticeably decline.[52] Instead of protesting the impact of the revolutionary land settlement on the financial resources of colleges, most towns that mentioned secondary education did so because they wanted to create such institutions. For example, the mayor and consuls of Die, where a Protestant academy and a Jesuit college had both been suppressed during the old regime, complained that the nearest colleges were twelve to twenty leagues away. Most of the inhabitants of this mountainous area were too poor to send their children to distant boarding schools. They needed a college at Die, where children could be educated at a reasonable cost.[53] As an old bishopric in a relatively isolated region, Die ressembled two other towns that expressed concern about the loss of educational establishments at the beginning of the Revolution, Saint-Gaudens and Entrevaux. More than two hundred inhabitants of the Pyrenean town of Saint-Gaudens signed a petition to protest rumors that their seminary and college, both attached to the nearby bishopric of Saint-Bertrand, would be suppressed. Such a fate would oblige them to educate their youths in rich towns of the plains, such as Toulouse. This would not only exceed their financial means but transform the mentalities of their children, who would return home with "a pronounced disgust for mountains covered in snow." Such youths would "desert this rough and savage country, which habit alone makes tolerable."[54] Townspeople from the Alpine town of Entrevaux, where the bishopric and seminary of Glandève were located, protested in like manner that students educated in the towns of lower Provence would acquire manners and attitudes out of harmony with the mountains where they were

---

[51] AN DIV bis 4:157 (Ardennes); DIV bis 4:158 (Ardennes); C 96:110, document 1 (Bernay); DIV bis 30:431 (Seine-et-Oise).

[52] AN DIV bis 18:295 (Vienne).

[53] Die also requested a royal lawcourt, AN DXVII:1.

[54] AN DIV bis 7:197 (Haute-Garonne).

born. "After having tasted the pleasures of a bountiful land, they would settle there," and Entrevaux, which had already lost one-third of its population in the past twenty years, would decline even more.[55]

Relatively few towns emphasized the loss of administrative institutions and fiscal agencies, although departments and directories would presumably replace most of these establishments. Many towns neglected even to mention that they used to have subdelegates, whose responsibilities ended abruptly with the collapse of the central government in the summer of 1789.[56] Even provincial capitals were careful not to boast of their intendancies. The once-powerful intendants now symbolized ministerial despotism. As for the agencies of tax farmers, petitioners often listed them without commentary, as proofs of institutional density rather than as demands for compensation. When townspeople did call attention to the hated officials who collected the salt tax, they ran the risk of supplying rival towns with rhetorical ammunition. "The bourg of Dun is groaning about the loss of its salt warehouse," wrote a special deputy from La Souterraine. "It ought to be celebrating this event with fireworks." Spokesmen for the little town of Ingrandes tried to disarm such criticism of their salt warehouse, customs agency, and bureau for indirect taxes by expressing "the most sincere desire that we will soon be entirely emancipated from all these fiscal establishments." In a parenthetical remark, petitioners from the Pyrenean town of Caudiès noted that their salt warehouse had recently been burned down in a popular insurrection. Urban elites needed to be cautious about singing the praises of fiscal agencies that people in towns and villages alike were determined to abolish.[57]

A handful of commercial towns did insist, however, that merchants needed direct access to the coffers of tax collectors in order to obtain cash. If the Revolution disrupted the complex flow of credit that joined merchants and tax collectors in the provinces to bankers and government treasurers in Paris, commerce and industry would suffer. Such was the fear of textile merchants at Reims and Laval, iron merchants at Saint-Dizier, and wine merchants at Cognac and La Rochelle. According to a memorial for Reims, merchants were accustomed to obtaining cash from the general receivers in the province of Champagne, who resided in this important town. As the accountants of government funds, these receivers, like private capitalists, needed to know personally the merchants whose paper notes they accepted. Receivers located in other towns would refuse to lend money to the textile manufacturers of Reims, who used this cash to pay their work-

[55] AN DXIX 25:396 (Entrevaux); DIV bis 3:155 (Basses-Alpes).

[56] Among the 656 seats of subdelegations that competed for districts and tribunals, only 120 mentioned this institution in their petitions.

[57] AN DIV bis 22:343 (Creuse); C 102:174 (Ingrandes); DIV bis 20:321 (Pyrénées-Orientales).

ers. Thus, Reims wanted a department to protect its business interests. In like manner, merchants at Saint-Dizier demanded a district, which they anticipated would replace their customs bureau, salt granary, bureau for indirect taxes, and water and forest court with a single tax agency. In the absence of such a public treasury, the iron and lumber merchants of Saint-Dizier would have to pay higher costs to transport cash from Paris or borrow it from private individuals. As a deputy from the textile town of Laval noted, tax funds provided a useful remedy for shortages of private capital. Without a departmental treasury to replace the accounts of agents of the General Farms at Laval, interest rates would increase and the commerce of the area would suffer. Petitioners from the highland town of Mende imagined an even worse fate unless they obtained a department for the province of Gévaudan. Cash would be "forever exported" to towns in lower Languedoc, and the commerce of Gévaudan would be "extinguished." Rivals from the town of Langogne countered sensibly that "it is not tax funds that attract the woolens industry, but on the contrary, commerce which attracts and makes cash circulate in an area." Yet private capitalism and public taxation were sufficiently interrelated to persuade merchants in several important towns that a large fiscal jurisdiction served the indispensable needs of commerce.[58]

Pleas for compensation were not limited to towns affected directly by institutional changes at the beginning of the Revolution. Around 150 towns and bourgs focused attention on a variety of other factors that undermined their vitality: earlier losses of royal courts; wars and natural disasters; changes in seaports, roads, and markets; and economic crises. Some of these communities had always been stagnant and obscure; others preserved memories of a golden age when they had once been populous and flourishing. Whatever their condition in the past, they now looked forward to a more promising future. The rhetoric of the National Assembly encouraged such hopes. As petitioners from the little market town of Avignonet explained, just as the National Assembly was concerned with the regeneration of France, so they wanted "the particular restoration" of their town. Still enclosed by "the precious remains of antiquity, such as ramparts and town gates," this former royal *châtellenie* needed only a district to regain its importance as a capital for nearby bourgs and villages. Thus, discontent mingled with ambition as impoverished towns and bourgs entered the competition for new establishments.[59]

Some jeremiads highlighted the enduring impact of unfortunate events on small towns. Memories of injustice still rankled townspeople at La

[58] AN DIV bis 10 (Marne); DIV bis 10 (Haute-Marne); DIV bis 10:234 (Mayenne); DIV bis 27:390 (Lozère); "Pétition du conseil général de la commune de la ville de Cognac," n.d., DIV bis 5:176 (Charente).

[59] AN DIV bis 7:197 (Haute-Garonne).

Ferté-Milon, whose royal *bailliage* had been transferred to Villers-Cotteret in 1703. The suppression of this lawcourt caused "irreparable harm" to their community, "which since that time has not been able to recover from the losses that it suffered." Less indignant than sorrowful, old families of proprietors at Villefranche, whose ancestors used to be judges, remembered the transfer of their royal court to Montmarault as a "fatal event, the source of a deluge of evils that have descended upon this town." According to petitioners at Vic, the end of the Thirty Years War marked the beginning of a "remarkable decadence." The bishop of Metz, who by the terms of the Treaty of Münster lost his sovereignty over Vic, ceased to reside here, and all the people attached to his court abandoned the town, too. As a result, the commerce and population of Vic declined substantially.[60] More often, townspeople complained about wars rather than peace treaties. According to municipal officials at the "unfortunate city" of Lescar, this old bishopic was ruined by the Goths in the year 845 and "has never been able to recover since that epoch." The army of the duke of Deux-Ponts destroyed Dun-le-Palleau in 1569, which took two centuries to become a town again; and wars ruined the markets and fairs of Baccarat, the bourg of Cassagnebère, and the barony of Le Donjon.[61] Natural disasters also figured in the litany of unhappy events that townspeople recalled. In 1773 a sudden flood drowned over sixty people at Châtelaudren and caused great damage from which the town had not yet recovered; in 1784 the Meuse River overflowed at Dun, destroying a bridge that needed to be repaired before the commerce of this town could be revived; and in 1787 two fires at Oisemont reduced much of the town to ashes and forced the inhabitants to contract enormous debts in order to rebuild their homes.[62] A few towns also blamed their poverty on the severe winter of 1788, which ruined the wheat and wine harvests at Cravant and destroyed three-quarters of the olive trees at Nyons. Between the arbitrary actions of rulers and the catastrophes of nature, small towns had ample cause for complaint.[63]

Other tales of woe described a long history of decline and stagnation. The Mediterannean town of Frontignan reached its peak in the eleventh century and remained an important fishing port until the sixteenth century, but then its jurisdiction was dismembered, its port neglected, its commerce transferred to the new port of Cette, and its fisheries ruined by a canal

[60] AN C 98:129 (La Ferté-Milon); DIV bis 21:331 (Cantal, commune in Allier mistakenly filed here); DIV bis 11:235 (Meurthe).

[61] AN DXIX 23:367 (Lescar); DIV bis 22:342 (Creuse); DIV bis 27:398 (Meurthe); C 102:173 (Cassagnebère); C 104:193 (Le Donjon).

[62] AN DXVII 1 (Châtelaudren); DIV bis 28:401 (Meuse); DIV bis 17:290 (Somme).

[63] AN DIV bis 18:301 (Yonne); DIV bis 22:348 (Drôme). Several Provençal towns, including Lambesc, Martigues, and Salon, emphasized the destruction of their olive trees during the winter of 1788.

along the coast. Bourgneuf suffered from the decline of the salt trade and the silting of its port; and La Haye-du-Puits blamed Richelieu and Louis XIV for driving its wealthy Protestants into exile and ruining its commerce and industry. "All the landowners have abandoned an area that has been handed over to pillage," wrote municipal officials from La Haye. With a substantial amount of cash being exported every year, never to return, the hamlets and farms were in ruins. "Three-quarters of the inhabitants, thrown back into a nearly savage condition, have no property left but the small plot of land where they will be buried." A spokesman for Le Malzieu told an equally depressing story of decline instead of progress: "This town amounted to something before the epoch of its disasters; since that time it has been almost nothing." First, the plague of 1632 wiped out two-thirds of its inhabitants, later the entire town burned down, and then the main road was transferred to a rival town, drying up forever the sources of wealth at Le Malzieu. "Everything was lost—commerce, communications, and relations with strangers." For the nadir of urban prosperity gone to ruin, nothing could compare with the little town of Solomiac, whose priest described its condition in 1789: a town hall and covered market-place threatened with imminent ruin; a parade ground eroded by stagnant water; prisons half-open, without walls, ready to collapse; aqueducts crammed with filth; fountains neglected and unhealthy; a royal road degraded and impassible during the rainy season; other roads useless all the time; fairs languishing; and markets in decay. Only a crushing burden of taxes remained as testimony to Solomiac's former wealth.[64]

Surprisingly few towns mentioned the economic crisis that accompanied the outbreak of the Revolution. Grain shortages did preoccupy large capitals such as Rouen and Besançon, whose municipalities took extraordinary measures to secure food supplies during the summer and fall of 1789. As late as November 13, special deputies from Rouen reported extensive obstacles to grain shipments from nearby towns that usually helped provision this city.[65] However, the Comité de Constitution of the National Assembly was not responsible for this problem, which towns tried to resolve through consultations with other municipalities, negotiations with grain merchants, and subsidies from the royal treasury.[66] Urban plans for departments sometimes took the geography of grain production into account, but alarming accounts of poverty and unemployment came primarily from

---

[64] AN DIV bis 25:366 (Hérault); DIV bis 26:383 (Loire-Inférieure); DIV bis 27:394 (Manche); DIV bis 27:391 (Lozère); DIV bis 7:198 (Gers).

[65] Ville de Rouen, *Analyses des délibérations de l'assemblée municipale et électorale du 16 juillet 1789 au 4 mars 1790* (Rouen, 1905), pp. 14–15.

[66] For example, municipal officials at Besançon tried to form a federation of towns in the Franche-Comté to regulate the grain trade in Nov. 1789. See Archives Municipales, Besançon, register 201, ser. D, vol. 1, fol. 169–79.

small towns that wanted districts or lawcourts. For example, the municipality of Saint-Pierre-sur-Dives described the sufferings of a population thrown out of work by the crisis in the textile industry; and spokesmen for Mamers noted that "since the month of June 1789, the textile industry [*manufacture*] has completely collapsed, plunging over 6,000 people at Mamers and its entire surroundings into the most cruel distress."[67] In a rare allusion to the social crisis triggered by the Great Fear in the summer of 1789, townspeople at Crémieu complained that most of the castles in this area of Dauphiné had been sacked or destroyed, and the nobles had fled, leaving a void in the urban economy. They admitted, however, that Crémieu had lost its position long ago as a frontier town on the main road to Italy. Like many other towns that bemoaned their poverty, it suffered more from commercial isolation than from a sudden collapse of industry and trade.[68]

Regardless of the historical roots of economic stagnation, townspeople expressed confidence that new establishments would restore prosperity. With a district or a lawcourt, Dompaire, whose royal jurisdiction had been drastically reduced in 1751, would be "reborn like the rest of the Empire"; Bonny-sur-Loire, which had lost everything over the years except its heavy taxes, would be "repopulated a second time"; and Ham, the victim of a fire around a hundred years ago that reduced its grain trade, would "soon regain its former splendor." Municipal officials at La Haye viewed the future with evangelical zeal: "Your wisdom and your foresight," they assured the National Assembly, "can regenerate with a word, just like the Supreme Being, this unhappy corner of the earth, which has been seized and devastated in turn by barons, fanaticism, taxation, and the favorites of the court." For Saint-Benoit-sur-Loire, whose fields were severely damaged when dikes along the river broke in 1788, a district would be the best means of "destroying even the memory of the evils that we have suffered." Municipal leaders at Le Donjon reflected a widespread mood of hope mingled with nostalgia when they thanked the National Assembly for locating a district in their town: "You are giving life to a vast area that has been miserable and stagnant for more than two hundred years. You are restoring the activity and splendor that it enjoyed in the thirteenth and fourteenth centuries, when Louis Bourbon, comte de Clermont, ordered the neighboring parishes to go to town for justice in the barony of Le Donjon."[69]

Petitioners from nearly 250 towns, bourgs, and villages affirmed that their communities would increase in size and wealth by becoming admin-

[67] AN DXVII 2 (Saint-Pierre-sur-Dives); DIV bis 30:429 (Sarthe).

[68] AN DIV bis 25:375 (Isère).

[69] AN DIV bis 32:446 (Vosges); DIV bis 26:381 (Loiret); DIV bis 17:290 (Somme); DIV bis 27:394 (Manche); C 103:183 (Saint-Benoit); C 104:193 (Le Donjon).

istrative or judicial seats in the new division of the kingdom. Many revealed ambitious plans for expansion in territorial influence, wealth, and population. In some petitions, declamations of community pride coexisted with cries of distress. In others, a message of boosterism altogether replaced demands for compensation. Bourgs with seigneurial courts wanted royal courts with larger jurisdictions; towns with minor royal courts submitted plans for *bailliages* courts; and those with *bailliages* aspired to more important appellate courts. At every level of the existing judicial system, communities wanted not only to maintain their relative position but to upgrade it. Several dozen of these contenders for new establishments were bourgs and villages that had never possessed any significant lawcourts. They hoped that wealthy men of law would settle in their communities and that numerous visitors would increase local trade. Some of these would-be towns also wanted lower taxes or more frequent markets and fairs to stimulate prosperity. As for established towns that emphasized their potential for growth, many were trying to increase the territorial jurisdiction of their lawcourts, although they often concealed this objective behind their pleas for help. Boosterism was the mirror image of sentimental rhetoric about decline and ruin. If the loss of old establishments would destroy a town, the acquisition of new ones would invigorate the urban economy or even bring a town into existence for the first time.

Ambitious leaders of little towns and bourgs often drew a contrast between the promise of development and a history of neglect. For the bourg of Selongey, an oppressive fiscal system had blocked development, but "a new order of things is going to give a new existence to this bourg and finally place it where it belongs in the political system"—at the center of a district. Spokesmen for Brienon blamed their seigneur, the archbishop of Sens, for never having done anything to improve the town, but now that seigneurialism had been abolished, they had "everything to hope from the present moment." Poor roads were the major cause of misfortune for Aubeterre, a little town in Angoumois, but with a district, these "horrible precipices" would be transformed into "safe and commodious highways," transport costs would fall, and farmers would grow cash crops instead of abandoning the land. Petitioners from L'Arbresle bemoaned their "lack of resources," while assuring the National Assembly that a lawcourt "would be for us an inestimable good." Those from the "poor and abandoned" little town of Limeuil reasoned from a different premise to a similar conclusion. Limeuil had fertile plains and a port at the confluence of the Dordogne and the Vézère rivers, but "by an inconceivable fate, this town is in a state of inertia which makes useless all the advantages that nature seems to have bestowed upon it." With a district, however, commerce would revive and the town would be raised to "the degree of prosperity for which it seems destined."[70]

Some communities were starting from scratch in their pursuit of urban rank and fortune: they lacked markets as well as lawcourts. Municipal officials at the village of Guignes, in the Brie, were especially ambitious. If Guignes obtained a district, "suddenly it would become a little town, very important by virtue of its pleasant site, its fine roads, its postal service, the fertility of its soil, its mineral waters, the nearby forests, and its healthy air." Of course, new buildings would be required to house the magistrates and lawyers who would settle in the burgeoning town. "In this way, craftsmen and merchants, whose work and business have slowed down considerably and nearly stopped since the Revolution, will find a resource not otherwise available." Guignes also requested a grain market, which would delight the farmers of the area because they would no longer have to lose time and money transporting their crops to markets four or five leagues away. In the past, "ministerial despotism, now happily annihilated," had blocked this request in order to protect the property rights of powerful noblemen who owned the markets in the nearest towns. Now the representatives of the commune of Guignes, "animated by the purest patriotism and the love of the public welfare," suggested that their village could become an entrepôt for the supply of Paris. After all, it was surrounded by twenty-eight parishes within a radius of two leagues, all closer to Guignes than to any town.[71]

Profits in real estate might be made if country towns became important centers of power. Empty lodgings could be rented to new residents, and buildings could be constructed on vacant land. The "ruined town" of Pérouges offered inexpensive lodgings to receive the new magistrates; and Cologne boasted of "many large houses available for sale or lease." Even the town of Ladavèze, which a spokesman admitted "is not presently inhabited," had "very beautiful houses within a quite short distance of its walls, not to mention those that are being constructed right now, and those that people would hasten to build if a district were located there." Of course, Ladavèze was an extreme case, but the defenders of quite small communities boasted of the prospects for new construction. The bourg of Herbignac, which possessed just over 80 houses "fit for habitation," had a favorable site "on a bedrock of stones that can be used for building"; the bourg of Jallais, numbering 150 households, had access to "the best limestone in France," with which to decorate new houses for the magistrates

---

[70] AN DIV bis 6:182 (Côte-d'Or); DIV bis 450:27 (Yonne); DIV bis 5:176 (Charente); C 94:92 (L'Arbresle); C 102:173 (Limeuil).

[71] Other examples of villages that sought markets as well as districts and lawcourts include Bouin, on an island off the coast of the Vendée, and Savigné-sur-Rille, north of Tours. AN DIV bis 17:286 (Seine-et-Marne); DIV bis 32:443 (Vendée); DIV bis 25:373.

who would settle there; and the "very small town" of Le Faou had land, stone, and wood available for expansion. Lest critics remark on the "mediocre extent" of the town of Le Faou, its memorialist affirmed that "the largest towns in the world were only hamlets until governments procured society for them."[72]

Proprietors stepped forward with specific plans to assist the growth of their towns. At Rozoy, where the "principal inhabitants" hoped to obtain a departmental seat, a spokesman announced proudly that "the patriotism of the townspeople is so strong that several of them have offered to advance the funds to construct new buildings." A proprietor at the market town of Montauban, in Brittany, made a similar offer. Monsieur Chantrel, who signed a petition from Montauban for a district, had just constructed a large town house, forty-two feet long and thirteen feet wide, on a "beautiful site" near the main highway. He would place this "multistory building," which had "excellent lighting" and "every sort of comfort," at the disposal of a district directory free of charge for two years. Then he planned to sell it to the officials. Several other "rich proprietors" at Montauban intended to invest in the construction of new houses if this settlement of five hundred inhabitants acquired a royal lawcourt. Existing dwellings could also be subdivided into more rentals. Petitioners from the little town of Montrevel listed eighteen residents who owned houses that had been constructed within the past ten years: a carpenter, a wheelwright, a shoemaker, a locksmith, a baker, a butcher, a pork butcher, an innkeeper, a tavern keeper, a hardware merchant, a process server, a bailiff, a schoolteacher, a surgeon, a notary, and two ladies. Each building could lodge several families, so the town could "grow fast very easily" to the benefit of house owners drawn from a variety of occupations.[73]

In requesting royal courts, many seigneurial towns and bourgs wanted to expand their jurisdiction over communities that used to possess separate lawcourts. For example, Courtalain proposed a royal *bailliage* with twenty-three parishes, as compared with the nine parishes in its existing seigneurial jurisdiction; Tannay submitted a plan that would expand its seigneurial *bailliage* of five parishes into a royal *bailliage* with twenty-eight parishes; and Dun-le-Palleau wanted to incorporate thirty-nine bourgs and villages into a jurisdiction that formerly contained only nine parishes. Such plans would replace the highly localized and splintered jurisdictions of ordinary seigneurial courts with a more extensive district for a royal court, based on a uniform conception of space. Each district would encompass all the parishes within a specified radius, which ranged from two to four leagues in a

[72] AN DIV bis 19:302 (Ain); DIV bis 24:362 (Gers); DIV bis 15:264 (Hautes-Pyrénées); DXVII 1 (Herbignac); C 97:119 (Jallais); DIV bis 23:352 (Finistère).

[73] AN DIV bis 90:1 (Seine-et-Marne); DIV bis 25:368 (Ille-et-Vilaine); DIV bis 3:146 (Ain).

majority of cases. Royal magistrates submitted comparable plans to increase their jurisidictions at the expense of seigneurial courts. The *prévôt* of Vermenton, who boasted of his "lively interest in the happiness and aggrandizement of our town," listed thirty-four *bailliages* and seigneurial justices within four leagues that could be joined to his royal court; and the officers of the royal *bailliage* at Neuville wanted to unite all the parishes within two leagues in their jurisdiction. Appellate lawcourts stimulated more ambitious proposals on the part of towns such as Quimper, in lower Brittany. Seeking a sovereign court as well as a department, municipal officials at Quimper assured the National Assembly that their town was capable of substantial growth, due to its maritime communications with Nantes, its direct access to stone, mortar, sand, and wood in the nearby countryside, and its proximity to fertile grainlands and fisheries along the coast. By contrast, the landlocked town of Carhaix would have to import building materials at great cost if it became a departmental seat.[74]

Around 150 towns and bourgs submitted plans for districts or tribunals that encompassed all the rural parishes within the radius of their weekly markets. Such plans were part of a larger strategy of emphasizing the vigor of markets, industry, or commerce. Some towns had a regional reputation for the importance of their weekly markets, which resembled fairs in attracting buyers and sellers from neighboring towns and adjacent *pays*. Others possessed quite ordinary markets that seemed impressive only in comparison with their lawcourts. In either case, townspeople had the option of justifying administrative and judicial institutions on the basis of their economic relationships with other communities. So did the residents of industrial towns and seaports that were engaged in long-distance commerce as well as local trade. Spokesmen for a total of 391 ambitious towns and bourgs chose to pursue this strategy of defining space in economic rather than institutional terms. Their petitions conveyed an impression of urban growth rather than decline, strength rather than vulnerability. In fact, some of these prophets of progress represented the interests of market towns that were just as small and stagnant as the *bailliage* seats or bishoprics whose petitions resounded with fears of ruin. Their claims to new institutions flowed from political opportunities as well as economic perceptions, the latter which were relative in any case to the circumstances of particular regions and communities.

Dozens of little towns in relatively isolated regions of the nation exaggerated the importance of their markets. For example, a correspondent from Verteuil, in the uplands of Angoumois, boasted of fourteen "considerable" fairs that "periodically bring the wealth of the surrounding area to

---

[74] AN C 112:277 (Courtalain); DIV bis 28:407; DIV bis 22:342; DIV bis 32:448; DIV bis 23:352 (Finistère).

us." On these fair days, strangers as well as merchants from the province displayed woolens and even silks under the large covered market of Verteuil, while every Wednesday, the inhabitants of neighboring towns arrived to buy all sorts of crops and foodstuffs. Left unspoken here is any mention of the poor roads that prevented townspeople at Vertueil from developing a significant export trade. Even on Wednesdays, Verteuil was only a primary market center. The rest of the time, it was a farming community that happened to possess a little barony, whose translation into a larger royal court was the goal of a few ambitious residents.[75] Townspeople at Bort, a small town that straddled the provinces of Limousin and Auvergne in the Massif Central, also exaggerated the scale of their economy when they described Bort as a "very commercial town" that served as the entrepôt for these two provinces. Its more modest functions were to provision peasants in the nearby mountains with grain and to serve as a point of transit for overland trade in cheese and livestock. Perhaps "extraordinary throngs of travelers" did use the "main highways" that crossed the Dordogne River at Bort, but such passersby would leave behind nothing but a little cash for the innkeepers in town.[76] Similarly, petitioners at the little town of Pouzauges, in the *bocage* country of lower Poitou, transformed their weekly markets into an "entrepôt" and their livestock fairs into "the only outlets" for trade with the neighboring province of Anjou and the more distant provinces of Brittany and Normandy. In fact, many livestock fairs existed in this region of dispersed settlements, and Pouzagues, like dozens of bourgs in Poitou, served primarily as a market center for nearby villages.[77]

Larger and more impressive market towns existed in provinces that had extensive commerce with seaports or major cities of the interior. In Normandy, for example, spokesmen for Gournay, a town of 3,000 inhabitants, had good reason to emphasize their weekly markets, which played an important role in supplying Paris with foodstuffs. Sales at these markets amounted to as much as 200,000 livres worth of all kinds of merchandise, including butter, eggs, fowl, fresh and salted fish, milk cows and other livestock. Farmers from a radius of ten or twelve leagues came to this "entrepôt for the entire *pays de Bray*," although such trips could not have been very frequent in a period when even men on horseback rarely covered a distance of ten leagues (forty kilometers) in less than a day. Some of the wealth generated by trade at Gournay had recently been invested in "establishments of utility and comfort, which equal in taste and solidity those in the

---

[75] AN DIV bis 5:176 (Charente).

[76] AN C 95:102 (Bort).

[77] AN C 93:89 (Pouzagues). On the dispersal of markets in this area, see Jean-Alexandre Cavoleau and A. D. de la Fontennelle de Vaudorée, *Statistique ou description générale du département de la Vendée* (Fontenay-le-Comte, 1844).

largest towns." Among these establishments were well-paved streets, new streetlights, fountains, promenades, fire pumps, and a public warehouse. The leaders of Gournay were urbanites who admired public emblems of prosperity and expected more wealth in the future. As they reasoned, the new highways that connected this part of Normandy to Paris guaranteed that markets in their town "can only increase in importance." A district and a royal lawcourt would confirm rather than generate wealth in such a town.[78]

In some regions, industrial production imparted unusual dynamism to towns that had never played an important role in the judicial system of the monarchy. For nearly two centuries, Saint-Etienne had been trying to obtain a royal *bailliage*, and just a year before the Revolution, the rapidly growing town of Cholet sent several memorials to royal officials, with the same goal in mind. Following the abolition of seigneurial courts, Saint-Etienne, Cholet, and dozens of other industrial towns emphasized their commercial prowess in petitions for new establishments. By defining commerce to include markets for the countryside as well as industrial exports, spokesmen for such towns based their claims on the relationship between urban growth and the rural economy. On the one hand, industrial exports favored local pride in the expansion of the urban economy. For example, Cholet, in western France, boasted of its commerce, "famed in the new world and the old"; Ganges, in Languedoc, praised its founding of "the most beautiful industry of stockings that exists," which "carries the commerce of a small country to the ends of Europe"; and Mazamet, also in Languedoc, applauded "the rapid and truly astonishing progress of its great commerce," worth more than three million livres a year. On the other hand, weekly markets connected these towns to peasants engaged in cottage industry. Various petitions from Cholet described this industrial "metropolis" as "the rendez-vous for 100 parishes"; the "soul and nursing mother" for all the parishes within a radius of over ten leagues; and "the unique center of an immense commerce in linens, handkerchiefs, thread, etc., produced in the countryside within a radius of three to four leagues, and brought to Cholet for sale to local merchants or to strangers." The leaders of rural parishes near Ganges agreed with urban spokesmen that this town played an indispensable role in the rural economy by distributing looms and raw materials to weavers in the countryside, and by extending cash and credit to these workers for the purchase of food. The same pattern of rural dependency on urban markets existed near Mazamet, where villages and hamlets were peopled by weavers who drew much of their subsistence from the town. With three grain markets a week, Mazamet was the "nourishing mother" for textile workers in the mountains. "We hear the

[78] AN DIV bis 27:284 (Seine-Inférieure).

cries of our brothers, our frightened neighbors," wrote urban patriots. "They are requesting through official deliberations that a district be located at Mazamet, their motherland, the center of relations for a population of 25,000."[79]

Few townspeople were more self-confident about their economic future than were the residents of rapidly growing industrial towns. Just as Cholet had grown from 4,000 to 9,000 inhabitants in the previous twenty years, so Bédarieux attracted "throngs of workers" to its weaving sheds, tanneries, copper founderies, and paper mills. At a town meeting, citizens agreed that Bédarieux was "the most commercial town of Languedoc, relative to its population."[80] Pride turned to arrogance at the textile town of Louviers, where over two hundred petitioners opposed the rival claims of Pont-de-l'Arche, a stagnant market town whose royal *bailliage* "derives from Gothic usages that must be abandoned today in favor of a better order of things." Louviers was "renowned for its manufacture of woolen cloth," and it also held three markets a week that attracted farmers and merchants from a radius of four or five leagues. In contrast to Pont-de-l'Arche, Louviers was "obviously going to grow in population and increase in force, establishments, and prestige." Such a town would always be of great utility to the surrounding area. Indeed, its markets provisioned the citizens of Pont-de-l'Arche with wheat and other foodstuffs such as fowl, butter, eggs, vegetables, and fruits. Inspired by a "lofty genius," the townspeople at Louviers greeted the Revolution as a new opportunity for growth, "just as a beautiful dawn is the harbinger of a splendid day." Their town was "destined to aggrandize itself and elevate its position by gathering the precious fruits of a great Revolution." As for Pont-de-l'Arche, it would always be "a town of the lowest rank," whose 1,500 inhabitants possessed "no means of growth at all."[81]

Not surprisingly, such self-confidence went hand in hand with an institutional heritage that provided little cause for celebration. For example, Louviers had nothing but a modest seigneurial court worth mentioning in its petition, while Pont-de-l'Arche had not only a royal *bailliage* but an *élection*, a *maîtrise particulier des eaux et forêts*, a subdelegation, and a *recette de la régie*, along with a salt granery and two convents. None of these establishments had a very extensive jurisdiction, but Pont-de-l'Arche ranked at level V on the institutional scale presented in table 1.10, which made it overinstitutionalized in comparison with its economic rank of only level VI. By contrast, Louviers ranked considerably higher on the economic

---

[79] AN DIV bis 30:423 (Rhône-et-Loire); DIV bis 26:389 and 67:2 (Maine-et-Loire); C 93:83 (Cholet); DXVII 1 (Cholet); DIV bis 8:207 and 25:366 (Hérault); DIV bis 17:291 (Tarn).

[80] AN DIV bis 25:366 (Hérault).

[81] AN DIV bis 23:349 (Eure).

scale (level IV) than on the institutional scale (level VI). Such contrasts can be correlated more generally with the rhetorical strategies adopted by townspeople. Among the 425 towns that emphasized the importance of lawcourts and other institutions for local prosperity, 38 percent ranked higher on the institutional than on the economic scale, 52 percent ranked equally on both scales, and only 10 percent ranked higher on the economic scale. Among the 340 towns that emphasized instead the vitality of their commerce and industry, 31 percent ranked higher on the economic scale, 56 percent ranked equally on both scales, and only 14 percent ranked higher on the institutional scale. Despite a national mood of crisis that encouraged townspeople to exaggerate their institutional losses and to disguise their commercial advantages, discrepancies in the institutional hierarchies and economic networks of the old regime did influence their pleas for compensation or their confidence in the future.[82] The tone and language of their petitions to the National Assembly revealed the distinctive anxieties and ambitions of an urban world shaped by the uneven development of both commerce and the state in eighteenth-century France.

[82] Towns with equal ranking on the two scales were more likely to express fears of decline if they had important institutions: 61/93, or 65 percent, of those above level VI adopted this rhetorical strategy, as compared with 158/316 (50 percent) of those at levels VI through VIII. The strongest contrast between optimistic and pessimistic rhetoric existed between towns at levels II through V on the economic scale that had a superior economic ranking (61/85, or 72 percent, boasted of their commerce), and towns at levels VI through VIII on the economic scale that had a superior institutional ranking (88/114, or 77 percent, emphasized their losses). This evidence is consistent with the fact that economic rank was strongly correlated with population size at higher levels, while institutional rank was correlated with population size only at lower levels of the hierarchy.

PART TWO

THE RHETORIC AND POLITICS
OF SPACE

IN A WIDE-RANGING polemic against a *bailliage* town, spokesmen for the flourishing seaport of Lorient dismissed the past: "Let us not be countered by the long history of the town of Hennebont, now that all the parchments have been torn up. We no longer judge men by the antiquity of their race, but by their talents and their virtues. Let us judge towns by their importance and their utility, and not by the dates of their foundation."[1] The voice of the Enlightenment and the ideology of the Revolution echoed in these words of contempt for tradition. Indeed, the abolition of the old regime confronted townspeople with a unique moment, when discourse seemed more powerful than institutions. To construct a new order, neither anxiety nor ambition would suffice. In the midst of revolution, the leaders of towns needed arguments that extended beyond their own walls to encompass a larger territory and even the nation itself. As special deputies from the old bishopric of Séez confessed, "We are aware that in the regeneration of a vast empire, all private interests must be swept aside by the general interest."[2] In this consciousness of a dramatic break with the past, townspeople struggled to find a new language that would impress the National Assembly. Appeals to the interest of rural populations countered pleas for the survival of towns; geographical analysis supplanted institutional description; and rhetoric acquired an ideological dimension. Through the arts of persuasion, the leaders of hundreds of towns aspired to become beneficiaries, not victims, of the new regime.

Their contentious discourse needs to be situated firmly in the context of political decisions that determined the boundaries and subdivisions of departments, and the location of capitals for the new administrative directories and lawcourts. Rhetoric can conceal as well as define relations of power. François Furet has argued that the Revolution "ushered in a world where mental representations of power governed all actions, and where a network of signs completely dominated political life."[3] A more plausible interpretation of the relationship between rhetoric and action during the Revolution would take into account the particular circumstances of actors as well as the general demands of ideology. Such a situational analysis

---

[1] AN DIV bis 27:392 (Lozère); ADXVI 53 (Lorient).

[2] AN DIV bis 12:249 (Orne).

[3] Furet, *Interpreting the French Revolution*, p. 48.

of the rhetoric surrounding the reconstruction of the French state highlights the influence of deputies and special deputies who represented towns in the National Assembly. In exercising power, these deputies responded to pressures from their hometowns and to the constraints that the Assembly itself imposed on the process of subdividing provinces into departments and districts. Yet they also acted in a legislative context that encouraged negotiations and compromises behind the grand scene of public debate. In the committees of the Assembly, deputies bargained for territory in defense of their constituents. Parochial loyalties ensured that the centrality of towns became the foremost issue that shaped both the language of townspeople and the decisions of deputies who redrew the map of France. The strategic importance of this issue helps explain why the institutional legacy of the past had a considerable influence on the formation of departments and districts. At the same time, the presence in the National Assembly of many deputies and special deputies from small and medium-sized towns ensured that the new territorial framework of the state would expand the jurisdictions of a substantial number of towns. In the contest over space, local demands converged with revolutionary ideology to foster territorial equality among towns.

Chapter 4

THE RHETORIC OF CONTENTION

THE FIRST ARTICLE of the beautiful declaration of the Rights of Man and Citizen declares men equal in rights, and states that social distinctions can only be founded on common utility." Thus did the revolutionary language of the National Assembly reappear in a municipal deliberation from Viane, formerly a town and now a "large village" in the mountains of upper Languedoc. Petitioners from Viane wanted a lawcourt in the district of Lacaune, a "vainglorious" little town whose inaccessible site contrasted with their own central location.[1] By invoking general principles in the context of local geography, they hoped to convince the National Assembly to change the distribution of establishments in this obscure corner of the kingdom. The spokemen for many towns and bourgs made a similar effort to translate parochial loyalties into a more general language of utility, equality, and patriotism. Their discourse was deeply rooted in the culture of the old regime, but it also expressed to varying degrees a new conception of the relationship between towns and the state. As provinces were subdivided into departments and districts, a more rational hierarchy of institutions would bring administrators and judges closer to the rural populations; spread the benefits of government more equally among towns and regions; and mobilize the energies of townspeople throughout the kingdom. None of these rhetorical themes—*rapprochement*, *vivification*, and patriotism—provided an adequate criterion for resolving disputes between towns. They can be interpreted instead as elements of a contentious discourse that related the particular interests of townspeople to more general perceptions of social order and political legitimacy.[2]

The principle of *rapprochement*, which revolutionaries in the National Assembly embraced in order to justify the partition of large provinces into smaller departments, became in the hands of many townspeople an argument for the proliferation of districts and lawcourts. A long history of jurisdictional conflicts in the old regime had familiarized petitioners with the idea that judges should reside at the center rather than the periphery of a *ressort*. From a central location, magistrates could investigate disputes between rural litigants more promptly, just as plaintiffs could appear in court

[1] AN C 101:162 (Viane).

[2] For a thorough analysis of the variety of geographical ideas expressed in this local discourse, see Ozouf-Marignier, *La formation des départements*, pp. 131–94.

more easily and at less expense. Each market town already attracted peasants from a well-defined area whose radius depended primarily on transport conditions. Thus, customary marketing relationships confirmed more abstract conceptions of centrality. By applying the idea of *rapprochement* to marketing areas, spokesmen for small towns and bourgs could develop a functional argument for the possession of royal courts. This line of reasoning first appeared in petitions that magistrates and men of law sent to the National Assembly after they learned that seigneurial courts would be abolished. For example, an address from the little market town of Ligueil proposed on August 11, 1789, that royal jurisdictions be formed around each town that held markets and fairs; and a memorial from the town and barony of Angles wanted royal or "national" courts created at intervals of four or five leagues so that nearby bourgs and villages which frequented the markets and fairs of this town would continue to be in its jurisdiction.[3] Debates in the National Assembly over the division of France encouraged a new wave of petitions that defended small districts as well as lawcourts. By the summer of 1790, a total of 1,059 towns and bourgs, of whom 87 percent had fewer than 5,000 inhabitants and 63 percent had fewer than 2,000 inhabitants, claimed that their central location within an area merited a new establishment. Spokesmen for 420 of these towns referred specifically to the social benefits of centrality, which followed from a utilitarian calculus that travel costs should be minimized. As emissaries from the small town of Torigny explained, litigants should be able to attend a lawcourt near their place of residence in order to save time and money. They proposed a jurisdiction with a radius of less than four leagues, "so that it is easy to go in the morning for one's legal business, and to return in the evening to sleep at home."[4]

Many petitioners tried to demonstrate their centrality by counting all the nearby villages, by measuring the distance to rival towns, or by submitting a map of the surrounding area. Most common were estimates of the number of rural communities in the vicinity of a town. A total of 716 *villes* and other contenders for districts or lawcourts presented such estimates, with 55 percent counting fewer than 30 nearby communities and only 16 percent counting more than 60 parishes or communes in their proximity. Nearly half of these towns also calculated the distance from outlying villages to their own location, using either an abstract measure of leagues or a concrete estimate of the number of hours that a traveler would need to reach them. The small scale of marketing and legal administration can be seen from the fact that only 117 towns mentioned a radius of at least four leagues or the equivalent distance in hours, as compared with 211 towns

---

[3] AN C 91:72, document 2 (Ligueuil); DXVII 1 (Angles); and DIV bis 18:295 (Vienne).
[4] AN DIV bis 5:172 (Manche).

that described an area with a radius of two or three leagues or hours of travel. To confirm their primacy over nearby villages, 516 towns also tabulated the distance to potential rivals. Typically, they listed three or four towns that were all located beyond a radius of a few leagues. By mentioning only the nearest royal *bailliage* instead of the nearest market center, some towns stretched their measure of interurban distance to six or more leagues, but a majority described at least one rival town within a range of three to five leagues. Of course, centrality within any network of localities is relative to the point of observation. As special deputies from one little town complained, "Centrality can be found wherever one desires; it suffices to indicate a circumscription for any town one chooses as a central point."[5] One town's centrality became another town's periphery, as mutually incompatible plans for districts and lawcourts reached the offices of the Comité de Constitution.

At least 159 towns tried to strengthen their case for a jurisdiction by submitting a map of their surroundings. A few of these maps were copied directly from sections of existing maps that Cassini and other cartographers had published, but a majority were drawn by surveyors or unknown amateurs for particular towns.[6] Such handmade maps often presented an abstract representation of the space around a town. Concentric circles would enclose the names of villages; rival towns would appear on the outer circumference of the plan or disappear from view altogether; and roads would be ignored. Colors as well as lines illustrated degrees of centrality in some of these "geometrical plans." More realistic maps that included rivers and roads had the same purpose of demonstrating the central location of a town. When the mayor of Avesnes submitted a plan for a district bordered by the Sambre River, special deputies from the rival town of Maubeuge complained that the map suppressed entire villages near their area while it filled the environs of Avesnes with the names of the smallest hamlets. The centrality of Avesne was an artifice of cartography: "It will always be easy to place any kind of town in the center of a district, if one starts from this town in order to draw the boundaries of the district."[7] Even a map as detailed as the one submitted by the town of Saint-Pourçain concealed such a prearranged conception of space. Bounded on the east by the river Allier and on other sides by straight lines that formed an irregular hexagon, Saint-Pourçain's plan relegated the small towns of Chantelle and Varennes to the very edge of its jurisdiction while carefully excluding the larger and

[5] *Mémoire* from the town of Saint-Macaire, AN DIV bis 8:202 (Gironde).

[6] Compare the "geometrical map" for Luxeuil (Haute-Saône), based on an extract of Cassini's map, with maps designed by Robinet, *géometre* at Lonjumeau (Seine-et-Oise); M. Boisseau, *avocat* at Neauphle (Seine-et-Oise); and Sébastiel le Jal, surveyor and *géometre* at Fontenay-le-Château (Vosges), in AN DXVII 1; DIV bis 32:446.

[7] AN DIV bis 29:410 (Nord).

more ambitious towns of Gannat and Cusset.[8] Such selective images became rarer after the National Assembly established the boundaries of districts, but some towns continued to submit maps that left blank spaces where roads would need to be traced in order to prove that rural populations could reach them more easily than a rival town.[9]

Instead of presenting an abstract model of space, many towns emphasized the social geography of their surroundings, the importance of commercial networks and population densities, or the relationship between *rapprochement* and social order. Rural as well as urban petitioners expressed a strong interest in establishing small jurisdictions for district directories and lawcourts. Bad roads, poor weather, and slow methods of transport imposed narrow limits on the distance that farmers could travel in less than a day. The radius of attraction for weekly markets rarely exceeded three or four leagues, although seasonal fairs might draw buyers and sellers from much longer distances. Under these circumstances, petitioners near Bonnétable expressed with polite exaggeration a common preference when they wrote, "Our dearest wish is to have a tribunal of justice in the nearest town, which is Bonnétable, the customary market center for our community." The municipal leaders of Bellafaire, a village in the Alps, embellished the same idea when they alluded to "numerous examples" of people who had drowned in the river Sasse while trying to reach the town of Sisteron, six leagues away. Bellafaire sold its livestock and crops at the smaller town of Seyne, only three leagues away on a passable road. Thus, Seyne would be the perfect center for a district and a lawcourt. Even peasants in the plains of Picardy, where transportation was easier than in the Alps, registered strong support for local towns. As petitioners near Roye argued, "The numerous and densely populated parishes neighboring the town of Roye are no further than two or three leagues from its walls, and we live with its townspeople and they with us. . . . Its position is very advantageous for the marketing of our crops; at little cost, and on passable roads, we can reach Roye quickly and complete our business." The somewhat larger town of Montdidier, located three to five leagues from most of these parishes, seemed "inaccessible in nearly all seasons," and grain farmers near Roye had "no contact" with Montdidier for the sale of their crops.[10]

From attachment to the market of a town, peasants acquired a broader

[8] Map in AN DIV bis 19:305 (Allier).

[9] See, for example, the map of the district of Evaux (Creuse), which suggests that neither Evaux nor the rival town of Chambon had any roads, AN DIV bis 6:184 (Creuse); and two maps of the district of Tarascon, submitted by a deputy from Saint-Rémy, in AN DIV bis 20:324 (Bouches-du-Rhône).

[10] Petitions from the parish of La Bosse, AN DIV bis 16:278 (Sarthe); the community of Bellafaire, DIV bis 3:154 (Basses-Alpes); and from farmers (*laboureurs*) in the district of Roye, DIV bis 17:290 (Somme).

interest in the services which they could obtain from townsmen. As petitioners near a market center in Burgundy remarked, "It is at Courson that we have our advisers, our solicitors, our notaries, our surgeons, blacksmiths, locksmiths, harness makers, bakers, butchers, shoemakers, and where we find the other artisans whom we need." With respect to legal counsel, peasants who owned land had reason to support their market town as a center for the drafting of notarial documents and the settlement of disputes over marriage contracts, wills and testaments, mortgages and other debts. Villagers at Boisemont praised the town of Andelys not only as the most flourishing market for the area but as the place where "we are all in the habit of drawing up our family documents; its magistrates, its officeholders have our confidence." In like manner, villagers near the small town of Donzy wrote, "This place is where all our inhabitants draw up their notarized documents, and, consequently, it is the town where all their secrets are kept." Through weekly visits to market centers, peasants also learned to appreciate the leadership qualities of townspeople and to seek their patronage. "Consider the bonds of habit which create a circle of friends among the inhabitants of the small area that surrounds each town," wrote a patriot from the little town of Conches. "They can find protectors against injustice, if need be, in the town that they are accustomed to visiting." Petitioners from Riez added that their market served as a "general rendezvous" for rural populations and fostered "a perfect and reciprocal knowledge of the virtue, the talents, the meritorious qualities of individuals, who are just like children within the same family; this permits better discernment in the choice of administrators and a more exact balance in the distribution of taxes and favors; it makes injustice nearly impossible."[11]

Towns favored by roads and commerce developed the argument that physical distances were less important than transport networks and commercial relationships in determining centrality. In the words of special deputies from the market town of Saint-Amour, "The central point is not the point which, measured geometrically, is in the center. . . . It is the point where correspondence with surrounding localities is the easiest, where commerce is the most naturally directed, where commodities arrive with the least difficulty."[12] Thus, Marle claimed that its position at the junction of four highways, leading in every direction, gave it a superior location to Vervins, whose geographical centrality in the *pays* of Thiérache could not compensate for an inferior road network; Cognac argued that its Saturday markets, which regulated the price of *eau de vie* throughout the provinces of Angoumois and Saintonge, attracted the parishes that were closer to the

---

[11] AN DIV bis 32:447 (Mouffy, in the Yonne); 23:349 (Boisemont, in the Eure); DIV bis 28:406 (Menou, in the Nièvre); DIV bis 62:3 (Eure); DIV bis 19:310 (Basses-Alpes).

[12] AN DIV bis 9:213 (Jura).

rival town of Jarnac; and La Rochelle insisted that its seaport, which exported and imported all kinds of commodities, made it "the moral and physical center of interests and affairs" for towns and villages of the interior.[13] The population of a commercial town might also counterbalance the geographical centrality of an administrative and judicial town. Deputies from Marseille pointed out that their great seaport contained nearly five times as many inhabitants as the old provincial capital of Aix-en-Provence and its rural surroundings. Spokemen for the port of Lorient agreed that "everything depends on population," which sustained their claim over the much smaller town of Hennebont; and the mayor of Dunkerque calculated that his town's population of 30,000, when combined with the 25,000 inhabitants of nearby cantons, substantially exceeded the 38,000 people who resided in the rival town of Bergues and its environs.[14]

Population estimates also supported the claims of towns that were located in rich and densely populated areas. Jurisdictions that combined mountains and plains generally had considerable internal variation in population densities, with the fertile lowlands containing more population than the highlands. This encouraged towns in the plains to redefine centrality in demographic terms. For example, petitioners from Nyons used the greater population densities in the plains of lower Dauphiné to counter the argument that Le Buis had a more central location in the mountains of the Baronnies. So did deputies from Villefranche-de-Rouergue, who rested their claim to a department on the soil conditions and population densities along the lower valley of the Aveyron, as compared with those of the highlands around Rodez: "It is for people and not for the immense deserts of the mountains in upper Rouergue that public establishments are made." In this case, however, spokesmen for Rodez replied that their town was not only located in the exact center of the department but was closer to territories that were just as populous as the areas around Villefranche. Only one-sixth of the population in the department was closer to Villefranche than to Rodez.[15] Such disputes over departmental seats sometimes led to elaborate calculations of centrality. After deputies from Saint-Omer demonstrated, map in hand, that a larger area of the Pas-de-Calais and more towns and bourgs were closer to their town than to Arras, deputies from this rival town replied that the countryside within seven leagues of Arras had the most wealth and population, while two-fifths of the area within seven leagues of Saint-Omer was not even located in the department. For Arras, which boasted of its own population of 24,000 inhabit-

---

[13] AN DIV bis 3:144 (Aisne); DIV bis 21:332 (Charente); DIV bis 21:333 (Charente-Inférieure).

[14] AN DIV bis 5:167 (Bouches-du-Rhône); ADXVI 53 (Lorient); DIV bis 29:410 (Nord).

[15] AN DIV bis 22:348 (Drôme); DIV bis 20:322 (Aveyron).

ants, demography provided a more realistic measure of centrality than did territory alone.[16]

Poor conditions of transport suggested the counterargument that *rapprochement* should be based on ecological rather than demographic conditions. The highlands of the southern Massif Central posed unusual obstacles to travelers, as the municipality of Pont-de-Camarès, a market center in Rouergue, emphasized in its request for a small district: "Distances that may appear short on a map increase infinitely in an area like this one, because of bad roads, steep mountains that have to be climbed and descended, and long detours around rivers that lack bridges and often block communications." Climate as well as terrain discouraged travel in the mountains of Gévaudan, where voters from the district of Saint-Chély dismissed the request of Le Malzieu for a tribunal: "In a *pays* where the length of the winters, the harshness of the climate, and the accumulation of snow make it very difficult, often perilous, and sometimes deadly to walk an extra two or three hours, the town with a central location must necessarily become the seat of justice." Forests created similar isolation in the *pays* of Othe, where the bourg of Aix-en-Othe protested its inclusion in the district of Ervy. "This locality is scarcely known; it is a species of continental island whose approach from our area is prevented by a thick forest of over 20,000 *arpents*, and by solitary hills and inaccessible marshes." As the center of thirty-five parishes, Aix-en-Othe deserved its own district in the department of Troyes. Even townspeople in relatively flat and open country sometimes used ecological arguments to justify small districts. Pertuis invoked the natural unity of the Durance River basin against plans to join its valley to the district of Apt, on the other side of the Luberon Mountains; and Riez protested that plans to attach the neighboring plateau to the mountains around Digne were "in opposition to nature itself. A different type of soil, striking contrasts in agricultural produce, in communities, in industry, in resources, everything will produce the most obvious confusion among heterogeneous parts that can never form anything but a shapeless and monstrous whole." Instead of defying natural regions, the National Assembly should follow the boundaries that climate and terrain had created in this part of Provence.[17]

Forms of land tenure and work routines also entered the debate over centrality. Several dozen towns argued that the principle of *rapprochement* should be applied, above all, to areas that had numerous legal disputes.

---

[16] Concerning this dispute between Saint-Omer and Arras, see Eugène Stevelberg, "L'influence de la perception et de l'organisation de l'espace sur la réforme administrative: Le cas du Nord et du Pas-de-Calais," in *Actes du 101e Congrès National des Sociétés Savantes*, vol. 2, *La France du Nord de 1610 à nos jours* (Paris, 1978), pp. 115–19.

[17] AN DIV bis 20:323 (Aveyron); DIV bis 27:392 (Lozère); DIV bis 4:162 (Aube); DIV bis 5:167 (Bouches-du-Rhône); DIV bis 19:310 (Basses-Alpes).

According to spokesmen for Château-Chinon, properties were minutely divided in the nearby mountains of the Morvan, leading to much litigation between small landowners. By contrast, the rival towns of Moulins-en-Gilbert and Corbigny were surrounded by big farms, where few peasants owned land and lawsuits were rare. From the town of Beaufort, near the valley of the Loire, came a similar argument that nearby estates were subdivided into small farms, which caused many lawsuits, while the area around the rival town of Baugé, with its infertile soil, was covered by heath and forest. According to municipal leaders at Meulan, in the valley of the Seine, rich and populated areas needed more districts than did thinly populated areas because they paid higher taxes and had more administative business. Higher population densities also implied more intensive work routines that might restrict opportunities for travel. According to townspeople from Belvès, any loss of time is harmful "in an area almost entirely planted in vineyards, where labor is by hand, and where the entire year barely suffices to take care of the vines." Petitioners from the town of Meung agreed that winegrowers needed to give the greatest care to their work and could not afford to lose time. The combination of farming and rural industry also resulted in heavy labor demands, which led a spokesman for the town of Condé-sur-Noireau to complain that industry would suffer if rural workers, "who leave their looms only to cultivate their small plots of land," were obliged to travel six or seven leagues for legal business. The defenders of several commercial towns applied this argument about the pressures of work to merchants. "Everyone knows," wrote deputies from Marseille, "that a businessman cannot abandon his countinghouse, his warehouses, his ships, his correspondence, his business, his daily accounts, without compromising his greatest interests and often his entire fortune." For professions that demanded constant attention, travel on administrative or legal business wasted not only time but money.[18]

Occasionally, townspeople defended *rapprochement* as a social cause of the poor rather than the rich. According to a committee at Bourgneuf, large jurisdictions would "increase the obstacles to justice for the indigent class of the people, and would place the poor and the weak even more at the mercy of the rich and the powerful." If a district lawcourt were located in a "foreign and unapproachable city," complained petitioners from Lormes, "the rich man" would profit, while "the poor man" would have to abandon his inheritance.[19] Such anticipations of democratic rhetoric were more than balanced, however, by stern demands for lawcourts that would

---

[18] AN DIV bis 28:406 (Nièvre); DIV bis 26:389 (Maine-et-Loire); DIV bis 30:431 (Seine-et-Oise); DIV bis 22:344 (Dordogne); DXVII 1 (Meung); DXVII 1 (Condé-sur-Noireau); DIV bis 5:167 (Bouches-du-Rhône).

[19] AN DIV bis 26:383 (Loire-Inférieure); DIV bis 28:407 (Nièvre).

repress crime and maintain social order. A total of 139 towns argued that local courts played an indispensable role in guarding society from a variety of dangers: anarchy and brigandage in the countryside; riots in market centers; labor conflicts in industrial towns; violent brawls in seaports. *Rapprochement* strengthened criminal justice, while distance from lawcourts fostered crime and disorder. In the dramatic language of municipal leaders from Gacé, "The sword of the law imprints terror, blunts the needle of crime, weakens the impulse towards wrongdoing. By contrast, when judges are far away, distance seems to serve as a rampart for crime, and multiplies the hope of impunity." Or as a postal director at the nearby town of Moulins-Lamarche announced, "The proximity of a judge makes rascals tremble with fear." In their punitive zeal, such advocates of lawcourts expressed the social anxieties of townspeople who perceived in their surroundings a perpetual threat of anarchy and violence.[20]

Mountainous and forested regions had a particular reputation for lawlessness in the old regime. Brigands were accused of taking refuge in remote highlands and deep forests; mountaineers were denounced for their brutal customs; and itinerant workmen were blamed for invading the forests and stealing wood. Entire populations who lived on the margin of agricultural settlements became a turbulent and irreligious multitude in the eyes of royal magistrates who were charged with enforcing Colbert's forest regulations in eighteenth-century France.[21] Urban elites did not have to visit the New World in order to find savages in the wilderness, although the brigands, scoundrels, malefactors, thieves, and murderers whom they denounced in their petitions shared little of the natural goodness attributed to Native Americans. Townspeople at Le Monastier, in the highlands of Forez, argued bluntly that "a lawcourt is of the greatest necessity in the midst of these mountains to restrain the evildoers, and to investigate and punish the violent deeds and murders committed around here all too often." Petitioners from Condat-en-Féniers also demanded a lawcourt to repress "disorder, crimes, and brigandage" in the highlands of Auvergne, and those from Felletin wanted a tribunal "to serve as a brake on the least obedient people" in the mountains of Combrailles. As officials at Le Buis explained, "In isolated areas of the mountains people are deprived of knowledge, little inclined to support public order, and easily persuaded to engage in seditious movements. It is useful to have authorities nearby to watch, repress, or help them, as the case may be." Located in the center of the

---

[20] AN DIV bis 12:249 (Orne); DIV bis 29:413 (Orne).

[21] See, for example, the dossier compiled by the *prévôté* and *maîtrise des eaux et forêts* of the principality of Château-Regnault, which includes letters in the year 1781 from priests and military commanders who denounced the "insults to religion" and the "*libertinage*" of populations in this forested area, AN DIV bis 19:315 (Ardennes).

highlands known as the Baronnies, Le Buis needed to exercise undivided authority over such ill-disciplined mountaineers.[22]

The turmoil of the Revolution created special problems of law enforcement in the forests around towns such as Darney (Vosges) and Haguenau (Alsace). A memorial for Darney complained that "immense forests," pressing in upon the town from all sides, had suffered "incalculable damage during the past year"; and voters in the district of Haguenau bemoaned "the nearly universal assault on communal forests that took place during the recent troubles."[23] Both these towns requested district tribunals in order to prevent such depredations. So did a few magistrates who were already responsible for policing forests, such as the *maître des eaux et forêts* at Château-Renault. As this magistrate explained, the surrounding forests supported a population of "laborers, lumbermen, nailmakers, ironsmiths, charcoal makers, gunsmiths, carters, boatmen, fishermen, glass workers, and slate quarriers, mixed together with all kinds of craftsmen." These workers owned nothing but little houses and gardens, and they exploited the forests to earn a living. According to the judge, who was the third member of his family to wage an unremitting struggle against hereditary rights of usage in these forests, the inhabitants were "trained from childhood in all kinds of misdemeanors, which they commit from the age of four to eighty, and to which they are drawn by habits transmitted from generation to generation." Without a tribunal on the spot, this border area would become the refuge of vagabonds from everywhere, and the forests, already seriously endangered, would be completely ruined.[24]

Restless and mobile populations also seemed to threaten social order in market towns, frontier towns, seaports, and industrial towns. Markets attracted "innumerable people" to Ligueil, and an "infinity of strangers" to Mirambeau. They gave rise to "a swarm of disputes" at Vouziers, facilitated "all kinds of crimes" at Auneau, and instigated "noise, clamors, and seditions" at Brou. Without a lawcourt, what would become of order and peace in towns such as La Française, whose markets and fairs brought "tumult and an indescribable fracas"? Towns along the eastern frontier, such as Héricourt, Lixheim, and Landau, wanted magistrates to "prevent contraband," repress "vagabonds and bandits," and guard against "fugitives, bankrupts, and criminals." From the seaport of Calais, "a place of transit, entry and exit from the kingdom, where a crowd of unknown people are found every day," petitioners feared that debtors would escape their creditors and crimes would go unpunished unless the town obtained a district court. Similarly, the port of Le Havre deserved a district tribunal because

[22] AN DIV bis 9:222 (Haute-Loire); DIV bis 29:416 (Cantal); DIV bis 108:8 (Creuse); DIV bis 6:190 (Drôme).

[23] AN DIV bis 76:4 (Vosges); DIV bis 29:422 (Bas-Rhin).

[24] AN DIV bis 19:315 (Ardennes).

it was "exposed to a perpetual coming and going of strangers from every nation, brought here by ships; and of men without any settled abode, attracted by maritime work and the appetite of gain. The variety of backgrounds and customs of all these people give birth to fights and misdemeanors; and the hope of impunity, through escape by sea, emboldens crime and multiplies violent assaults."[25]

According to spokesmen for several industrial towns, workers posed an equal threat to social order. Back in the 1660s, the aldermen of Saint-Etienne had petitioned the king that the workers and craftsmen in their town "would become a populace of scoundrels and brigands if the most severe law enforcement did not prevent great crimes by rigorously punishing the smallest misdemeanors." In 1790, their descendents again insisted that Saint-Etienne needed a lawcourt to maintain order, which had recently been troubled by "several insurrections." Municipal officials at Ganges, a small industrial town in Languedoc, expressed similar anxiety about textile workers when they requested a district tribunal: "If the stern eye of justice were more distant, it would exercise less restraint over license; especially in manufacturing towns, the presence of an active judge is a necessity at every moment."[26]

Such arguments amounted to a plea for lawcourts in each and every town. The idea of *rapprochement* seemed to dissolve into a welter of local interpretations, as distances shrank to the radius of country markets, the territory of distinctive *pays*, or the walls of separate towns. Political slogans, derived from revolutionary discourse, accentuated these centrifugal tendencies. Many townspeople hoped that the National Assembly would stimulate economic development by restructuring the hierarchy of institutions in accordance with egalitarian ideals. They invoked moral arguments in support of distributing directories and lawcourts to many central places rather than concentrating all the resources of government in a few towns. Their idea of *vivification*, which echoed the rhetoric of deputies who defended the plan of the C.C. in the National Assembly, combined social resentments against large and prosperous towns with physiocratic theories of wealth and revolutionary slogans of equality. Townspeople called for emancipation from the "aristocratic despotism" of provincial capitals, and they promised to spread the advantages of the Revolution to the country-

---

[25] AN C 91:72, document 2 (Ligueil); DIV bis 21:334 (Charente-Inférieure); DIV bis 19:315 (Ardennes); DIV bis 9:221 (Eure-et-Loir, mistakenly filed under Loiret); DIV bis 23:351 (Eure-et-Loir); DXVII 1 (La Françoise-en-Quercy); DIV bis 30:426 (Haute-Saône); DIV bis 27:398 (Meurthe); DIV bis 16:268 (Bas-Rhin); DIV bis 29:415 (Pas-de-Calais); DIV bis 17:282 (Seine-Inférieure).

[26] *Mémoire* cited by André Coron, *Essai sur la sénéchaussée de Saint-Etienne dans ses rapports avec le bailliage de Forez* (Lyon, 1936), p. 138, n. 5; AN DIV bis 30:425 (Rhône-et-Loire); DIV bis 25:366 (Hérault).

side. A few advocates of small towns presented new images of family relationships as well as new arguments about political rights. Just as the idea of *rapprochement* implied the fragmentation of urban regions, so the principle of equalizing the benefits of government implied the breakdown of urban hierarchies. Through closer association with the state, small towns would acquire the same means of prosperity that large towns had tended to monopolize during the old regime.

Urban interests and egalitarian ideology first converged in the rhetoric of townspeople who welcomed the division of large provinces into smaller departments. In Dauphiné, for example, the mayor of Gap hailed "the new order of things" as the "best means to fertilize the countryside, make small towns flourish, and regenerate the entire kingdom. At last, all commerce, all cash, all resources will no longer be concentrated in a few capitals. Now small localities can hope to share these great advantages and exercise proportionate influence over the political administration of the state."[27] While Gap hoped to obtain a department for the high Alps, the town of Valence, in the Rhône River valley, had designs on the rich lowlands of Dauphiné. Its leaders protested the efforts of the intermediate commission of the provincial estates, meeting at Grenoble, to mobilize public opinion around the existing institutions of the province. Asking the rhetorical question of why Grenoble alone opposed the division of the Dauphiné into three departments, spokesmen for Valence replied:

> The victories over ministerial power have now begun to challenge the mentality that used to reign in the capital cities and their administrative bodies. Lower-ranking towns and the countryside, emancipated from the influence of these capitals, now want to preserve for themselves or in nearby localities the resources that used to give such abundance and life to the principal towns. It is this spirit of equality, this desire for a wise distribution of important establishments throughout the provinces, which explain the changes underway.[28]

Similarly, a general assembly of townspeople at Vienne, who also hoped to obtain a department in Dauphiné, praised the abolition of provincial privileges and criticized any effort to preserve the aristocratic influence of towns such as Grenoble. Their own province, with its several mountainous areas and relatively unimportant commerce, needed to be revitalized by a division that brought justice closer to litigants and reduced the distance between administration and the people. Dismissing fears of Parisian domination, they insisted that if any capital were to be feared in Dauphiné, it would be the town of Grenoble.[29]

---

[27] AN DIV bis 19:311 (Hautes-Alpes).
[28] AN C 101:162 (Valence).
[29] AN DIV bis 8:211 (Isère).

Once the partisans of a division into relatively small departments became victorious, public attention shifted to the rivalries between various towns for departmental seats, district directories, and lawcourts. Now a variety of towns embraced the ideas of *vivification* and equality. Some continued to denounce provincial capitals and other large towns for oppressing the countryside. Others decried the wealth and ambition of commercial towns, which threatened to monopolize all power in an area by becoming departmental or district seats. Still others defended small towns against large ones, or one small town against another one, or the countryside against all towns. After district seats were chosen in February 1790, equality became an important theme in the disputes concerning lawcourts, which might be assigned to different towns in accordance with the principle of sharing establishments. Finally, the completion of judicial reform in August 1790 provoked new controversies over the survival or suppression of small districts and lawcourts, whose *ressorts* often reduced the jurisdictions of towns that had possessed *présidiaux* and royal *bailliages* during the old regime. Here again, the ideal of equality supported small towns against the efforts of larger neighbors to aggrandize territory at their expense. As a result of these successive conflicts, a total of 227 towns appealed explicitly to the egalitarian ideals of the National Assembly, and another 127 towns defended the logic of apportioning establishments to central places that had the greatest need for revitalization, rather than to those which had the most population, commerce, and wealth. As the leaders of small and vulnerable towns became increasingly familiar with debates in Paris, they learned to translate their grievances into revolutionary discourse. The mayor of Avesnes stated the new political principles with especial clarity: "The system of the National Assembly is not to take benefits away from those who have too little, in order to give benefits to those who have too much; its purpose, on the contrary, is to revitalize all parts of the empire and to restore balance by redistributing wealth equally and by sharing the means of power and abundance."[30]

This new political consciousness derived much of its strength from social attitudes and beliefs that originated in the old regime. To begin with, many towns resented the concentration of tax revenues in provincial capitals, where the government lavished its attention on roads, buildings, and other public works. If the intendants of eighteenth-century France promoted monumental projects in the capitals where they resided, such as Aix-en-Provence, Bordeaux, and Montpellier, they paid much less attention to the development of other towns.[31] "Urbanism" became a grandiose symbol of

[30] AN DIV bis 12:245 (Nord).

[31] On urbanism in the old regime, see Pierre Lavedan, *Histoire de l'urbanisme: Renaissance et temps modernes* (Paris, 1941); and Duby, *Histoire de la France urbaine* 3:439–82.

political favoritism. In describing this "reign of abuses," petitioners from Lambesc called attention to the "sumptuous monuments, superb promenades, magnificent edifices, costly roads, and ostentatious avenues" that the government had constructed with their tax monies for the "particular embellishment" of the capital of Provence. Similarly, municipal officials at Viviers denounced the large towns of Languedoc for viewing them only as tributaries during the old regime: "The splendid monuments erected at our expense for the vanity of administrators, that superb public square which cost so many millions, that quay which bears the name of a famous prelate, that canal constructed for the town of a parliamentary president, those scientific collections and professors of physics, those unmerited subsidies, those lavish displays of every sort, all testify to the fact that association with these large towns will never suit our needs." Such attitudes mingled hostility toward the culture of large towns with resentment of the government. As a special deputy from the Burgundian town of Nuits complained about the capital of Dijon, "All the arts are united there to embellish it with monuments whose luxury and magnificence have ruined the inhabitants of the small towns and the countryside who have had to cover the costs: bishopric, seminary, college, public schools, university, academy, spectacles . . . are supported and paid for by those who are forced to go there to educate their children or obtain justice."[32]

Inequities in the burden of taxation compounded the grievances of small towns. Petitioners from Montluçon complained that "we are bent under the weight of taxes, while in the capitals, taxes are nothing or almost nothing in proportion to wealth, commerce, and population. . . . For the past twenty years and more, our tax monies have been used to provide them, at our very great prejudice, with all kinds of objects of decoration and luxury." An anonymous resident of Is-sur-Tille, a bourg in Burgundy, emphasized that towns had grown during the old regime by offering fiscal privileges to rich landowners, who deserted the countryside in order to squander their revenues on urban luxuries. "It is by concentrating in large towns all the tribunals, all the points of administration, all kinds of establishments, all sorts of encouragement, that the sources of prosperity, industry and activity in the countryside have been exhausted." The larger the town, the more proprietors benefited from fiscal exemptions, due to the sale of offices and other fiscal privileges. Spokesmen for the *pays* of Vic-en-Carladès, in Auvergne, commented that the provincial capital of Clermont-Ferrand paid lower taxes in proportion to its wealth and population than did the medium-sized towns of Aurillac and Saint-Flour, which in turn were taxed less heavily than was the small town of Maurs. All hope of

---

[32] AN DIV bis 59 (Bouches-du-Rhône); DIV bis 19:312 (Ardèche); DIV bis 22:337 (Côte-d'Or).

equality in the provinces would soon vanish if these same privileged towns, having fattened themselves on the juices of the countryside through an unequal apportionment of taxation, succeeded in monopolizing all the new establishments. Municipal officials at the small town of Rue, in Picardy, agreed that a long history of fiscal oppression justified popular fears of "the powerful men who inhabit large towns." If the principal towns in the provinces monopolized establishments in the districts, the new division would perpetuate an urban aristocracy forever, and the people of the countryside would always be overtaxed and oppressed.[33]

Critics of urbanization argued that large towns were accumulating wealth and population at the expense of small towns and the countryside. According to municipal officials at Condé-sur-Noireau, in Normandy, cities in the old regime were "bottomless pits which swallowed up the output of the countryside and small towns, along with the human species itself." Petitioners from Blesle, in Auvergne, blamed the principal towns, with their privileges, opulence, roads, commerce, and lucrative employments, for the fact that market towns and rural communities in their province were suffering from "ruinous emigration." So did a spokesmen for Montaigut, also in Auvergne, who argued that for the past forty years, towns of the first and second rank had been destroying those of an inferior class. Against this background of migration to provincial capitals and other important towns, the division of the kingdom afforded an opportunity to restore a healthy equilibrium to French demography. In the words of petitioners from Maurs, yet another Auvergnat town, "The National Assembly has constantly expressed the most formal desire to redirect to small towns and the bountiful countryside the flow of population that luxury and despotism have been piling up in the principal towns of the kingdom." A critic of Lyon added that the simple countrymen of the province of Forez needed to be protected from the corrupting influence of Lyon:

> It is by frequenting this great city that our petty merchants and rural workers have learned about odious pleasures, invented by egoism and disorder. Insulting nature, they dare to calculate, to limit the number of their children, suffocating the future generation in the very arms of the hymen. Everyone knows that this plague, the greatest enemy of population, has spread to the smallest villages.

He concluded that to stop such dangerous abuses, it was essential to establish a separate department for Forez.[34]

[33] AN DIV bis 19:307 (Allier); DIV bis 108:6 (Côte-d'Or); DIV bis 2:48 (Cantal); DIV bis 31:440 (Somme).

[34] AN DIV bis 5:172 (Calvados); C 92:76 (Blesle); DIV bis 14:256 (Puy-de-Dôme); DIV bis 21:331 (Cantal); Printed *Réflexions patriotiques présentées par un habitant du Forez à l'Assemblée Nationale*, n.d., DIV bis 16:272 (Rhône-et-Loire). For a more general analysis of these antiurban sentiments, see Ozouf-Marignier, *La formation des départements*, pp. 110–21.

In contrasting urban vice with rural virtue, such critics drew on a cultural tradition that equated conspicuous consumption, or *luxe*, with decadence and immorality.[35] For townsmen at Vertus, in Champagne, peasants would become corrupted if they had to travel to large towns for justice and administration. The "display of luxury" in such places would undermine their "rustic and patriarchal customs," teach them lessons of "fiscal greed and legal chicanery," and show them "the dangerous principles of egoism and falsehood." Sharing with physiocratic thinkers the assumption that farming is the primary source of wealth, notables at the market town of Craponne drew a sharp contrast between commercial towns and the countryside. Agriculture, "first among all the arts because it feeds mortals," would be neglected if establishments were all concentrated at the large town of Le Puy, "absolutely devoted to business and commercial speculations." Tenant farmers near Craponne would be plunged back into a state of "inertia, distress and oppression" if they had to support the "pride and luxury" of Le Puy. Petitioners from Luçon distinguished more generally between the impact of large and small towns on rural society: "It is a recognized truth that if large towns, through their luxury, impoverish and dessicate the countryside, small towns stimulate it, favor circulation, encourage agriculture, and preserve domestic morality." Finally, the mayor of Solliès, a bourg in Provence, criticized all towns for monopolizing power: "In accumulating great wealth and its accompanying vices in towns, pride has left nothing but discouragement and misery in the countryside."[36]

Some men of letters in eighteenth-century France had developed a very different moral perspective on luxury by identifying wealth with civilization, and social pleasures with economic progress. Their reevaluation of luxury in the context of a market economy suggested that the greater the private demand for goods and services, the higher the level of public prosperity.[37] By linking this concept of market demand to the location rather than the size of towns, some petitioners succeeded in praising urban wealth while defending small towns. For example, officials at Château-du-Loir reversed the physiocratic equation between agriculture and wealth by arguing that crops and livestock remained "sterile objects" until they entered circuits of consumption and exchange with towns. As meeting places for

[35] Jean-Jacques Rousseau exemplified this tradition in eighteenth-century France, whose wider context is discussed by Jean Sekora, *Luxury: The Concept in Western Thought, Eden to Smollett* (Baltimore, 1977), pp. 23–131.

[36] AN DIV bis 27:395 (Marne); DIV bis 9:222 (Haute-Loire); DIV bis 18:294 (Vendée); DIV bis 18:293 (Var).

[37] André Morizé, *L'apologie du luxe au XVIIIe siècle et "Le Mondain" de Voltaire* (Paris, 1909). See also the general analysis of capitalism and moral thought in eighteenth-century Europe, by Albert O. Hirschman, *The Passions and the Interests: Political Arguments for Capitalism before Its Triumph* (Princeton, 1977).

commerce and the arts, towns stimulated the surrounding countryside by reason of their population, their wealth, their consumption, their commerce, and their industry. It followed that the greater the distance of rural communities from towns, the less the value of their properties, the marketing of their crops, the activity of their labor, and the resources of their inhabitants. To reduce misery, towns needed to be spread throughout the interior of the kingdom. Petitioners from Roye confirmed that "villagers near towns are necessarily more opulent, more populated than those far away, because their existence is assured by the ease of selling their crops." Thus, establishments that revitalized small towns would also spread prosperity to the countryside. As a special deputy from a little market town in the Bourbonnais concluded, "The interest of an agricultural nation is not to melt the population of several towns into a single one so it can become larger." Instead, the goal of territorial reform needed to be to equalize the population of towns by sharing establishments among them.[38]

Many spokesmen for market towns believed that this principle of *partage* should exclude commercial and industrial towns from competition for new establishments. The more resources a town already possessed, the weaker its moral claim to compensation for the abolition of existing lawcourts and administrative agencies. An implicit image of natural equilibrium between different types of towns, derived from the culture of the old regime, influenced this argument. Just as towns that depended on lawcourts were ill-equipped to become commercial centers, so towns that thrived on commerce should not become judicial centers. Magistrates in towns that lacked navigable waterways or other commercial facilities had long defended such a geographical differentiation of commercial and judicial functions. For example, a memorial from the *présidial* of Riom argued in 1763 that "people are born as businessmen at Clermont, and as magistrates or men of letters at Riom. To protect the establishments of justice at Riom and to extend the resources and branches of commerce at Clermont is to use for the general good of the state a superior portion of the genius and habits of each citizen."[39] Such a division of labor implied that both types of towns would suffer from jurisdictional changes. Alongside the obvious losses that judicial towns would face, commercial towns confronted more subtle dangers. Their merchants, lured by the prospects of social mobility, would retire from trade in order to become magistrates and lawyers. Thus did municipal officials at the little market town of Courpière oppose the industrial town of Thiers. "You would misunderstand badly the sensibility of Frenchmen," they informed the National Assembly, "if you believed that

[38] AN DIV bis 89:2 (Sarthe); DIV bis 16:279 (Sarthe); DIV bis 31:439 (Somme); DIV bis 19:306 (Saint-Gérand-le-Puy, Allier).

[39] Cited in Everat, *La sénéchaussée d'Auvergne*, p. 124.

in a small town, where the highest honors would go to magistrates, the son of a rich businessman would continue the commercial activities of his father. . . . He would abandon commerce for a legal career in the hope of one day being honored by the commission of a judgeship, by the voters of his province, or by the choice of the monarch." The commerce of Thiers, which helped the entire nation by exporting goods to foreign countries, would be ruined if this town acquired a royal *bailliage*.[40]

Such disingenuous concern for the prosperity of commercial towns expressed the social contradictions of the bourgeoisie in eighteenth-century France: Avid for honors as well as wealth, merchants aspired to enter more prestigious occupations as soon as they became successful businessmen. Thus did municipal officers from the Burgundian town of Nuits diagnose the economic decline of the rival town of Seurre. Unlike Nuits, which had no navigable river, industry, or commerce except the sale of its wine, Seurre possessed the great advantage of a port on the Saône River. Yet the townspeople of Seurre profited little from the immense commerce in grain, wine, hay, wood, coal, and all sorts of merchandise that flowed through their port. Why were they such "tranquil spectators" of this bustling trade? "The principle cause of this inertia," explained the spokesmen for Nuits, "can be found in the creation of a subordinate jurisdiction by the seigneurs of the town. They gave free offices to everyone who wanted to become a solicitor. These legal specialists withdrew from the risks of profitable commerce to enjoy the emoluments attached to judicial office." The moral of this story was clear: "It is against their own interests that the inhabitants of Seurre are seeking a royal court." To this charge, a special deputy from Seurre replied rather lamely that his town had, indeed, seen better days. At the beginning of the century, the merchants of Seurre had supplied magistrates to the *parlement* of Dijon and daughters to impecunious noblemen. To restore this time of vigor, Seurre needed a more important lawcourt of its own. The deputy neglected to mention how this would revive the merchants, who had seemed to vanish with the wealth that earlier generations took to Dijon.[41]

If commercial success was incompatible with judicial offices, then lawcourts should be located in towns that did not have any commerce at all. According to special deputies from Bâgé, a little town whose rival, Pont-de-Vaux, had large markets and fairs, a flourishing commerce, manufactures, several major roads, a river, and a canal under construction, "It has always been a wise policy to place courts in the least commercial localities, and Bâgé fits this description." After insisting that the town of Bourgoin

---

[40] AN DIV bis 29:416 (Puy-de-Dôme). For a similar discussion of this theme, see Ozouf-Marignier, *La formation des départements*, pp. 232–37.

[41] AN DIV bis 22:337 (Côte-d'Or); DIV bis 21:334 bis (Côte-d'Or).

would be harmed if it obtained a district tribunal, because "lawcourts are the ruin of business and industry," petitioners assured the National Assembly that "this inconvenience is not to be feared at La Tour-du-Pin, where there has never been any commerce." When spokesmen for Cholet, an industrial town in Anjou, boasted of their extensive commerce, rivals at Mortagne replied, "Experience shows that it is not in the interest of commercial towns to have royal lawcourts."[42] In this case, however, the leaders of Cholet tried to refute their adversaries:

> The officers of our little seigneurial town and our salt granary have always engaged in commerce whenever they had funds to invest. In order to save appearances and concede something to prejudice, they do not personally appear in the markets, and they do not ordinarily stock merchandise in their homes. But they have business interests anyway. Thus, we have reason to believe that the air of the new court that we are seeking will not be any more contagious than that of the old one.[43]

Yet these comments revealed that public opinion viewed commerce and the magistrature as incompatible professions. From this moral belief it was easy to infer that merchants and judges should reside in different towns, so the former would not be tempted to leave business or the latter to enter it.

Revolutionary ideology helped to justify the view that towns lacking the resources of commerce deserved preferential treatment in the distribution of new establishments. To begin with, the Declaration of the Rights of Man proclaimed the principle of equality: "Men are born and remain free and equal in rights."[44] By extending this principle to the territorial division of the kingdom, patriots in the National Assembly agreed that areas of equal size had the same rights to directories and lawcourts, regardless of their population and wealth. Finally, deputies endorsed the idea of sharing establishments among rival towns. From this cluster of ideas it was easy to legitimize the demands of weak and vulnerable towns against more prosperous and powerful neighbors. Deputies from Aix-en-Provence set an example of such reasoning when they opposed the effort of Marseille to become the capital of a department for western Provence. If Marseille had "all the gold and nearly all the inhabitants of Provence," if this great port corresponded with "all the nations of the universe," if the annual commerce of Marseille approached 600 million livres, these were so many reasons not to increase its power by giving it a departmental directory and lawcourt. "The National Assembly wants to foster equality and spread its

[42] DIV bis 1:7 (Ain); DIV bis 25:374 (commune of Saint-Victor, near La Tour-du-Pin, Isère); DIV bis 18:294 (Vendée).
[43] AN DXVII 1 (Cholet).
[44] Text published by Georges Lefebvre, *The Coming of the French Revolution*, trans. R. R. Palmer (Princeton, 1947), p. 189.

benefits everywhere," argued Charles-François Bouche, an influential deputy from Aix. His hometown, dependent throughout history on political
institutions, without commerce or industry, burdened with debts and
taxes, deprived of its *parlement*, and confined to an area one-third the size
of its former province, faced misery and depopulation unless it obtained
the departmental seat. Contrasting the "luxury, opulence and ambition" of
Marseille with the vulnerability of Aix, Bouche concluded, "It is a question
of helping the weak against the strong."[45]

Spokesmen for many towns used comparable arguments against their
own rivals. For example, municipal officials at Rochechouart, a little town
in Poitou, explained that the National Assembly could not approve inequality among towns after having proclaimed the principle of the equality
of the Rights of Man. Instead of favoring towns that already enjoyed prosperity, it should rescue towns that have been unjustly neglected. Rivals at
the neighboring town of Saint-Junien, who benefited from a much better
road than did Rochechouart, "should rest content with this advantage instead of trying to monopolize everything." Similarly, a municipal official at
Le Buis invoked the proposition that "men are equal in rights, so towns
must share in this equality." Therefore, opulent towns in Dauphiné, favored by major roads and waterways, should stop boasting of all their advantages, stop insulting less fortunate towns, and stop trying, like parasitical branches sucking juices from their roots, to join Le Buis to their own
jurisdictions. A special deputy from the little town of Tannay, impressed
by decrees that reserved lawcourts for towns that did not obtain directories, announced rather naively that "according to the principles of the National Assembly, as exemplified in over fifty decrees, all towns must participate equally in public establishments." Because Tannay was a poor town
without any commerce, it, not Clamecy, deserved the tribunal, because
Clamecy, a commercial town, already had the district.[46]

As an active goal of public policy, the principle of equality acquired a
social dimension that foreshadowed the democratic ideals of Jacobins and
sans-culottes. New establishments should redress the balance between rich
and poor, privileged and neglected towns. A deputy from a small town
near Bordeaux drew an explicit connection between individual rights and
social equality when he wrote that "The spirit of the national Assembly is
no more to accumulate all the advantages in a single place, at the price of
impoverishing and degrading an entire *pays*, than it is to sacrifice a crowd
of neglected citizens to a small number of privileged people. In a word, the
truly social principle that it has adopted applies no less to towns than to
individuals." A special deputy for the town of Allanche, in Auvergne, went

---

[45] *Mémoire* in AP:11, 2d annex to session of Nov. 5, 1789, pp. 702–3.
[46] AN DIV bis 18:297 (Haute-Vienne); DIV bis 22:348 (Drôme); DIV bis 28:409
(Nièvre).

still further in advocating the redistribution of wealth: "In the division of benefits, poverty alone has rights, and wealth must be repulsed; legislators must remove all the means that can produce extreme wealth and extreme poverty. Equality must be the goal of all their institutions and all their laws, because from equality alone is born happiness, which is the purpose of all societies." Equally expressive of democratic values were denunciations of the aristocracy. Here many petitioners transposed the popular belief in an "aristocratic plot" into an attack on rival towns. "If you destroy the *châtellenie* of Bouchain," warned a deputy from this area, "people here will believe that the National Assembly has destroyed the Flemish theocracy and the aristocracy of priests and nobles only to establish an aristocracy of large towns at the expense of the countryside and small towns." "What is the aristocracy that we have proscribed," asked the mayor of Quintin, "if not the ascendancy of the few over the many? But what a monstrous aristocracy a town would impose on an entire department if all the useful establishments were placed there."[47]

Alongside these public references to an aristocracy of towns, some petitioners expressed egalitarian principles in the private imagery of the family. In doing so, they may have been inspired by a new ideal of family relationships, based on sentiment rather than authority, which some historians have traced to eighteenth-century England and France.[48] This ideal implied affection between parents and children, and equality between husbands and wives, brothers and sisters, older and younger siblings. By applying such relationships of affection and solidarity to the nation, provinces, and towns, patriots could replace the patriarchal obligations of subjects to their king with new moral values based on equality. For example, the mayor of Pamiers praised the division of the kingdom for transforming "all of France into a single family of brothers who, all being equal in rights, and all having the same interests, will always be united for the common happiness, without ever being disunited by any principle of rivalry." A deputy from Maubeuge agreed that because "all Frenchmen are brothers, all the towns of France have incontestable rights to find their happiness in the operations of the National Assembly." For municipal officials at Brest, who approved of dividing Brittany so they could obtain a department, sisterhood inspired the same ideal of equality: "All the provinces are sisters and must be of a single mind; there should be no more

[47] AN DIV bis 1:18 (Gironde); DIV bis 21:331 (Cantal); DIV bis 2:49 (Nord); DIV bis 22:340 (Côtes-du-Nord).

[48] See, especially, Laurence Stone, *The Family, Sex, and Marriage in England, 1500–1800* (London, 1977). For an analogous trend in France, see Annik Pardailhé-Galabrun, *La naissance de l'intime: 3,000 foyers parisiens, XVIIe–XVIIIe siècles* (Paris, 1988), pp. 181–87. For a more skeptical view, see André Burguière, ed., *Histoire de la famille*, vol. 2, *Le choc des modernités* (Paris, 1986), pp. 111–40.

distinctions among them."[49] Townspeople at Châteauneuf-du-Faou symbolized the principle of equalizing prosperity among towns by declaring that all children of the fatherland were equally dear in the eyes of the National Assembly. For a memorialist from Is-sur-Tille who wanted to preserve districts in small towns, maternal images of affection justified equality:

> All the new establishments are the children of the same mother, and they must be equally dear in her eyes. She guards and supervises with all the more tenderness and solicitude those who seem to have a weaker constitution; and her fear that they will not reach adolescence, far from suggesting the barbarous example of those peoples who suffocate sickly or ill-formed individuals at birth, only redoubles her cares and affections.

According to a spokesman for Saint-Loup, paternal authority should also be tempered by love: "A good father, if he cannot share his fortune equally among his children, still leaves none without the signs of his tenderness." In like manner, the National Assembly should cast its benevolent regard on Saint-Loup by establishing a lawcourt in this bourg. For municipal officials at Montlhéry, writing later in the Revolution, primogeniture was a "barbaric custom" that enabled the eldest son to invade the totality of the heritage of a common father. "May the rival town of Corbeil, in preserving the district directory, cede the tribunal to its sister, the town of Montlhéry." Thus, the domestic spirit of the modern family, strengthened by customs of partible inheritance, could serve the cause of equality among towns as well as individuals.[50]

Countering all this rhetoric, however, were spokesmen for prosperous towns who denied that weaker neighbors deserved any special rights. For one thing, the proliferation of districts and tribunals would increase the costs of administration. As Dupont de Nemours pointed out, expenditures of public funds on directories and lawcourts might benefit towns, but they would burden the countryside with higher taxes.[51] Why squander the hard-earned money of taxpayers on towns that were falling into ruins or on bourgs that had never amounted to anything? Deputies from the seaport of Blaye, outvoted in a departmental assembly by partisans of the declining little town of Bourg, could not restrain their indignation.

[49] AN DIV bis 20:317 (Ariège); DIV bis 29:410 (Nord); letter from the municipality (hereafter "Mun.") of Brest, quoted in Louis Delourmel and Louis Esquieu, *Brest pendant la Révolution: Correspondance de la municipalité de Brest avec les députés de la sénéchaussée de Brest aux Etats-Généraux et à l'Assemblée Constituante, 1789–1791* (Brest, 1909), p. 65.

[50] AN DIV bis 23:352 (Finistère); DIV bis 108:6 (Côte-d'Or); DIV bis 30:426 (Haute-Saône); *pétition* from the *conseil général* of Montlhéry, Nov. 11, 1792, DIV bis 90:2 (Seine-et-Oise).

[51] Dupont de Nemours, "Observations sur les principes qui doivent déterminer le nombre des districts et celui des tribunaux dans les départements," AP 11:606, annex to session of Feb. 15, 1790.

Is it really necessary to restore at great cost a town that has no port, no roads, and no commerce? . . . These little towns without commerce are parasitical bodies that devour the countryside without providing any advantage to the state. They should be left to go straight to ruin instead of being revived at immense expense.[52]

Furthermore, wealthy and important towns were essential to economic growth.

It would be ridiculous to imagine, wrote deputies from Clamecy, that the National Assembly intended to reduce towns, like individuals, to the equality of nature. Capitals and central places, which develop the arts and put money into circulation, will always preserve their superiority for the general welfare. Not surprisingly, deputies who favored the port of Nantes agreed: "Large towns are necessary for the prosperity of knowledge, the arts, and commerce; small towns do not present any such advantages." In addition, large towns contained more men of talent than did small towns, and they fostered more patriotism and enlightenement. As spokesmen for the port of Toulon explained, "The most important administrative institutions should be placed in large towns, which are more favorable to the preservation of liberty, to impartial and mild administration, to the development of enlightened activity, and to the combination of many kinds of assistance." Finally, the argument for equality resulted in absurdity. If deputies from little towns could justify establishments on the basis of their helplessness and obscurity, so could the smallest villages. Where would the proliferation of establishments end? Deputies from the seaport of Harfleur concluded that "the surface of the earth would be filled with towns, if there were agreement to support them by artificial means."[53]

Yet little towns and bourgs already covered the surface of France with a dense array of central places whose magistrates exercised authority over the countryside. The abolition of the old regime created an opportunity to strengthen the bonds between such communities and the state. Officeholders in the *bonnes villes* that belonged to the royal domain had long been accustomed to defending the interests of the king. Through new establishments, their royalism could be transformed into a deeper sense of obligation to the nation. As for the men of law who once governed seigneurial towns, their sense of public duty could be changed even more dramatically into devotion to national laws and institutions. Officials in the new regime could provide moral leadership for fellow townspeople and nearby villagers, too. The more directories and lawcourts were established, the more widespread patriotism might become. Target had this in mind when he defended the establishment of districts as well as departments: "Adminis-

[52] AN DIV bis 8:202 (Gironde).
[53] AN DIV bis 28:409 (Nièvre); DIV bis 9:218 (Loire-Inférieure); Printed *mémoire* for Toulon, p. 6, in ADXVI:78; DIV bis 30:433 (Seine-Inférieure).

tration is a school of patriotism and public law. Its branches should be multiplied, if you want to spread the spirit of liberty, inspire love for the Constitution, and prepare worthy representatives for the nation."[54] Thus, patriotism, like *rapprochement* and *vivification*, implied that the National Assembly should take into account the interests of small towns in the distribution of establishments. Otherwise, townspeople might become indifferent or even hostile to the new regime. A spokesman for the C.C. recognized this danger when he announced on January 19, 1790, that the National Assembly "intends to reward the patriotism of towns, and to encourage this patriotism through the sharing of establishments."[55] The mayor of Quintin expressed himself more bluntly: "To multiply the seats of the new establishments is to extend and propagate public spirit; it is to interest many towns in the success of the work that the National Assembly has undertaken. If, on the contrary, you concentrate public spirit in a few towns, you will soon suffocate it."[56]

In the old regime, patriotism and privilege had formed dual aspects of a relationship between towns and the monarchy that might be characterized as an implicit contract involving reciprocal obligations. Just as towns had mustered troops and raised cash to defend French kings, so these rulers had confirmed the institutional rights and fiscal privileges of towns. After the Revolution, petitioners continued to recall historical proofs of loyal service to the monarchy. As a reward for loving their kings, Issoudun had received exemption from the *taille*, and Lauzerte had preserved its royal *sénéchaussée* from envious rivals.[57] The "very old town" of Saint-Maixent contrasted its constant devotion to the Crown with the more doubtful patriotism of Poitiers. Charles VII had rewarded Saint-Maixent with "great privileges," including the right to place the royal crown and fleur-de-lis on its coat of arms.[58] But now that towns were obliged to renounce their privileges and obtain new establishments from the National Assembly, they began to displace their loyalty from the king to *Messieurs les députés*. Having learned that their seigneurial court would be suppressed, petitioners from Ussel wrote on August 20, 1789, that they were "trembling with the most intense joy at this important news." Consternation rather than joy more than likely expressed their mood, but they concluded their *adresse* for a royal court with the confident words that "the citizens of Ussel . . . are beginning to feel the impact of the happiness that you are preparing for them."[59] Townspeople from Langres opened their *adresse* for a departmen-

---

[54] Speech by Target, Nov. 11, 1789, AP 9:746.
[55] Speech by Gossin, Jan. 19, 1790, AP 11:234.
[56] AN DIV bis 22:340 (Côtes-du-Nord).
[57] AN DIV bis 8:209 (Indre); DIV bis 26:385 (Lot).
[58] AN DIV bis 17:288 (Deux-Sèvres).
[59] AN DXVII 2 (Ussel).

tal seat and a lawcourt with a more formal declaration of allegiance to the National Assembly: "The citizens of the town of Langres have the honor of expressing their adhesion to the wisdom of your decrees, their inviolable respect for your persons, and their deepest gratitude for the work that you are devoting to the regeneration and happiness of the state."[60] Some towns forwarded even more sophisticated *adresses* that avoided any mention of their own demands, which would have contradicted their lofty rhetoric of devotion to the nation.[61] In many cases, however, petitioners coupled their declarations of submission to the decrees of the National Assembly with requests for departments, districts, or lawcourts. The *adresse* was a text that often represented in its introductory encomium and its subsequent details the loyalty that townspeople offered the National Assembly, and the favors that they expected in return.[62]

Patriotism involved action as well as words. Here towns described their services to the state, which ranged from the payment of ordinary taxes and extraordinary assessments to the policing of the grain trade and the recruitment of national guards. A few towns even boasted of their contribution to the international power of France, but more commonly they emphasized their gifts and other payments to the national treasury. Their patriotic zeal, which expressed a willingness to make sacrifices for the state, also justified demands for new establishments. Whether townspeople welcomed the loss of their fiscal privileges, offered to render justice free of charge, made patriotic gifts, or pledged to pay higher taxes, they continued to expect rewards for their patriotism. Their defense of social order also affirmed local interests as well as national concerns. Grain riots and other popular disorders threatened the property rights and commercial profits of urban elites. Assaults on tax collectors also endangered municipal finances in towns that shared the proceeds of *octrois*, or sales taxes, with the central government. In equating patriotism with social discipline, urban leaders agreed with their deputies in the National Assembly that decrees for the maintenance of property rights, the protection of the grain trade, and the collection of taxes must be enforced. Townspeople who volunteered to serve as national guardsmen symbolized the renewal of a traditional alliance between towns and the state. Thus, military service in the cause of order, like taxes and patriotic gifts, became a motive for recompense in the form of directories or lawcourts. Some townspeople denounced their rivals

[60] AN DIV bis 10 (Haute-Marne).

[61] See, for example, the *adresse* from the town of Péronne, read to the National Assembly on Jan. 8, 1790, which reported a *contribution patriotique* of 92,605 livres and concluded with a discreet allusion to "all the hopes that the year just ended has permitted us to conceive," in AP 11:118.

[62] At least 375 towns affirmed their patriotism in *adresses* and other petitions that included requests for new establishments.

for riots, factional conflicts, or aristocratic sympathies that disqualified them from acquiring new establishments, while others admitted that they would be unable to guarantee submission to the National Assembly unless their demands were granted. Urban rivalries threatened to polarize public opinion around enthusiastic patriots and disillusioned counterrevolutionaries. In this process of politicization, the rhetoric of townspeople anticipated the deepening crisis of legitimacy that patriots would confront in their heroic effort to replace the old regime with a new constitution.

Nearly 300 towns boasted of their financial contributions to the state. Foremost were 106 towns that compared their customary burden of direct and indirect taxes with the smaller fiscal payments of their rivals and 94 towns that emphasized their patriotic gifts and pledges of extraordinary taxes to resolve the budgetary crisis that confronted the government. Estimates of the financial sacrifices of townspeople were as varied as the complexity of the fiscal system. The seaport of Granville, which enjoyed exemption from the *taille*, collected an annual average of 131,000 livres in taxes on tobacco, 120,000 in taxes on salt, 111,000 in other indirect taxes, and 30,000 in taxes on the registration of official documents; the river town of Meung paid only 23,000 livres in *taille* and *capitation*, but its fiscal bureaus collected another 125,000 in wine taxes, duties on leather and other goods, *vingtièmes*, and registries for notaries, bailiffs, and solicitors; the industrial town of Longuyon paid 20,000 livres in duties on iron production, as well as 8,000 in personal property taxes and 4,000 for the lease of Crown lands; and the market towns of Charmes, in Lorraine, and Chambon, in the Massif Central, paid 8,794 and 5,426 livres, respectively, in direct taxes.[63] Whether towns collected indirect taxes for the state obviously had a much greater impact on such estimates than whether their citizens paid a substantial share of their incomes in direct taxes. Generally speaking, the larger the town, the more impressive its fiscal contribution to the state but the smaller its per capita burden of property taxes. While the port of Fécamp, with 6,500 inhabitants, supposedly paid six times as much money to the royal treasury as did the *bailliage* town of Cany, with 1,400 inhabitants, over 90 percent of the fiscal revenues collected at Fécamp came from indirect taxes.[64] In the matter of ordinary taxation, the payments of commercial towns included large sums of money collected from nonresidents.

Extraordinary taxes and donations also reflected the general wealth of towns, but here the notables of small towns could make a special effort to impress the National Assembly with their patriotism. Following the ex-

---

[63] References to official documents about taxation in AN DIV bis 27:394 (Manche); DIV bis 26:382 (Loiret); DIV bis 11:242 (Moselle); DIV bis 18:298 (Vosges); DIV bis 6:184 (Creuse).

[64] Certificates from tax officials at Fécamp and reply to a deputy from Cany, AN DIV bis 33:433 (Seine-Inférieure).

ample of a group of Parisian women who made the first *dons patriotiques* to the National Assembly on September 7, 1789, the citizens of small towns began to donate jewels and other valuables to a special treasury for the redemption of the government debt.[65] The Breton town of Hennebont opened a public subscription for a patriotic gift on September 15, and many other towns followed suit in the next several months.[66] Most patriotic gifts were presented to the National Assembly as pure acts of altruism, but special deputies from Chauny indicated the ulterior motives that persuaded many towns to include precious objects with their *adresses*: "Following the example of an immense number of towns in the kingdom, and for the success of their demand for a district, they believe that in addition to the patriotic gifts of jewelry and silver that they have already brought to Paris, the municipality should also offer to renounce a portion of the value of the offices that it purchased for 20,000 livres, and to pay the special tax imposed on formerly privileged individuals during the last six months of this year." In a deliberation on December 15, the municipality of Chauny expressed its "eagerness to accept these propositions."[67] Deceived by the results of a similar initiative, the chevalier de la Varignière, special deputy for a town in Normandy, published a letter to his constituents explaining how he arrived at the National Assembly on January 26 at ten o'clock in the morning, bearing a patriotic gift. This gift consisted of a "superb gold box, studded with diamonds and wrapped in a little document that stated the demands of the town of Torigny." M. de la Varignière was told to return at six in the evening to read the document aloud, but first he had to attend a meeting of deputies from his province, where he watched helplessly as they drafted a decree that rejected Thorigny's request for a district. "I took this decree to the person who had given me the golden box, and asked him if he still wanted to make his patriotic gift. He replied that he would reserve it for the assistance of the most destitute inhabitants of Thorigny, who would be ruined by the suppression of their *bailliage*."[68]

The surge of patriotic sentiment that townspeople calculated would ad-

[65] The first patriots to make financial sacrifices were twenty-one wives and daughters of artists, including Mme. David and Mme. Fragonard. Their *adresse* of Sept. 7, which alluded to the patriotism of women in ancient Rome, donated their personal jewelry, which they "would blush to wear now that such sterile pleasures should be sacrificed to the state." They proposed that "all true friends of the fatherland" follow their example by making voluntary donations to a *caisse* that would amortize the national debt. It is noteworthy that these ladies had a *présidente*, Mme. Moitte, and formed a deputation that appeared in person in the National Assembly, although they had to rely on M. Bouche to read their discourse. AP 8:591.

[66] Declaration from the town of Hennebont (Morbihan), read aloud to the National Assembly on Sept. 15, 1789, AP 8:641.

[67] Letter and municipal deliberation cited by R. Hennequin, *La formation de l'Aisne*, p. 138, n. 1.

[68] Printed *Lettre à mes Constituents*, pp. 1–2, AN ADXVI 49 (Thorigny).

vance their own ambitions also persuaded the government to couch new fiscal demands in the language of voluntary sacrifice. Following the advice of Necker, who portrayed the desperate financial state of the kingdom in convincing details, the National Assembly voted on October 6, 1789, to raise 160 million livres in new revenue through the imposition of an extraordinary tax known as a *contribution patriotique*. This tax was supposed to equal one-quarter of the earnings of taxpayers during the year 1790, but its success would depend on voluntary pledges rather than fiscal coercion. Each taxpayer would declare his personal revenues to municipal officials, whose register of pledges would measure less the real wealth than the patriotic fervor of local citizens.[69] Townspeople responded by interpreting the *contribution patriotique* as an opportunity to demonstrate both their eagerness to serve the state and their worthiness to receive favors in return. Writing on October 25, 1789, ten citizens from a little town in Berry assured *nosseigneurs*, the deputies, that true Frenchmen everywhere would answer the cry of the fatherland in danger: "Had we been asked for our lives, we would have been ready to sacrifice them. To contribute a quarter of our revenues is a patriotic act." Following this peroration, they requested a lawcourt and a district.[70] The leaders of a revolutionary committee at Nîmes voiced their concern that towns would be judged by the size of their *contribution patriotique*: "When throughout France the principal towns are distinguishing themselves by their generous efforts, this city, which has described so truthfully its importance, its population, its commerce, and its just rights to all sorts of public establishments, would not want, through the parsimony of its sacrifices, to expose itself to the accusation of infidelity in its promises, or exaggeration in its discourse."[71] In a competition that ressembled an auction, towns large and small boasted of their voluntary effort to raise taxes: 600,000 livres from Le Havre; 303,265 from Lorient; more than 117,000 from Fontainebleau; 85,000 from Rochefort; 41,082 from Arbois; 19,000 from Mortagne; 11,686 from Nogaro.[72] As townspeople from Saint-Brieuc explained, their gift of over 100 marcs of silver and their *contribution patriotique* of 120,000 livres proved that they were in the forefront of the Revolution. By contrast, the rival town of Quintin had raised only 15,000 livres for the state.[73]

[69] Necker, "Rapport sur l'état annuel des finances," Sept. 24, 1789, AP 9:139–46; Necker's project for a *contribution patriotique*, Oct. 1, 1789, AP 9:228–31; the decree to this effect, Oct. 6, 1789, AP 9:351–54.

[70] *Adresse* from Mézières, AN DIV bis 8:210 (Indre).

[71] AN C 97:119 (Nîmes).

[72] AN DIV bis 17:282 (Seine-Inférieure); C 204:192 (Lorient); DIV bis 31:435 (Seine-et-Marne); DIV bis 5:178 (Charente-Inférieure); DIV bis 25:376 (Jura); DIV bis 32:443 (Vendée); DIV bis 24:361 (Gers).

[73] AN ADXVI 32 (Quintin).

According to notables from Pont-l'Abbé, towns formed "powerful columns of general police," whose decline would endanger the state.[74] Petitioners from nearly 150 towns agreed that they were uniquely equipped to defend the cause of order, either because of their moral self-restraint, their patriotic zeal, or their military organization. Especially noteworthy were townspeople who provided details about their behavior during the grain riots and other disorders that accompanied the outbreak of the Revolution in the spring and summer of 1789. Some vaunted their mild manners and peaceful character, or contrasted their own efforts to preserve order with the agitation that swept other communities. For example, the citizens of Châtelaudren demonstrated their "patriotic sentiments" by preventing disorder, those at Fécamp enjoyed "perfect tranquillity," and those at Bonnétable remained calm "in the midst of the storms that raged elsewhere."[75] Only rarely did petitioners follow the lead of a notable at Montlhéry who complained that events were out of control. According to M. Loyal, formerly a provincial administrator, grain riots on August 31 and September 7, 1789, had created an acute shortage of grain for local bakers and consumers at Montlhéry. The local judge, who was also the subdelegate, had fled for his life, the *maréchaussée* had withdrawn, and the bourgeois guard had collapsed. The town desperately needed a new lawcourt to put an end to this "horrible anarchy."[76] Much more commonly, townspeople bragged of their efforts to protect the grain trade. Market towns near Paris, such as Anet, Arpajon, Houdan, and Epernon, took "incredible pains" to keep grain flowing to the nation's capital, even though their own citizens were sometimes "threatened with famine."[77] In several provinces, the municipal leaders of neighboring towns agreed to form military alliances in order to guarantee free trade in grain.[78] However modest the amount of grain in circulation, notables in small towns were proud to describe their role in provisioning larger towns. Those at Nesle even argued that by serving as a storehouse for the entire province of Picardy, their town deserved to obtain the same establishments as the largest towns of the kingdom.[79] The grain trade symbolized the interdependency of urban elites and their com-

[74] AN DIV bis 23:353 (Finistère).

[75] AN DXVII 1 (Châtelaudren); DIV bis 17:282 (Seine-Inférieure); DIV bis 16:277 (Sarthe).

[76] Letter to a deputy in the National Assembly, Sept. 9, 1789, forwarding a *mémoire* for a lawcourt at Montlhéry, AN DXVII 1.

[77] AN DIV bis 30:431 (Seine-et-Oise); DIV bis 17:281 (Seine-et-Oise); DIV bis 7:193 (Eure-et-Loir); C 102:173 (Anet).

[78] For example, in Normandy, Vire organized a confederation that included Vire, Bayeux, Isigny, Carentan, Périers, and Saint-Lô; and in Burgundy, Nolay joined "a contract of union and fraternity" with Autun, Arnay-le-Duc, Beaune, and Châlon. AN DIV bis 5:172 (Manche); DIV bis 21:335 (Côte-d'Or).

[79] AN DIV bis 31:439 (Somme).

mon subordination to the national government in Paris. As such, the shipment of grain, like the payment of taxes, became an act of patriotism.

To preserve order, most towns relied on their own militia, although the royal army, which withdrew from Paris after the storming of the Bastille, still garrisoned some provincial capitals and fortified towns, especially along the frontiers. The Great Fear, which historians have usually interpreted as a peasant uprising, involved an equally significant military mobilization in hundreds of small towns.[80] Militia that had been moribund for decades were hastily reorganized, officers appointed, and volunteers recruited to defend townspeople against unknown assailants. Many market towns appealed for aid from nearby villages, which helps explain why these mobilizations involved so many peasants. Yet urban militia quickly took control of most armed gatherings, and they even marched against bands of peasants in the few regions where the Great Fear evolved into popular revolts against seigneurs. Following the example of Paris and other cities, townspeople formed committees to preside over their local militia, which increasingly became known as a "national guard." Awareness of the common interests of all towns helped inspire federations of national guards, first in small areas, then in entire provinces, but each town retained its separate military organization. Petitioners from 104 towns described with pride their officers and troops. For example, the "patriotic legion" of Ernée contained 510 men; the "national militia" of Selongey formed eight companies, each with 45 riflemen dressed in Parisian uniforms; and the national guard of Arbois consisted of 1,200 men. A spokesman for Beaune mocked rivals at the little town of Boiscommun, where in their eagerness to form a national militia, everyone wanted to become an officer, leaving practically no one to serve in the ranks. If only the townspeople of Boiscommun could borrow soldiers from Beaune, which already had nearly 300 guardsmen! As this anecdote suggests, petitioners assumed that the larger their militia, the greater the evidence of their patriotism. The national guard was not only a military institution; it was an agency of civic pride and political consciousness.[81]

As demonstrations of patriotism became increasingly important, towns began accusing rivals of indifference or disloyalty to the new regime. Like the rhetoric of Jacobins in Paris, such denunciations relied heavily on the technique of guilt by association. A few royal towns tried to associate their rivals with seigneurial traditions. For example, the municipality of Mo-

---

[80] For the standard interpretation of this event, see Georges Lefebvre, *The Great Fear: Rural Panic in Revolutionary France*, trans. Joan White (New York, 1973).

[81] AN C 90:69, document 4 (Ernée); DIV bis 6:182 (Côte-d'Or); DIV bis 25:376 (Jura); DIV bis 9:219 (Loiret). For a good study of the organization of the national guard in small towns and bourgs, see Roger Dupuy, *La Garde Nationale et les débuts de la Révolution en Ille-et-Vilaine, 1789–mars 1793* (Paris, 1972).

lières argued that "ancient feudal prejudices have left profound traces" at Montpezat and Castelnau, little towns that used to depend on private lords. Spokesmen for La Fère went further still in criticizing the old castle town of Coucy for its feudal past: "It is not at the moment when liberty has just been born that we would make the inhabitants of the countryside tributaries of such a town, and force them to support the walls inside which the shackles of their ancestors were forged, and the towers where so many victims bemoaned their fate."[82] Other petitioners made invidious comparisons between their own patriotism and the aristocratic sympaties of rival towns: La Rochelle welcomed the "auspicious Revolution," while Saintes remained "a center of aristocracy" because so many priests and noblemen lived there; Issoudun, with its many poor laborers, had a stronger interest in putting into operation "the new order of things" than did Bourges, with its many clergy and rich nobles; and Marvéjols possessed "more equality" than Mende, so heavily influenced by its bishop and clergy.[83] Sharing the aversion to factionalism that would make Jacobins such critics of political parties, a few towns compared their own unity with the divisiveness of their neighbors. According to patriots at the little Breton town of Rochefort, rivals at Questembert were rent by factionalism. If Questembert obtained the district lawcourt, the inhabitants of Rochefort "would be punished for their zeal, while those who followed the party contrary to the interests of the nation would be rewarded." By politicizing such factional divisions, patriots would soon be accusing their adversaries in other towns of being "counterrevolutionaries." For example, the president of a "provisional council" at Carhaix used such language to denounce "influential families" at the rival town of Rostrenen in January 1790.[84]

Patriots sometimes expressed their own disillusionment with the Revolution at news that their demands were being disregarded by the National Assembly. As soon as the active citizens of Riez learned that their bishopric would be transferred to Digne, they reported that townspeople were turning against the Revolution: "In our country desolation is at its height, and soon despair will be boundless." Responding to plans for the creation of only three districts in upper Auvergne, municipal officials at Maurs wrote that "the inhabitants of this country, instead of blessing providence for the benefits that the new constitution is procuring for them, would be exposed to regret the old regime. . . . Inertia and discouragement would gradually replace the emulation that has begun to germinate in everyone's mind." Petitioners who favored the town of Mortagne, in Poitou, complained that the rival town of Montaigu was "trying to establish an ascendancy that

[82] AN DIV bis 10:224 (Lot); DIV bis 3:148 (Aisne).
[83] AN DIV bis 5:177 (Charente-Inférieure); DIV bis 8:209 (Indre); DIV bis 27:390 (Lozère).
[84] AN DIV bis 28:402 (Morbihan); DIV bis 23:352 (Finistère).

would reduce our patriotism, because we would see ourselves humiliated and forgotten." Some townspeople intimated that they would not be able to pay taxes unless they received compensation for the loss of earlier establishments. After all, if towns lost their trade as well as their lawcourts, their taxable revenues would decline along with the value of their properties. "It is only by preserving the same advantages as other towns that Puiseaux can support her share of tax payments to the state," wrote a memorialist for this little town. The mayor of a town in Languedoc even threatened a tax revolt: "If Anduze does not obtain anything, I can no longer answer for the docility of the people; I can no longer offer assurances for the successful collection of taxes that have been raised to incredible levels." Indeed, petitioners from forty-three towns expressed fears that people would be driven to violence by the denial of their just demands. "Who would be the first victims of the insurrection?" asked municipal officials at Auxerre, after having informed their deputies in the National Assembly that failure to obtain a departmental seat would have "unfortunate consequences" in the *pays*. "It might be us, or perhaps you."[85]

Of course, such threats were not likely to impress deputies from rival towns. If patriotism implied self-sacrifice, then towns should be prepared to renounce their own claims in deference to the larger interests of the nation. Anticipating complaints from unsuccessful contenders for establishments, Rabaut Saint-Etienne called on all citizens to "take guard against themselves, their passions, their rivalries, and those particular interests, so often misconstrued, that might be called the vanity of towns."[86] The *conseil général* of Saint-Palais, in the Basque country, expressed the mood that patriots appreciated: "We swear on the altar of the fatherland that in all circumstances and whatever the outcome of our just demands, we will sacrifice all that we hold dearest in order to maintain the constitution, and that we will always remain equally faithful to the nation whose happiness you are assuring, and to the king whom we cherish."[87] But such rhetoric itself had ulterior motives. However many townspeople endorsed the general principles of *rapprochement*, *vivification*, and patriotism, their demands for new establishments expressed parochial concerns. The Revolution was supposed to advance the general welfare. In the cacaphony of voices that reached the National Assembly from provincial towns, who would speak for the nation as a whole? Were most deputies the "impartial

[85] AN DIV bis 3:155 (Basses-Alpes); Dec. 28, 1789, DIV bis 21:331 (Cantal); DXVII 1 (municipal deliberation [henceforth "Mun. Delib."] of Evrones, in support of Mortagne); DIV bis 9:219 (Loiret); DIV bis 7:195 (Gard); *observations* from Mun. Auxerre, Nov. 17, 1789, reprinted by Charles Porée, *La formation du département de l'Yonne en 1790* (Auxerre, 1910), p. 147.

[86] *Nouvelles Réflexions*, AP 10:39.

[87] AN DIV bis 29:419 (Basses-Pyrénées).

men" who would disregard the interests of their own hometowns in reorganizing the state? Far from it. In the territorial division of the kingdom, rhetoric necessarily furthered the claims of some towns at the expense of others. Appeals to the unity of the nation would not eliminate "the jealousy of towns" that revolutionary politics unwittingly encouraged in replacing the old regime with a new hierarchy of institutions.[88]

[88] Phrases cited from Rabaut Saint-Etienne, *Nouvelles Réflexions*, AP 10:38–40.

Chapter 5

THE POLITICS OF PAROCHIALISM

URING the French Revolution, new forms of political representation clashed with earlier traditions of aristocratic patronage, factional intrigue, and corporate rivalry. In compelling Louis XVI to acknowledge the constituent authority of the National Assembly, deputies originally elected to present the grievances of separate orders to the Estates-General became the de facto rulers of the kingdom. No longer would courtiers be able to modify royal decrees through personal access to the king and his ministers. Factions at the Court, like councillors in the royal government, were powerless to halt the course of the Revolution. Corporate institutions such as *parlements* and provincial estates had no greater success in blocking reforms. Indeed, the destruction of all corporations became a rallying cry among the patriots who dominated the National Assembly. While these deputies were preparing to regenerate the kingdom, many townspeople were trying to reorganize local institutions of government. At both the national and the local level, new leaders emerged to voice public opinion. Such patriots disavowed the factions and corporations of the old regime. They aspired to enlighten the people by representing its true interests in public discourse. At the heart of their revolutionary project was the belief that elected officials, unlike venal officeholders or royal bureaucrats, would defend the rights of individuals and the unity of the nation.

Revolutionaries were inclined, however, to exaggerate their break with the past. In theory, deputies in the National Assembly served as representatives of the entire nation rather than as spokesmen for particular provinces, communities, or social classes. Similarly, townspeople who gathered together to petition their deputies expressed the general will of "the people," whose unanimity constituted the legitimizing principle of revolutionary politics. In practice, hundreds of deputies in Paris remained attentive to the needs of their hometowns, just as tens of thousands of petitioners in the provinces continued to affirm local interests at the expense of rival towns. The territorial reorganization of the kingdom had the paradoxical effect of stimulating parochial loyalties that the new departments and districts were supposed to destroy. Through the legislative committees that formulated plans for the division of provinces, deputies fought over territory as if they were ambassadors from competing lands. A host of special deputies arrived in Paris to lobby on behalf of hundreds of towns that lacked direct representation in the National Assembly. Petitions filled with the signatures of townspeople and villagers also reached the C.C., whose commissioners were supposed to reconcile conflicting demands for establishments in accordance with the general interest. As a rule, however, these commissioners ratified the decisions that deputies from each province and department had already reached in committee meetings. Despite much rhetoric about disregarding local interests, towns fortunate enough to have skillful and determined advocates within these committees generally triumphed over their adversaries. The division of France revealed the influence of lobbyists behind the solemn decrees of the National Assembly and the strength of parochial sentiments beneath the grandiose discourse of nationalism.

The count of Choiseul d'Aillecourt, a deputy from the Second Estate of Chaumont-en-Bassigny, reported to his constituents in 1791:

> A map of the kingdom was divided into squares; each deputation from the provinces was convoked to distribute territory; each deputy, with a pin and a piece of thread, came to mark his department, make his district, choose his canton. Each calculated the advantage of his town, the vanity of his village. Many special deputies arrived from the provinces to combine their local passions with these fantasies of conquest. Everyone wanted to have a large department and a fine district, or wanted his town to become the *chef-lieu*, or anticipated judicial establishments, which led to mutual concessions. I have seen deputies squabbling over vast territories, compass in hand, insisting on villages, ceding them, signing treaties of exchange, making deals, and marking the frontiers of their sovereignty.[1]

As a court noble who commanded a regiment and maintained a residence in Paris, Choiseul d'Aillecourt observed with disdain the attachment of many deputies to provincial towns. By contrast, André-Marie Merle, the mayor of Mâcon and a deputy from the Third Estate, wrote to friends in his hometown on January 20, 1790, "Today is our great day when the departmental seat will be chosen. For the past two days, we have been meeting until midnight at the office of the Comité de Constitution, where the bishop of Autun, by the greatest of misfortunes, is the presiding officer, judge, and devilish adversary of us. I haven't slept a wink during this past night of anguish and fear."[2] When Mâcon finally obtained the permanent seat of administration in exchange for granting Chalon-sur-Saône the criminal tribunal of the department, Merle wrote home to announce, "Everything has been decided. . . . The matter was handled well. Good-bye,

---

[1] Printed *Comte-rendu par M. Choiseul d'Aillecourt à ses commettants* (Paris, 1791), in AN ADXVI 50.

[2] Letter of Jan. 20, 1790, cited by F. Siraud, "Etude sur la formation du département de Saône-et-Loire," *Annales de l'Académie de Mâcon*, 2d ser., vol. 11 (1894), p. 226, n. 1.

my friends, I don't want to say more about it now; I believe I'm going to die of joy."[3]

In their opposing attitudes toward the politics of parochialism, the count of Choiseul d'Aillecourt and the mayor of Mâcon reflected the views of two kinds of deputies, those aloof from the details of territorial reorganization, and those committed to the interests of particular towns. Generally speaking, deputies from the Third Estate had closer social ties to urban communities and more professional involvement in administrative and legal institutions than did deputies from the nobility or the clergy. Magistrates in royal courts, who numbered 178 deputies from the Third Estate and only 25 deputies from the nobility of the robe, were especially likely to represent small and medium-sized towns in the National Assembly, as table 5.1 shows.[4] Seventy-four percent of these judges came from towns that had fewer than 10,000 inhabitants, as compared with 43 percent of all the deputies whose place of residence on the eve of the Revolution can be traced. A majority of the other officials and men of law who represented the Third Estate also came from small and medium-sized towns, and only 6 percent resided in the countryside. This group of deputies included 195 barristers (*avocats*), the largest single occupational group in the National Assembly, and 55 municipal leaders, some of whom were also lawyers by profession. A third social category from the Third Estate, comprising merchants and other businessmen, had relatively few deputies outside the largest towns. At the opposite extreme, 47 deputies from other occupations who represented the Third Estate (in the fourth row of table 5.1) resided in the countryside. These included 32 farmers and 11 "bourgeois" or proprietors, whose rural communities had no chance of obtaining districts or lawcourts.[5]

The magistrates and lawyers who represented *bailliages* in the Third Estate often began their political careers in 1789 by drafting *cahiers de doléance* for their hometowns and by serving as delegates to *bailliage* assemblies. Just as they helped shape the general *cahiers* in accordance with the

---

[3] Letter of Feb. 12, 1791, cited in ibid., p. 233, n. 1.

[4] Especially numerous were magistrates from royal *bailliages* and *sénéchaussées*, who accounted for 129 deputies from the Third Estate and only 5 deputies from the Second Estate at the end of 1789. On their role in the National Assembly, see Dawson, *Provincial Magistrates*, pp. 193–240.

[5] This data about occupations and places of residence is based primarily on Brette, *Les Constituants*, which lists the deputies elected from each electoral constituency, indicates whether they died or resigned before the end of 1789, and lists *députés suppléants* who replaced them. I have included only those deputies who were serving in the Assembly between Nov. 1789 and Feb. 1790, when the basic decrees on departments and districts were drafted in committees and approved by the Assembly. In several dozen cases where information about the occupation or the place of residence of a deputy is missing from this source, I have found further details in Brette, *Recueil de documents*, vol. 2.

TABLE 5.1
Social Origins of Deputies to the Estates-General

Social Background of Deputies	Nucleated Population of Places of Residence							
	40,000 and Over	20,000–39,999	10,000–19,999	5,000–9,999	2,500–4,999	Under 2,500	Rural	Total
3d Estate, royal judges	6 (3%)	11 (6%)	28 (16%)	50 (28%)	49 (28%)	32 (18%)	2 (1%)	178
3d Estate other law	27 (10%)	32 (12%)	30 (12%)	49 (19%)	39 (15%)	66 (26%)	15 (6%)	258
3d Estate business	25 (32%)	8 (10%)	11 (14%)	7 (9%)	9 (12%)	10 (13%)	7 (9%)	77
3d Estate other	8 (8%)	5 (5%)	4 (4%)	8 (8%)	15 (14%)	19 (18%)	47 (44%)	106
3d Estate totals	66 (11%)	56 (9%)	73 (12%)	114 (18%)	112 (18%)	127 (21%)	71 (11%)	619
2d Estate (nobels)	82 (49%)	15 (9%)	11 (7%)	7 (4%)	7 (4%)	8 (5%)	39 (23%)	169*
1t Estate (clergy)	28 (9%)	18 (6%)	34 (12%)	24 (8%)	35 (12%)	33 (11%)	124 (42%)	296
All deputies	176 (16%)	89 (8%)	118 (11%)	145 (13%)	153 (14%)	169 (16%)	234 (22%)	1084*

Sources: The place of residence of most deputies is given by Armand Brette, *Les Constituants: Liste des députés et des suppléants élus à l'Assemblée Constituante de 1789* (Paris, 1897); some missing information can be found in Brette, *Recueil de documents relatif à la convocation des Etats Généraux de 1789* (Paris, 1896), vol. 2; and in a "Liste de Messieurs les députés à l'Assemblée Constituante, dressée par ordre alphabétique de départements," July 1791, AP 33:67–87. The classification of towns by size of nucleated population is based on the data used in tables 1.1–1.9. The category "rural" refers to communites that did not have markets or any of the other establishments used to classify towns in these tables.

* Data about place of residence is missing for 103 of the nobles who sat in the National Assembly at the end of 1789.

views of their fellow townspeople, so they obtained election to the National Assembly as the representatives of particular towns within regional coalitions of voters. Such alliances of urban delegates were especially common in electoral assemblies that grouped several "secondary" *bailliages* or *sénéchaussées* around a primary one. At Cahors, for example, where delegates gathered from six *sénéchaussées*, they chose one deputy from the largest town in each of these judicial districts. At Forcalquier, delegates from the *sénéchaussées* of Forcalquier and Sisteron formed an alliance against those from the *sénéchaussée* of Digne and chose two deputies from Sisteron, one from Forcalquier, one from a village near Forcalquier, and none from Digne.[6] Where electors from a single *bailliage* formed the final stage of elections, those from the chief town of the *bailliage* sometimes obtained both deputies, but more often they had to share the deputation with either a second town or a rural community. Once elected to the National Assembly, deputies from the Third Estate usually corresponded with friends and compatriots in the town that had originally delegated them.[7] Such political allegiances became all the more important once departments and districts were destined to replace the *bailliages* as electoral districts. Deputies from the Third Estate often joined provincial and departmental committees on the basis of the location of their hometowns, whose municipal leaders provided a vital element of continuity in the midst of institutional collapse.[8]

Cultural identities often reinforced the political relationship between deputies and provincial towns. Many leaders of the Third Estate agreed with François Buzot, a lawyer from Evreux who wrote unabashedly to his fellow townspeople, "I will not conceal the fact that I love my *pays* with passion, that I have done everything within my power to make it happy and flourishing, and that I will continue to do so."[9] For such deputies, the town and surrounding countryside that formed their *pays* deserved affection, loyalty, and support. Even the victims of such bias conceded its moral force. Municipal officials at Riez, opposed by deputies from rival towns in

[6] These electoral alliances of delegates at Cahors and Forcalquier are discussed by Eugène Sol, *La Révolution en Quercy, 1788–1791*, 2d ed. (Paris, 1932), pp. 117–18; and Jules Viguier, *La convocation des Etats Généraux en Provence* (Paris, 1896), pp. 286–92.

[7] For examples of such correspondence, see H. Carré and P. Boissonade, *Correspondance inédite du constituant Thibaudeau, 1789–1791* (Paris, 1898); Daniel Ligou, *La première année de la Révolution vue par un témoin, 1789–1790: Les "bulletins" de Poncet-Delpech, député du Quercy aux Etats Généraux de 1789* (Paris, 1961); and Francisque Mège, *Gaultier de Biauzat, député du Tiers-Etat aux Etats Généraux de 1789: Sa vie et sa correspondance*, vol. 1 (Paris, 1890).

[8] For the relationship between the towns where deputies resided and their membership on departmental committees, see the "Liste de Messieurs les députés à l'Assemblée Constituante, dressée par order alphabétique de départements," July 1791, AP 33:67–87.

[9] Letter from Buzot to Mun. Evreux, Feb. 2, 1790, in C. Dauban, ed. *Mémoires inédits de Pétion et mémoires de Buzot et de Barbaroux* (Paris, 1866), lx–lxi.

their request for a district, wrote with mixed feelings, "We applaud very sincerely their love for their homeland [*patrie*], but the result is unjust." Similarly, a special deputy from Mortagne described the "praiseworthy zeal" of two deputies from the rival town of Montaigu to serve their homeland, though he added that "they should not use their influence against justice and equity." The sentiment of local patriotism might also be directed toward an "adopted town," where a judge had purchased an office or a lawyer had married into a local family. Thus, spokesmen for Fontainebleau complained that both deputies from their area were judges at the *bailliage* court of Melun and had settled in recent years in this rival town. "They could not prevent themselves from favoring their adopted *pays*." Even if deputies tried to be impartial, they would be subjected to moral pressure from their compatriots at home. As petitioners from the town of Saint-Valéry-en-Caux explained, they could not expect M. Cherfils, the deputy from this area, to support their request for a district. "He would compromise himself in the eyes of the inhabitants of Cany, his fellow citizens." Special deputies from Fécamp, another town in competition with Cany, wrote less sympathetically that M. Cherfils favored "his ordinary place of residence" because he occupied a judicial post there which he wanted to keep. Some critics even accused deputies of favoring a town where they owned property or where they had relatives who hoped to profit from a district or a tribunal. After assuring the municipality of Vence that he supported its request for a district, Mougins de Roquefort, the mayor of Grasse, arranged instead for a district at Saint-Paul-les-Vence, where he owned land. To neutralize the rivalry of Vence, which was entirely surrounded by this district of Saint-Paul, he placed it in the district of Grasse. Nonetheless, such imputations of corruption were less significant than acknowledgments of the moral obligations that deputies felt toward their hometowns. For many representatives of the Third Estate, the *patrie* did not yet mean the French nation. It meant their homeland, the town and nearby *pays* where they possessed family and friends, office and land, moral reputation and political influence.[10]

Unlike the deputies from the Third Estate who defended provincial towns in the National Assembly, relatively few noble deputies had social ties or political obligations to such communities. To begin with, deputies from the Second Estate had been elected not by delegates from towns and villages but exclusively by fellow noblemen in the *bailliage* constituencies. Furthermore, most nobles elected to the National Assembly had no administrative experience outside the army, which was the chosen profession for

[10] AN DIV bis 19:310 (Basses-Alpes); DXVII 1 (Mortagne-en-Poitou); DIV bis 31:435 (Seine-et-Marne); DIV bis 30:433 (Seine-Inférieure); DIV bis 17:433 (Seine-Inférieure); *mémoire* for Vence, DIV bis 18:292 (Var).

two-thirds of them.[11] Finally, their social origins and professional qualifications resulted in a distinctive residential pattern that discouraged the urban loyalties so common among deputies of the Third Estate. Nobles on active duty as military officers were often stationed in garrison towns, far from the country estates or town houses where other members of their families might reside. Such officers comprised 70 of the 103 nobles whose residence on the eve of the Revolution is unknown. Among the 169 noble deputies who did declare a residence, 49 percent lived in Paris and other large towns, 23 percent in the countryside, and only 13 percent in towns of fewer than 10,000 inhabitants (see table 5.1).[12] Some court nobles possessed honorific offices in provincial towns, as *gouverneurs* and *grands baillis*, but typically they resided in Paris. Only a small number of these high-ranking nobles, such as the duc de la Rochefoucauld, played an active role in the division of the kingdom, and relatively few of the lower-ranking nobles who resided in the provinces gave proofs of their devotion to a hometown. Even the *chevalier* Cazalez, who was born in the small town of Grenade, waited until he received two separate requests for a district before writing to assure the local inhabitants that "I will not forget their interests."[13] Noblemen, whose urban patronage derived less from their social activities than from their ownership of seigneurial rights and landed estates, were called upon to assist provincial towns much less often than were deputies from the Third Estate. As table 5.2 shows, only 19 towns in the entire kingdom depended exclusively on a noble deputy for support, as compared with 186 towns that relied on a single deputy from the Third Estate.

The First Estate of the clergy gave a more balanced representation to urban and rural communities than did either the Second or the Third Estate. Table 5.1 indicates that 42 percent of the clerical deputies resided in the countryside, nearly always as parish priests, while 31 percent came

[11] Among the 272 deputies from the Second Estate still in the Constituent Assembly at the end of 1789 (a few dozen had resigned or never taken their seats), 139 held a military rank, including 64 *maréchals de camp* and 30 colonels; 41 were former military officers; 25 were magistrates or former magistrates in royal court; and most of the remaining 67 deputies were seigneurial lords who gave no profession. Tabulation based on Brette, *Les constituents*. Using other sources, Timothy Tackett has found that 78 percent of all the nobles who sat at any time in the National Assembly had a military background: "Nobles and Third Estate in the Revolutionary Dynamic of the National Assembly, 1789–1790," *American Historical Review* 94, no. 2 (Apr. 1989): 277.

[12] Tabulation based on Brette, *Recueil de documents*, vol. 2. This analysis confirms the findings of Timothy Tackett, who used the *Almanach de Paris* to trace the residences of noble deputies, "Nobles and Third Estate," p. 276. See also James Murphy and Patrice Higonnet, "Les députés de la noblesse aux Etats Généraux de 1789," *Revue d'histoire moderne et contemporaine* 20 (Apr.–June 1973): 230–47.

[13] Letter from Cazalez to his brother-in-law, the mayor of Grenade, Dec. 25, 1789, cited by R. Rumeau, *Formation du district de Grenade* (Toulouse, 1897), p. 9.

TABLE 5.2
Number of Deputies from Towns, by Size of Towns

Number of Deputies	Nucleated Population of Towns						
	40,000 and Over	20,000– 39,999	10,000– 19,999	5,000– 9,999	2,500– 4,999	Under 2,500	Total
Towns with 4+ deputies	11	15	13	19	12	2	72
Towns with 2–3 deputies	0	8	21	38	34	26	126
Deputy from 3d Estate only	2	2	10	29	48	95	186
Clerical deputy only	0	0	0	5	17	30	52
Noble deputy only	0	0	1	1	9	8	19
TOTAL	13	24	45	92	120	161	455

Sources: Included are all towns and market bourgs where deputies resided on the eve of the Revolution, according to Brette, *Recueil de documents*, vol. 2. I have added seven towns patronized by nonresident nobles, two towns aided by clerical deputies who resided elsewhere, and fourteen towns not mentioned in Brette's dictionary but described as the residence of a deputy in a "Liste de Messieurs les députés à l'Assemblée Constituante," AP 33:67–87.

from towns with fewer than 10,000 inhabitants, and 27 percent came from larger towns. These urban deputies included 43 bishops and 123 priests, whose political role in the National Assembly became transformed under the pressure of events. While some bishops and priests clung to their original task as defenders of the interests of the Church, others joined with deputies from the Third Estate in the secular mission of regenerating the kingdom. Generally speaking, deputies from the lower clergy became more actively engaged in the provincial and departmental committees that settled the fate of towns than did deputies from the higher clergy. The example of Thomas Lindet, a priest from the textile town of Bernay, proves how effectively such committee work could advance the interests of a particular town. Bernay had long been obliged to share its royal *bailliage* with the nearby town of Orbec. After admonishing his fellow townspeople that Bernay had no chance of acquiring a department for itself, Lindet developed a plan for the division of Normandy that would include Bernay in the department of Evreux, where it would be certain to obtain a district, while relegating Orbec to the department of Caen, where it would have to compete with Lisieux. The final agreement of deputies from Normandy to create five departments in this province, reached after numerous debates behind closed doors, vindicated Lindet's strategy. As he happily informed townspeople at Bernay, "We are irrevocably separated from Orbec. . . . The Assembly of deputies from the province has assured our tranquillity by getting rid of neighbors whose constant pretentions had become burdensome and embarrassing."[14] Other clerical deputies who defended small towns in the National Assembly included the abbé Rolland, who agreed to represent his hometown of Gap, although he had been elected from the constituency of Forcalquier; Jean-Gaspard Gassendi, a priest from a village near Digne; and Paul-Augustin Pous, a priest from Mazamet. Like Lindet, these priests corresponded with local townspeople and wrote memorials to the C.C.[15] Only a small number of towns depended exclusively, however, on such clerical deputies to argue their cause. Table 5.2 shows that fifty-two towns had a bishop or priest as their only deputy in the National Assembly, fewer than one-third the number of towns that relied on a single

[14] Letter from Lindet cited by Boivin-Champeaux, *Création et formation du département de l'Eure, 1789–1790* (Paris, 1868), p. 3. Lindet's role in the division of Normandy is fully documented in his correspondence published by Amand Montier, ed., *Correspondance de Thomas Lindet pendant la Constituante et la Législative, 1789–1792* (Paris, 1899), pp. 8–107.

[15] For Rolland's correspondence with Mun. Gap, see "Origines du département des Hautes-Alpes et l'abbé Rolland, député à l'Assemblée Constituante," *Annales des Alpes* (July–Aug. 1911): 5–15; the *abbé* Gassendi wrote a "Mémoire sur le chef-lieu du département du Nord de la Provence" (misfiled in AN F2 I:496) that convinced the Constitutional Committee to support Digne; and Pous responded to a petition from Mun. Mazamet for a district by publishing some *observations* in an unsuccessful defense of his hometown, AN DIV bis 17:291 (Tarn).

deputy from the Third Estate, and just over one-tenth the total number of towns and market bourgs that had a resident in the Assembly.

Of course, not all deputies had equal success in patronizing their hometowns. A few came from market centers that had so little chance of acquiring districts or lawcourts that no one submitted any petitions on their behalf to the National Assembly. For example, Jean-François Campmas, a doctor from a bourg of only 620 inhabitants in the mountains of Albigeois, devoted his energies to the departmental ambitions of Albi. Campmas viewed with skepticism the efforts of small towns in his province to obtain districts and lawcourts: "It is not the disinterested love of the fatherland [*patrie*] that guides all our towns of the second rank. They have a strong desire to take care of their own welfare by figuring out how to bag the poor litigants from the countryside."[16] Thirty-six little towns and bourgs that had deputies like Campmas in the Assembly resigned themselves to the modest rank of cantonal seats. At the opposite extreme, deputies from over two hundred towns became involved in the competition for departmental directories and appellate lawcourts, and many seemed bound to fall short of such ambitious goals. For example, Pierre-François Barbié, the *lieutenant-général* of the *bailliage* of Vitry, reported to a fellow magistrate back home that plans for an appellate court were unlikely to succeed. When municipal officials learned of his pessimism, they accused him of neglecting their rights. Barbié replied indignantly that "the interests and the glory of Vitry are extremely dear to my heart," and a few days later he explained that "we are in a moment of crisis for our town; I am trying to preserve what it has and even to improve its fate."[17] The most he could accomplish, however, was to prevent the neighboring town of Saint-Dizier from forming a district at the expense of Vitry.

Michel-René Maupetit, a judge at the ducal court of Mayenne, found himself under similar suspicion when he failed to prevent the larger town of Laval from besting Mayenne in the contest for a departmental seat. Denounced by a revolutionary committee at Mayenne, Maupetit insisted that he had sketched four different maps that would have made Mayenne more centrally located than Laval. Privately, however, he confessed to a friend that he did, in fact, prefer Laval. Mayenne, with a population of 8,000 inhabitants as compared with 15,000 at Laval, shared the vice of most small towns: an absence of social unity. "Narrow pretensions and passions reign there, always opposed to the general welfare, and I would not predict a very long existence for any important administration concentrated in localities that are too small." Faithful to his own town, Maupetit had, it is

---

[16] Letter cited by Emile Appolis, "La formation du département du Tarn," *Revue du Tarn*, n.s., 13 (1938): 78.

[17] Letters of Oct. 25, Nov. 3, Nov. 7, 1789, published in E. Jovy, ed., *Le spicilège de Vitry* (Vitry-le-Francois, 1899), 1:727–33.

true, proposed in a committee meeting to make Mayenne rather than Laval the capital, but his fellow deputies burst out laughing at the idea. "I had difficulty restraining myself from laughing, too," he wrote. "It is evident that only at Mayenne can anyone think differently."[18]

Yet the population of a town alone did not determine whether it became a departmental seat. Among the 91 towns with at least 10,000 inhabitants, only 51 achieved this goal, along with 32 smaller towns. Of course, some departments did not contain any large towns, but deputies on the provincial committees were able to propose changes in the boundaries that determined which towns would be included in each department. Through shrewd negotiations, some of them succeeded in improving the centrality of their hometowns while neutralizing dangerous rivals. For example, Pierre-François Gossin, the lieutenant-general of the *bailliage* of Bar-le-Duc, recognized that the duchy of Bar would need to obtain territory from a neighboring province in order to form the requisite area for a department. Unable to expand southward into Champagne, where deputies from Chaumont-en-Bassigny insisted on preserving their own centrality in relation to Langres, Gossin looked northward toward Verdun and the *généralité* of Metz. He offered his colleagues from Metz and Nancy a more central location in their respective departments, persuaded deputies from Verdun to withdraw from the department of Metz in order to preserve their bishopric, and agreed to share either an appellate lawcourt or a departmental directory with Saint-Mihiel.[19] Gossin was not only an effective negotiator, but a *rapporteur* for the C.C., and he took the floor of the National Assembly on January 30, 1790, to announce, "with moving emotion," that he was going to "defend his homeland" (*patrie*) against the pretensions of Verdun. The deputies from this town, berated by their municipality for abandoning any claim to a department, were now trying to violate their promises to Gossin. Such conventions among deputies, which resembled contractual obligations, carried much weight among the magistrates and lawyers in the Assembly, who rallied to Gossin's support.[20] Indeed, public debates rarely had any serious effect on the decrees that the C.C. submitted to the Assembly for approval.[21] These decrees usually con-

---

[18] "Lettres de Michel-René Maupetit, député à l'Assemblée nationale constituante, 1789–1791," *Bulletin de la Commission historique et archéologique de la Mayenne*, 2d ser., 19 (1903): 377–78; 20 (1904): 84–91.

[19] On Gossin's role in the formation of the department of the Meuse, with its seat at Bar-le-Duc, see Jean Louis Masson, *Histoire administrative de la Lorrain: Des provinces au départements et à la région* (Paris, 1982), pp. 144–45, 157–69, 248–52.

[20] *Le point du jour* 6:201, p. 241; and AP 11:395.

[21] A total of 28 proposals of the C.C. for departmental seats and 54 proposals for district seats or tribunals were disputed on the floor of the National Assembly; in only two of the former cases and four of the latter did the Assembly overrule the C.C. by transferring a de-

formed to the views of deputies on the departmental committees, although unresolved disputes were sometimes referred to voters in the departments.[22] Thus, coalitions of deputies shaped not only the boundaries of departments but the rights of towns to acquire departmental establishments. It was surely no coincidence that among the 116 towns that obtained departmental seats or alternates in February 1790, 108 had direct representation in the National Assembly.

Departmental committees also recommended how many districts to create and which towns to select as the seats of directories and tribunals in these districts. Here, too, the size of a town was only one factor that influenced its probability of acquiring one of these establishments. Table 5.3 shows that among all the towns contending for new establishments, 96 percent of those assisted by a royal judge who sat in the National Assembly succeeded in obtaining a district or a tribunal; so did 83 percent of those supported by another deputy from the Third Estate and 62 percent of those dependent exclusively on a clerical deputy or a noble patron. By contrast, 44 percent of the towns that had only special deputies to plead their cause and only 17 percent of those which simply forwarded petitions to Paris proved successful. The smaller the size of a town, the more its likelihood of becoming a district seat depended on the persuasive powers of local residents who sat in the National Assembly. Only towns with more than 10,000 inhabitants had a 100 percent rate of success, regardless of whether they had hometown deputies to defend their cause. Among towns with fewer than 5,000 inhabitants, the presence of a royal judge or other deputy from the Third Estate made a dramatic difference in success rates, as did, to a lesser extent, that of a local priest or nobleman in the Assembly.

Map 5.1 displays this striking correlation between the geographical origins of deputies and the distribution of districts and district tribunals. The many circles on this map signify successful contenders for districts or tribunals that had at least one local resident in the National Assembly, while the relatively few solid triangles signify unsuccessful towns that also had a local resident in the Assembly. The dense distribution of large and small circles indicates that in many departments, nearly every town that had a deputy acquired a district or a tribunal, regardless of its size. Such a geographical pattern reflects the political alliances that deputies from various towns formed on provincial and departmental committees. Not all deputies were included, however, in such coalitions. Thus, two relatively large triangles near the Mediterannean coast signify the failure of deputies from the towns of Pézénas and Clermont-l'Hérault to gain any establishments

---

partmental seat, district, or tribunal to another town. Tabulation based on scattered debates reported in AP, *Le point du jour*, and *Journal des Etats Généraux*, Jan.–Nov. 1790.

[22] A total of 29 conflicts over departmental seats or alternates and 38 conflicts over districts or tribunals were referred to departmental or district assemblies of voters.

TABLE 5.3
Success Rate of Towns with Deputies

Social Background of Deputy	Nucleated Population of Towns				
	10,000 and Over	5,000–9,999	2,500–4,999	Under 2,500	Total
Town with royal judge from 3d Estate as deputy	32/32 (100%)	40/40 (100%)	39/41 (95%)	24/28 (86%)	135/141 (96%)
Town with other deputy from 3d Estate only	47/47 (100%)	41/44 (93%)	43/51 (84%)	43/67 (64%)	174/209 (83%)
Town with deputy from 1st or 2d Estate only	3/3 (100%)	7/8 (88%)	18/24 (75%)	15/34 (44%)	43/69 (62%)
Special deputy only	7/7 (100%)	13/22 (59%)	38/70 (54%)	67/181 (37%)	125/280 (44%)
No deputies or special deputies	2/2 (100%)	9/16 (56%)	31/74 (42%)	93/717 (13%)	135/809 (16%)
TOTAL	91/91 (100%)	110/130 (85%)	169/260 (65%)	242/1,027 (24%)	612/1,508 (40%)

Sources: Place of residence is given in Brette, Recueil de documents, vol. 2, supplemented by "Liste de Messieurs les députés." Evidence about contending towns and special deputies is compiled from the documents in AN DIV bis and related archival series. The seats of departments, districts, and district tribunals in 1790 are listed in Almanach royal (Paris, 1791).

Note: This table displays the ratio between towns that obtained departments, districts, or tribunals and all towns seeking such establishments, for each category of representation: towns with a royal judge from the Third Estate serving as a deputy; other towns represented by a deputy from the Third Estate; towns represented only by a deputy from the clergy or the nobility; towns lacking regular deputies who sent special deputies to Paris; and towns that did not have any deputies or special deputies in Paris. Included in the table are towns patronized by nonresident nobles and clergy. Excluded are 36 little towns and market bourgs whose deputies and municipal leaders made no effort to obtain districts or lawcourts; only 2 of these localities were represented by royal judges.

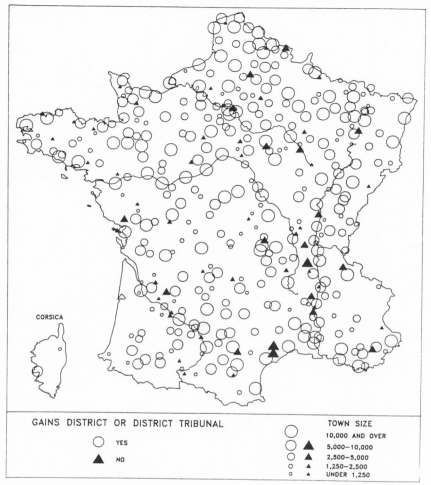

Map 5.1. Success of Towns with Regular Deputies, 1789–1790

in the department of the Hérault, where deputies from Montpellier and Béziers insisted on forming only four districts. Behind nearly every triangle on this map is a drama of intrigue in the National Assembly, whereby ambitious deputies refused to make concessions to colleagues from other towns.

Among the tactics of deputies who triumphed in committee meetings, some involved preliminary bargaining over the boundaries of departments, while others concerned how many districts should be created, what kinds of towns should be chosen as district seats, and whether districts and lawcourts should be shared by rival towns of the same district. When provincial committees traced the boundaries of departments, deputies from border towns often joined forces with colleagues who represented one of the towns in contention for a department. The quid pro quo of such an alliance would be a promise to grant the border town a district. As special deputies from Toucy, near the town of Auxerre, complained,

> In the new projects of division, the towns that have the ambition of becoming departmental seats are trying to extend their jurisdictions as far as possible. It is impossible to conceal the fact that to realize their pretensions, they are willing to make compromises only with the secondary towns that are farthest away from the center. These towns consent to join with the principal town on the condition of obtaining a district. . . . To give this arrangement a superficial appearance of justice, these frontier towns are given a narrow strip of territory, and by this stratagem, such towns attempt to pass for central places.[23]

Thus did spokesmen for the small town of Saint-Fargeau agree to enter the department of Auxerre. Similarly, a deputy from the bourg of Montguyon, on the border of Saintonge, played skillfully on the rivalries between several towns in this region for departments. First, he insisted that Montguyon wanted to join a department at Libourne or Bordeaux rather than Angoulême, but then he agreed to enter the department of Saintes, where Montguyon obtained a district tribunal.[24] Even after departments had been formed, such maneuvers sometimes succeeded. When the municipality of Revel discovered that deputies from Albi and Castres would not grant them a district in the department of the Albigeois, they instructed their deputy, the marquis de Vaudreuil, to arrange for their transfer to the department of Toulouse. Here they acquired a district, as did six other small towns that allied themselves with deputies from Toulouse.[25]

Once such border disputes were resolved, conflicts over departmental seats continued to create opportunities for the deputies of small towns to press their claims for districts or lawcourts. Thus, the king's magistrates at the *châtellenies* of Montmarault and Cérilly wisely opposed the effort of Montluçon to compete for a departmental seat with Moulins, although their little towns were closer to Montluçon. Grateful for their votes against a rotation of the departmental seat, a deputy from Moulins included Montmarault and Cérilly in a plan for seven districts, which a majority of the departmental committee adopted against the strenuous objections of special deputies from Montluçon.[26] Similarly, deputies from Angers outmaneuvered Saumur by agreeing to form eight districts in their department,

[23] AN DIV bis 32:449 (Yonne).
[24] Letter from Ratier de Montguyon, in AN DIV bis 5:177 (Charente-Inférieure).
[25] AN DIV bis 17:291 and 24:557 (Haute-Garonne).
[26] Several documents in AN DIV bis 19:306–7 (Allier).

and deputies from Clermont-Ferrand followed the same strategy against their rivals from Riom.[27] The early resolution of such conflicts opened the way for deputies to restrict districts to a smaller number of towns. In Picardy, for example, where Amiens obtained a departmental seat without opposition, deputies from Abbeville, Montdidier, and Péronne joined with those from Amiens to recommend that only four districts be created, one for each of their hometowns.[28] Similarly, deputies from Aurillac and Saint-Flour, who agreed to rotate the departmental seat of the Cantal, voted for only three districts, and so did deputies from Le Puy and Brioude, in the Haute-Loire.[29]

Still another tactic involved conceding the administrative seat of a district to a rival town in exchange for a guarantee that one's own town would obtain the district tribunal. Thus, Lescurier de la Vergne, the lieutenant-general of the *bailliage* of Salers, agreed to transform the *élection* of Mauriac into a district, but he allied himself with deputies from Aurillac, who wanted some of this territory for their own district. In exchange, they agreed to place the tribunal of the district of Mauriac at Salers.[30] The particular decrees on the formation of departments reserved tribunals to a second town in thirty-three districts, largely in response to pledges that deputies such as Lescurier obtained either from their colleagues on departmental committees or from members of the Comité de Constitution.[31]

Not all deputies pursued such negotiations or brought them to a successful conclusion. For example, a deputy from Saint-Pol-de-Léon, a Breton bishopric that had a higher institutional rank than did the commercial town of Morlaix during the old regime, agreed to the incorporation of his hometown into the district of Morlaix.[32] Divided loyalties seem to have influenced Pierre-Florent Masson, a lawyer elected from Roye who actually resided at Péronne. He made no complaint when deputies from Mont-

[27] AN DIV bis 26:388 (letter of complaint by deputies from Saumur, Maine-et-Loire); and Mège, *Formation du Puy-de-Dôme*, pp. 113–25.

[28] *Réflexions* by the députés from Picardy, AN DIV bis 17:289 (Somme). In this case, the C.C. overruled them and recommended a fifth district at Doullens, which the National Assembly approved.

[29] Complaints of Vic-en-Carladès and Allanche, AN DIV bis 21:331 (Cantal); and Mège, *Formation du Puy-de-Dôme*, pp. 232–63.

[30] *Adresse* of protest from Mauriac, AN DIV bis 82:3 (Cantal).

[31] Decrees from Jan. 19–Feb. 17, 1790, combined with minor changes into the general decree of Feb. 26, 1790, AP 11:716–24. In the final decree of Aug. 26, 1790, on the location of tribunals, 67 towns that were not district seats obtained a tribunal instead. *Réimpression de l'ancien Moniteur* 5:478–79.

[32] *Considerations* for Saint-Paul-de-Léon, protesting a printed memorial by some deputies of Brittany which asserted that Saint-Paul had renounced its claims in the general interest, AN DIV bis 23:353 (Finistère).

didier and Péronne drew up a plan to incorporate the *bailliage* of Roye in districts for their own towns. Belatedly, under pressure from special deputies sent by the municipality of Roye, M. Masson did try to obtain *partage* with Montdidier, but the National Assembly only agreed to permit voters in the first district assembly to discuss this issue. Having been placed on the edge of the district, Roye had no chance of gaining majority support at this gathering, and Montdidier ended up with both the district and the tribunal.[33]

M. Perrée Duhamel, a merchant who represented the seaport of Granville, complained with more justice that deputies from rival towns had "permitted themselves to be seduced by the project of creating within their hometowns many inns and cabarets that would enrich their constituents at the expense of distant towns, bourgs and hamlets." Lacking an *élection*, Granville was excluded from a coalition that deputies from such administrative towns of the Cotentin, in lower Normandy, formed among themselves. M. Pain, a councillor at the *bailliage* court of Torigny, also failed to revise the plan of these deputies. When matters came to a vote in committee, M. Pain proved "too timid to mount the podium and oppose the draft of a decree for only seven districts."[34] No such charge of irresolution could have been directed against M. Hennet, a royal judge from Maubeuge who submitted a series of lengthy memorials to the C.C., first requesting a district, then seeking the tribunal in the district of Avesnes. In this case, the peripheral location of Maubeuge near the Austrian frontier and its reputation for industry rather than for litigation hampered competition with the *bailliage* town of Avesnes, whose district would fit easily into the plans of a deputy from Le Quesnoy for a district in *his* hometown.[35] Such disputes proved that the commissioners responsible for drafting decrees for the National Assembly could not reconcile all the demands of deputies. Too many small towns, located near each other, wanted districts and tribunals.

Indeed, the work of the C.C. was greatly complicated by the arrival of special deputies from hundreds of provincial towns. Unlike the regular deputies, who were susceptible to the moral pressure of colleagues in the Assembly who appealed to the general interest, special deputies had the exclusive task of defending the interests of particular towns. These *députés extraordinaires* applied to the National Assembly a system of representation that municipalities and other corporations of the old regime had long em-

[33] AN ADXVI 77 (pamphlet by the deputies from Picardy); DIV bis 31:439 (Somme, *mémoire* by special deputies from Roye and *exposé* by Liénart, deputy from Montdidier).

[34] *Réclamation* in AN DIV bis 10:231 (Manche) and printed *Lettre à mes commetants*, by the chevalier de la Varignière, AN ADXVI 49.

[35] *Mémoires* by M. Hennet and M. Gossuin (deputy from Le Quesnoy), AN DIV bis 12:244 and 29:411 (Nord).

ployed. In response to royal centralization, municipal authorities had developed the practice of appointing ad hoc deputies to defend their rights and privileges at Court and in the councils of the king. Colbert had tried to prohibit such deputations, on the grounds that municipal officers were misappropriating local taxes in order to finance trips to Paris for private business.[36] More objectionable perhaps were the opportunities for influence-peddling in the corridors of power. Yet municipalities did have legal cases to defend in royal councils, and even Colbert had been unable to prevent them from employing legal counsel for special missions to Paris. In the eighteenth century, formal procedures existed for giving a *procuration*, or power of attorney, to such ad hoc deputies, whose travel costs and per diem expenses could, under certain circumstances, be financed through municipal funds. Even if the intendants refused to authorize such expenditures, municipal leaders might still travel at their own expense to Paris, where interviews with ministers and other dignitaries of the realm often seemed essential for the satisfactory resolution of disputes. Effective lobbyists needed to prepare legal briefs, or *mémoires*, for circulation among the relevant officials, but they also needed to cultivate relationships of patronage within the royal government.[37] A bureaucratic system of representation did exist for merchants in a few cities, whose chambers of commerce employed permanent deputies in the bureau of commerce as well as ad hoc deputies whom they sent to Paris on special occasions.[38] Municipalities never succeeded, however, in establishing such institutional channels for the representation of urban interests. Each appeal to the central government implied a separate lobbying campaign, whose success depended on personal diplomacy as well as written documentation.

A memorial by Abbé Ganault de la Rochevisé, submitted to the National Assembly on September 1, 1789, describes a typical mission by an ad hoc deputy on the eve of the Revolution. The *abbé* presented himself as the "agent" of the commune of Cholet, which first authorized him in May 1788 to request a royal *bailliage*. He began his task by corresponding with the intendant of Tours and with Lamoignon, the minister of justice (*garde des sceaux*), to whom he forwarded a series of *mémoires*. On July 15, 1788, municipal officials at Cholet gave him a *procuration* to represent them in

[36] Edict of 1683, cited by Charles Normand, *Etude sur les relations de l'etat et des communautés aux XVIIe et XVIIIe siècles: Saint-Quentin et la Royauté* (Paris, 1881), p. 155.

[37] Individuals acting on their own behalf experienced the same difficulty gaining access to powerful officials in Paris. See the letter from Félix Faulcon to his cousin, July 19, 1782, describing his interminable efforts to receive authorization to purchase an office at the *présidial* court of Poitiers, in Debien, *Correspondance de Félix Faulcon* 1:129.

[38] Frederick L. Nussbaum, "The Deputies Extraordinary of Commerce and the French Monarchy," *Political Science Quarterly* 48 (Dec. 1933): 534–55. Concerning the bureaucratic system of the Bureau of Commerce, see Harold T. Parker, *The Bureau of Commerce in 1781 and Its Policies with Respect to French Industry* (Durham, N.C., 1979).

Paris, where he met with Lamoignon. He also consulted with the bishop of Blois, the mayor of Tours, and the chief president of the *cour des aides* in Paris, who interceded on his behalf. But Lamoignon fell from power, the intendant of Tours wrote an unfavorable report, and the case was forgotten in the ministry. The municipality of Cholet renewed the *abbé's* power of attorney on May 4, 1789, so that he could undertake another mission to Paris. Unable to obtain any reply from the new minister of justice, he turned his attention to the National Assembly, whose decision in August to abolish seigneurial courts encouraged him to give the president of the Assembly a new memorial for a *bailliage* court. Abbé Ganault disappears from view after this request; this narrative of events suggests both the obstacles that lobbyists encountered in the ministries of the old regime and the ease with which they redirected their appeals to the National Assembly after the outbreak of the Revolution.[39]

Following news that the provinces would be divided into departments and districts, towns began authorizing special deputies to present plans for these new jurisdictions. Some did so in response to the advice of regular deputies. For example, municipal officials at Niort sent two special deputies to Paris as soon as Charles Filleau, a *conseiller* at the *sénéchaussée* of Niort who sat in the National Assembly, asked them for "the reasons and means that would permit him to plead their cause." These special deputies, the *lieutenant-criminel* of the *sénéchaussée* and a medical doctor, joined with M. Filleau to draft a memorial for a threefold division of the province of Poitou, so Niort could obtain its own department.[40] More commonly, municipalities sent deputations on their own initiative, either to advocate plans that regular deputies might not present with as much knowledge and energy or to represent the interests of towns that lacked their own spokesmen in the National Assembly. A *comité des représentants de la commune de la ville d'Agen* illustrates the former tendency to supplant regular deputies with ad hoc deputies. This *comité* estimated that "MM. the deputies of the *sénéchaussée* [of Agen] in the National Assembly, preoccupied with the general interest, would not, without inconvenience, be able to neglect these tasks in order to devote themselves to the details demanded by the discussion of particular and local petitions; their votes might even inspire less confidence in the Assembly if they were accused of conflicts of interest." Lobbyists from Agen, charged with the specific task of "defending and justifying the interests of the town," would not suffer from such inhibitions, so the *comité* chose two special deputies, whom they instructed to enlist the support of two citizens from Agen who were already residing in

[39] AN C 93:83 (Cholet).
[40] Louis Merle, *La formation territoriale du département des Deux-Sèvres: Etude de géographie historique* (Niort, 1938), pp. 32–34.

Paris.[41] The municipality of Thann, in Alsace, dramatized the concern of towns that had no regular deputies in the Assembly. On January 10, 1790, after approving a memorial for a royal *bailliage*, its members appointed two special deputies to go to Paris, "considering that the salvation or the ruin of the inhabitants [of Thann] depends on the success of this mission, and that in such a difficult situation, no measures should be left untried, both to preserve their personal security and to protect them from the reproaches and curses of their children and all their posterity."[42]

As the competition for establishments intensified, increasing numbers of towns resolved to send lobbyists to Paris. Many municipalities responded to the example of real or imagined rivals. For Clermont-Ferrand, it was the surreptitious passage of two special deputies from Brioude, en route to Paris, that sparked action. Fearing that Brioude wanted to secede from the province of Auvergne in order to form its own department, the *comité permanent* of Clermont called a general assembly of the town on November 19, 1789, to choose ad hoc deputies of its own. "The first lines of our instructions," these deputies later wrote, "were to guard against the intrigues of the Brivadois." Along with Clermont-Ferrand and Brioude, several other towns of the Auvergne that wanted departmental seats—Riom, Saint-Flour, and Aurillac—sent special deputies to join their regular deputies in Paris. Ten smaller towns in the province followed their example in the hope of obtaining districts or tribunals.[43] In Picardy, where the towns of Amiens, Beauvais, Laon, and Soissons sent special deputies to compete for departments, fourteen smaller towns did so to reinforce their claims to districts.[44] By the first week of January, 1790, a Parisian newspaper reported that more than eight hundred special deputies from the provinces were trying to gain admission to the sessions of the National Assembly, which had only sixteen seats reserved for them.[45] News that lawcourts would be based on the districts, which reached many towns during this month, stimulated more missions to Paris. As mentioned in chapter 2, Dupont de Nemours announced at the end of January that "all the towns of the kingdom have sent special deputies to Paris to ask for district seats; 1,824 of these deputies are already surrounding the Comité de Constitution and new ones are arriving every day."[46] Rivalries over district tribunals

[41] Mun. Agen, Nov. 14–15, 1789, cited by Louis Desgraves, *La formation territoriale du département de Lot-et-Garonne* (Nérac, 1956), p. 22.

[42] AN DIV bis 29:421 (Haut-Rhin).

[43] Documents quoted in Mège, *La formation du Puy-de-Dôme*, pp. 90–93, 261; and dossiers in AN DIV bis 29:416 (Puy-de-Dôme).

[44] Hennequin, *La formation de l'Aisne*, pp. 126–31; H. Baumont, "Le département de l'Oise: Sa formation en 1790," *Bulletin de la Société des Etudes Historiques et Scientifiques de l'Oise* 1 (1905): 54–57; and dossiers in AN DIV bis 17:290 and 31:439 (Somme).

[45] *Journal des Etats-Généraux*, Jan. 7, 1790, 7:269.

[46] Dupont de Nemours, "Observations," AP 11:606.

set in motion yet another wave of lobbyists in the spring and summer of 1790, as some towns entered the competition for the first time, while others sent new deputations to argue for or against the sharing of establishments. For several months, hundreds of special deputies were present in Paris, and at times they outnumbered the regular deputies who came from provincial towns.

In its entirety, this lobbying campaign involved at least 391 towns, of which 280 had no other spokesmen for their cause in the National Assembly.[47] Small towns were especially dependent on ad hoc deputies: 82 percent (251/303) of the towns with fewer than 5,000 inhabitants that sent special deputies did not have a regular deputy in the National Assembly, as compared with only 21 percent (19/88) of the larger towns that sent such spokesmen. Map 5.2 displays the geographical distribution and relative size of towns that relied exclusively on lobbyists in Paris. The alternating pattern of high and low densities on this map confirms the phenomenon of contagious example: In some departments, neighboring towns imitated each other by sending deputies to Paris, while elsewhere few, if any, towns took the trouble of authorizing such missions. Small towns in the Paris region, the Loire River basin, and parts of the Massif Central were considerably more involved in this movement than were their counterparts in Brittany, the Midi, and the eastern provinces.

Variations in the cost of travel to Paris help explain these regional contrasts. Unlike regular deputies, who voted themselves a subsidy in 1789, special deputies had to depend on municipal funds to supplement their own resources. The greater the distance from Paris, the more money such delegates needed. Thus, Coucy-le-Château, a little town in Picardy, financed three deputies for only 600 livres, while Les Sables d'Olonne, a small port on the edge of Poitou, spent 1,200–1,300 livres on two deputies, and Vic-Fézensac, a small town in Gascogny, authorized 2,400 livres for two deputies. This latter municipality could afford such an expenditure only because a local notable donated 600 livres as a patriotic gift and advanced another 1,800 livres in anticipation of tax receipts due four months later.[48] The costs of special deputations were decisive obstacles to action in some towns. The municipality of Langeac, in Auvergne, decided to avoid the expenses of a deputation by corresponding instead with regular deputies from other towns; and petitioners at Pérouges, in Bresse, confessed that they were too poor to follow the example of a neighboring town that

---

[47] On the basis of signed documents by special deputies in the archives of the C.C. (DIV bis) and of all the published accounts of the formation of departments, I have tabulated 746 special deputies from these 391 towns. Additional special deputies may have been sent from other towns, but no trace of them exists in the National Archives or in local publications.

[48] Hennequin, *La formation de l'Aisne*, p. 129, n. 1; AN DIV bis 18:294 (Vendée); DIV bis 7:200 (Gers).

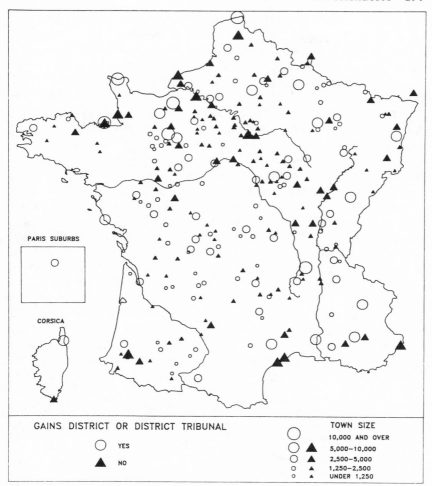

Map 5.2. Success of Towns with Special Deputies Only, 1789–1790

was funding such a mission.[49] Yet many small towns in relatively impoverished regions of the Massif Central and southwestern France did send ad
hoc deputies to Paris, as map 5.2 shows. These regions had been more
integrated into the fiscal system of the monarchy before the Revolution
than had *pays d'état* such as Brittany and Languedoc, or frontier provinces
such as Alsace and Lorraine. Institutional traditions as well as financial resources explain why so many towns in the old *pays d'élection* sent special

[49] AN DIV bis 26:380 (Haute-Loire); DIV bis 19:302 (Ain).

deputies to Paris, while relatively few towns on the periphery of the kingdom did so.

In choosing these deputies, either by majority vote or by co-optation
within a narrow circle of notables, townspeople usually followed the social
traditions of the old regime, whereby men of law, clerics, and even noblemen seemed more impressive spokesmen for most communities than merchants. Among the 279 special deputies whose occupations can be identified, only 6 were *négociants* or *marchands*, as compared with 63 *avocats*, 49
royal magistrates, 39 nobles or other military officers, and 24 ecclesias-
tics.[50] The reluctance to choose businessmen as special deputies can be illustrated in reverse by the case of Montauban, whose municipality did authorize wealthy merchants to represent its interests in Paris. When these
special deputies agreed to unite Montauban with Toulouse in a single department, a general assembly of townspeople, dominated by attorneys, disavowed their plan. Whatever the commercial ties between these two
towns, the famous barristers of Toulouse would threaten the clientele of
lawyers at Montauban.[51] In territorial disputes involving the jurisdiction
of lawcourts, towns needed men of law to defend them. The private interests and public talents of magistrates and lawyers also made these notables
more willing than other townspeople to undertake such missions. Like 70
percent of the regular deputies who represented the Third Estate in the
National Assembly, 69 percent of the special deputies had some legal or
administrative experience. In keeping with their municipal origins, however, 26 percent of the ad hoc deputies were mayors or municipal officials,
as compared with only 9 percent of the regular deputies. Taking into account the decision of many towns to send more than one notable to Paris,
the typical deputation included at least one judge, lawyer, or municipal
official. For example, Vic-Fézensac chose a royal judge as well as a retired
military officer; Beaugency delegated its mayor, who was a barrister by
profession, along with a nobleman; and Gisors sent a barrister and a
priest.[52] A few towns also enlisted the support of compatriots who were
already residing in Paris. Coucy-le-Château asked a barrister in the Paris
parlement and a former mayor who directed the academy of surgery in Paris
to join forces with its mayor, who was also the lieutenant-general of its
bailliage; Montmarault authorized a lawyer residing in Paris to assist its

[50] This tabulation is based on documents from special deputies who gave their occupations,
a few municipal deliberations describing the appointment of such special deputies, and published sources on the formation of departments.

[51] AN DIV bis 10:224 (Lot); and speech by M. Viguier, deputy from Toulouse, session of
Jan. 16, 1790, AP 11:210.

[52] AN DIV bis 7:200 (Gers); DIV bis 26:381 (Loiret); C 101:168 (Gisors). Out of 147
towns in which the social origins of at least one special deputy can be identified, 119 sent a
judge, barrister, other man of law, or municipal official.

regular deputy in the National Assembly; and Ruffec took the unusual step of issuing a power of attorney for its seigneur, the comte de Broglie, who resided in Paris.[53] As a general rule, however, special deputies were local notables, eager to compete for establishments in the National Assembly.

Thomas Lindet, whom we have already encountered as the shrewd and effective deputy from Bernay, greeted with alarm the arrival of so many envoys from provincial towns.

> A great mistake has been committed in the procedure for dividing the kingdom, that of waiting for special deputations that regular deputies from every area have encouraged. Ad hoc deputies with the least worthy pretensions have put much heat into their solicitations, and they are returning home very discontented. All these envoys are men attached to positions in the old regime, and they are combating for house and hearth [*pro aris et focis*].

Lindet himself turned a deaf ear to special deputies from several towns near Bernay, but he predicted in January 1790 that some envoys would succeed in multiplying establishments.[54] Table 5.3 confirms that among towns which had no regular deputies in the National Assembly, 44 percent obtained either a district or a tribunal if they sent special deputies, as compared with only 16 percent otherwise.[55] Most of this variation occurred among towns with fewer than 2,500 inhabitants, whose rate of success was only 13 percent if they lacked any spokesmen in Paris, and 37 percent if they relied on special deputies. Maps 5.2 and 5.3 illustrate the importance of envoys from little towns. The smallest circles on map 5.2, which refer to towns of fewer than 2,500 inhabitants whose special deputies achieved success, are relatively common in some areas; the same symbols on map 5.3, which indicate success among small towns that had no spokesmen at all in Paris, are extremely rare. By contrast, the larger circles, which denote successful towns of 2,500–4,999 inhabitants, 5,000–9,999, or 10,000 and over, are nearly as widespread on map 5.3 (towns without either deputies or special deputies) as they are on map 5.2 (towns with special deputies). The less important a town already seemed to be, the more its political fate depended on envoys who could justify its demands and neutralize its critics.

---

[53] AN DIV bis 3:144 (Aisne); DIV bis 19:307 (Allier); and Du Chambon, *La formation de la Charente*, pp. 148–49. I have identified a total of 26 special deputies who resided in Paris.

[54] Letters of Jan. 11 and 13, 1790, in Montier, *Correspondance*, p. 51.

[55] These calculations exclude towns that had regular deputies as well as special deputies in Paris. This latter group of 110 towns had a success rate of 81 percent, as compared with a success rate of 85 percent for the 308 contending towns that had only regular deputies to defend their interests. The rate fell slightly because towns that learned of opposition to their demands were more likely to send special deputies than were towns assured of a district by their regular deputies.

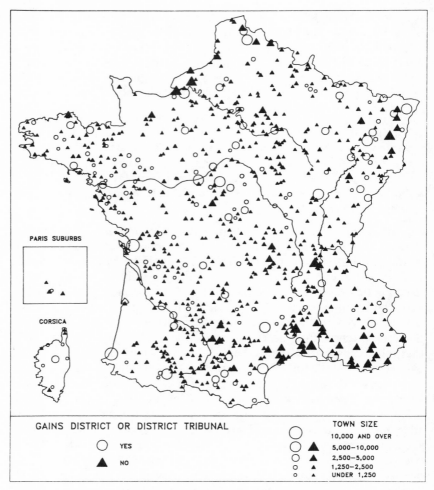

Map 5.3. Success of Towns without Any Deputies, 1789–1790

Successful lobbying required shrewd tactics and a fortunate combination of circumstances. To begin with, special deputies who arrived before departmental committees had completed their deliberations were often able to gain access to these committees. Here lobbyists from small towns tried to persuade the regular deputies to multiply the number of districts and tribunals. In the committee for the Sarthe, deputies originally agreed on a plan for six districts, but after special deputies from several towns arrived, they held another meeting, at which the comte de Tessé proposed to conciliate everyone by creating nine districts and five tribunals, allocated among eleven different towns. By a majority of five to four, the deputies endorsed this plan, and special deputies helped them draw up the list of district seats. Similarly, the committee for the Oise voted at first for only six districts, but envoys from Compiègne and Breteuil persuaded them to add two more districts for these towns.[56] Even if deputies refused to multiply districts, envoys might form alliances to share establishments. On the committee for the Haute-Loire, where special deputies outnumbered regular deputies, those from Yssingeaux and Monistrol agreed to share the directory and tribunal in one district. A special committee of envoys from nine small towns in the Seine-et-Marne endorsed a similar compromise between Moret and Montereau. In the department of the Ain, it was regular deputies who tried to reconcile the conflicting demands of envoys from Châtillon-les-Dombes and Pont-de-Veyle by offering the former a district and the latter a tribunal. Deputies from the Bouches-du-Rhône proposed instead to rotate district directories between three pairs of rival towns in their department. Finally, if departmental committees were unwilling to mediate such disputes or failed to satisfy one town or another, then special deputies could appeal to the C.C. In the Aveyron, the regular deputies asked envoys from Sévérac and Saint-Geniez to submit their rivalry to this higher authority, but in most departments, spokesmen with unfulfilled demands for districts or tribunals took this initiative themselves.[57]

Indeed, appeals to the C.C. became extremely numerous in January and February 1790, after departmental committees submitted their plans for districts. The eight members and four commissioners of this committee had the authority to modify these plans and to insert additional clauses for *partage* in the decrees that they prepared for a vote in the entire National Assembly. The commissioners, who served as *rapporteurs* for the C.C., could also advise the Assembly to refer disputes to departmental or district assemblies of voters. Much lobbying centered on the precise wording of the decrees that these *rapporteurs* proposed. At one extreme, a town rebuffed by a departmental committee might be included on the list of districts after all; at the other extreme, its demands might be explicitly rejected by the *rapporteur*. Between complete success and total failure, a gradation of conciliatory wording might stipulate a tribunal for the town in question, or permit it to share unspecified establishments, or refer its demands to the

[56] L'Hermitte, "L'assemblée administrative du département de la Sarthe," in *La Révolution dans le Sarthe* (1922), pp. 76–79; and AN DIV bis 16:277 (Sarthe); *mémoire* for Beauvais, DIV bis 29:412 (Oise).

[57] Josanne Pothier, "Création du département de la Haute-Loire, 1789–1790," *Almanach de Brioude et de son arrondissement* 56 (1976): 109–10; AN DIV bis 17:285, 287 (Seine-et-Marne); Eugène Dubois, *Histoire de la Révolution dans l'Ain* (Bourg, 1930), 1:135–41; AP 11:519 (decree on district seats); DIV bis 4:165 (Aveyron).

voters. While regular deputies had the right to introduce amendments to such decrees on the floor of the National Assembly, special deputies were excluded from these public debates. Some lobbyists published pamphlets to publicize their views in the National Assembly, but few deputies paid close attention to parochial disputes outside their own departments. It was the *rapporteurs* themselves whom lobbyists needed to convince. The memorials that these envoys submitted, their rejoinders to the arguments of rivals, their proofs of popular support at home, all became a mass of documents that accumulated in the offices of the C.C. As special deputies from Clermont-Ferrand reported on December 12, 1789, even before lobbying reached its peak, "One thing is certain: The Comité de Constitution has received a crowd of memorials that it does not have time to read, because it is completely overwhelmed with work." Under these circumstances, success depended less on written materials than on personal interviews. In the perceptive words of the envoys from Clermont, "It is by arranging for private meetings, where arguments are presented in a strong and effective manner, that favorable decisions can be obtained."[58]

Only fragmentary evidence exists about these consultations, which resembled intrigues rather than debates. In a few departments, the *commissaires* responded to the pressure of lobbyists by singling out one town for preferential treatment. Thus, they added a fourth district to the Aisne for Doullens and a fourth district to the Cantal for Murat, after envoys from these towns appealed to them.[59] Much more frequently, however, the C.C. refused to permit more districts than the regular deputies wanted. After the departmental committee in the Seine-et-Oise rejected the agreement between Montereau and Moret for a sixth district, the C.C. disregarded the strong objections of envoys from both these towns. Here one of the *commissaires*, Dupont, took the side of his hometown of Nemours, which wanted to incorporate Montereau and Moret into its own district.[60] In the neighboring department of the Yonne, the C.C. even overruled a committee of regular and special deputies that voted eleven to three in favor of nine districts. Its *rapporteur* agreed instead with a memorial by a regular deputy from Auxerre, who played on the continuing rivalry between envoys from three small towns in order to advocate only seven districts.[61] As for the numerous requests that the C.C. received concerning the sharing of directories and lawcourts, here, too, the objections of regular deputies

[58] Letter of Dec. 12, 1789, published in Mège, *Formation du Puy-de-Dôme*, p. 249.

[59] Printed *observations* for Doullens, AN DIV bis 17:290 (Somme); Printed *réclamation* for Murat, AN DIV bis 5:174 (Cantal); *rapports* by Gossin on the departments of Picardie and Haute-Auvergne, Jan. 26 and 28, 1790, AP 11:326, 362.

[60] *Rapport* of Gossin on the department of Brie et Gatinais, Jan. 30, 1790, AP 11:395; and speech of Dupont de Nemours, Jan. 27, AP 11:350–51.

[61] Charles Porée, *La formation du département de l'Yonne en 1790* (Auxerre, 1910), pp. 59–63.

carried more weight than did the pleas of ad hoc deputies. Only if opposition came primarily from other special deputies did the C.C. sometimes agree to reserve the tribunal for a town that failed to become a district seat.[62] More commonly, however, such disputes were referred to the voters. This was the easiest concession for the C.C. to make, and the one that appears most often in the decrees of the National Assembly.[63]

Thus, the politics of parochialism, discussed mainly behind closed doors in the National Assembly, returned to its origins in provincial towns. Following the advice of the C.C., deputies agreed to refer disputes involving a total of 182 towns to electoral assemblies in the departments and districts.[64] These consultations implied that local populations were in a better position to judge their interests than were the deputies in Paris. Such had been the argument of tens of thousands of petitioners all along. As soon as the National Assembly had abolished seigneurial courts, townspeople had begun to mobilize public opinion in favor of new establishments, and their petitioning campaigns became increasingly vigorous as rivalries for departments and districts intensified in the winter of 1789–90. As expressions of community support, *adresses* from small towns to the National Assembly were often endorsed by a variety of signatories, drawn from crafts and commerce as well as from the legal profession. Public meetings involving as many as 675 petitioners were held in several hundred towns, and a total of nearly 40,000 townspeople signed their names to documents requesting lawcourts and directories. Even illiterate residents were sometimes listed as participants in the general assemblies that municipal leaders, old and new, convoked in response to the territorial reorganization of the kingdom. Equally impressive were the petitions that townspeople circulated in nearby villages. A total of 508 towns collected signatures from rural communities in order to prove that the inhabitants of the surrounding countryside supported their demands. Over half of these towns received endorsements from more than ten rural parishes or municipalities, and 157 of them obtained the help of peasant leaders in over twenty communities. In response to the territorial reorganization of the kingdom, petitioners in nearly 9,000 villages voiced their support for a nearby town as the vital center of their legal and administrative affairs.[65]

Townspeople submitted two types of documents that were designed to

[62] Examples of *partage* in response to the lobbying by special deputies include Gisors in the district of Les Andelys, Orbec in the district of Lisieux, and Wassy in the district of Saint-Dizier.

[63] In 38 districts, rivalries over tribunals were referred to voters, as compared to 33 districts where *partage* was decreed or implied.

[64] Tabulation based on decrees on particular departments, Jan. 19–Feb. 17, 1790, AP 11:234–621, *passim*; and the royal *lettres patentes* on the division of France, Mar. 4, 1790, *Réimpression de l'ancien Moniteur* 4:3–340, *passim*.

[65] Tabulations based on a computerized analysis of all relevant documents in AN series DIV bis, C, ADXVI, DXVII.

represent public opinion: the *adresse* and the municipal *délibération*. Neither of these documents conformed precisely to the conception of a petition as a grievance or request signed by individuals in their capacity as citizens of the nation. An *adresse* expressed the views of a general assembly of inhabitants from a particular community or group of communities; and a *délibération* registered the results of a town meeting convoked in the traditional manner by municipal authorities. Because *adresses* were often signed by municipal officers as well as by ordinary citizens, they combined official and unofficial, collective and individual dimensions of public opinion.[66] So did *délibérations* that listed men from a variety of occupations who participated in a general assembly of the community. Where the two documentary forms differed was in the relative emphasis that they placed on officially authorized expressions of opinion. *Délibérations* were relatively common in areas of southern France where small towns had strong municipal institutions that survived the initial phase of the Revolution unchallenged by public committees. *Adresses* were more characteristic of towns and bourgs in western and central France where municipal institutions had been weak before the Revolution, where revolutionary committees often exercised power in 1789, and where judges as well as municipal officers or committee members presided over general assemblies. In most provinces of northern and eastern France, committees played a lesser role in local politics than they did in the west, but townspeople submitted more unauthorized *adresses* there than they did in the south.[67]

Magistrates and men of law obviously had the strongest personal interest in the success of such mobilizations of local opinion. Judicial *compagnies* took the initiative of petitioning the National Assembly in several dozen towns, and royal magistrates joined with other petitioners in many towns. Thus, *les officiers de justices et municipaux* as well as *la communauté des habitants* endorsed a memorial from the town of Argenton-en-Berry; and *bailliage* magistrates at Beaumont-le-Royer signed an *adresse* from the inhabitants of this town.[68] Seigneurial judges played an equally conspicuous role in the petitions of many towns that did not possess royal courts. For example, the *officiers* of a seigneurial court organized a town meeting at Sau-

[66] All documents bearing the signatures of ordinary inhabitants can be described as *adresses*, although some were called *requêtes*, *suppliques*, *mémoires*, or even *lettres* by townspeople themselves.

[67] On regional variations in the role of revolutionary committees in small towns, see Daniel Ligou, "A propos de la révolution municipale," *Revue d'histoire économique et sociale* 30 (1960), 146–77. Lynn Hunt has shown that provincial traditions were less important than socioeconomic structures in determining the outcome of political conflicts in large towns during the summer and fall of 1789. See her article "Committees and Communes: Local Politics and National Revolution in 1789," *Comparative Studies in Society and History* 18 (July 1976): 321–46.

[68] AN DIV bis 8:209 (Indre); DIV bis 6:192 (Eure).

gues; and seigneurial judges presided over the *comité permanent* in the town of Pons, a general assembly in the bourg of Apchon, and a municipal deliberation in the town of Saint-Chinian. At Le Lude it was the seigneur, M. le comte de Lavienville, who served as president of a local *comité*, and his seigneurial judge, M. Lenoir de la Cochetière, who convoked the town meeting that agreed to submit a memorial for a district and a lawcourt.[69] Barristers, solicitors, and notaries also led petitioning campaigns in some communities. M. Vacquier, the mayor who presided over a town meeting at Sévérac, was also an *avocat en parlement*; so was M. Jean-Marie Viguier, the mayor and first consul of Rieux, who urged his fellow townspeople to seek a district and a lawcourt. Two officers of the salt granary at La Haye-Descartes, both lawyers, wrote a cover letter for the *supplique* that residents of this town signed; and two solicitors as well as a seigneurial judge presented arguments for a lawcourt in a public meeting that notaries convoked in the bourg of La Tourblanche.[70] Men of law also figured prominently on the commissions that some towns chose to write *mémoires* for new establishments, following the precedent of assemblies of the Third Estate that had appointed *commissaires* to draft *cahiers de doléances*. Among such commissioners were a barrister and a solicitor at Mussy-l'Evêque; three barristers at Uzès; a royal magistrate, a seigneurial judge, a barrister, and a solicitor at Vézelay; and two magistrates, two barristers, and two notaries at Grenade.[71] Regardless of whether old mayors, *échevins*, and *officiers municipaux* retained their authority, men whose social position depended on lawcourts became the foremost advocates of districts and tribunals in many towns.

With respect to the collective dimension of urban politics, many *adresses* and *délibérations* referred to public meetings, which were more common in small towns than in large ones. Only fourteen of the ninety-one municipalities and committees that governed towns of over 10,000 inhabitants held general assemblies to endorse requests for new establishments, as compared with nearly half the towns of fewer than 2,500 inhabitants whose leaders sent documents to the National Assembly. Map 5.4 illustrates the proliferation of town meetings in small towns throughout the Paris basin, the plains of the Loire River, the Massif Central, and the southwest. Only along the eastern and southeastern periphery of the kingdom were such assemblies rare, either because townspeople displayed less enthusiasm for new establishments or because municipalities formulated de-

---

[69] AN DIV bis 9:222 (Haute-Loire); DIV bis 21:333 (Charente-Inférieure); C 93:87 (Apchon); DXVII 1 (Saint-Chinian); C 102:173 (Le Lude).

[70] AN DXVII 2 (Sévérac); DIV bis 24:356 (Haute-Garonne); (Indre-et-Loire), Nov. 25, 1789, DXVII 1 (La Haye-Descartes); DIV bis 5:176 (Dordogne, misfiled in Charente).

[71] AN DIV bis 20:319 (Aube); DXVII 2 (Uzès); DIV bis 32:448 (Yonne); Rumeau, *Grenade*, pp. 6–9.

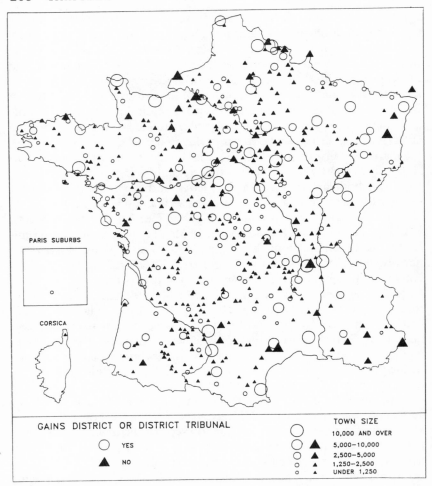

Map 5.4. Success of Towns that Hold Public Meetings, 1789–1790

mands without seeking a broader base of public support. The map includes a few large towns such as Nîmes, Poitiers, and Toulouse, where urban leaders organized general assemblies of delegates from the various corporations instead of inviting all townspeople to attend. Such representative institutions were a traditional method of canvassing public opinion in towns where the authorities feared tumultuous gatherings of the laboring poor.[72] On the basis of royal policy and customary practices, some medium-sized

[72] Bordes, *L'administration provinciale*, pp. 199, 254–79.

towns also restricted general assemblies to a small number of delegates. At Châteaudun, for example, only forty-four men, representing four religious chapters, eight professional corporations, and twenty guilds of merchants, shopkeepers, and artisans, attended a meeting on November 24, 1789, to endorse a request for a department.[73] Furthermore, municipal leaders in large and medium-sized towns often took responsibility for signing the *adresses* or *mémoires* that such deputies approved. This helps explain why only forty-six of the contending towns that numbered at least 5,000 inhabitants forwarded documents signed by over twenty-five people.

More democratic assemblies, based on parishes rather than on occupational groups, were held in many small towns and bourgs that lacked corporate institutions.[74] A total of 414 market towns that numbered fewer than 2,500 inhabitants held such assemblies, and 129 of them collected signatures from over fifty local residents. In such communities, political rights were restricted less by class than by age and sex. Only in one little town of Brittany did fourteen women, all merchants or shopkeepers, join with sixty-four men in signing an *adresse* for a lawcourt.[75] Of course, a hierarchy of social rank and precedence also existed among the men of small towns. Municipal registers often mirrored this hierarchy by listing magistrates and lawyers first, then other professional men and bourgeois proprietors, followed by wholesale merchants, shopkeepers, artisans, and farmers.[76] Illiterate participants in public meetings were sometimes excluded from mention in these registers, which implied that only literate townspeople possessed individuality as citizens.[77] Literacy was an even more obvious criterion of social discrimination in towns that submitted *adresses*, for only inhabitants who could sign their names appeared at the bottom of these documents. As if to symbolize the community of the literate, petitioners in some towns of the Paris basin neglected to write their occupations on these *adresses*.[78] A stronger sense of social rank characterized magistrates, lawyers, and other professional men in towns of central and western France, where they were careful to write their *titres* as well as their names on petitions for lawcourts. Merchants in such communities

---

[73] M. Rabouin, *Châteaudun pendant la Révolution* (Châteaudun, 1904), pp. 13–16.

[74] On the rarity of guilds in the small towns, see P. Boissonnade, *Essai sur l'organisation du travail en Poitou depuis le XI siècle jusqu'à la Révolution*, 2 vols. (Paris, 1900), 2:1–36.

[75] *Adresse* from Gourin (Morbihan), AN C 113:277.

[76] Examples include Mun. Delibs. at Montereau, Castellanne, and Sévérac, AN DIV bis 17:285 (Yonne); DIV bis 3:153 (Basses-Alpes); DXVII 2.

[77] See, for example, the reference to "an infinity [of citizens] who do not know how to write," in Mun. Delibs. Vieillevigne, AN DIV bis 26:383 (Loire-Inférieure).

[78] For example, among 53 signatories of an *adresse* from Beaumont-le-Roger, only the *bailliage* magistrates gave their occupations, and among 57 petitioners at Albert, none gave their occupations. AN DIV bis 6:192 (Eure); DIV bis 17:289 (Somme).

often noted their occupations, too, but artisans sometimes neglected to do so, even if they were literate.[79]

While the size of the public that attended assemblies can be estimated in many towns, the occupational profile of participants is usually incomplete. Table 5.4 presents evidence from twenty-eight towns where such information does exist for over two-thirds of the participants. Generally speaking, men of law and other urban notables turned out in disproportionate numbers to support requests for new establishments, but the larger the gathering, the higher the proportion of merchants, shopkeepers, and artisans whose occupations appear in *adresses* and *délibérations*, too. These averages conceal substantial variations in the social background of petitioners from particular towns. For example, men of law accounted for thirty-five of the participants in a town meeting at Bort, twenty-eight at Sévérac, and twenty-five at Château-Chinon, but only nine of them attended a meeting at Bourgueil, seven at La Châtre, and two at Apchon.[80] Differences in the relative importance of lawcourts within small towns and bourgs help explain such contrasts. So do alternative political tactics on the part of ambitious leaders, who tried in some towns to mobilize individuals from all social groups and elsewhere to compile a selective list of notables who endorsed their demands. At one extreme, petitions affirmed the self-consciousness of literate elites; at the other extreme, they signified the solidarity of entire communities.

In competition with other towns for the honor and profit of acquiring lawcourts and directories, many urban leaders turned to the countryside for additional support. Arguments based on the interests of an entire region or *pays* might disarm criticism that men of law and shopkeepers wanted to acquire establishments for their own selfish purposes. In the words of municipal officials at Gacé, a small town of Normandy, "If we had only the demands of our own town to present to our Lords in the National Assembly, we would remain silent. . . . But we are presenting the demands of all the parishes that surround us."[81] To confirm such assertions, some townspeople encouraged rural inhabitants to attend their meetings and sign their *adresses*, while others requested the formal adhesion of rural communities to their demands. The former tactic of joint meetings and petitions characterized the actions of around one hundred towns where a

---

[79] Examples include a *placet* from "the inhabitants of the town of Lassay," signed by 13 men of law, 6 other notables, 24 merchants and shopkeepers, and 34 individuals with unknown occupations, probably weavers and other artisans; and a *mémoire* from Donzy (Nièvre), signed by 18 men of law, 13 other notables, 12 merchants, only 6 artisans, 2 farmers, and 15 unknown residents. AN DXVII 1 (Lassay); DIV bis 28:407 (Nièvre).

[80] AN C 95:102 (Bort); DXVII 2 (Sévérac); DXVII 1 (Château-Chinon); DIV bis 25:372 (Indre-et-Loire); DIV bis 25:370 (Indre); C 93:87 (Apchon).

[81] *Mémoire*, AN DIV bis 29:413 (Orne).

TABLE 5.4
Occupational Distribution of Participants in Town Meetings

Number of Petitioners	Men of Law		Other Notables		Merchants, Tradesmen		Artisans		Farmers		Unknown		Total
Over 100	116	(15%)	157	(20%)	195	(25%)	180	(23%)	69	(9%)	68	(9%)	786
51–100	219	(22%)	173	(18%)	202	(20%)	222	(22%)	68	(7%)	103	(10%)	987
26–50	107	(34%)	87	(28%)	47	(15%)	43	(14%)	2	(1%)	28	(9%)	314
TOTAL	442	(21%)	417	(20%)	444	(21%)	445	(21%)	139	(7%)	199	(10%)	2,086

Sources: Adresses, délibérations and other requests for districts and lawcourts, from the following towns, in series AN DIV bis, C. ADXVII: over 100 participants: Bort (Corrèze), Castellanne (Basses-Alpes), Montereau (Yonne), Nesle (Somme), Sévérac (Aveyron), Valence-d'Agen (Lot-et-Garonne); 51–100 participants: Annot (Basses-Alpes), Bourgueil (Indre-et-Loire), Château-Chinon (Nièvre), Cologne (Gers), Donzy (Nièvre), Gourin (Morbihan), La Châtre (Indre), Lormes (Nièvre), Pamiers (Ariège), Rochefort-en-Montagne (Puy-de-Dôme), Saint-Gaudens (Haute-Garonne), Saint-Germain-Lembron (Puy-de-Dôme), Saint-Pierre-le-Moutier (Nièvre), Verdun-sur-Garonne (Haute-Garonne); 26–50 participants: Aigre (Charente), Apchon (Cantal), (Creuse), Blesle (Haute-Loire), Corbigny (Nièvre), Le Lude (Sarthe), Montpont (Dordogne), Rochechouart (Haute-Vienne), Saint-Vallier (Drôme).

variety of institutions facilitated direct appeals to notables in the countryside. The jurisdiction of a royal *bailliage* served this purpose at Bouzonville; a barony at Montignac; a subdelegation at Guingamp; a *viguerie* at Apt; and an *élection* at Barbezieux.[82] Sometimes townspeople convoked delegates from rural communities, but more often they invited the "principal inhabitants" of the countryside to sign their petitions. These leaders of rural opinion included nearly 600 priests, syndics, merchants, seigneurs, and yeomen farmers from 50 parishes in the *bailliage* of Saint-Sauveur-le-Vicomte; 122 priests, seigneurs, syndics, and men of law from 23 parishes near Rochechouart; and 120 mayors, aldermen, and electors from 65 communities in the *châtellenie* of Bouchain.[83] By indicating their social rank and place of residence on the same documents that townspeople signed, such notables symbolized the community of interests that bound litigants to lawcourts and rural elites to urban magistrates and administrators.

Over four hundred towns followed the more formal procedure of asking village leaders to sign separate documents for submission to the National Assembly. Several dozen towns that wanted departmental seats or appellate lawcourts set a precedent for such action by trying to persuade other municipalities to endorse their plans. For example, a special commission at Toulouse sent eighteen delegates throughout the hinterland of this provincial capital, seeking adhesions for a large department. These delegates visited at least fifty towns and bourgs, carrying official letters from the authorities of Toulouse. The document that two solicitors from Toulouse brought on December 8, 1789, to the town of Grenade promised "all the particular satisfactions that will be within our power to grant and that can be reconciled with your respective localities." Despite the impersonality of this letter, which the delegates probably showed to other towns, municipal officials at Grenade replied that they would be happy to enter the department of Toulouse—but only if they obtained a district and a tribunal. After receiving assurances on this score, they responded to delegates from Auch and Montauban, who arrived later in the month with rival plans for departments, that Grenade had committed itself to Toulouse.[84] Not all municipalities were so steadfast in their commitments. Townspeople at Montluçon, who complained of being "assailed by deputies from most of the surrounding capitals," put in their own bid for a department and persuaded nearby towns to withdraw their support for Guéret. Municipal officials at two little towns of lower Berry, deceived at first by emissaries from Issoudun who raised the imaginary danger of transfer to a department in

[82] AN DIV bis 11:242 (Moselle); DXVII 1 (Montignac); DXVII 1 (Guingamp); DIV bis 5:167 (Bouches-du-Rhône); C 97:117 (Barbezieux).

[83] AN DIV bis 27:393 (Manche); DXVII 2 (Rochechouart); DIV bis 12:246 (Nord).

[84] Rumeau, *Grenade*, pp. 5–9. On the general campaign of Toulouse, see Claude Devic and Joseph Vaissette, *Histoire générale de Languedoc*, 2d ed. (Toulouse, 1876), 13:1399–1404.

Touraine, retracted their adhesions and endorsed the town of Châteauroux.[85] As these cases proved, however, municipalities took their deliberations seriously when they opted for one department rather than another.

The election of new municipalities throughout the kingdom at the end of January 1790 greatly encouraged towns to solicit formal adhesions from rural communities. A few towns had already begun to ask general assemblies in the countryside to endorse their demands. When a *comité permanent* of electors from the *bailliage* of Bar-sur-Seine resolved on November 19, 1789, to seek a district, it sent delegates with copies of its *délibération* to rural communities. A total of nineteen parishes held general assemblies that voted in favor of Bar-sur-Seine, and from ten to thirty-seven literate members of each parish signed *délibérations* that repeated the same arguments that the *comité permanent* had used. The parishioners of Balnot-le-Châtel even held a second assembly on December 5 to affirm their earlier resolution against Les Riceys, an ambitious bourg whose vineyards offered none of the resources that the grain markets of Bar-sur-Seine provided.[86] In 1790, such *délibérations* became widespread, as towns in competition for districts and tribunals appealed to rural municipalities. Frequently, townspeople supplied the arguments and even copies of the documents that they wanted villagers to sign. For example, elected officials at Cosne received endorsements from twenty rural communes by sending them "models already prepared, which they had only to copy and sign"; the municipality of Hennebont circulated a letter whose phrases reappeared in the *délibérations* of thirteen rural parishes; and the mayor of Pont-de-Vaux personally visited three nearby parishes, where he wrote in his own hand the documents that officials signed.[87] Within a few weeks, and sometimes on the very same day, a number of different municipalities in districts such as Pont-de-l'Arche, Saint-Chély, and Corbigny approved nearly identical texts.[88] Just as townspeople had circulated model *cahiers de doléances* for rural parishes to imitate during the elections to the Estates-General, so they orchestrated rural *délibérations* on their own behalf.[89] In form, however,

[85] AN DIV bis 19:307 (Allier); Mun. Cluis and Mun. Aigurande, AN DIV bis 25:370 (Indre).

[86] AN DIV bis 4:161 (Aube).

[87] Complaints of Mun. Donzy, Lorient, and Saint-Trivier, and Mun. Delibs. for Cosne, Hennebont, and Pont-de-Vaux, in AN DIV bis 28:407, 409 (Nièvre); ADXVI 53 (Lorient) and DIV bis 36:580 (Morbihan); C 121:380 (Saint-Trivier) and DIV bis 56:7 (Ain).

[88] 51 Mun. Delibs. supporting Pont-de-l'Arche, signed mainly on Jan. 11, 1790; 27 Mun. Delibs. supporting Corbigny, nearly all signed on Feb. 7, 1790; and 22 Mun. Delibs. supporting Saint-Chély, usually on Feb. 14, 1790. AN DIV bis 23:349 (Eure); DIV bis 28:409 (Nièvre); DIV bis 27:392 (Lozère).

[89] On the diffusion of model *cahiers* in 1789, see Henri Sée, "La rédaction et la valeur historique des cahiers de paroisse pour les Etats-Generaux de 1789," *Revue historique* 102

these documents were authentic acts of independent municipalities, each signed by a small number of literate officials and each offered as proof that public opinion in the countryside favored a particular town.

Not all towns tried to canvass rural officials. Some dismissed the very thought as beneath their dignity. "Intrigue is the recourse of weakness," wrote the leaders of Lorient. "We have not entered upon a career where there is more profit than honor to acquire. We are, it is said, new men, but we have the pride of old townspeople. We have awaited justice and we have not gone to beg for it among those who owe it to us." Others denounced such methods as odious, shameful, or iniquitious. For townpeople at Moustiers, the "secret, sinister and insidious maneuvers" of their rivals at Riez could only arouse "the indignation of all respectable people." Such language intimated that conspirators were at work. Spokesmen for Carentan blamed "intriguers" who had formed "a kind of cabal" in rival bourgs to collect the signatures of country dwellers. According to municipal officials at Le Malzieu, a powerful conspiracy had been formed in the *pays*, consisting of several country priests who were born at Saint-Chély, nobles who possessed fiefs in the area, and privileged persons who resided in this town. A special deputy from Le Malzieu denounced by name three seigneurs, two seigneurial judges, five priests, and a doctor who had used their influence to collect signatures from rural parishes. For example, Breschet, from Saint-Chély, estate agent and judge in the parish of Prunières, "disposes at his will of the votes of everyone in this parish"; another Breschet, also a native of Saint-Chély, is the priest as well as the mayor of Saint-Pierre-le-Vieux and "lets his parishoners do only what he wants." Ignorant and impoverished peasants were no match for such intriguers. From Château-Chinon came reports that a bailiff and a clerk from the little town of Moulins-Engilbert were making the rounds of parishes in the district, assembling parishoners after mass and haranguing them with false promises of great tax reductions if they would sign ready-made declarations of support for Moulins-Engilbert. Petitions containing such flagrant offenses against the law should be prohibited by the National Assembly.[90]

Thus, complaints about petitioning campaigns raised basic issues about political legitimacy in the countryside. For the municipality of Doullens, *délibérations* favoring rival towns were "nothing but the fruit of the most outrageous deception, envy and malice"; for Montlhéry, they were testimonials of "rustic men who signed blindly"; for Semur-en-Brionnais, they

---

(1910): 292–306; and Roger Chartier, "Culture, lumières, doléances: Les cahiers de 1789," *Revue d'histoire moderne et contemporaine* 29 (Jan.–Mar. 1981): 68–93.

[90] AN ADXVI 53 (Lorient); DIV bis 3:153 (Basses-Alpes); DIV bis 27:393 (Manche); DIV bis 27:391 (Lozère); DIV bis 28:406 (Nièvre).

were adhesions of "simple and illiterate men."[91] One town's demonstration of rural support became another town's evidence that "timid and credulous peasants" had been surprised and seduced.[92] Magistrates at the *bailliage* court of Bouzonville even undertook a formal investigation of charges that emissaries from Sarrelouis were illegally gathering signatures in the countryside.[93] Neither traditional practice nor the new political theory of the Revolution could justify such efforts to manipulate public opinion. As one critic reasoned:

> These signatures, sometimes begged for, sometimes ordered, partly denied afterward by retractions, are so many proofs of the deception practiced on the good faith and the carelessness of the countryside. Far from being the guarantors of a reasoned will, whose object is generally salutary, they attest only to sordid intrigue and a self-interest disturbed by its own nullity. . . . By what right could a mayor, a municipal official, a town clerk suddenly become the organ of the general will, without having consulted that will on such an important matter, in a preliminary assembly, and without having been legally authorized to demonstrate it? . . . To recall these signatures is to denounce the illegality and the worthlessness of the document on which they are written.[94]

However, not all the townspeople who denounced their rivals for circulating petitions had neglected to use such methods themselves. Longuyon submitted a petition signed by 229 residents of 26 rural communities before dismissing a petition from Longwy that contained 450 signatures from 76 communes; and Donzy collected 16 parish deliberations before complaining that rivals at Cosne had "extorted" support from 20 municipalities.[95] In many cases, moral indignation expressed the failure of townspeople to compete on equal terms with their adversaries. Some were too disdainful of the peasantry, but others learned to their regret that petitioning campaigns, like elections, have losers as well as winners. In this respect, the politics of parochialism foreshadowed the deeper dilemma of the French Revolution: How could the will of the people be discovered amidst the clash of interests and opinions?

High rates of illiteracy in the countryside made systematic surveys of rural opinion impossible to undertake, but townspeople who succeeded in

---

[91] AN DIV bis 31:440 (Somme); DIV bis 30:431 (Seine-et-Oise); DIV bis 30:427 (Saône-et-Loire).

[92] Mun. Delib. Phalsbourg, AN DIV bis 27:398 (Meurthe).

[93] "Réquisitoire et plainte" and "Information" containing testimony from 51 witnesses who accused the police commissioner of Sarrelouis of carrying around petitions to rural communities, AN DIV bis 28:404 (Moselle).

[94] Printed *Observations pour la ville de Longuyon* (Paris, n.d.) [by a special deputy], pp. 42–43; AN ADXVI 53.

[95] AN C 103:181 (Longuyon) and DIV bis 28:405 (Moselle); DIV bis 28:407 (Nièvre).

collecting more municipal deliberations or more signatures than their opponents did naturally emphasized this fact. Considerable variations did exist in the scale of petitioning. Two hundred and twenty-nine towns gathered signatures in fewer than eleven communes, while forty-one towns submitted documents to prove that over forty communes supported them. Generally speaking, towns ranging in size from 2,500 to 5,000 inhabitants were the most likely to gain rural support, but nearly two-thirds of all the towns that collected rural signatures had fewer than 2,500 inhabitants, as table 5.5 shows. As for large towns, which exercised economic influence over entire regions, their leaders rarely circulated petitions in nearby rural communities. Instead, they sought support from lesser towns for departments and appellate courts. By contrast, the leaders of market towns, who were competing primarily for districts and tribunals, tried to demonstrate their primacy as central places for the countryside. Thus, the circulation of petitions in rural communities became primarily a small-town phenomenon. Map 5.5 illustrates the geographical distribution of this phenomenon. In some departments, so many towns mobilized rural support that some were bound to fail, as the solid triangles on the map indicate. Nonetheless, small towns that mustered considerable rural support did improve their chances of obtaining a district or a lawcourt. Among towns numbering fewer than 2,500 inhabitants, 49 percent (46/94) of those endorsed by over twenty rural communes gained their objectives, as compared with only 18 percent (128/704) of those that did not obtain any signatures from other communities.[96]

A comparison of maps 5.4 and 5.5 suggests, however, that many petitioning campaigns, like many towns meetings, failed to influence the National Assembly. The smallest triangles on both maps signify the many little towns, numbering fewer than 1,250 inhabitants, that lost hope of gaining either a district or a tribunal. Indeed, petitions had little effect unless towns also had deputies or special deputies to advocate their cause in Paris. Rural endorsements that towns simply forwarded to the National Assembly were far too numerous for the C.C. to pay them close attention. Furthermore, the *commissaires* of the C.C. tended to discount such petitions as expressions of urban rather than rural opinion. As M. Gossin explained to the National Assembly on September 23, 1790,

> The inhabitants of the countryside have, in general, viewed with indifference the pretensions of towns and the efforts to obtain lawcourts. They have scarcely ex-

[96] This correlation is weaker among towns with 2,500–5,000 inhabitants: 67 percent (120/178) of the towns without rural petitioners were successful, as compared with 77 percent (27/35) of the towns endorsed by residents of over twenty rural communes. Among larger towns, rural support made no consistent difference in the rate of success: 90 percent (124/138) of those without rural petitioners succeeded, as compared with 98 percent (54/55) of those with support from 1 to 20 communes, but only 82 percent (23/28) of those with support from residents in over 20 communes.

TABLE 5.5
Number of Rural Communes Supporting Urban Petitions

	Nucleated Population of Towns Gaining Rural Support				
	10,000 and Over	5,000– 9,999	2,500– 4,999	Under 2,500	Total
Number of rural communes with petitioners					
Over 40	4 (10%)	7 (17%)	11 (27%)	19 (46%)	41
21–40	7 (6%)	10 (9%)	24 (21%)	75 ((65%)	116
11–20	3 (2%)	13 (11%)	24 (20%)	82 (67%)	122
1–10	19 (8%)	20 (9%)	42 (18%)	148 (65%)	229
All communes with rural support	33 (6%)	50 (10%)	101 (20%)	324 (64%)	508
No rural signatures	58 (6%)	80 (8%)	158 (16%)	704 (70%)	1,000
All contenders	91 (6%)	130 (9%)	259 (17%)	1,025 (68%)	1,508

Sources: Documents from rural communes and documents signed by rural residents that support a particular town as the seat of a district or a lawcourt, 1789–1790, AN C:90–123; DIV bis 1–34, 56–76; ADXVI 18:81.

Note: The number of rural communes with petitioners is an estimate that includes (1) the number of separate *déliberations* from other communes and (2) the number of parishes, communities, or communes mentioned by signatories of urban petitions as their places of residence.

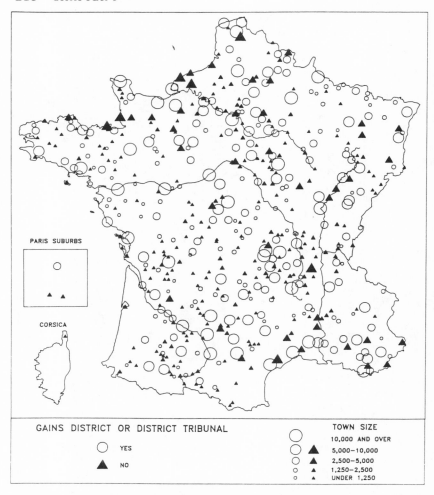

Map 5.5. Success of Towns with Rural Petitioners, 1789–1790

pressed their views in favor of one town or another except when country lawyers [*praticiens*] incited them by going round the villages with *délibérations* prepared in advance. The Comité de Constitution has often had reason to judge that most of these demands were the result of particular interests and intrigues.[97]

Perhaps this dismissal was unfair to the thousands of villagers who signed petitions. Rural proprietors had good reason to prefer a district and

[97] Printed *Décret de l'Assemblée nationale rendu sur la protestation de la municipalité et du district de Corbigny*, by M. Gossin, AN ADXVI 54.

a tribunal in the nearest market center, where they could defend their interests without spending money on travel to a more distant town. Many petitioners did not imitate a common text, and even rural inhabitants who did so were less ignorant than critics averred. A *délibération* from the parish of Plouay, in Brittany, distinguished clearly between imitation and ignorance: "Taking into consideration the reasons stated in the letters of Messieurs the municipal officials of the town of Hennebont, we declare unanimously our adherance to the edict that they took for the definitive establishment of the district in that town."[98] If the C.C. brushed such documents aside, it was less because they seemed inauthentic than because they cluttered up the process of making decisions in the National Assembly. Rural petitions might carry weight if deputies or special deputies vouched for their reliability. Otherwise, they disappeared amidst thousands of other documents that little towns mailed to the National Assembly. Towns needed politicians and lobbyists to translate local demands into national institutions. The voice of the people alone would fall on deaf ears.

Even departmental and district assemblies of electors were not permitted to resolve disputes over the location of directories and lawcourts. When the National Assembly passed its decrees on the formation of particular departments, some deputies expected that decisions would be delegated to these assemblies. Instead, the C.C. proposed in mid-February that all such decrees be restated so that final decisions would remain with the National Assembly: "It is important that no changes be made in the state except by the authority of the legislature," argued Dupont de Nemours, *rapporteur* for the general decree on the division of the kingdom. "The people have given power to this body as a function that cannot be delegated."[99] With such reasoning did the National Assembly claim the power that used to reside in the person of the king. Following the abolition of provincial privileges and seigneurial lawcourts, public establishments belonged to the entire nation. Towns alone could not possess them, nor could assemblies of voters in the provinces determine their location. Fearing that parochial demands and antagonisms would jeopardize the new organization of the state, the National Assembly affirmed its exclusive authority over all decisions about departmental and district seats. Furthermore, once it had passed definitive decrees on this subject, electoral assemblies would have to refer any proposals for change to the next legislature. Royal absolutism had ceased, but legislative pretensions to sovereignty had just begun.[100]

[98] AN DIV bis 36:580 (Morbihan).

[99] *Rapport* by Dupont de Nemours, Feb. 15, 1790, AP 11:604–5.

[100] See articles 1 and 2 of the decree of Feb. 16, 1790, AP 11:609–10. On the theoretical foundations of the authority exercised by the National Assembly, see Baker, *Inventing the French Revolution*, pp. 224–51.

Chapter 6

URBAN RIVALRIES AND THE FORMATION

OF DEPARTMENTS

THE MOST important decisions about the division of the kingdom concerned the transformation of provinces into departments. This process of departmentalization created a territorial framework of administration that all subsequent regimes would preserve. In like manner, the new map of France restructured the administrative hierarchy of towns around departmental capitals. Henceforth, intermediate agencies of government, along with their numerous staffs of functionaries and employees, would become concentrated in the seats of departments. Many deputies anticipated this relationship between the formation of departments and the destiny of administrative towns. They viewed the plan of division from an urban perspective. Which town in each department had the best claim to administrative primacy? How might the boundaries of departments be modified or completely redrawn in order to improve the chances for a particular town to become a capital? What compromises with other towns might reduce the risks of competition for establishments? The answers to such questions involved geographical plans and political stratagems. Using a variety of arguments about central places, provinces, natural regions, and commercial networks, deputies tried to redraw departmental boundaries in accordance with urban interests. After intensive negotiations and prolonged debates, the National Assembly agreed to transform thirty-two departments completely and to modify the boundaries of another thirty-five departments. Urban ambitions explain nearly all the controversies over departments, whose final boundaries depended on alliances among the spokesmen for towns in the Assembly.

The C.C. provided a point of departure for negotiations by sketching departmental boundaries on a detailed grid map of the kingdom. Map 6.1, which is a schematic copy of that original map, shows that the plan of the Committee represented a compromise between geometrical and historical conceptions of space.[1] Each department would be roughly equal in area,

[1] As noted in chapter 2, this was the second map prepared by L. Hennnequin, a copy of which has been preserved in the Bibliothèque Nationale, C 4925 Res. The earlier map, with its geometrical pattern of "large squares," was probably posted in the offices of the committee on Oct. 3. See the letter from Michel-René Maupetit, dated Oct. 3, 1789: "I went to the Committee to see which large square we were in," in "Lettres de Michel-René Maupetit,"

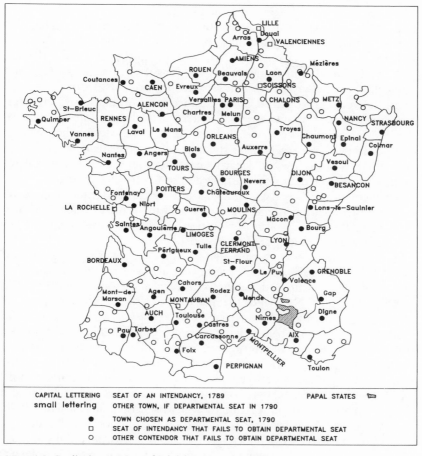

Map 6.1. Preliminary Map of Division, October 1789

but the boundaries of these new jurisdictions would vary from straight lines that ignored history to sinuous contours that followed the frontiers of existing *généralités* or *gouvernements*. While most of the departments in the Ile-de-France, Champagne, Burgundy, and Lorraine would disregard the administrative geography of the old regime, departments located in Auvergne, Brittany, Franche-Comté, Normandy, Languedoc, and Provence would carefully preserve the borders of these historic provinces.

Bulletin de la Commission historique et archéologique de la Mayenne, 2d ser., 19 (1903): 362–63. The departmental committees formed in November used the later and more realistic map as a basis for discussion. See Bourdon, "La formation des départements de l'Est," pp. 190–91.

New boundaries, based on the principle of territorial equality, would be traced only within the existing contours of these large provinces. The committee remained even more faithful to history by recommending that nine smaller provinces—Flanders and Artois in the north; Limousin, Marche, Quercy, Périgord, and Rouergue in the Massif Central; and Béarn and Roussillon in the Pyrénées—form separate departments. Its map made no effort, however, to construct administrative space around provincial capitals or other administrative towns. Eighteen of the former capitals of intendancies, including large towns such as Caen, Metz, Montpellier, Nancy, and Toulouse, were placed near the edge of a department. So were the largest towns in twenty-one departments that did not contain any seats of intendants. Fewer than one-tenth of all the towns that tried to become departmental capitals had a favorable location near the center of a department on this preliminary map. The names of the former capitals and new departmental seats, as well as the locations of other towns that sought departmental seats, are indicated on map 6.1.

As soon as deputies from particular provinces began examining the plan of the C.C., they brought the issue of central places into the forefront of discussion. For example, deputies from Caen and Coutances opposed a fourfold division of Normandy that placed their towns at the opposite ends of the same department; those from Albi and Castres wanted to combine their dioceses into a separate department instead of joining the same department as Toulouse; and those from several towns in the southwest tried to escape from the domination of Bordeaux and Agen by forming an intermediate department between these two towns.[2] In the Paris region, where the Committee had proposed to attach Versailles and Melun to the department of Paris, deputies from these towns insisted on restricting Paris to its own walls. This brought into question the division of other departments around Paris, as deputies from a dozen towns, including Meaux, Château-Thierry, and Provins to the east, and Beauvais, Compiègne, Noyon, and Soissons to the north, disputed six different plans that would favor or harm their respective claims to centrality.[3] In nearly every province that the C.C. proposed to subdivide, deputies confronted alternative plans that would locate rival towns in separate departments or shift one town toward the center of a department at the expense of its rivals.

Like territorial equality, centrality was an abstract criterion that needed

---

[2] Comparison of the original plan with the demands of Caen and Coutances, as described by special deputies from Carentan in a printed *mémoire*; *mémoires* for Castres and Albi; and unsigned *observations* concerning departments in the southwest. AN ADXVI 27 (Carentan); DIV bis 17:291 and 31:441 (Tarn); and DIV bis 10:225 (Lot-et-Garonne).

[3] Mun. Versailles, AN DIV bis 30:432 (Seine-et-Oise) and ADXVI 74; *mémoire* by deputies from Melun, DIV bis 17:287 (Seine-et-Marne); and R. Hennequin, *La formation de l'Aisne*, pp. 85–98.

to be reconciled with a variety of historical and geographical circumstances. Only a few spokesmen for towns tried to justify a department simply by measuring distances on a map. Petitioners from Compiègne did calculate that they were located eighteen leagues north of Paris, which would place them at the center of a department with a radius of nine leagues; a revolutionary committee at Montluçon discovered by tracing squares on a copy of de Hesseln's map that they were precisely in the center of a department to the south of Paris, with eighteen leagues to a side; and deputies from Etampes used triangular measurements to prove that Etampes, Meaux, and Mantes were the most appropriate localities to form departments around Paris. The geometrical plans of Compiègne and Etampes disregarded the ambitions of larger towns in the Paris region, such as Beauvais, Orléans, Soissons, and Versailles, and they had no chance of success; that of Montluçon generated more interest by calling attention to the *pays* of lower Bourbonnais and Combrailles, which were nearly large enough to form a separate department between Moulins and Guéret.[4] In this respect, the spokesmen for Montluçon resembled their counterparts in many towns who tried to justify departmental plans by describing historical, topographical, or commercial features of an area. With even Abbé Sièyes conceding that geometry provided only an ideal model of space, it became obvious that deputies in the National Assembly would not be impressed by calculations of radiuses, rectangles, or triangles. They favored concrete representations of space, as embodied in historical provinces, natural *pays*, or economic regions.[5]

Urged by many townspeople to preserve the territorial integrity of existing provinces, a substantial number of deputies tried to exploit the deference already shown by the C.C. for provincial boundaries. Some pleaded that provinces as large as Dauphiné and Poitou should not be partitioned into smaller departments, while others insisted that provinces as small as Aunis and Bugey should not be incorporated into larger departments. These contrary views about the appropriate size of departments expressed a common tendency to defend historical conceptions of space. The spokesmen for provincial capitals led this campaign for continuity with the past. According to the *comité permanent* of Clermont-Ferrand, the capital of Auvergne, a division that neglected history—the varied customs, laws, and usages that centuries of development had imparted to the peoples of France—would become an enterprise so contrary to nature that it could not succeed. Any sudden transformation of thirty-two provinces into

[4] AN DIV bis 29:412 (Oise); DIV bis 19:307 (Allier); DIV bis 17:280 (Seine-et-Oise); DIV bis 3:149 (Allier).

[5] For a concise analysis of this point, see M. V. Ozouf-Marignier, "Territoire géometrique et centralité urbaine: Le découpage de la France en départements, 1789–1790," *Annales de la recherche urbaine* 22 (1984): 58–70.

eighty departments would turn province against province and town against town by obliging them to make conflicting demands. Petitioners from Mende, the capital of Gévaudan, expressed alarm at the Committee's plan to combine Gévaudan and Velay into a single department. Their province had always been a corporate body, separated from other provinces by its usages, its customs, and its civil, political, and ecclesiastical administration. Municipal officials at Poitiers were equally distressed at the plan to subdivide Poitou into three departments. Poitiers would no longer be the heart of the entire province, and its *sénéchaussée*, one of the oldest and most extensive in the kingdom, might suffer a drastic decline in jurisdiction. Townspeople at Le Dorat struck a more hopeful note in their request for a provincial assembly. As the former residence of the counts of the Marche, Le Dorat had a historical claim to primacy in the lower Marche, which was a distinct province with its own royal *sénéchaussée*, a number of towns and large bourgs, and a great quantity of parishes, fiefs, and seigneurial justices. Pierre-François Gossin described with similar confidence the "sacred rights" of the Barrois to form a separate department, based on its institutional unity within the larger *généralité* of Lorraine. Governed by provincial estates until its annexation by France, and still possessing its own system of taxation, the Barrois looked to its capital, Bar-le-Duc, as the depository of its archives, the seat of its fiscal administration, and the proud possessor of one of the oldest Chambre des Comptes in the kingdom. This capital represented the will of the entire province in demanding a department that would perpetuate a millennial tradition of self-administration.[6]

The Roman *civitates* that had governed the various tribes of Gaul in late antiquity still survived in some regions as dioceses of the Catholic church.[7] Provinces such as Anjou, Périgord, Quercy, and Rouergue derived historical unity from their bishoprics as well as their secular rulers. This suggested that departments might be organized around the capitals of dioceses, not only in the oldest provinces but in bishoprics established by medieval and early modern popes. A deputy from Reims adopted this approach to the division of Champagne into three departments, based on the dioceses of Reims, Troyes, and Châlons-sur-Marne. So did three *commissaires* at Narbonne, who proposed that the *sénéchaussée* of Carcassonne be divided into two departments, one centered on the diocese of Narbonne and the other on the diocese of Castres. In Brittany, townspeople at Quimper and Vannes both invoked ecclesiastical geography in defense of sepa-

[6] Letter cited in Mège, *Formation du Puy-de-Dôme*, p. 87; AN DIV bis 27:390 (Lozère); DIV bis 18:295 (Vienne); DIV bis 18:297 (Haute-Vienne); "Opinion de M. Gossin," AP 10:703–4.

[7] On the continuity between *civitatas* and medieval dioceses, see Duby, *Histoire de la France urbaine*, vol. 1, *La ville antique* (Paris, 1980), pp. 72–137.

rate departments. Quimper was the capital of the bishopric of Cornouaille, with a beautiful cathedral, a newly remodeled episcopal palace, a vast college, and one of the foremost seminaries in Brittany; and Vannes was the capital of a diocese that ranked second only to the diocese of Nantes in the taxes that its numerous towns, bourgs, and rural parishes paid to the estates of Brittany. In Normandy, special deputies from Lisieux drew up a plan for a sixth department in the hope of preserving their bishopric; and in Provence, the consuls of Apt proposed a fourth department, based on the historic role of their town as the capital of a Gallic tribe, a Roman colony, and an episcopal see. Petitioners from Saint-Gaudens objected strenuously to news that the diocese of Comminges would disappear in the department of Toulouse, and they made repeated efforts to obtain a department of their own. Even a group of citizens from Alet, a town that contained only 1,100 inhabitants, pleaded for a department that would save their bishopric, founded three hundred years earlier by Pope John XXII.[8]

In the conjunction of historical traditions with local geography, some townspeople perceived moral sentiments of loyalty and affection that distinguished the inhabitants of each province from their neighbors. "Throughout history men have had a predilection for the soil where they were born," wrote a deputy from Mur-de-Barrez, a small town in the province of Rouergue that resisted transfer to a department in upper Auvergne. These two *pays*, separated by high mountains, possessed different legal regimes and systems of measurement. Their respective populations, who shared very few relations of friendship and kinship, lived like strangers to one another. Departments should reaffirm the solidarity of provincial communities instead of creating conflict and confusion: "In the present situation," explained members of the bourgeois militia of Poitiers, "all Poitevins are brothers and friends, but the division of their province into two or three departments would soon make them strangers to one another, and perhaps even enemies and rivals." Townspeople who were tempted to disrupt provincial boundaries in order to acquire more important establishments should remember their moral obligations. Thus reasoned delegates from the province of Saintonge, meeting at the capital of Saintes, when they learned that the inhabitants of Saint-Jean-d'Angély, "misled by the seductions of La Rochelle," had expressed a willingness to abandon their motherland. "In coming here, they visit their own brothers and friends. Their customs and habits are the same as ours. We have nearly the same principles and laws. Like us, they are Saintongeais, courageous and patri-

[8] AN DIV bis 10 (Marne); DIV bis 20:321 (Aude); DIV bis 23:352 (Finistère); DIV bis 28:402 (Morbihan); DIV bis 5:172 (Calvados); DIV bis 20:324 (Bouches-du-Rhône); DIV bis 7:197 (Haute-Garonne); ADXVI 22 (Alet).

otic. How could they abjure an ancient union which they should honor, just as we do?"[9]

Even more than laws and customs, language distinguished the populations of a few provinces from their neighbors. This cultural phenomenon influenced departmental plans in Alsace, Lorraine, Brittany, Roussillon, and the Basque *pays* of the Pyrénées. All of these areas were located on the periphery of the kingdom, and they all contained many inhabitants who did not speak or comprehend the French language. The initial plan of the C.C. recommended two departments for Alsace, one for German-speaking Lorraine, and one for Roussillon, but elsewhere it ignored linguistic boundaries. Special deputies from the Breton port of Saint-Malo pointed out that a fivefold division of their province would include French and Breton speakers in the same department of Saint-Brieuc, and it would also group together the northern and southern coasts of lower Brittany, whose populations spoke mutually unintelligible dialects of Breton, in the department of Quimper. Such a plan resulted from the purely geometrical operations of engineers who overlooked the danger of combining peoples who did not understand each other and who would not be able to present their grievances to administrators. A more realistic plan would divide the province into six departments, including one for Saint-Malo and its French-speaking hinterland and two for the Breton speakers of lower Brittany.[10]

In southwestern France, the linguistic particularism of the Basques interfered with the plan of the C.C. to join the *pays* of Labourt, Navarre, and Soule to the same department as towns in the Adour River valley. Petitioners from Dax, one of these river towns, objected that different customs and languages required particular and distinct regimes: the Basques had "an unintelligible idiom which seems necessarily to make them forever strangers to all the other peoples of the universe." The mayor of the Basque town of Saint-Jean-Pied-de-Port agreed that customs, habits, and, above all, language formed an absolute barrier between the Basques *pays* and neighboring areas. Labourt, Navarre, and Soule wanted to regenerate themselves by forming their own department, with a sovereign tribunal to restore the "national lawcourt" that Louis XIII had transferred from Navarre to the *parlement* of Pau. Yet this *parlement* created an institutional precedent for attaching the Basques *pays* to the province of Béarn. According to deputies from Pau, the customary laws of the Basques were written in the dialect of Béarn, which proved that language was a "chimerical obstacle" to administrative unity. Municipal leaders of Bayonne, a seaport surrounded by the *pays* of Labourt, took language more seriously, only to reject the separatist

[9] AN DIV bis 4:165 (Aveyron); DIV bis 32:444 (Vienne); DIV bis 5:177 (Charente-Inférieure).
[10] AN DIV bis 8:208 (Ille-et-Vilaine).

ambitions of the Basques: "Already isolated by their character, by their customs, and essentially by their language from Frenchmen, who are like strangers in their midst, the Basques would only double this wall of separation if they were left to themselves. Now that the National Assembly has the essential goal of destroying the solidarity of provinces, how can it agree to tolerate and even to foment the particularism of the Basques?"[11]

To such arguments, deputies from Labourt protested that the Basques were French in their heart and soul but needed their own department in order to participate in administrative assemblies. In the words of Garat, *ainé*, "If you joined men who spoke a hundred different languages, what would you expect them to say to each other? Astonished to find themselves united, they would end up by separating from each other like the people in the Tower of Babel." Of course, the Basques would not have such an easy time seceding from a department, and Garat warned the National Assembly, "If you join us to Béarn, you will be handing us over to the aristocracy of those, among the Basques, who understand French." Another deputy from Labourt added that while Basques who leave their *pays* learn French easily, "plowmen do not go elsewhere to take language courses." In this debate over the Basque *pays*, language raised questions about the social as well as the territorial basis of political representation.[12]

If geographical conditions distinguished a province from its neighbors, townspeople were likely to invoke nature as well as history in defense of separate departments. Mountains obstructed communications within the interior of the Massif Central, the Alps, and the Pyrénées, especially during the winter months. This suggested that mountainous provinces had been created by nature. Thus, petitioners from Mende delivered a lecture on geography: "Travel through Gévaudan and contemplate the lofty barriers that nature has so majestically placed around it. These are immovable and will defy until the end of time the vain efforts of mortals to change them." Enclosed within their mountains, the Gévaudans had a distinctive economy based on livestock and woolen production that attached them to their native soil. "Never will it be possible to strip them of their affection for the land where they were born." Municipal officers at Millau, who hoped to acquire the seat of a department for the province of Rouergue, drew a similar connection between geography, economic conditions, and cultural cohesion: "The high mountains that surround Rouergue, the temperature of its climate, the nature of its agricultural produce, the characteristics of its commerce, everything, even language, customs, the genius of its inhab-

---

[11] AN C 99:155 (Dax); C 100:156 (Saint-Jean-Pied-de-Port); speeches of Jean-François Mourot and Louis-Jean-Henry Darnaudat, both from Pau, Jan. 12, 1790, *Le point du jour*, 182:6, pp. 17–19; DIV bis 14:258 (Basses-Pyrénées).

[12] Speeches of Garat *ainé* and M. de Macaye, deputies from the *bailliage* of Ustaritz (*pays* of Labourt), Jan. 12, 1790, *Le point du jour*, 182:6, pp. 16–19.

itants, isolates it from neighboring provinces. These are limits posed by the hand of nature, relations fortified by habit."[13]

In comparison with mountains, river valleys usually fostered territorial unity, but several large rivers did separate provinces. Thus, the Rhône River flowed between Dauphiné and Vivarais, and the Loire River divided Nivernais from Berry. Here, too, townspeople described natural barriers to communication that justified the preservation of historic boundaries. Of Dauphiné, commissioners for the estates of this province wrote, "Nature has traced its limits—the Alps and the Rhône." Spokesmen for the town of Viviers agreed that "nature has placed a considerable barrier between Vivarais and Dauphiné which it is not always possible to cross."[14] Such geographical obstacles implied commercial rivalries and conflicts of interest over road construction. Indeed, almost no one advocated that the two banks of the Rhône River become joined in the same department.[15]

By defining space in the context of topography rather than history, it also became possible to propose new boundaries for departments. In the central Pyrénées, for example, several small towns competed for territorial influence over a series of little *pays*—Bigorre, Comminges, Couserans, Nebouzan, and the county of Foix. While Tarbes, Saint-Gaudens, and Saint-Girons each tried to fashion a department for one of these historic *pays*, the citizens of Foix submitted a plan that would join foothills and plains in the neighboring province of Languedoc to the mountainous county of Foix. Through the river basin of the Ariège and its tributaries, all the localities in such a department could communicate with Foix, whose location midway between the high valley of the Ariège and the plains of Languedoc made it the natural center of this area. By contrast, inaccessible mountains separated Foix from the headwaters of the Garonne River, where the original plan of the C.C. traced the boundaries of a department that would join the county of Foix to Comminges and Couserans.[16] In the Alps, townspeople at Gap raised similar objections to a plan of division that would attach them to Grenoble. Isolated from "the rest of the universe" during the winter and neglected by the previous administration, the high country of Dauphiné deserved its own department. "By granting our wishes," wrote a *bailliage* magistrate from Gap, "the National Assembly will have the glory of giving a new birth to all the inhabitants of a vast country, who lack only an instrument and some means of activity to draw themselves out from under the weight of misery that they bemoan." Although the town of Em-

---

[13] AN DIV bis 27:390 (Lozère); DIV bis 20:323 (Aveyron).

[14] AN DIV bis 25:374 (Isère); DIV bis 19:312 (Ardèche).

[15] The only exception was Vienne, whose *comité général* proposed a department with some territory on the other side of the Rhône, in Lyonnais and Forez. Letter of Nov. 24, 1789, AN DIV bis 8:211 (Isère).

[16] AN DIV bis 20:317 (Ariège).

brun rivaled Gap for leadership of this area, its municipality agreed that the *bailliages* of upper Dauphiné should secede from the rest of the province, whose wealth and luxury contrasted so greatly with the poverty of the mountains.[17]

Many townspeople shared the belief that an enlightened administration could overcome geographical obstacles to economic growth. On the one hand, they emphasized regional inequalities in productivity and wealth, but on the other hand, they confidently affirmed that administrators could reduce such inequalities. In this manner, the concept of a homogeneous region, based on soil, climate, and topography, acquired a dynamic dimension. Poverty originated in nature, but through administrative institutions, scarce resources could be transformed into wealth. In this movement from nature to history, townspeople expressed not only the ideals of the Enlightenment but their own experience of the relationship between public works and economic growth during the eighteenth century. According to municipal officials at Auch, the capital of Gascogny, this hilly and arid province, bereft of navigable waterways, remained backward and impoverished until its roads improved dramatically under the administration of an energetic intendant, M. D'Etigny. The transport network that this intendant created brought life to the region and improved the revenues of the state dramatically. Now the *généralité* of Auch, which covered an area of over eight hundred square miles, needed to acquire its own provincial assembly and appellate court, instead of being incorporated into the wealthy province of Guyenne, as nobles at Bordeaux had proposed.[18] Townspeople at Périgueux, who lamented the attachment of their province to the *généralité* of Bordeaux during the old regime, made a similar argument about regional poverty and economic development. Suffering from inadequate natural resources and administrative neglect, the province of Périgord lacked roads, navigable rivers, industry, and commerce. To improve its economy, Périgord needed "a patriotic and energetic administration, concentrated in its midst and uniquely devoted to its interests." Otherwise, the Périgordins would be forced to compete with the Bordelais for influence in a department that joined together disparate regions, one agricultural and the other commercial. What common language could the administrators of such a department speak? Either the province of Périgord would have to bend its neck beneath the yoke of Bordeaux, whose power and prestige would crush it, or there would be perpetual conflict.[19]

The departmental ambitions of Montbrison, in the province of Forez, whose boundaries the original map ignored, also revolved around the idea

---

[17] AN DIV bis 1:6 and DIV bis 3 (Hautes-Alpes).
[18] AN ADXVI 38 (Auch).
[19] AN DIV bis 6:187 (Dordogne).

that areas with different natural resources and economic activities should possess separate administrative institutions. Deputies and special deputies from Montbrison contrasted the region of Forez with that of Lyonnais. Forez was an agricultural *pays*, formed naturally by the Loire River basin and surrounded on all sides by mountains, while Lyonnais was a commercial *pays*, centered on the city of Lyon. Attached to the *généralité* of Lyon during the old regime, the inhabitants of Forez had seen their taxes misused for the benefit of this wealthy capital. Their economy, though capable of development, would never receive the slightest assistance as long as they remained under the domination of Lyon.[20]

Commerce encouraged a conception of space that subordinated the homogeneous characteristics of a particular area to the functional relationships between towns and a variety of geographical settings. From this perspective, urban regions were more important than natural *pays*. Among the economic activities that defined these regions, none was more important in eighteenth-century France than the production and distribution of grain. This raised the question of whether the grain trade should be taken into account in defining departments. This question aroused considerable controversy in several provinces, including the Ile-de-France. Paris had formed a separate constituency in the elections to the Estates-General, while the *prévôté* and *vicomté* of Paris "outside the walls," joined by the *bailliages* of Versailles and three smaller towns, had elected its own deputies.[21] This precedent suggested that Paris should preserve its electoral identity as a separate department. Otherwise, the city would be surrounded by rural districts whose voters might exclude Parisians from the departmental administration and even from the National Assembly. Yet such a plan would eliminate Parisian administrative surveillance of nearby river ports and grain markets that played an important role in provisioning the enormous population of the city. When deputies from other towns in the Ile-de-France agreed in mid-December to create a department for Versailles that would entirely surround Paris, several members of the Paris Commune expressed grave concern about the implications of this plan for the Parisian economy. "Isn't it a veritable mockery to tell us that by restricting Paris to its *banlieu*, we are being done a favor?" asked the *abbé* Fauchet, the leading advocate of a large Parisian department, with a radius of nine leagues. "It would be a rare privilege indeed to be at the mercy of all our surroundings, without any jurisdiction or police rights, without movement, without foodstuffs, without bread." What would happen if the vast departments at the gates of Paris refused to help the city? "The price of grain would rise enormously, the city would become uninhabitable for

---

[20] AN DIV bis 16:272 (Rhône-et-Loire).
[21] Brette, *Les Constituants*, pp. 3–10.

most people, and at the least apprehension of a poor harvest, famine would destroy in a few days whoever remained." As for free trade in grain, which Dupont de Nemours had assured the National Assembly would guarantee supplies to Paris, the *abbé* Fauchet dismissed this panacea. "Because the buyers of wheat in the three neighboring departments will be free to transport it wherever they want, they will drive up the price of bread as high as they please."[22] Such an alarming prospect, which reflected the experience of many Parisians who had suffered from high bread prices during the previous winter, convinced a majority of districts in the city to petition the National Assembly for a large department.[23]

Like members of the Paris commune, townspeople at Besançon and Grenoble also objected to plans that threatened to reduce their food supply. The province of Franche-Comté contained mountains to the east and plains to the west of Besançon, whose population usually relied on grain imported from the plains around Gray and Dôle. What would happen if Besançon were confined to a mountainous department in the middle of the province, while Gray and Dôle entered the departments of upper and lower Franche-Comté, respectively, as deputies from these towns proposed? On the assumption that departments would follow the example of entire provinces at the beginning of the Revolution, Besançon would lose access to the grain markets in the plains. As a special deputy explained, "Last spring we saw the inhabitants of Lorraine and Champagne use force to prevent the transfer of their wheat to Franche-Comté; we saw the Francs-Comtois oppose for their own sake the export of grain to Savoy. If the departments of the upper, middle, and lower parts of the province became as estranged from each other as Franche-Comté is today from Champagne and Lorraine, is there not reason to fear that in years of grain shortage, the upper and lower departments would conduct themselves in the same manner as the Lorrainers and the Champenois have just done?" If the province could not be preserved as a single department, as deputies from Besançon first demanded in November, then each of its subdivisions should contain portions of the plains as well as the mountains. Following this logic, the special deputy from Besançon submitted a plan that would include the entire *bailliage* of Gray and the fertile lowlands near Dôle in the department of Besançon.[24]

With similar motives in mind, deputies from Grenoble looked toward the Rhône River valley when they lost hope of transforming the entire

[22] AP 10:701, 3d annex, Dec. 21, 1789.

[23] On the debate over the department of Paris, see Fernand Bournon, *La création du département de Paris et son étendue, 1789–1790* (Paris, 1897).

[24] General assembly of Mun. Besançon, Dec. 7 and 26, 1789, in Archives Municipales de Besançon, register 201, ser. D, pp. 193–94, 206–8; AN DIV bis 9:212 (Jura); DIV bis 6:188 (Doubs).

province of Dauphiné into a department. Although Grenoble served as the gateway to the mountains, they denied that its commerce led in this direction. The plan of the C.C. to attach Grenoble to the high Alps ignored the fact that these arid lands, fertile only in minerals, contributed nothing to the food supply of the capital. Only two leagues from the plains of Dauphiné and thirty leagues by carriage from the Alpine town of Briançon, Grenoble drew its grain and most of its wine from the diocese of Vienne. It also supplied these lowlands with iron and plaster produced in the mountains. Lacking any resources of their own for food production except a small valley, the townspeople of Grenoble had the greatest need to include the most fertile part of the province in their department. As for a plan that deputies from Vienne submitted to transform this diocese into a small department of its own, this would consign half the territory and population of the entire province to the department of Grenoble. Such a "monstrous disproportion" should be avoided by joining Vienne to Grenoble and by creating a separate department for the Alpine *bailliages* of Gap, Briançon, and Embrun.[25]

Townspeople confident of their food supplies presented other arguments for forming departments in accordance with commercial relationships that cut across the boundaries of provinces and natural *pays*. Commerce facilitated the movement of people as well as goods from Limousin and neighboring provinces to Limoges; unified the populations in the basin of the Yonne River and its tributaries around Auxerre; brought life to the hinterlands of Marseille, Saint-Malo, and La Rochelle; linked the interior of Artois and coastal seaports to Saint-Omer; and stimulated the development of rural industry around Laval, Saint-Quentin, and Sedan. Apart from Laval, none of these towns had a central location on the departmental map presented by the C.C. Their spokesmen presented a variety of plans, some combining territory from two or three provinces, others demarcating a coastal area or small industrial region within a larger province or *généralité*. What such plans had in common was a conception of space as an extension of urban commerce. Relationships of exchange rather than historical traditions or characteristics of nature defined the kinds of departments that leaders of these commercial towns proposed.

Limoges and Auxerre, though differing greatly in size and administrative importance, had in common a central position in transport networks and a peripheral location on the map of provinces. Deputies from Limoges boasted of their town's large population of 25,000–30,000, its numerous establishments as a provincial capital, and its extensive commercial relations, sustained by major roads that converged from every direction. Located on the edge of Limousin and lower Marche and near enclaves of

---

[25] AN DIV bis 8:208 (Isère).

Poitou, Limoges wanted a circular department that contained territory from all of these provinces. Its deputies offered to divide Limousin into two departments and to form a department for Limoges out of the multiple jurisdictions that used to separate the plains of lower Marche, to the north of the Vienne River, from the mountains of upper Limousin, to the south.[26]

Auxerre had its own distinguished past as the seat of a medieval diocese and a county on the northern edge of Burgundy, but its population numbered only 12,000, and its *bailliage* and *présidial* court had a relatively small jurisdiction. Located not far from a patchwork of territories in Nivernais, Gâtinais, and Champagne, the leaders of this town, like those of Limoges, perceived in their transport network and their commerce an opportunity to form a department. The Yonne River, which became navigable at the outskirts of Auxerre, flowed northward into the Seine, permitting shipments of wine, lumber, and other goods all the way to Paris. A major highway led from Auxerre through the mountains of Burgundy to Lyon and the Midi, so the port of Auxerre functioned as an entrepôt for merchandise brought overland by wagon and then shipped downriver. Just as the merchants of Auxerre received goods from towns to the south for shipment northward, so municipal officials emphasized this pattern of commerce in their plan for a department. Towns of upper Burgundy such as Semur and Saulieu had daily relations with Auxerre; so did the town of Clamecy, in Nivernais, whose merchants floated lumber down the Yonne River to Auxerre. The markets and fairs of Auxerre also attracted residents of small towns and bourgs to the north, in Champagne, and to the west, in Gâtinais. A department centered on the roads that radiated outward from this town and the river that flowed through its port would combine agricultural diversity—grain fields, vineyards, forests, and meadows—with commercial and administrative unity.[27]

Seaports that faced directly toward the ocean had less favorable prospects of becoming departmental seats than did ports located above the confluence of major rivers with the sea. For example, Marseille, La Rochelle, and Saint-Malo would necessarily be on the edge of any department that reached into the interior, while Bordeaux, Nantes, and Rouen had access to extensive territory on both sides of the rivers that they bridged. The former wanted to exclude rival towns of the interior from coastal areas that their merchants dominated, while the latter confidently sought land in every direction. The leaders of Marseille, who took pride in the long history of their free port, tried at first to preserve their administrative autonomy within Provence by forming a separate department, just as Paris had. As

[26] AN DIV bis 18:296 (Haute-Vienne).

[27] Porée, *La formation de l'Yonne*, pp. 33–36, 146–52; AN DIV bis 18:300–301 (Yonne).

the third largest city in the kingdom, with a port that benefited the entire nation, Marseille deserved its own administrative regime. When this proved impossible to achieve, deputies from Marseille submitted a plan for a maritime department that would include the seaport of Toulon. Marseille and Toulon shared an interest in commerce rather than agriculture, and they communicated easily with each other by sea. According to this plan, the interior of eastern Provence, including the judicial center of Draguignan, would be attached to the department of upper Provence. Whatever the obstacles to travel between Draguignan and the mountains to the north, the ports along the coast belonged under the jurisdiction of Marseille. Here departmental space would be defined by coastal shipping rather than by the topography of the land.[28]

Spokesmen for La Rochelle and Saint-Malo also objected to the initial plan of the C.C. and proposed alternatives more consistent with the economic influence of these seaports. Although La Rochelle had been the seat of an intendant who administered both the provinces of Aunis and Saintonge, its location in the northwestern corner of the *généralité* was so unpromising that deputies urged the National Assembly to form a separate department for Aunis. The expanding agricultural economy of Aunis, based on the drainage of salt marshes along the coast and the planting of vineyards on the hills of the interior, compensated for the small size of this province, which covered only 130 square leagues. Merchants at La Rochelle, who outfitted ships for voyages to the New World, also invested capital in the production of eau-de-vie and exported crops from Aunis and coastal areas of lower Poitou. By constructing a canal from La Rochelle to Niort, this economic region could expand still further in scale and prosperity. But if La Rochelle lost its credit facilities, which depended on the fiscal agencies of the state, the rural economy would collapse. "Destroy the commerce of La Rochelle," wrote petitioners from this port, "and industrious activity would disappear at the same moment from these provinces." Thus, the interdependency of seaport and coastal region became a justification for attaching the lowlands of lower Poitou to a department of Aunis. In like manner, special deputies from Saint-Malo argued that their seaport spread "circulation and life to all its surroundings within a distance of twelve to fifteen leagues." The provisioning of ships attracted large numbers of rural inhabitants who found a ready market for their crops at Saint-Malo. Furthermore, carpenters, caulkers, and all kinds of rural workers were employed by merchants in the port, and the families of fishermen and sailors resided nearby. Here, too, a maritime department would reinforce the economic unity between a seaport and its hinterland.[29]

[28] AN DIV bis 5:167 (Bouches-du-Rhône).
[29] AN DIV bis 5:178, 177 (Charente-Inférieure); DIV bis 8:208 (Ille-et-Vilaine).

A network of canals linked ports along the coast of Flanders to towns in the province of Artois. The administrative geography of this area had been complicated during the old regime by a series of *pays*, each centered on a seaport, that stretched down the coast from Flanders to Picardy. Instead of regrouping Flanders, Artois, and the *pays* of Calaisis, Boulonnais, and Montreuil into two departments, the C.C. proposed in its initial plan to preserve the existing boundaries of Flanders and Artois, and to form a third department by detaching the coastal area to the south from the *généralité* of Amiens. A fourth department would preserve the *généralité* of Valenciennes to the east of Flanders and Artois, which included the provinces of Hainaut and Cambrécis. But after deputies from Amiens insisted on incorporating the mouth of the Somme River into their department, those from Arras agreed to extend the department of Artois to the sea. As for Flanders, Hainaut, and Cambrécis, which used to make up the jurisdiction of the *parlement* of Douai, deputies from these provinces agreed to form a narrow department that reached all along the northern frontier of the kingdom from Dunkerque to Valenciennes.[30]

It would be difficult to imagine a less symmetrical division of territory, which contradicted both rectangular and circular conceptions of space. Seeking to justify a different plan of division that combined the entire coastline from Dunkerque to Montreuil with the western part of Artois, townspeople at Saint-Omer described the canals that cut across provincial boundaries in this region. By doing so, they inverted the spatial relationship between coast and hinterland that deputies from seaports such as La Rochelle had emphasized. Now a town of the interior would dominate the coast. Saint-Omer seemed destined to play this role by virtue of its location along a canal that linked rivers of the interior to the sea. In the direction of maritime Flanders and the channel ports, canal boats linked Saint-Omer to Bergues, Gravelines, Bourbourg, Dunkerque, Calais, Guines, and Ardres, while in the interior of Artois, canals and rivers led to Aire, Saint-Venant, Merville, Estaires, and Béthune. Public stagecoaches, traveling on paved roads, reached all points on the circumference of the department that Saint-Omer envisaged. Here was a conception of space as a linear system of communications around a central place. Just as transportation facilities stimulated the commerce of Saint-Omer, whose townspeople boasted of their famous industrial enterprises, so canals, rivers, and roads provided an infrastructure for a common administration.[31]

The organization of the textile industry in eighteenth-century France favored yet another conception of space as an extension of urban influence over the rural populations of a surrounding area. From this perspective,

---

[30] R. Hennequin, *La formation de l'Aisne*, pp. 79–83; and Berlet, *Les provinces*, pp. 266–73.
[31] AN DIV bis 12:246 (Pas-de-Calais).

transport networks that connected towns to each other were less important than the capillary movement between a central place and a dispersed zone of textile production. Spokesmen for Saint-Quentin, Sedan, and Laval requested departments modeled on such relationships of interdependency between town and countryside. According to municipal officials at Saint-Quentin, merchants in their town attracted a large number of clothiers (*fabricants*) on a daily basis from villages within ten leagues round. These commercial ties, based on the common interest, would become even stronger and would facilitate communications, reduce costs, and increase administrative efficiency if Saint-Quentin became the seat of a department. A deputy from Sedan also called attention to the industrial leadership of his town in requesting a department along the German frontier. As the center of a manufacturing *pays*, Sedan employed 30,000 textile workers and exported fine woolens worth eight or nine million livres per year. Its commerce, aided by navigation on the Meuse River, made Sedan the principal town for 300,000 people within nine or ten leagues. This area, whose extension along the river basin formed a narrow arc rather than a circle, included portions of two provinces, Champagne and the duchy of Bar, which Sedan proposed to unite. As for Laval, its deputy described three ways in which his town functioned as the commercial and industrial center of lower Maine, an area that the preliminary map of the C.C. traced as a department. First, the linen industry of Laval interested all the inhabitants of the province: farmers who supplied raw materials, capitalists who invested funds, and artisans and workers of all ages and sexes who found employment. Next, the markets of Laval served as an entrepôt for the supply of grain to areas in short supply. Finally, the town's port, located at the highest point of navigation along the Mayenne River, handled a variety of goods that merchants imported or exported. In sum, Laval functioned as the center of an urban region, coordinating production, purchasing commodities, and redistributing supplies throughout the *pays* of lower Maine.[32]

The various descriptions of space that spokesmen for towns presented to the National Assembly did little to resolve conflicts over the division of the kingdom. Many plans either contradicted the general principle that departments should be roughly equal in area or failed to take the formation of neighboring departments into account. Arguments about the importance of commercial realities clashed with those based on historical traditions. Nature vindicated economic exchange as well as geographical isolation. So many voices were raised in disputation that no single map could represent all the conflicting plans, which overlapped to form a chaotic pattern rather than a coherent division of space. Most of the provincial

---

[32] AN DIV bis 3:145 (Aisne); DIV bis 4 (Ardennes); DIV bis 10:234 (Mayenne).

committees that deliberated from November 1789 through January 1790 had to choose among two or three basic plans of division, whose differences expressed rival urban ambitions as well as opposing geographical conceptions. The decisions of these committees followed no consistent theory of spatial organization, for arguments emphasizing history, or nature, or commerce succeeded in some cases and failed in others. Through a process of decision making that depended primarily on urban alliances, the National Assembly based some departments on a single province, others on the highland or lowland areas of a province, and still others on arbitrary partitions or amalgamations of historic provinces and geographical *pays*. Sometimes commercial towns improved their centrality and sometimes they lost all hope of becoming departmental seats. Despite much rhetoric about geography, decisions to modify the initial map of departments subordinated the weight of history, the force of nature, and the power of commerce to the influence of towns in the National Assembly.

Successful plans for departments needed to take three political factors into account: (1) the effort of the C.C. to apply the principle of territorial equality to the subdivision or consolidation of provinces; (2) the interdependency of plans for the creation of separate departments within provinces or groups of provinces; and (3) the rivalries between various towns that a given plan assigned to the same department. These factors established a political framework for negotiations that improved the chances of success for some plans at the expense of others. Just as each part of a jigsaw puzzle must fit into a larger pattern, so the formation of any particular department depended on a more general context of national policy, regional alignments, and local rivalries or alliances.

Although the C.C. agreed to preserve the external limits of provinces whenever possible and to consult with deputies about the internal division of these provinces, its members refused to approve any plans that violated the spirit of the decree of November 11, which required a division into 75–85 departments. Such a target implied an average area of 300–350 square leagues per department. No decree stipulated that *all* departments must fall within this range, and the C.C. itself proposed a separate department for Rouergue, with 474 square leagues, and one for Roussillon, with only 212 square leagues.[33] Nonetheless, a division that tolerated still greater variations, such as a giant department for Dauphiné, with 848 square leagues, counterbalanced by lilliputian departments for Aunis (100 square leagues) and the Basques *pays* (140 square leagues), would contradict the rationale for the entire operation. Sièyes and Thouret had con-

---

[33] These are the areas of the departments of Aveyron and Pyrénées-Orientales, which corresponded closely to the original plan of the C.C. See L. Prudhomme, *Dictionnaire géographique et méthodique de la République française en CXX départements* (Paris, an VII), vol. 1, appendix, "Tableau général du nombre des départements."

ceived the new territorial division as a means of equalizing electoral constituencies, consolidating national unity, and increasing administrative efficiency. In voting for 75–85 departments, a majority of deputies had voiced their approval of these goals. Departments as large as Dauphiné might rebel against the authority of the National Assembly; those as small as Aunis and the Basques *pays* might ignore it; and both extremes would encourage deputies in other provinces to request similar concessions. Unless the National Assembly affirmed the principle of territorial equality in its particular decrees on departments, enormous discrepancies in the size of provincial jurisdictions would survive to the detriment of legislators, administrators, and the nation as a whole.[34]

Deputies who opposed the pretensions of provincial capitals aided the C.C. in its resolve to divide large provinces. In Franche-Comté, deputies elected from every *bailliage* except Besançon insisted on a threefold division of their province; in Brittany, deputies on the provincial committee accused their colleagues from Rennes of "trying to prevent the Revolution" by refusing to cooperate in drafting a plan of division; and in Dauphiné, deputies from towns in the Rhône River valley outvoted those from Grenoble who wanted to preserve the integrity of their province.[35] In this latter case, when the minority appealed to the National Assembly, the *rapporteur* for the C.C. dismissed its argument that any separation of mountains from plains would interrupt the grain trade and burden the highlands with excessive costs for the maintenance of roads. Alluding to the majority opinion within the deputation, he described the "very considerable disadvantages" of forming a single administration for the entire province, which contained contrasting climates and peoples with divergent customs and needs. Nothing in the geography of Dauphiné could justify an exception to the political principles that the Assembly had already consecrated.[36] As special deputies from Clermont-Ferrand explained to their fellow citizens at home, "All the operations of the National Assembly are founded on the metaphysical and moral principle that France, to be regenerated, must necessarily experience a total revolution." Instead of resisting the inevitable, Clermont-Ferrand should endorse a plan that gave its own department of lower Auvergne 380 square leagues, while enclosing the mountains of up-

---

[34] See the objections of M. Gossin, *rapporteur* for the C.C., to departments for Dauphiné, Aunis, and the *pays* Basques, session of Jan. 12, 1790, AP 11:170.

[35] Summary of letter from M. D'Arçon, special deputy to Mun. Besançon, session of Jan. 1, 1790, Archives Municipales Besançon, register 201, ser. 3, vol. 1, pp. 209–10; letter from Lanjuinais, Defermon, and Varin, deputies from Rennes, to Mun. Rennes, Dec. 30, 1789, Municipal Archives Rennes, #1008, "Pièces relatives à la Révolution française"; Marcel Blanchard, "Contribution à l'étude de la formation du département de l'Isère," *Recueil des travaux de l'Institut de géographie alpine* 2 (1914): 412–13.

[36] M. Gossin, speech of Jan. 12, 1790, AP 11:170.

per Auvergne in a department of only 240 square leagues.[37] Thus, negotiating over the terms of the division became more sensible than trying to reopen the debate over provincial unity.

Deputies from each province were supposed to undertake these negotiations, but their efforts to organize themselves into committees were complicated by the fact that provinces often did not coincide with the *généralités* of the old regime. Some provinces could be traced back to the ecclesiastical geography of the late Roman empire, others to the feudal heritage of the Middle Ages, and still others to the codification of customary laws during the sixteenth century. The terms "province" and "*pays*" were often used interchangeably, although many *pays* derived their identity from a market town or a natural area rather than from institutions such as bishoprics, duchies, or *bailliages*. By contrast, intendancies were relatively easy to define, but they often incorporated several provinces or *pays*, and their boundaries sometimes overlapped with each other in a confusing manner.[38]

To accommodate customary as well as administrative definitions of space, the Constituent Assembly created three types of provincial committees: (A) committees for intendancies that followed closely the boundaries of a single province; (B) committees for intendancies that contained more than one province; and (C) committees that combined two or three intendancies and a varying number of provinces.[39] Committees for a single intendancy and province were the easiest to create, and their external boundaries usually conformed to the departmental map that the C.C. had originally proposed. This implied that deputies would need to rearrange only the internal boundaries of departments within their own province. A comparable task confronted a few committees of the second type, whose intendancies comprised well-defined provinces such as Quercy and Rouergue, which the C.C. had already proposed to transform into departments. By contrast, committees of the third type usually needed to cope with a variety of boundary disputes between intendancies and provinces. Whether the initial plan of the C.C. traced departments in such regions on the basis of provincial frontiers, administrative divisions, natural features of the landscape, or abstract criteria of territorial equality, urban rivalries were likely to bring several lines of division into question simultaneously. Negotiations on such committees often involved a sequence of agreements

---

[37] Letter from three special deputies to Mun. Clermont-Ferrand, Nov. 24, 1789, cited by Mège, *Formation du Puy-de-Dôme*, pp. 94–95.

[38] Brette, *Les limites et les divisions territoriales de la France*, pp. 57–84, 109–14.

[39] This typology expands the Constitutional Committee's own classification into two kinds of committees, those based on a single province and those combining several provinces (Berlet, *Les provinces*, pp. 233–35). A third type of committee existed in practice: one that combined several *généralités*.

that progressively limited the opportunities for towns to become departmental capitals.

Table 6.1 presents some systematic evidence about the urban alliances formed in the three types of committees. Each numbered line refers to the capital or capitals of intendancies that were represented on a committee, along with the names of the provinces or *pays* that deputies mentioned in their negotiations. The lines headed by small letters list the towns that formed a successful alliance, separated by the symbol *vs.* (versus) from a list of unsuccessful rivals. If more than one combination of towns occurred in the process of subdividing the area under dispute, these are indicated by additional lettered lines, with a maximum of four combinations (lines a through d) in the case of the intendancy of Montpellier. Towns whose deputies agreed to join the same department are separated by commas; those involved in multidepartmental alliances are joined by the symbol for addition (+); towns that played a role in such coalitions although their deputies were on a different committee are listed in brackets. As for the unsuccessful towns, their deputies often failed to present a coherent plan for dividing the territory under dispute. Such towns are listed together with the conjunction "or" to indicate that they presented isolated and often mutually incompatible objections to the plan of the majority coalition. Finally, the large towns, numbering at least 20,000 inhabitants, are named in capital letters to distinguish them from smaller towns.

The table confirms the greater complexity of urban alliances in areas where overlapping administrative jurisdictions had to be sorted out before departmental boundaries could be formed. This was the case for six of the eight committees that grouped together deputies from two or three intendancies (category C), as compared with only four of the thirteen committees that were based on a single intendancy (categories A and B). These latter cases include Montpellier, which could be classified in category C because it consisted of two separate *généralités*, centered on Montpellier and Toulouse, as well as several *pays* that possessed their own administrative traditions. The subdivisions of the intendancies of Châlons-sur-Marne and Clermont-Ferrand were also complicated by negotiations with deputies from neighboring provinces. All the other committees in categories A and B operated within well-defined administrative boundaries and simply had to decide how to subdivide their own *généralités*. By contrast, most of the committees in category C had serious difficulty amalgamating the territory of neighboring intendancies into departments. As the table shows, different kinds of urban alliances emerged as these disputes were progressively resolved. In the Paris region, for example, deputies from the intendancy of Orléans agreed to form three departments, centered on the three largest towns of this area, while deputies from Versailles were leading a successful campaign against a large department for Paris. Following the resolution of this dispute, deputies from Soissons organized an elaborate coalition among towns that still hoped to gain departments to the north, northeast, and southeast of Paris. In like manner, the subdivision of the intendancies of Bordeaux and Auch, in the southwest, involved intricate and shifting coalitions of deputies as far north as Périgueux and as far south as Pau and Bayonne.

The evidence presented in table 6.1 also suggests several characteristics of successful alliances. First, these coalitions usually included a majority of the contending towns within an area under dispute. Among the thirty-six alliances that played an influential role in forming departments, nineteen involved deputies from at least four towns, and another ten grouped together deputies from three towns. In only four cases did deputies from a minority of contending towns carry the day. Second, agreement among the deputies from two large towns nearly always guaranteed success for the plan of division that they advocated. Examples include Montpellier and Nîmes, in lower Languedoc; Rouen and Caen, in Normandy; Metz and Nancy, in Lorraine; Rennes and Nantes, in Brittany; and Tours and Angers in the *généralité* of Tours. While size alone did not guarantee a departmental seat, as the case of Marseille proved, only seven of the thirty-two former seats of intendancies were on the losing side of an interdepartmental alliance. Two further points involve the role of small towns in negotiations over the formation of departments. As table 6.1 indicates, some victorious coalitions included several towns that agreed to join the same department. Examples include Vesoul, Gray, and Dôle, in Franche-Comté, and Châlon-sur-Saône, Mâcon, and Charolles, in Burgundy. In both cases, deputies supported plans that would place their hometowns in a different department from the former provincial capital. Those in the southern part of Franche-Comté also agreed to rotate the departmental directory among several towns, a strategy that deputies from several dozen small and medium-sized towns adopted.[40] Towns that remained aloof from such agreements often ended up on the losing side, however. Thus, table 6.1 includes twelve cases in which a single town tried in vain to change a plan of division that deputies from several towns supported. In another twelve cases, towns that wanted their own departments failed to present a coherent plan of division that took each other's interests into account.

If deputies from some towns were more effective than others in shaping the formation of departments, some also had a better hand to play in committee negotiations. Three aspects of urban geography influenced the general outcome of political negotiations: the role of towns in the administrative and judicial hierarchies of the old regime; the historic association of

[40] A total of 72 towns made such agreements, of which 55 had fewer than 10,000 inhabitants.

TABLE 6.1
Urban Alliances That Shaped the Division of Provinces into Departments

A. Committees for a single intendancy and province
  1. Aix-en-Provence (Provence)
     a. AIX-EN-PROVENCE + TOULON, Brignoles, Draguignan, Grasse + Forcalquier,
        Gap, Sisteron *vs.* MARSEILLE
  2. Bastia (Corsica)
     a. Bastia *vs.* Ajaccio or Corte
  3. Besançon (Franche-Comté)
     a. Vesoul, Gray + Dôle, Lons-le-Saulnier, Poligny, Salins *vs.* BESANCON
  4. Châlons-sur-Marne (Champagne)
     a. CHALONS-SUR-MARNE + Chaumont + Rethel, Mézières, Charleville + TROYES
        + [Bar-le-Duc, Verdun] *vs.* REIMS or Langres or Vitry or [Sedan]
  5. Clermont-Ferrand (Auvergne)
     a. CLERMONT-FERRAND + Saint-Flour, Aurillac *vs.* Brioude or Issoire
     b. CLERMONT-FERRAND + [MOULINS] + Brioude, [Le Puy] *vs.* Riom + Saint-
        Flour, Aurillac
  6. Grenoble (Dauphiné)
     a. GRENOBLE + Valence + Gap *vs.* Vienne
  7. Rennes (Bretagne)
     a. RENNES + NANTES + Quimper + Saint-Brieux + Vannes *vs.* Saint-Malo
  8. Strasbourg (Alsace)
     a. STRASBOURG + Colmar
B. Committees for a single intendancy that had more than one province
  1. Dijon (Bourgogne, Bresse, Bugey, Charolais, Mâconnais)
     a. DIJON + Chalon/sur-Saône, Mâcon, Charolles *vs.* Autun or Châtillon-sur-Seine
     b. Bourg, Nantua *vs.* Belley
  2. Lyon (Beaujolais, Forez, Lyonnais)
     a. LYON, SAINT-ETIENNE *vs.* Montbrison, Roanne + Villefranche
  3. Montauban (Quercy, Rouergue)
     a. Cahors, Figeac + Rodez, Millau *vs.* MONTAUBAN
  4. Montpellier (Comminges, Couserans, Gévaudan, Languedoc, Vivarais, Velay)
     a. MONTPELLIER + NIMES + Caracassonne *vs.* Béziers or Narbonne + Alais
     b. MONTPELLIER + NIMES + Privas, Aubenas, Villeneuve-de-Berg *vs.* Mende, Mar-
        véjols + Annonay, Le Puy
     c. MONTPELLIER, Béziers, Lodève, St. Pons + NIMES, Alais, Uzès + Le Puy,
        [Brioude] + Mende, Marvéjols + Privas, Annonay, Aubenas, Bourg-Saint-Andéol,
        Tournon
     d. Castres, Albi, Lavaur + Carcassonne, Castelnaudary *vs.* TOULOUSE
  5. Tours (Anjou, Maine, Saumurois, Touraine)
     a. TOURS + ANGERS + Le Mans + Laval, Mayenne *vs.* Saumur
C. Committees for more than one intendancy and province
  1. Bordeaux, Auch (Béarn, Bigorre, Gascogne, Guyenne, Labourd, Landes, Navarre, Soule,
     Périgord)
     a. BORDEAUX + Périgueux, Bergerac, Sarlat *vs.* Lisbourne or Sainte-Foy
     b. BORDEAUX + Auch + Mont-de-Marsan + Agen *vs.* Dax + Bazas or La Réole or
        Condom or Lectoure or Nérac
     c. Pau + Tarbes *vs.* Bayonne or Dax or Saint-Jean-Pied-de-Port

TABLE 6.1 (*cont.*)

2. Bourges, Moulins (Berry, Bourbonnais, Haute Marche, Nivernais)
   a. Moulins + Guéret *vs.* Montluçon
   b. Bourges + Nevers + Châteauroux *vs.* Issoudun
3. Lille, Amiens, Valenciennes (Artois, Boulonnais, Cambrésis, Flandres, Hainaut, Picardie, Valenciennes
   a. ARRAS + LILLE, DOUAI, VALENCIENNES + AMIENS *vs.* Boulogne or Cambrai or Saint-Quentin
   b. ARRAS + LILLE *vs.* SAINT-OMER + DOUAI, VALENCIENNES
4. Metz. Nancy (Barrois, Lorraine, the Trois Evêchês)
   a. METZ + Bar-le-Duc, Verdun + [Châlon-sur-Marne + Chaumont] *vs.* Sedan
   b. METZ + Lunéville + Bar-le-Duc, Saint-Mihiel, Verdun + Mirecourt, Epinal *vs.* Sarreguemines or Sarrelouis
5. Paris, Orléans, Soissons (Ile-de-France, Auxerrois, Orléanais, Soissonais and associated *pays*)
   a. ORLEANS + Blois + Chartres *vs.* Montargis, Gien
   b. VERSAILLES + Melun, Meaux + Senlis *vs.* PARIS + Etampes
   c. VERSAILLES + Beauvais + [AMIENS] + Melun + Soissons + Auxerre *vs.* Laon + Noyon, Senlis + Meaux + Sens or Provins
6. Perpignan and parts of the intendancies of Auch and Montpellier
   a. Perpignan + Foix, Pamiers + [Toulouse] *vs.* [Saint-Gaudens]
7. Poitiers, Limoges, La Rochelle (Augoumois, Aunis, Basse Marche, Limousin, Poitou, Saintonge)
   a. LIMOGES + [Gueret] + Tulle + Angoulême *vs.* POITIERS or Le Dorat or Montmorillon
   b. Niort, Saint-Maixent, Parthenay *vs.* POITIERS + Fontenay-le-Comte
   c. Angoulême + Saint-Jean-d'Angély, Saintes *vs.* LA ROCHELLE
8. Rouen, Alençon, Caen (Normandie, Perche)
   a. ROUEN + CAEN + Alençon + Coutances + Evreux *vs.* Lisieux + Avranches + Vire

Sources: *Mémoires, adresses*, and other documents from townspeople in AN DIV bis; published correspondence of deputies; secondary works on the division of France.

Notes: The symbols in the table signify the following:

CAPITAL LETERS		A town with at least 20,000 inhabitants in 1789
+	(plus sign)	Links allied towns that became located in separate departments
,	(comma)	Links allied towns that became located in the same department
Or	(conjunction)	Separates towns that did not support each other's plans for different departmental boundaries
[ ]	(brackets)	A town located in an area that was under the jurisdiction of a different committee

towns with provinces large enough to preserve a separate identity as departments; and the extent to which commercial and industrial towns had a favorable location within a rural hinterland. Deputies from the seats of important *généralités* were usually in the strongest bargaining position, once they agreed to subdivide their former jurisdictions. They could make concessions to relatively distant towns while isolating nearby towns that tried to encroach on the territory of their own departments. Deputies from the capitals of medium-sized provinces that had been incorporated into larger *généralités* often achieved comparable success by mobilizing provincial loyalties. Spokesmen for the capitals of small provinces or *pays* were in a much weaker position, and only in a few mountainous areas, where topography limited the prospects for territorial integration, did such towns have any chance of becoming departmental seats. Elsewhere, their only hope rested in mutual concessions involving the rotation of departmental directories and assemblies. As for commercial and industrial towns, they also had trouble influencing plans of division unless they were already important administrative capitals. Even a few seats of intendancies that specialized in commerce lost out in competition with old rivals. Commercial wealth provoked envy among the deputies from less fortunate towns. Generally speaking, the new departmental map of France favored administrative and judicial centers of the old regime over seaports and other commercial towns that tried to parlay their economic influence into larger territorial jurisdictions.

To analyze the outcomes of committee deliberations, the departmental map that deputies approved in January and February 1790 can be compared with the initial plan of division back in October 1789. Map 6.2 shows the boundaries of the new departments, along with the locations of the towns that became the initial seats of departmental assemblies and directories in 1790.[41] Moving around the maritime facade of the kingdom, we can see that major changes occurred in three coastal areas: in the extreme north, where a fivefold division of the intendancies of Lille, Valenciennes, and Amiens was replaced by a fourfold division that eliminated a separate department along the Atlantic coast; in Normandy, where a fourfold division, each including a coastal area, gave way to a fivefold division that created a separate department for the interior between Caen and Alençon; and in the extreme southwest, where a department for Bayonne and

---

[41] This map is based on an original map of departmental and district boundaries in the Bibliothèque Nationale, "Carte de la France divisée en Départements et Districts . . . par les auteurs de l'Atlas national de France [corrigée in 1792]," Bibliothèque Nationale, GE CC 1097. The boundaries of departments in southeastern France have been modified, however, to include the papal states of Avignon and Comtat Venaissan, not annexed to France until 1792. The map does not include Corsica, whose administrative division into one or two departments continued to be a matter of dispute throughout the revolutionary era.

Map 6.2. Departments and Departmental Seats, 1790

the Adour River basin disappeared. By contrast, the boundaries of departments in Provence, Brittany, and Poitou remained essentially intact, despite the efforts of deputies from the seaports of Marseille, Saint-Malo, and La Rochelle, respectively, to change them.

In most of these coastal areas, towns that had lawcourts with extensive rural jurisdictions during the old regime formed successful alliances against seaports that remained isolated from other towns. In Brittany and Provence, coalitions revolved former seats of *parlements*. Rennes was threatened by Saint-Malo's plan for a sixfold division of the province that would detach this seaport, along with the surrounding coastline, from its department. In like manner, Marseille's plan for a narrow, coastal department in

Provence would restrict Aix-en-Provence to a smaller department of the interior. Deputies from Rennes and Aix, who had tried in vain to oppose the subdivision of their provincial jurisdictions, were determined to resist any further losses of territory and fiscal resources.[42] They gained unwavering support from colleagues who represented other towns that wanted departmental seats. The bishopric of Saint-Brieuc would lose its central location in the division sponsored by Saint-Malo; and the departments of Quimper and Vannes would shrink considerably in area. Furthermore, Quimper aspired to become the judicial capital of lower Brittany, which a partition of this area into two departments might prevent.[43] Even the naval port of Brest, hostile to the pretensions of Quimper, opposed Saint-Malo's plan for a separate department along the northwest coast. Such an arrangement would favor the seaport of Morlaix, a more dangerous rival than Quimper because of its location in the most densely populated and commercial part of lower Brittany.[44]

In Provence, deputies from the seaport of Toulon were no more enthusiastic about the plan of Marseille for a maritime department. They hoped to obtain the departmental seat in eastern Provence, which included towns of the interior that Marseille proposed to attach to the mountainous department of upper Provence. Deputies from these other towns, who also wanted a share of departmental establishments, were strongly opposed to union with towns of upper Provence, whose deputies reciprocated their sentiments exactly. They joined with Aix in isolating the deputies of Marseille from the rest of the committee for Provence, whose views easily persuaded the C.C. to leave Marseille in the same department as Aix.[45]

Deputies from Pau led the opposition to a separate department for Ba-

[42] Rennes also wanted access to the sea via the port of Saint-Malo. See Léon Dubreuil, *La Révolution dans le département des Côtes-du-Nord* (Paris, 1909), p. 14.

[43] On the ambition of Quimper, see letters from deputies from the *sénéchaussée* of Brest to Mun. Brest, cited in Delourmel and Esquieu, *Brest pendant la Révolution*, p. 65, n. 1, and p. 70, n. 3.

[44] In mid-November 1789, the deputies from Brest supported a plan for a department in northwestern Brittany, but the municipality preferred to compete with Quimper rather than with Morlaix. Letters cited in Delourmel and Esquieu, *Brest pendant la Révolution*, pp. 67–69.

[45] See the *mémoire* by Charles-François Bouche, deputy from Aix-en-Provence, annex to session of Dec. 9, 1789, AP 10:455–59. Similar rivalries between the seaports of Dunkerque and Boulogne, along with fears that Saint-Omer would displace them as the commercial center of this coastal area, help explain the failure of Saint-Omer's plan of division. The main support for this plan came from Douai and Valenciennes, who resented the effort of Lille to monopolize the administration of the department of the Nord. When deputies from maritime Flanders switched their support from Lille to Douai, the plan of Saint-Omer, already rejected by the National Assembly, lost its political support within the deputation from the Nord. On these intrigues, see Zeni, "Urban Networks and the French Revolution in the Nord," pp. 100–104; and the dossiers in AN DIV bis 12:244, 246; and DIV bis 36:581.

yonne and the Adour River valley. The Basques themselves were disunited because the little towns of Mauléon and Saint-Palais feared the ambition of Saint-Jean-Pied-de-Port. Spokesmen for both of these towns, hoping to obtain districts in a larger department, broke ranks with their fellow Basques and welcomed the decision of the National Assembly to amalgamate the *pays* of Labourt, Navarre, and Soule with the province of Béarn. Meanwhile, deputies from Bordeaux and Auch opposed every effort to create two departments for the area between the Garonne River and the Adour River. The ambitions of Dax and Mont-de-Marsan, along with those of Bazas, Agen, Condom, and La Réole, in the Garonne River basin, canceled each other out, and Bordeaux ended up with the largest and most densely populated department in the southwest, a fitting tribute to its influence as an administrative and judicial capital in the old regime. As for Bayonne, its municipality, shunned by all the other towns in the area, reluctantly entered the department of the Basses-Pyrénées, despite its commercial ties with the Adour River basin.[46]

To the north of Bordeaux, the seaport of La Rochelle encountered similar opposition from towns of the interior, despite its previous administrative role as the capital of an intendancy. The formation of departments along the entire coast between the Garonne and the Loire rivers was complicated by the fact that the *généralités* of Poitiers, La Rochelle, and Limoges overlapped with each other and with older provincial boundaries. Deputies from these *généralités* had to appoint commissioners to work out a plan of territorial exchange among the provinces of Poitou, Limousin, Aunis, Saintonge, Angoumois, and lower Marche. "I have never seen so much confusion," reported one of these commissioners. "Everyone was trying to take from his neighbors and no one wanted to give anything in return."[47] Deputies from Poitou finally agreed to abandon their enclaves in the *généralité* of Limoges, which opened the way for this town to attach the *pays* of lower Marche to its department, but they refused to make any concessions to La Rochelle. Even Niort, an industrial town of Poitou that wanted to construct a canal to La Rochelle, expressed no interest in joining the same department as this seaport. Instead, the deputy from Niort joined with four colleagues who supported an intermediate department for the

---

[46] Debate in session of Jan 12, 1790, *Le point du jour* 6:182, pp. 16–20; AN DIV bis 14:258 (*syndic* of estates of Soule, Basses-Pyrénées); DIV bis 29:419 (Saint-Palais, Basses-Pyrénées). On the protracted conflict over the division of the intendancies of Bordeaux and Auch, see Louis Desgraves, *La formation de Lot-et-Garonne*, pp. 16–27; AN DIV bis 8:203 (Gironde); DIV bis 9:216 (Mont-de-Marsan, Landes); DIV bis 9:214 (Dax, Landes); *rapport* of Gossin and debate, sessions of Jan. 14–15, 1790, AP 11:188, and *Journal des Etats Généraux* 7:374–88.

[47] Letter from René-Antoine Thibaudeau, deputy from Poitiers, cited by Merle, *La formation des Deux-Sèvres*, p. 47.

plains and wastelands between upper and lower Poitou. This area had no natural or historic unity, and its most central town, Parthenay, had only 3,000 inhabitants, but the C.C. insisted that a province as large as Poitou must be divided into three departments. The formation of a department for Niort and Parthenay confirmed the failure of La Rochelle to extend its political influence into an area of Poitou only a short distance away. Despite impassioned appeals to the C.C. and the National Assembly, La Rochelle and its little *pays* of Aunis were incorporated into the same department as Saintes and the larger *pays* of Saintonge.[48]

In Normandy, an extensive coastline also gave rise to disputes, but in this province, the largest towns with access to the sea—Rouen and Caen—were also the most important administrative and judicial capitals. Hardpressed to obtain districts, not to speak of departments, spokesmen for the smaller but more rapidly growing seaports of Le Havre and Cherbourg played no role in the decision of deputies from Normandy to abandon the initial plan of division. Here controversy centered on the efforts of Lisieux and Vire, both textile towns of the interior, to carve departments for themselves out of the *généralités* of Caen, Alençon, and Rouen. Deputies from these three *généralités* battled in committee for nearly a month over whether to create five or six departments. A fivefold division would improve the centrality of Caen and Alençon as well as Coutances and Evreux, both seats of bishoprics and *présidiaux*. Alternatively, a sixfold division would permit Lisieux and Vire to encroach on the territory of Caen and Rouen, while eliminating Evreux from contention in upper Normandy and favoring Avranches over Coutances in lower Normandy.[49] As Thomas Lindet, the shrewd partisan of Evreux, reported on December 4, 1789, "Those from Avranches and Vire are putting a great deal of heat into supporting a division that would be quite harmful to us. Those from Rouen are trying to preserve their advantage, as well as those from Caen." Several competing maps were drafted and discarded, as deputies fought for their particular interests with "more passion than relatives over the division of an inheritance." A spokesman for Lisieux submitted a plan that would partition the landlocked *généralité* of Alençon among three coastal departments; deputies from Rouen and Caen insisted on dividing the entire channel coast of Normandy among themselves; and Lindet struggled to include the mouth of the Eure River in a department for Evreux, but not for Lisieux. It was Lindet's map, modified in its details but not its overall design, that attracted the most support, satisfying as it did the interests of

---

[48] Eugène Desgranges, *La formation territoriale du département de la Haute-Vienne, 1789–an X* (Paris, 1942), pp. 41–60; AN DIV bis 31:437 (Niort, Deux-Sèvres); letter from Thibaudeau, Nov. 17, 1789, in Carré and Boissonnade, *Correspondance du Constituante Thibaudeau*, pp. 40–45; session of Jan. 12, 1790, AP 11:170.

[49] A. Lebaindre, *La formation du département de la Manche* (Caen, 1911), pp. 31–33.

the three former capitals. As Lindet wrote on January 5, "This division has preserved as much as possible the traditional habits and commercial relations" of the province. All the victorious towns, he noted, "had the advantage of being the seats of the former establishments."[50]

Although Languedoc bordered the Mediterannean Sea, disputes in this large province, which lacked any major seaports, centered exclusively on administrative and judicial capitals. If Nîmes, one of the largest textile towns in the kingdom, could boast of an important *sénéchaussée* and a large diocese, much smaller seats of bishoprics or *sénéchaussées* in Languedoc and its associated *pays* also wanted departments of their own. Formerly, the fiscal administration of the estates of Languedoc had been located in the capitals of each diocese. Now these twenty-three dioceses would have to be amalgamated into six or seven departments. As the municipality of Lavaur complained, most of the "leading towns" that used to serve as diocesan capitals would be reduced to an inferior rank as "secondary towns."[51] The danger seemed greatest to towns that would be located in the same departments as Montpellier and Toulouse, the former capitals of the entire province, but throughout the plains and mountains of Languedoc, towns competed for departmental seats. To mitigate such rivalries, Rabaut Saint-Etienne, the influential deputy from Nîmes, proposed the rotation of establishments among important towns in each department. Deputies from the southern towns of Vivarais, who feared the transfer of the northern town of Annonay to the neighboring *pays* of Velay, were quick to welcome this compromise. Their colleagues from Gévaudan, where the Protestant town of Marvéjols had long rivaled the bishopric of Mende for provincial leadership, reached a similar agreement to rotate departmental assemblies between these two towns. In lower Languedoc, where the much larger towns of Montpellier and Nîmes needed allies in order to avoid being squeezed into the same department, Rabaut Saint-Etienne and his colleagues from Nîmes offered alternates to Alais and Uzès, and deputies from Montpellier reluctantly conceded as much to Béziers, Lodève, and Saint-Pons. Even deputies from Albi and Castres, in upper Languedoc, promised an alternate to Lavaur, although they broke this agreement afterward and fought among themselves for primacy in a department based on the old *pays* of Albigeois. A total of nineteen towns in Languedoc formed intradepartmental alliances on the basis of *alternats*.[52]

[50] Letters from Lindet, in Montier, *Correspondance de Thomas Lindet*, pp. 27, 39–40.
[51] AN DIV bis 31:441 (Tarn).
[52] Speech by Rabaut Saint-Etienne on Dec. 9, 1789, AP 10:453; and letters from special deputies from Montpellier, Nov. 24 and Dec. 3, 1789, in Charles D'Aigrefeuille, *Histoire de la ville de Montpellier* (Montpellier, 1882), 4:667–69. As a comparison of maps 6.1 and 6.2 shows, these alliances resulted in two major changes in the plan of division for Languedoc: Mende achieved its goal of forming a separate department for the *pays* of Gévaudan, aided by

In most of the intendancies within the interior of the kingdom, historic capitals of provinces or *pays* that also had important lawcourts were in the best position to influence the formation of departments. Whether the deputies from these towns supported the original plan of division naturally depended on where their jurisdictions were situated on the departmental map. For example, Cahors and Rodez, both seats of bishoprics and *présidial* lawcourts, were happy to endorse the plan, which used the frontiers of their historic *pays* of Quercy and Rouergue to subdivide the *généralité* of Montauban. Cahors was particularly eager to displace Montauban as the administrative capital of Quercy, and its municipality obtained endorsements from all the secondary towns of the province. Despite the commercial importance of Montauban, this town suffered from its location on the border between Quercy and Languedoc. Caught between Toulouse and Cahors, Montauban finally opted to stay in the same department as Cahors, where it failed to become the departmental seat. Despite having a considerably larger *sénéchaussée* than Rodez, Villefranche-de-Rouergue suffered a comparable fate. Having obtained a provincial assembly back in 1779 because of its location near the center of the *généralité* of Montauban, this town now found itself on the border of two departments. Its deputies did not protest, however, until Rodez refused to share the establishments of the department of Rouergue with Villefranche. By then it was too late.[53]

Other towns of the interior that supported the general outline of the initial plan of division included Tours, Angers, Laval, and Le Mans, in the *généralité* of Tours; and Bourges, Moulins, Châteauroux, and Nevers in the *généralités* of Bourges and Moulins. Except for Laval, which rested its case, as we have seen, on its role in the textile industry of lower Maine, all of these towns had important institutions in the old regime. Angers, Bourges, Le Mans, and Tours were the capitals of historic provinces, with large dioceses, extensive *sénéchaussées* or *bailliages*, and military *gouvernements*; Moulins was the seat of the only *sénéchaussée* in the Bourbonnais, and it had a *gouvernement* as well as an intendant; Châteauroux had a larger *bailliage* jurisdiction than did any other town in the province of Berry, including the capital of Bourges; and Nevers was the capital of the duchy of

---

the success of Le Puy in persuading the Auvergnat town of Brioude to join a department for the *pays* of Velay; and Toulouse had to expand its jurisdiction southward into the Pyrénées after deputies from Albi, Castres, and Lavaur refused to join its department. Its annexation of the *pays* of Comminges took place in the larger context of agreements to create two departments in the Pyrénées between Pau, to the west, and Perpignan, to the east: one for the *pays* of Bigorre, centered on Tarbes, and one for the *pays* of Foix and Couserans, centered on Foix.

[53] Copies of seven Mun. Delibs. from small towns supporting Cahors; letter from Poncet-Delpech, deputy from Montauban, complaining that his "codeputies" favored Cahors, AN DIV bis 10:223–24 (Lot); and "*observations*" from Andrand, deputy from Villefranche, AN DIV Bis 20:322.

Nivernais, with a large seigneurial jurisdiction, a bishopric, and a *gouverne-ment*. None of the other towns in these provinces could rival them. The garrison town of Saumur, which did have more commerce than Angers, could not muster any support outside its little *pays* of Saumurois for a fifth department in the *généralité* of Tours; deputies from Bourges and Châteauroux countered the ambitions of Issoudun by subdividing the province of Berry in a manner that left Issoudun near the border of the two departments; and Moulins allied itself with Guéret to uphold a division between the provinces of Bourbonnais and Marche that left Montluçon in a corner of the same department as Moulins. This outcome had not been a foregone conclusion, because emissaries from Guéret had approached the municipality of Montluçon with an offer to unite the *pays* of lower Bourbonnais and upper Marche in a single department. Fearing the prospect of sending grain in times of shortage to the infertile *pays* of upper Marche, the townspeople of Montluçon turned down this offer. As a result, they ended up competing for a departmental seat with the larger town of Moulins instead of with the smaller town of Guéret.[54]

In contrast to these areas where boundary readjustments did not affect the basic plan of division, significant changes occurred in the boundaries of departments in Champagne, Lorraine, Burgundy, Franche-Comté, Dauphiné, the *généralité* of Lyon, and the *généralités* of Paris, Orléans, and Soissons, as a close comparison of maps 6.1 and 6.2 shows. In nearly every case, coalitions of towns that wanted to improve their centrality took the initiative of redrawing the map of division. For example, a deputy from Chaumont worked closely with Gossin and other deputies from Bar-le-Duc to form departments centered on these towns. Even Langres agreed to modify the initial map of division, which had placed this town in the same department as Dijon. Deputies from Châlons-sur-Marne ratified Chaumont's plan for a department along the upper Marne River, which would preserve the centrality of Châlons in its own department along the middle Marne. So did deputies from the southern part of Lorraine, who welcomed a plan that preserved the traditional frontier between Champagne and the uplands of the Vosges mountains. Pressed from towns to the west and the south, deputies from Metz and Nancy agreed to expand their departments eastward, where the German-speaking area of Lorraine had only two defenders in the National Assembly, both rural priests. The final map of Lorraine and Champagne improved the centrality of Metz, Nancy, Bar-le-Duc, Epinal, Chaumont, Troyes, and Mézières, all destined

---

[54] *Procès-verbal* of the *comité* of Montluçon, Dec. 10, 1789, AN DIV bis 19:307 (Allier). On the rivalry between Saumur and Angers, see "Lettres de Maupetit" 19:96. Saumur appealed in vain to the National Assembly, which refused to grant it a department, AP 11:184. On the alliance between Bourges and Châteauroux, see Marcel Bruneau, *Les débuts de la Révolution dans les départements du Cher et de l'Indre, 1789–1791* (Paris, 1902), pp. 113–20.

to become departmental seats. As for the flourishing textile towns of Reims and Sedan, which had unfavorable locations on the original map of division, they remained on the edge of departments after the process of territorial revision had been completed. Sedan was too close to the German frontier, and deputies from Reims miscalculated their prospects of gaining a large department in competition with Chaumont and Mézières as well as Châlons-sur-Marne.[55]

Deputies from Lyon were more fortunate than their counterparts from Reims and Montauban. Finding their *généralité* split into two departments on the preliminary map of division, they insisted on preserving the *pays* of Beaujolais, which included the fertile plains of the Saône River to the north of Lyon. Deputies from Mâcon, reluctant to enter the same department as towns of Beaujolais, aided Lyon by opting for a large department in southern Burgundy.[56] As for the plan that deputies from Montbrison submitted to create a separate department for the *pays* of Forez, spokesmen for Saint-Etienne would have nothing to do with it. For two centuries, the judges of Montbrison had preserved a monopoly of royal justice in Forez, despite the repeated efforts of Saint-Etienne to obtain a *bailliage* court.[57] Now that "despotism, aristocracy and the feudal regime" had finally been overthrown, Saint-Etienne would fulfill its ambition, but only if it escaped from the jurisdiction of Montbrison. Municipal leaders denied that the province of Forez consisted primarily of an agricultural plain. The densely populated mountains to the east of the Loire Valley and toward the south comprised an important industrial region, centered on the large and flourishing town of Saint-Etienne itself. The rural populations of these mountains were employed by the tens of thousands in the ribbon-weaving and metal-working trades known as the "manufactures" of Saint-Etienne. This part of Forez had close commercial ties with Lyon, but it was isolated from Montbrison. Consequently, either the region of Saint-Etienne should be-

[55] On the negotiations behind the subdivision of the *généralités* of Châlons, Metz, and Nancy, see Bourdon, "La formation des départements de l'Est en 1790," pp. 187–217; Mettrier, *La formation de la Haute-Marne*, pp. 69–81, 279–86; and Masson, *Histoire administrative de la Lorraine*, pp. 133–291.

[56] On negotiations over the subdivision of the province of Burgundy, in which deputies from Mâcon and Châlon-sur-Saône prevented Autun, allied momentarily with Dijon, from forming two departments on a north/south axis, one for the plains of the Saône, and the other for the mountains to the west, see F. Siraud, "Etude sur la formation de Saône-et-Loire" 11:224–26; *réponse* of Mâcon, Châlon-sur-Saône and Charolles to a printed *mémoire* from Autun; *mémoire* by Arnould, deputy from Dijon; and *observations* by special deputies from Autun, AN DIV bis 16:275 (Saône-et-Loire); and DIV bis 6:182 (Côte-d'Or). A third department in the *généralité* of Dijon was formed to the east of the Saône River valley for the *pays* of Bresse and Bugey, following the failure of Belley to muster any support from other towns of Bugey to create a separate department for this mountainous *pays*.

[57] On the history of this rivalry, see Coron, *Essai sur la sénéchaussée de Saint-Etienne*.

come a separate department or it should remain attached to the department of Lyon, which shared its interest in the development of commerce. Deputies from Lyon played on this rivalry between Saint-Etienne and Montbrison by offering to rotate the departmental assembly between both of these towns, as well as with Villefranche and Roanne, the other seats of *élections* in its *généralité*. This offer persuaded deputies from Villefranche to drop their objections to a unified department, leaving only Montbrison to protest that "of all the despotisms, the hardest to bear is that of a great city against a town or province weaker than itself."[58]

In Dauphiné and Franche-Comté, contrasting types of urban alliances explain why conflicting geographical principles triumphed in the committees for these provinces. Just as Vienne challenged Grenoble in the Dauphiné, so Dôle opposed Besançon in Franche-Comté. Located in the lowlands of their respective provinces, these towns had a similar goal: to confine their old rivals to mountainous departments. Vienne could appeal to the initial plan of division, which placed Vienne and Valence in one department for the plains of the Rhône and placed Grenoble and Gap in another department for the mountains of the Alps. Dôle seemed to have the more challenging task of revising the plan for Franche-Comté, which located it in the same department as Besançon. Yet Vienne failed, while Dôle succeeded.[59] Simply put, spokesmen for Vienne ignored the interests of other towns, while the deputy from Dôle allied himself with all the towns of Franche-Comté that feared the influence of Besançon. In Dauphiné, deputies from Grenoble took the initiative of appealing to Valence, the most important town in the Rhône Valley to the south of Vienne. Their tripartite plan of division would not only form a separate department for Gap, in the high Alps, but it would partition the southern half of the province in a manner that improved the centrality of Valence, otherwise relegated to the extreme southern edge of the same department as Vienne. Against this plan, spokesmen for Vienne belatedly but without success devised a plan for combining all the lowlands of Dauphiné, along with the mountains to the southeast, into a single department.[60] By contrast, Dôle joined with Poligny and Salins, *bailliage* towns that also found themselves assigned to the same department as Besançon, to offer Lons-le-Saulnier,

[58] Mun. Delib. Saint-Etienne, AN DIV bis 30:423; *observations* by the deputies of Lyon; Mun. Delib. Montbrison, DIV bis 16:270; other documents in DIV bis 30:423 (Rhône-et-Loire).

[59] Report of a general assembly at Vienne, Dec. 27, 1789, AN DIV bis 8:211 (Isère); and *pétition* of 188 residents of Dôle, protesting the abolition of *alternats* in June 1791, DIV bis 9:213 (Jura).

[60] *Mémoire* by the *comité permanent* of Vienne, AN DIV bis 6:190 (Isère); Printed *observations* by a deputy who opposed Vienne, DIV bis 8:208 (Isère); "Observations sur la division du Dauphiné," unsigned, DIV bis 8:211 (Isère).

farther south, a larger and more fertile department for the southern part of Franche-Comté. The town of Gray, with its grain port on the Saône River, also resisted the entreaties of Besançon and bargained successfully for a share of establishments with Vesoul, the dominant town in the northern half of the province. As a result of these alliances, Besançon lost all the territory in the plains between Vesoul and Lons-le-Saulnier, despite the strenuous objections of its special deputies in Paris. By accepting the promise of an *alternat*, deputies from Dôle and Gray, like those who represented other *bailliage* towns in Franche-Comté, achieved a rare victory over a provincial capital whose commercial orientation toward the plains of Franche-Comté rather closely paralleled the relations of exchange between Grenoble and the plains of Dauphiné.[61]

Nowhere in the kingdom were negotiations over the formation of departments more complicated than in the Paris region. Despite the protest of the Paris Commune, the National Assembly voted on January 14, 1790, to create a miniature department for Paris, with a radius of at most three leagues.[62] But by this time, several *généralités* in the Paris basin had already been divided. Instead of starting from Paris and forming other departments accordingly, as the *abbé* Sièyes had originally proposed, the C.C. began with outlying areas and worked toward Paris.[63] This placed increasing pressure on towns near Paris, whose departmental plans had to take into account the agreements that deputies from other provinces had already reached. For example, when Montargis and Gien, who agreed to form a single department, were attached instead to the department of Orléans, this ruined a plan of deputies from Sens to add Montargis to *their* department.[64] With at least fifteen towns trying to become departmental seats in an area reduced to only four departments, negotiations became painful and protracted. All six of the plans that deputies examined would dismember the *généralités* of Soissons and Amiens as well as that of Paris. A majority of commissioners from the region finally selected plan number four, which gave a central location to Versailles in a department that entirely surrounded Paris. This plan also favored the industrial town of Beau-

---

[61] Letter from J. N. Laloy to Mun. Chaumont, reporting the views of deputies from Dôle, cited in Mettrier, *La formation de la Haute-Loire*, pp. 76–791; and Jean Girardot, *Le département de la Haute-Saône pendant la Révolution* (Vesoul, 1973), 1:170–73.

[62] Most deputies from Paris agreed with the majority that no ordinary department could provision such an enormous city, which deserved its own electoral representation and administrative assembly. *Rapport* of Gossin and brief debate, session of Jan. 14, 1790, AP 11:180; Bournon, *La création du département de Paris*, pp. 13–16.

[63] Bureaux de Pusy, "Rapport sommaire sur la nouvelle division du royaume," session of Jan. 8, 1790, AP 11:120.

[64] Porée, *La formation de l'Yonne*, pp. 42–46; AN ADXVI 75 (*précis* for Etampes). Orléans allied itself with Chartres and Blois to create three departments in its former *généralité*, centered on these three towns.

vais, to the north, the *bailliage* town of Melun, to the east, and the river port of Auxerre, to the southeast. It differed most from competing plans, however, in shifting southward the boundary of the department that contained Soissons, which improved the centrality of this former administrative capital. As deputies from the rival town of Laon complained afterward, "We have strong reasons to believe that the pretensions of Soissons to be *chef-lieu* had much to do with the choice of plan number four."[65]

By dint of extraordinary effort, all the provincial committees either resolved their disputes or referred them to the National Assembly, which decided on January 15, 1790, to divide the provinces into precisely eighty-three departments.[66] The new map of the kingdom, which departmental committees drew in the next few weeks, expressed, as we have seen, an equilibrium of urban interests. While a few medium-sized provinces had been transformed directly into departments, more commonly *généralités*, provinces, and *pays* had been amalgamated or divided in accordance with the relative size, institutional importance, and political influence of towns. The C.C. recognized this fact in its preliminary draft of a general decree on the division, when it used the names of towns to designate the new departments.[67] Yet the final version of this decree introduced a new system of nomenclature, based on rivers and mountains.[68] This famous policy, which seemed to symbolize the role of nature in the division of the kingdom, served the more immediate task of disguising urban rivalries in many departments. As one commissioner of the C.C. explained, "Your committee thinks that you must cease to accord supremacy to one town over another, and I agree that the means of destroying this supremacy is not to name departments after their *chef-lieux*."[69] So the terminology of depart-

---

[65] Printed *comte-rendu* (Paris, 1790), AN ADXVI 18. On the division of the Paris region, see R. Hennequin, *La formation de l'Aisne*, pp. 85–98; and L. Berthoumeau, *La formation du département de Seine-et-Marne* (Dijon, 1914), pp. 32–45.

[66] The basic plan of division was completed by Jan. 8, 1790, when Bureaux de Pusy gave a "Rapport sommaire sur la nouvelle division du royaume" in the name of the C.C., AP 11:119–25. Disputes that deputies appealed to the floor of the National Assembly were settled in the next week, and "a final decree on the departments," listing the number of departments per province, was passed on Jan. 15, AP 11:189.

[67] General decree read by De Cernon for the C.C., Feb. 17, 1790, AP 11:621. The earlier decrees on particular departments had named 27 of them after their chief town, and the rest after provinces, geographical subdivisions of provinces, or *pays*.

[68] Session of Feb. 26, 1790, AP 11:717–24.

[69] Speech of Bureaux de Pusy, session of Feb. 16, 1790, AP 11:711. De Cernon added that the existence of *alternats* made it impossible to designate all departments with the name of a single town, AP 11:711. See also Thomas Lindet's caustic judgment, "You will be amazed by the scientific denomination of our departments, or you will laugh at this ridiculous nomenclature, that the committee of division took upon itself to fabricate on the pretext that the seats of a few departments have not yet been determined pending the choice of the voters." Letter of Mar. 8, 1790, in Montier, *Correspondance de Thomas Lindet*, p. 107.

ments referred to the permanency of nature rather than to the primacy of towns. In this manner, deputies acknowledged that only a minority of the new *chef-lieux* dominated all the space enclosed within these departments. Just as the fragmentation of space into a variety of jurisdictions and *pays*, each centered on a different town, encouraged the proliferation of plans for departments, so the redefinition of space within a unified nation-state required a new language, neither provincial nor urban in origin. The National Assembly agreed not only to transpose historical space into abstract departments but to symbolize the subordination of towns to nature. Yet deputies continued to battle in departmental committees over the seats of departments and districts. Within the new spatial order of departments, towns remained as contentious as before.

Chapter 7

DISPUTES OVER THE SEATS OF DEPARTMENTS

D ECREES OF THE National Assembly left in question the capitals of nearly half the departments, either by granting alternates to rival towns or by referring disputes to electoral assemblies in the departments. The precise wording of these decrees opened a new arena of contention, as some deputies tried to name permanent seats of departmental administration while others disputed the choice of provisional capitals or alternates. Efforts to postpone such decisions raised the issue of which town should host the first meeting of voters in a department, and whether these voters should express their views about alternates as well as permanent seats. Once electors in the departments began their deliberations, still another range of issues, involving rural as well as urban perspectives, emerged to complicate the decisions of the National Assembly. Territorial conflicts threatened in some cases to displace historic capitals in favor of obscure little towns that happened to enjoy the advantage of centrality. In several instances, the National Assembly decided to overrule a majority of voters in order to place the departmental directory in the larger of two contending towns. Deputies registered a growing awareness that many urban ambitions would have to be sacrificed in the interest of administrative rationality, and before completing their deliberations in 1791, they voted to abolish all the alternates that they had approved back in January and February of 1790. Now eighty-three towns became the definitive seats of departments. The outbreak of counterrevolution in some regions of the nation added a political dimension to urban rivalries that continued to plague the Legislative Assembly and the Convention. Neither the triumph of the Montagnards over federalist revolts in 1793 nor the decision of the Thermidorians to strengthen the departments at the expense of the districts brought these disputes to an end. Indeed, the abolition of district directories and tribunals in 1795 caused a new wave of agitation over departmental establishments. Not until the Napoleonic empire did the departmental system achieve its final form. The Restoration Monarchy preserved unchanged the capitals of each department, despite a resurgence of demands for the transfer of prefectures in 1814–15. After a generation of upheaval, towns that had failed to become the *chef-lieux* of departments were obliged to accept their subordinate rank in a government more centralized than the old regime had ever been.

In dividing the provinces into departments and districts, the National

Assembly followed the procedure of passing a separate decree for each department, which permitted considerable variation in the policy of choosing capitals. Some deputies fought on the floor of the National Assembly for a decisive vote on a permanent *chef-lieu*. For example, when Gossin reported on February 1, 1790, that the C.C. favored the convocation of voters at Lambesc to mediate between the claims of Marseille and Aix-en-Provence to the departmental establishments of western Provence, François Bouche rose to plead the cause of his hometown of Aix. His contrast between the poverty of Aix and the opulence of Marseille may have struck a responsive chord in the Assembly, but when he launched into a tedious description of the fifty and more plagues that had appeared at Marseille since the invasion of the Turks, other deputies insisted that he return to the point. Bouche hastily concluded that the capital and all the establishments of the department should immediately be awarded to Aix. His discourse on the plague seems to have lured the following speaker, a businessman from Marseille, into making the farfetched claim that only a departmental administration in this seaport could save the health of the nation: "The plague requires that Marseille become the seat of an administration to guard incessantly against this scourge. You are not determining the interests of Marseille, but your own, and those of France." The archbishop of Aix argued more convincingly that a majority of the population in the department resided outside the city and territory of Marseille, whose peripheral location compared unfavorably with the centrality of Aix. It was also unreasonable to force administrators and electors to hold their deliberations at Marseille, where living costs were extremely high. The principle of *rapprochement*, as well as the National Assembly's "constant desire to favor less wealthy *pays*," implied a prompt decision in favor of Aix. Impressed by the archbishop's brief and well-organized speech, the deputies voted by a large majority to place the *chef-lieu* at Aix rather than at Marseille.[1]

More frequently, deputies who had been outvoted in committee preferred to postpone any final settlement of disputes over departmental seats by appealing to the voters. The first such case appeared on January 19, the day that the National Assembly began debating decrees on particular departments. The C.C. wanted to make Charleville the capital of the department for northern Champagne, but the deputation from this province favored Mézières. Following the advice of Gossin, *rapporteur* for the C.C., the National Assembly decreed that the first electoral assembly would meet "provisionally" at Mézières, where the voters would decide by a plurality of votes which town "must become the definitive seat of the department." Later that day, Gossin proposed a similar procedure for suspending judgment on an alternate between Angers and Saumur. He reported that the

---

[1] Speeches reported in *Journal des Etats-Généraux* 8:161–62; and AP 11:408.

C.C. opposed such an arrangement because Angers was much more centrally located in its department than was Saumur and possessed the advantages of a larger population, better communications, and more establishments under the old regime. Unfortunately, the Committee had previously assured the deputies from Saumur of an alternate, so Gossin now advised an appeal to the voters. His decree, passed without objections by the Assembly, stated that "Angers is the *chef-lieu* of the department, which nonetheless will rotate with Saumur, unless the departmental assembly [of electors] judges that this alternate is contrary to its interest, in which case the seat will remain fixed at Angers." On January 21, Gossin introduced another variant on this theme by proposing that voters gather at Châlons-sur-Marne, the provisional capital of a department in Champagne, where they would decide, by majority vote, whether to rotate the *chef-lieu* or leave it fixed at Châlons. In this case, deputies from Reims, who sought a departmental administration so merchants from this town would not lose access to government tax funds, failed to obtain any guarantees from the C.C. The decree on the department of the Marne, though conceding the possibility of an alternate, left the voters to choose which towns, if any, would benefit from such a compromise. Deputies from Villefranche-de-Rouergue were even less fortunate in challenging the terms of a decree that assigned to Rodez the departmental seat of Rouergue. On January 25, the only concession they could wrest from the Assembly was a clause permitting the first assembly of voters to decide whether Rodez should "remain" the capital of the department.[2]

By February 17, when the National Assembly passed its last individual decree on the organization of departments, a total of twenty-eight electoral assemblies had been authorized to vote on the location of capitals, alternates, or other departmental establishments. In twelve of these decrees, the National Assembly ruled out any compromise involving alternates and instructed the voters to name a single capital; in another six decrees, it asked them to choose between a list of alternates or a permanent seat; in nine decrees, it permitted discussion of unspecified towns that might participate in alternates; and in one decree, it authorized discussion of the location of departmental lawcourts.[3] These variations in the role of voters expressed the conciliatory policy of the C.C. in early 1790, whose members preferred interim agreements that hastened the organization of the new departments rather than final judgments that risked alienating public opinion in rival towns. Of course, this risk of disaffection seemed relatively low in departments that contained a large provincial capital such as Toulouse or Rennes,

[2] AP 11:234–35, 266, 316.
[3] Tabulation based on the *lettres patentes du roi*, Mar. 4, 1790, sanctioning the decrees of Jan. 15, Feb. 16 and 26, 1790, *Réimpression de L'ancien Moniteur* 4:3–340, *passim*.

whose deputies triumphed easily over spokesmen for the much smaller towns of Saint-Gaudens and Saint-Malo, respectively. Yet half the towns with over 20,000 inhabitants and nearly one-third of the seats of intendants failed to become definitive seats of departments in January–February 1790. Even Lyon, the second-largest city in France, received only the first assembly of the department of the Rhône-et-Loire, pending a vote of the electors on whether to approve an alternate with Montbrison, Roanne, Saint-Etienne, and Villefranche. Among the towns that had to await the judgment of voters in the summer of 1790 were provincial capitals such as Arras and Grenoble, seaports such as La Rochelle and Toulon, and commercial towns of the interior, such as Niort and Soissons. Several dozen less important administrative towns and marketing centers also presented their candidacy to voters in the departments, including the supposedly neutral communities of Aire, Moirans, and Navarrenx, which the National Assembly had chosen to host the first electoral assemblies in the departments of the Pas-de-Calais, Isère, and Basses-Pyrénées, respectively. A total of eighty-five towns and bourgs competed for the twenty-eight capitals about which voters were asked to deliberate.

Map 7.1 displays the location of these towns and indicates their population size and their success or failure in obtaining voter support for alternates. The map also shows, in solid rectangles and triangles, which towns became departmental seats or alternates in eleven other departments where the National Assembly introduced the system of alternates without appealing to the voters.

Urban rivalries persisted in many departments that the Constituent Assembly had formed out of large and medium-sized provinces such as Auvergne (Puy-de-Dôme), Burgundy (Saône-et-Loire), and Dauphiné (Drôme, Hautes-Alpes, Isère).[4] It is noteworthy that only three of the twelve former administrative capitals in such provinces (Châlons-sur-Marne, Clermont-Ferrand, and Grenoble) faced the voters. Conflict persisted near the periphery rather than at the center of large *généralités* such as Dijon and Rennes, where towns of subordinate rank during the old regime now competed for primacy. A second category of disputes involved towns in disparate provinces or *pays* that were amalgamated into a single department: Béarn and the Basques country (Basses-Pyrénées), Chalosse and the Landes (Landes), Artois and parts of Picardy (Pas-de-Calais), Aunis and Saintonge (Charente-Inférieure), Lyonnais and Forez (Rhône-et-Loire). In all these heterogeneous departments, deputies in the National

---

[4] Other examples include Berry (Indre), Brittany (Finistère), Champagne (Ardennes, Marne, Haute-Marne), Ile-de-France (Aisne, Oise, Seine-et-Marne), Languedoc (Aude), Lorraine (Vosges), Normandy (Manche), Poitou (Deux-Sèvres), and Provence (Var).

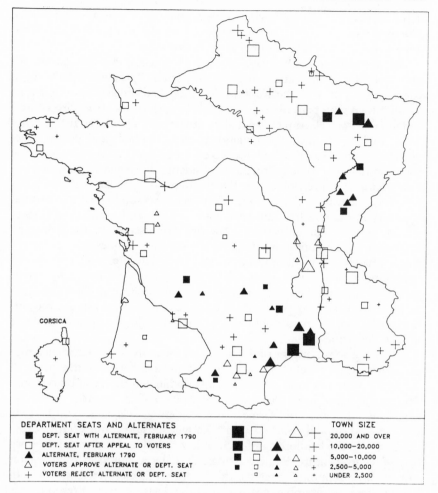

Map 7.1. Alternates and Appeals to Voters for Departmental Seats, 1790

Assembly failed to reach agreement about the location of the new capitals. Map 7.1 indicates the importance of rivalries among medium-sized towns, ranging in size from 5,000 to 20,000 inhabitants. Such towns accounted for fifty-four of the candidates for departmental seats and alternates in the summer of 1790, as compared with twenty-three smaller towns and eight larger towns. The presence of small towns among the ranks of contenders usually signified a fragmented urban network that encouraged several towns to join the competition. Such multipolar rivalries existed in sixteen departments, as compared with bipolar conflicts in twelve departments. The map also shows that alternates rarely appealed to the voters, who endorsed this compromise in only four departments.[5]

The departmental assemblies, or electoral colleges, that debated the location of capitals consisted of delegates chosen by "primary" assemblies of voters in the cantons. The National Assembly had restricted voting rights to adult men who paid the equivalent of three days' wages in direct taxes, and its two-stage electoral system prevented most of these "active citizens" from participating directly in national, departmental, and district elections.[6] Yet the Assembly had also taken precautions to ensure that rural communities would choose their own residents as delegates to the electoral colleges instead of relying on the leadership of absentee landlords and lawyers from the towns. The average department was subdivided into around eighty cantons, which meant that many bourgs and even some villages would serve as cantonal seats for the primary assemblies. Each of these small cantons, averaging only five and a half square leagues in area, elected approximately 1 percent of its active citizens as delegates, and a residential requirement excluded townspeople from becoming *électeurs* in the numerous rural cantons.[7] Despite considerable local variation in the calculation of wage levels and tax payments, a rough equality existed in the proportions of urban and rural populations represented in the electoral colleges of each department.

As for the social origins of the delegates themselves, local evidence suggests that farmers were often chosen to represent rural communities. Of course, this does not mean that peasants dominated the electoral colleges. The cost of attending an electoral college, which often lasted for more than a week, would deter poor farmers from becoming delegates. Nor did men who worked the soil possess as much knowledge and administrative experience as did the landlords and men of law found in every country bourg of eighteenth-century France. Nonetheless, large numbers of delegates from rural communities attended the departmental electoral assemblies. In the Finistère, for example, nearly half of the delegates were Breton-speaking cultivators, and in the Landes, 110 rural proprietors, plowmen, and

[5] The Aude (all the district seats), the Lot-et-Garonne (Aiguillon), the Rhône-et-Loire (all the district seats), and the Deux-Sèvres (Parthenay and Saint-Maixent).

[6] Session of Oct 22, 1789, AP 9:479. The requirement for eligibility for election to the administrative assemblies of districts and departments was payment of a higher tax, worth ten days' wages. Sessions of Oct. 29, 1789, AP 9:597; and Nov. 18, 1789, AP 10:88. These eligibility requirements, which applied to the elections held in 1790, were modified in 1791. See Jacques Godechot, *Les Institutions de la France sous la Révolution et l'Empire* (Paris, 1951), pp. 73–74.

[7] This residential requirement was specifically introduced to prevent townspeople from voting in a village where they owned property. Session of Oct. 22, 1789, AP 9:478–79; constitutional article adopted Nov. 18, 1789, AP 10:88.

cultivators served as delegates, alongside 63 "bourgeois" proprietors, 48 lawyers, 20 notaries, and 16 magistrates. It is the exclusion of artisans rather than cultivators that marked the oligarchical tendencies of electoral colleges in 1790. Only three artisans in the Landes and one artisan in the Finistère served as delegates. Equally noteworthy are the small numbers of clergymen and military officers in these electoral colleges. Rural proprietors and farmers had considerably more voting power in the electoral colleges than did nobles and priests, who made up less than 5 percent of the delegates in the Finistère and Landes. As for merchants and shopkeepers, they comprised around one-sixth of the members in these colleges, which is probably typical of their representation in most areas of the kingdom. Only a minority of these merchants were engaged in wholesale trade, and such *négociants*, like their counterparts in the National Assembly, were heavily outnumbered by men of law. In their geographical origins and occupations, most delegates to the electoral colleges were deeply involved in landed society.[8]

As a consequence, urban rivalries at the departmental level often acquired a territorial dimension that brought townspeople and rural notables into political alliances. Debates over the location of capitals produced conflicts between various districts or *pays*, as the spokesmen for each contending town appealed to delegates from the countryside. In these conflicts, the commercial role of a town usually carried less weight than its geographical location near the center or periphery of a department. For example, delegates from Soissons, a river town whose *généralité* had been dismantled to form two departments, argued in vain that their grain commerce with Paris justified administrative primacy in the department of the Aisne, despite the more central location of Laon. This argument had already provoked a controversial reply when deputies from the *bailliage* of Laon published an open letter to the *electeurs* in the department, denouncing the mayor of Paris for writing to a commissioner of the C.C., "Bear in mind, Monsieur, that Soissons furnishes Paris with a third or a quarter of all the grain necessary for its subsistence and that, consequently, our lives depend on Soissons; if I can obtain for her what I believe in any case to be a just request, the municipality of Soissons will be obligated to us in the future."[9] These deputies reported that they had countered such intrigues by accusing officials at Soissons of speculating in grain during the severe food shortages of 1789. Why had the executive commission of the province purchased grain at 290 francs per *muid* for redistribution to other towns in the *généralité*,

[8] List of *electeurs* in the minutes of the departmental electoral assembly of the Finistère, June 7–28, 1790, AN DIV bis 61:1; and printed *tableau* of the delegates chosen by primary assemblies in the Landes, AN DIV bis 6:6.

[9] Letter from Bailly, Jan. 11, 1790, published in Hennequin, *La formation de l'Aisne*, pp. 203–4.

and then sold it for 330 francs per *muid*? Why had much of this grain been shipped to Paris, when markets in the province had already been stripped clean by merchants acting on behalf of Paris, and when desperate towns and villages had been pleading with little success for a share of the reserves at Soissons? Forestalling, monopoly, corruption: these were the charges that deputies from Laon had first leveled against Soissons in the committees of the National Assembly and were now publicizing among the voters authorized to decide the issue at the neutral town of Chauny. Over six hundred delegates gathered on May 20, 1790, to hear a violent attack on the grain merchants of Soissons: "They have sucked the blood of the entire province," thundered one orator from Laon, as pandemonium broke out in the assembly. Nearly two hundred delegates from Soissons and the south of the department withdrew in protest, but an overwhelming majority of those remaining voted 411 to 37 to place the *chef-lieu* permanently at Laon. In this manner, an old judicial town that lacked any navigable waterway or grain trade wrested administrative leadership from Soissons, whose commerce with Paris seemed to harm the interests of rural populations in the central and northern districts of the department.[10]

Anxieties about the grain trade may have also discouraged support for Charleville, in the Ardennes, and Langres, in the Haute-Marne. While spokesmen for the river port of Charleville argued that their grain markets attracted farmers every week from the districts of Rethel and Vouziers, the partisans of Rethel answered that the export trade of Charleville would drain away foodstuffs from the countryside. Charleville did supply the industrial town of Sedan with grain, but its orientation toward this northern borderland of the department reduced its appeal to the southern districts. Mézières, a garrison town just across the river from Charleville, seemed less threatening to the south. At the electoral assembly of the Ardennes, delegates from Charleville, anticipating defeat, threw their support to Mézières in exchange for the district and tribunal in that area. This compromise thwarted the ambitions of both Sedan and Rethel, whose locations at the opposite ends of the department rendered any coalition against Mézières unlikely.[11]

As for the rivalry between Chaumont and Langres, here resentment over the grain trade simply accentuated the geographical advantage of Chaumont. When 250 delegates from the four northern and central districts of the Haute-Marne voted to fix the *chef-lieu* permanently at Chaumont, 43 residents from the southern districts of Langres and Bourbonne joined

[10] Printed *comte-rendu* by deputies from Laon, AN ADXVI 18; speech by M. Lebrun, in AN DIV bis 75; and Hennequin, *La formation de l'Aisne*, pp. 165–208, 344–47.

[11] Charles Gailly de Taurines, *La formation territoriale du département des Ardennes en 1789–1790* (Paris, 1933), pp. 20–23, 48–53; and documents supporting Charleville, Mézières, Rethel, and Sedan, in AN DIV bis 4:157–58.

them. Langres was the center of the grain trade with neighboring provinces, but its municipality, fearing a popular uprising, had refused to sell
flour to the nearby bourg of La Ferté-Amance in May 1790. The mayor of
this bourg had succeeded, however, in obtaining provisions from Chaumont, whose municipality had been purchasing grain on its own account
during the winter. Delegates from La Ferté-Amance and its environs broke
ranks with their historic capital of Langres in order to reward Chaumont
for its generosity.[12] Yet the fact that only 163 delegates had been chosen
from this area proved that Chaumont was bound to triumph by mobilizing
the much larger contingent of delegates from the four central and northern
districts. Indeed, a deputy from Chaumont had arranged to shift the departmental boundary northward before agreeing to refer the issue of an
alternate to the voters. Reasoning that "departments are being created for
the advantage and convenience of their inhabitants, and not at all for
towns," he inferred correctly that a majority of *électeurs* in the Haute-
Marne would vote for Chaumont because of its central location.[13]

The principle of centrality shaped the outcome of deliberations in two-
thirds of the electoral assemblies that were authorized to discuss the capitals of departments. Sometimes centrality favored a historic capital such as
Angers, in the Maine-et-Loire, where delegates from the former province
of Anjou dominated the assembly and voted 532 to 104 against an alternate with Saumur. On a smaller scale, Châteauroux parlayed its central location in the Indre into a decisive vote of 262 to 47 against an alternate
with Issoudun; and Guéret consolidated its geographical advantage over
Aubusson, in the Creuse, by gaining the unanimous support of delegates
from four out of seven districts. Châlons-sur-Marne, the old capital of the
généralité of Champagne, withstood the challenge of Reims, a much larger
and more commercial town, by a vote of 262 to 210. In the Charente-
Inférieure, where the seaport of La Rochelle was supposed to rotate the
administration with Saintes, delegates from the countryside agreed to rule
out this compromise, although they fell short of endorsing Saintes as the
permanent seat. Reims and La Rochelle typified commercial towns that
électeurs refused to support against smaller but more centrally located rivals. Involvement in long-distance trade rarely helped townspeople muster
support from rural *électeurs*, who were much more interested in locating
administrative agencies in a town that they could easily reach.[14]

The most complicated deliberations occurred in areas where a historical

---

[12] Mettrier, *La Formation de la Haute-Marne*, p. 168, n. 1; Charles Lorain, *Les subsistances
en céréales dans le district de Chaumont de 1788 à l'an V* (Chaumont, 1911), 1:92–93.

[13] Letters published by Mettrier, *La formation de la Haute-Marne*, pp. 279–86.

[14] O. Desme de Chavigny, *Histoire de Saumur pendant la Révolution* (Vannes, 1892), p. 77;
procès-verbaux, electoral assemblies of the Indre, Marne, and Charente-Inférieure, AN C 118–
119, 345, 350–52.

division existed between the various *pays* that formed a department or where several towns could claim an equal rank as administrative centers during the old regime. Regional conflicts became especially severe in the Basses-Pyrénées and the Finistère, where urban ambitions were superimposed on linguistic and cultural differences. Deputies from the Basses-Pyrénées had not even been able to agree on a town where the *électeurs* would deliberate on the location of the first administrative assembly. The Basques had proposed Saint-Palais, but the Béarnais had convinced the C.C. to recommend Navarrenx, which happened to be in the center of the department. Presumably, neither Pau nor Bayonne, at opposite ends of the department, was acceptable to a majority of the deputation. Yet many citizens of Pau were determined to make their presence felt at Navarrenx. With a population of nine hundred active citizens, Pau was entitled to only nine delegates, but its national guard accompanied this deputation to Navarrenx at the beginning of August 1790. Arriving fully armed, these patriotic troops found the gates of Navarrenx closed by a hostile municipality. After this inauspicious show of force, the *électeurs* of Pau tried to strike a bargain with Bayonne, offering this seaport an alternate if the first session of administration were held at Pau. Such a compromise was anathema to delegates from the Basques country, who threw their votes to Navarrenx, which also gained the support of many delegates from the Béarnais districts of Oloron and Orthez. Partisans of an alternate argued in vain that this would be the best means of fashioning "a truly French people" by "merging the customs, habits, and languages of the Béarnais and the Basques." Their opponents replied that a permanent capital equidistant from the heartlands of these two peoples would better accomplish such a purpose. As for the fact that Navarrenx had fewer than 1,500 inhabitants, its defenders replied that the wealth and commerce of a town was a good reason *not* to place a capital there. After a lengthy debate on August 12, 1790, three-fifths of the delegates voted for Navarrenx. Anticipating this outcome, which a twelve-man commission of delegates had recommended, 148 *électeurs* from the district of Pau had refused to vote, so the count was actually 290 for Navarrenx and 38 for an alternate.[15]

Yet this victory proved short-lived. The mayor of Pau departed for Paris to inform the National Assembly of the "unpatriotic sentiments" of Navarrenx and of "irregularities" that should invalidate the vote of the electoral assembly.[16] On October 4, 1790, Gossin took sides with Pau in the name of the C.C. Ridiculing the pretensions of Navarrenx, a tiny fortress that

---

[15] Session of Feb. 17, 1790, AP 11:621; *mémoire* for Navarreins, AN DIV bis 29:418; printed *Rapport des douze commissaires à l'assemblée électorale des Basses-Pyrénées* (Pau, 1790).

[16] Letter of Aug. 28, 1790, DIV bis 14:258 (Basses-Pyrénées).

lacked even a post office, a stagecoach service, or a printing press, Gossin denounced the political culture of small towns:

> It is not in such localities that administrative assemblies should be placed, or rather exiled. Not without great inconveniences can these assemblies be isolated from the sight of other men, who can stimulate their ambition or supervise their zeal for a difficult career. To remove administrators from great theaters of action is to expose them to discouragement, boredom, and abuses of authority. There is no public opinion in small towns, or, if it exists, it is petty just like its center; it shrinks intelligence and enlightenment, it destroys patriotism and courage.

By contrast, the town of Pau, with a population that Gossin very generously estimated at 15,000–18,000, possessed "a crowd of public buildings and establishments" on the eve of the Revolution, including a *parlement*, a *cour des aides*, a *chambre des comptes*, a *cour des monnaies*, a university, and a seminary. Its citizens had renounced all their fiscal privileges, rallied the estates of Béarn around the cause of the National Assembly, and formed a national guard in the cradle of Henry IV. How could the National Assembly agree to place the capital of the Basses-Pyrénées in Navarrenx instead of Pau? Gossin insisted that the will of 290 *électeurs* must not triumph over the will of reason. As for the argument from centrality, he pointed out that Pau had a more central location in its department than did several towns that the National Assembly had already chosen as capitals of other departments. Two deputies followed Gossin to the podium in an effort to defend Navarrenx, but they overlooked the vital point that a majority of *électeurs* had chosen this town as a compromise between the interests of the rural populations in the Basques *pays* and Béarn. In any case, for a National Assembly dominated by deputies from towns, Gossin's image of urban primacy proved irresistible, and Pau gained the coveted decree that made it the capital of the Basses-Pyrénées.[17]

Territorial rivalries shaped debate over the capital of the Finistère, too. The northern and southern districts of this department were isolated from each other by mountainous terrain, and the rural economies and urban networks of each area differed appreciably. The north had a reputation for greater wealth, based on the fertility of its soil, the industry of its inhabitants, and the importance of its towns. The great naval port of Brest stimulated the economy of this area with its demand for foodstuffs and naval provisions. So did the commercial port of Morlaix, whose merchants financed a thriving cottage industry in the countryside and exported large quantities of linen cloth to Spain. As for the southern districts, here large stretches of wasteland left an impression of poverty and underdevelop-

---

[17] AP 19:430; and defense of Pau in the year IV, with details about Gossin's report, AN ADXVI 59.

ment, although parts of the diocese of Quimper, known as the *pays* of Cornouaille, were close to the sea and densely populated. As the chief town of this region, Quimper took pride in its lawcourts rather than its commerce, which seemed negligible in comparison with that of either Brest or Morlaix. None of these towns was near the department's center, where the town of Carhaix, the only settlement of any importance, numbered fewer than 2,000 inhabitants. Under these circumstances, the issue of choosing a capital split the deputation of the Finistère along regional lines.[18] Deputies from Brest, unable to muster any support from their colleagues for a department of Brest, rallied to the nearby town of Landerneau, which stockpiled supplies for the navy in time of war. Landernau, which had the advantage of a more central location than either Brest or Morlaix had, therefore became the main rival of Quimper. Although a majority of the Breton deputation, impressed by the superior judicial rank of Quimper during the old regime, tried to fix the *chef-lieu* of lower Brittany permanently in this town, the National Assembly followed the conciliatory advice of the C.C. and referred the controversy to the first electoral assembly of the Finistère.[19]

Delegates from Brest and Landernau led the north against Quimper when this assembly gathered on June 26, 1790. With its larger population and fiscal resources, the north had more *électeurs* than the south had, and after two days of debate, the assembly voted 251 to 219 against making Quimper the permanent seat of the department. But in a third day of debate, the majority failed to choose another capital and decided instead to refer the dispute back to the National Assembly.[20] This surprising stalemate expressed the devious policy of delegates from the district of Carhaix, whose notables had already drafted two memorials requesting a department. Now they calculated that the National Assembly would favor Carhaix because of its location midway between the northern and southern coasts. Delegates from Morlaix, their own appetites whetted by the defeat of Quimper, seem to have abandoned Landernau, too.[21] The main effect of such intrigue was to strengthen the position of Quimper, whose partisans convinced the National Assembly to overrule Gossin when he proposed, in the name of the C.C., to transfer the *chef-lieu* to Landernau. Members of the clerical party, who sympathized with the old bishopric of Quimper, allied themselves with lawyers who suspected the ambition of

---

[18] On these geographical contrasts, see printed *Observations* for Quimper, AN DIV bis 62:1; and *procès-verbal* of an assembly held by delegates from the northern districts on Oct. 3, 1790, AN DIV bis 23:353 (Finistère).

[19] Session of Jan. 22, 1790, reported in *Journal des Etats-Généraux* 8:11.

[20] *Procès-verbal* of the departmental electoral assembly, June 7–28, 1790, AN DIV bis 62:1.

[21] Documents from Carhaix in AN DIV bis 23:352 and 36:577 (Finistère). On the ambivalent role of delegates from Morlaix, see an unsigned note for the C.C., in AN DIV bis 62:1.

the naval port of Brest. In the words of Abbé Béradier, a deputy from Paris who challenged the Committee's advice, "If Quimper loses the *chef-lieu*, you would be pronouncing its total ruin." Thus, the right wing of the National Assembly embraced, if only for a moment, the egalitarian principle of spreading the benefits of the Revolution to poor as well as rich towns. With other deputies clamoring for an amendment in favor of Quimper, the National Assembly voted on August 20, 1790, to make this town the permanent capital of the Finistère.[22]

In several departments, a profusion of urban ambitions compounded the problems of historical and geographical disunity. For example, threats of violence, intrigues, boycotts, and confusion characterized deliberations in the electoral assembly of the Deux-Sèvres, where regional antagonisms intersected with conflicting plans to rotate the *chef-lieu* or fix it in a single town. To the southwest, Niort dominated a *pays* of fertile plains, while to the north, the market town of Parthenay boasted of its role as the capital of Gâtinais, a *pays* of hedgerows and cattle farms. Between Niort and Parthenay stood Saint-Maixent, an old Protestant town that retained only remnants of the woolen industry that used to flourish in this area of Poitou. *Electeurs* from each of these towns pursued a different tactic when debate began on June 23, 1790. Parthenay, which enjoyed the advantage of perfect centrality in the department, opposed an alternate in the hope of becoming the permanent seat; Saint-Maixent, fearing this ambition, voted for the alternate; and Niort, resting on the right of possession, abstained. That night, however, delegates from the districts of Parthenay and Saint-Maixent joined forces with those from the district of Thouars, in the northeastern corner of the department. They agreed to eliminate Niort from the alternate and divide the spoils among themselves: Parthenay and Saint-Maixent would rotate the administration, unless one of them obtained the departmental lawcourt instead; Thouars would get the bishopric; and Niort would be left with the college, poor consolation for a town of more than 12,000 inhabitants.[23]

Needless to say, the partisans of Niort reacted angrily when their compatriots from the north sprang this plot on them the next day. Townspeople gathered in the streets to protest—*electeurs* from the district of Parthenay later heightened the drama by describing a barricade of old barrels, stacked on rotting planks, that miraculously prevented the demonstrators from bursting into the assembly room. Partisans of Niort had great difficulty speaking amidst the tumult, and they refused to vote when their adversaries pushed through the motions that had been secretly prepared. Further disputes broke out over the wording of the assembly's minutes, which

[22] Session of Aug. 20, 1790, AP 18:172–73.
[23] Merle, *La formation des Deux-Sèvres*, pp. 89–109.

were never ratified, and *électeurs* from Niort withdrew to draft a protest at the town hall. When delegates from the districts of Parthenay and Thouars gathered a few weeks later to elect their district administrators, they countered with complaints about the "horrible ruckus" that had greeted every effort to deliberate about issues that seemed "contrary to the local interests of Niort." *Electeurs* from the district of Thouars added, "We were viewed with an evil eye by most of the citizens [of Niort]." Only "fear of disorder" had prevented them from voting to transfer the departmental seat immediately to another town.[24]

These tumultuous scenes, which probably involved countrymen who had never visited Niort before in their lives, were all for naught. Under the influence of a deputy from Niort, the C.C. had rewritten its original decree on the Deux-Sèvres to authorize the first *administrative* assembly, not the first electoral assembly, to deliberate on an alternate. Yet the *électeurs* from Parthenay had obtained seven positions on this administrative assembly to only five for Niort, and they mustered a majority of eighteen votes to fix the *chef-lieu* permanently at Parthenay. This success was incomplete, however, because their alliance with Saint-Maixent had broken down, and six administrators voted for this town instead of Parthenay, along with eight who favored Niort and three who abstained. This rupture, which followed a decision of the National Assembly to place the bishopric of the department at Saint-Maixent, was all the more serious because this town had two deputies in the National Assembly, while Parthenay had none. Meanwhile, special deputies from Niort hurried to Paris, where they protested the vote of the administrative assembly and drew an invidious comparison between the large population, excellent communications, and commercial vigor of their own town, and the small size, isolation, and unproductive soil of Parthenay. They added prophetically that Niort also had a national guard of 1,800 men "to help impose respect for the laws." While the northern districts of the department would be swept into the counterrevolutionary uprising of the Vendée, Niort did, in fact, become an outpost of Republican defense. Of course, the National Assembly could not have anticipated this future when it decided on September 16, 1790, that Niort would become the permanent capital of the Deux-Sèvres.[25]

The presence of several competing towns produced similar intrigue in the Var, where voters failed to decide whether to rotate the departmental directory. An earlier decree of the National Assembly had already autho-

[24] Printed *mémoire* for Niort, AN DIV bis 74:2; *arrêté* of the district electoral assembly of Parthenay, and *procès-verbal* of the district electoral assembly of Thouars, AN DIV bis 31:438 (Deux-Sèvres).

[25] *Note* in AN DIV bis 31:436 (Deux-Sèvres); letter from M. Chabot, DIV bis 17:288 (Deux-Sèvres); Printed *mémoire* for Niort, DIV bis 74:2; Merle, *La formation des Deux-Sèvres*, p. 187; AP 19:20–21.

rized the rotation of administrative assemblies among all the district seats in this department, following a precedent suggested by deputies from Dauphiné.[26] The rotation of the directory, which would execute policy while the assembly was not in session, raised the issue of administrative continuity in its most acute form. Spokesmen for Toulon, a naval port of 26,000 inhabitants that expended more government revenues in a year than the interior of Provence collected in a decade, argued that rotation would violate contemporary customs, deter older men from serving as officials, increase administrative costs, and risk the loss of precious documents. As a large town of the "second rank," Toulon had all the facilities required for the directory, including private bankers to facilitate the transfer of tax funds from the districts. An administration in this seaport could also supervise the grain trade, regulate the collection of customs dues, and assist the provisioning of the navy. Its industrious population had "none of the passions of small towns, nor the cold indifference of excessively large cities."[27] But Toulon was in the southwestern corner of the department, far from the northeastern district of Grasse, whose delegates argued strenuously in favor of an alternate. Grasse boasted of a population of 12,000, which made it the second-largest town of the Var, and its royal *sénéchaussée*, *viguerie*, and bishopric had been just as important as the comparable establishments of Toulon during the old regime. The ambitions of Grasse conflicted, however, not only with those of Toulon but also with those of Brignoles and Draguignan, smaller towns of the interior that used to possess *sénéchaussées* and *vigueries*, too. Draguignan was located near the geometrical center of the department, but Brignoles was closer to the most densely populated area around Toulon. While delegates from Draguignan used the argument of centrality to seek the provisional headquarters of the department, leaving open the question of permanency or rotation, delegates from Brignoles joined with Toulon in voting against the alternate, but only so they could claim the permanent seat for themselves. The contradictory tactics of these several towns resulted in a stalemate, and after three days of debate in July 1790, a plurality of delegates voted to refer the matter back to the National Assembly.[28]

This dispute gave the C.C. an opportunity to take a firm position on the question of alternates. The idea of rotating administrative assemblies had originally been conceived as a political expedient, designed to reconcile the ambitions of towns whose deputies were opposing any realistic plan of division into departments. By granting electoral assemblies the right to discuss such concessions, some deputies anticipated that a majority of del-

---

[26] Decrees of Feb. 3 and 10, 1790, AP 11:420, 540.

[27] Printed *mémoire* and manuscript *précis* for Toulon, AN ADXVI 78.

[28] *Mémoire* for Grasse, AN DIV bis 31:442 (Var); and *délibération* of the departmental electoral assembly, July 17–20, 1790, AN DIV bis 18:292 (Var).

egates would vote to end them. Although this did not always happen, the C.C. tried to avoid any extension of the practice of alternates, on the grounds that it reduced the efficiency and increased the cost of administration. For example, it ignored a vote in the electoral assembly of the Aude to imitate the neighboring department of the Hérault by rotating the *chef-lieu* among all the district seats; and it took no action on a vote in the electoral assembly of the Tarn to rotate administrative sessions between Castres, Albi, and Lavaur every two years instead of every four.[29] After the departments had been formed in February 1790, the C.C. submitted only one decree that sanctioned an alternate—between Beauvais and Compiègne, in the Oise. By September, when it addressed the case of Toulon, it had adopted the policy of favoring permanent capitals, even in the face of opposition from the voters.[30] Gossin embraced the entire argument of special deputies from Toulon in condemning alternates: "The Comité de Constitution has adopted the principle of fixing the seat of administration, and this principle must triumph over all the considerations that have been raised against it." This issue settled, he proceeded to defend Toulon, whose naval installations protected the entire Mediterranean coast of France, as the largest, most commercial, and most enlightened town in the Var. A deputy from Grasse took the podium to argue prophetically that the directory should not be placed in a naval port exposed to foreign attack, but the National Assembly ratified Gossin's proposal, making Toulon the capital of the Var.[31]

As the National Assembly drew to a close in September 1791, Gossin moved to eliminate all the alternates that had been decreed back in 1790. This "conciliatory expedient," he insisted, "is not only a deformity that you need to erase; it is a real evil that you must redress. . . . What is more ridiculous and burdensome than such gyrating administrations, which require the movement of papers and clerks from town to town, the multiplication of buildings to receive them, and the doubling of their costs of operation?" In the old regime, it might have been tolerable to rotate the meeting places of provincial estates, but the new constitution had established a hierarchy of institutions that brought all points of the empire under the direct supervision of administrators. With directories and assemblies in every district,

[29] *Délibération* protesting the vote in the Aude, AN DIV bis 58:5; Emile Appolis, *La rivalité administrative entre Castres et Albi, 1789–1823* (Albi, 1938), p. 31.

[30] Decree of May 21, 1790, on the Oise, when the C.C. rejected a vote in the departmental electoral assembly to locate the *chef-lieu* permanently at the smaller but more centrally located town of Clermont, AP 15:632; and AN DIV bis 86:4. In the session of July 28, 1790, the C.C. advised against this compromise in the Pas-de-Calais, where voters had sided with the small town of Aire against Arras. Robespierre was among the deputies from this town who helped persuade the National Assembly to overrule the *électeurs* and make his hometown the *chef-lieu*. *Journal des Etats-Généraux* 14:61–62; and AP 17:387.

[31] Session of Sept. 4, 1790, AP 18:558–59.

it had become useless and even shocking to move the superior level of administration around from place to place. Gossin himself had helped arrange an alternate between his hometown of Bar-le-Duc and Saint-Mihiel, but now he declared that he had always fought against this "defective institution." Elections were about to be held to replace half the members of the departmental assemblies, so alternates would soon be implemented unless the National Assembly acted promptly. The moment was all the more propitious because the deputies would not have to respond to the inevitable petitions from disgruntled townspeople. In just a few weeks they would hand over power to a new Legislative Assembly. Gossin proposed that the departmental assemblies and directories be fixed in the towns where the directories now resided. Any changes would have to be made by subsequent legislatures. His draft of a decree, which had been discussed in committee for over four months, passed without any debate on the floor of the Assembly. It seemed to mark the triumph of administrative rationality over the special interests of all the towns that were awaiting their turn to become *chef-lieux*.[32]

Yet deputies from the department of the Cantal had persuaded Gossin to slip an extra clause into his decree, authorizing the town of Aurillac to exercise the *alternat* before a subsequent legislature decided whether to leave it there or return it to the town of Saint-Flour. Other deputies had tried to gain the same exemption, but Gossin explained the following day that this special clause did *not* apply to any other departments.[33] Townspeople from Saint-Flour naturally complained bitterly about their fate, and the abolition of alternates revived disputes between rival towns in nearly all the departments where this compromise had originally been approved. In the Haute-Saône, the towns of Vesoul and Gray had already been quarreling over their alternate, and anonymous pamphleteers had denounced the grain merchants of Gray for forestalling, speculation, and usury. Also in Franche-Comté, petitioners at Dôle had reacted sharply at earlier news that the C.C. was planning to abolish alternates: "Are the principles of equality and justice that have dictated rotation of the *chef-lieu* among all the principal towns of the Jura going to be abandoned? Will we see, as in the old regime, proud towns monopolize all the favors?" On September 6, 1791, just before alternates were abolished, an electoral assembly in the Lot-et-Garonne had voted to transfer the next session of the departmental council to the small town of Aiguillon, whose central location made it a more convenient meeting place than the provisional capital of Agen.[34] These incidents foreshadowed more serious challenges to the existing cap-

---

[32] Gossin's *rapport* and subsequent decree, Sept. 11, 1791, AP 30:559.

[33] Article 4 of the decree of Sept. 11, 1791, and session of Sept. 12, 1791, AP 30:563–64.

[34] Girardot, *Le département de la Haute-Saône* 1:176–81; *pétition* from Dôle, June 1790, AN DIV bis 9:213 (Jura); printed *exposé* and *pétition* for Aiguillon, Dec. 1791, DIV bis 66:3.

itals in several of the departments where alternates had originally been established: Marvéjols tried to displace Mende, in the Lozère; Lunéville nearly obtained the directory of the Meurthe from Nancy; Dôle and Lons-le-Saulnier fought for control of the Jura; Saint-Etienne, Montbrison, and Roanne seceded from the Rhône-et-Loire; and Albi triumphed over Castres in the Tarn. Unresolved conflicts also erupted in several departments where the National Assembly had chosen a permanent capital in 1790: Marseille invaded Aix and seized the departmental administration of the Bouches-du-Rhône; Langres tried to do the same against Chaumont, in the Haute-Marne; Landernau wrested temporary control of the Finistère away from Quimper; Oloron came close to victory over Pau, in the Basses-Pyrénées; Saint-Lô replaced Coutances in the Manche; and first Grasse, then Brignoles, and finally Draguignan supplanted Toulon as the capital of the Var. The decrees of 1790–91 proved to be less definitive than the National Assembly had hoped.

It would be misleading, however, to attribute these administrative changes to the will of the voters, or even to the lobbying efforts of townspeople. From 1792 onward, revolutionaries and counterrevolutionaries battled for supremacy throughout the nation. Their intense struggles widened the context of urban rivalries and increased the arbitrary power of the national government over local institutions. Representatives on mission from the Convention revoked elected officials and appointed temporary commissions in departments that resisted the Convention, and they punished several federalist capitals by transferring departmental administration to other towns. After Robespierre fell from power, towns victimized by the Montagnards tried to recoup their losses by denouncing erstwhile capitals of patriotism as centers of terrorism. Counterrevolutionary excesses brought a new round of complaints about murder gangs that made towns such as Castres and Lons-le-Saulnier unfit to serve as departmental capitals. Gradually, however, political rhetoric subsided during the Directory, as rival towns competed for civil lawcourts and central schools as well as for administrative institutions. The ideological combat of the Jacobin phase of the Revolution gave way to older expressions of urban pride and self-interest, although the theme of egalitarianism continued to influence debate over the division of establishments among contending towns.

The rhetoric of denunciation became a fundamental aspect of urban rivalries after the civil constituton of the clergy provoked an open split between patriots and counterrevolutionaries. This ideological transformation can be illustrated in the case of the town of Pamiers, whose municipality had not mentioned political issues at all in 1791 when it first requested the transfer of the capital of the Ariège from Foix. A year later, 135 citizens of Pamiers signed a petition that denounced the directory at Foix for "constantly favoring the refractory priests and aristocrats of Pamiers, even to the point of lighting the fires of civil war against the patriots of this town." Having intervened in municipal elections to protect fanatical priests, the Directory was now spreading false rumors that Pamiers was a haunt of brigands where public security was endangered and where, as a consequence, any public establishments would be compromised. Such charges would obviously jeopardize the continuing efforts of Pamiers to obtain the departmental administration, which helps explain why the patriots began their petition by attacking the Directory, whose officials, they added, were all from Foix. Only after this denunciation did they repeat the geographical arguments that their municipality had deployed against Foix the previous year.[35]

The first protest that led to the transfer of a departmental seat occurred in the town of Mende, where an electoral assembly was convoked on February 26, 1792, to choose a new bishop. Many of the delegates refused to take an oath supporting the new constitutional organization of the clergy, and the national guard of Mende joined with rioters to expel troops of the regular army who were trying to restore order. At word of this counter-revolutionary uprising, the Legislative Assembly decided to transfer the administration of the Lozère to Marvéjols, whose Protestants had been rivals of the Catholics at Mende since the sixteenth century. Following threats against the judges on the criminal tribunal of the department, who were responsible for investigating murders committed during the uprising, this lawcourt was also transferred to Marvéjols.[36] A more extensive revolt in May 1793, organized by royalist bands in the countryside of Lozère, captured Marvéjols as well as Mende, and Republican officials took refuge in the district town of Florac. The insurrection proved short-lived, however, as troops from neighboring departments arrived to drive the rebels back into the mountains. The restoration of Republican authorities raised the issue of the seat of administration anew, and a *commissaire* from Saint-Flour proposed a dramatic change that would eliminate the Lozère altogether. His goal was to attach enough territory to the eastern districts of Cantal so his hometown could form its own department. If Saint-Flour could not dominate the western districts around Aurillac, let the Cantal and the Lozère be amalgamated into two departments along the mountain range that separated Aurillac from Saint-Flour. This plan came to naught because Châteauneuf-de-Randon, formerly a deputy from the *sénéchaussée* of Mende and now a representative on mission for the Convention, restored the administration of the Lozère to its former capital. Yet the townspeople of Saint-Flour rallied support from all the primary assemblies of

[35] *Pétition*, Mar. 1792, DIV bis 58:3. On the factional rivalries behind this denunciation, see Arnaud, *La Révolution dans le département de l'Ariège*, pp. 191–214, 255–85.

[36] Abbé P. J. B. Delon, *La Révolution en Lozère* (Mende, 1922), pp. 179–239.

voters in their district and petitioned the Convention to emancipate their area from the control of Aurillac. "To try to unite what nature has divided," they insisted, "would be to attack the natural and imprescriptible rights of man." Instead, Châteauneuf-de-Randon treated the townspeople of Saint-Flour themselves as counterrevolutionaries, and Aurillac retained the *chef-lieu* of the Cantal.[37]

The overthrow of the monarchy on August 10, 1792, precipitated a regional bid for power on the part of Marseille, whose national guard had already demonstrated its will to dominate the rival town of Aix-en-Provence earlier in the year. On February 26, a detachment of eight hundred guardsmen from Marseille had entered Aix to disarm a garrison of "counterrevolutionary" Swiss guards, and its leaders would have brought the administration of the Bouches-du-Rhône back to Marseille if the members of the directory had not gone into hiding. On August 22, sparked by rumors that patriots from the town of Manosque had been captured by counterrevolutionaries at Aix, another force of eight hundred guardsmen from Marseille hastened to the rescue. Invading the town hall and prison of Aix, they killed a gendarme and a soldier, and they forced the directory and criminal court of the department to return with them to Marseille. That evening, the administrative council of the Bouches-du-Rhône, dominated by partisans of Marseille, voted to sanction this violent transfer of authority. Its public proclamation praised "the burning patriotism of the citizens of Marseille" and accused Aix of lacking sufficient military force to oppose a "Saint Bartholomew's massacre."[38] This reference to the religious wars presaged a violent denouement to the factional conflict in lower Provence. Indeed, the Jacobin Club of Marseille, which reigned supreme for several months in the winter of 1792–93, succumbed in the spring of 1793 to a federalist uprising in the city. The federalists themselves were crushed by the Convention, whose representatives on mission imposed a reign of terror on Marseille.[39] Throughout this succession of events, the departmental administration, buffeted about by Jacobins, Federalists, and Montagnards alike, remained at Marseille. With the triumph of the Thermidorians, however, 550 members of the "regenerated popular society" of Aix moved to restore their town's rightful rank as capital of the department. They denounced Marseille for having seized "by terror and force of arms" the administration and lawcourt of the department, and they commented ironi-

[37] Ibid., pp. 339–44; *procès-verbal* of the authorities at Saint-Flour, July 28, 1793, AN DIV bis 108:1; printed *pétition* from Saint-Flour, year III, AN ADXVI 27.

[38] Michael L. Kennedy, *The Jacobin Club of Marseille, 1790–1794* (Ithaca, 1973), pp. 99–101; Alexandre Arizzoli, *Le chef-lieu du département des Bouches-du-Rhône* (Aix-en-Provence, 1901), pp. 20–37; *arrêté* of the departmental council, AN DIV bis 59:4.

[39] Kennedy, *The Jacobin Club of Marseille*, pp. 119–48; William Scott, *Terror and Repression in Revolutionary Marseille* (New York, 1973), pp. 71–164.

cally that the Marseillais, having thrown themselves into a "revolutionary career," had pursued federalism and counterrevolution with equal impetuosity. But now that these times of calamity and terror were over, Aix deserved the return of its establishments. Fearful of a revival of Jacobinism at Marseille, the Thermidorian Convention granted this request on January 27, 1795.[40]

On the very same day that national guardsmen from Marseille burst into Aix, patriots at Langres launched a similar expedition against Chaumont, only this one became a comedy of errors. Langres and Chaumont, true to their long-standing rivalry, had taken opposing sides of the political conflict that raged throughout the nation in the summer of 1792. While a large and active society for the defense of the constitution at Langres had been affiliated with the Jacobins in Paris since February 1791, an analogous society at Chaumont, only recently founded, lacked popular support and did nothing for the Jacobin cause. The directory of the Haute-Marne at Chaumont, expressing the moderation of this town, tried in July 1792 to suppress the Jacobins of Langres. These patriots replied by denouncing the directory for distributing royalist propaganda, and they were overjoyed to learn on August 22 that the new Republican government in Paris had suspended this bastion of reaction. Around three hundred men resolved to seize the departmental administration by force and bring it back to Langres. Armed with two cannon and commanded by officers of the national guard, they set off during the night. A visiting townsman from Chaumont who had witnessed their preparations raced ahead to alert his compatriots, and when the men of Langres arrived in battle order, they found a detachment of the army garrison guarding the gates and the national guard of Chaumont deployed on the town square. The mayor of Chaumont, who had taken these precautions, permitted the Langrois to enter the city and state their mission. The sight of troops and guardsmen had tempered the ardor of these militants, and they now averred that they had come only to assist in the suspension of the directory. Their suddenly modest goal had already been fulfilled by the mayor of Chaumont, who read them the order that he had issued to that effect. It remained for the men of Langres to return home again, where they were greeted by an unsympathetic mayor, who had warned them not to depart. A hundred years later, a local saying still existed at Langres that whenever anyone did something foolish, "he has returned from the campaign of Chaumont."[41]

At the height of the federalist crisis in 1793, several departmental capitals were transferred by representatives on mission, operating with the ar-

---

[40] Arizzoli, *Chef-lieu*, pp. 39–47; *pétition* from Aix, 15 brumaire, year III, AN DIV bis 82:1.

[41] Mettrier, *Formation de la Haute-Marne*, pp. 170–74.

mies of the Republic in zones of civil war. The fate of Lyon was exemplary. To isolate the city in preparation for a military siege, the agents of the Convention resolved to cut the administrative links between Lyon and its department, the Rhône-et-Loire. This was all the more necessary because armed bands from Lyon were operating in the industrial town of Saint-Etienne, where their heavy-handed methods of dissolving popular societies, searching private homes for weapons, and requisitioning grain provoked strong popular opposition. A similar foray into Montbrison gained some support among the landlords and magistrates of this conservative town, but it also triggered resistance farther to the north, where the little town of Fuers welcomed district officials who were in flight from Montbrison. On August 12, four representatives on mission in the area decreed that the districts of Saint-Etienne, Montbrison, and Roanne would become a separate department of the Loire, with its administrative seat at Feurs.[42] Most of this area had formed the province of Forez during the old regime, and its secession from Lyon fulfilled old ambitions as well as the immediate needs of revolutionary warfare. Yet ironically, the notables of Montbrison, who had led the unsuccessful campaign of Forez to constitute a separate department back in 1790, were not the initial beneficiaries of the new administration. According to Javogues, the Montagnard representative who used terror to organize the new department, "Since the beginning of the Revolution, the royalists in the town of Montbrison have constantly oppressed the countryside." In a grandiose edict issued on October 29, 1793, he commanded that the fortifications of the town be razed and a column erected with the following inscription: "The town of Montbrisé [broken mountain] made war on liberty; it no longer exists."[43] All the constituted authorities of Montbrison were suppressed, and its district seat and tribunal were transferred to the little town of Boen, whose inhabitants, the "sans-culottes" directory later boasted, "have always marched with a firm and ardent pace on the road of the Revolution."[44]

Not to be left behind, Montbrison founded its own popular society, which petitioned the Paris Jacobin Club in November 1793 to help return the district seat to a town that was now composed "only of true sansculottes."[45] This confession of militancy led nowhere, but six months later, after Javogues had been recalled to Paris in disgrace, new representatives on mission agreed to transfer the district to Montbrison, whose "moderates" were back in power. A year later, the political atmosphere began to

[42] E. Brossard, *Histoire du département de la Loire pendant la Révolution française* (Paris, 1904) 2:100–63; *arrêté* in AN DIV bis 84:3.

[43] *Arrêté* of Oct. 29, 1793, cited by Brossard *Histoire de la Loire* 2:237–41.

[44] *Délibération* of 12 prairal, year II, AN DIV bis 72:2.

[45] Letter from the correspondence committee of the Paris Jacobin Club to the Convention, 23 frimaire, year II, AN DIV bis 84:3.

favor the deeper ambitions of the Montbrionnais, who had never forgotten that their town used to be the capital of the province of Forez. With the Convention in the hands of anti-Jacobins and with local officials turning a blind eye to royalist murder gangs, the municipality of Montbrison decided on May 30, 1795, to denounce the town of Feurs for its role in the Terror and to ask the representative on mission at Lyon to transfer the departmental seat to Montbrison. Yet the fate of the new department had not been settled in the Convention, where deputies from Lyon were arguing that their own department of the Rhône, reduced to only two districts, was excessively small for such an important city. Indeed, they nearly persuaded the Commission des Onze, a committee of eleven members of the Convention, which drafted a new constitution for the Republic in August 1795, to restore the Rhône-et-Loire. At this critical moment, the town of Saint-Etienne, which had supported Lyon back in 1790, intervened to oppose the "insatiable needs" of this large city. Lyon had allegedly misused its electoral power to dominate the earlier departmental administration for its own advantage. Now Saint-Etienne posed its own candidacy for the *chef-lieu* of the Loire, based on its large population, extensive commerce, and important armaments works. The pride of industrialists echoed in the petition that district administrators at Saint-Etienne sent to the Convention: "If the government protects the industry of Saint-Etienne, as the interests of the Republic demand, the population of this city will soon exceed 100,000. . . . With so many local advantages, will we continue to remain the shameful tributaries of England and Germany? . . . No! No! . . . The government will make our commune the Birmingham of France."[46] Such grandiose ambitions carried less weight in Paris than an edict that officials at Montbrison secured from the departmental directory at Feurs, supporting Montbrison rather than Saint-Etienne as the permanent seat of the Loire. This document gave decisive weight to deputies from the department who convinced the Commission des Onze to preserve the department, with its *chef-lieu* at Montbrison.[47]

Riots and civil wars in western France also introduced a political dimension to urban rivalries over the capitals of departments. In April 1793, a Republican society at Lorient denounced the pusillaminity of officials in the town of Vannes, where the directory of the Morbihan had failed to take decisive action against rebellious peasants. The national guard of Lorient, by contrast, had sprung to the defense of the Republic: "Already our batallions have carried death and terror to the hordes of brigands that fanaticism and aristocracy had assembled." The Convention should order ad-

---

[46] Letter of 6 thermidor, year III, AN DIV bis 65:3.
[47] Broussard, *Histoire de la Loire* 2:360–64, 433–36; letters and petitions in AN DIV bis 65:2.

ministrative sessions to be held inside the walls of Lorient, which sheltered the purest and most constant patriotism.[48]

In November 1793, another outpost of Republicanism in the west, the town of Les Sables-d'Olonne, mounted a similar attack against Fontenay-le-Compte, the capital of the Vendée. Like Lorient, Les Sables was a seaport that had fought against rebels from the countryside. But its special deputies to the Convention described a longer history of administrative neglect and political subversion in the Vendée. Because Fontenay-le-Compte was located on the extreme southern edge of the department, none of the patriots in the districts of Les Sables and Challans could afford to serve in the departmental administration, whose posts all fell into the hands of men from Fontenay. These officials refused to fund any public-works projects for roads, bridges, and canals in the north, and they ignored the pleas of local administrators for troops to suppress the first riots that broke out in the districts of Challans and Les Sables. According to petitioners from Les Sables, "For over two years, these districts constantly requested military force to control all their parishes, and they would have succeeded with several hundred men, dispersed at various points. But the department turned a deaf ear to them; its political principles were not in harmony with those of its districts. This is the source of our misfortune, and the reason why the blood of our patriots has everywhere been spilled." Furthermore, Fontenay put up no resistance when it came under direct attack, despite its garrison of 6,000–7,000 troops. By contrast, Les Sables resisted two sieges by large armies of brigands. Located midway between the northern and southern borders of the department, this seaport claimed the support of over eighty municipalities. As for La Roche-sur-Yon, another contender for the *chef-lieu*, its centrality was purely artificial. According to the emissaries from Les Sables, this *bourgade* of at most 150 households was completely inaccessible for much of the year.[49]

Trusting in the judgment of its representatives on mission in the west, who used Vannes and Fontenay as military bases in hostile territory, the Convention paid no attention to the petitions of Lorient and Les Sables. In the Finistère, however, army commanders seconded the efforts of civilians in the northern districts to triumph over the southern capital of Quimper. The city of Brest had never forgiven Quimper for using its influence in the National Assembly to capture the *chef-lieu* despite the negative vote of the electoral assembly in 1790. "This is not the first time that the blacks, the ultrablacks, the fanatics of the Assembly have been our enemies," municipal officials at Brest had written angrily on August 25, 1790, to their

[48] Letter of Apr. 3, 1793, AN DIV bis 85:13.

[49] Two *mémoires* and a *précis* by special deputies from Les Sables-d'Olonne, 12 and 25 frimaire, year II, AN DIV bis 91:4. In fact, La Roche-sur-Yon had important cattle fairs, despite its small size.

deputies in the National Assembly. "We should have expected defeat, because the enemies of the public welfare wanted to place the capital in a locality where they would encounter less resistance and more followers."[50] In the fall of 1792, when new primary assemblies and departmental electoral assemblies were convoked, municipal officials at Brest renewed their opposition to Quimper and organized petitioning campaigns in favor of Landernau. To buttress their case, they approached civilian functionaries and army officers in the city, who agreed to write personal letters in support of Landernau, which was much closer than Quimper to their base of operations. General Conclaux, the highest-ranking military officer at Brest, even presented their arguments to three representatives on mission in February 1793. Another departmental electoral assembly held that month split along regional lines, but Quimper mustered nearly as much support from five southern districts as Brest and Landernau did from four northern districts. It was the federalist revolts in the summer of 1793 that finally precipitated action in Paris. A decree of August 19, 1793, motivated by the federalist sympathies of the departmental administration at Quimper, replaced this elected body with a provisional commission at Landernau.[51]

But this was not the end of the matter. Quimper had its functionaries, just like Brest, and it also had its Jacobins. More important still, it had four deputies in the Convention, who used the letters and petitions that townspeople forwarded to reverse the earlier decision. From the clerks and receivers of the stamp tax came complaints about the living costs at Landernau: "It is notorious that proximity to Brest makes vital necessities so rare and difficult at Landernau that no *pensions* at all can be found." According to twenty clerks, employees, commissioners, and functionaries attached to the departmental administration, so many soldiers and naval agents were crowding into town that no office space could be found. The president of the popular society at Quimper forwarded a memorial in defense of the town's loyalty and patriotism, and the municipality, the district directory, the committee of surveillance, and the criminal court of the department all joined their voices to an address from this society that boasted, "Not a single city in the department of Finistère took a position against federalism sooner than Quimper." Copies of old petitions from four district directories and seven municipalities were refurbished and sent to the Convention, along with a printed reply to the machinations of delegates from the four northern districts in February 1793. Armed with all these documents, the deputies from the southern districts of the Finistère secured a new decree that transferred the provisional administration back to Quimper. This unleashed a new round of petitions from popular societies in the northern

---

[50] Letter on Aug. 25, 1790, in Delourmel and Esquieu, *Brest pendant la Révolution*, p. 190.
[51] See the petitions and correspondence in AN DIV bis 62:1.

towns and bourgs, but it was obviously impossible to satisfy both regions. Administrative continuity triumphed, as Quimper again became the capital of the department.[52]

Religious rivalries and social conflicts help explain why a similar regional division in the Tarn had a more lasting impact on the administrative organization of this department after the Terror. Castres and Albi, the two main contenders for the *chef-lieu* of the Tarn, differed not only in their regional bases of support but in their religious and economic history. Castres was a flourishing textile town with a Protestant elite of merchants during the eighteenth century. Albi was a Catholic town with a landed elite that shunned industry. At the beginning of the Revolution, deputies from Castres boasted of their commerce and cautioned the National Assembly that local Protestants, who had been expelled from office after the revocation of the Edict of Nantes, would continue to be excluded from civil employment unless Castres obtained the departmental seat: "They would not dare move to a town where there have never been any Protestants, and where fanaticism still preserves much energy."[53] Events later in the Revolution confirmed the patriotism of Protestants at Castres, but the town itself changed dramatically from a Montagnard stronghold during the Terror to a refuge for counterrevolutionaries after Thermidor. The presence of a Catholic majority of textile workers does much to explain this dramatic shift in political loyalties at Castres, whose royalists took over the national guard, dominated the electorate, and launched a White Terror against local Republicans during the year 1797. On September 17, the *commissaire* who represented the central government in the Tarn fled for his life to Albi, followed by twenty-seven Republican notables whose relatives and friends had been massacred by royalist bands. The army was deployed to occupy Castres, but the *commissaire*, aided by townspeople at Albi who had already circulated petitions for the *chef-lieu* throughout the northern cantons of the department, now urged the government to transfer the seat of administration permanently to Albi. In a lobbying campaign that emphasized the counterrevolutionary tendencies of Castres, deputies from the region of Albi convinced the legislative assemblies to grant this request. No representatives from Castres were present to defend their town, and the law of 27 brumaire in the year VI (November 17, 1797) made Albi the capital of the Tarn.[54]

The coup of 18 fructidor (September 4, 1797), which tried to halt the drift toward royalism in the legislature, sparked a similar campaign against

---

[52] Letters from government clerks, 15 and 30 fructidor, year II; *adresse* from Quimper, 21–22 fructidor, year II; and other petitions and correspondence, all in AN DIV bis 62:1.

[53] *Observations* for Castres, AN ADIV bis 1:10.

[54] *Rapport* by Ysabeau to the Conseil des Anciens, 27 brumaire, year 6, AN ADXVI 77; and Appolis, *La rivalité administrative*, pp. 33–53.

Lons-le-Saulnier, in the Jura. Petitioners from Dôle denounced this departmental seat as "a den of cyclops whose walls and pavements are still stained with the blood of innocent Republicans." Lons-le-Saulnier owed its violent reputation to a federalist uprising in 1793, followed by a bloody Thermidorian reaction against the Jacobin Terror. According to Republicans at Dôle, over thirty heads of family were murdered in the streets of Lons-le-Saulnier and at least fifty families were forced to flee "this town of cannibals" in the months before the coup of fructidor.[55] Back in 1793, a representative on mission had even transferred the administration and lawcourt of the department to Dôle, but after Thermidor, the Convention had restored Lons-le-Saulnier as the *chef-lieu*, following news that Dôle had become a haven for terrorists. The antiroyalist context of fructidor seemed to promise yet another shift in the administrative geography of the Jura.[56] This time, however, administrative continuity counted for more than did ideological conformity. The *rapporteur* for a special commission of the Council of Five Hundred, appointed to investigate the controversy over the capital of the Jura, argued that changes in the location of administration were always costly, disruptive, and harmful to *administrés*. Stability was the supreme value now. Concessions to one town would only inspire new demands elsewhere: "Woe to transitory legislation that inspires hope for every ambition and every system."[57]

Indeed, experience proved that changes in the location of departmental capitals rarely settled controversies among rival towns. In the year IV, the Commission des Onze that reorganized the administrative and judicial system of the Republic tried to conciliate the rival claims of Nancy and Lunéville to leadership in the department of the Meurthe by placing the directory at Nancy and the civil and tribunal lawcourts at Lunéville. Deputies from Nancy immediately protested this decision, so the Convention agreed to place the lawcourts at Nancy and the directory at Lunéville! This compromise aroused even more opposition from Nancy, which finally gained all the departmental establishments.[58] Similar controversy greeted decisions to share establishments in other departments as well. Coutances mounted an extensive petitioning campaign to obtain the directory as well as the lawcourts of the Manche after the Commission des Onze decided to transfer the departmental seat to Saint-Lô; special deputies from Pau besieged the legislative assemblies after regular deputies from Oloron persuaded the Commission des Onze to locate the directory in their town;

---

[55] Printed *Pétition* by 516 Republicans at Dôle, undated [year VI], AN ADXVI 43; Jean Brelot and Gustave Duhem, *Histoire de Lons-le-Saulnier* (Lons-Le-Saulnier, 1957), pp. 241–56.

[56] Brelot and Duhem, *Histoire de Lons-le-Saulnier*, pp. 241–56.

[57] Printed *rapport* by Rous, deputy from the Aveyron, 4 germinal, year VI, AN ADXVI 43.

[58] See the pamphlets from Nancy and Lunéville in AN ADXVI 50–51.

and special deputies from Clermont-Ferrand protested the decision of the Convention to locate the civil and criminal courts of the Puy-de-Dôme at Riom.[59] Following the abolition of district directories and lawcourts in 1795, some towns complained that they no longer possessed any important establishments, while others coveted a monopoly of departmental institutions. Under these circumstances, the legislative assemblies of the Directory tried to preserve the status quo, which varied from one department to another. In eight departments, they upheld the location of directories and lawcourts in rival towns; in another dozen departments, they turned down requests to share such establishments; and in only four departments—the Meurthe, Basses-Pyrénées, Tarn, and Var—did they pass laws to transfer these departmental establishments from one town to another.[60] The contradictory claims of rival towns, the complexity of legislative procedures, and, above all, the search for administrative stability explain why nearly all the departmental capitals of 1791 remained the seats of departments under the Directory.

The Constitution of the Year VIII, which laid the foundations for the Napoleonic empire, strengthened the departmental framework of administration by establishing prefectures in each department.[61] Like the intendancies of the old regime, these prefectures defined the most important administrative towns in the empire, which numbered 130 departmental seats at the height of Napoleon's military power on the European continent. Within the borders of prerevolutionary France, however, Napoleon created only one new department—the Tarn-et-Garonne—and transferred five departmental seats. These changes did elevate the administrative rank of several commercial towns in response to the recommendations of prefects, the lobbying efforts of townspeople, and the political calculations of Napoleon himself. In 1800, the prefect of the Bouches-du-Rhône insisted on residing at Marseille, where he would earn a higher salary than at Aix-en-Provence, and deputies from Marseille persuaded the first consul, who already suspected Aix of royalist sympathies, to transfer the *chef-lieu* permanently to their town.[62] Napoleon's subsequent decisions to elevate the administrative rank of Lille (1803), Montauban (1808), and La Rochelle (1810) followed triumphal visits to these former intendancies, whose notables contrasted the disastrous impact of the Revolution with the flourish-

[59] A. Lebaindre, *La formation du département de la Manche* (Caen, 1911), pp. 158–67; pamphlets for Oleron and Pau in AN ADXVI 59; and Mège, *Formation du Puy-de-Dôme*, pp. 198–206.

[60] Tabulations based on pamphlets by *rapporteurs* for legislative commissions during the Directory, in AN ADXVI 19–81.

[61] Jean Bourdon, *La Constitution de l'an VIII* (Rodez, 1941), pp. 85–117.

[62] Arizzoli, *Chef-lieu*, pp. 43–47.

ing condition of their commerce and trade during the old regime.[63] The emperor found it easy to agree that administrative power would restore the fortune of these important towns. At the conclusion of a splendid reception offered by the municipality of Montauban on July 29, 1808, he declared:

> I am satisfied with the love for me that my faithful subjects in my *bonne ville* of Montauban have expressed. I have seen with sorrow the losses that this town has suffered. I will restore it to its rights; you can regard it as the seat of a department, and I will raise it to the rank of the principal towns in my empire.[64]

In moving the capital of the Vendée from Fontenay-le-Compte to La Roche-sur-Yon in 1804, Napoleon expressed similar confidence in the power of the state to foster urban growth. Here the army as well as the administration would transform La Roche-sur-Yon into the strategic center of a department whose rebellious peasants seemed beyond the reach of troops at Fontenay.[65] Finally, Napoleon patronized his hometown of Ajaccio, which became the exclusive capital of the island of Corsica in 1811.[66] Thus, the few modifications that he made in the departmental system of the Directory were designed less to locate prefectures in the most dynamic centers of commerce than to reward loyal towns with the favors of the state.

The Restoration Monarchy inherited eighty-six departments from the empire, whose capitals remained unchanged despite petitions from a dozen towns that claimed a more central location, a more prosperous economy, or a more fervent royalism than their rivals. Although nearly all the prefects of Napoleon were replaced after his brief return to power in 1815, their successors inherited control over a variety of administrative agencies that would be costly to transfer to other towns. Furthermore, Louis XVIII relied on his ministers to decide such questions, and ministerial procedures for changing the location of capitals became time-consuming and inconclusive, as prefects had to consult with departmental councils and munici-

---

[63] On the efforts of La Rochelle, Lille, and Montauban to obtain prefectures, see the correspondence in AN F2 I:498–501.

[64] Cited in Daniel Ligou, ed., *Histoire de Montauban* (Toulouse, 1984), p. 247.

[65] Decree of 5 prairial, year XII (May 27, 1804), AN F2 I 502. On the failure of Napoleon's grandiose objectives at "Napoleon-Vendée," as the new capital of the Vendée was called during the empire, see John Merriman, *The Margins of City Life: Explorations on the French Urban Frontier, 1815–1851* (New York, 1991), pp. 101–12.

[66] Corsica had been subdivided into two departments in 1793, but Napoleon's decree of Apr. 24, 1811, suppressed the department of Golo, with its prefecture at Bastia, and transferred the appellate court of Corsica from Bastia to Ajaccio. Bastia regained the appellate court at the beginning of the Restoration Monarchy, but the prefecture remained at Ajaccio. Antoine Albitreccia, *La formation du département de la Corse de 1801 à 1811* (Paris, 1938), pp. 1–16.

palities. These consultations proved that any change in administrative geography would foster discontent. As the prefect of the Saône-et-Loire reported, if Mâcon lost the prefecture, it would turn against the government.[67] Finally, the decision to transfer one departmental seat would revive ambitions elsewhere in the kingdom. Towns that had fallen from departmental rank during the Revolution, such as Castres and Toulon, would naturally attempt to acquire prefectures, and so would towns that had tried and failed to become departmental seats back in 1790, such as Reims and Soissons. If some ambitions proved temporary, others were only dormant, and each change of regime—1800, 1814, even 1830—would awaken the same old arguments about centrality, commerce, and administration.[68] Discrepancies continued to exist between the administrative rank and the commercial importance of some towns in the departmental system invented during the Revolution and preserved by Napoleon, but demands for the transfer of prefectures threatened to disrupt urban interests and bureaucratic routines that became increasingly sacrosanct with the passage of time. Even the process of industrialization in nineteenth-century France brought only one change in the network of prefectures, as Saint-Etienne became the capital of the Loire in 1855. Territorial acquisitions during the Second Empire added the prefectures of Nice, Annecy, and Chambéry, while losses in the Franco-Prussian war removed Colmar, Metz, and Strasbourg. Yet on the eve of World War I, eighty-two prefectures remained unchanged from the First Empire. Administrative continuity had triumphed over the urban rivalries that marked the period of the French Revolution.[69]

[67] Letter from prefect to minister of the interior, Sept. 25, 1814, AN F2 I 501.

[68] For petitions and administrative correspondance concerning requests for changes in the location of prefectures between 1800 and 1832, involving seventeen departments, see the dossiers in AN F2 I:496–502.

[69] Mirot, *Manuel de géographie historique* 2:417–34.

Chapter 8

THE STRUGGLE FOR DISTRICTS AND TRIBUNALS

D ISTRICTS rather than departments shaped the rivalries of the great majority of towns that competed for establishments at the beginning of the Revolution. Not only would the districts be much more numerous than the departments, their administrative boundaries would also define the jurisdictions of new lawcourts that the C.C. intended to create for civil litigation. This combination of administrative and judicial powers brought more than 1,100 towns and bourgs into contention for district seats. Despite the principle of *rapprochement*, which expressed the fragmentation of space and the density of institutional networks in the old regime, only a minority of contending towns were likely to succeed. Even the original plan of Sièyes called for only 720 districts, and after the National Assembly agreed to vary from 3 to 9 the number of districts in each department, its committees approved only 544 districts. This average of 6.5 districts per department conceals considerable variety: at one extreme, 25 departments were subdivided into 8 or 9 districts, while at the other extreme, 17 departments obtained fewer than 6 districts. Institutional traditions, urban ambitions, and political alliances explain much of this variation. Once towns were assigned to a district, a new round of competition began over district tribunals. The National Assembly sparked such rivalries by authorizing the sharing of establishments in some of its decrees on the division of departments. Such proposals for *partage* usually encountered resistance, however, from district seats that wanted to profit from a lawcourt as well as from an administrative directory. They also inspired other towns to request tribunals. During the spring and summer of 1790, more than 200 towns competed with around 170 district seats for the lawcourts that the National Assembly finally distributed in its decree of August 26, 1790. Local pride and contempt for outsiders intensified many of these disputes. Townspeople not only boasted of their own advantages, which might range from commercial prosperity to abundant markets, plentiful supplies, respectable lodgings, and well-educated elites. They also drew invidious comparisons with neighboring towns and bourgs, which supposedly languished in poverty and isolation or suffered from inferior establishments and a shortage of magistrates and lawyers. Debates about the sharing of districts and tribunals highlighted the economic foundations of urban influence over the countryside and the sociocultural preconditions of rank and power within the apparatus of the state.

When the National Assembly abandoned the idea of dividing every department into nine districts, it opened the way for an arbitrary policy of allocating districts in accordance with conflicting principles of political ideology and administrative rationality. On the one hand, some deputies embraced the principle of *rapprochement* and affirmed the egalitarian goal of spreading the benefits of the Revolution to small towns and the countryside. As a deputy from the Lot-et-Garonne explained, a plan for only four districts would discriminate against the townspeople and rural populations in the uplands of this department, where roads to the main towns of the lowlands were impassable for two-thirds of the year. Communities in these relatively isolated areas would lack adequate representation in the departmental assembly, and they would fail to get the new roads that they needed: "The four privileged towns . . . would hold the rest of the department under their empire and would deprive them of all hope of participating in the general regeneration that is the object of the decrees of the National Assembly." Similarly, in the Bouches-du-Rhône, a deputy invoked egalitarian ideals to defend a division into nine districts, which favored the interests of the countryside against an "aristocracy" of large towns that wanted districts only for themselves. If this department were subdivided into only five districts, "the spirit of the old regime would still subjugate us. The big fish would continue to eat the little ones, and small towns would remain the prey of large towns."[1]

On the other hand, many deputies began to question the egalitarian principle of *rapprochement*, especially after Dupont de Nemours gave a speech to the Assembly on January 27, 1790, that criticized the proliferation of districts. The fewer these administrative jurisdictions, the lower the costs of administration and justice and the greater the range of choice for the new officials and magistrates. Dupont calculated that if nine districts were created per department, each of them would contain, on average, around 36,000 inhabitants, of whom 540 would be needed to serve as municipal councillors, justices of the peace, officials on the directories, and magistrates on the tribunals. Such a ratio of around seventeen adult males for each official seemed much too low. "How can this be sufficient in a society where most men have too little leisure, education, or independence to become officials?" In a printed version of his speech, Dupont added that small jurisdictions would multiply the number of solicitors while reducing their clientele.

This was the disadvantage of seigneurial justices and very small royal *bailliages*, which had been multiplied to excess in some provinces for shameful fiscal rea-

[1] *Observations* by Renaut, deputy from Agen, AN DIV bis 10:225 (Lot-et-Garonne); and *mémoire* by Durand de Maillane, deputy from Saint-Rémy, AN DIV bis 20:324 (Bouches-du-Rhône).

sons. It is this unfortunate necessity to live off small jurisdictions that has made the country lawyers so disreputable in a large part of the kingdom: many doctors, many illnesses; many solicitors, many lawsuits.

Thus, the public interest required large districts that reduced administrative costs and increased the pool of talent and experience. Dupont did concede that districts might be as small as 36 square leagues in mountainous areas, where transport costs provided a real obstacle to administrative and judicial services. Nonetheless, he insisted that in the plains, where good roads linked villages to the major towns, districts should have an average size of 108 square leagues. He recommended a policy of increasing the size of districts where conditions of transport were favorable and reducing the size of districts only where communications were difficult.[2]

But the reasoning of Dupont de Nemours overlooked the relationship between conditions of transport, economic growth, and cultural development. His utilitarian principle of minimizing the cost and maximizing the quality of administration implied that the lower the tax base and the smaller the pool of qualified recruits, the greater the disadvantages of small districts. Yet regional variations in fiscal revenues and population densities were positively correlated with the density of transport networks. Relatively isolated areas of the kingdom, such as the Massif Central, had less fertile soils, lower agricultural revenues, and fewer educated townspeople than did areas covered with navigable waterways and all-weather roads, such as the Ile-de-France and upper Normandy. From the point of view of public finance and administrative recruitment, departments in the impoverished highlands should have the *smallest* number of districts and tribunals, while those in the fertile lowlands should have the *largest* number of such establishments. If the inhabitants of relatively isolated areas suffered from high transport costs, they would also have more difficulty paying the taxes and supplying the talent necessary for public administration. By contrast, the urban economy imparted more dynamism to the countryside in areas that had access to regional trade and long-distance commerce. Small towns in these areas also tended to have more vigorous markets and more cultivated elites than did their counterparts in the highlands. Here districts could be multiplied without harming the public interest, which many deputies equated in any case with the needs of their hometowns. As a subcommittee of deputies from the Seine-et-Oise pointed out, a large number of towns, all meriting "respect and consideration," were requesting new establishments in this rich and densely populated department near Paris. Here tax revenues were so large that the administrative costs of nine districts would not even be noticeable. Furthermore, litigants would be

---

[2] *Observations* by Dupont de Nemours, published at the end of Jan. 1790, reprinted in AP 11:606–9.

obliged to travel more often to the district seats now that all the seigneurial courts had been abolished. To save time and expense, they wanted small districts that would strengthen their relationship to nearby towns.[3]

Thus, Dupont de Nemour's arguments for economy could be turned against plans for large districts in the plains and small districts in the mountains. While deputies from the Seine-et-Marne followed his advice and formed only five districts, their colleagues from the Seine-et-Oise persisted in their plan for nine. With similar inconsistency, deputies from the mountainous department of the Haute-Loire created only three districts, while those from the equally small and isolated department of the Lozère established seven. In the nation as a whole, the C.C. made no effort to impose one pattern of division in the lowlands and another in the highlands. Among the seventeen departments that the National Assembly agreed to subdivide into fewer than six districts, nine were in the mountains of the Alps, the Pyrénées, and the Massif Central, but another six were in the fertile plains along the Mediterannean coast, the valleys of the Rhône and the Rhine, and the Paris basin. As for the twenty-four departments that its decrees subdivided into eight or nine districts, these ranged from the mountains of the Massif Central, the Vosges, and the Jura, to the Mediterannean coast, the valleys of the Garonne and the Loire, and the plains of Artois and Flanders. Striking contrasts existed in the distribution of districts within adjacent departments that shared similar geographical characteristics. Thus, four were created in the Hérault and eight in the Gard; five in the Somme and nine in the Oise; three in the Cantal and nine in the Aveyron.

Systematic analysis of departmental variations in the size of districts does reveal a correlation between relatively small districts and relatively high population densities and per capita levels of direct taxes.[4] As Dupont de Nemours himself complained, deputies tended to ignore his reasoning. This can also be seen in the fact that variations in the density of roads and navigable waterways were not correlated with the size of districts after controlling for population densities and per capita taxation.[5] Furthermore, departments themselves varied considerably in size, which encouraged deputies to multiply or restrict the number of districts. At one extreme, the

[3] *Rapport*, Jan. 26, 1790, AN DIV bis 17:280 (Seine-et-Oise).

[4] These two variables are both negatively correlated with the size of districts and together explain 15 percent of the variance in a regression equation ($R = .44$ and adjusted R square $= .15$). For the population size, amount of direct taxes, and area of each department, I have used a table published by Prudhomme, *Dictionnaire géographique*, vol. 1, appendix.

[5] In a regression equation with departmental measures of population densities and per capita direct taxes, a transport index of departmental transport networks in the early nineteenth century, developed by Bernard Lepetit, has a partial correlation with the average size of districts per department of only $-.05$, which is not statistically significant. For the index, see Lepetit, *Chemins de terre et voies d'eaux*, table 6, p. 92.

Hautes-Alpes contained only 251 square leagues and 120,000 inhabitants, while at the other extreme, the Gironde had 537 square leagues and 500,000 inhabitants. It is scarcely surprising that deputies formed only three districts in the Hautes-Alpes, as compared with seven districts in the Gironde. A regression analysis of the number of districts on variables that measure the area, population, and tax yields of departments yields a multiple correlation coefficient of .52. Yet this statistical correlation can only explain around 25 percent of the variance in the number of districts per department.[6] Obviously, other factors had a preponderant influence on the subdivision of departments into districts.

Foremost among these other influences were the institutional heritage of the old regime and the conflicting pressures of townspeople to multiply or restrict the number of districts. The extraordinary variety of jurisdictions that distinguished one province from another helps explain why deputies approached the division with contrasting ideas about administrative geography. Although departmental committees were responsible for recommending district seats to the C.C., several provincial deputations favored a fixed number of districts in each of the departments that they formed. Such uniformity expressed general views about the existing jurisdictions throughout a province. For example, the Breton deputation approved an egalitarian solution to the extreme contrasts in size and the overlapping jurisdictions of the dioceses and royal *sénéchaussées* in their province. They agreed to form nine districts in each department, which made room for some important seigneurial towns that possessed neither bishoprics nor royal lawcourts in the old regime. A division of Brittany into a total of forty-five districts also seemed a happy medium between the twenty-five royal *sénéchaussées* and the sixty subdelegations that existed in this province on the eve of the Revolution. The provincial committee of Lorraine and the Trois Evéchés (Metz, Toul, and Verdun) also opted for nine districts per department, but here they followed the precedent of the numerous *bailliages* that had been created in these provinces back in 1751. By contrast, deputies from Normandy favored a sixfold subdivision, based primarily on the medium-sized *élections* that already provided a rational basis for fiscal administration in the *généralités* of Caen and Alençon. Even the departmental committee for the Eure, which contained nine *élections* and nine royal *bailliages*, insisted on following the example of their colleagues in the Calvados, where the six *élections* became the framework for only six districts. Deputies from Franche-Comté also chose a sixfold subdivision for each department in their province, although here they had in mind the twelve *bailliage* towns that wanted to preserve their jurisdictions in the Doubs and the Jura. Finally, deputies from Alsace adopted a tripar-

---

[6] *R* square in this equation is .27, but adjusted *R* square is only .24.

tite division based on the six districts that the provincial assembly of this province had created in 1787. They assigned three districts to the Haut-Rhin and three to the Bas-Rhin, to which they added a fourth district for Strasbourg.[7]

In like manner, some of the departmental committees followed particular institutional traditions that help explain variations in the number of districts. Deputies from the Var used the framework of *vigueries* in order to form nine districts, while their counterparts in the Basses-Alpes rejected the *vigueries* in favor of their five *sénéchaussées*, whose capitals each acquired a district. The committee for the Rhône-et-Loire favored the five former seats of *élections* in their large and densely populated department, and the committee for the Marne transformed their six *élections* into so many districts. In Languedoc, where dioceses had served as fiscal jurisdictions during the old regime, deputies from the Tarn formed five districts by adding one extra district to their four dioceses, while deputies from the Hérault partitioned one of their five dioceses in order to create four districts. These kinds of subdivisions or amalgamations of existing jurisdictions became an easy means of accommodating or excluding rival towns. In the Ain, deputies subdivided the *élection* and *bailliage* of Belley after spokesmen for Nantua and Saint-Rambert insisted on their own districts; while in the Côte-d'Or, several small *bailliages* were suppressed in favor of the towns of Dijon, Saint-Jean-de-Losne, Semur, and Arnay-le-Duc. Indeed, the precise boundaries of earlier jurisdictions played a much less important role in the deliberations of deputies than the location of the towns that wanted new establishments. Departmental committees did not trace the limits of districts until after the National Assembly ratified their decisions on how many districts to create. Towns rather than territories usually fixed their attention as they chose the number of districts. In many departments, they had to mediate between the claims of towns that possessed different types of jurisdictions, and whether they opted for continuity or change in the seats of districts as compared with earlier institutions, urban ambitions were often at stake.

The basic pattern of rivalry over the subdivision of departments involved conflicts between relatively important towns that wanted extensive jurisdictions and lesser towns that sought districts for themselves. Foremost among the advocates of large districts were frustrated contenders for departmental seats, such as Mayenne and Saumur. Special deputies from the town of Mayenne, unable to displace Laval as *chef-lieu*, strenuously opposed a plan for seven districts in the department of Mayenne. A division into only three districts, they argued, would reduce administrative costs by

---

[7] These generalizations and those in the following paragraph are based primarily on a comparison of the previous jurisdictions with the districts formed in these various departments.

half and guarantee more qualified officials and magistrates. But special deputies from the little town of Lassay accused Mayenne of trying to dominate "all the neighboring towns and parishes and even the entire department." A regular deputy from Mayenne admitted that it was "impossible to support a division that would give the district of Mayenne alone at least 130–140 parishes, many a long distance away." Deputies from Laval had already conceded districts to other small towns, whose examples undermined the opposition of Mayenne to Lassay.[8] A similar structure of contention took place in the Maine-et-Loire, where deputies from Saumur sought a large district as compensation for their failure to transform the *pays* of Saumurois into a separate department. They complained in vain that a plan for eight districts, favored by deputies from Angers and several smaller towns, would reduce their own *bailliage* of 206 parishes to a district of only 66 parishes.[9]

More successful demands for large districts came from Brioude and Béziers, whose deputies tried at first to obtain their own departments and then shifted tactics in order to swallow up the jurisdictions of smaller towns. Brioude had its eyes on the royal *prévôté* of Langeac, whose municipality unwisely relied on deputies from other towns to defend its interests in the National Assembly.[10] When Le Puy offered to include Brioude in its department, both towns reached an agreement to cede part of the *pays* of Langeac to the Puy-de-Dôme and attach the rest to the district of Brioude. A fifteen-year-old girl from Langeac, ardent in defense of her homeland, protested bitterly that Brioude and Le Puy "were profiting from the spoils of others who have been blindly sacrificed." Langeac failed to obtain a district only because of "the secret machinations [*travail souterrain*] of Brioude, which wanted to be at the head of a large district."[11] Of course, the quid pro quo of this intrigue was an even larger jurisdiction for Le Puy, whose district ended up with 45 percent of the inhabitants in the entire department.[12]

In the Hérault, Béziers negotiated a similar deal with Montpellier, whose municipality had taken the initiative in proposing a plan of division into only four districts. This plan hinged on the partition of the diocese of Agde, whose municipal officials learned much to their chagrin that a deputy from Pézénas was trying to incorporate them into a district for *his*

---

[8] Printed *mémoires* for Mayenne and *adresse* for Lassay, AN DV bis 10:234 (Mayenne); letter from Maupetit, in "Lettres de Maupetit," p. 185.

[9] *Réflexions* by deputies from Saumur, AN DIV bis 26:388.

[10] Mun. Delib. Langeac, AN DIV bis 26:380 (Haute-Loire).

[11] Letter from Jeanne du Rival, "enfant de 15 ans," Feb. 7, 1790, AN DIV bis 9:222.

[12] For the population size of districts, based on the census of the year II, see the table in M. J. Guillaume, ed., *Procès-vervaux du Comité d'instruction publique à la Convention Nationale* (Paris, 1904), 5:672.

hometown. The quarrel between Agde and Pézénas opened the way for Béziers to claim the entire diocese, whose wealthy vineyards and numerous inhabitants would counterbalance the large population of Montpellier and its environs. By conceding the port of Cette to Montpellier, deputies from Béziers consolidated their claim over the rest of the diocese. Among the ten other towns in the department that requested districts, only the bishoprics of Lodève and Saint-Pons succeeded, but they had to settle for much smaller districts, which together contained fewer inhabitants than the district of Béziers alone.[13]

Opposing the political alliances of towns that wanted large districts were coalitions of other deputies and special deputies who favored small districts. In the Puy-de-Dôme, where eight towns had spokesmen on the departmental committee, a majority voted on January 26 for eight districts despite the opposition of Riom, which sought a fivefold division. The minority returned to the charge at a second meeting, called after Dupont de Nemours's speech impressed the National Assembly with the disadvantages of so many districts. Here spokesmen for Billom and Besse defended their districts against the partisans of Riom while deputies from Clermont-Ferrand remained on the sidelines. But when the C.C. decided to recommend only five districts, Gaultier de Biauzat, the most influential deputy from Clermont-Ferrand, intervened to persuade its *rapporteur* to endorse the original plan. Gaultier feared the enmity of the deputy from Billom, who had supported Clermont-Ferrand in all its previous disputes with Riom over the departmental seat.[14]

In the Cher, Sallé de Chou, a deputy from Bourges, had to make similar concessions to small towns. Having approved a plan for eight districts, he developed second thoughts at news that the C.C. intended these same districts to serve as judicial circumscriptions. Eight new tribunals would "bastardize the holiest of institutions" in a department that used to have only five *bailliages*, four of which had little business. But Sallé de Chou admitted to his constituents at Bourges that a division into five districts would arouse "great resistance on the part of the other towns, which all have an interest in obtaining a public establishment." Confronted by eleven candidates for districts, he settled for seven districts and then offered tribunals to another three towns that would share establishments with their district seats. This compromise still left the district of Bourges with over 50,000 inhabitants, as compared with fewer than 25,000 inhabitants in most of the other districts, whose capitals had possessed even smaller jurisdictions during the old regime.[15]

---

[13] Documents from Agde and Béziers, AN DIV bis 8:206 (Hérault); and *Observations* for Montpellier, reprinted by D'Aigrefeuille, *Histoire de la ville de Montpellier* 4:678.

[14] Mège, *Formation du département du Puy-de-Dôme*, pp. 115–18.

[15] Letter from Sallé de Chou reprinted in M. D. Mater, "Formation du département du

But some deputies invoked cogent arguments against little towns and bourgs that wanted new establishments. Thomas Lindet, who played a key role in forming the department of the Eure, pointed out that fourteen different towns wanted a district or a tribunal in this department. To heed all of these requests, "we would have multiplied to infinity officials and men of law at the very moment when it is necessary to simplify financial and judicial administration." Despite the advantage of bringing justice closer to the people, tribunals needed to attract enough lawsuits to justify their existence. The suppression of feudal dues and tithes, along with procedural reforms in the law, would reduce the number of trials in the future. Furthermore, numerous justices of the peace would settle many disputes before they reached the district courts. "It would be absurd to lavish the taxes of the people on useless tribunals." Lindet and his colleagues drafted a plan for only six districts, in only one of which the tribunal and the district seat would be located in different towns. Five former *bailliages* were among the victims of this plan, but the *rapporteur* of the C.C. dismissed their protests: "All the additional subdivisions are being sought only by small towns that are too close to each other, and that are only concerned about their own interests."[16]

The pressure for districts certainly became excessive in many departments. In the Haute-Garonne, where the municipality of Toulouse had roused many somnolent bourgs in its campaign for a large department, a total of twenty-seven communities petitioned the National Assembly for a district and another eleven asked for a royal lawcourt. At least twenty towns and bourgs also entered bids for districts in the Ardèche, Dordogne, Gard, Gers, Loiret, Puy-de-Dôme, Rhône-et-Loire, Seine-et-Oise, Var, and Yonne, and at least ten localities did so in another sixty-one departments. Regardless of how many districts the deputies on a departmental committee agreed to form, they always faced additional demands. Generally speaking, the smaller the number of districts, the higher the ratio of disappointed contenders, but even ninefold divisions could not satisfy everyone. Indeed, the location of district seats in little towns and bourgs inspired envious neighbors to challenge such good fortune. The more the districts, the more the complaints that the wrong town had gained the ear of deputies in the National Assembly. Many intense rivalries involved obscure localities that found themselves competing for establishments in the same little district. Other conflicts erupted when a vigorous market town or even a seaport searched in vain for its name on the list of districts. Some deputies tried to calm such rivalries by permitting the division, or *partage*,

Cher," *Mémoires de la Société historique, littéraire, et scientifique du Cher*, 4th ser., 14 (1899): 175–76; Bruneau, *Les débuts de la Révolution*, pp. 124–25.

[16] Letter from Lindet reprinted in Montier, *Correspondance de Thomas Lindet*, p. 42; session of Feb. 1, 1790, AP 11:408.

of establishments between two towns. As mentioned in chapter 5, decrees on the formation of departments stipulated such arrangements in thirty-three districts. However, the wording of these decrees was sometimes ambiguous, and only thirteen of the district seats involved in such compromises accepted their fate. A majority insisted on obtaining the tribunal as well. Furthermore, the example of *partage* in a few districts inspired many more towns to request equal treatment vis-à-vis rivals who had triumphed in the contest for district seats. The most vociferous of these towns persuaded the C.C. to refer their claims to the voters, who were asked to mediate disputes in twenty-six districts. But many towns submitted demands for *partage* after the departments were formed, including fifty towns that had not even requested districts. Lawcourts seemed more advantageous to many townspeople than directories, and the location of tribunals generated passionate debate in the provinces as well as protracted lobbying in Paris.

By August 1790, a total of 375 towns and bourgs in 168 districts were competing for tribunals.[17] Map 8.1 shows that neighboring towns were locked in such disputes throughout the nation. Claims and counterclaims spread to at least one district in seventy-four departments, and to three or four districts in twenty-six departments. Towns in every kind of geographical region were involved, although more rivals were concentrated in the Massif Central than in the mountains of eastern France. This pattern reflects the greater density of little towns in the former region, where seigneurial as well as royal courts attracted men of law during the old regime. The map also displays the relative size of contending towns, which varied from a few large towns of over 10,000 inhabitants to many small towns and bourgs of fewer than 2,500 inhabitants. In general, towns of more than 10,000 inhabitants exercised enough regional influence during the old regime to secure a district and a tribunal without challenge from lesser towns. Only a handful of large seaports and industrial towns had to struggle for recognition as judicial centers.

Table 8.1, which analyzes more precisely the relationship between the size of towns and their involvement in district rivalries, shows that 85 percent of the towns that disputed the sharing of establishments (row 3) had fewer than 5,000 inhabitants. However, three-quarters of the smallest towns requested a royal court or a district between August 1789 and January 1790 and then dropped out of the struggle instead of insisting on *partage* (480 cases in rows 1 and 2). Over half of the communities that contained a central agglomeration of 1,250–2,500 inhabitants also resigned themselves to a cantonal seat and a justice of the peace. Nonetheless,

---

[17] This tabulation includes 26 towns, located in 13 districts, that ceased in Feb. 1790 to protest departmental decrees that assigned one of them the tribunal and the other the district. In all the other cases of *partage*, protest continued into the spring and summer of 1790.

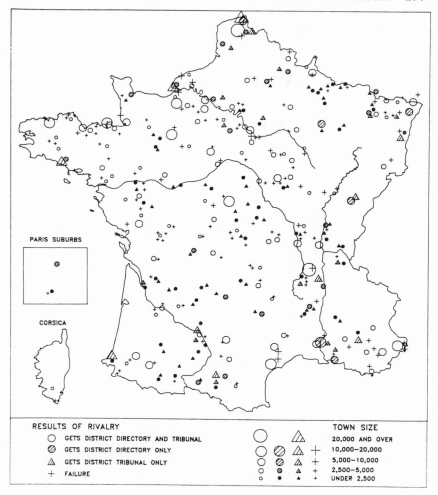

RESULTS OF RIVALRY

○	GETS DISTRICT DIRECTORY AND TRIBUNAL
◎	GETS DISTRICT DIRECTORY ONLY
△	GETS DISTRICT TRIBUNAL ONLY
+	FAILURE

TOWN SIZE

○		△		20,000 AND OVER
○	⊘	△	+	10,000–20,000
○	◎	△	+	5,000–10,000
○	●	△	+	2,500–5,000
○	●	▲	+	UNDER 2,500

PARIS SUBURBS

CORSICA

Map 8.1. Rival Towns Seeking District Tribunals, 1790

105 of the smallest towns, 109 of those with 1,250–2,500 inhabitants, and 106 of those with 2,500–4,999 inhabitants continued to dispute the location of district tribunals. Equally noteworthy is the fact that only a minority of small towns gained both a district seat and a tribunal without encountering any opposition after January 1790 (row 4). By contrast, 62 percent of the towns with 5,000–9,999 inhabitants and 85 percent of the towns with at least 10,000 inhabitants monopolized establishments at the district level without any rivals. Disputes over *partage* took place primarily in districts that did not have any large or medium-sized towns.

TABLE 8.1
Size and Role of Towns in District Rivalries

| | Size of Nucleated Population | | | | | |
	10,000 and Over	5,000– 9,999	2,500– 4,999	1,250– 2,499	Under 1,250	Total
1. Seeks lawcourt only	0	2 (1%)	11 (4%)	70 (22%)	228 (73%)	311
2. Seeks district only	0	6 (1%)	47 (10%)	145 (32%)	252 (56%)	450
3. Disputes *partage*	14 (4%)	41 (11%)	106 (28%)	109 (29%)	105 (28%)	375
4. Monopoly unopposed	77 (21%)	81 (22%)	94 (25%)	76 (20%)	44 (12%)	372
TOTAL	91 (6%)	130 (9%)	258 (17%)	400 (26%)	629 (42%)	1,508

Sources: Petitions and other documents in AN C:90–123; DIV bis 1–32, 108–110; ADXVI 18–81; and listing of the seats of districts and district tribunals, *Almanach royal* (Paris, 1791).

Note: Partage refers to the location of the district tribunal in a town different from the location of the district directory.

The success or failure of contending towns is also indicated on map 8.1 and analyzed in table 8.2. The symbols on the map distinguish between towns that failed to obtain *partage* (crosses), towns that gained a tribunal (hatched triangles), towns that were confined to a district seat (hatched circles), and towns that preserved both a district and a tribunal (empty circles). The two main outcomes of rivalry—*partage* or monopoly of district establishments—are signified by the proximity of a hatched circle and a hatched triangle, or an empty circle and a cross. In addition to the pairs of symbols for bipolar rivalries, a few clusters with additional crosses signify multipolar conflicts involving three, four, or even five rivals for a tribunal. In the Deux-Sèvres, for example, four bourgs competed with the district seat of Melle for a tribunal, and in the Haute-Loire, the town of Yssingeaux abandoned its district seat for a tribunal in conflict with four other market centers. By examining the size of the symbols on the map, which vary as a function of the population size of towns, the outcomes of two basic patterns of rivalry can be compared: symmetrical pairs of towns in the same size category and asymmetrical pairs of towns in different size categories.[18] The larger empty circles near smaller crosses on the map stand out as examples of asymmetrical pairs in which the larger town gained both the district seat and the tribunal.

Table 8.2 sets forth two dimensions of urban rivalries that help explain whether towns succeeded in challenging the district seats chosen in February 1790: economic primacy and institutional rank. Towns that were substantially more important than their rivals from an economic point of view nearly always emphasized this fact in their petitions. Because the scale of the urban economy varied from district to district, such comparisons involved a variety of particular circumstances, such as the presence of seaports, industrial towns, river ports, or local market towns. Towns engaged in differing degrees of commerce usually varied enough in population size, however, to use population ratios as a standard measure of relationships of economic dominance, equality, and inferiority. Table 8.2 uses a threshold of 2.0 to distinguish between two patterns of asymmetrical rivalries, depending on whether the challenger was more than twice as large as the district seat (a dominant relationship) or less than half as large (an inferior relationship). In a few districts where the ratio of population was less than 2.0, rival towns nonetheless had quite differing degrees of economic influ-

---

[18] If towns are classified on the basis of geometrical size intervals (under 1,000; 1,000–1,999; 2,000–3,999; etc.), asymmetrical pairs can be defined more precisely as cases in which one town was at least two size intervals larger than the other (over 2,000 as compared with under 1,000, etc.). In 42 of these cases, the larger town monopolized the district and tribunal, but in 22 cases, both towns shared the establishments, and in 8 cases, the smaller town monopolized the establishment. Symmetrical pairs (adjacent intervals or the same size category) were equally likely to result in *partage* (46 cases) or monopoly (46 cases.)

TABLE 8.2
Proportions of Contending Towns That Gain *Partage*

Institutional Dominance	Economic Dominance			
	Dominant	Equal	Inferior	Total
1. Superior rank	1/1 (100%)	8/10 (80%)	4/9 (44%)	13/20 (64%)
2. Equal rank, *bailliage*	8/11 (73%)	24/41 (59%)	7/28 (25%)	39/80 (49%)
3. Equal rank, *bailliage*	2/4 (50%)	3/11 (27%)	1/9 (11%)	6/24 (25%)
4. Inferior rank	4/6 (67%)	5/21 (24%)	2/17 (12%)	11/44 (25%)
TOTALS	15/22 (68%)	40/83 (48%)	14/63 (22%)	69/168 (41%)

Sources: Economic dominance or inferiority is defined on the basis of whether the nucleated population of a contending town was at least twice as large as the population of its rival. Institutional dominance or inferiority is defined on the basis of the rank of the royal courts, if any, that towns had on the eve of the Revolution. For demographic sources, see appendix 1; for sources about lawcourts, see chapter 1.

Note: Dominance or inferiority is defined from the perspective of the *challenger,* i.e., the town did *not* obtain the district set in the decrees of February 1790. *Partage* refers to the location of the district tribunal in a town different from the location of the district directory.

ence, and have been classified accordingly. Much more commonly, how-ever, lower demographic ratios indicate similar ranges of economic influ-ence among rival towns, which have then been classified in the intermediate category of "equality." Pairs of towns within each district have been defined from the perspective of the challenger, that is, the largest town of a district that sought a tribunal after failing to obtain the district seat in February 1790.[19] The proportions in the table indicate the rates of success among such challengers. The importance of the economic dimen-sion emerges clearly from a comparison of the aggregated rates in the col-umn totals: 68 percent of the challengers that dominated their rivals from an economic perspective obtained tribunals, as compared with only 22 per-cent of the challengers that were inferior in population and commerce to their rivals.

But table 8.2 also shows that the judicial rank of towns in the old regime influenced the probability of success. Just as some townspeople took pride in their population size and economic importance, so others called atten-tion to their lawcourts and their magistrates. Indeed, the smaller the town and the less vigorous the urban economy, the more weighty the presence of judicial institutions and men of law seemed in the minds of petitioners. Among the many lawcourts that they described, *présidiaux* ranked highest, followed by royal *bailliages*, although townspeople sometimes tried to ele-vate their seigneurial courts to the rank of *bailliages*, too. Royal *présidiaux* and *bailliages* not only derived prestige from their appellate jurisdiction over lesser courts but often acquired disproportionate political influence as the seats of constituencies for deputies from the Third Estate. It stands to reason that these deputies would defend the primacy of *bailliage* seats in the new districts, all the more so because their hometown loyalties so often coincided with such institutional continuity. By amalgamating the terri-tory of small *bailliages* into larger districts, some deputies also arranged to expand the jurisdiction of their towns. Thus, table 8.2 distinguishes be-tween four types of contention involving the judicial hierarchy of the old regime: districts in which the challenger had a higher-ranking court than did the town originally selected as the district seat (row 1); districts in which neither town had a *bailliage* court (row 2); districts in which both towns had a *bailliage* court (row 3); and districts in which only the defend-ing town had a *bailliage* court (row 4). The row totals confirm the influ-ence of judicial rank at both extremes of the judicial hierarchy: superior-ranking challengers had a success rate of 65 percent, as compared with a rate of only 25 percent for inferior-ranking challengers. These totals also indicate the political vulnerability of *bailliage* towns that were initially in-

[19] To simplify the analysis, additional contenders in districts that had multipolar rivalries have not been included.

corporated into the district of a nearby town that also had a *bailliage*: *partage* took place in only 25 percent of these districts, as compared with 49 percent of the districts where neither contender possessed a *bailliage* court.

Finally, the crosstabulation of success rates reveals the interplay of both dimensions of rivalry: A higher rank on either scale increased the rate of success, while a lower rank on either scale reduced it. Towns that scored low on both scales had the lowest probability of success, although three of them did gain *partage*.[20] Four of the six challengers that had a dominant economic role and an inferior judicial rank succeeded, but so did four of the nine challengers that had a superior judicial rank and an inferior economic role. Thus, deputies followed an inconsistent policy of sometimes sharing establishments among towns that had contrasting roles to play in the commercial and judicial networks of the old regime and sometimes concentrating all the establishments in a single type of town. As for the several dozen districts where towns were equally balanced in their judicial rank and economic influence, here *partage* was over twice as likely to occur among non-*bailliage* towns as among *bailliage* towns. Yet seventeen out of the forty-one non-*bailliage* towns that equaled their rivals in economic importance still failed to gain *partage*. The more equal the rank of towns in the old regime or the more specialized their dependency on either lawcourts or commerce, the greater the margin of uncertainty that surrounded contests over lawcourts.

Geographical conditions also complicated urban rivalries, as the spokesmen for rival towns presented contradictory arguments about their centrality in marketing and communications networks or appealed for the support of rural populations in mutually isolated parts of a district. Whether conflicts centered on ambiguities in the economic role of towns, variations in institutional traditions, or differences in geographical settings, attempts to resolve them were likely to seem arbitrary to one side or the other. Particular examples of these several aspects of conflict will illustrate what a perplexing task the National Assembly confronted in either sharing establishments among contentious towns or awarding the tribunal as well as the district seat to a single town.

The relationship between seaports and the countryside was an especially problematical feature of administrative geography at the beginning of the Revolution. We have already noted the failure of several important seaports, including Marseille and La Rochelle, to translate their commercial

---

[20] The seigneurial town of Mirepoix gained a district seat as the price of its agreement to join the same department as the more important *présidial* town of Pamiers, which opted for the tribunal; the little seigneurial town of Wassy gained the tribunal in the district of Saint-Dizier, an important commercial town as well as the seat of a *bailliage*; and so did the little *bailliage* town of Bouzonville in the district of Sarrelouis, a garrison town with a *présidial* court.

power into departmental leadership. The same difficulty confronted ten seaports that failed to obtain district seats, including Bayonne, Dunkerque, Le Havre, and Lorient.[21] These four ports were placed in the districts of much smaller towns that benefited from closer proximity to rural inhabitants and more active spokesmen in the National Assembly.[22] Bayonne was attached to the district of Ustaritz, Dunkerque to Bergues, Lorient to Hennebont, and Le Havre to Montivilliers. Of these district seats, only Bergues numbered over 5,000 inhabitants, and even it was only one-fourth the size of Dunkerque; Montivilliers and Hennebont, both old *bailliage* towns, each numbered around 2,500 inhabitants, as compared with over 18,000 at Lorient and Le Havre; and Ustaritz, the former seat of the Basque tribunal in the *pays* of Labourd, contained fewer than 1,000 inhabitants, as against over 11,000 at Bayonne. Not surprisingly, petitioners from Le Havre complained that their town had been treated "in the same manner as certain individuals, certain corporations were by the good old government of France: the same injustice, the same disrespect, the same sacrifice to men who know how to make a fuss." They also pointed out the flagrant prejudice of the Assembly against their fellow seaport of Bayonne: "Although Bayonne provides a livelihood for the entire Basque country, it has been subordinated to a town whose existence was probably not even suspected by ten members of the National Assembly."[23] Municipal officials at Lorient expressed equal indignation at their fate: "We are being treated like the parvenus at the former royal Court, whom the nobility and even the bourgeoisie despised." The electors of the Morbihan had refused to support Lorient in its quarrel with Hennebont. Electors in the districts of Dunkerque and Le Havre rendered the same verdict against these seaports. As an anonymous petition from Dunkerque protested, all three towns were victims of injustice.[24]

Merchants who had dealings with the entire world refused to concede that jurisdictions as small as a district should be centered outside their walls. Spokesmen for Bayonne emphasized the "great inconvenience" that businessmen would suffer if they had to abandon their countinghouses to attend administrative assemblies at the isolated bourg of Ustaritz; and merchants at Le Havre stated flatly that their business affairs would prevent

[21] The other seaports in question were Antibes, Bonifacio, Blaye, Fécamp, Granville, and Honfleur. Two further seaports, Montreuil and Martigues, obtained district seats but not tribunals.

[22] The electors from Bayonne and Dunkerque had been outvoted by rural electors in the *bailliage* constituencies, so these ports had no deputies in the National Assembly; Lorient and Le Havre were represented by wholesale merchants who were outmaneuvered by the deputies from Hennebont and Montivilliers, both *bailliage* court magistrates by profession.

[23] *Réclamation*, AN DIV bis 17:282 (Seine-Inférieure).

[24] AN DIV bis 36:580 (Morbihan); DIV bis 29:410 (Nord).

them from serving on any administrative body located outside the city. Their reluctance to travel even a few leagues on country roads suggests, however, the insularity of seaports. Wholesale merchants transacted business with a wide network of clients, and they relied on agents to handle shipments to and from the interior. The long-distance commerce of these ports did not depend on social interaction with the surrounding countryside. Although Lorient defended its East Indian Company as a source of prosperity for the entire province of Brittany, and Le Havre praised its warehouses for supplying raw materials to the textile industry throughout upper Normandy, this trade did not require intensive contacts with nearby rural populations. It was agricultural markets, not wholesale supplies, that attracted farmers on a regular basis. Of course, the population of a seaport had to eat, and its demand for food could benefit farmers in the hinterland. Petitioners from Le Havre argued that their main markets, held every Tuesday and Friday, filled the town with "a large number of inhabitants from the countryside," bringing goods to sell from a distance of four to six leagues away. But defenders of Montivilliers pointed out that Le Havre possessed no grain markets. Farmers from a hundred different parishes brought their grain instead to the markets of Montivilliers. Wheat sold in this town was then ground into flour for the provisioning of Le Havre. They concluded that Le Havre was not a center of agricultural trade at all. It served only as an entrepôt for merchandise imported from abroad and redistributed throughout the kingdom. Consequently, farmers had no reason to go there, whether to sell their crops and livestock or to pay their taxes.[25]

The site of Lorient, on an estuary that blocked access by land to the interior of Brittany, had never favored local trade, and the seaport did not hold any markets at all. Petitioners from twenty-one rural parishes in the district of Hennebont complained that they had little contact with this isolated port, which sometimes took several hours to reach when the sea was dangerous. Food and lodgings at Lorient were "extraordinarily expensive"; visitors had to submit to inquisitorial customs agents who searched them "with the last indecency"; and once inside this duty-free port, they had difficulty finding anyone who could understand their language. Lorient was a French town on the edge of a Breton-speaking countryside. By contrast, Hennebont had a big market, low living costs, and many citizens who spoke Breton. These parish testimonials, ratified by general assemblies and signed by literate minorities, suggest that Lorient had few friends in

[25] *Mémoire* for Bayonne, AN DIV bis 29:419 (Basses-Pyrénées); printed letter from *Les électeurs de la ville de l'Orient,* AN ADXVI 53; *réclamation* for Le Havre, AN DIV bis 17:282 (Seine-Inférieure); *réponses* for Montivilliers, AN DIV bis 17:284 (Seine-Inférieure).

the countryside.[26] Created by the government only a century earlier for foreign trade, the port seemed to have grown at the expense of Hennebont, whose leaders rallied public opinion against its "dangerous ascendency." When Lorient offered them the tribunal in exchange for the district, municipal officials at Hennebont rejected any thought of compromise: "They want the honors of the fiscal administration so they can take the tribunal away from us later." Of course, Lorient denied any such intention and accused Hennebont of being a small and faction-ridden town, unable to provide all the new administrators and judges. Hennebont offered only men of law, while Lorient had men of every profession, and especially those best qualified to serve as administrators. In this rivalry between the merchants of Lorient and the lawyers of Hennebont, mutual isolation bred contempt and animosity.[27]

Despite the rural support that Bergues, Hennebont, and Montivilliers mustered against their larger and wealthier rivals, the National Assembly voted in August 1790 to give these seaports the district tribunals. In the case of Montivilliers, controversy persisted until the last minute. The deputies from Rouen, who feared the growing competition of Le Havre with their own port, helped convince the C.C. to support Montivilliers, which had the advantage of centrality. But the deputy from Le Havre carried the debate to the floor of the National Assembly, where he emphasized the commercial destiny of Le Havre to become "the foremost port in the empire." It would surely be unjust to strip such a large town of its tribunal in favor of a mere *bourgade*. Now the deputy from Montivilliers, who took the podium, failed to mention the agricultural markets of his town, or the vote of district electors in its favor. Instead he boasted of the famous woolens industry that Montivilliers used to possess and asked the Assembly to revive the town's economy by giving it the tribunal as well as the district. This argument proved singularly ineffectual, and a rural priest near Montivilliers did not help matters either by mentioning the importance of the religious establishments in this town. In this unique instance, the National Assembly overruled the advice of the C.C. and voted to place the tribunal of the district at Le Havre.[28] The deputies who had favored Bergues and Hennebont did not rise to challenge the advice of the Committee to place the tribunals of these districts at Dunkerque and Lorient, respectively. Nor did defenders of the Basques *pays* of Labourt complain when Bayonne

---

[26] See, especially, Delibs. Languidic, Saint-Gilles-les-Champs, and Plouhinec, AN DIV bis 36:580 (Morbihan).

[27] Mun. Hennebont, AN DIV bis 36:580 (Morbihan); and printed letter for Lorient, AN ADXVI 53.

[28] Session of Aug. 19, 1790, AP 18:161. Deputies tried and failed to reverse the Constitutional Committee in another seventeen cases, AP 18:115–18, 138, 160–61, 215–17; *Le point du jour* 13:403, p. 196.

gained the tribunal over Ustaritz, whose economy was so weak that its municipal officials tried to rest their case primarily on the language difference between Basques in the countryside and French-speaking notables in the seaport.[29] Yet the district tribunals that Bayonne, Dunkerque, Le Havre, and Lorient acquired soon became largely redundant when the National Assembly also established commercial tribunals in these seaports to meet the needs of their merchants.[30] As for the smaller *bailliage* towns whose primary concern all along had been to preserve their lawcourts, they ended up with nothing but the district seats.

Like seaports, textile towns in eighteenth-century France had a strong orientation toward interregional and even international commerce, and they often contained a larger population than did typical market towns. As centers for the spread of rural industry, however, such towns differed considerably from seaports in the vigor of their interaction with the countryside. Some were already regional capitals of commerce and administration, such as Amiens, Lille, and Troyes; such contenders for departmental seats had no difficulty monopolizing the establishments of a district. Others were relatively large towns, such as Saint-Quentin and Sedan, with important *bailliages*, dioceses, or *élections* that guaranteed them a district seat and a tribunal. In the third rank were smaller industrial towns, such as Bernay and Montdidier, whose previous *bailliages* helped them fend off rivals. But a few dozen industrial towns that played a less prominent role in the institutional life of the old regime also sought districts and tribunals. These included rapidly growing textile towns that lacked royal *bailliages* and less dynamic industrial towns whose existing jurisdictions were too small to form a district. Such towns nearly always emphasized the importance of their rural industry, but only Cholet, Louviers, and Saint-Geniez became district seats. All the rest were assigned against their will to the districts of other towns, where most of them tried in vain to obtain tribunals. With rare exceptions, unless centers of industrial production already possessed important jurisdictions, they failed to compete effectively with rival towns.

Merchants rather than lawyers formed the local elite in most of these industrial towns, and they were proud of their commerce and their markets. By calling attention to the vital influence that industry played in the rural as well as the urban economy, they tried to demonstrate the community of interest that linked their towns to parishes in the countryside. Descriptions of rural industry served as rhetorical devices to defend a sep-

[29] Mun. Delib. Ustaritz, AN DIV bis 71:1.

[30] By a decree on Aug. 11, 1790, the National Assembly agreed to establish *tribunaux de commerce* in towns that obtained the support of departmental directories. Particular decrees authorizing such lawcourts in 154 towns were passed during the following year. AP 17:721–24.

arate district and jurisdiction. As a deputy explained in defense of Condé-sur-Noireau, in the *bocage* country of lower Normandy,

> Condé is, so to speak, the capital of a *fabrique* of linen and cotton cloth which is of major importance for this part of the province. The individual workshops for this activity are in most of the parishes that seek union with the town, which feeds and supports them. Workers distributed throughout these villages are, properly speaking, only the passive agents of the rich *fabricants* who reside at Condé. If these *fabricants* stopped supplying materials to all these workers and stopped advancing cash for the piecework of a large number of them, this branch of commerce in all kinds of coarse woolen cloth, figured linen napkins, and heavy twilled cottons would perish totally.[31]

Petitioners from Yvetot, trying to wrest the district seat away from Caudebec, created a similar image of rural dependency on their town, whose markets served as the center for exchange among merchants and weavers throughout the *pays* of Caux, in upper Normandy.

> There are almost no family heads or even single persons working for themselves who are not obliged to come every week or at least every month to Yvetot to provision themselves with raw materials and to sell their finished goods. Yvetot alone has a covered market for itinerant merchants; it is the only repository of the materials necessary for textile workers. Thus, Yvetot is the natural and essential rallying point for all the *administrés* and, consequently, the political as well as the geometrical center of the district.[32]

Such descriptions filled memorials from Cholet, Ganges, Mazamet, Orbec, Saint-Chamond, Saint-Génies, and Tinchebray, as well.[33]

In four respects, however, the relationships of exchange that created such dependency might not advance the political goals of townspeople. To begin with, a thriving textile industry in the town and its immediate environs might be coupled with a very limited radius of influence over the countryside. Mazamet and Saint-Chamond are examples of towns whose merchants employed workers mainly in the town, *faubourgs*, and nearby villages. When the leaders of these towns tried to collect petitions for a district, they obtained support from no more than fourteen rural parishes. This fell far short of the dozens of parishes that less-commercial towns

---

[31] Letter from Louis Lamy, *négociant* from Caen who patronized Condé unsuccessfully, May 4, 1790, AN DXVII:1.

[32] *Pétition* from the popular Republican Society of Yvetot, in 1793, AN DIV bis 74:1A.

[33] AN DXVII 1 (Cholet); DIV bis 25:366 (Hérault); DIV bis 17:291 (Tarn); AF III 33 (Orbec); DIV bis 30:423 (Rhône-et-Loire); DIV bis 20:322 (Aveyron); DIV bis 29:413 (Orne).

sometimes mobilized in defense of existing royal and seigneurial courts.[34] Secondly, towns were often closely spaced together in areas where rural industry encouraged population growth. Only a few leagues separated El-beuf from Louviers, Saint-Chamond from Saint-Etienne, and Mazamet from Castres. Thirdly, the *fabricants* in small textile towns often depended on merchants in the larger towns to supply them with capital and raw ma-terials. These relationships sometimes encouraged townspeople to opt for one department rather than another on strictly economic grounds. For ex-ample, the *fabricants* of Ganges opted for the department of Montpellier rather than Nîmes because they borrowed capital from the former city and encountered competition from the latter. Only after the municipal leaders of Ganges discovered that they would not even obtain a tribunal in the district of Montpellier did they regret their earlier refusal to join the de-partment of the Gard, a decision "contrary in every respect to our true interests."[35]

Finally, rural industry often spread across the boundaries of existing ju-risdictions and brought ecologically distinct *pays* or microregions into closer contact with each other. Townspeople needed skillful negotiators in Paris to disentangle commercial spheres of influence from boundaries based on historic institutions or natural *pays*. In the highlands of Ro-uergue, for example, the tracing of district boundaries harmed the textile town of Saint-Génies, whose special deputies failed to prevent the transfer of the area known as the *causse de Sévérac* to a separate district for the little market town of Sévérac. Many peasants in this highland area wove cloth for the merchants of Saint-Géniez, but special deputies from Sévérac con-vinced the C.C. that the soil and climatic conditions around their town were completely different from those in the valley of the Lot, where Saint-Géniez was located. As a result, district boundaries bifurcated the market area of Saint-Géniez, and this town of 3,000 inhabitants found itself near the edge of its district, protesting to no avail a decree that assigned the district tribunal to the smaller but more centrally located town of Espa-lion.[36]

Commerce in grain and other agricultural commodities involved hier-archies of urban dominance and subordination that became focal points of

---

[34] *Observations* for Saint-Chamond, mentioning 12 rural petitions, AN DIV bis 30:423 (Rhône-et-Loire); Mun. Delibs. from 14 rural communities for Ganges in DIV bis 8:206 (Hérault); Mun. Delibs. from 7 rural communities for Mazamet, in DIV bis 17:291 (Tarn). Compare with the 51 Mun. Delibs. in favor of Pont-de-l'Arche, a *bailliage* town of only 1,500 inhabitants, AN DIV bis 23:349 (Eure).

[35] Letter from the *corps des fabricants*, Nov. 29, 1789, AN DIV bis 25:366 (Hérault); and Mun. Delib., Nov. 9, 1790, AN DIV bis 63:5.

[36] See the *rapport* for the C.C. on this dispute, AN DIV bis 4:165 (Aveyron); and a *mémoire* for Saint-Geniez, AN DIV bis 20:322 (Aveyron).

controversy in a few dozen districts. At one extreme, towns of differing size and market functions disputed their role in the grain trade, while at the other extreme, small towns conceded their economic inferiority but invoked countervailing arguments, such as superior lawcourts. The districts of Tarascon and Carentan illustrate conflicts over agricultural marketing, while the districts of Langeais and Marcigny point to the salience of institutional traditions.

The leaders of Tarascon, an important Provençal town on the Rhône River, boasted of their grain trade with Languedoc and Burgundy, and contrasted their population of 12,000 and their rank as the most heavily taxed town in Provence with Saint-Rémy, a town whose 3,000 inhabitants paid less than half as much in taxes and possessed neither commerce nor industry.[37] But Saint-Rémy had a deputy in the National Assembly who denied that Tarascon exercised economic leadership within the area. The merchants of Tarascon were only wholesalers whose imported grain was redistributed to the rural populations through the Wednesday markets at Saint-Rémy. Wine, vegetables, lambs, sheep, and oxen were also bought and sold at these markets, which attracted such a crowd that even people from Tarascon came regularly to display their merchandise and their handicrafts. Consequently, the villagers who flocked to Saint-Rémy had little occasion and less desire to visit Tarascon. They were rural folk, with simple habits and plain clothes, and they felt at ease in the small town of Saint-Rémy, where they never risked becoming "the objects of laughter and contempt."[38] Not only cultural barriers but economic rivalries separated the rural populations of the area from the merchants of Tarascon, who had refused to supply grain to the market of Saint-Rémy at the height of the food shortages in 1789. Having orchestrated rural protest against Tarascon at that time, the municipality of Saint-Rémy now succeeded in mobilizing support from fifteen of the twenty-one villages in the district. These rural petitions, presented by the deputy from Saint-Rémy, became the basis of a successful appeal to the C.C. for the tribunal.[39]

In the large district of Carentan (Manche), a complex system of exchange between pastoral and grain-producing areas underlay disputes between Carentan itself, a coastal town of 2,500 inhabitants, and two smaller bourgs of the interior, Périers and La Haye-du-Puits. Grain flowed from local markets in bourgs such as La Haye, which contained only 300 inhabitants, to intermediate markets such as Périers, with a population of around 1,600 inhabitants, and onward to the markets of larger towns, such as Carentan. Where was the center of this marketing network? Municipal offi-

[37] *Adresse* for Tarascon, AN DIV bis 5:168 (Bouches-du-Rhône).
[38] *Note* for Saint-Remy, AN DIV bis 20:325 (Bouches-du-Rhône).
[39] Documents in AN DIV bis 20:324 (Bouches-du-Rhône).

cials at La Haye, seven leagues away from Carentan, announced that they
were at the center of eight markets, held on different days of the week at
La Haye and seven other bourgs. Electors in nearby parishes confirmed
that farmers in this area subsisted on dark bread and sold all their wheat at
La Haye, which exported 10,000 sacks of grain every year, including 2,000
sacks to feed Carentan. But a general assembly of inhabitants at Périers
presented *their* markets as "the principal outlet for the production of the
entire area and the entrepôt for the neighboring towns." Testimonials from
parishes near Périers confirmed that this bourg held a very important grain
market where all the crops sold in the neighboring bourgs, including La
Haye-du-Puits, were brought for export to towns as far away as Bayeux,
Caen, and even Paris. One parish in the area added that Périers also had an
"immense commerce in oxen, cows, sheep, butter, chickens, game, and all
sorts of merchandise." As for Carentan, its municipal officers insisted that
their town was the center of marketing throughout the district, with a considerable commerce in grain, livestock, and butter.[40]

If over forty municipalities in the district supported La Haye or Périers,
this was not only because they did all their marketing in these bourgs. They
also feared the reputation Carentan had for deadly fevers, which people
generally attributed to the marshes near this town. Petitioners from one
village protested that visitors to Carentan were constantly attacked by fevers and epidemic diseases. "Strangers are afraid to spend any time there.
. . . Out of five hundred men from the army regiment of Rohan Soubise
who were stationed there, all but thirty became sick." Similarly, a group of
rural electors who supported La Haye wrote that no one from outside the
town of Carentan would agree to serve there as an administrator or a magistrate. They did not want to run the risk of dragging out their lives in a
listless condition, undermined by fevers and torn by attacks of colic. Special deputies from La Haye added that the fevers at Carentan caused mental
damage to their victims. "Judges would be exposed to delirium."[41] Of
course, the citizens of Carentan denied these charges. They submitted rec-
ords to prove an excess of births over deaths in recent years and to show
that sixty-eight residents of the town were over seventy years old. Heading
this list of old folks were Pierre Hébert Herbager, age eighty-four, "still
performing guard duty like a young man," and Marie le Roy, *veuve* Dar-
tenay, age ninety-three, "still walking in the streets to receive her daily
bread from charitable people." In any case, municipal officials at Carentan

[40] Letter from Mun. La Haye-du-Puits and *adresse* from *électeurs*, AN DIV bis 27:394
(Manche); *rémonstrances* from Périers and letter from Sainte-Opportune de Lessay, DIV bis
10:230 (Manche); *adresse* from Mun. Carentan, DIV bis 27:393 (Manche).

[41] *Adresse* from parish of Tribehou, AN DIV bis 27:393 (Manche); *adresse* and letter for
La Haye in AN DIV bis 27:394 (Manche).

added, marshes existed throughout the district.[42] At the first district electoral assembly, Carentan managed to get a plurality of votes for both the
district seat and the tribunal, but only because the majority, which insisted
on *partage*, split its votes between Périers and La Haye. This indecisive
outcome led to further intrigues in Paris until Périers, the former seat of a
royal *bailliage*, finally obtained the tribunal in August 1790.[43]

No one disputed the mediocre role of Langeais in agricultural trade, but
spokesmen for this district seat tried to turn their weakness to advantage
when challenged by the larger and more flourishing market town of Bourgueil. The notables in both these towns of the Loire River valley owned
vineyards that formed their chief source of income, but Langeuil also possessed a royal *bailliage*, while Bourgueil had only a small seigneurial court.
Lacking an institutional heritage to compare with that of Langeais, special
deputies from Bourgueil drew a sharp contrast between the commercial
scope of their own markets and the strictly local influence of the markets at
Langeais. According to them, the commerce of Bourgueil revolved around
the export of twelve thousand tubs of butter every week to towns in the
neighboring province of Poitou and the import of provisions from larger
towns along the Loire, such as Saumur and Tours. Sales at each weekly
market included an average of three hundred cattle, twenty-five thousand
tubs of butter, wheat and all kinds of grains, chickens, peas, coriander, lic-
orice, hemp and hempseed, flax, linen, muslin, and other cloth. This market catered to the needs of the entire area, which included many vineyards.
Over twenty large parishes within three leagues did all their marketing at
Bourgueil, and three or four thousand people entered town on every market day. By contrast, the smaller town of Langeais, farther upstream on the
Loire, had a market useful only for its own consumption of butter, eggs,
vegetables, and other foodstuffs. "No strangers go there," claimed the
spokesmen of Bourgueil. "Nothing in the way of commerce exists there to
distinguish its market and give it the slightest importance."[44] How did special deputies from Langeais reply to this invidious comparison? They accused Bourgueil of profiting from so much commerce that it did not need
a district or a tribunal! Langeais, on the other hand, would be completely
destroyed if it failed to replace its royal *bailliage*. They also emphasized that
Langeais had a more central location in the district than did Bourgueil,
whose market area included parishes in the neighboring department of the
Maine-et-Loire. Indeed, a majority of the rural municipalities in the district
endorsed Langeais as the seat of both the directory and the tribunal, al-

[42] "Etat des personnes anciennes existantes dans la ville de Carentan," and *adresse* from
Mun. Carentan, AN DIV bis 27:393 (Manche).

[43] On the indecisiveness of the district electors, see a letter by a special deputy from Carentan, in AN DIV bis 27:393 (Manche).

[44] *Précis* for Bourgueil, AN DIV bis 25:372 (Indre-et-Loire).

though the C.C. decided to maintain an earlier decree that guaranteed for Bourgueil the tribunal of the district.[45]

Agricultural trade in the district of Marcigny gave even less reason for the *bailliage* seat of Semur-en-Brionnais to gain *partage*, and here rural opinion tended to favor the larger market town. Marcigny enjoyed a favorable position on the Loire River, and its port stimulated a "very flourishing commerce in grain, wine and timber" with Paris and even Nantes. By contrast, Semur had neither markets nor fairs, and during the food crisis of May 1789, not a grain of wheat remained in its storehouse. The 400 inhabitants of this "paltry settlement" survived that crisis only by drawing supplies from Marcigny, whose markets normally provisioned all the parishes of this small district. Worse still, the "town" of Semur, on the summit of a steep hill that was very difficult to reach during the winter months, consisted of only forty-two houses. How could such an isolated locality, which amounted to "absolutely nothing," compete with a commercial town of 4,000 inhabitants? Municipal officials at Marcigny, defying a signed "treaty" in which their special deputies and those of Semur had agreed to share the establishments of the district, set about to mobilize the countryside against any compromise with Semur. In May 1790, they forwarded the adhesions of twenty-seven rural parishes and insisted that if *partage* were unavoidable, they should get the tribunal.[46]

To this campaign, a special deputy from Semur angrily replied that the merchants of Marcigny had themselves created the food shortages of the previous year by buying up all the grain in the countryside, storing it until prices rose, and then reselling it to the poor peasants who had produced it in the first place. Now they were peddling petitions in the countryside by tricking ignorant men—and even women—into believing that grain supplies, not lawcourts, were the issue. Such "odious and puerile maneuvers" deserved nothing but contempt, although the town agent (*procureur*) of Semur was careful to submit seventeen adhesions for *his* town, including four municipalities that retracted earlier commitments to Marcigny. Egalitarian rhetoric embellished this counteroffensive. With their "aristocratic pretensions," the townspeople of Marcigny, greedy to monopolize everything, were trying to "raise themselves on the ruins of their neighbors." Yet it was a nobleman in the National Assembly, the marquis de Digoine, whose patronage for Semur may have been decisive. Brushing aside the

---

[45] *Précis* for Bourgueil, *observations* for Langeais, 23 Mun. Delibs. for Langeais, 8 for Bourgueil, and letter by a special deputy from Bourgueil, in AN DIV bis 25:372, 8:210, and 25:373 (Indre-et-Loire).

[46] *Observations*, letter, *adresse*, and Mun. Delibs. in AN DIV bis 30:428 (Saône-et-Loire). A letter by special deputies from Semur emphasized the earlier agreement, DIV bis 30:427 (Saône-et-Loire).

objections of Marcigny, the C.C. agreed to uphold its original decree for *partage* by assigning the tribunal of the district to Semur.[47]

Wealth and poverty involved shifting rhetorical strategies as petitioners invoked the moral logic that the weak deserved assistance from the state while the strong could take care of themselves. At Beaumont-sur-Oise, for example, royal magistrates tried to preserve their *bailliage* in December 1789 by boasting of their town's river port and its grain and flour trade with Paris. But after Beaumont was placed instead in the district of Pontoise, municipal officials contrasted the grain mills and extensive commerce of this rival town with their own indigent population, which supposedly needed a tribunal in order to grow and flourish.[48] This plea went unanswered, like many others from small *bailliage* towns confronted by larger ones, but the argument for compensation raised concern among the adversaries of little towns. Even spokesmen for Bourgueil, having denigrated Langeais for its negligible market, developed second thoughts after this town made a virtue of its weakness: Langeais was rich after all, they explained in a subsequent memorial. Its abundant harvests of high-quality wine and its location on a main highway along the Loire River were advantages enough, but if Bourgueil failed to get a district and a tribunal, its markets would be deserted and it would be "absolutely annihilated."[49]

The partisans of Saint-Chély, a market town in the Lozère, also changed their tune after spokesmen for the smaller and more isolated judicial seat of Le Malzieu pleaded for help. In early January, they had submitted a certificate from a government inspector to prove that Saint-Chély was the center of the textile industry in upper Gévaudan. But the more they boasted of their numerous population, better roads, and greater commerce, the more spokesmen for Le Malzieu emphasized their poverty, losses during the Revolution, and need for compensation: "The town of Saint-Chély confesses that it is rich because of its commerce, so Le Malzieu has the right to prosper because of its establishments." To counter such an argument, special deputies from Saint-Chély assured the National Assembly in August 1790 that their town was not commercial after all: "Its markets are only the rendezvous for peasants from all the surroundings, who come to sell the *serges* and *cadis* that they have woven to agents of merchants from other towns, such as Mende and Marvéjols." These peasants did not even spend any money at Saint-Chély; they brought their own food, settled their business during the day, and returned home the same evening. In trying to preserve advantages inseparable from its central lo-

---

[47] Letters and *adresse* from Semur, AN DIV bis 30:427 (Saône-et-Loire). On the patronage of M. De Digoine, see the complaint of a special deputy from Marcigny, in DIV bis 30:428 (Saône-et-Loire).

[48] *Adresse*, Dec. 22, 1789, and *adresse*, Aug. 8, 1790, DIV bis 30:432 (Seine-et-Oise).

[49] *Précis* by special deputies from Bourgueil, AN DIV bis 25:372 (Indre-et-Loire).

cation in the district, Saint-Chély was working "less for its own happiness than for the general utility." Backed up by deliberations from nearly two-thirds of the parishes in the district, and by a vote of thirty-four to five at the district assembly of electors held in June, these deputies succeeded in forestalling the danger of *partage* with Le Malzieu.[50]

In a few dozen districts, townspeople disputed who would suffer most unless they obtained new establishments. For contradictory prophecies of ruin, it would be difficult to match the conflict between Chauny, Coucy, and La Fère, in the department of the Aisne. These three towns, which ranged in size from only 700 at Coucy to 2,500 at La Fère and 3,200 at Chauny, each possessed a small *bailliage* that together made up a single district along the Oise River, where La Fère and Chauny both had ports. The formation of this district had followed nearly a month of wrangling among deputies from the larger towns of Laon and Soissons, whose conflicting ambitions for the departmental seat had given special deputies from Chauny, Coucy, and La Fère just enough leverage to block a plan that would have attached them all to neighboring districts. The price of this separate district had been an agreement to consult the voters about an equitable division of establishments among the three towns.[51] Although its *bailliage* had been the smallest and least important in the area, Coucy insisted on either the district seat or the tribunal. Its electors to the district assembly were happy to concede the economic superiority of Chauny and La Fère:

> If only our town were placed, like those of Chauny and La Fère, on a navigable river, which always offers such abundant resources! But no, situated on top of a hill, its existence depends solely on attracting people inside its walls. If it does not obtain one of the two establishments to compensate it for the three that it is losing [a *maîtrise des eaux et forêts* and a salt granary as well as a *bailliage*], it will be totally annihilated. It would be just as well to level it.[52]

But deputies from Chauny, though boasting of their population and their local markets, were not about to acknowledge any profits from trade, which would jeopardize their own claim for compensation: "Chauny, which has no commerce to speak of, derived very great benefit from its jurisdiction; reduced to a cantonal seat, it would be left without any resources and ruined."[53] Nor did La Fère accept the argument of its rivals that this town did not deserve any new establishments because it had a cavalry regiment, an arsenal, and a school of artillery: "Where are the prof-

---

[50] *Adresse* from Saint-Chély; speech, *adresse*, and *précis* for Le Malzieu; *Mémoire* and Mun. Delibs. for Saint-Chély, in AN DIV bis 27:391 (Lozère).

[51] Hennequin, *La formation de l'Aisne*, pp. 154–64, 218–23.

[52] *Observations* by 12 *électeurs*, AN DIV bis 3:148 (Aisne).

[53] *Mémoire* for Chauny, AN DIV bis 3:144 (Aisne).

STRUGGLE FOR DISTRICTS 315

its for the inhabitants of La Fère? Might they be in industry? Everyone knows that a regiment has its own artisans and craftsmen. People also know that soldiers are often employed as common laborers, and that they work for cheap wages because, already paid by the army, they need less than day laborers who are burdened with a family." Furthermore, troops set a "fatal example" of prodigality and luxury, which brought "misery to local residents." Finally, by increasing the population of consumers, they caused food shortages and inflated the cost of living.[54]

Although this self-serving argument convinced no one from Coucy, La Fère did succeed in attracting support from a faction of magistrates and lawyers at Chauny, who opposed any deal with Coucy that would leave this town with the tribunal. As a result, the electoral assembly of the district broke up in confusion, and the National Assembly decided to place the directory at Chauny and the tribunal at Coucy, as a majority of electors from these towns had momentarily agreed.[55] A year later, a group of merchants from La Fère cast the dispute about compensation in a somewhat different light when they sought a *tribunal de commerce*: La Fère, they explained, was the entrepôt for a thriving rural textile industry, whose commerce "entirely dominated" the canton of Chauny![56] Such belated revelations about commerce were not infrequent among townspeople who made every effort to conceal such wealth while they were lamenting the loss of their *bailliages* in 1790.

In districts that suffered from poor communications, petitioners often claimed that a rival town was inaccessible. Of course, the quality of roads depended on the eye of the beholder. When petitioners from Evron argued that Saint-Suzanne was on top of a steep rock and nearly inaccessible, the notables of this town replied that Evron was only a "stinking, unhealthy sewer" and just as difficult to reach: "stones here, mud there, bad roads everywhere."[57] Similarly, when a deputy from Longwy described the mountainous terrain, covered with forests, that blocked communications with Longuyon, spokesmen for this town replied, "Does Longwy imagine that the difficulties which supposedly fatigue the traveler headed for Longuyon would disappear upon his return route toward Longwy?"[58] Yet obstacles to communication were sometimes serious enough to convince ru-

---

[54] Printed *opinion*, AN DIV bis 3:146 (Aisne).

[55] On the intrigues at the electoral assembly, see the letter and *mémoire* by two special deputies from Coucy, AN DIV bis 3:144 (Aisne); and Hennequin, *La Formation de l'Aisne*, pp. 348–50.

[56] *Pétition*, May 6, 1791, AN DIV bis 57:9 (Aisne).

[57] AN C 93:84 (Evron); DIV bis 27:397 (Mayenne). Evron failed to prevent Saint-Suzanne, the seat of a little royal *bailliage*, from getting the tribunal in its district.

[58] *Pétition* and printed *observations*, AN ADXVI 53. Longuyon gained the tribunal in the district of Longwy.

ral as well as urban notables that they deserved a separate district. Townspeople from Pertuis insisted that the plains of the Durance Valley, which supplied Aix-en-Provence with grain, were almost completely isolated by the Luberon Mountains from the basin of Apt to the north. They gathered petitions from sixteen villages to prove that these mountains were "rude, steep, covered by snow for part of the year, with roads as impassable as they are dangerous for travelers." In this case, however, spokesmen for Apt replied that the main road through the mountains had recently been improved: "All kinds of vehicles—*cabriolets*, carriages, carts—pass through these mountains every day and in all seasons of the year without the slightest difficulty." When electors from Pertuis presented their case for a separate district to the departmental assembly of the Bouches-du-Rhône, they suffered a resounding defeat, and the National Assembly placed the tribunal as well as the directory of the district at Apt.[59]

A similar conflict had a different outcome in the district of Martel, where rivers instead of mountains separated Martel from the rival town of Saint-Céré. Municipal officials at Saint-Céré forwarded a certificate from the local commander of the *maréchaussée* to prove that the roads to Martel, seven leagues to the north, were "impassable in nearly every season of the year because of the frequent flooding of the Dordogne and Sère rivers, as well as the torrents of Bourdalou, Petayrols, Latourmente, and La Sourdoyre." When the departmental assembly of the Lot rejected their request for a separate district, they rallied support from communities to the south of the river and requested the tribunal. According to a petition from electors at Saint-Céré and nearby cantons, some villages in this area were an entire day's journey from Martel. Two-thirds of the inhabitants in the district could not reach the district seat at some times of the year without running the risk of drowning, and they ran an equal risk of dying of thirst at other times of the year, when water disappeared from the surface of the limestone plateau where Martel was located. Water in this little town was often rarer than wine. The larger population and higher tax burden of Saint-Céré convinced a majority of deputies from the Lot to grant this town *partage*. Now it was the turn of municipalities on the north side of the Dordogne River to protest that Saint-Céré was far at the other end of the district, while Martel was close to the center. In the event, municipal officials at Martel opted for the tribunal, so the district seat was transferred to Saint-Céré.[60]

Beyond the problem of communications, these debates about centrality raised the issue of territorial identity among rural as well as urban populations. Through petitions and municipal deliberations, village notables in

---

[59] *Observations* for Pertuis, Mun. Delib. Peipin d'Aigue, and *Mémoire* for Apt, AN DIV bis 5:167, 3:154, 20:324 (Bouches-du-Rhône).

[60] Documents for Saint-Cére and note by six deputies, AN DIV bis 26:385 (Lot); and *pétitions* for Martel, Sept.–Nov. 1790, AN DIV bis 85:1.

mutually isolated parts of a district often registered a strong preference for their customary market town in the competition for district seats and tribunals. Such loyalties took an especially dramatic turn in the department of the Aisne, where Guise and Vervins pursued a bitter struggle for control of two disparate areas, the upper valley of the Oise and the *pays* of Thiérache. Guise dominated the rich plains around the Oise valley and possessed a panoply of old-regime institutions: *bailliage*, ducal court, *maîtrise*, *élection*, customs bureau, military governor, chapter of canons, and convents. Vervins had nothing but a seigneurial court, a few fiscal agents, and a small garrison, but it was the historic capital of Thiérache, a relatively infertile *pays* covered with forges, glassworks, and *fabriques* for the production of stockings and linenware. In this area, municipal officials calculated voting rights on the basis of a daily wage of only ten sols, as compared with fifteen to twenty sols in the area near Guise. The modest incomes and social egalitarianism of rural electors near Vervins aroused the contempt of special deputies from Guise, who accused them of making the rounds of châteaus back in 1789, forcing seigneurs to renounce their rights. Now these men from "the most despicable class" were campaigning in the cantonal assemblies of Thiérache, rousing sentiments against Guise.[61] Indeed, nearly two-thirds of the electors in the district did sign a petition in May against holding the first electoral assembly at Guise, where they had been authorized to discuss the transfer of the district to Vervins. When this meeting was held despite their protest, the delegates voted seventy to sixty in favor of Vervins.[62]

But no sooner had they cast their ballots than angry demonstrations broke out in the streets of Guise. Fearing for their lives, many delegates who supported Vervins withdrew from town. This left the field clear for the municipality of Guise to organize a meeting of the rump, which voted seventy-two to two in favor of concentrating all the establishments at Guise. The following afternoon, as these partisans of Guise were preparing to pack the slate of administrators for the new district, rumor suddenly spread that thousands of armed peasants were about to invade the town. The fugitive electors from Vervins had roused their national guard and were marching to the rescue of compatriots who had allegedly been trapped inside the town! Swelled by peasant recruits all along the path of its march, this makeshift army numbered as many as 3,000 men when it halted near the walls of Guise, whose national guardsmen were preparing to defend themselves. Fortunately, negotiations soon resolved the immediate crisis—no citizens from Vervins were still inside the town—and everyone dispersed, but the municipalities of Vervins and nearby villages has-

---

[61] Printed *observations* for Guise, AN DIV bis 19:304 (Aisne).
[62] *Pétition* forwarded May 24, 1790, AN DIV bis 57:11.

tened to denounce these events to the National Assembly: violent crowds at Guise had nearly massacred their electors; the sacred rights of man as well as decrees of the Assembly had been outrageously violated; and the deliberation of the rump in favor of Guise should be rendered null and void. These petitions, debated on the floor of the Assembly on June 16, 1790, resulted in a decree that awarded the district seat to Vervins. After further confusion and protest, the C.C. decided to place the tribunal at Guise, whose leaders had forwarded fifty-two petitions from communities that wanted a separate district for their town. This compromise did not satisfy either town, but it enabled the Assembly to avoid forming yet another district, which many deputies believed were already too numerous.[63]

These events at Guise, though exceptional in their violence, were symptomatic of the urban-rural alliances that emerged around distinct *pays* and market areas within many districts. For the C.C., such alliances magnified urban rivalries instead of resolving them. Electoral assemblies that were supposed to resolve disputes often split into factions around competing towns; if a majority opted for one town as the district seat and tribunal, a vocal minority nearly always protested that another town deserved at least the tribunal. As Gossin reported to the National Assembly on August 17, 1790: "The confidence that the Assembly placed in the electoral assemblies has not been justified everywhere. The Assembly had thought that at a moment when the towns seemed to share their conquest of the countryside, they would defend its interests. Unfortunately, particular interests have nearly everywhere suffocated public spirit in these assemblies." Instead of taking such deliberations into account, the C.C. proposed to avoid further "dangerous rivalries" by making prompt decisions, based on the earlier decrees on the formation of districts. Unless the tribunal had been explicitly "reserved" for a different town, it should be placed in the district seat.[64]

Such a policy meant disregarding not only the votes of electoral assemblies but also the petitions that towns were soliciting from rural communities. Indeed, we have seen that in several districts, such as Montivilliers, Hennebont, Langeais, and Saint-Céré, the Assembly disregarded rural opinion against *partage*. It also paid no attention to petitioning campaigns against *partage* in 25 districts, and it refused to grant *partage* to towns that submitted petitions from rural communities in another 26 districts. As for 31 districts where rival towns mobilized rural support for or against *partage*, the Assembly granted *partage* in 17 of them but denied *partage* in the other 14. This policy may have been inconsistent, but it responded to the

[63] For a narrative of these events, see Hennequin, *La Formation de l'Aisne*, pp. 352–59; for the opposing views of Guise and Vervins, see documents in DIV bis 19:304 (Aisne) and 57:6–7.

[64] AP 18:161.

experience that geographical divisions were impossible to reconcile by majority vote. If towns themselves were not prepared to compromise, how could rural notables be expected to mediate their disputes? This became the task of the National Assembly, which followed its earlier decrees for *partage* in 42 districts, intervened to impose *partage* on quarreling voters in another 10 districts, and extended *partage* to towns in 17 districts where this possibility had not been mentioned in earlier decrees. Only two towns, Auxonne and Orbec, failed to obtain tribunals that had been guaranteed to them back in February.[65] Thus, political continuity, tempered in a few dozen cases by lobbyists who gained access to the C.C. during the spring and summer, triumphed in the decrees on district tribunals, passed hastily in four brief sessions of the Assembly between August 17 and 22. Deputies challenged the seats of only nineteen tribunals on the floor of the Assembly, and only those favoring Le Havre succeeded in gaining *partage* against the advice of the *rapporteur* for the Committee.[66]

What had the Assembly wrought in its decisions on tribunals? It had reduced to the rank of cantonal seats a large number of market towns that used to host more important lawcourts than the justices of the peace they would now receive. These included 68 seats of royal *bailliages*, of which 29 continued the struggle for *partage* into the summer of 1790. But the Assembly had also promoted to the rank of district tribunals 259 towns that had not been *bailliage* seats on the eve of the Revolution. Some were as poorly supplied with legal personnel as Lormes, whose eleven men of law seemed impressive only in comparison with the three lawyers who supposedly made up the entire bar at the neighboring town of Corbigny; or Saint-Trivier, whose two canon lawyers would have to be supplemented by several men of law whom the municipality reported were willing to settle here.[67] The presence on the list of ninety-nine towns that had fewer than 1,250 inhabitants residing inside their walls or built-up area speaks for the low level of urbanization in some districts of the nation. But the proliferation of lawcourts during the old regime had encouraged a few people in even the most obscure market towns to acquire a smattering of legal training. Towns with as many as two or three thousand inhabitants often had several dozen families dependent in one way or another on lawcourts. It is

[65] They were outmaneuvered by deputies from the rival towns of Saint-Jean-de-Losne and Lisieux, respectively.

[66] These tabulations are based on the "Decréts relatifs à la division du royaume," annex to session of Feb. 26, 1790, AP 11:716–24; the debates on the seats of tribunals, Aug. 17, 19, 20, and 22, 1790, AP 18:115–217 *passim*; and the decree of Aug. 23, 1790 on the seats of tribunals, AP 18:239–44. Included among the district seats is Martigues, which obtained the transfer of this seat from Salon by a decree on Dec. 1, 1790; Salon retained the tribunal in this district. See Mun. Delib. Salon, Dec. 12, 1790, AN DIV bis 59:5.

[67] *Réponse* by a special deputy from Lormes, AN DIV bis 28:408 (Nièvre); and *mémoire* by Gueidan, deputy from Saint-Trivier, AN DIV bis 56:8.

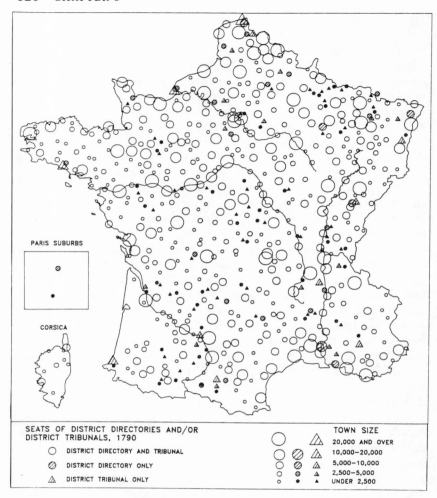

Map 8.2. District Directories and Tribunals, 1790

this broad social base of legal personnel, dispersed in hundreds of small towns, that explains both the intensity of lobbying for district seats and tribunals, and the success of 245 towns that numbered fewer than 2,500 inhabitants in acquiring one or both of these establishments.

Map 8.2, which shows the location of district directories and tribunals in 1790, confirms the importance of such little towns as central places in the new administrative and judicial system. The map also illustrates the tendency for the smallest towns to obtain only a directory (indicated by hatched circles) or a tribunal (hatched triangles), while larger towns often monopolized both of these establishments (empty circles). In comparison with that of the old regime, the institutional hierarchy of towns had been dramatically compressed. Henceforth, only three levels of administration existed, with most towns of any consequence ranking as the seats of district directories. The role of district tribunals would not be clarified until the summer of 1790, but townspeople expected that these establishments would equal in importance the former royal *bailliages*. Here, too, a substantial promotion of small towns seemed likely. A total of 266 towns that ranked below level V on the institutional scale presented in chapter 1 gained districts or tribunals. Among towns that ranked at level VI, 23 percent became district seats and another 6 percent obtained district tribunals. Even 11 percent of the towns at level VII of the prerevolutionary hierarchy of institutions attained the same rank in the new system of departments and districts as many level IV and V towns. Among towns at the lowest three levels of the previous institutional hierarchy, economic rank had a higher correlation with success than did institutional rank, which confirms that superior markets in microregional settings gave them a competitive advantage over little seats of subdelegations and minor royal courts.[68] Of course, success and failure would be relative to the benefits that districts and tribunals brought to the towns where they were located. In this respect, most urban notables had a larger stake in lawcourts than in directories. They would calculate the prospects for the future on the basis of the still uncertain policy of the National Assembly concerning judicial reform. Would the deputies preserve the higher rank and more extensive jurisdictions of towns that used to have *parlements* and *présidiaux*, or would they create an egalitarian system of lawcourts, centered on the districts? This became the most dramatic issue that polarized public opinion around the conflicting interests of large and small towns during the process of territorial reorganization that began in 1789.

[68] Among towns at levels VI through VIII of the institutional scale, 30 percent (34/112) of those with a higher economic ranking gained a district or a tribunal, as compared with 22 percent (41/190) of those with a higher institutional rank and 18 percent (137/744) of those with an equal rank on both scales.

PART THREE
THE FATE OF SMALL TOWNS

THE INSTITUTIONAL role of small towns waxed and waned with the fortunes of the Revolution. After considerable debate in 1790, the National Assembly decided to favor small towns in its judicial as well as its administrative reforms. A coalition of deputies from subordinate towns within the old judicial hierarchy refused to establish special courts of appeal for towns that used to possess *parlements* and other superior jurisdictions. Instead, the Assembly authorized the district lawcourts to hear appeals from each other. This egalitarian system provoked a movement to reduce the number of districts, whose costly proliferation would elevate many little towns to the same judicial rank as large and medium-sized towns. But the campaign for fewer districts threatened to undermine the political loyalty of newly elected officials in the districts destined for suppression. Henceforth, defenders of the Revolution discovered the advantages of a dense network of administrative institutions in small towns. At the height of the Terror, the Montagnard faction of the Convention even increased the powers of the district directories at the expense of the departments. For a time, the cause of democracy seemed to coincide with the fate of small towns as centers of administration. Such democratic energies quickly vanished, however, during the Thermidorian reaction against the Montagnards. In 1795, the Convention ratified a new constitution that abolished all the district directories and tribunals. Only one town in each department would retain a lawcourt to settle property disputes. As for local administration, it would be vested in several thousand cantonal municipalities, each with a *commissaire* appointed by the central government. This system dispersed instead of concentrated administrative authority, and its inadequacies help explain the collapse of the Directory in 1799.

In establishing the prefectoral corps at the beginning of the Consulate, Napoleon returned to the tripartite institutional hierarchy of the Constituent Assembly, but he excluded two-fifths of the former seats of directories from the rank of subprefectures. Napoleon also introduced a hierarchy of lawcourts that shifted the institutional balance from small to medium-sized and large towns. In both respects, territorial reorganization lost its close connection with the egalitarian ideology that had supported urban ambitions at the beginning of the Revolution. Henceforth, townspeople who aspired to recover the jurisdictions that they had lost in 1789 or 1795 would need to modify their rhetoric in accordance with the authoritarian regime of Napoleon. Their efforts rarely achieved success, either during the Consulate and the Empire, or after Napoleon's fall from power, when many urban leaders ostentatiously embraced the royalist cause. For some notables, monetary instability and economic crisis in the 1790s had already led to disillusionment with the ability of the government to generate economic prosperity through institutional reform. Indeed, the Revolution had the paradoxical effect of reducing the resources of the central government at the very time when local populations expected great benefits to flow from the regeneration of the state. Over the longer run, however, many notables retained their confidence in the power of lawcourts and other public establishments to stimulate the urban economy. With respect to small towns, the history of postrevolutionary France throws a skeptical light on such optimism, which exaggerated the benefits of lawcourts and misconstrued the relationship between administration and urban growth. Nonetheless, the territorial settlement of the First Empire did shape the urban development of nineteenth-century France by consolidating administrative authority in the prefectures and subprefectures. In preserving the departmental map of revolutionary France, Napoleon ensured that towns promoted to the rank of departmental seats would maintain their institutional advantages for many decades. In the demographic history of nineteenth-century towns, the extent of those advantages can be evaluated. If relatively few small towns achieved major territorial gains during the revolutionary era, those few would exemplify the relationship between the state and urban development in modern France.

Chapter 9

JUDICIAL REFORM AND THE POLITICIZATION
OF URBAN RIVALRIES

PERHAPS NO ASPECT of the old regime aroused more unanimous opposition in the National Assembly than the judicial system, with its hereditary corporations of magistrates, its costly procedures of civil litigation, its complicated hierarchy of appeals, and its flagrant violations of the rights of the accused. By confusing private property with public service, venal judgeships undermined professional standards, hampered efficiency, and burdened litigants with heavy court fees. At the two extremes of the judicial hierarchy—the *parlements* and the seigneurial courts—deputies saw ample evidence of privilege and corruption. The legislative pretensions of magistrates in the *parlements* seemed especially dangerous to patriots in the National Assembly, who retaliated against the counterrevolutionary sentiments of nobles of the robe in several provincial towns by suspending the regular sessions of *parlements* in November 1789.[1] As for the seigneurial courts, the Assembly not only abolished them in August 1789 as remnants of feudalism but criticized the spirit of chicanery that these courts had allegedly fostered in the countryside during the old regime. By coupling a new kind of institution, the justice of the peace, with changes in legal procedure that encouraged the prompt settlement of disputes, reformers hoped to undermine the baneful influence of country lawyers and practitioners on rural society.[2]

It might be expected that an Assembly numbering 127 *bailliage* court magistrates within its ranks would view the intermediate-level courts of the old regime with more sympathy. Yet here, too, venality of office condemned existing institutions, and so did the historical legacy of jurisdictions that varied greatly in size and importance from one province to the next. The same rationalizing tendency that encouraged the National Assembly to abolish *généralités*, *élections*, and subdelegations also convinced it to redraw the boundaries of legal jurisdictions throughout the kingdom. As early as August 17, 1789, a spokesman for the C.C. called for an "ab-

[1] Decree of Nov. 3, 1789, AP 9:666. On the conflict between the National Assembly and the *parlements* in 1789, see Henri Carré, *La fin des parlements, 1788–1790* (Paris, 1912), pp. 101–34, 155–68.

[2] On the background of this movement for reform, see Carey, *Judicial Reform in France*; and Mackrell, "Criticism of Seigniorial Justice," pp. 123–44.

solute revolution" in the entire system of justice. When Thouret presented a detailed plan of judicial organization in December 1789, he agreed that "regeneration must be complete." And when debate on this plan began in March 1790, the Assembly swept aside the objections of the marquis de Cazalès, sole defender of the *parlements*, and voted overwhelmingly to "reconstruct the entire judicial order."[3]

Yet the C.C. adopted a traditional approach to civil litigation and appellate jurisdictions, despite its revolutionary proposals to to elect all judges, eliminate court fees, and establish juries in criminal cases. All disputes over real property, as well as disputes over personal property worth more than one hundred livres, would be settled by panels of judges, following customary written procedure. Furthermore, a complicated hierarchy of appeals, ranging from district and departmental tribunals to superior courts with jurisdiction over several departments, would be calibrated in accordance with the monetary value of lawsuits. The departmental courts would even function as district courts for the particular districts in which they were located, just as *présidiaux* in the old regime had combined the functions of *bailliage* courts with larger appellate jurisdictions. In like manner, the idea of "superior" courts, with rights of appeal over "inferior" courts in the districts and departments, implied the same kind of unequal relationship that used to exist between the *parlements* and other lawcourts. Indeed, judges on the superior courts would have to meet more stringent conditions of eligibility, and they would presumably receive higher salaries than the other judges, although Thouret's plan was silent about this issue. Finally, the personnel of the lawcourts would double at each level of the system, with five district judges, ten departmental judges, twenty supradepartmental judges, and thirty-six judges on a Supreme Court of Review. In sum, the C.C. recommended a hierarchical system of lawcourts that would preserve the institutional superiority of large towns over small ones.[4]

This plan did stimulate the ambition of deputies who hoped to elevate their hometowns to the rank of superior courts. As Thibaudeau, a deputy from Poitiers, explained to his constituents, "I count on the establishment of a superior court at Poitiers to compensate this town for the losses that

---

[3] AP 8:445–449; session of Dec. 22, 1789, AP 10:718; session of Mar. 24, 1790, AP 12:348. For a general analysis of the judicial reforms of the Constituent Assembly, see Jean Bourdon, *La réforme judiciare de l'an VIII*, vol. 1, *Les institutions* (Rodez, 1941), pp. 153–77. For a detailed history, see Emile Giraud, *L'oeuvre d'organisation judiciare de l'Assemblée Nationale Constituante* (Paris, 1921).

[4] "Précis de l'organisation du pouvoir judiciare, proposé à l'Assemblée nationale par le Comité de Constitution," submitted by Thouret on Dec. 22, 1789, AP 10:726–31. For a general discussion of the debate over this plan, see Edmond Seligman, *La justice en France pendant la Révolution* (Paris, 1901), 1:280–328.

it will suffer as a result of the changes underway."[5] In like manner, special deputies from Montpellier accepted a departmental alternate with Béziers in order to improve their chances of gaining a superior court, which they supposed would be much more advantageous to their town than an administrative assembly.[6] But such deputies ran the risk of being outmaneuvered by the partisans of rival towns. De Chou, whose fellow magistrates at Bourges feared the loss of their extensive *présidial* jurisdiction, recognized that whether Bourges obtained a superior court would depend on "various combinations." If Clermont-Ferrand obtained one, then Moulins would depend on it, so Bourges would be in a natural position to include the departments of the Nièvre, the Indre, and even the Creuse in its jurisdiction. But if Moulins instead of Clermont triumphed, then Bourges would be in danger of falling under its jurisdiction. On March 10, 1790, after consulting with deputies from neighboring departments, De Chou endorsed a project for superior courts at Riom, Limoges, and Bourges, but he warned his constituents that deputies from Moulins and Nevers, who wanted these courts for their own towns, were on intimate terms with one of the most influential members of the C.C. Some deputies were also talking about creating only one sovereign court for every ten or twelve departments, while others wanted every department to have its own final court of appeals. Under the circumstances, De Chou described his own intrigues as shadowboxing. Nothing had yet been settled in the National Assembly.[7]

Indeed, critics of the French legal system, inspired by the English example of itinerant judges who presided over jury trials, brought the entire plan of the C.C. into question at the end of March 1790. First Adrien Duport, a former magistrate on the Paris *parlement*, and then Jean-Baptiste Chabroud, a barrister from Vienne, presented alternative plans that would dispense altogether with a hierarchy of lawcourts. Duport argued that *any* permanent lawcourts, consisting of judges appointed for life, would dominate the people by elaborating obscure and complicated traditions of jurisprudence. Such "gothic edifices" should be replaced by juries, chosen at random from the citizenry, to ascertain the facts of a case, and by itinerant judges, elected for fixed terms of office, to render verdicts on the basis of clear and simple laws. In Duport's system, each district would have one jury and two judicial officers, serving alternately as the director of the jury and as a judge on the assizes held in other districts. In this manner, judges would never pass sentence on their fellow townspeople, unlike sedentary judges, who were always exposed to the pressure of local opinion and the

[5] Letter of Nov. 7, 1789, in Carré and Boissonnade, *Correspondance de Thibaudeau*, p. 31.
[6] Letter from special deputies to Mun. Montpellier, Dec. 3, 1789, in d'Aigrefeuille, *Histoire de Montpellier*, p. 669.
[7] Letters of Jan. 6 and Mar. 10, 1790, in Mater, "Formation du département du Cher," pp. 178, 187.

bias of friends and relatives. Rotating assizes, consisting of district judges, had the further advantage of preventing the kind of social inequality that used to exist among judges at various levels of the old judicial hierarchy. Proclaiming that all judges are "essentially equal," Duport, the noble *parlementaire*, appealed to the former *bailliage* magistrates in his audience by explaining that in his system, judges "will no longer be humiliated by this hierarchy of tribunals, of superior and inferior judges, of sovereign courts, *présidiaux*, and *bailliages* that raised up some in order to lower others." He also rejected any effort to perpetuate the kinds of monetary thresholds that distinguished *présidiaux* from *bailliages* in the old regime. It would be a "great and solemn injustice" to substitute an "aristocracy of wealth" for that of nobles, and to permit the rich to appeal their lawsuits to higher courts while obliging the poor to settle their disputes in courts of first instance. Indeed, Duport opposed any courts of appeal, which would preserve "the superiority of some towns over others." By relying instead on itinerant panels of "great judges" to review the decisions of district judges, his plan would restore "perfect equality among all towns."[8]

Repeated applause greeted Chabroud's defense of a similar plan, but partisans of the French legal system, with its written procedures of litigation and its professional judges, launched a successful counterattack against jury trials in civil lawsuits. Experienced men of law from all kinds of towns, including Tronchet, the president of the Paris bar, Defermon, an attorney at the *parlement* of Rennes, Gossin, a *bailliage* judge at Bar-le-Duc, Mougins de Roquefort, a magistrate from Grasse, and Brillat-Savarin, a lawyer from the little town of Belley, joined with Thouret to condemn civil juries as impractical, dangerous, and unnecessary innovations. Such juries were impractical because of the extraordinary variety of customary laws that regulated property transactions in different provinces of the kingdom and because of the inextricable relationship between fact and law in the French legal tradition. At the very least, a new and uniform civil code would have to be written before juries could be introduced. In all probability, ordinary citizens would never understand enough about the law to render verdicts in accordance with French civil procedure, which required documentary proofs rather than oral testimony. Yet to abandon judicial scrutiny of written evidence would threaten the private interests of a great many citizens who customarily recorded their property rights in notarial documents that served as legal evidence. As Thouret argued, the French tradition of documentary proofs had become deeply embedded in social mores. Suddenly to introduce completely different procedures borrowed from the English would provoke massive discontent with the new judicial system. While

---

[8] AP 12:420–26. For more details on Duport's views, see Georges Michon, *Essai sur L'histoire du parti Feuillant: Adrien Duport, 1789–1792* (Paris, 1924), pp. 135–80.

nearly all the deputies agreed that jury trials should be introduced in criminal cases, a large majority voted on April 30, 1790, to exclude juries of any kind from civil lawsuits.[9]

Just as the corollary of jury trials would be assizes courts, so the rejection of juries implied permanent tribunals. Many deputies agreed that the customs of French family life ruled out any imitation of the English institution of assizes. "I ask you," declaimed a lawyer from Nancy, "do you think that respectable and settled citizens, honored by the esteem and confidence of their compatriots, would accept positions that required them to travel all the time?" No *bon père de famille* would leave behind "everything that fills his soul with sweet affections" in order to run from town to town for a large part of the year. Another critic from Nancy added that ambulatory judges would "arrive like postilions, appear like charlatans." Instead of studying their lawbooks after courtroom sessions, they would constantly be on the road, reading the postal guide. Tronchet, whose attack on civil juries had precipitated the vote against this innovation, also capped the debate on assizes by insisting that judges must be enlightened scholars rather than ignorant travelers: "I will never have confidence in a judge who arrives, carrying all his knowledge in his saddle bag, to decide my fortune." French bourgeois ideals of domesticity and professionalism triumphed as the National Assembly voted on May 3, 1790, that all judges must be sedentary.[10]

Permanent lawcourts that judged on the basis of written documents implied, in turn, the right of appeal. But Duport and Chabroud convinced many deputies that the C.C. had proposed "too many appeals, too many lawcourts, and too many judges." Even Thouret, who feared the political ambition of appellate judges, abandoned the plan for an elaborate hierarchy of lawcourts. A large majority of deputies voted for only two degrees of jurisdiction above the level of justices of the peace.[11] To implement this decision, a new plan of organization would have to be devised. Thouret tried and failed to convince the Assembly that departmental judges should hold assizes in neighboring departments. This plan violated the principle of sedentary lawcourts. A few deputies argued that departmental courts should hear all appeals, but others objected that such courts would infringe on the jurisdiction of district courts and employ too many judges. As special deputies from Clermont-Ferrand reported, "Everyone seems in agreement not to establish departmental tribunals, and to reinforce the district

[9] Speeches by Chabroud and Thouret, AP 12:443–56, 555–56; and general debate, Apr. 5–8, 28–30, AP 12:543–92, *passim*, and 13:317–43, *passim*.

[10] Speeches by Régnier, Prugnon, and Tronchet, May 2, and session of May 3, 1790, AP 15:359–62, 370.

[11] Chabroud's speech on Apr. 8, 1790, AP 12:587; and decree of May 1, 1790, AP 15:353–54.

tribunals instead."[12] Trying to accomodate this demand for simplification, the C.C. submitted a new plan on July 5 that excluded appellate judges from any direct jurisdiction over lawsuits. All disputes over real property would be adjudicated in the first instance by panels of three judges in the districts. Appeals from these decisions would then go to panels of eight judges with jurisdiction over three or four departments. Responding to the egalitarian rhetoric of critics, the committee affirmed that "all judges are equal" and carefully avoided describing the supradepartmental tribunals as "superior" courts. Yet this plan did nothing to equalize the benefits that townspeople expected to receive from the presence of new lawcourts. Those few towns that became the seats of appellate courts would attract many more lawyers and litigants than would the hundreds of towns that gained district tribunals. In the competition for appellate courts, the losers would vastly outnumber the winners.[13]

Pétion de Villeneuve and Chabroud seized upon this imbalance to re-open the entire question of appellate jurisdictions on July 20, just as the National Assembly was about to decide how many judges to establish for each district court. "Large courts of appeal will preserve the spirit of chicanery, increase the distance that plaintiffs have to travel, multiply men of law and, with them, lawsuits," insisted Pétion. "Soon you will see the departments disputing among themselves over these establishments, which they will view as a source of riches." It would be far better to "annihilate the impolitic and dangerous hierarchy of lawcourts" by permitting appeals from one district lawcourt to another. Chabroud followed Pétion to the podium with a systematic defense of such a plan. Point by point, he appealed to deputies who feared a revival of powerful lawcourts, a hierarchy of superior and inferior judges, jealous rivalries between towns and departments, unnecessary encouragment of litigation, and pretentious claims to domination on the part of judicial capitals. Tumultuous applause greeted his allusion to *villes parlementaires*, where everyone was a judge, a barrister, a solicitor, a clerk, a pettifogger; where the "immoral industry" of litigation replaced all "useful industry"; and where citizens found themselves reduced to "an odious and precarious existence." The inhabitants of such towns were the "true adversaries" of any plan that would destroy the kinds of "grandiose establishments" that they used to possess. For Chabroud, all "preferential treatment" should be abolished. Instead, he proposed to establish a salutary emulation among all district tribunals, which would be authorized to receive appeals from litigants anywhere in the kingdom. Special rules would be drafted to specify which district court

[12] Thouret's speech of Apr. 6, 1790, AP 12:557; and letter from special deputies to Mun. Clermont-Ferrand, reprinted in Mège, *Formation du Puy-de-Dôme*, p. 279.

[13] For the complete text of the C.C.'s plan, submitted on July 5, 1790, see AP 10:735–41.

would receive an appeal when the plaintiffs themselves were unable to agree on this matter. Thus, freedom of choice, allied with the principle of equality, would unite all the lawcourts into "a single totality."[14]

Chabroud's remarkable speech provoked consternation on the part of deputies from several provincial capitals. In their zeal to refute his plan, they expressed a pride in appellate judges and a contempt for small towns that only strengthened opposition to supradepartmental courts. Oblivious to the presence in the National Assembly of hundreds of deputies from small towns, Irland de Bazôges, the former lieutenant-general of the huge *sénéchaussée* of Poitiers, insisted that "few district judges would have the talent, education, and professional esteem to adjudicate appeals. Nearly all of these courts will be located in small towns, and many will even be in bourgs or villages. Experienced lawyers, who are now concentrated around the major lawcourts, will be unwilling to leave their friends and families to settle in such localities." Lanjuinais, a law professor from Rennes, mingled arrogance with naïveté when he tried to illustrate this point: "There will always be a great difference between the judges of Rennes and those of Vannes. You will never be persuasive in arguing that a better judgment can be obtained by going from the center of enlightenment to the sojourn of inexperience. The great majority of the deputation from Brittany support the plan of the Committee." Several deputies from this province sprang to their feet immediately to contradict him. Le Guen de Kerengall, from the little *bailliage* of Lesneven, announced defiantly, "The will of the deputation is not contrary to reason; consequently, it conforms to the plan of M. Chabroud." Le Chapelier, another lawyer from Rennes, rushed to the support of M. Lanjuinais, but his words only made matters worse: "The greatest talents are found in large towns; it is in the midst of great affairs that great judges and juriconsultists are formed. . . . In small towns there are only petty interests."[15]

It was no wonder that deputies from many towns rallied around Chabroud. "Let us be frank, messieurs," said a priest from Carcassonne. "You see that these demands for appellate courts are being supported here only by deputies from large towns, who want to revive the effects of aristocracy. They speak to the advantage of only twenty cities against the entire kingdom."[16] In this clash of interests, deputies from small and medium-sized towns turned against the spokesmen for provincial capitals, and so did some deputies from Paris. According to Thibaudeau, who viewed Chabroud's plan with dismay, "All the inhabitants of the towns that had no hope of obtaining supreme courts, and they were a very large majority,

---

[14] Speech of July 20, 1790, AP 17:208–11.

[15] Debate on July 23, 1790, AP 17:309–10.

[16] Cited by Felix Faulcon, letter of July 23, 1790, in Debien, *Correspondance de Felix Faulcon*, pp. 274–75.

adopted this new system." He added that the C.C. abstained from the debate because its Parisian members, such as the lawyer Target, agreed with the political arguments of Chabroud against large appellate courts.[17] This left the field open for deputies such as Brillat-Savarin, Delay d'Agier, and Mougins de Roquefort, all from district towns of middling importance, to pose as defenders of the countryside against large towns. Chabroud himself came from Vienne, which had long resented the dominance of Grenoble in the province of Dauphiné. On July 23, he delivered an impassioned reply to Lanjuinais and Le Chapelier. It is true, he conceded, that great juriconsultists are found in large towns. "But who consults them? Who employs these eloquent lawyers? Rich men, who can afford to pay them. Such lawyers do not exist for the poor." Applause from "a very large part of the assembly" followed this speech, and "a very large majority" promptly passed a decree in favor of Chabroud's simple plan for district judges to serve also as appellate judges.[18]

This startling triumph for the partisans of equality among towns had the paradoxical effect of raising fresh doubts about the decisions already taken to create a large number of districts. Thouret had addressed this issue back in March by suggesting that the number of district judges should range from three to five, depending on how many districts had been formed in each department.[19] Now that district courts would exercise appellate powers, he abandoned this proposal. Every tribunal would need five judges. Furthermore, the salaries of district judges would have to be increased. But this implied considerable government expenditures at a moment when the budgetary crisis of the state was growing more serious every day. Why not restrict tribunals to some districts, or better yet, why not suppress some of the districts, which would reduce administrative as well as judicial expenses?[20] These contradictory pressures to pay judges more and to spend less money opened the way for a reversal of urban alliances in the Assembly. Henceforth, deputies from large and medium-sized towns who coveted larger jurisdictions would try to force the taxpayers in neighboring districts to request the suppression of their own tribunals and administrative directories.

[17] Letter from Thibaudeau to Mun. Poitiers, July 24, 1790, in Carré and Boissonnade, *Correspondance de Thibaudeau*, pp. 113–14.

[18] AP 17:310–12. Chabroud refined his plan subsequently in collaboration with Thouret. See his speech of July 27, 1790, introducing the specific articles that would regulate appeals, in AP 17:382.

[19] Speech of Mar. 24, 12:347.

[20] Sentetz, a former royal prosecutor at the *sénéchaussée* of Auch, proposed on July 20 that tribunals be established in only the two largest towns of each department. On the same day, Tronchet advised the Assembly to make its decrees on the location of tribunals provisional instead of permanent so that it could reduce the number of districts and tribunals after it consulted public opinion in the departments. AP 17:203–5.

The budgetary issue was veiled at first by political passions in the Assembly, as defenders of the Revolution insisted on paying large salaries to all judges. The C.C. did propose a sliding scale of salaries, in accordance with the idea that large towns had higher living costs than did small towns, but it recommended a minimum salary of 1,800 livres, which judges in all towns numbering fewer than 20,000 inhabitants would receive. Two months earlier, clerical spokesmen in the Assembly had tried in vain to raise the minimum salary of priests from 1,200 to 1,500 livres.[21] Now right-wing deputies showered the Assembly with amendments to reduce the salaries of judges. It was like an auction, reported the *Journal des Etats-Généraux*—600 livres, 800 livres, 1,000 livres, 1,200 livres. But M. de Menou, a liberal nobleman, declaimed that "only those who want to overthrow the Constitution oppose the salaries recommended by the Committee. If you want good judges, you must pay them enough so they will not be tempted to pillage or steal." Applause from the left greeted these words, to which the marquis d'Ambly replied, "Judges have the same honor as we do: that of serving the fatherland. Money is not needed for that." "Yes," retorted another deputy, "when one has 20,000 or 30,000 livres in rents like you do; but men who are not so rich must not be excluded from the honor of serving as judges. Since the only distinctions that we recognize are talents and virtues, the fatherland must certainly pay its own functionaries and place them beyond material cares."[22] The same conflict between left and right recurred two days later, when the Assembly debated whether to fix the minimum salary of district administrators at 1,200 livres, as the C.C. advised, or only 600 livres, as M. d'André, a former councillor in the *parlement* of Aix-en-Provence, proposed. M. Guillaume, a lawyer from Paris, accused the supporters of d'André's motion of wanting to restore "the aristocracy of the rich," and M. Lanjuinais denounced the right wing of the Assembly for its niggardly approach to salaries at a moment when immense work needed to be undertaken in the departments and districts.[23]

Yet in the midst of these debates, M. Démeunier, a member of the C.C., revealed a different reason for paying high salaries to all judges: "The distribution of districts is very unequal and too many have been created in some departments. The C.C. thinks that the best means of getting fewer districts is to burden them with the cost of their establishments." According to the editor of the *Journal des Etats-Généraux*, these words brought forth repeated applause in the Assembly, proving how much the Committee had anticipated the views of many deputies. If the operation of dividing the departments into districts were started all over again, the Assembly

[21] Session of June 17, 1790, AP 16:239–41.
[22] Session of Aug. 30, 1790, in *Journal des Etats-Généraux* 15:143–44; and AP 18:415–16, which cites only De Menou's speech.
[23] Session of Aug. 31, 1790, in *Le point du jour*, Sept. 1, 1790, 415:397.

would be careful not to permit so many districts. "Everyone senses today that three or four districts per department would suffice."[24] No one paid any attention to M. De Montcalm-Gozon, a nobleman from the poor province of Rouergue, who made the perfectly sensible suggestion that districts and departments be consulted about salary scales that would be consistent with local needs and resources.[25] As Thomas Lindet explained in a letter to his fellow townspeople at Bernay, Thouret was insisting on high salaries for all judges in order to encourage a reduction in the number of districts. "It seems to me that the Committee, repentant for having left too much latitude in the subdivision of departments, hopes that the spirit of economy that many people share will force a reduction to three districts per department. I fear, for our town, this insinuation, which has gained many votes."[26]

Indeed, no sooner had the Assembly voted to set the minimum salary of judges at 1,800 livres than Thouret submitted the following draft of a decree: "The Legislative Body will impose on each district the annual expenses of the tribunal and the administrative body established there." At this surprising motion, M. Couppé, a former seigneurial judge from the small town of Lannion, exclaimed that "justice is a debt of the state, and all citizens should contribute equally to the debts of the state." After all, district judges were authorized to hear appeals from throughout the kingdom, just as district administrators were obliged to collect taxes for the national government. The Assembly had already agreed to put all village priests on the state payroll. Why, then, should judges and administrators be paid exclusively by local taxpayers? Because the Committee had an ulterior motive: to impose higher per capita taxes on small and thinly populated districts than on large and densely populated ones, so that taxpayers would urge the Assembly to suppress the small districts. In the words of M. Regnaud, a lawyer from the ambitious town of Saint-Jean-d'Angély, "During the division of the kingdom, you saw each little town demand a district or a tribunal. It has been impossible to reduce these districts, but the Committee feels that everyone should appreciate the necessity for such a reform. . . . What is at stake here is not a constitutional rule, but a momentary measure to bring about the reduction of districts." Barnave, an eloquent lawyer from Grenoble, did point out that local pride and hope of gain would discourage townspeople from supporting the elimination of their own districts. A better strategy would be to impose the cost of districts on the departments, which would inspire a larger number of citizens to demand a reduction. But Thouret convinced a wavering Assembly to

---

[24] *Journal des Etats-Généraux* 15:142.
[25] *Le point du jour*, 414:387.
[26] Letter of Aug. 30, 1790, in Montier, *Correspondance de Thomas Lindet*, p. 215, n. 2.

punish only those who mistakenly imagined that they would benefit from little districts. No matter that this expedient would contradict the principle of spreading the benefits of the Revolution to poor areas of the kingdom, where government subsidies were needed to finance an adequate infrastructure of administrative and judicial services. Having invoked the slogan of equality to block the ambitions of provincial capitals, a majority of deputies now turned against the country towns and bourgs that had just acquired district tribunals. Let the rural electors feel the pain of higher taxes, and supposedly they would abandon these little towns, too.[27]

Barnave was right. Not only did townspeople oppose the abolition of their own districts, but very few rural notables supported the transfer of a nearby district seat to a more distant town. Pressure for reductions came instead from departmental administrators, aided by townspeople who wanted to expand their own districts at the expense of neighboring ones. Even in the few departments where petitions for reductions circulated in the countryside, plans to suppress particular districts provoked more conflict than agreement. The only successful movement for fewer districts took place in the Ardèche, where the first departmental electoral assembly, meeting back in June, had decided to reduce administrative costs by replacing seven districts with only three. Yet this decision provoked considerable controversy as soon as townspeople discovered that only one tribunal would be created for each district. A decree to this effect, passed by the National Assembly on August 18, seemed a blatant example of favoritism. Deputies from the towns of Annonay and Villeneuve-de-Berg had arranged for these former judicial capitals to recover nearly all their jurisdictions as the seats of district tribunals. Officials at rival towns reported angry protests at local fairs, and several district directories petitioned the Assembly to modify its decree. Deputies from the Ardèche insisted, however, that reductions expressed "the will of the people" and "the interests of the countryside." The National Assembly followed their advice on September 18 by scheduling new elections for officials who would replace all the existing district directories of the Ardèche. This decision to disrupt the existing administrative system served as a doubtful precedent for other departments, whose electoral assemblies had either approved the existing districts or neglected to discuss the issue.[28]

Nonetheless, several departmental directories took up the issue of reductions in September, and others followed suit later in the year.[29] Budgetary

[27] Debate on Aug. 30, 1790, AP 18:417.

[28] Jolivet, *Ardèche*, 197–99; petitions in AN DIV bis 19:312–14; printed *Court exposé sur la réduction des districts du département de l'Ardèche*, signed by six deputies, in AN ADXVI 20; AP 19:66.

[29] Paul Meuriot, "Les districts de 1790, comment ils sont devenus les arrondissements de

calculations played an important role in their deliberations. In the smaller districts that were prime candidates for suppression, judicial and administrative salaries would cost the taxpayers 23,700 livres. For a department with nine districts, these costs would amount to around 9 percent of tax revenues.[30] Obviously, officials in such departments could reduce expenses significantly if several districts were suppressed. For example, the *procureur-général-syndic* of the Sarthe estimated that a reduction from nine to five districts would save 140,000 livres, or the equivalent of 3 sols per livre (15 percent) on the land tax. In the Var, where nine districts had also been established, a special commission of the directory complained that administrative costs were higher than in the neighboring department of the Bouches-du-Rhône, whose larger and wealthier population had to pay for only six district directories and tribunals. A reduction from nine to five districts in the Var would save taxpayers 125,000 livres. Similarly, departmental directories in the Ain, the Doubs, the Maine-et-Loire, and the Morbihan concluded from an analysis of administrative costs that the number of districts should be reduced.[31]

Great variations in the population size of districts also encouraged consolidation. In the nation as a whole, 102 districts had fewer than 30,000 inhabitants, 340 had between 30,000 and 70,000 inhabitants, and 92 had over 70,000 inhabitants. As table 9.1 indicates, these variations were greatest in departments that had more than six districts. The table classifies departments on the basis of the number of districts into which they were subdivided. Its index of inequality, which is based on the ratio of population in the largest and smallest district of each department, rises from an average of 1.6 in departments with three districts to an average of 3.4 in departments with seven or eight districts.[32] Such variations resulted in glaring inequities in administrative costs, which ranged from less than 0.33 livres per capita in the most populated districts to more than 1.2 livres per

l'an VIII," *Séances et travaux de l'Académie des Sciences Morales et Politiques*, n.s., 81 (Jan.–Feb. 1921): 457–61.

[30] Estimates based on districts where the seats of directories and tribunals had fewer than 20,000 inhabitants. For example, see the salary tables for the department of the Ain, in AN DIV bis 48. Average tax revenues per department based on "Tableau général," in Prudhomme, *Dictionnaire géographique*, vol. 1, appendix.

[31] *Circulaire* in the Sarthe, AN DIV bis 89:2; Delib. Directory of the Var, Sept. 29, 1790, DIV bis 75:2; documents in DIV bis 56:2 (Ain), 76:2 (Maine-et-Loire), 108:10 (Doubs), and Désiré Jouany, *La formation du département du Morbihan* (Vannes, 1920), pp. 74–75.

[32] Variation in this index is greater still within individual departments: from only 1.1 in the Ardèche and the Ariège to a maximum of 9.5 in the Saône-et-Loire, where the district of Châlon-sur-Saône, with 193,300 inhabitants, towered above that of Bourbon-Lancy, with 20,400 inhabitants. Population data for districts based on Guillaume, *Procès-verbaux du d'instruction publique* 5:665–79.

TABLE 9.1
Population Size of Districts, by Number of Districts per Department

	Number of Districts per Department							
	Nine	Eight	Seven	Six	Five	Four	Three	Total
Population 70,000 or over	11	16	19	22	4	11	9	92
Population 30,000–70,000	103	30	53	115	16	14	9	340
Population under 30,000	39	10	26	19	5	3	0	102
Index of inequality	3.0	3.4	3.4	2.4	2.4	1.8	1.6	2.7
Number of departments	17	7	14	26	5	7	5	81

Sources: The population size of districts is given in "Tableau de la population des départements et districts de la République," M. J. Guillaume, ed., Procès-verbaux du Comité d'instruction publique à la Convention Nationale (Paris, 1904), 5:665–79. Population data for districts in Corsica is missing. Districts in the Seine have been excluded because the population of Paris was so much larger than that of the two other districts.

Notes: The index of inequality is calculated by dividing the population of the largest district in each department by the population of the smallest district in that department, rounding off the quotient to a single decimal point, and taking the average of the quotients across each category of departments in the columns of the table. For example, taking the five departments that were subdivided into three districts, the quotients that measure the relationship between the populations of the largest and smallest districts are 1.1, 1.1, 1.5, 1.9, and 2.3; averaging these five quotients gives an index of inequality of 1.6 for this category of departments.

capita in the least populated districts.[33] A reduction in the number of districts offered the prospect of equalizing these tax rates, as the *procureur-général-syndic* of the Morbihan pointed out. The elimination of the smallest districts would also give more equal weight to each district in departmental elections. According to commissioners in the Var, electors from the small districts of Saint-Paul, Fréjus, and Saint-Maximin, who were outnumbered three to one by those from the large districts of Draguignan, Toulon, and Grasse, had almost no influence in the departmental electoral assembly held in 1790. The goal of political as well as fiscal equality could be achieved in this department by establishing only four districts, each with approximately the same number of active citizens.[34]

Of course, districts could also be equalized by reducing the size of the largest ones, but this would not lower the overall burden of taxation. The most influential critics of existing districts promised lower taxes rather than more equality. For example, a deputy from the Breton town of Pontivy instigated a petitioning campaign against the district of La Roche-Bernard by arguing that its tribunal would burden local taxpayers with "enormous expenses." Municipal officials in the canton of Musillac voiced alarm at such a prospect. One-quarter of the inhabitants in this impoverished and isolated area could not afford to pay any taxes at all. Why should the landowners of Musillac help pay for the salaries of officials in the little town of La Roche-Bernard if they could join the district of Vannes, a much larger and more commercial town? Three deputies to the National Assembly from rural communities in the Finistère played on similar fears of higher taxes when they insisted that too many districts had been created in Brittany. Municipal officials at Kernilis even retracted an earlier endorsement of the district of Lesneven after receiving nine letters from their deputy, Le Guen de Kerangall, preaching the cause of fiscal economy. Now they wanted only only two districts in the northern Finistère, at the large towns of Brest and Morlaix. A total of twenty-seven municipalities and cantonal assemblies in this department joined the campaign for fewer districts. Similarly, anonymous propagandists in the Mayenne convinced the leaders of fourteen communities that administrative costs would "fall upon the countryside to enrich only the inhabitants of the towns." Petitioners from Vieuvy voiced shock at the news that salaries would cost taxpayers 25,000 livres in the district of Ernée, which contained only thirty-five parishes. On

---

[33] Estimates based on districts of over 70,000 and under 30,000 inhabitants, in which the seats of districts and tribunals had fewer than 20,000 inhabitants. The salaries of judges and administrators would increase by as much as 63 percent in districts headed by a town of over 60,000 inhabitants, but per capita costs would still be lower than in predominantly rural districts with fewer than 30,000 inhabitants.

[34] AN DIV bis 68:3 (Morbihan); DIV bis 75:2 (Var).

top of this, the townspeople of Ernée were planning to build a "sumptuous palace of justice" with public funds![35]

Yet even in these departments of northwestern France, where critics of the new administrative and judicial system encouraged rural resentment of urban wealth, townspeople were often more eager than villagers to suppress particular districts. For example, antiurban rhetoric concealed the ambition of townspeople at Mayenne, still smarting from their failure to prevent the little towns of Evron and Villaines from acquiring separate districts. Similarly, municipal officials at Vannes encouraged the movement for fewer districts in the Morbihan; and those at Morlaix favored efforts to dismantle neighboring districts in the Finistère. While townspeople developed specific plans for territorial aggrandizement, villagers were often vague about which districts should be eliminated. They found it easy to request transfer to a district seat where they already had business dealings. Thus, anonymous electors from the district of Doullens favored the suppression of this district because the much larger town of Amiens served as the center of their grain and textile commerce.[36] But customary marketing relationships often favored small towns. The argument from *rapprochement*, which drew its strength from the high costs of transport in rural France, continued to influence rural notables. If they wanted lower taxes, they also wanted easy access to the district seat. Consequently, petitioners who signed petitions for fewer districts often imagined that their own district would survive. In the Sarthe, for example, many rural parishes that called for a reduction were already located in the district of Le Mans, the departmental seat.[37] In departments where petitioners discovered that their customary market center might lose its district seat, they often sprang to its defense. Generally speaking, public campaigns for or against particular districts became struggles between rival towns instead of conflicts between townspeople and villagers.[38]

Responding to the threat of suppression, officials in small towns were quick to denounce the "aristocratic" ambitions of their rivals. In the Ain, for example, where the former provincial capital of Bourg seemed behind a plan for only four districts, the directory of Châtillon-les-Dombes complained that "all the powers" used to be concentrated at Bourg: provincial

---

[35] For these and other examples of rural support for fewer districts, see the dossiers in AN DIV bis 10:234 (Mayenne), 67:6, 68:3, and 109:4.

[36] Printed *mémoire*, AN ADXVI 77.

[37] See the documents in AN DIV bis 89:2; and Gossin's report on this petitioning campaign, which fell into disarray when the departmental council tried to choose which districts would be preserved, AP 20:725–26.

[38] For examples of rural petitions that defended small towns, see those from the districts of Cérilly and Le Donjon, in the Allier; Barjols, in the Var; and Challans, in the Vendée, in AN DIV bis 57:16, 75:2, 76:1.

council, *bailliage*, *présidial*, *élection*, subdelegation, and *maréchausséee*. The inhabitants of this town, who had benefited from "revolting injustices" in the expenditure of public funds and the allocation of taxes, still possessed a "spirit of superiority." If the smaller districts were suppressed, Bourg would restore its position as the "dominant town," and all the cash would end up there again, instead of flowing back to the taxpayers elsewhere in the province. In justifying such a policy on fiscal grounds, "the enemies of the people" were covering themselves with "the specious veil of the general welfare." The *procureur-syndic* for the district of Montluel, who argued that the 7,350 inhabitants of Bourg paid less taxes than the 3,731 townspeople and farmers of Montluel, concluded that "such injustices will continue unless small towns retain their new administrative power."[39] In like manner, the district directory of Cérilly, threatened by a circular from the departmental directory of the Allier, fought back by informing the National Assembly that "the large towns, which for too long have oppressed the countryside," would monopolize all the establishments if some districts were eliminated." The mayor of Bourbon-l'Archambault, whose town had received the tribunal in the district of Cérilly, agreed that a reduction of districts would "revive the old regime." For the past fifteen years, considerable taxes had been raised in the area for highway construction, but these funds had been used only to embellish the three principal towns of the Allier and to open roads for them. "None of the small towns or the countryside profited from these expenditures; they always paid taxes without getting anything in return." If four of the seven districts were suppressed, the largest towns would regain "the same despotism that has just been taken away."[40]

Thus, defenders of small towns turned fiscal arguments against their adversaries. They also rejected arguments about the superior qualifications of notables in more important towns. Electors from the little town of Neuville, in the Loiret, affirmed both their democratic sentiments and their political loyalties when rivals at Pithiviers tried to suppress their district. These critics had accused Neuville of lacking "any of those citizens whom one meets in larger localities under the denomination of nobles and bourgeois, whose fortune, education, and free disposal of their time permit them to sacrifice their leisure to public service." To this arrogant comparison, the fledgling democrats of Neuville replied ironically:

> We must confess that Neuville does not enjoy the honor of having among its inhabitants any nobles, or any newly created nobles, or any bourgeois enjoying an excessive amount of wealth. It does have the good fortune, however, of pos-

[39] Letters from the district directory of Châtillon-les-Dombes, and printed *Esquisse des vexations de l'Ancien Régime*, by the *procureur-syndic* of the district directory of Montluel, AN DIV bis 56:20–21.

[40] Letters in AN DIV bis 57:17; DIV bis 3:149 (Allier).

sessing many excellent citizens, a substantial number of whom are ready, by virtue of their industry, their labor, and their frugality, to be useful to their fatherland and to their fellow citizens, without expecting any personal gain.

Because of their new district, the citizens of Neuville, who used to be subordinated to the *élection* of Pithiviers, were now the equals of the residents in this town, who could not bear to concede the loss of their "imaginary superiority." It was the plain folk of Neuville who took the lead in forming a national guard and pledging funds to the *contribution patriotique*. Surely such patriots deserved the support of the National Assembly![41]

Not all the partisans of small towns were as disingenuous about their personal ambitions as those from Neuville. The municipality of Ornans voiced alarm at word that the departmental directory of the Doubs wanted to eliminate the district seat and tribunal in this town. Earlier in the year, an "infinite number" of citizens, filled with zeal for public affairs, had done everything, spending time and money, in order to preserve local opportunities for employment. It would be unfair if they lost all hope of obtaining, through their civic spirit and their virtue, "the new positions that the Revolution has promised as recompense to good Frenchmen." Most of these respectable families would fall into decline if the district of Ornans were suppressed. On a more threatening note, the district directory of Cusset, in the Allier, tried to refute the argument that suitable candidates could not be found for all the new tribunals.

> Imagine how many citizens, having lost their offices, are left with no hope but to become judges. If they are employed, they will defend the constitution. If there are too few positions for them to obtain, they will fall into despair and curse a revolution that will have reduced them to misery. What will become of this legion of judges whose courts have been suppressed, and of all the men of law reduced to unemployment? What will happen to their families? Will they not increase the ranks of the army of the discontented, already too large?

Similarly, a memorialist for the district of Saint-Rambert warned of a "great commotion" in nearly three hundred towns if the National Assembly, having just completed the new edifice of the state, began to tear it down again by suppressing districts and tribunals. "A universal insurrection would not fail to be supported by those losing out in the revolution." However exaggerated such fears of popular revolt, any reduction in the number of districts risked undermining support for the National Assembly. In the words of a deputy who reported intense opposition to reductions on the part of small towns in the Sarthe, "The more districts we would suppress, the more malcontents we would create."[42]

[41] Printed *réponse*, ADXVI 46 (Neuville).

[42] Mun. Delib. Ornans; printed *Proclamation du district de Cusset*; *mémoire* for the district

The National Assembly first confronted such resistance in mid-October, when special deputies from small towns in the Ain arrived, bearing numerous petitions against a decision by the directory of this department to request a reduction from nine to four districts. For the C.C., which now decried the concessions made earlier to spokesmen from small towns, these petitions were a disagreeable surprise. If townspeople alone would benefit from the higher taxes needed to pay for little districts, then why did the leaders of so many rural communities sign these petitions? Gossin, speaking for the Committee, tried to convince the Assembly on October 15 that officials in the directories and municipalities were misusing their authority by circulating petitions. Their efforts to rally public opinion only proved that townspeople still viewed the countryside as a domain to conquer. Unless the Assembly took immediate measures to stop these "great disorders," administrative bodies would develop the "very dangerous habit" of forming leagues (*coalitions*) with a "mass" of individuals. Announcing that the C.C. wanted to prepare a general decree for the elimination of at least 137 districts and tribunals, Gossin moved that the members of district directories and municipalities be prohibited from soliciting petitions and that all the departmental councils, meeting in November, be authorized to propose reductions.[43]

But preparations for a general decree would rekindle all the urban rivalries that had interfered with the earlier division of the departments into districts. "You are going to throw the kingdom into a morass of disputes," warned M. Bouche. "You should preserve what has been done instead of risking even worse results." M. d'André, often in disagreement with his fellow townsman from Aix, rose to affirm that such a decree would turn the kingdom upside down. Only particular decrees for reduction should be considered, on the basis of requests from districts that wanted to merge with each other. With equal vigor, Abbé Bourdon, from the little district seat of Evaux, challenged the right of departmental directories to speak for the taxpayers (*administrés*), who should be consulted directly before the National Assembly took any action. Expressing a groundswell of opinion against disrupting the administrative institutions that had so recently been established, these critics convinced the Assembly to reject the general clauses of Gossin's decree. Only the departmental council of the Ain would

---

of Saint-Rambert; and "Réflexions" by Pelisson de Gennes. AN DIV bis 108:10; DIV bis 57:15; DIV bis 56:14; DIV bis 89:2.

[43] *Rapport*, AP 19:646. The departmental councils, or *conseils généraux*, consisted of twenty-eight delegates in addition to the eight members of the directories that formed the permanent executive organs of departmental administration. See Godechot, *Les institutions*, p. 98.

be ordered to express its opinion about the particular plan of reduction submitted by the directory in this department.[44]

Just two days later, Gossin renewed his skepticism about petitioning campaigns, but this time he objected to unauthorized deliberations from nearly three hundred municipalities in the Sarthe that wanted fewer districts. These petitions had been solicited by the *procureur-général-syndic* of the department without the permission of the directory of the department. Alluding to Rousseau's theory of the general will, Gossin argued that "a majority of the municipalities certainly does not form the will of a majority of *administrés*, especially when there are suspicions that this will has been manipulated, as the directory has complained." Following his advice, the Assembly referred the dispute to the departmental council of the Sarthe.[45] But this council, like its counterpart in the Ain, could not decide which districts to suppress, and nearly half the delegates petitioned the National Assembly not to make any changes. Elsewhere in the nation, most of the departmental councils either ignored the issue of reductions or voted to uphold the status quo. On November 24, Gossin reported that the C.C. had completely reversed itself. Now its members believed that it would be impolitic and harmful to suppress *any* districts. Even in the Var, where the general council ratified the Directory's plan of reduction, not a single commune in the districts of Barjols, Fréjus, and Hyères favored the suppression of these districts, and many were clamouring against any innovation. According to Gossin, "the same thing has taken place in every department where the administrators have proposed any reductions whatsoever."[46]

Many deputies were increasingly worried by reports of counterrevolutionary uprisings in the provinces, which seemed to prove the need for administrative stability. Agrarian protest against feudal dues, food riots in market towns, and, above all, growing Catholic opposition to the Civil Constitution of the Clergy seemed to threaten the new regime.[47] Officials in the districts would bear much of the responsibility for enforcing the decrees of the National Assembly. Gossin alluded to this political reality when he warned, "To reduce the districts at a moment when the constitution has so many enemies, and when the organization of national guards has not yet been completed, is to incite great fermentation." Fewer patriotic administrators and judges would be employed, and new officials

[44] Speeches of MM. Lavie, Bouche, D'André, and Abbé Bourdon, and decree of Oct. 15, 1790, AP 19:647.

[45] AP 19:672–73.

[46] AP 20:725–27.

[47] On the emergence of counterrevolutionary protests among Catholics in 1790, see D. M. G. Sutherland, *France, 1789–1815: Revolution and Counterrevolution* (New York, 1986), pp. 107–11.

would have to be elected at a moment when people were tired of elections. As the strongest columns of the constitution, administrative bodies should be reinforced, not undermined. Consequently, Gossin advised the Assembly to reject any changes in the districts of the Ain, Sarthe, and Var. From the left of the Assembly, François Buzot, who would later rebel against the Convention, took the floor to denounce "the internecine divisions that some men have an interest in creating and maintaining in our provinces." He proposed that *all* requests for reductions be referred to subsequent legislatures, and the National Assembly promptly agreed to leave to its successors the problem of consolidating small districts into larger ones.[48]

The Legislative Assembly, which replaced the National Assembly on October 1, 1791, made no effort to reorganize the districts. Nearly two-thirds of its members had begun their political careers during the Revolution as administrators or judges, including 236 members of district councils, directories, and tribunals.[49] Loyalty to former colleagues and sensitivity to local political pressures help explain why these former officials from small towns, who dominated the Comité de Division of the Assembly, confined their attention to boundary readjustments.[50] Despite rumors in the spring of 1792 that as many as 270 districts would be suppressed, this committee buried all requests for fewer districts, which came mainly from departmental directories and councils.[51] Such plans for reductions sparked petitioning campaigns in defense of the status quo. For example, when the directories of Argenton and La Châtre learned that they might be suppressed, they forwarded petitions from dozens of municipalities to the Comité de Division. In like manner, the municipal councils of Mortagne, in the Orne, and Hyères and Saint-Maximin, in the Var, came to the aid of their district directories when the assemblies of these departments asked the Legislative Assembly for reductions. So did 146 administrators, judges, and other townspeople from Carhaix, and 70 officials and fellow citizens from Châteaulin, in the Finistère. Petitioners from a few towns, such as Châteaubriant and Guerande, in the Loire-Infèrieure, and Beaucaire and Le Vigan, in the Gard, did acknowledge the need for reductions,

[48] Session of Nov. 24, 1790, AP 20:727.

[49] Tabulation based on the biographical information in August Kuscinksi, *Les députés à l'assemblée législative de 1791* (Paris, 1900).

[50] This committee took over responsibility for boundary disputes and other issues concerning the territorial division of France. Among the twenty-seven deputies who served on it during the period of the Legislative Assembly, only three came from towns of over 10,000 inhabitants, while twenty came from smaller towns that had districts or tribunals, two came from other small towns, and two came from rural communes. Membership lists in AP 34:450 (Oct. 27, 1791), and AP 39:393 (Mar. 5, 1792); places of residence in Kuscinski, *Les députés*.

[51] The directories of the Aube and Hautes-Alpes, and the councils of the Lozère, Orne, and Basses-Pyrénées requested fewer districts in 1791. AN DIV bis 57:4, 11; DIV bis 58:4; DIV bis 70:1; F2 I:503; Delon, *La Révolution en Lozère*, pp. 17–18.

but they naturally wanted to preserve their own district seats. Typically, the directory of Le Vigan endorsed the idea of suppressing the neighboring districts of Saint-Hippolyte and Sommières while complaining of a plan to incorporate the districts of Le Vigan and Sommières into that of Saint-Hippolyte. Instead of trying to choose among such contradictory plans, the *Comité de Division* quietly ignored all the petitions that it received for the expansion of some districts at the expense of others.[52]

Under the Legislative Assembly, the districts became increasingly important agencies of government, which also explains why pressures to reduce them came to naught. Their officials—a *procureur-syndic*, a four-member directory, and a twelve-member council—mediated between departmental administrations and local municipalities. In the district seats, they joined with other "constituted authorities," such as municipal councils, district judges, and military commanders, to preside over public ceremonies that celebrated the unity of the nation. From these central places, the *procureurs-syndics* communicated legislative decrees and administrative circulars to the municipalities, which were then obliged to submit new tax roles to the district directories, along with a variety of other information. These directories in turn apportioned taxes among the communes and forwarded statistical tables and reports to the departmental *procureurs-généraux-syndics*. When the legislature authorized departments to spend money on public works and charitable activities, district officials decided how to allocate these funds to local communities. They also played a vital role in the sale of church lands and the supervision of the clergy, two sensitive political issues. As inflationary pressures deepened in the winter of 1791–92, these officials took measures to provision local markets and maintain public order. Finally, with the outbreak of war in April 1792, district administrators supervised military recruitment in the villages, helped organize detachments of volunteers, and even clothed and equipped these soldiers for service at the front. When the Legislative Assembly proclaimed a national emergency on July 12, 1792, all the members of each district council were called into permanent session. Henceforth, they would bear the main burden of mobilizing the countryside for warfare.[53]

Military defeats undermined the authority of the Legislative Assembly

---

[52] AN DIV bis 110:1; DIV bis 65:4. On the general policy of the committee, see Meuriot, "Les districts de 1790," pp. 462–63.

[53] On the administrative functions of district directories, see Godechot, *Institutions*, pp. 101–3. For examples of their activities, see Louis Biernawski, *Un département sous la Révolution française: L'Allier de 1789 à l'an III* (Moulins, 1909), pp. 167–268; Madeleine Dériès, *Le district de Saint-Lô pendant la Révolution, 1787–an IV* (Paris, 1922); and Eugène Corgne, *Pontivy et son district pendant la Révolution, 1789–Germinal an V* (Rennes, 1938). For an excellent essay on local administration during the early years of the Revolution, see Alison Patrick, "French Revolutionary Local Government, 1789–1792," in Baker, *The French Revolution and the Creation of Modern Political Culture* 2:399–420.

and doomed the monarchy, which collapsed after Parisian rebels stormed the royal palace and imprisoned the king on August 10. In the crisis of legitimacy that followed this violent insurrection, a Convention of newly elected deputies replaced the Legislative Assembly on September 21. This Convention took prompt action to maintain the existing authorities in the departments, but it also abolished the monarchy, proclaimed a unitary Republic, and prepared to draft a new constitution for popular ratification. The debates over this constitution reopened the question of territorial organization. A constitutional committee, dominated by deputies from Paris and Bordeaux, submitted a plan on February 15, 1793, to abolish all the districts and district tribunals.[54] Its spokesman, the marquis de Condorcet, endorsed a new version of Abbé Sièyes's old project for *grandes communes*, which would incorporate towns and villages into the same basic units of administration. Combining the ideas of Turgot and Sièyes, Condorcet estimated that the radius of each *grande commune* should not exceed two and a half leagues, or the distance people could walk to and from a central place in a single day. This implied an average of around fourteen administrative subdivisions per department.[55] Urban and rural municipalities would be reduced to sections of the *grandes communes*, each with a single agent in charge of local administration. Justices of the peace would also be concentrated in these *grandes communes*, and departmental tribunals, with civil juries, would replace the district tribunals. Thus, Condorcet's plan called for a drastic reduction in the number of municipal officials, justices of the peace, and civil judges. As for the departmental administrations, they would be subordinated more closely to an Executive Council in Paris, which would appoint its own agents instead of relying on elected *procureurs-généraux-syndics* in each department. For Condorcet, the administrative institutions of the state needed to be transformed in accordance with rational principles of spatial organization.[56]

But many deputies paid only lip service to the cause of perfecting the constitution. They judged Condorcet's plan on political grounds and found it either too authoritarian in its basic outline or too disruptive in its practical effects. While Montagnard deputies from Paris took the lead in defending the Paris Commune against Girondin attacks, deputies from provincial towns questioned whether institutions that had proven their value to the Republic should be hastily suppressed. Deputies from 415

[54] Of the nine members and six *suppléants* chosen on Oct. 11, 1792, ten were deputies from Paris, two from Bordeaux, one from Marseille, one from Lyon, and one from Bayeux. AP 52:455; and Kuscinksi, *Dictionnaire des Conventionnels* (Paris, 1917).

[55] Calculation based on hexagonal subdivisions, each with an apothem of two-and-a-half leagues and an area of twenty-three square leagues, in accordance with central place theory.

[56] *Rapport* in AP 58:592–93. On the political context of Condorcet's constitutional ideas, see Baker, *Condorcet*, pp. 316–30.

different towns, including 357 seats of districts and tribunals, sat in the Convention, and over 200 of them had previously served on district councils or lawcourts.[57] Hometown loyalties as well as administrative experience discouraged such deputies from supporting Condorcet's ideal system. Many would have agreed with Louis-Joseph Charlier, a former district administrator at Châlons-sur-Marne, who defended the districts for rendering "very great services" as "the guardians of liberty." Furthermore, as word of food riots and counterrevolutionary uprisings reached Paris during the spring of 1793, even leaders of the Girondin faction developed second thoughts about dismantling the existing administrative system. In the words of Pétion de Villeneuve, "To change the territorial division at a moment when anarchy is spreading and civil war has blazed forth to threaten us, is to run the risk of disorganizing everything." Michel-Edme Petit, who also sympathized with the Girondins, agreed that a new division would cause "shocks, divisions, conflicts throughout France, which we certainly do not need." Finally, the merger of existing municipalities into *grandes communes* would undermine local government in the countryside. Drawing on his own experience as a municipal officer, Petit concluded his critique of *grandes communes* on this note: "The municipal sash is everywhere the sustenance of revolutionary courage, the stimulus to probity, a vehicle of honor." Most deputies agreed that local identities fostered effective municipal administration. When they voted overwhelmingly on May 21 to preserve all the existing communes, plans to eliminate the districts collapsed. Lanjuinais, a Girondin who had reported earlier that "suppression is the general will," introduced a motion on May 25 to divide each department into districts. The motion carried unanimously.[58]

In these debates over the constitution, Montagnard deputies voiced opposition to the concentration of administrative power in departmental directories.[59] Confirming their worst fears, many officials on these directories protested against the expulsion of Girondin leaders from the Convention at the beginning of June. The federalist movements that challenged the Convention in provincial cities such as Bordeaux, Lyon, and Caen rarely gained much popular support in smaller towns.[60] Consequently, the tri-

---

[57] Places of origin and previous administrative experience of deputies are derived from Kuscinski, *Dictionnaire des Conventionnels*.

[58] Speeches on Apr. 24 (Lanjuinais), Apr. 26 (Petit), May 15 (Charlier and Pétion), May 21 (Petit), and May 25 (Lanjuinais), AP 63:194–95, 408–9, 64:699–700, 65:149–50, 156. On the political sympathies of particular deputies for the Girondins or the Montagnards, I have followed Alison Patrick, *The Men of the First French Republic: Political Alignments and the National Convention of 1792* (Baltimore, 1972), appendix 2, pp. 315–39.

[59] Prolonged murmurs of discontent from the upper seats of the Convention—the Mountain—accompanied the passage of a decree for "a central administration in each department" on May 15, AP 64:701.

[60] On the urban geography of federalism, see Bill Edmonds, " 'Federalism' and Urban Re-

umphant Montagnard faction of the Convention began to strengthen the authority of the districts as a counterweight to the departments. This trend culminated in the law of 14 frimaire (December 4, 1793), which abolished the departmental councils, presidents, and *procureurs-généraux-syndics* and stripped the departmental directories of all political responsibilities. Henceforth, the district directories, headed by "national agents," would correspond directly with the governing committees in Paris, relay orders to the municipalities, and supervise every aspect of the Terror. In the eyes of Billaud-Varenne, who presented the law of 14 frimaire to the Convention, districts had the advantage of being too small to challenge the central government. Their officials would function as "levers of execution, passive in the hands of the power that moves them, lifeless and inert in the absence of any [external] impulse." Even more hostile than Billaud-Varenne to political initiative from below, Danton urged the Convention to appoint "men of the Republic" instead of relying on "local men" to carry out its orders. The Committee of Public Safety, caught between its democratic rhetoric and the exigencies of power, hesitated for a few weeks and then accepted an amendment to purge the *procureurs-syndics* in the districts and to appoint national agents in their place. Drawing a sharp distinction between local officials and the people, Couthon, speaking on behalf of the Committee, had no difficulty rationalizing this violation of the principle of free elections: "While the revolutionary machine is still in motion, you would harm it by permitting the people to elect public functionaries, because they would run the risk of naming men who would betray them."[61]

But what if the people themselves opposed the revolutionary government? Unlike Montagnards in the Convention who were quick to blame officials for perverting the popular will, patriots in some provincial towns accused entire communities of aristocratic tendencies. They projected urban rivalries into revolutionary politics. In a few cases, townspeople in district seats politicized earlier demands for the tribunal that a rival town had been awarded. For example, special deputies from Monistrol and Saint-Didier denounced Yssingeaux in April 1792 for organizing an uprising against patriots in the Haute-Loire. They argued that the populace of this town, "entirely corrupted by the clergy and by numerous societies of pious laymen," must be deprived of the "particular benefits of the Revolution, and especially of the lawcourt, a favor which it has repeatedly shown that it is unworthy to enjoy, and which it never should have obtained." A few

---

volt in France in 1793," *The Journal of Modern History* 55, no. 1 (Mar. 1983): 22–53; and Alan Forrest's essay, "Federalism," in Baker, *The French Revolution and the Creation of Modern Political Culture* 2:309–29. Forrest has published an excellent local history of this movement in Bordeaux and the department of the Gironde: *Society and Politics in Revolutionary Bordeaux* (Oxford, 1975).

[61] Speeches of 23 brumaire, 3 frimaire, and 14 frimaire, year II, in AP 79:455, 80:71, 636.

months later, spokesmen for Haguenau denounced Saverne, the judicial seat of their district, as an "entirely fanatical town" whose inhabitants, devoted to refractory priests and aristocratic lawyers, were "enemies of the Revolution." Following the proclamation of the Republic, municipal officials at Mauriac used similar rhetoric against the judicial center of Salers, "the home of aristocracy and fanaticism." Members of a popular society returned to the charge in July 1793, this time describing Salers as a town that "has constantly abhorred the Revolution, while Mauriac has always distinguished itself by its patriotism." None of these denunciations had any effect, but in September 1793 a representative on mission decided to punish the town of Le Buis by transferring its tribunal to the district seat of Nyons. At the end of the following year, the municipalities of these rival towns were still disputing charges that Le Buis had falsely been denounced for rebelling against the Convention. At the very least, the partisans of Nyons contrasted "the cold indifference of the inhabitants of Le Buis with the revolutionary conduct of our fellow citizens."[62]

Much more frequently, townspeople demanded the district directory, whose administrative functions included such important tasks for local communities as the sale of national lands and the stockpiling of grain.[63] Especially in the Montagnard phase of the Revolution, directories monopolized the attention of rival towns. Between June 1793 and July 1794, a total of twenty-eight towns sought a directory, as compared with only two towns that wanted a tribunal.[64] Even in districts where establishments had been divided, only towns that possessed the tribunal took the initiative of challenging the status quo. The rivalry between Espalion and Saint-Geniez illustrates the primacy of administrative concerns after the Montagnards encouraged the sale in small lots of national lands and imposed price controls on grain and other commodities. According to the popular society of Espalion, bidders at the district seat of Saint-Geniez were buying properties at deflated prices in order to resell them for a large profit. The members of this society also boasted that their town, which had a central location in the district, served as a supply depot for fodder needed by the army of the Pyrénées. Back in 1790, the "rich egoists" of Saint-Geniez had gained the

[62] Letters against Yssingeaux in AN DIV bis 65:3; *observations* for Haguenau, DIV bis 88:1; *adresse* and *pétition* for Mauriac, DIV bis 82:3; *pétition* for Le Buis and *mémoire* for Nyons, DIV bis 82:14.

[63] On the administrative functions of district directories during the Terror, see Babeau, *Histoire de Troyes* 2:215–33; Deriès, *Le district de Saint-Lô*, pp. 80–86; and the documents in Lorain, *Les subsistances en céréales* 1:390–538.

[64] Districts continued to be the main goal of towns during the Thermidorian period (Aug. 1794–Sept. 1795), when the Convention received another seven requests for district seats. By contrast, between Jan. 1792 and May 1793, eight towns requested a district, seven wanted a tribunal, and one asked for both. Tabulation based mainly on documents in AN DIV bis 81–91.

district only because they had possessed enough gold to send special deputies to Paris. "How could poor sansculottes, whose patriotism was nearly their only possession, expect to triumph over a commune that has the advantage of an extensive, brilliant, and lucrative commerce?" But now that the Republic had triumphed, "reason, justice, and all the Republican virtues are the order of the day."[65]

Faced with accusations of "aristocracy, fanaticism, and egoism," the popular society of Saint-Geniez replied indignantly that this textile town had always marched in the forefront of the Revolution. Its members joined with the municipality to provide the Convention with a detailed narrative of the town's patriotic feats: 150 volunteers for the army in 1792; several campaigns of national guardsmen against draft resisters and counterrevolutionaries in the mountains of the Lozère; organized resistance to the federalists of Bordeaux in the summer of 1793; unanimous agreement during the Terror to ban all public religious ceremonies and to do without priests and vicars; and admirable patience in the face of a deplorable famine that continued to ravage the town. Like the sansculottes of Espalion, the patriots of Saint-Geniez did not mention the tribunal that both towns had formerly disputed. In the midst of famine, they had lost interest in attracting magistrates and lawyers to their town. Instead, they lamented the territorial boundaries of their district, which excluded several nearby villages that used to supply their market with grain. In 1794, when towns needed the sanction of district administrators in order to requisition grain from villages, such discrepancies between administrative boundaries and traditional marketing areas could be disastrous. Not surprisingly, these defenders of Saint-Geniez ended their petition to the Convention by criticizing "the abuses that have slipped into the territorial division of France." In the year II, only administrators, not lawcourts, could guarantee the provisioning of towns.[66]

The administrative demands of foreign and civil war made the government in Paris and representatives on mission more concerned about the precise location of directories, too. If a district seat seemed exposed to enemy attack or lacked access to good roads, another town might become a more appropriate center of military supply. In like manner, if counterrevolutionaries gained control of a district seat, a rival town that pledged its loyalty to the Convention might deserve to gain the directory. The Legislative Assembly had already authorized the provisional transfer of district administration from towns threatened by invasion, such as Montmédy, in the Meuse, and Benfeld, in the Haut-Rhin.[67] The rump of this Assembly,

[65] AN DIV bis 81:12.
[66] Letter in AN DIV bis 81:12, reprinted in AP 90:420–21.
[67] AN DIV bis 68:2; DIV bis 88:1.

still meeting while elections to the Convention were being organized, also set a precedent for political sanctions by shifting the district seat of Châtillon to Bressuire on September 5, 1792. This decision followed reports that 6,000 brigands had invaded the town of Châtillon and burned the registers of the directory, while the same rebels had later been repulsed with heavy losses when they tried to capture the town of Bressuire. The directory itself had taken refuge at Bressuire, which convinced the Assembly that this town would offer better security for administrators than Châtillon, whose inhabitants had done nothing to oppose the rebels.[68]

The Convention followed this precedent during the federalist crisis of June 1793 by voting to transfer the district seat of Evreux to the smaller town of Vernon. District as well as departmental officials at Evreux had tried to organize resistance to the Convention in the department of the Eure. In particular, the directory had issued orders on June 15 for the farmers in the district to bring all their reserves of grain to Evreux, where the federalists were concentrating troops. This measure posed a direct threat to the subsistence of Vernon, whose municipality responded by denouncing rather belatedly a federalist proclamation that the departmental directory had issued back on June 6.[69] Fearing, above all, the requisitioning powers of the district directory, Vernon hastened to send special deputies to Paris, carrying a petition signed by 283 townspeople who pledged their loyalty to the Convention. These emissaries arrived on the eighteenth, when their alarming report provoked a stern decree that not only prohibited anyone from obeying the rebellious administrators at Evreux but also rewarded Vernon for its loyalty by making it the provisional seat of the district.[70]

Representatives on mission issued orders on their own authority to transfer the seats of eleven districts during the period of the Terror, when the authority of the Convention threatened to disintegrate entirely in some departments. Military operations explain some of these decisions, such as the transfer of the district of Hyères to Solliès during the siege of Toulon.[71] Equally important were punitive actions directed against real or alleged

[68] AP 49:121. For a description of this revolt, which foreshadowed the much larger insurrection of the Vendée, see Tilly, *The Vendée*, pp. 306–8.

[69] A deputation from the popular society and surveillance committee of Vernon had already appeared in the Convention on June 13 to denounce the federalist movement in the Eure, but the *conseil général* of the commune refused to act until it received the requisitioning order on the fifteenth. See AP 66:472–73.

[70] Mun. Delib., *Adresse*, and decree of June 18, AP 66:678–72.

[71] *Adresse* of protest by Mun. Hyères, which regained the district seat a year later, AN DIV bis 91:2. Other examples include the transfer of the district seat of Benfeld to Schlestadt, an important garrison town in the Bas-Rhin; and the attachment of the district of Boulay to that of Sarrelouis, a fortified town in the Moselle, near the German frontier. See the dossiers on these affairs in AN DIV bis 88:1.

opponents of the Convention. In the region around Lyon, for example, where the terrorist Javogues wreaked vengeance on the bourgeoisie of his hometown of Montbrison, militants at Autun also persuaded this swaggering proconsul of the Republic to eliminate the district of Bourbon-Lancy.[72] Denounced as aristocrats, the administrators and judges in this small town fought back by accusing "the ambitious city of Autun" of coveting their territory for the past three centuries. Javogues brushed aside such ancient rivalries, arrested the magistrates, and issued an edict on December 3, 1793, to attach their district to Autun, due to its "counterrevolutionary tendencies." Fortunately for Bourbon-Lancy, Javogues was recalled to Paris in disgrace, and when a new representative on mission arrived, he released the officials and restored the district.[73]

An even more flagrant example of high-handed intervention against a district seat occurred just north of Toulouse, in the district of Grenade. Here the townspeople of Beaumont, having tried in vain to acquire a directory as well as a tribunal back in 1790, renewed their campaign for the district in October 1793 on the pretext that Grenade had become a "center of aristocracy." To these "calumnies engendered by ambition, cupidity, and greed," the municipality of Grenade retorted with proofs of its eagerness to execute the laws of the Republic. Four hundred townspeople, it assured the Convention, were serving in the armies along the frontiers. Volunteers from Beaumont had joined instead the revolutionary army of the Haute-Garonne, led by their former mayor, Hugueny, who had made a career for himself as a terrorist in Toulouse. Armed with an edict from a representative on mission named Paganel, Hugueny and his troops occupied the town of Grenade on November 5, 1793, ostensibly to enforce orders for the requisitioning of grain. The hapless citizens of Grenade reported afterward that Hugueny's men had terrorized the population for forty-two days, pillaging houses in the town, raiding nearby villages, and making off with silver, mirrors, clocks, jewels, lace, and fancy ornaments of ladies' clothing. Such accusations only convinced Hugueny to exact more vengeance on Grenade. He persuaded Paganel to transfer the district seat in an edict of January 21, 1794, that declared, "The commune of Grenade is marching today more than ever in the opposite direction from the Revolution, since its general council and committee of surveillance are infected with aristocracy and the most extreme egoism." Beaumont, by contrast, "has never ceased to keep pace with circumstances." Paganel later admitted that he no idea which town had a more suitable location in the district, and the Thermidorian directory of the department reported in May 1795 that

---

[72] On Javogues's unsavory reputation as a terrorist, see Colin Lucas, *The Structure of the Terror: The Example of Javogues and the Loire* (Oxford, 1973).

[73] Pamphlets and petitions from Autun and "Bellevue-les-Bains" (Bourbon-Lancy), and *arrêtés* of Javogues and Gouly, 13 frimaire and 18 nivoise, year II, in AN DIV bis 89:1.

the markets and roads of the area favored Grenade. Two months later, another representative on mission returned the district seat to this town.[74]

Political intrigues in Paris account for a decree of the Convention that transferred the district seat of Caudebec to Yvetot.[75] The rivalry between these two towns exemplifies the uses of political rhetoric during the Terror. Caudebec, an old *bailliage* town with a small port on the Seine, had the misfortune of sending two deputies to the Convention who were both expelled as Girondins in June 1793. Yvetot thrived on the textile industry of upper Normandy, and its artisans and weavers became enthusiastic Montagnards in the year II. They wanted the district seat because of the "granary of abundance" that would accompany it. But the special deputies from Yvetot who presented their demands to the Convention in October 1793 were careful not to mention local concerns about food supply. Instead, they boasted of protecting all the grain shipments to Paris that passed through Yvetot along the main road from Le Havre, and they denounced Caudebec as a town governed by a "judgocracy" (*robinocratie*) of moderates, even federalists, a veritable "swamp that can never produce any patriotism." Petitioners from the popular society of Caudebec fought back by describing their patriotic ceremonies in honor of Marat and Le Peletier, their arrests of suspects, especially Englishmen, and their 180 citizens who were serving in the armies of the Republic—to no avail. A militant from Yvetot gained the ear of the Jacobin Club in Paris, obtained a provisional decree transferring the district seat, and then secured his own appointment as the national agent for the Committee of Public Safety at Yvetot.[76]

Caudebec tried to regain the district in May 1794, but its special deputies triggered a chorus of denunciations from the popular societies of Yvetot and nearby bourgs. "Ask them," demanded the militants of Yvetot in a letter to the Jacobin society in Paris. "Ask them if some of their members didn't bemoan the execution of Capet and approve the murder of Marat; ask them if three-quarters of the commune didn't refuse to attend the funeral ceremony for this martyr of liberty." If Yvetot accused Caudebec of federalism, Caudebec accused Yvetot of Hébertisme. A military agent of

---

[74] Petitions and other documents from Beaumont and Grenade in AN DIV bis 63:2 and 83:3; Rumeau, *Formation du district de Grenade*, pp. 15–18; Richard Cobb, *Les armées révolutionnaires des départements du Midi* (Toulouse, 1955), pp. 29–33; and Axel Duboul, *L'armée révolutionnaire de Toulouse* (Toulouse, 1891).

[75] The Convention also transferred the district seat of Vilaines-la-Juhel to Lassay on July 24, 1793, after the mayor of Vilaines refused to attend a ceremony proclaiming the new constitution; and it transferred the district seat of Mirepoix to Pamiers on May 21, 1794, following the arrival of special deputies who boasted of Pamier's mobilization of over 1,000 sansculottes to fight at the sieges of Toulon and Lyon and against the tyrants of Sardinia and Spain. AN DIV bis 85:8; DIV bis 81:9, and decree of 2 prairial, year II, AP 90:511.

[76] Dossiers in AN DIV bis 74; and L. P. Lefevre, *Yvetot pendant la Révolution de 1788 à 1815* (Yvetot, 1908), pp. 156–160.

the Convention at Rouen denounced "intriguers" at Yvetot for using Hé-bert, Danton, and other "scoundrels" to trick the Convention into transferring the district seat to Yvetot. He added that the new guard of the granary there was refusing to obey orders to send grain to Rouen. The Comité de Division decided to resolve this dispute once and for all in favor of Yvetot, whose patriotic defense of the Convention, more than its central location, earned it the "prize" of the district seat. The municipality of Caudebec made one last effort in 1795, after the political winds had changed dramatically. Yvetot, it informed the Legislative Committee of the Convention, had been a hotbed of terrorism: everywhere the name of Robespierre, and the words "guillotine" and "Montagnard" had resounded in the streets of this town. Caudebec, of course, had always been the home of the purest patriotism. But the Convention was about to abolish all the districts, and the petition from Caudebec, like so many others, was quietly filed away and forgotten.[77]

Among the fruitless requests for a district seat, those from insurrectionary areas of western France offer remarkable testimony to the persistent ambition of small-town notables.[78] After the district of Machecoul had been completely overrun by the Vendean rebels, Republicans at Bourgneuf, who coveted the district seat in this area, reported that their town had always been distinguished by its civic spirit. "It is here that the insurrectionary movement coming from Machecoul and the Vendée halted." Admittedly, everyone at Bourgneuf had fled to Nantes, but the town would be a suitable center for the restoration of government authority in the district. As for Machecoul, "misled by fanaticism and aristocracy, and depopulated by death and terror, bound with few exceptions to the counterrevolutionary conspiracy, and covered with the blood of patriots," that town did not deserve to possess "the establishments of patriotism and revolution." But sixty refugees from Machecoul, many of them widows of Republicans slain in the uprising, wrote from Nantes that three-quarters of the townpeople were patriots. With a garrison of 3,000 troops, Machecoul could become a defensive outpost against the Vendée and regain its commercial role as a grain market for Nantes.[79]

No such voices were raised in defense of Saint-Florent, a town reduced

[77] Dossiers in AN DIV bis 74:1A and DIV bis 90:3; AP 91:509–10, 527; and Lefevre, *Yvetot*, pp. 156–60.

[78] Other towns that requested district seats without success during the Terror include Auxonne, Bagnols, Bourg-St.-Andéol, Brienne, Fontainebleau, Maiche, Martel, Montereau, Montlhéry, Bourg-St-Andéol, St-Germain-les-Belles, and Vaucouleurs. In the Thermidorian phase of the Convention (Aug. 1794–Sept. 1795), Coulommiers, Dunkerque, Landrecies, Le Grand-Pressigny, and Tournus sent unsuccessful petitions to the Convention for districts.

[79] Letter from refugees of Bourgneuf, Sept. 2, 1793, and undated *adresse* from refugees of Machecoul, AN DIV bis 84:5.

to rubble by the avenging armies of the Republic. In this district, however, the municipal officials of Montrevault, who had fled to Angers, petitioned the Convention in April 1795 to give their little town the district seat. "Although all the communes have been burned down, Montrevault still preserves the castle of its former seigneur, which has become a national property now that its owner has emigrated. The town also has many houses, while nothing at all remains at Montgloire, formerly called Saint-Florent." The new commissioners of the district confirmed in June that Montgloire had become uninhabitable. Everything had been burned to the ground, and troops had pillaged the commune even after these officials had returned. No civil administration worthy of the name could function here, but in the midst of disaster, townspeople from Montrevault hoped to restore their own fortunes in alliance with the state. If new buildings were needed, they explained to the Comité de Division, "Montrevault is in the center of woods that can be used for construction, and it contains earth and quarry stones suitable for building."[80]

Of course, the Convention had no intention of sponsoring the urban development of Montrevault. In 1795, its leaders faced an economic crisis of unparalleled dimensions. Having abandoned the price controls of the Montagnards in December 1794, the government lost control of its currency, the famous assignats, which were depreciating at a catastrophic rate. Tax revenues covered a smaller and smaller fraction of expenditures as the treasury frantically issued more and more assignats.[81] This accelerating collapse of the currency provoked so much uncertainty that many farmers stopped supplying urban markets altogether. Poor harvests and military requisitions reduced the supply of food in the countryside, too. District directories and urban municipalities had more and more difficulty provisioning the towns, even by force. In Paris, the government continued to subsidize the sale of bread, but in some provincial cities, where municipal authorities had to reduce bread rations drastically, people starved. Even army contractors had difficulty supplying troops along the frontiers, which helps explain the drive to conquer foreign lands.[82] As for the tens of thousands of civilians who depended on the revolutionary government for a job, they were being paid, if at all, in a nearly worthless currency. The Montagnards, true to their centralizing tendencies, had abolished local financing of essential government functions. By the decree of 21 floréal (May 10, 1794), all the expenses of administrative bodies would be cov-

---

[80] *Adresse* from Mun. Montrevault, letters from district *commissaires* and the national agent, AN DIV bis 85:4.

[81] On the monetary crisis of 1795, see S. E. Harris, *The Assignats* (Cambridge, Mass., 1930), pp. 186–205.

[82] On the food shortages and starvation in provincial towns during the year III, see Richard Cobb, *Terreur et subsistances, 1793–1795* (Paris, 1965), pp. 151–78, 211–342.

ered by the national treasury.[83] These expenses included indemnities to nonsalaried members of departmental and district councils, who were obliged to meet in permanent session with the salaried directors. Members of the committees of surveillance that operated in every district seat were also on the government payroll. So were a host of clerks and minor officials. In principle, the state financed the revolutionary machine of government; in practice, its payments were often in arrears and failed to keep pace with the cost of living.[84]

These economic circumstances would have undermined even the most unified of governments, but the Convention was torn by factional conflicts, fearful of royalist opposition, and intolerant of Catholic religious beliefs.[85] Political passions even countermanded the need for administrative retrenchment. On February 22, 1795, the Convention did agree to suppress daily sessions of the district councils, abolish most of the revolutionary committees in district seats, and reduce from eight to five the number of departmental administrators. This would save nearly twenty million livres.[86] On April 16, however, the Girondin deputy Lesage, expelled from the Convention by the Montagnards and welcomed back by the Thermidorians, opened an attack on the administrative charter of the Terror, the law of 14 frimaire. Alluding to recent accounts of riots and seditions in various localities, Lesage denied that food shortages were the true cause of these revolts. Liberty and order depended on effective administration, and under the system created by the Montagnards, "The interior of the Republic is not being administered at all." Lesage blamed the district officials for raising themselves above their "natural superiors" in the departmental capitals; for supporting the "tyrannical domination" of evil men; and for refusing to take any initiative in repressing the current disorders. Too numerous and too dispersed throughout the territory of France, these authorities lacked moral influence or physical force. Restore full powers to the administrators of the departments, Lesage urged his fellow deputies; they will extirpate fanaticism, outmaneuver the royalists, crush seditions, and pacify the interior. Inspired by this speech, which rallied critics of *chouannerie* (anti-Republican bands in the countryside of western France) as well as enemies of the Montagnards, the Convention restored the orig-

---

[83] Ramel, "Rapport sur les contributions directes," in *Réimpression de l'ancien Moniteur* 20:461–69. The law was supposed to go into effect on 1 vendémiaire, year III (Sept. 22, 1794).

[84] On the misery of judges in the year III, see Bourdon, *Réforme judiciare* 1:203–4.

[85] For a sympathetic history of the Thermidorian Convention, see M. J. Sydenham, *The First French Republic, 1792–1804* (Berkeley, 1973), pp. 26–82; for a hostile analysis, see Georges Lefebvre, *The Thermidorians*, trans. by Robert Baldick (London, 1964).

[86] *Rapport* of Thibault, 4 pluviose, year III (Jan. 23, 1795), and decree of 4 ventôse, year III, *Réimpression de l'ancien Moniteur* 23:287–88, 509–10.

inal functions of the departmental directories and increased their size again to eight members, regardless of the added cost.[87]

For the Thermidorians, who wanted to strengthen executive authority and consolidate social order, this decree of April 16 did not go far enough. It left the district directories in place and even ratified the additional powers that they had acquired during the Terror. Two months later, Boissy d'Anglas, a long-time critic of the districts, introduced the draft of a new constitution that would abolish the districts altogether and replace them with cantonal municipalities. Lesage was also a member of the Therimodorian Commission des Onze that prepared this constitution, but Boissy and Daunou, the former constitutional bishop of Paris, took the lead in persuading the Convention to adopt it. Memories of the Terror as well as rhetoric about budgetary savings entered into their defense of a new administrative system. In the words of Boissy, "The 547 districts, the 44,000 municipalities, were a dangerous superfluity. This immensity of administrations, all acting at the same time, too often in contrary directions, almost always without subordination, was in the political body a germ of anarchy and death." His plan, which he had already sketched back in the spring of 1793, called for every canton to form a "municipality" that would administer subordinate communes. Towns with over 5,000 inhabitants would form separate municipalities, but smaller towns would elect only a municipal agent and an *adjoint*, just as did rural communes. These agents would form the cantonal municipality, headed by an elected president and a commissioner appointed by the executive directory in Paris. Like municipal officials in the previous system, the cantonal officials would not receive salaries. Consequently, administrative costs would be reduced by dropping from the government payroll all the functionaries in the districts. With the districts gone, the district tribunals would also disappear, eliminating another "crowd of idle functionaries." All appeals from cantonal justices of the peace would be directed to a single civil tribunal in each department, where judicial authority would be concentrated in the hands of a smaller number of distinguished magistrates. For Boissy, civil judges, like salaried administrators, would fortify the authority of the government by residing in departmental capitals, not district seats.[88]

The idea of cantonal municipalities provoked considerable opposition from the floor of the Convention. In a debate that lasted two days, several deputies with administrative experience denied the feasibility of such a sys-

[87] Speech of Lesage and decree of 27 germinal, year III, *Réimpression de l'ancien Moniteur* 24:236–37.

[88] *Discours* by Boissy d'Anglas, 5 messidor, year III (June 23, 1795), *Réimpression de l'ancien Moniteur* 25:106; and Boissy's earlier *Projet de Constitution*, annex to session of Apr. 17, 1793, AP 62:289–308. On the background and main features of the Constitution of the Year III, see Sydenham, *The First French Republic*, pp, 56–82.

tem. Eschassériaux the elder, a lawyer and departmental administrator from Saintes, asked where the government would find enough officials to run fifty or sixty cantonal municipalities in each department, when it had scarcely been able to recruit enough qualified men to serve on one-tenth as many district directories. If the cantonal agents were not salaried, very few citizens would be willing to undertake such burdensome tasks. Only proprietors with sufficient revenues would become communal agents, and they would have to travel to the cantonal seat in order to deliberate. This would prevent the kind of continuity that sedentary officials imparted to the administration of the districts. Furthermore, all these cantonal municipalities would have to employ clerks, so their administrative costs might easily exceed those of a much smaller number of districts. Boudin, who had presided over the district administration of Châteauroux, declared bluntly, "In my department, the execution of the new project is impractical. You will certainly not be able to find candidates for the cantonal municipalities, or else those who are enlightened enough to be good administrators will not be wealthy enough to serve. Thus, you will have nothing but an incoherent administration, or rather, you will have nothing at all." Dormay, formerly a district administrator at Vervins, added that the work of a dozen officials and clerks in the average district would have to be dispersed among forty cantonal officials and clerks. The budgetary savings that Boissy d'Anglas promised were illusory. As for the activity of the government, Dormay contrasted the professionalism of the district directories with the inexperience of amateurs in the cantons: "A single administration, composed of several educated men, continually employed, operates in a more uniform and prompt manner than ten or twelve administrations, composed for the most part of citizens who are insufficently trained as administrators and who can only concern themselves with public affairs momentarily, and after a disagreeable and expensive trip."[89]

To these cogent arguments for administrative continuity, Boissy and his colleagues replied that political and social considerations condemned the district directories. For Boissy, these administrations were not only useless wheels but dangerous corps. For Daunou, they disrupted the unity of the government and weakened the departmental administrations. Unable to control the municipalities in large towns, they dominated those in rural communes. For Charles Delacroix, a former member of the departmental administration of the Marne, they had the incurable vice of representing the interests of job hunters in small towns:

Experience has proven that these administrations are nearly always composed exclusively of citizens in the small towns where they are established; the modest salaries accorded to district administrators do not permit educated men who have settled in the countryside by taste or business affairs to serve as district officials. Such posts will necessarily circulate among a small number of families and individuals who treat them as a patrimony. Anyone who has inhabited the countryside knows how impatiently rural people have always borne the yoke of the scribblers [*hommes de plume*] who are so numerous in small towns. It is time to put these men out of operation.

Delacroix denied that only rich men would be willing to serve in the cantonal municipalities. Pecuniary sacrifices would be negligible for administrators who would always have relatives or friends in the cantonal seat to offer them hospitality. Berlier, a former member of the departmental directory in the Côte d'Or, voiced confidence that intrigue would end now that public functionaries, no longer salaried, were animated exclusively by honor. He added that the cantonal municipalities would not have much work to do anyway, apart from apportioning taxes.[90]

Thus, the Thermidorians had a social conception of administration that excluded the ambitious notables of small towns who had played such an active role in defense of the Republic. On the one hand, the central government would pay generous salaries to the members of the departmental directories, whose wealth made them suitable defenders of law and order. On the other hand, it would rely on landed proprietors in the countryside to administer the rural populations. In this project for government on the cheap, officials in small towns would be reduced to the same minor and unsalaried functions as notables in thousands of bourgs and villages that also functioned as cantonal seats.[91] Montagnard deputies such as Goupilleau, formerly the *procureur-syndic* of a district in the Vendée, decried in vain a plan that would "eliminate a respectable class of men from public functions."[92] Boissy and his colleagues did not intend to employ men of mediocre fortune who lived in little towns. They viewed the state from the perspective of departmental capitals, where most of them had served as departmental administrators during the Revolution.[93] Even Eschassériaux,

[90] Ibid., pp. 175, 189–92.

[91] A total of 4,872 cantons existed in the 87 departments of the year III. Tabulation based on Gérard Walter, *Répertoire de l'histoire de la Révolution française, travaux publiés de 1800 à 1940*, vol. 2, *Lieux* (Paris, 1951), entries for departments, which give the number of districts and cantons.

[92] Speech of 19 messidor, *Réimpression de l'ancien Moniteur* 25:176. Goupilleau, Eschassériaux, and Génissieux, another defender of the districts, were former Jacobin Club members and Montagnards. Among critics of the district, Berlier and Delacroix had supported the Montagnard faction, but they had not joined the Jacobin Society in Paris. See Patrick, *Men of the First French Republic*, appendix 2, pp. 315–39.

[93] Among the seven deputies who spoke against the districts, four had been departmental administrators, and two of the others came from departmental capitals. None had been district officials. Among the seven defenders, only one had been a departmental administrator,

who had a similar background, conceded that the number of districts should be reduced. So did Boudin. Daunou seized upon this equivocation among the partisans of the status quo. "If you reduce, you provoke incalculable protests, you call to Paris ten thousand special deputies. If you suppress, you create a stronger government, a more co-ordinated administration."[94] Political circumstances were finally ripe to accomplish what neither the Legislative Assembly nor the earlier Convention had dared: the reduction of most towns to the rank of cantonal seats.[95]

The plan to suppress all the district tribunals, which would have aroused a storm of controversy back in 1790, passed nearly unnoticed into the Constitution of the Year III. Only one deputy published a pamphlet in defense of these lawcourts, and no one protested when the clauses establishing a single civil tribunal in each department were approved on July 28, 1795.[96] In part, this inertia followed from the decision to abolish the districts, but it expressed a deeper disillusionment with the judicial system inherited from the Constituent Assembly. The Montagnards had suspected judges of harboring counterrevolutionary sentiments, and they had reduced their salaries, eliminated their qualifications, and talked of replacing them with compulsory arbitrators. During the Terror, men of law had fallen into disfavor as well. Corporations of *avoués* had been dissolved, and customary procedures of civil litigation had been abolished. In a note that revealed the mood of Montagnard deputies, a former district judge from the little town of Bouzonville had written across a petition for a district tribunal in November 1793, "Because the Convention will not fail to second the will of the people, which aspires only to abolish lawcourts, I invite the city of Dourdan to remain patient a little longer, and I remind the Convention that it would do a great service to the people by getting rid of these ruinous institutions."[97] As for the Girondins, they had been associ-

---

two others came from departmental capitals, and four came from small towns. These deputies included three district administrators and a district judge. Patrick notes that district administrators who sat in the Convention were disproportionately favorable to the Montagnards. *Men of the First French Republic*, p. 219.

[94] Ibid., p. 190. Daunou was responding to Delecloy, who warned that a large number of citizens would be discontented if the districts were suppressed.

[95] Yet partisans of the districts were powerful enough in the Convention to convince the *rapporteur* for the Commission des Onze not to risk a specific vote on the issue of cantonal municipalities. Following Delacroix's speech, he simply passed on to the next clause of the Constitution. Session of 21 messidor, *Réimpression de l'ancien Moniteur* 25:195.

[96] P. J. D. G. Faure, *Touche légère sur la Constitution des Onze* (Paris, year III); session of 10 thermidor (July 28, 1795), *Réimpression de l'ancien Moniteur* 25:365.

[97] Note by Couturier, dated 29 brumaire, year II (Nov. 19, 1793), written on a letter from the Popular Society of Dourdan, AN DIV bis 90:2. On the attack on professional lawyers during the Terror, see Michael P. Fitzsimmons, *The Parisian Order of Barristers and the French Revolution* (Cambridge, Mass., 1987), pp. 90–110; and Isser Woloch, "The Fall and Resur-

ated with Condorcet's constitutional plan for a single civil lawcourt in each departmental seat, with a jury chosen by the plaintiffs themselves.[98] The Legislative Committee of the Therimidorian Convention returned to the idea of a professional magistrature, which implied a concentration of talent in fewer lawcourts. Between Montagnard contempt for all men of law and Thermidorian disdain for small-town magistrates, the existing district tribunals were doomed. Henceforth, large departmental tribunals, each consisting of at least twenty judges, would handle all disputes over landed property and all appeals from justices of the peace. They would also hear appeals from neighboring departments. In a word, departmental tribunals would monopolize all the functions of the former district tribunals.[99]

The Constitution of the Year III established only one intermediate jurisdiction between the departments and the cantons: correctional tribunals. Here, too, the Thermidorians favored more centralization than did the Constituent Assembly, whose tripartite system of criminal justice had included police tribunals in each commune, correctional courts in each canton, and a criminal tribunal in each department. Fearing a revival of Jacobinism in urban municipalities, the architects of the new constitution stripped the communes of police powers, placed a single police tribunal in each canton, and located from three to six correctional lawcourts in each department. The presiding judge of each correctional court would be delegated from the criminal tribunal of the department, whose judges were recruited from the civil tribunal. By attaching a commissioner appointed by the Directory in Paris to each correctional court, the Thermidorians hoped to strengthen the influence of the government over the prosecution of misdemeanors (*délits*), which fell under the exclusive jurisdiction of these courts. Like the former correctional courts in the cantons, the new correctional courts would render verdicts without a jury, and they would be empowered to impose sentences of up to two years in prison for first offenders, and four years in prison for recidivists. Following the precedent of the Constituent Assembly, only felonies (*crimes*) would be referred to the criminal tribunals of the departments for indictments and convictions by a jury. Thus, the Thermidorians retained distinct levels of prosecution for petty offenses, misdemeanors, and felonies, while shifting the locus of correctionary authority from the cantons to intermediary lawcourts.[100]

The Convention asked its Comité de Division to demarcate the jurisdic-

---

rection of the Civil Bar, 1789–1820s," *French Historical Studies* 15, no. 2 (Fall 1987): 246–49.

[98] On the Girondin orientation of the Constitutional Committee that approved Condorcet's plan, see Sydenham, *The First French Republic*, p. 13.

[99] On the judicial system of the Constitution of the Year III, see Godechot, *Institutions*, pp. 414–18; and Bourdon, *Réforme judiciare* 1:186–93.

[100] Bourdon, *Réforme judiciare* 1:173–74, 189–91.

tions of these new lawcourts and to choose the towns where they would be located. This committee made its decisions on the basis of population as well as topography. Having already undertaken a census of districts in response to the Montagnard Constitution of 1793, which called for single-member constituencies of equal population, it used this census to combine districts into correctional jurisdictions. Generally speaking, the committee amalgamated districts of fewer than 30,000 inhabitants into correctional jurisdictions with over 50,000 inhabitants. As a result, it reduced from 544 to 350 the total number of intermediate jurisdictions. Following this procedure of incorporating smaller districts into larger ones, it tended to select towns in the more populous districts as the seats of correctional courts. Thus, none of the thirteen capitals of districts populated by fewer than 20,000 habitants obtained correctional courts. Above that threshold, the proportion of district seats that gained these courts rose from 30 percent for districts with 20,000–29,999 inhabitants to 53 percent for districts with 30,000–39,000 inhabitants; 69 percent for districts with 40,000–49,999 inhabitants; 76 percent for districts with 50,000–59,999 inhabitants; 85 percent for districts with 60,000–69,999 inhabitants; and 97 percent for districts with over 70,000 inhabitants.[101]

The most populous districts tended to have the largest towns, so this geographical operation also discriminated against the smaller seats of districts and tribunals. While 89 percent (184/206) of the former district towns numbering over 5,000 inhabitants obtained correctional tribunals, this rate of success fell to only 26 percent (50/191) of the former capitals numbering fewer than 2,000 inhabitants. Taking into account towns that had benefited from the *partage* of district establishments, only 57 percent of the former district towns became the seats of correctional courts. A total of 262 towns, most of them small, suffered a demotion to the rank of cantonal police courts. Map 9.1 illustrates the contrasting fate of large and small towns in 1795. Only a few district towns were promoted to the rank of civil tribunals (indicated by hatched circles). Most of these lawcourts, like the criminal tribunals formed by the Constituent Assembly, were placed in large and medium-sized departmental seats (hatched rectangles). In like manner, only a handful of former cantonal seats gained correctional tribunals (solid triangles). Typically, these lawcourts were placed in medium-sized towns that used to possess district directories or tribunals (open circles). A few departmental seats also received correctional courts instead of civil tribunals (open rectangles). As for the small district towns, a majority of them were reduced to police tribunals in the cantons (crosses).

[101] Calculations based on the table in Guillaume, *Procès-verbaux du Comité d'instruction* 5:665–79; and the listing of correctional courts in *Almanach national* (Paris, year IV). See also Meuriot, "Les districts de 1790," pp. 469–71.

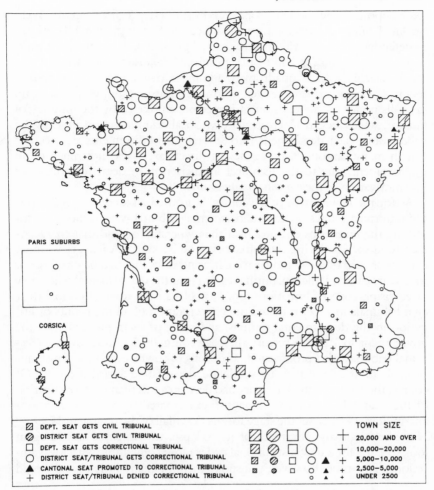

Map 9.1. Civil and Correctional Tribunals in 1795, by Department and District Seats

This redistribution of lawcourts would set a precedent for the restoration of intermediate administrative and judicial institutions in 1800. The Thermidorian constitution created too many agencies of administration in the cantons and not enough civil tribunals in the departments. As late as July 1797, many cantonal administrations had not yet been formed, and those in operation rarely met.[102] Nor did the cantonal *commissaires*, who

[102] Godechot, *Institutions*, p. 413. For local studies of administration during the Directory, see G. Lameire, *Les municipalités de canton dans le département du Rhône sous le Directoire*

were appointed by the Directory, fare much better as fiscal agents. Well-qualified and loyal *commissaires* were difficult to find in many rural cantons, as defenders of the district directories had predicted. To stimulate recruitment, the government had to place cantonal *commissaires* on the government payroll, which quadrupled administrative costs in the departments.[103] *Commissaires* were even promised bonuses if they would draw up tax rolls under the supervision of inspectors employed by the ministry of finance, which began to create its own local administration in 1797 by subdividing each department into several "arrondissements de recette." But in many cantons, this "agency of direct taxes" was not much of an improvement, due to the technical inexperience, inadequate funds, and low motivation of the cantonal *commissaires*.[104]

As for the new system of lawcourts, it aroused all kinds of complaints. Only thirteen judges on each departmental tribunal were responsible for settling the numerous disputes over the ownership of land that characterized rural society during the Directory. The backlog of cases grew longer every year, and by 1799 judges were hearing cases that had begun three or four years earlier. Unless plaintiffs resided near the departmental seats, they faced rising costs of litigation, too. Notables in the towns that lost their civil tribunals in 1795 resented the concentration of all the profits of litigation in the departmental capitals, and some of them pleaded with the government in Paris to restore their lawcourts.[105] Rivalries over correctional tribunals also proliferated, as dozens of towns urged the legislative councils of the Directory to subdivide the existing jurisdictions.[106] Of course, the failure of the Directory had deeper causes than the Constitution of the Year III. Political factionalism, exacerbated by religious divisions and military defeats, set the stage for the downfall of the regime in 1799.[107] Nonetheless, in the aftermath of its collapse, townspeople would again look to Paris for a new institutional order more compatible with local ambitions. This time, however, the spokesmen for many little towns would

---

(Lyon, 1941); and Marcel Reinhard, *Le département de la Sarthe sous le régime directorial* (Saint-Brieuc, 1935).

[103] Law of 21 fructidor, year III (Sept. 7, 1795), *Réimpression de l'ancien Moniteur* 25:692–93.

[104] Godechot, *Institutions*, p. 437; Marcel Marion, *Histoire financière de la France depuis 1715* (Paris, 1927), 4:83–87.

[105] On these complaints, see Bourdon, *Réforme judiciare* 1:273–303; Bergier, *Esquisse d'un nouveau plan de l'ordre judiciare* (Paris, nivose, year 8); and Vasse, *Opinion du représentant du peuple Vasse* (Paris, year 8).

[106] Petitions in AN AF III:33, and dossiers mentioned in the catalogue of ser. C, Robert Anchel, et al., *Les papiers des assemblées du Directoire aux Archives Nationale, Inventaire de la série C* (Paris, 1976).

[107] On the general history of the Directory and its collapse, see Martin Lyons, *France under the Directory* (New York, 1975).

have no success. In replacing the former districts with new "arrondisse-ments," based on correctional jurisdictions and fiscal *recettes*, Napoleon and his advisors would vindicate the critics of the original subdivision of many departments into more than five or six districts. For the typical small town that had gained a district, a district tribunal, or both of these establish-ments back in 1790, the Thermidorian reaction of 1795 marked the end of a brief epoch of institutional equality.

Chapter 10

THE NEW URBAN HIERARCHY

"C ITIZENS," proclaimed the consuls of the Republic on December 15, 1799, "the Revolution is anchored on the principles that began it; it is over."[1] With these words, Napoleon Bonaparte, whose coup d'état of 19 brumaire (October 10, 1799) had swept aside the Directory and Legislative Councils established in 1795, promised that yet another constitution would bring to a close the revolutionary era. In fact, the Constitution of the Year VIII lasted no longer than its predecessor of the year III. Inspired to a large extent by Abbé Sièyes, who wanted to reconcile a stronger executive power with legislative institutions, the new text alluded only vaguely to the territorial organization of the state. Napoleon quickly transformed its complicated system of electoral assemblies and appointed officials into a facade for his own power, which culminated in a new constitution that made him the hereditary emperor of the French in 1804. The foundations of the modern French state were designed not by Sièyes but by Napoleon and his advisors in the Conseil d'Etat. They created a new and enduring hierarchy of administrative and judicial institutions in the laws of 28 pluviôse (February 17, 1800) and 27 ventôse (March 17, 1800). The former law, "concerning the division of the territory of the Republic and the organization of local administrations," subdivided the departments into arrondissements and established a corps of prefects and subprefects, appointed by Napoleon, to enforce the administrative policies of the central government. The latter law, "on the organization of tribunals," restored a hierarchy of civil lawcourts, with a "tribunal of first instance" in each arrondissement and an appellate court in every three or four departments. The Conseil d'Etat also decided which towns would obtain the prefectures, subprefectures, and lawcourts. With very few exceptions, it placed lawcourts in the same towns that it selected as administrative capitals. Despite considerable pressure from other towns to modify these decisions, the territorial settlement of the Consulate survived with only minor modifications until the twentieth century. It founded an urban hierarchy in the long *durée* of French history.[2]

This reconstruction of space around a hierarchy of appellate lawcourts, departmental capitals, and arrondissement seats expressed a compromise

[1] Jacques Godechot, ed. *Les Constitutions de la France depuis 1789* (Paris, 1970), p. 162.

[2] On these laws, see Bourdon, *La Constitution de l'an VIII*, pp. 85–98; and Bourdon, *La réforme judiciaire de l'an VIII* 1:273–420.

between the needs of the state and the interests of towns. Napoleon and his councillors wanted, above all, to strengthen the authority of the central government over local administration, whose fragmentation into thousands of cantonal municipalities had undermined the power of the Directory. From this perspective, territorial reform involved the consolidation of cantons into larger "communal arrondissements." By contrast, many townspeople were more interested in the promise of judicial reforms that would restore their former lawcourts. But instead of restoring the districts, which varied greatly in territory and population, the government could use the existing jurisdictions of correctional courts for the new tribunals of first instance. Such a policy of territorial continuity would appeal to the interests of nearly three hundred towns. By forming arrondissements in the same manner, the government could also fulfill its goal of consolidating the cantons. An intermediate level of administration and justice, based on correctional jurisdictions, would reconcile the centralizing demands of the government with the decentralizing ambitions of townspeople.[3]

The language of the Constitution of the Year VIII seemed to exclude such a compromise. In its brief clauses about local administration, it implied that the officials in each communal arrondissement would exercise joint responsibility for an area larger than a canton but smaller than a district. Both Sièyes and Daunou, who helped to draft this constitution, opposed the tripartite administrative system of the Constituent Assembly. Sièyes revived his old idea of *grandes communes*, each with an area of 36–40 square leagues, which implied at least 650 arrondissements. Daunou, as an architect of the Constitution of the Year III, wanted even smaller arrondissements, no more than 700 square kilometers in area, or around 28 square leagues.[4] The Conseil d'Etat decided instead to distinguish clearly between three levels of administration. Each commune would form a separate municipality, with a mayor responsible for executing the orders of the government and a council authorized to deliberate on the communal budget. Between the prefects in the departmental seats and the mayors in the communes, an intermediate echelon of subprefects would be responsible for surveillance rather than routine administration in each arrondissement. This functional differentiation between subprefects and mayors made it possible for the government to consolidate the cantons into much larger jurisdictions than Daunou and Sièyes had proposed. Preserving the terminology but not the meaning of "communal arrondissements," the ap-

---

[3] A lobbyist from the small town of Vic-sur-Seille, a correctional seat but not a former district capital, first publicized the idea that arrondissements should be based on correctional jurisdictions rather than districts. *Opinion* of Vignon, cited by Bourdon, *La Constitution de l'an VIII*, p. 91.

[4] Ibid., pp. 88–94.

pendix to the legislative text enumerated only three to six arrondissements in each department, with an average size of 1,500 square kilometers, or nearly 60 square leagues.[5] When Daunou, who had opposed the districts and communes back in 1795, defended the idea of only one level of administration below the departments, Roederer, the spokesman for the Conseil d'Etat, replied scornfully, "The frivolous and chimerical pretension of reducing administration to two degrees led to the division of France into six or seven thousand cantons."[6] The new hierarchy of prefectures, subprefectures, and communes would maximize the authority of the state while minimizing administrative costs.

It would also lay the foundations for a coherent territorial organization of justice and taxation as well as administration. The law called for a total of 359 arrondissements within the original territory of the French Republic, a number that compared closely with the 370 correctional jurisdictions and 380 fiscal *recettes* established in these same departments by the Convention and the Directory.[7] As Roederer explained, the new division was "traced in large part on the one that experience has established for correctional police, and which can also serve for the new lawcourts of first instance; it is also very similar to the division of the *recettes* for direct taxes. Thus, the interests of finance and justice recommend it to the government for administration."[8] Of course, the Conseil d'Etat had to decide whether to follow the boundaries of correctional jurisdictions or *recettes* in departments where these subdivisions were not identical. Such decisions were complicated by the fact that in forty departments, the number of tribunals differed from the number of *recettes*. For example, the Ain, the Gard, and the Moselle had five tribunals but only four *recettes*, while the Lot-et-Garonne, the Meuse, and the Seine-et-Marne had five *recettes* but only four

---

[5] *Projet de loi* and speech by Roederer, AP 2d ser., 1:148–171; Bourdon, *La Constitution de l'an VIII*, pp. 91–92.

[6] Speech by Daunou, as *rapporteur* for the committee of the Tribunat that examined the legislative project, 23 pluviôse (Feb. 12, 1800), AP 2d ser., 1:179–87; and *Réponse du citoyen Roederer*, in Roederer, *Oeuvres* 7:102–11. On Roederer's constitutional ideas, see Kenneth Mergerison, *Pierre-Louis Roederer: Political Thought and Practice during the French Revolution* (Philadelphia, 1983), pp. 133–53.

[7] "Tableau des départements et des arrondissements communaux de la République française," AP 2d ser., 1:150–69. A total of 402 arrondissements are listed, including 45 in territories annexed after 1795 and lost in 1814–15. The total of 370 correctional courts takes into account changes in the location and numbers of correctional tribunals between 1795 and 1800, as indicated by comparing the lists in the *Almanach National* for the years IV and VIII. The estimate of 380 fiscal *recettes* is based on the original "Tableau du nombre de préposés aux recettes" in the law of 22 brumaire, year VI, *Bulletin des lois* (Paris, year VI), no. 1543, pp. 23–24, to which were added three *recettes* in year VII, as mentioned in *Bulletin des lois*, nos. 2980, 3123, and index. On the extent of continuity with the correctional jurisdictions originally formed in 1795, see Meuriot, "Les districts de 1790," pp. 474–75.

[8] AP 2d ser., 1:169.

tribunals. In thirty-two of these departments, the Conseil d'Etat standardized arrondissements by eliminating the extra tribunals or *recettes*.[9] It also
suppressed five arrondissements in departments that had equal numbers of
both jurisdictions, while adding only two extra arrondissements on the
basis of former districts instead of correctional jurisdictions or *recettes*. As
Roederer later explained, "A rule was followed rather generally of forming
the fewest divisions possible."[10]

This method of procedure implied that several dozen seats of correctional tribunals or *recettes* would not become the seats of arrondissements,
and it obviously doomed the hopes of many towns that had been reduced
to the rank of cantonal seats back in 1795. The Conseil d'Etat tried to
avoid complaints from such towns by postponing its decisions about the
location of prefectures and subprefectures. It assigned only numbers to the
new arrondissements and listed their cantons in alphabetical order. Speaking on behalf of a committee of the Tribunate, Daunou expressed surprise
at this "omission" of capitals and warned that the government lacked the
constitutional authority to establish administrative centers without the
sanction of a law. Another tribune, Sédillez, insisted on lifting the veil of
mystery surrounding the new capitals. Otherwise, a "guilty silence" might
"conceal injustice or mask unconstitutional enterprises." Roederer replied
to such criticism that "the project aims to combine justice, administration,
and fiscal *recettes* in the same capitals, so that it will be easy for the inhabitants of the countryside to undertake in a single visit all the business that
might call them to town." Thus, the plan for the location of administrative
seats could be announced later, when the law on judicial organization was
ready for debate.[11]

This disingenuous statement overlooked the fact that by adopting the
correctional jurisdictions as a framework for arrondissements, the Conseil
d'Etat was anticipating continuity between the seats of lawcourts in the
Directory and subprefectures in the Consulate. This is probably what Sédillez feared. He wanted arrondissements to be based on the former districts, which would favor his hometown of Nemours instead of Fontainebleau. But neither Sédillez nor other tribunes who complained about the
correctional jurisdictions could accuse the government of favoritism toward particular towns.[12] By avoiding any mention of capitals, Roederer

[9] In this manner, a total of 13 correctional jurisdictions and 23 fiscal arrondissements were
suppressed (excluding the Seine, which had 14 *recettes* in 1797).

[10] Copy of letter from the Conseil d'État to the minister of the interior, 14 messidor, year
8 (July 2, 1800), in dossier Nogaro, AN F2 I:510.

[11] Speeches on 23 pluviôse (Feb. 12, 1800), AP 2d ser., 1:184–87; and Roederer, "Réponse," in *Oeuvres* 7:103–4.

[12] When the district of Nemours had been abolished in 1795, Fontainebleau had gained
the correctional tribunal in this area, instead of Nemours. The other critics were Duchesne,

and his colleagues on the Conseil d'Etat succeeded in deflecting attention from urban rivalries. As one of their supporters in the Tribunat argued, if capitals had been listed in the legal text, "the clash of particular interests, needs, and affections would have often monopolized our discussion to the detriment of public interests." Debate remained on a more abstract plane, where the deficiencies of the existing cantonal system convinced a substantial majority of the Tribunate to approve the bill.[13]

The government published its list of prefectures and subprefectures on 11 ventôse (March 1, 1800), the same day that it submitted its plan of judicial reform to the Tribunate.[14] These two texts confirmed its strategy of locating administrative and judicial institutions in towns that already possessed correctional tribunals. A total of 334 prefectures and subprefectures were located in such towns, as compared with only 25 seats of arrondissements that were promoted from the rank of cantonal seats.[15] Having made these decisions, the Conseil d'Etat then proposed that 333 out of 359 tribunals of first instance also be located in former correctional seats. According to its plan, only ten arrondissements would have different seats of subprefectures and tribunals, as compared with 67 cases of *partage* between district directories and tribunals back in 1790. Map 10.1 illustrates the manner in which correctional tribunals shaped the distribution of subprefectures, while map 10.2 shows the extent to which the prefectoral system overlapped with the new hierarchy of lawcourts. The crosses on map 10.1 indicate seats of correctional tribunals that lost their separate jurisdictions, while the solid circles indicate cantonal seats that were promoted to the rank of subprefectures in 1800. These 36 demotions and 25 promotions were scattered about in departments where the Conseil d'Etat had either reduced the number of correctional jurisdictions or favored the seats of fiscal *recettes* that did not have these lawcourts. By contrast, 250 towns that possessed correctional tribunals also obtained subprefectures (empty circles). The squares on the map indicate the seats of prefectures, all of which had civil and criminal tribunals or correctional courts during the Directory. As for map 10.2, it shows other elements of continuity: be-

---

from the Drôme, where the town of Romans had been attached to the same arrondissement as Valence, and Caillemer, from the Manche, where the new plan eliminated a separate arrondissement for Cherbourg. AP 2d ser., 1:189–92, 205–7.

[13] Speech by Chauvelin, 24 pluviôse (Feb. 13, 1800). The vote on the next day was 71 to 25; the Corps Législatif ratified the law without debate three days later (Feb. 17, 1800). AP 2d ser., 1:203, 208–12.

[14] *Arrêtés* of 11 and 17 ventôse, year VIII, naming the prefects and subprefects, *Bulletin des lois* 8:61 and 13:90; and *projet de loi*, presented 11 ventôse. On the decision to name administrative capitals without a law, see Roederer, "Rapport fait au conseil d'état . . . sur la désignation des chefs-lieux," *Oeuvres* 7:111–14.

[15] In addition, two prefectures were located in towns that had possessed criminal and civil tribunals but not correctional tribunals in 1800 (Mézières and Foix).

tween subprefectures and tribunals of first instance (empty circles); departmental capitals and criminal tribunals (empty triangles); and the seats of sovereign courts before the Revolution and appellate courts in 1800 (empty squares). The few solid symbols on this map indicate patterns of discontinuity: the ten towns, usually quite small, that obtained a tribunal of first instance instead of a subprefecture (solid circles); the eight towns that displaced prefectures as the seats of criminal tribunals (hatched triangles); the eight prefectures that did not obtain criminal tribunals (crosses inscribed in circles); and the eleven towns, usually large, that were promoted to the rank of appellate courts (hatched squares).[16]

The interests of towns justified the government's deliberate policy of continuity in judicial institutions. As Emmery, the *conseiller d'état* who presented the project of judicial reform to the Tribunate, explained on March 5, "The project leaves the tribunals of first instance in the localities where the laws had placed the tribunals of correctional police; the rights of towns to possess these kinds of establishments, which they are extremely jealous to preserve, have been respected as much as possible." He added that the new appellate courts, numbering twenty-seven within the territorial boundaries of prerevolutionary France, would be located in towns that used to possess sovereign courts or other major lawcourts. These towns had suffered the most from the Revolution, and they contained the most qualified candidates for appellate judgeships.[17] Map 10.2 shows how this policy sometimes took priority over the principle of centrality in distributing appellate courts. The space to the east of Paris obtained four appellate courts that were bunched together in pairs: Metz and Nancy, and Dijon and Besançon, all former *villes parlementaires*. Montpellier and Nîmes, in lower Languedoc, formed a similar pair of appellate courts, each near the edge of its jurisdiction. By contrast, the towns that gained appellate courts within the immense jurisdiction of the *parlement* of Paris were distributed in a much more regular pattern, in keeping with the novelty of their appellate jurisdictions.

The committee of the Tribunate that examined this project applauded the new hierarchy of civil tribunals for making justice more accessible to the people and less costly to the government. Its *rapporteur*, Caillemer, anticipated that if any objections were raised in debate, "they will only be directed against a few irregularities in the distribution of lawcourts." But such "vices of locality" could not be corrected by the Tribunate, which lacked the constitutional power to amend bills. A critic like Sédillez, who objected to the concentration of subprefectures and tribunals in the same

---

[16] In this map, like all the subsequent ones for the period from 1800 to 1815, the classification of large as well as small towns by population size is based on the *Enquête dite 1,000*, undertaken by the prefects between 1809 and 1812. AN F20: 428–29.

[17] Speech to the Tribunate, 14 ventôse, an VIII, AP 2d ser., 1:304–7.

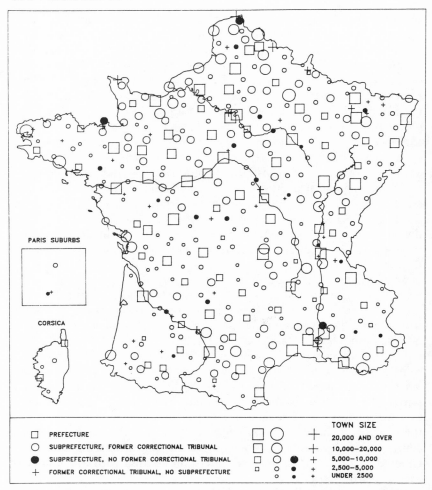

Map 10.1. Prefectures and Subprefectures, by Correctional Tribunals, 1800

towns, could complain only that he had to approve the bill entirely or reject it entirely.[18] This meant that influence had to be exercised behind the scenes while the Conseil d'Etat was still drafting legislation. Such surreptitious lobbying did take place in the weeks before Emmery made his report. For example, the tribune Grenier joined with emissaries from Riom to compete with Clermont-Ferrand for an appellate court. Lobbyists from

[18] *Rapport* on 21 ventôse and debate on 23 ventôse (March 12 and 14, 1800), AP 2d ser., 1:349, 381–82.

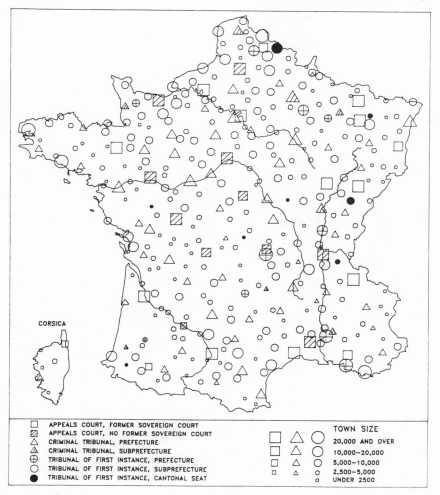

Map 10.2. The Hierarchy of Lawcourts, 1800

both of these towns circulated memorials and countermemorials to all the members of the Conseil d'Etat. Riom finally triumphed when Lady Désaix, a relative of one of Napoleon's generals, persuaded the first consul to have the text of the law changed at the last minute.[19] Similar rivalries pitted Cahors against Agen, Strasbourg against Colmar, and Blois and Tours against Orléans. Many small towns also petitioned for additional arron-

[19] Mège, *Formation du Puy-de-Dôme*, pp. 207–222. For other rivalries over appellate courts, see Bourdon, *Réforme judiciare* 1:354–62.

dissements and tribunals.[20] At the end of his speech to the Tribunate, Emmery dismissed all this agitation: "The establishment of justice in France cannot be delayed until final resolution of the thousands of disputes that have arisen between neighboring departments, communes, and towns over the location of tribunals." A majority of the Tribunate agreed that the moment of decision had arrived. After listening to only four speakers debate the bill, they endorsed it by a margin of 59 to 23. The Legislative Corps followed their example a few days later by an even more lopsided vote of 232 to 41.[21]

Yet to gain this victory, supporters of the bill had been obliged to concede that changes in the location of some lawcourts might be necessary. "Do not imagine," Caillemer assured the Tribunate, "that the government will close its eyes to reality; it will be eager to propose any measures that are in the interest of petitioners [réclamants]." Even Emmery, speaking in the name of the Conseil d'Etat, promised the Legislative Corps that the government would soon "perfect" the new law.[22] Such conciliatory language encouraged towns to request the transfer of subprefectures and tribunals or the creation of additional arrondissements. Indeed, another round of urban rivalries began as soon as the government implemented the new administrative and judicial system. Petitions of complaint reached the ministry of the interior from nearly one hundred towns during the Consulate. Not surprisingly, most of these candidates for arrondissement seats had served as the capitals of districts until 1795, and some of them had lost correctional tribunals in 1800. Several dozen towns renewed demands for subprefectures or tribunals during the Empire. Pressures for territorial changes peaked after the Empire collapsed in 1814. Over a hundred towns tried to convince the new royalist government to elevate them above the rank of cantonal seats, often as compensation for losses suffered during the Revolution. Of course, such demands threatened the position of existing capitals, which replied with petitions in defense of the status quo. Between 1800 and 1823, a succession of ministers of the interior received petitions and administrative correspondence involving around two hundred towns that disputed the boundaries and capitals of arrondissements.[23]

Map 10.3 indicates the location of these contenders for subprefectures and tribunals. It distinguishes between unsuccessful towns (crosses);

---

[20] The archives of the Conseil d'État were destroyed by fire during the Paris Commune, but dozens of petitions from small towns also reached the ministry of the interior, where they have been preserved in AN F2 1:504–23.

[21] AP 2d ser., 1:307, 412, 447.

[22] Ibid., pp. 350, 447.

[23] Dossiers in F2 I:504–23. The terminal date of 1823 has been chosen because Valenciennes obtained a subprefecture in that year, which was the last change in the location of administrative or judicial capitals during the Restoration Monarchy.

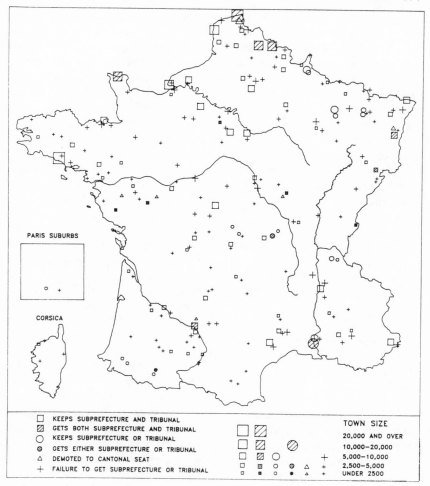

Map 10.3. Rivalries for Subprefectures and Tribunals of First Instance, 1800–1823

towns demoted to the rank of cantonal seats after 1800 (triangles); towns that retained an arrondissement seat (empty squares) or *partage* (empty circles); and towns promoted to an arrondissement seat (hatched squares) or *partage* (hatched circles). In comparison with the distribution of towns that competed for district tribunals back in 1790 (map 8.1), map 10.3 shows a sparser array of rival towns after 1800. Cases of *partage* became much rarer, and in some departments, no towns at all disputed the capitals of arrondissements. Very small towns became especially discouraged, although towns of all sizes disappeared from the ranks of contenders. This general trend paralleled the waning prospects of success for towns that sought subprefectures and tribunals after 1800: only two towns gained *partage*; three that already had one establishment added the other one; four obtained a new arrondissement; and three replaced rivals towns as the capitals of arrondissements.[24] Population size does help explain these few examples of success: nine out of fourteen successful towns had over 2,500 inhabitants, as compared with only three of the nine towns that were demoted. Yet eighteen towns with over 5,000 inhabitants failed to obtain an arrondissement seat, and so did another forty-two towns with over 2,500 inhabitants. Some of these frustrated ambitions can be traced back to 1790, but others emerged for the first time in 1800, when towns that had previously been in different districts now competed within the same arrondissements. In either case, success was equally rare for small and medium-sized towns that challenged the status quo.[25]

Nonetheless, some urban leaders persisted for years in their demands, trying to find arguments that would convince the government. In a few dozen cases, they even succeeded in gaining the support of prefects and departmental councils of notables, only to be overruled in Paris. Under these circumstances, local notables appealed directly to the first consul himself, who seemed to have final authority over all matters of state, including the location of subprefectures and tribunals. Increasingly during the Empire, municipal officials returned to the political tactics of the old regime, trying to gain personal access to Napoleon and offering fulsome praise to this absolute ruler. At the beginning of the Restoration, many townspeople added a counterrevolutionary dimension to the rhetoric of contention. As their language and tactics changed, the political culture of France seemed to return full circle to its monarchist traditions. Thus, a closer examination of struggles for arrondissement seats can reveal significant patterns of change in the political mentality and practices of urban elites. In like manner, analysis of government policy toward these urban rivalries can illustrate important features of the larger project for political and social stabilization that officials of the Consulate, Empire, and Restoration shared.

Municipal officials quickly discovered that legislative councils in the new regime had no power to redress grievances about the location of subprefectures or tribunals. At the beginning of February 1800, the Tribunate even refused to discuss petitions "of local interest," which it referred hence-

[24] Tabulation based on dossiers in F1 I:504–23; and comparisons of the lists of subprefectures and tribunals in the *Almanach national* for the year IX and the *Almanach Royal* for the year 1816.

[25] Counting pairs or triads of rivals, 41 had been in the same district in 1790, but 28 had been in different districts.

forth to the government without any observations.[26] As soon as the prefectoral corps was established, townspeople who tried to correspond directly with the ministry of the interior were also rebuffed: the ministry followed a standard procedure of returning their petitions to the prefects, sometimes with a note instructing these officials to reprimand the municipal authorities for not following "the hierarchical order of correspondence."[27] Townspeople must direct their complaints to the prefects, who were authorized to consult with the councils of municipalities, arrondissements, and departments about local issues. On the basis of these consultations, the prefects would then report to the ministry about requests for changes in the boundaries of arrondissements and the location of subprefectures.

This procedure, which the government began to implement in the summer of 1800, seemed to place prefects in a strategic position to decide the fate of towns. Astute municipal officials naturally concluded that criticism of existing arrondissements should be cast in a manner that emphasized the administrative needs of the state. The principle of *rapprochement*, which implied earlier in the Revolution that justice and administration should be brought closer to the people, now acquired a new meaning: smaller arrondissements would improve administrative efficiency. Townspeople had begun to complain about the excessive size of some correctional jurisdictions during the Directory, arguing that additional tribunals would increase surveillance of the evil-minded while reducing the cost of investigating crimes. These arguments had carried enough weight to convince the legislative councils of the Directory to establish twenty new correctional courts.[28] After the law of 27 ventôse, which extended the principle of *rapprochement* from criminal to civil justice, advocates of extra tribunals continued to follow this line of reasoning.[29] Townspeople also followed another precedent from the Directory, when fiscal *recettes* had been established to reduce the danger of transporting tax funds from distant communes to the seat of a department. Just as smaller arrondissements would minimize the costs of criminal justice, so they would increase the security of tax funds. Finally, petitioners added that communications between the prefectoral corps and local officials would be hampered unless arrondissements were based on existing road networks and marketing arrangements.

[26] Sessions of 7 and 18 pluviôse, year VIII, AP 2d ser., 1:132–35, 174–177.

[27] Letters from minister of the interior to prefects of the Finistère and the Gers, 22 germinal and 19 vendémiaire, year XI, returning petitions for new arrondissements from L'Isle-Jourdain and Rostrenen, AN F2 I:507, 510.

[28] AN, series C, dossiers catalogued in Robert Anchel, et al., *Les papiers des assemblées du Directoire*.

[29] For examples, see the dossiers of Rosternen, Verneuil, Argenton, and Bourmont, in AN F2 I:507, 508, 511, 514.

For example, the municipality of Sézanne, shocked to learn that its former district and correctional jurisdiction had been attached to the arrondissement of Epernay, emphasized the negative impact on the government of this "great error": orders and dispatches could not be sent promptly from Epernay to Sézanne because roads between these two towns were so poor; tax collectors would have to transport funds through a large forest, at considerable risk; witnesses convoked by the tribunal at Epernay in criminal cases would have to be reimbursed for their travel expenses; the public treasury would suffer heavy losses from the absence of competitive bids at Epernay for timber rights to national woods near Sézanne; and mayors and assistant mayors from rural communes who frequented the markets of Sézanne would not be able to seek enlightenment from the subprefect. "As obstacles to administration multiply, lax enforcement of the laws will necesssarily follow, and the public good will suffer great prejudice." Only by restoring the former district of Sézanne could distances between communes and the *chef-lieu* be arranged "for the convenience of public service." The position of Sézanne was so useful for the general administration that the prefect had been obliged to delegate authority to the mayor of this town in some matters that the subprefect normally handled. In their published brief for a separate arrondissement, the mayor and assistant mayors of Sézanne concluded, "Thus, the interests of the government, as well as those of all the communes in the former district of Sézanne, have been injured by the operation that has ignored this town."[30]

The prefect of the Marne, seconded by the departmental and arrondissement councils, agreed that administration in the arrondissement of Epernay was "infinitely difficult and, especially, very costly." He recommended a new subdivision that would reconstitute the district of Sézanne and compensate Epernay with four cantons that had been transferred from its former correctional jurisdiction to the arrondissement of Reims in 1800.[31] At least twelve other prefects, impressed by complaints about the disproportionate size of an arrondissement or the deficiencies of a *chef-lieu*, proposed changes in the administrative geography of their departments between 1800 and 1804. The prefect of the Eure made such a persuasive case for restoring the district of Verneuil that the minister of the interior agreed on September 19, 1800, to forward his request, along with those of several

[30] *Réclamation*, Archives Départementales de la Marne (hereafter "AD"), 118 M2. For similar arguments about the need to reduce the expenses of judicial administration and to minimize the danger of robbery to tax collectors, which towns had begun to use during the Directory to justify additional correctional jurisdictions and fiscal *recettes*, see the dossiers of Verneuil, Nogaro, Tartas, and Bourmont, AN F2 I:508, 510, 512, 514.

[31] "Avis du préfet," written across the printed *réclamation* of Mun. Sézanne and dated 13 frimaire, year IX (Dec. 3, 1800), AD Marne, 118 M2.

other prefects, to the consuls for a decision.[32] But the Conseil d'Etat, whose section of the interior had subdivided the arrondissements without paying close attention to local geography, persuaded Napoleon to ignore the advice of these prefects. The new institutions had scarcely been implemented, and time alone would prove whether the current subdivision of departments should be modified. Even useful changes in administrative geography might encourage less justifiable demands. Opposing the formation of additional arrondissements on budgetary grounds and fearing that transfers of *chefs-lieux* would intensify urban rivalries, the Conseil d'Etat upheld the status quo, however defective it might appear to be in the eyes of prefects as well as local notables. On October 14, 1800, Napoleon and his councillors signed a statement that "it would be impolitic and dangerous to overturn precipitously the state of things established by the organic laws on civil administration and the judicial order."[33] Three months later, the consuls issued an edict that rejected all demands for changes in the boundaries or capitals of arrondissements.[34]

On July 15, 1803, however, the Conseil d'Etat issued an edict, exclusively on the advice of Napoleon, to transfer the subprefecture of Bergues to the much larger seaport of Dunkerque. Senator Herwyn, who had skillfully arranged for his hometown of Bergues to become the arrondissement seat in 1800, learned of this surprising event from the other two consuls, Cambacérès and Le Brun, who made a point of denying any responsibility for Napoleon's decision. Herwyn protested in vain to the first consul, who had recently visited Dunkerque to inspect military preparations for war with England. Lamenting the decline of their commerce, the merchants of Dunkerque had persuaded Napoleon to restore the fortunes of their town at the expense of Bergues, whose patron in Paris now found himself decisively outmaneuvered.[35] A week later, on July 22, Napoleon issued a comparable decree moving the prefecture of the Nord from Douai to Lille. Several months passed before the Legislative Councils ratified a special law that transferred the tribunal of Bergues to Dunkerque, following the insistence of the minister of justice that the government could not change the location of tribunals without legislative approval. After Napoleon became emperor of the French, he disregarded such constitutional niceties, signing edicts to move tribunals from Barr to Schlestadt, Montaigu to Napoleon-Vendée, and Moulins-en-Gilbert to Château-Chinon. Such unilateral actions, although preceded by elaborate administrative inquiries, encouraged

---

[32] *Rapport* of the minister of the interior, in dossier Verneuil, AN F2 I:508.

[33] Copy dated 23 vendémiaire, year IX, in dossier Montfort, AN F2 I:521.

[34] *Arrêté* of 25 nivoise, year IX, cited in a draft letter from the minister of the interior to the prefect of the Creuse, AN F2 I:507

[35] Letters from Herwyn and Mun. Bergues to the first consul, 28 messidor and 13 thermidor, year XI. AN F2 I:517.

other townspeople to hope that Napoleon would take their side, too, in disputes over subprefectures and tribunals.

From the beginning of the Consulate, a few petitioners voiced unbounded admiration for this man of destiny. "How much the heavens would be praised," wrote the national agent of Beaumont to Lucien Bonaparte on March 12, 1800, "if the hero whose blood flows in your veins had long ago executed the project of saving France. . . . Just imagine how many victims he would have rescued, how many injustices he would have prevented. . . . May this great man receive from all Frenchmen and from all of Europe the tribute of praise justly merited; may he live eternally for the happiness of mankind." As the minister of the interior, Lucien would presumably convey these sentiments of joy to Napoleon and add a word in favor of Beaumont's request for a sixth arrondissement in the department of the Haute-Garonne.[36] Such obsequious rhetoric became more widespread after Napoleon revealed his imperial ambitions in 1804. "It is at the feet of this hero, this prodigy of virtues and glory, that the inhabitants of L'Isle Jourdain come to present their humble supplications and the claims that they have to his justice," wrote twenty-five petitioners from this market town of the Gers on May 23, 1805. Denied a separate arrondissement in 1800, they now invoked the name of "Napoleon the Great—the greatest of Conquerors and the best of Princes" in order to wrest a *chef-lieu* away from the rival town of Lombez, "so little that it has never been worthy of the slightest attention at any time whatsoever."[37] Municipal officials from Saint-Dizier, in the Haute-Marne, expressed equal zeal for Napoleon: "What can the town of Saint-Dizier not expect from a new Charlemagne who, warrior and legislator, encompasses with his genius the different parts of administration in the Empire; who recently, while visiting his provinces, in developing great projects for the glory of France, transferred from Douai to Lille the departmental seat of the Nord, and from Bergues to Dunkerque that of a communal arrondissement?" To flesh out this rhetoric, they enclosed a memorial describing the superiority of Saint-Dizier, a commercial and industrial town of 6,000 inhabitants, over the arrondissement seat of Wassy, an isolated commune of only 2,200 inhabitants, "without any communications or any kind of industry." Neglecting to mention the central location of Wassy in the arrondissement, they blamed its acquisition of a tribunal and a subprefecture on the intrigue of a former deputy. The interest of the government demanded that the *chef-lieu* be placed at Saint-Dizier, with its strategic location on a major road to Germany.[38]

Documents of this sort probably never crossed Napoleon's desk. In an

[36] AN F2 I:509.
[37] *Adresse* to minister of the interior, 4 prairial, year XIII, AN F2 I:510.
[38] Letter on 4 frimaire, year XIII (Nov. 24, 1804), AN F2 I:514.

authoritarian regime that increasingly resembled an absolute monarchy, townspeople needed direct access to the emperor, whose will so obviously determined affairs of state. The municipal council of Lesneven recalled how the king of France had graciously received deputies from this Breton town in 1535 and had preserved their tribunal. In a deliberation on August 8, 1806, the town fathers decided to follow the example of their ancestors by sending a deputation to Paris. These emissaries would "expose, at the feet of the throne, the sentiments of gratitude, fidelity, love, respect, and admiration that all the inhabitants shared for the sacred person of the august leader of the state and hero of the century." They would also beg His Royal and Imperial Majesty to restore to his faithful town of Lesneven the establishments that the Revolution had destroyed: an Ursuline convent, a tribunal, and the arrondissement of a subprefecture. They returned empty-handed, however, to Lesneven, having been told in Paris that "demands of this sort could not be heard at the present moment."[39] Gaining an audience with the emperor was no easy task. Some municipal officials succeeded in conveying their wishes to Napoleon while he was traveling in the provinces. As early as 1803, when Dunkerque capitalized on such a visit, the mayor of Sézanne went first to Paris and then to Reims, where he presented the first consul with a petition. Glancing briefly at the manuscript, Napoleon handed it to the minister of the interior, who supposedly agreed that the complaints of Sézanne were justified. Napoleon himself must have been unimpressed, for this polite reply led nowhere, despite the mayor's subsequent letter to a patron in Paris, asking him to prod the minister into action.[40] In like manner, the hopes of Verneuil rose when Napoleon traveled through this town in 1811, en route to Cherbourg. In the words of the bishop of Evreux, who intervened afterward on behalf of Verneuil, the emperor spoke with "such kindness" to the mayor, municipal council, and "all the people" that they "dared present him with a petition for an arrondissement." But as the minister of the interior explained to the bishop, Napoleon did not issue any order for such an arrondissement, and there the matter rested.[41]

Cherbourg, the large naval port that Napoleon visited after passing through Verneuil, had a stronger case to make for a separate arrondissement in the department of the Manche. With a strategic military role to play in the war with England, a population of 14,000 inhabitants, and a correctional jurisdiction until the rival town of Valognes eliminated it in 1800, Cherbourg ressembled Dunkerque in its position. Yet all the pro-

[39] Letter to the minister of the interior, Aug. 8, 1806, AN F2 I:509.

[40] Letter from mayor to unspecified notable in Paris, 25 messidor, year XI (July 14, 1803), AD Marne, 118 M:2.

[41] Letters from the bishop to the minister, Aug. 6, 1811, and from the minister to the bishop, Aug. 22, 1811, AN F2 I:508.

testations of its municipality, which the prefect and the departmental council consistently supported, led nowhere until Napoleon's visit. The emperor must have been impressed by what he heard from the local authorities; on July 11, 1811, he issued a decree to form the arrondissement that they had so long desired.[42]

Having broken a long-standing policy not to add any subprefectures or tribunals, Napoleon took the opportunity to create a second arrondissement on the same day. This one was specifically designed for the little town of Rambouillet, where he had turned the former royal château into an imperial residence. The mayor of this town, M. Delorme, had mounted an artful campaign to persuade the Emperor that the seat of his château deserved a higher rank within the state than a mere cantonal seat. How else could a functionary of suitable dignity be present on all occasions to greet His Majesty? A subprefecture and a tribunal would also indemnify the town of Rambouillet for its heavy taxes and enforce more rigorously the laws against poaching in the surrounding forests. For nearly four years, at every opportunity, M. Delorme invoked such arguments on behalf of his town. Not surprisingly, the nearby towns of Etampes and Versailles, which stood to lose a substantial portion of their own jurisdictions, resisted his plan, and so did most of the rural communes in the area. But Napoleon was flattered by the thought of turning Rambouillet into a more impressive setting for his court. He not only ruled in favor of this little town but made M. Delorme the subprefect of the new arrondissement.[43]

The hierarchy of imperial dignitaries that Napoleon created in conscious imitation of the old regime suggested indirect avenues of political influence for townspeople. When the duke of Massa passed through the little town of Langeais on August 12, 1808, municipal officials handed him a sycophantic address to Napoleon in the hope of gaining a separate arrondissement. In like manner, Longwy used the patronage of General Chasseloup, an inspector general in the engineering corps, who wrote in 1808 from Milan to assure the minister of the interior that this fortified town had a larger population than the arrondissement seat of Briey. According to the general, Longwy also had a permanent garrison, two splendid highways, beautiful inns, important fairs, active commerce, forges, mines, and woolen works. Unfortunately, the mayor of Longwy, seeking to arouse the sympathy of the minister, wrote in a separate letter that troops had not been stationed in the town for ten years, wholesale trade had disappeared, and the population had declined from 3,000 in 1790 to only 2,168 in

---

[42] Earlier documents from Cherbourg are in AN F2 I:514, but the dossier prepared in 1811 must have been forwarded to the Conseil d'Etat, whose archives were burned in 1871.

[43] On this affair, see the detailed correspondence in AD Seine-et-Oise, 8 M1; and AN F2 I:521.

1806. As for the prefect, who also supported Longwy, he explained to the minister that the two rivals were at the opposite ends of the arrondissement, but that Longwy had better roads and resources for a *chef-lieu*. In the Haute-Vienne, Maréchal Jourdan agreed to patronize Saint-Junien in its rivalry with the smaller town of Rochechouart, and so did General Dalesme, a member of the legislative body. Even a lady of the court, Madame la duchesse de Dalmatie, intervened on behalf of Lacaune. The minister of the interior politely expressed regret at not being able to create a fifth arrondissement in the department of the Tarn for her protégé. From the files of the ministry of the interior, it would appear that military officers and other dignitaries of the Empire had no more success than prefects and mayors in convincing the government to create new arrondissements or to move existing *chef-lieux*.[44]

In adopting the forms of subservience and the practices of patronage that used to characterize the political culture of the old regime, townspeople anticipated the resurgence of royalism that accompanied the restoration of the Bourbons in 1814. Even the municipal council of Rambouillet, which had gained so much from Napoleon, announced in May 1814, "This nascent town, which lost everything with the overthrow of the monarchy, . . . has everything to hope from a wise and truly paternal government."[45] Other towns, with more cause to complain about their losses than Rambouillet had, greeted the advent of Louis XVIII enthusiastically. Municipal officials at Uzerche, for example, had sought Napoleon's patronage in vain. After appealing in 1811 to "this magnanimous sovereign who, similar to Providence, assures the well-being of simple hamlets as well as the splendor of great cities," they turned in 1814 to Louis XVIII.

> Sire, the town of Uzerche, enriched by the benevolence of your predecessors, was, so to speak, dispossessed at the same time as your august family. For twenty years, it lamented the fate of her legitimate princes and of yourself. During the past month, it has rejoiced at the return of your majesty to the throne of his ancestors, with all the more reason because soon the heir of the virtues of Louis XII and Henry IV will erase all the evils of the past. May the town of Uzerche, injustly despoiled, occupy your thoughts for an instant, and a new act of justice and benevolence will signal your reign!

[44] Letters in AN F2 I:511 (Langeais); F2 I:516 (Longwy); F2 I:523 (Saint-Junien); F2 I:522 (Lacaune). Only one town, Schlestadt, may have used the influence of military commanders successfully. The subprefect of Barr was transferred temporarily to Schlestadt to oversee the mobilization of supplies along the German frontier, and a decree of Feb. 10, 1806, made this transfer permanent. See the incomplete correspondence in F2 I:519.

[45] Mun. Delib., May 10, 1814, AD Seine-et-Oise, 8M 2. The town fathers were following the example of M. Delorme, who offered his services to Louis XVIII and retained his post as subprefect.

They coupled this petition with a municipal deliberation that told how a poor laborer from Uzerche, "sharing the sadness and profound indignation of his fellow citizens" at news of the death of Louis XVI, had courageously said, while working in the countryside, that an innocent man had perished. Denounced, arrested, and condemned to death by strangers, this father of six children had been executed on the public square of Uzerche to terrorize the royalists who were so numerous in the town. From this tragic event, the municipality concluded that the royalist sympathies of the inhabitants of Uzerche, always proudly affirmed, explained why this town had failed to obtain an arrondissement in the year VIII.[46]

Looking back on the history of the Revolution, a spokesman for Joinville dated this town's fall from favor to 1793, when it had refused to support the constitution of the Montagnards; so did deputies from Le Buis, whose inhabitants had lost their tribunal for refusing to accept this "anarchistic and sanguinary" constitution and for shouting "Long live the king!"[47] Emissaries from Verneuil traced their town's misfortunes to the time of the Directory, when townspeople had supported "those who were trying to restore the old monarchy."[48] Petitioners from Romans accused Napoleon of a "blind predilection" for Valence, while as late as 1821, those from Calais were decrying Napoleon's hatred for this town, "doubtless because he knew of its attachment to the Bourbon dynasty."[49] Such charges of political favoritism often acquired a decidedly counterrevolutionary tone. Delegates from Hesdin argued that their town had been victimized by the "revolutionary furies" of Montreuil; a spokesman for Guise denounced the "gangrened" *pays* of Vervins for continuing to support a former deputy of the Convention who had persecuted Guise throughout the Revolution for its royalism; and petitioners from Martel claimed that the rival town of Gourdon had obtained the *chef-lieu* because "the great majority of inhabitants in the town of Martel were opposed to the Revolution." In this case, however, the municipality of Gourdon protested that this town had rebelled against "the principles of the Revolution" in 1793, while "enraged demagogues" had continued to frequent the popular society of Martel.[50] Similarly, when spokesmen for Arles attributed this town's failure to get any establishments in 1800 to "the hatred that it had shown for the Revolution," rivals at Tarascon retorted that their town had mus-

[46] *Pétition* and Mun. Delib., May 12, 1814, AN F2 I:506.

[47] *Mémoire* for Joinville, Aug. 16, 1816, AN F2 I:514; and printed *Mémoire* for Nyons, F2 I:508.

[48] Letter to the Minister of the interior, Apr. 22, 1814, AN F2 I:508.

[49] *Réclamations* from Romans, AN F2 I:508; and *pétition* for Calais, Mar. 21, 1821, F2 I:518.

[50] *Mémoire* for Hesdin, July 10, 1815, AN F2 I:518; letter for Guise, June 5, 1816, F2 I:504; undated *pétition* for Martel, letter from Mun. Gourdon, May 19, 1816, F2 I:513.

tered six hundred soldiers for the duc d'Angoulême in 1815, while Arles had done nothing for the royalist cause. Indeed, ultraroyalists became so active at Tarascon that they rioted on February 13, 1816, when the subprefect ordered the arrest of a man accused of murdering a proprietor during the White Terror. The government had to intervene with the army to restore order, and the king issued an ordinance on February 22 to punish the populace of Tarascon by transferring the subprefecture and tribunal to Arles. Here royalism outdid itself and played into the hands of a rival town.[51]

This example was unique because it brought a local rivalry to the direct attention of the king. Unlike Arles, most towns that wanted changes in the administrative and judicial organization of the kingdom had to rely on a combination of elaborate administrative channels and informal contacts within the royal entourage. Like their predecessors during the Consulate and Empire, the prefects of the Restoration were consulted by the ministry of the interior, but their views carried little weight unless they supported the status quo. Discontented townspeople sought more impressive patrons in the duke of Angoulême, nephew of Louis XVIII; Madame the duchess of Angoulême; the duke of Richlieu, who became the minister of foreign affairs; Madame the duchess of Richelieu; the prince of Condé; the marquis of Dreux Brezé, grand master of ceremony of the king, and so forth. To judge from petitions for subprefectures and tribunals, the duke of Angoulême was the most popular courtier at the beginning of the Restoration. The towns of Argenton, Dol, Guerande, Hennebont, and Joinville all sought his aid, while Martel and Uzerche beseeched the duchess of Angoulême to intercede with the king. Although the duke transmitted a favorable note for Joinville to the minister of the interior, neither he nor his wife seem to have paid much attention to the pleas of other towns.[52]

More noteworthy were the efforts of the duke and duchess of Richelieu on behalf of Verneuil. The duke himself was not especially impressed by the letter that the mayor of Verneuil, M. Saint-Aignan, addressed to him on January 11, 1816. Alluding to his former acquaintance with Monsieur de Vaublanc, now the minister of the interior, Saint-Aignan concluded his entreaty, "I very much hope that something can be done to help him [the minister] envisage the request of Verneuil from a favorable point of view." The duke had simply written across the top of this letter the following phrase—"the object concerns the special attributions of the minister of the interior"—and passed it on to the minister. Two weeks later, however, he wrote a personal letter to his colleague, insisting that "very serious reasons

<hr/>

[51] *Précis* for Arles; *rapport* for Tarascon; and voluminous dossier about the political background of this dispute, AN F2 I:505.
[52] See dossiers in AN F2 I:506, 511, 512, 513, 514, 516.

seem to demand this change." The spirit of Verneuil has always been good, he explained, and Madame de Richelieu and her family took refuge there during the Terror, where they found protectors. Trained in the manners of the old regime, the duke of Richelieu was more willing to oblige his wife than the mayor of Verneuil. From behind the scenes, it was the duchess who had taken this affair in hand.[53]

In a letter as polite as it was discouraging, the minister of the interior replied to the duke on February 5:

> Please be assured, Monsieur le duc, that I could not overlook the interest that you have for the town of Verneuil, and that I would have much pleasure in making on behalf of its inhabitants a decision that was agreeable to you. But I must say to your excellency that the present circumstances and the system of economy that the king has adopted will not perhaps permit me to consider this affair at the moment, and that it will be advisable to postpone it.[54]

Four years later, the duke and duchess de Richelieu were still trying in vain to arrange for Verneuil to obtain a separate arrondissement. Their failure, and that of nearly everyone else who requested changes in administrative geography during the Restoration, confirms the determination of the government to avoid the fate of the monarchy in 1789 by balancing the budget. Economy, not patronage, became the watchword of Louis XVIII's reign. Only two additional arrondissements were created, one in 1814 for the little *pays* of Gex, following changes in the frontier with Switzerland, and one in 1823 for the large town of Valenciennes, which already had a separate tribunal of first instance.

A few prefects of the early Restoration urged the minister of the interior to create additional arrondissements for towns such as Carhaix, Chauny, Pont-à-Mousson, Sézanne, and Verneuil, all former royal *bailliages*, but in each case, budgetary objections prevailed. A tribunal of first instance would cost around 10,000 francs in salaries for the judges and clerks, and a subprefecture would add another 6,000 francs a year to the operating expenses of the government.[55] A courthouse, jail, and office space for the subprefecture would also need to be provided by the state, although municipalities sometimes agreed to finance the purchase or repair of public buildings. During the Empire, Bressuire, Château-Chinon, Cusset, and Lourdes all obtained the transfer of establishments because they offered

[53] Letters in AN F2 I:508.

[54] Letter of Feb. 5, 1816, AN F2 I:508.

[55] See the estimates in "Tableau des dépenses à la charge du Gouvernement pour la creation d'un 6e arr. dans le dept. de l'Eure, dont Verneuil chef-lieu" [around June 1820], AN F2 I:508.

better facilities than had rival towns.[56] But once investments had been made and functionaries housed in decent premises, further changes were considered wasteful and unnecessary. As a memorial for Bressuire argued in 1814, the town house of the subprefecture had cost 34,000 francs and the palace of justice had cost 15,000 francs. To construct comparable buildings at Châtillon or Thouars, the rivals of Bressuire, would cost over 100,000 francs. In like manner, the prefect of the Nièvre defended Cosne against La Charité on the grounds that the former town had spent at least 80,000 francs to house the subprefecture and the tribunal. Major expenses would be required to move these establishments to La Charité, whose municipality was heavily in debt.[57] Despite repeated demands from towns such as Thouars and La Charité, the government of Louis XVIII consistently refused to transfer arrondissement seats. Only two towns—Montbéliard in 1814, and Arles in 1816—gained a subprefecture at the expense of rivals, and even Arles had to return the tribunal to Tarascon in 1821.

Instead of trying to accomodate townspeople who lamented the disappearance of *bailliages* and other institutions of the old regime, the Restoration Monarchy made a serious effort to suppress many of the tribunals that it had inherited from the Empire. On January 15, 1817, following approval by a ministerial council, Louis XVIII signed a legislative proposal that would abolish eight of the appellate courts and reduce the number of tribunals of first instance in many departments.[58] A special commission, headed by the minister of justice, had recommended an even more drastic policy of preserving only thirteen appellate courts, one for each of the former *parlements*, and eighty-six tribunals, one per department. According to this commission, the principle of *rapprochement*, which had shaped the movement for judicial reform during the revolutionary and imperial epoch, should be abandoned. In multiplying lawcourts in small towns, "where men of talent are rare and means of instruction negligible," reformers had undermined the prestige and authority of magistrates, who needed to deploy an imposing apparatus of justice in order to intimidate the common people. The Napoleonic system had tried to reconcile *rapprochement* with hierarchy by varying the numbers and salaries of magistrates in accordance with the size of towns and the functions of tribunals. The tribunals of first instance in small towns had only three judges, whose salaries of 1,000 francs often proved insufficient to attract well-educated recruits. Even appellate courts ranged in size from twelve to thirty-three judges, and the salaries of these judges exceeded 3,000 francs only in cities of over

[56] For a detailed history of the rivalry between Château-Chinon and Moulins-Engilbert, which turned on the question of a courthouse, see A. Jary, *Notice sur le tribunal de Château-Chinon* (Château-Chinon, 1905), pp. 15–62.

[57] AN F2 I:521 (Bressuire); F2 I:517 (La Charité).

[58] *Projet de loi*, AN BB5 362.

50,000 inhabitants.[59] For the minister of justice and his colleagues on the commission, who included the president and two councillors on the *cour de cassation*, this system dispersed judicial authority, reduced professional standards, and even corrupted public morality. To discourage chicanery and reconstitute the legal profession, tribunals should be concentrated in "truly important towns."[60]

In its more modest project of January 1817, the government tried to take into account the views of *procureurs-généraux*, prefects, and departmental councils. A year earlier, the minister of justice had issued secret orders for the *procureurs-généraux* to prepare lists of tribunals that could be suppressed within the jurisdictions of their respective appellate courts.[61] While some of these officials obliged by singling out little towns that lacked the resources to attract distinguished magistrates, others defended nearly all the seats of lawcourts within their jurisdictions, and several of them criticized ministerial policy vigorously.[62] At Rouen, for example, the *procureur-général* argued that any reductions in his area would overwhelm the remaining tribunals with litigation and reduce the efficiency of criminal justice. More important still, such decisions would create strong opposition from towns that depended on such public establishments for their prestige, wealth, and very existence. As proof that lawcourts were assets for the towns that possessed them, he pointed out that "if the inhabitants of these arrondissements were consulted, they would not agree to lose their tribunals."[63] Indeed, when the minister of the interior did ask the prefects to consult the departmental councils about this issue in the summer of 1816, many reported opposition to any suppressions. Departmental councils defended at least twenty-three of the sixty-nine tribunals that various *procureurs-généraux* listed as candidates for suppression.[64] In the minority of departments where the councils did approve of reductions, the small towns in question usually protested. So did the leaders of fourteen important towns that feared the loss of their appellate courts, including all eight of those listed in the government's project. It was becoming obvious that many deputies in the Chamber of Deputies would also object to reductions that their constituents opposed.[65]

[59] Bourdon, *La Réforme judiciare de l'an VIII*, 1:338–48, 366–71, 395–420.

[60] Notes summarizing the reasoning of the commission, drafted by Ollivier, councillor at the Cour de Cassation, Apr. 4, 1817, AN BB5 362.

[61] Circular of Jan. 22, 1816, AN BB5 362.

[62] A total of eight *procureurs-généraux* defended the status quo, seven proposed only one or two suppressions, six wanted three or four suppressions, and seven proposed from five to eight suppressions. Reports in AN BB5 362–65.

[63] Letter to the minister of justice, Feb. 20, 1816, AN BB5 365.

[64] Tabulation based on reports in AN BB5 362.

[65] The ministry tabulated a total of 53 towns whose municipalities objected to its project, AN BB5 362. Many of their letters and petitions are in BB5 362–65.

This mobilization of public opinion revealed that the tribunals and appellate courts of the Empire had come to symbolize social stability for many townspeople. After the shocks of the revolutionary epoch, urban leaders wanted assurances that institutions would cease to change with every passing regime. The *procureur-général* of Paris expressed this longing for stability when he wrote to the minister of justice:

> I would fear, I must confess, that in the present circumstances it would be rather imprudent to turn the new judicial order upside down when the immediate effect would be to throw out of work an entire population of bailiffs, *avoués*, judicial agents and others who depend on tribunals for a livelihood. We have learned too often at our own expense how costly it is for nations to let themselves be carried away by all these ideas of perfection that often produce only evils and destruction.[66]

At the beginning of the Revolution, lawyers and magistrates had expressed fears of urban depopulation and ruin because their royal *bailliages* and other institutions of the old regime had been abolished. Now their successors, the functionaries of the Empire and the early Restoration, looked back instead to the prefectures, subprefectures, and tribunals created in 1800. The earlier theme of *vivification*—that public establishments brought prosperity to towns—became a justification for preserving the new capitals of justice and administration. As the municipality of Le Vigan explained, the transfer of its arrondissement seat to the rival town of Saint-Hippolyte would bring "incalculable upheavals." Entire families would be obliged to move and to sell at a loss the properties that they had purchased or improved because of the public establishments granted to the town. Others whom family circumstances prevented from seeking employment elsewhere, including worthy magistrates, *avoués*, and bailiffs, would be forced to abandon their functions or careers (*états*). If the government changed the location of the subprefecture and tribunal, it would inflict irreparable harm on Le Vigan.[67]

The larger the town, the more frightening the project to suppress tribunals appeared in the eyes of local notables. When the municipality of Caen learned that the government planned to eliminate the appellate court in this town, it protested bitterly that Caen had lost many establishments during the Revolution. A large number of inhabitants would abandon the town if its appellate court were also abolished. The prefect of the Calvados agreed that this lawcourt remained the "principle resource" of a capital that lacked industry and commerce: "It produces much good because of the judges, lawyers, and law students who reside here and because of the large

[66] Letter of Aug. 28, 1816, AN BB5 362.
[67] *Mémoire*, Dec. 3, 1818, AN F2 I:509.

number of litigants that it attracts." The suppression of this *cour royale* would create discontent in "all classes of society," including the laboring poor who were already suffering from high food prices. In a letter to the minister of general police, the prefect predicted "very dangerous consequences" if the government persisted in its plans. The prefect at Orléans, although less fearful of popular protest, voiced similar anxiety about the economic consequences of abolishing the appellate court in this town. Following the loss of Santo Domingo and the collapse of trade with Constantinople, the sugar refineries and stocking-frame industry of Orléans had been ruined. As the municipality of Orléans insisted, the *cour royale* was "the only important establishment" that this town still possessed. Even the leaders of Nîmes, a major commercial and industrial town, argued that the abolition of their appellate court would deliver a devastating blow to the local economy. The magistrates, lawyers, *avoués*, and all the lesser personnel of the court would carry off a principal part of the mobile wealth that stimulated commerce, and litigants who brought considerable profits to local merchants would cease to frequent the town. As a result, Nîmes would lose 500,000 francs a year in income from salaries, rents, and retail trade.[68]

Such fears persuaded many deputies in the Chamber of Deputies to defend the status quo, and the government, anticipating a legislative defeat, decided to abandon its project. In a note of explanation, an official in the ministry of justice calculated that 308 judgeships would have been suppressed and another 1,000–1,200 officials of the courts and lawyers would have lost their jobs or been obliged to move with their families to another town. "It is easy to understand how much the suppression of the *cours* would afflict towns that, in losing [these establishments], would lose at the same time a considerable number of inhabitants and many people obliged by lawsuits to visit them frequently." The state itself would have realized almost no budgetary savings from the operation, because some judges would have been transferred to the remaining appellate courts, others would have been entitled to pensions at half pay, and *avoués* and *huissiers* would have been reimbursed for the caution money that they had paid to obtain these official positions. As for the fate of tribunals of first instance, which the original project would have suppressed by royal *ordonnance*, the Chamber of Deputies insisted on its prerogative to approve or reject any such measures in particular legislation.[69]

Plans for the consolidation of lawcourts continued to be discussed in the ministry of justice, but the July Monarchy opted instead for a modest increase in the salaries of magistrates. The provisional Republican govern-

---

[68] Mun. Delibs. and correspondence in AN B5 362 (Caen), 365 (Orléans), 364 (Nîmes).
[69] Unsigned note justifying the adjournment of the *projet de loi*, AN BB5 362.

ment in 1848 set up a commission to examine the issue. Its recommendations, which followed the same lines as the project of Louis XVIII's government, aroused another storm of protest. More than three hundred petitions from the department of the Hérault, many signed by dozens of residents, urged the National Assembly to preserve the appellate court at Montpellier. It would be contrary to the principles of a Republican government to reconstitute immovable judicial corporations with excessive jurisdictions: "Surely the Republic does not want to restore the *parlements* and to concentrate justice in a few places at the expense of litigants." From Agen, over nine hundred artisans and shopkeepers, deploring rumors that the appellate court in their town was about to be suppressed, covered a petition with their names and occupations. "Such a measure would not only be disastrous for this town; it would deliver a mortal blow to all the industries in the department and to the destiny of the workers." Suppression of the tribunals in the arrondissements would be "equally fatal to the arrondissement seats and to our brothers, forcing them to come to our town in search of resources that we ourselves will have lost." Instead of democraticizing France, the commission's plan would bring back the arrogant influence of the aristocracy. "You will help the large cities, but you will reduce to misery the workers in the small localities." According to municipal officials at Senlis, the project was "anti-Republican and anti-democratic." It would "ruin three-quarters of the towns of France," not to speak of Senlis itself, which would be "reduced to the condition of a village." Faced with such an outcry of public opinion, the National Assembly in 1848, like the governments of Louis XVIII, Charles X, and Louis Phillippe, decided not to tamper with the lawcourts created by Napoleon.[70]

Louis Napoleon Bonaparte, following in the authoritarian tradition of his illustrious uncle, did issue a few decrees that transferred the seats of subprefectures and lawcourts from small towns to larger and more commercial rivals. Mulhouse, one of the most important industrial cities in France, displaced the much smaller town of Altkirch in 1857; that same year, Cholet, a bustling textile town that had been nearly destroyed during the counterrevolutionary uprising of the Vendée, finally triumphed over Beaupréau, a little town whose stubborn loyalty to the Legitimist cause endangered the government's management of elections in the area; and in 1868 Saint-Nazaire, a new seaport at the mouth of the Loire, obtained the subprefecture and the tribunal in the former arrondissement of Savenay. Louis Napoleon's minister of police, Persigny, also recommended that the large industrial city of Saint-Etienne be transferred to the department of

---

[70] Printed copies of the petition from the Hérault and manuscript petitions from Agen and Senlis, AN C:2254. On the legislative debates over judicial reform between 1815 and 1848, see Alfred Hiver de Beauvoir, *Histoire critique des institutions judiciares de la France de 1789 à 1848* (Paris, 1851).

the Rhône, where police agents at Lyon would have direct authority over its turbulent work force. Instead, the government decided in 1855 to move the prefecture of the Loire from Montbrison to Saint-Etienne, although it did leave the assize court at Montbrison. During the Second Empire, France also gained three more departments with the annexation of Nice and Savoy, but then its defeat in the Franco-Prussian war led to the loss of three much more prosperous departments in Alsace and Lorraine. As for the conservative coalition of Orléanists and Legitimists that governed France after the fall of the Second Empire and the Paris Commune, it did nothing to change the administrative and judicial system, despite long-standing complaints among royalists about the excessive centralization of the French state.[71]

When Republican politicians returned to power in the 1880s, some of them criticized the prefectoral system and talked of returning to the cantonal municipalities of the Thermidorian constitution. Nothing came of such nostalgia for the administrative institutions of the Directory.[72] Not until the eve of World War I did advocates of supradepartmental regions make a serious effort to overhaul the French administrative system.[73] As one prefect wrote, however, in a confidential report to the ministry of the interior, the government would encounter "insurmountable obstacles" if it tried to deprive this or that little town of its subprefecture and its tribunal. "Electoral interests will always intefere with the general interest and nothing will be done."[74] He was well-informed. Provincial newspapers and politicians mounted a successful defense of the existing arrondissements and lawcourts until 1926, when Poincaré, armed with decree powers, suppressed 106 subprefectures and 227 tribunals of first instance. Even this draconian measure aroused so much local opposition that most of the tribunals were restored in 1929.[75] In essential respects, the judicial hierarchy

[71] On the transfers of *chef-lieux* during the Second Empire, see Mirot, *Géographie historique* 2:424–25. For the political motives behind the transfer of the subprefecture of Béaupreau to Cholet in 1857, see the *note* in the files of the minister of the interior, Oct. 26, 1857, AN F2 I:513; on Persigny's plan in 1852, see the memoirs of the prefect de Romand, published in Bruxelles in 1855 and cited by Siraud, "Etude sur la formation du département de Saône-et-Loire," p. 241, note 1.

[72] See the reference to a project by M. Goblet, minister of the interior in 1882, in type-written draft of a project for cantonal organs of administration in 1921, minister of the interior, AN F2 2000.

[73] On this movement of regionalism, see Nordman and Revel, "La formation de l'espace français," in Revel, *L'espace français*, pp. 146–49.

[74] *Rapport* by prefect of the Charente, in reply to a ministerial *circulaire* of Sept. 15, 1910, asking the prefects for their views about an official project of administrative reorganization that would suppress many subprefectures. AN FIB I:913.

[75] Some of the subprefectures were also restored either in 1933 or 1940–44. See the map of the administrative reform of 1926 and the subsequent changes, in Stéphane Sinclair, *Atlas de géographie historique de la France et de la Gaule* (Paris, 1985), 148–49. For a list of the

of the First Empire survived until the Fifth Republic.[76] The administrative hierarchy of prefectures and subprefectures still exists today, although a higher level of regional institutions has recently been added. Behind this continuity are the same forces that brought the system into existence in the first place: the needs of the central government and the interests of local populations, as expressed by the leaders of cities and towns.

complicated judicial changes between 1926 and 33, see Mirot, *Géographie historique* 2:478–85. The history of these reforms and the local opposition that they generated has not been written, although ample sources exist in the Parisian and provincial press of the period.

[76] On the contemporary period, see Henri Rolland, *Les institutions judicaires*, 2d ed. (Lyon, 1983). An *ordonnance* of Dec. 22, 1958, replaced the 354 remaining tribunals of first instance with 175 *tribunaux de grande instance* (in mainland France), which no longer corresponded to the administrative arrondissements in most departments.

Chapter 11

THE FRENCH REVOLUTION AND URBAN
GROWTH IN THE NINETEENTH CENTURY

WHAT KIND of an impact did the institutional changes of the
French Revolution have on towns in nineteenth-century
France? As we have seen, many contemporaries believed that
towns faced a bleak future of poverty and decline unless they became the
seats of departments, arrondissements, and lawcourts. Would such beliefs
be vindicated by events or would the rhetoric of *vivification* become a cultural anachronism in an industrializing age? This problem involves two
distinct issues: (1) the extent to which changes in the institutional hierarchies of the state had a short-term impact on urban prosperity and growth;
and (2) the extent to which the stabilization of those hierarchies created
long-term advantages for administrative towns. Underlying the first issue
is the straightforward idea that changes in the jurisdiction of towns over
rural populations would influence prospects for urban employment and
trade during or shortly after the revolutionary era. This idea can be tested
by comparing the variance in population growth rates of towns that gained
or lost administrative jurisdiction and lawcourts between 1789 and 1815.
Two levels of the urban hierarchy need to be distinguished, depending on
whether towns were more likely to be affected by the formation of departments in 1789 or the consolidation of arrondissements in 1800. With respect to the subdivision of provinces into departments, the former capitals
of intendancies often suffered territorial losses at the beginning of the Revolution even if they became departmental seats. By contrast, other towns
that became the capitals of departments often expanded their jurisdictions
dramatically. The later subdivision of departments into arrondissements
brought gains and losses to a different set of towns, depending on the
importance of their old jurisdictions as compared with the new subprefectures and tribunals of first instance. Over the long run, however, urban
economies would adjust to these changes in jurisdiction. If administrative
rank influenced urban prosperity or decline later in the century, it would
depend on whether appellate lawcourts, prefectures, subprefectures, and
tribunals of first instance brought enduring advantages to towns.

This issue of long-term growth is complicated by the fact that administrative agencies and lawcourts were not the only establishments that towns
gained or lost during the revolutionary era. Ecclesiastical, educational, and

military hierarchies all changed dramatically, and so did the location and functions of commercial institutions sponsored by the state, such as chambers of commerce. Most of these institutions became more widespread later in the nineteenth century, unlike the stable hierarchy of prefectures and subprefectures. Furthermore, transport networks changed dramatically from the 1840s onward, with fundamental consequences for the process of urbanization.[1] Generally speaking, departmental capitals benefited more than other towns from these changes. They did so in part because the egalitarian premises of the departmental framework of administration continued to influence government policy during the nineteenth century. When applied to military garrisons, transport facilities, and even banking institutions, the principle of territorial equality implied that at least one town in every department, usually the departmental seat, would obtain institutions and commercial opportunities that stimulated urban growth. As for arrondissement seats, a majority of them were small towns whose shopkeepers and craftsmen depended on trade with the countryside. Such towns would be vulnerable to agrarian depression and rural depopulation, although improvements in transportation might extend the radius of their markets. Their greatest advantage was the presence of a social elite of functionaries, professional men, and landlords. This might stabilize their population, even if it did not stimulate much growth.

With respect to the immediate impact of the French Revolution on urban demography, Bernard Lepetit has shown that the size of towns was inversely correlated with population growth during the period from the early 1780s to 1806.[2] His study is restricted to towns with over 5,000 inhabitants, but my own data confirm that during the first two decades after the outbreak of the Revolution, small towns were growing more rapidly than medium-sized or large towns.[3] Warfare, emigration, food shortages, and the collapse of overseas trade took a heavy toll on many provincial capitals of the old regime. So did the abolition of the *généralités* and the dispersal of administrative institutions and fiscal agencies to other

---

[1] For studies of this process in nineteenth-century France, see Marcel Roncayolo, "Logiques urbaines," in Duby, *Histoire de la France urbaine*, vol. 4, *La ville de l'âge industriel* (Paris, 1983), pp. 17–71; P. Aydalot, L. Bergeron, and M. Roncayolo, *L'Industrialisation et croissance urbain dans la France du XIXe siècle* (Paris, 1981); Dupeux, "La Croissance urbaine," pp. 173–89; and Charles A. Pouthas, *La population française pendant la première moitié du XIXe siècle* (Paris, 1956).

[2] Lepetit, *Les villes dans la France moderne*, pp. 224–33.

[3] Using the demographic data discussed in the appendix 1, I have calculated that towns with a nucleated population of fewer than 5,000 inhabitants in 1809 had increased between 1789 and 1809 by an average of 21 percent, as compared with 14 percent for towns with a nucleated population of 5,000–9,999 inhabitants (127 cases), −1 percent for towns with 10,000–19,000 inhabitants in 1789, and −8 percent for towns with at least 20,000 inhabitants in 1789.

towns. Out of eighty-six departmental seats at the beginning of the Empire, only twenty-seven had been capitals of intendancies on the eve of the Revolution. These towns had lost, on average, around three-fifths of their administrative jurisdiction. Another four seats of *généralités* had been reduced to the rank of subprefectures, and one had even been denied that modest establishment.[4] By contrast, fifty-nine other towns had increased their jurisdiction dramatically by becoming the seats of prefectures. If we compare population trends between the old and new administrative capitals, we find that the former towns lost, on average, 4 percent of their population between 1789 and 1809, while the latter increased their population, on average, by 7 percent.[5]

By estimating the number of cantonal seats contained within the administrative and fiscal jurisdictions of each town at the beginning and the end of this period, we can correlate territorial changes more precisely with demographic trends.[6] Table 11.1, which classifies the capitals of *généralités* and/or departments on an aggregate scale of cantonal seats gained or lost, shows a consistent tendency for annual growth rates to increase or decline as jurisdiction expanded or declined. Regression analysis confirms that this correlation remains statistically significant when the size of towns is taken into account.[7] Just as the abolition of the *généralités* helps explain the stagnation of large towns during the revolutionary era, so the formation of departments helps account for the growth of smaller towns.[8]

At the intermediate level of the administrative hierarchy, jurisdictions remained unstable until the formation of arrondissements in 1800. Only

[4] Bastia, Soissons, Montauban (which received a separate department only in 1808), La Rochelle (which gained the departmental seat of the Charentes-Maritimes only in 1810), and Valenciennes (which did not obtain a subprefecture until 1823).

[5] Calculations based on whether towns were departmental seats at the beginning of the Empire. Saintes and Fontenay-le-Compte are included, while Montauban and La Rochelle are classified as arrondissement seats.

[6] To make these calculations, I subtracted the aggregate number of cantonal units of administrative jurisdiction that a given town possessed in 1815 from the aggregate number of cantonal units of administrative jurisdiction that the town possessed in 1789. For the methods used to tabulate these cantonal scales of jurisdiction, which take into account several types of administrative institutions, see appendix 1.

[7] The partial correlation between jurisdictional change and growth rates is positive (.24), while that between town size and growth rates is negative (− .33). Together, these variables explain 24 percent of the variance in growth rates among towns that lost intendancies and/or gained departmental seats between 1789 and 1808 (multiple R = .49).

[8] This correlation between changes in the scale of administrative jurisdictions and variations in the growth rates of departmental seats disappears between 1809 and 1836. However, Lepetit has shown that twenty-eight prefectures that improved their institutional rank on a seven-point scale during the revolutionary era had a higher average growth rate during this period than did fifteen prefectures that declined in rank on this scale. Lepetit, *Les villes dans la France moderne*, pp. 234–36.

TABLE 11.1

Annual Rates of Population Change of Major Administrative Capitals, by Changes in Administrative Jurisdictions between 1789 and 1808/9

Changes in Jurisdiction	Average Annual Rates of Change per 1,000 Inhabitants, 1789–1809		
	Mean	Standard Deviation	Number of Cases
Gains 50 or more on cantonal scale	5.6	6.9	37
Gains 25–49 on cantonal scale	2.5	6.4	8
Stable (-25 to 25) on cantonal scale	-0.5	7.1	15
Loses 25–49 on cantonal scale	-2.9	8.9	7
Loses 50 or more on cantonal scale	-3.7	8.6	19

F score $= 5.2$

Level of significance $= .00$

Sources: The scale is based on aggregate gains or losses of administrative jurisdiction, as measured in cantonal units. Annual growth rates are based on estimates of the total population in 1789 and on the total population around 1809, as given in the *Enquête dite 1,000*. On these calculations, see appendix 1.

Note: Major administrative seats are defined as towns that had intendancies in 1789 or prefectures in 1808. This analysis excludes Paris, as the nation's capital, and Périgueux, Ajaccio, Bastia, and Mont-de-Marsan because of unreliable population data in 1789. It classifies Montauban and La Rochelle as subprefectures, and Saintes, La Roche-sur-Yon, and Lille as prefectures. Versailles is classified with towns that suffered the greatest losses of jurisdiction (50 or more), because the royal court attracted residents from all over the kingdom before the Revolution.

from this point forward does it become meaningful to analyze the relationship among subprefectures and cantonal seats between urban growth rates and changes in the scale of jurisdictions. If we compare the 755 towns and bourgs that used to have a subdelegation, *élection, recette* for direct or indirect taxes, *maîtrise des eaux et forêts*, or salt tribunal in 1789 with the 294 towns that acquired a subprefecture by 1815, we might conclude that 64 percent were demoted, 32 percent stayed at the same level, and only 4 percent were promoted in rank.[9] However, many subdelegations, fiscal *re-*

[9] Among the 755 administrative seats in 1789 (excluding intendancies), 458 were reduced to the rank of cantonal seats and 52 to the rank of simple communes; 265 obtained subpre-

cettes, and administrative tribunals had much smaller jurisdictions than did the average arrondissement. Furthermore, hundreds of little towns and bourgs had only one or two administrative institutions in 1789, while nearly all the seats of arrondissements had intermediate fiscal agencies for the collection of direct and indirect taxes and had subprefectures, as well. By measuring change in the size of jurisdictions, a more realistic analysis of promotions and demotions can be developed. Table 11.2, which uses a cantonal scale of jurisdictional gains and losses, suggests that the administrative influence of nearly half the towns in question remained stable, while it expanded substantially more often than it contracted for towns at the extremes of the scale.[10] The table classifies towns into four categories, depending on the probability that their administrative and fiscal institutions in 1789 would be translated into subprefectures and the equivalent tax agencies in 1815. All but one of the twenty-nine towns in rank IV, which had no significant administrative institutions in 1789, gained at least ten cantonal units of jurisdictions by obtaining subprefectures and tax agencies at the level of arrondissements. Nearly three-quarters of the towns in rank III, by contrast, had no appreciable gains or losses in jurisdiction, although only 14 percent (58/405) of these former seats of subdelegations, salt granaries, and/or *recettes* of the *régie* obtained arrondissement seats. Structural change in the size of jurisdictions characterized a much larger proportion of towns in ranks I and II, with fewer gains and more losses at the extremes (10 +/−) among towns that used to have *élections* and *directions* for indirect taxes. Promotions were more common among the seats of fiscal *recettes,* whose former jurisdictions had been considerably smaller, on average, than their new arrondissements.

Map 11.1 shows regional patterns in the structural transformation of these intermediate networks of administration. The map distinguishes between towns that gained jurisdiction (figures with crosshatching) and those that lost jurisdiction (empty figures). Substantial changes are signified by squares (at least 10 cantons of aggregate jurisdiction gained or lost), and more modest changes by circles (5–9 cantons).[11] It is easy to perceive the contrast between the old heartland of the monarchy—the provinces of the Ile de France, Normandy, Champagne, and the Loire River valley, where administrative rationalization reduced the jurisdiction of many towns—and the more peripheral areas of western and southern France, where the same process often expanded the jurisdiction of towns.

---

fectures, and 29 towns that did not previously have any of these institutions were promoted to subprefectures.

[10] See appendix 1 for an explanation of this cantonal scale.

[11] It should be emphasized that these are not literally cantons but that this is an abstract scale, based on the total estimated number of cantonal seats within several administrative and fiscal jurisdictions.

TABLE 11.2

Changes in Jurisdiction of Lesser Administrative Towns, 1789–1815

Rank in 1789	Losses or Gains in Jurisdiction							Total	Number of Subprefectures
	Loses 20 or More	Loses 10–19	Loses 5–9	Stable (−4 to 4)	Gains 5–9	Gains 10–20	Gains 20 or More		
Rank I	14	32	26	36	21	17	2	148	108 (73%)
Rank II	6	29	53	53	22	30	9	202	79 (39%)
Rank III	0	1	67	284	3	34	16	405	58 (14%)
Rank IV	—	—	—	—	1	13	15	29	29 (100%)
TOTAL	20	62	146	373	47	94	42	784	274

Sources: For sources and computational procedures, see appendix 1.

Notes: Gains or losses in jurisdiction are measured as the difference in the aggregate numbers of cantonal seats within administrative and fiscal jurisdictions in 1789 and 1815. Towns that had *élections* and/or *directions* for the *régie générale* or the *fermes générales* are classified in Rank I; other towns with *recettes* for direct taxes, *recettes des fermes générales*, and/or *maîtrises particuliers des eaux et forêts* are classified in Rank II; towns that had only a subdelegation, a *grenier à sel*, and/or a *recette* of the *régie* are classified in Rank III; and those that obtained subprefectures although they did not have any of these institutions are classified in rank IV.

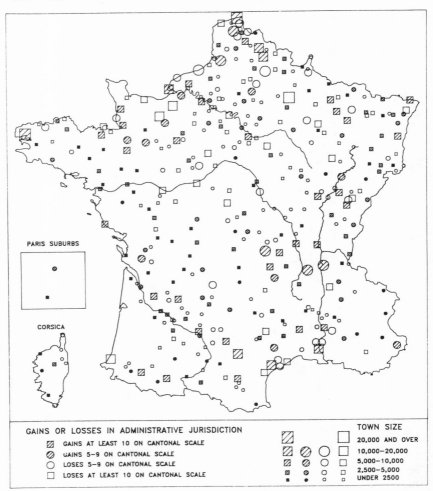

Map 11.1. Lesser Administrative Seats that Gain or Lose Jurisdiction, 1789–1815

The varying densities of administrative lawcourts and fiscal agencies in the old regime, as compared with the more uniform system of arrondissements after the Revolution, help explain this contrast. In the north, a plethora of administrative lawcourts and *recettes* for indirect taxes were replaced by a smaller number of arrondissements, while in the west and south, the abolition of provincial institutions and fiscal immunities set the stage for the central government to draw a larger number of towns into its administrative network. A closer inspection of the map indicates, however, that in many areas institutional changes had contrary effects on the jurisdictions of nearby towns. Even in the Paris basin, some towns succeeded in expanding their territorial influence while others declined as administrative centers. Clusters of towns whose jurisdictions waxed or waned can also be found in parts of Brittany, Languedoc, Dauphiné, Burgundy, Franche-Comté, Alsace, Lorraine, and Flanders, all provinces on the periphery of the kingdom. Indeed, seventy departments had both winners and losers, and thirty-eight departments, scattered through nearly every region, contained towns at both extremes of the scale of jurisdictional gains and losses.

If the formation of arrondissements stimulated the population of towns that expanded the size of their administrative jurisdictions, then rank on this cantonal scale should be correlated with urban growth rates in the years following the Consulate. To test this hypothesis, growth in the nucleated population of towns can be calculated for the period from 1809 to 1836, whose relatively stable features of urban demography have been demonstrated by Lepetit and Royer.[12] Table 11.3 presents the distribution of growth rates by change in the size of jurisdictions. It shows, to begin with, that the growth rates of all categories of towns were positive, which belies the worst fears of townspeople that institutional losses would result in demographic decline. In a period of rural population growth and expanding agricultural production and exchange, even the towns least favored by the new administrative system grew, on average, at a slow but appreciable rate of 2.4 per thousand per year. Yet the towns that benefited most from the jurisdictional changes grew at a much more rapid pace. Those ranking highest on the scale (+ 20) had an average growth rate of 8.1 per thousand per year, nearly three times as fast as those ranking lowest (2.4 per thousand). A less dramatic contrast in growth rates characterized towns that gained or lost from ten to nineteen cantonal units of jurisdiction. Below this threshold, however, jurisdictional changes had no effect on growth rates. It is variance at the extremes that explains why the cantonal scale is significantly correlated with growth rates. Another qualification needs to be made, as the table shows. Only the growth rates of small towns, numbering fewer than 5,000 inhabitants, accelerated or decelerated as jurisdictions expanded or contracted. The administrative reforms of Napoleon helped to increase the population of some small towns at the expense of others, but they had no appreciable effect on larger towns. Above a threshold of 5,000 inhabitants, other economic forces outweighed the

[12] Bernard Lepetit and Jean-François Royer, "Croissance et taille des villes," *Annales: E.S.C.* 35 (1980): 987–1010. My procedure differs from theirs because I use the nucleated population of towns to calculate urban growth rates in the nineteenth century. I do so because my analysis includes all cantonal seats with at least 1,500 nucleated inhabitants in 1836. Only the nucleated population of these communes was published in the *Bulletin des lois*, unless they also had a total population of at least 3,000 inhabitants.

TABLE 11.3
Annual Rates of Population Change of Minor Administrative Seats between 1809 and 1836, by Changes in Administrative Jurisdictions, 1789–1815

| | Average Annual Rates of Change per 1,000 Inhabitants, by Size of Towns | | | | | | | | |
| | All Minor Administrative Seats | | | Under 5,000 Inhabitants | | | Over 5,000 Inhabitants | | |
Changes in Jurisdiction, 1789–1815	Mean	Standard Deviation	Number of Cases	Mean	Standard Deviation	Number of Cases	Mean	Standard Deviation	Number of Cases
Gains 20 or more on cantonal scale	8.1	8.1	40	9.3	8.7	29	5.1	5.0	11
Gains 10–19 on cantonal scale	5.9	6.1	85	7.0	5.4	56	3.7	8.8	29
Gains 5–19 on cantonal scale	4.4	8.5	45	4.3	7.8	29	4.4	10.0	16
Stable (−4 to +4) on cantonal scale	5.3	7.6	226	5.7	7.6	190	2.8	7.4	36
Loses 5–9 on cantonal scale	4.1	5.9	93	4.6	5.5	72	2.6	7.2	21
Loses 10–19 on cantonal scale	3.6	6.2	52	3.6	5.3	38	3.9	8.3	14
Loses 20 or more on cantonal scale	2.4	5.5	18	1.4	4.1	10	3.6	6.9	8
	F score = 2.62			*F* score = 3.44			*F* score = 0.23		
	Level of significance = .02			Level of significance = .00			Level of significance = .97		

Sources: Growth rates are based on the nucleated population, as listed in the *Enquête dite 1000*, using prefectoral reports from 1809–1812, in AN F20:428–429; and the *Bulletin des lois* (Jan.–June 1837), pp. 69–140. Towns with fewer than 1,500 nucleated inhabitants in 1836 are missing from the latter source and not included in the analysis.

Note: Minor administrative seats are defined as towns that had administrative institutions below the level of intendancies in 1789 and below the level of prefectures in 1815. Changes in jurisdiction are measured as the differences in the aggregate numbers of cantonal seats within administrative and fiscal jurisdictions in 1789 and 1815. For computational procedures, see appendix 1.

importance of gaining the modest administrative personnel of a subprefecture.

Turning to the judicial reforms of the Empire, we can measure changes in rank more easily than in the case of administrative capitals, although here, again, we need to examine changes in the scale of jurisdictions. Table 11.4 distinguishes between four groups of towns, depending on their judicial rank on the eve of the Revolution: (I) towns with sovereign courts; (II) those with *présidiaux*; (III) those with royal *bailliages* or *sénéchaussées*; and (IV) those with only ordinary royal courts or seigneurial courts. Within each group, towns are then classified in accordance with their rank in 1815, depending on whether they obtained appeals courts, assize courts, tribunals of first instance, or no lawcourts above the level of justices of the peace. Within each row of the table, shifts in the territorial jurisdiction of these twelve categories of towns are measured in terms of cantonal seats gained or lost.[13] The table indicates considerable movement at the bottom of the hierarchy between low-ranking towns and royal *bailliages*: while 124 towns that used to be inferior in dignity to *bailliage* towns acquired tribunals of first instance and 8 even became seats of assize courts, 163 *bailliage* towns were stripped of all jurisidiction over civil lawsuits. Indeed, only 125 of the 288 towns with simple *bailliages* or *sénéchaussées* gained tribunals of first instance, including 16 that were promoted to the rank of assize courts. Mobility in rank also characterized the towns that used to have *présidiaux*: while 7 fell to the bottom of the hierarchy, 11 ascended to the heights by obtaining appellate courts. In between these extremes, 32 *présidiaux* towns gained assize courts and 40 became seats of tribunals in the arrondissements. Only at the top of the hierarchy, among seats of sovereign courts, did a majority of towns retain the same rank, including all 13 of the former *villes parlementaires*. Even here, 4 towns that once had *conseils souverains* or *chambres des comptes*, including Montauban and Nantes, had to settle for assize courts, and another 3, including Clermont-Ferrand, gained nothing but a tribunal of first instance. If we equated *bailliage* courts with tribunals of first instance and *présidiaux* courts with assize courts, we could conclude that two-thirds of all these towns moved up or down the judicial hierarchy between 1789 and 1815.

The evidence about changes in the size of circumscriptions suggests, however, that half of these towns experienced relatively small shifts in the number of cantons that were subordinated to the jurisdiction of their lawcourts. Many former *bailliages* encompassed so little territory that ninety-five of them were suppressed but did not lose jurisdiction over more than a single canton. Only one-tenth of all the former seats of *bailliages* and *présidiaux* lost jurisdiction over an area as large as five cantons, and only a handful lost jurisdiction over at least ten cantons. By far the greatest terri-

---

[13] See appendix 1 for an explanation of these measurements.

TABLE 11.4
Changes in Jurisdiction of Royal Lawcourts between 1789 and 1815, by Judicial Rank in 1789 and 1815

Judicial Rank in 1789/1815	Losses or Gains in Jurisdiction							
	Loses 20 or More	Loses 10–19	Loses 5–9	Stable (−4 to 4)	Gains 5–9	Gains 10–20	Gains 20 or More	Total
I. Sovereign court								
Appeals	8	0	0	1	1	0	6	16
Assize	2	0	0	1	0	0	0	3
Tribunal	3	0	0	0	0	0	0	3
II. Présidial								
Appeals	0	0	0	0	0	0	11	11
Assize	0	0	0	0	1	8	23	32
Tribunal	0	5	2	32	1	0	0	40
No Tribunal	0	1	2	4	0	0	0	7
III. Royal bailliage or sénéchaussée								
Assize	0	0	0	0	1	3	13	16
Tribunal	0	2	4	76	26	1	0	109
No Tribunal	1	2	20	140	0	0	0	163
IV. Low rank in 1789								
Assize	0	0	0	0	0	0	8	8
Tribunal	0	0	0	20	87	17	0	124
TOTAL	14	10	28	274	116	29	61	532

Sources: Gains and losses of jurisdiction are measured in cantonal seats. For computational procedures, see appendix 1.

torial losses occurred among a small number of *villes parlementaires* and other seats of sovereign courts. As the counterpoint to these losses, a few towns made impressive territorial gains by acquiring appellate courts. Nearly all the seats of assize courts also increased their territorial jurisdiction substantially, irrespective of their former rank in the judicial hierarchy. It is doubtful, however, whether these criminal courts attracted as many litigants to towns as the *présidiaux* or *bailliage* courts of the old regime would have: they had no civil jurisdiction and their responsibilities for criminal justice were limited to the small proportion of offenses that required trial by jury. Only towns in one category consistently expanded their territorial influence as judicial centers: former seigneurial towns and low-ranking royal towns that acquired tribunals of first instance; 112 of these towns gained at least five cantons of jurisdiction. Map 11.2 shows that such promotions were more widespread than demotions of *bailliage* towns to the rank of cantonal seats or simple communes. The uneven distribution of royal *bailliages* in the old regime explains why demotions were concentrated in the provinces of the Paris basin, Lorraine, and Burgundy, which had the highest densities of *bailliages* on the eve of the Revolution.

Just as changes in administrative jurisdictions help explain variations in the growth rates of small towns between 1809 and 1836, so the judicial reforms of the Empire also had demographic implications for towns. Table 11.5 shows, first, that towns promoted to the rank of civil tribunals grew more rapidly than towns that lost *bailliages* or *sénéchaussées*; second, that the greater the loss of jurisdiction, the slower the rate of growth among these former seats of *bailliages*; third, that towns with fewer than 3,000 inhabitants were especially sensitive to gains or losses of jurisdiction; and finally, that shifts in the location of lawcourts had no effect on the growth rates of towns numbering over 5,000 inhabitants. These trends may be misleading, however, because tribunals were usually located in the same towns as subprefectures. By using the technique of multiple regression, we can examine the relative effect of changes in both jurisdictional networks on urban growth rates. This analysis shows that changes in administrative jurisdictions had a stronger short-term impact on growth rates than did changes in judicial institutions. Restricting our analysis to small towns that experienced significant gains or losses in either institutional sphere, we find that the administrative changes account for considerably more of the variance in growth rates between 1809 and 1836 as the judicial changes.[14]

---

[14] Multiple R = .26; adjusted R square = .06; partial correlation coefficient between changes in administrative jurisdictions and growth rates = .17; partial correlation coefficient between changes in judicial jurisdictions and growth rates = .07. Analysis based on 228 towns with a nucleated population of fewer than 5,000 in 1809 that (1) gained or lost at least 10 cantons of administrative jurisdiction or (2) gained civil tribunals or lost *bailliages*. The

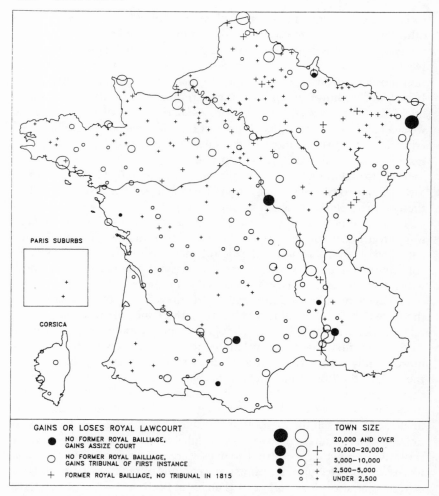

Map 11.2. Towns that Gain or Lose Royal Courts, 1789–1815

However, if all cantonal seats with over 1,500 nucleated inhabitants in 1836 are included in the analysis, even the administrative changes account for only 1 percent of the total variance in growth rates during this period. Demographic expansion and economic growth in the countryside probably explain why so many small towns and bourgs were growing rapidly

correlation coefficient between these two types of towns is .53, indicating some overlap among winners and losers in both institutional spheres.

between 1809 and 1836, regardless of whether they were subprefectures or cantonal seats.[15]

In the middle decades of the century, the growth rates of small towns decelerated as the rural population of France reached its peak and then leveled off. Subprefectures and cantonal seats that numbered fewer than 3,000 inhabitants experienced a similar downward trend in growth rates.[16] However, these subprefectures were more resistant than small cantonal seats to population decline later in the century. Between 1861 and 1896, they had an average growth rate of 3.6 per thousand, as compared with 0.7 per thousand for small cantonal seats.[17] It is during this period that towns providing administrative services to the countryside differed most in their demographic profile from market bourgs. Contemporaries attributed this stability of small administrative towns to a distinctive social structure. In 1876, for example, one-quarter of the labor force in the average subprefecture of fewer than 5,000 inhabitants consisted of functionaries and employees of the government, lawyers and other professional men, retail merchants, and landlords.[18] Administrative services were coupled with more specialized kinds of shops than consumers could find in the typical cantonal seat. Subprefectures were especially likely to have more fabric stores, booksellers, watchmakers, and hotel keepers. Insurance agents nearly always resided in the *chef-lieu*, too.[19] As Bernard Lepetit has emphasized, functionaries set the cultural tone of small subprefectures, attracted landlords from the countryside, and patronized urban fashions in clothing and even personal hygiene. Lepetit points out that public baths, which became fashionable during the July Monarchy, were much more common in subprefectures than in cantonal seats.[20] Savings banks were another in-

---

[15] Ranging in size from 1,500 to 3,000 nucleated inhabitants, 455 cantonal seats that had not possessed *bailliage* courts in 1789 had an average annual growth rate between 1809 and 1836 of 8.1, as compared with 9.5 for the towns of this size that gained tribunals.

[16] The average annual rate of growth for the 76 subprefectures that had fewer than 3,000 nucleated inhabitants in 1809 was 7.2 per thousand between 1809 and 1836 and 2.0 per thousand between 1836 and 1861, as compared with rates of 7.5 and 2.3 per thousand for the 508 cantonal seats in this size classification. Because population data for 1836 is limited to towns and bourgs with at least 1,500 agglomerated inhabitants, this is the lower threshold of town size for all calculations of growth rates between 1809 and 1836 and 1836 and 1861. See appendix 1 for sources.

[17] $F = 5.80$, sig $F = .02$. All 89 subprefectures and 2,079 cantonal seats that had fewer than 3,000 agglomerated inhabitants in 1809 are included in this analysis.

[18] Paul Meuriot, "La petite ville française," *Journal de la Société de Statistique de Paris* 49 (1908): 238–39, 250–51.

[19] See the the commercial directory of Didot-Bottin, *Annuaire-Almanach du Commerce*, vol. 2, *Départements* (Paris, 1861), which provides a detailed listing of shopkeepers, insurance agents, bankers, etc., in all the subprefectures of France and many cantonal seats.

[20] Lepetit, *Les villes dans la France moderne*, pp. 240–54. On small administrative towns

TABLE 11.5

Annual Rates of Population Change of Towns between 1809 and 1836, by Changes in Judicial Rank and Jurisdiction between 1789 and 1815 and by Town Size

| | Average Annual Rates of Change per 1,000 Inhabitants, by Size of Towns | | | | | |
| | All Towns | | | Towns with 1,500–2,999 Inhabitants | | |
Changes in Jurisdiction	Mean	Standard Deviation	Number of Cases	Mean	Standard Deviation	Number of Cases
Gains tribunal	6.5	7.0	121	9.5	7.0	48
Loses *bailliage* and 1 canton or less	5.5	7.4	51	6.2	7.7	35
Loses *bailliage* and 2–4 cantons	2.9	6.1	32	4.9	6.1	19
Loses *bailliage* and 5 or more cantons	2.4	7.8	14	2.7	9.0	8

F score = 3.14
Level of significance = .03

F score = 3.46
Level of significance = .02

	Towns with 3,000–4,999 Inhabitants			Towns with 5,000 or More Inhabitants		
	Mean	Standard Deviation	Number of Cases	Mean	Standard Deviation	Number of Cases
Gains tribunal	5.6	5.4	34	3.6	7.0	39
Loses *bailliage* and 1 canton or less	3.7	6.0	11	4.3	8.1	5
Loses *bailliage* and 2–4 cantons	1.2	2.6	10	-3.7	10.2	3
Loses *bailliage* and 5 or more cantons	0.4	3.0	3	3.8	9.5	3
	F score = 2.61 Level of significance = .06			F score = .96 Level of significance = .42		

Sources: Calculations of rates of population change are based on the nucleated population of towns, as published in the *Enquête dite 1,000*, and the *Bulletin des lois*, Jan.–June 1837, pp. 69–140. Because communes with a nucleated population of fewer than 1,500 inhabitants were not listed in the latter source, they have been excluded from the analysis. Estimates of jurisdictional changes in royal lawcourts are based on the number of cantonal seats gained or lost, as described in appendix 1.

dicator of bourgeois cultural values. By 1864, nine-tenths of the subprefectures, along with almost all the prefectures, had a *caisse d'épargne*. Only a small minority of cantonal seats, located mainly in northern France, also had branches of this officially sponsored institution.[21]

These social and cultural differences between administrative towns and cantonal seats are consistent with the fears expressed by leaders of many small towns during the Revolution. In losing their lawcourts, these towns often did become indistinguishable from bourgs. Except for a single justice of the peace, a bailiff, a tax collector, and perhaps a notary, hundreds of former seats of royal and seigneurial justice lost their magistrates and men of law. As spokesmen for Vierzon complained in 1821, this former *bailliage* town "has fallen into obscurity and become assimilated to a country bourg."[22] Yet as the case of Vierzon itself shows, the concentration of professional elites in subprefectures did not always imply stagnation for towns demoted to the rank of cantonal seats. Vierzon became an important industrial town, with a canal port and major railroad junction, later in the century. Its population grew at a rate of 13 per thousand inhabitants between 1836 and 1896, which was faster than most of the former *bailliage* towns that obtained subprefectures.[23] Indeed, tribunals of first instance had no effect on long-term growth rates among former *bailliage* towns that numbered fewer than 5,000 inhabitants at the beginning of the century. If we look at the period from 1861 to 1896, when population data on all the cantonal seats that used to have *bailliages* were published, we find that variations in growth rates depended more on the initial size of these towns than on their functions as judicial centers.[24]

Nor did larger towns that obtained appellate courts or assize courts benefit as much from these higher-level lawcourts as many townspeople expected. We can isolate the effect of lawcourts by comparing discrepancies

during this period, see also Jean Vidalenc, *Le département de l'Eure sous la Monarchie constitutionnelle, 1814–1848* (Paris, 1952), pp. 378–99.

[21] A total of 253 out of 285 subprefectures and 87 out of 89 prefectures, as compared with only 220 out of 2,376 cantonal seats, had *caisses d'épargnes* by this year, according to the entries in Joanne, *Dictionnaire des communes de la France* (Paris, 1864). On the more rapid diffusion of this savings institution through the urban network of northern France between 1817 and 1848, see Lepetit, *Les villes dans le France moderne*, pp. 346–65.

[22] *Mémorial*, AN F2 I:506.

[23] Among former *bailliage* towns with a nucleated population of fewer than 5,000 inhabitants in 1809, only three had a faster rate of growth during this period: Saint-Dié (17.1), Epernay (20.1), and Cognac (26.7).

[24] Among former *bailliage* towns with a nucleated population of fewer than 2,500 in 1809, the 97 cantonal seats had an average growth rate between 1861 and 1896 of 1.9, as compared with 1.6 for the 21 seats of tribunals; among larger *bailliage* towns, numbering from 2,500 to 4,999 nucleated inhabitants in 1809, the 34 cantonal seats had an average growth rate between 1861 and 1896 of 4.6 per thousand, as compared with 3.7 for the 55 seats of tribunals.

in the administrative and judicial hierarchy after the Revolution. With respect to appellate courts, four were located in subprefectures: Aix-en-Provence, Bastia, Douai, and Riom. Far from causing these towns to grow faster than other subprefectures, courts of appeal did nothing to forestall the stagnation of Aix, Douai, and Riom during the nineteenth century. The population of Aix increased by only 22 percent between 1809 and 1861, that of Douai grew by only 13 percent, and that of Riom declined by 37 percent, as compared with an average increase of 59 percent for all subprefectures. As for Bastia, it owed its dramatic population growth (an increase of 155 percent between 1809 and 1896) to its commercial and military role as the main seaport and garrison town on the island of Corsica. Assize courts had no effect, either, on the growth rates of the nine subprefectures that obtained these establishments. A few of these towns lost population during the century, and the average population increase for all nine towns was 52 percent, slight less than the average for all subprefectures.[25]

If contemporaries exaggerated the importance of lawcourts, they had more reason to anticipate that departmental seats would grow faster than other towns. This contrast first emerged during the middle decades of the century. Between 1836 and 1861, prefectures had an average growth rate of 6.6 per thousand, as compared with 3.6 per thousand for subprefectures. Later in the century, the average growth rate of prefectures accelerated to 8.4 per thousand, while it fell slightly to 3.3 per thousand among subprefectures. Meanwhile, the average rates for cantonal seats declined from 2.8 to 0.7 per thousand.[26] Over the long run, the higher the rank of towns within the administrative hierarchy, the greater the increase in population.

Prefectures benefited, of course, from the hierarchical organization of all administrative services, whose supervisory personnel generally resided in the same town as the prefect. For example, even a small departmental seat such as Foix had the *direction* and *inspection* of three fiscal bureaucracies: for direct taxes and the *cadastre*, or land-tax registry; for the registry of

[25] The declining towns were Coutances (− 20 percent between 1809 and 1896), Saint-Flour (− 10 percent), and Saint-Omer (− 6 percent). At the other extreme, the nucleated population of Reims increased by 220 percent, but this can be explained by the importance of industry in this city.

[26] Analysis of variance: 1836–61, $F = 6.10$, sig. $F = .00$; 1861–96, $F = 44.63$, sig. $F = .00$. Comparisons for the period from 1836 to 1861 are based on 86 prefectures, 264 subprefectures, and 666 cantonal seats that had at least 1,500 nucleated inhabitants in 1836 (Nice and Savoy excluded); for the period from 1861 to 1896, 86 prefectures and all 277 subprefectures and 2,227 cantonal seats are included. If only cases for which data also exist in 1836–61 are included in the latter period, the results would not differ significantly (average growth rates of 8.5 for 83 prefectures, 3.3 for 256 subprefectures, and 0.7 for 619 cantonal seats (excluding towns lost to Germany in 1871). $F = 35.64$, sig. $F = .00$.

documents (*enregistrement*); and for indirect taxes. Several agents of the treasury resided in town: the *receveur-général* and *receveur particulier*; the *receveur-entreposeur*; the *payeur*; and the *conservateur des hypothèques*. There were also an *inspecteur* and *sous-inspecteur* attached to the forest administration, and several civil engineers in the government department of roads and bridges (Ponts et Chaussées).[27] Each of these offices naturally employed government clerks. As the central bureaucracy of the French state expanded in the course of the century, so did this subordinate personnel in the departmental seats. However, the salary scale of functionaries was graduated in accordance with the size of the towns where they were posted. Bureaucratic ambition led from smaller subprefectures to larger ones and to Paris, which mitigated against any general relationship between the purchasing power of functionaries and the growth of the smaller departmental seats. More significant in the long run were two other characteristics of government policy that favored prefectures: (1) the modeling of other institutional hierarchies of the state on the administrative hierarchy; and (2) the creation of a new transport infrastructure, based on the railroad, that increased the commercial importance of administrative towns in the interior of France.

The reconstruction of the French state between 1789 and 1815 brought dramatic changes to ecclesiastical, educational, military, and commercial institutions, which became increasingly centered on departmental capitals in the course of the nineteenth century. With respect to the ecclesiastical hierarchy, the Constituent Assembly made the fundamental decision to establish a single diocese for each department. Its Civil Constitution of the Clergy tried to preserve continuity with the past by locating most of the new bishoprics in towns that used to have such establishments. Nonetheless, sixty-two bishoprics were suppressed in 1790. After the collapse of the new ecclesiastical hierarchy during the Revolution, Napoleon's concordat with the pope in 1801 reduced to only fifty the number of bishoprics within the permanent frontiers of France. The Restoration Monarchy added another thirty bishoprics in 1822, even subdividing two departments into dioceses so that Marseille and Châlons-sur-Marne would regain their bishoprics, alongside Aix-en-Provence and Reims. Through all these changes, departmental capitals preserved an advantage over other towns, accounting for 71 percent of the bishoprics in 1790, 78 percent of those in 1801, and 71 percent of those in 1822. Map 11.3 shows the distribution by administrative rank of bishoprics in this latter year, when fifty-four departmental capitals (crosshatched squares), seventeen subprefectures (circles with inscribed crosses), and only five cantonal seats (empty circles) still

[27] See the entry for Foix in Joanne, *Dictionnaire des communes*, p. 810. In 1861, Foix had a nucleated population of 3,915, a population counted separately of 549, and a total population of 5,507.

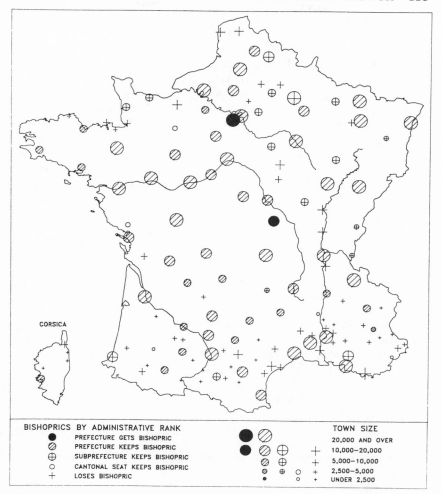

Map 11.3. Towns that Keep or Lose Bishoprics, by Administrative Rank, 1789–1822

had bishoprics. By contrast, twenty-five cantonal seats, thirty-six subprefectures, and only three prefectures were among the towns that lost their bishoprics. As the uncircled crosses on the map indicate, these losses were concentrated in the south, where the density of bishoprics had been unusually high at the end of the old regime.[28]

During the Revolution, the abolition of the tithe, the sale of church

[28] On these changes in the location of bishoprics, see Mirot, *Géographie historique de la France* 2:324–33.

lands, the suppression of chapters and regular orders, and the persecution of refractory priests had serious repercussions on cathedral towns. Olwen Hufton has shown how much the town of Bayeux suffered after the clergy of this bishopric lost their landed revenues and ceased to provide employment or charity for the laboring poor. The municipal leaders of Bayeux waged a successful lobbying campaign in 1790 to gain the new bishopric in the department of the Calvados, but far from compensating the town for its losses, this institution collapsed during the Terror.[29] Bayeux was typical of cathedral towns, whose population tended to stagnate during the revolutionary era regardless of whether their bishoprics were suppressed in 1790 or preserved until Republicans abandoned the constitutional clergy in 1793–94.[30] The reconstruction of the Catholic church during the Empire and the Restoration Monarchy had no effect on urban growth rates between 1809 and 1836, but later in the century, the population of towns that regained their bishoprics did increase more rapidly than that of other administrative centers.[31] However, prefectures with bishoprics did not grow any faster in the later decades of the century than prefectures that had never been the seats of dioceses. This suggests that bishoprics did not have an independent effect on urban growth rates.[32] Yet their social influence is undeniable. Diocesan centers were at the forefront of the extraordinary proliferation of female congregations during the nineteenth century. By fostering female celibacy, of course, these congregations would not have contributed to the demographic vitality of the towns where they were especially numerous.[33]

The revolutionary attack on the Church undermined the educational as well as the ecclesiastical institutions of the old regime. The teaching orders were suppressed, the universities abolished, and the colleges stripped of their endowments.[34] This set the stage for dramatic changes in the urban

[29] Olwen Hufton, *Bayeux in the Late Eighteenth Century: A Social Study* (Oxford, 1967), pp. 162–203.

[30] Using population estimates for 1789–93, I have located population data during the revolutionary era for 125 former bishoprics, which had an average annual growth rate between 1789–93 and 1809 of 0.5 per thousand, as compared with an average of 5.3 per thousand for 237 other towns that became prefectures or subprefectures during the Empire.

[31] The 78 towns that regained bishoprics had an average rate of growth of 6.3 per thousand inhabitants between 1836 and 1861 and 7.7 between 1861 and 1896; the 49 former bishoprics with a nucleated population of at least 1,500 in 1836 had average growth rates of 3.9 and 1.2 during these respective periods.

[32] Between 1861 and 1896, the 59 prefectures that had bishoprics had an average annual growth rate of 8.9 per thousand, as compared with 8.0 for the 24 prefectures that never had been the seats of bishoprics.

[33] For an analysis of the urban diffusion of these congregations, see Claude Langlois, *Le catholicisme au féminin: Les congrégations françaises à supérieure générale au XIXe siècle* (Paris, 1984), pp. 479–511.

[34] Godechot, *Institutions*, pp. 383–89.

map of higher education. Some revolutionaries proposed a new geometry of public instruction, based on districts as well as departments, but the Convention decided in 1795 to establish only one Central School in each department.[35] This policy implied a brutal contraction of educational opportunity: the Central Schools of the Directory were located in fewer than one-third of the towns that used to have colleges, and they enrolled only one-quarter as many students.[36] Napoleon increased still more the elitist character of state education when he replaced the Central Schools with fewer than half as many lycées in 1802. Most of the twenty-seven appellate court jurisdictions received only one lycée, and these same territorial divisions became the basis of academies and faculties when Napoleon founded an Imperial University in 1808. As a result, twenty-three seats of appellate courts obtained lycées or faculties, as compared with only ten other towns, including eight prefectures.[37] Napoleon did encourage towns to finance their own secondary schools, which became "communal colleges" in 1808, but he tried to prevent private boarding schools from competing with the lycées. Often Catholic in inspiration, these schools replaced the colleges of the old regime in many towns that could not afford to support communal colleges. Their proliferation complicates the task of comparing educational networks before and after the Revolution. Nonetheless, by investing resources of the central government exclusively in faculties, lycées, and a few professional schools, Napoleon created an educational hierarchy that privileged only one-fifth of the towns that used to have universities or *collèges de plein exercise*. The postrevolutionary system of secondary and higher education also favored the most important judicial and administrative capitals of the state, unlike the prerevolutionary distribution of colleges that varied in accordance with historical traditions and local needs.

Subsequent regimes concentrated faculties in Paris and the largest provincial cities. Map 11.4 shows the distribution of faculties, royal colleges (formerly lycées), and communal colleges in 1831, when only eleven cities still had faculties of law, medicine, letters, or science.[38] This map also contrasts the small number of other towns that had royal colleges with the dense array of communal colleges. During the Restoration Monarchy, Church schools competed effectively with both types of public secondary

[35] Dominique Julia, *Les trois couleurs du tableau noir: La Révolution* (Paris, 1981); and R. R. Palmer, "The Central Schools of the First French Republic: A Statistical Survey," *Historical Reflections* 7, no. 12–13 (Summer–Fall 1980): 223–47.

[36] Bonin, *Atlas de la Révolution française*, 2:40.

[37] Tabulation based on the list of lycées and faculties in *L'Almanach Impérial* (Paris, 1812). See also, Bonin, *Atlas de la Révolution française* 2:28–31, 70–77.

[38] This map is based on a listing of royal and communal colleges in the *Almanach royale et nationale* (Paris, 1831). The state-funded lycées were called royal colleges only during the July Monarchy. Note that the size intervals of towns are based on the census of 1836.

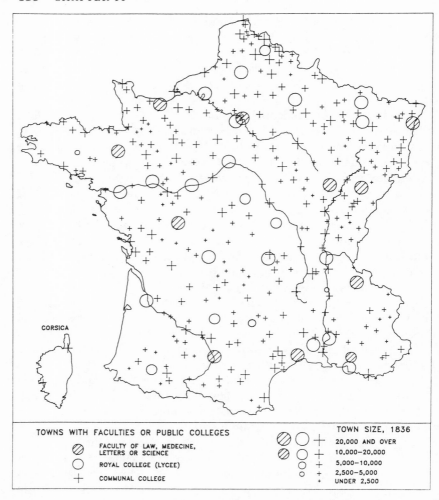

Map 11.4. Faculties, Royal Colleges, and Communal Colleges, 1831

schools, which were not correlated at all with urban growth rates between 1809 and 1836. Starting with the July Monarchy, however, governments placed renewed emphasis on state schools and expanded the number of royal colleges (renamed lycées after 1848), which included a majority of departmental seats by 1861. They also restored some of the faculties of letters and science that had been suppressed by the Restoration Monarchy, laying the foundations for modern universities later in the century. As a result of these changes, the upper levels of the educational system lost their close association with the highest level of the judicial system. Only thirteen seats of appellate courts, along with three other cities, gained universities during the early Third Republic.[39] By contrast, seventy-one of the prefectures, along with thirty-six subprefectures and only four cantonal seats, had lycées by 1910. The upgrading of some communal colleges into lycées and the disappearance of several dozen others, left this intermediate level of education concentrated mainly in the subprefectures. By the eve of World War I, the hierarchy of public secondary schools overlapped closely with the administrative hierarchy.[40]

Until the 1880s, enrollments expanded more rapidly in the lycées than in the universities, which still had only 27,817 students at the end of the century, as compared with 52,372 *lycéens*. Enrollments in the lycées increased by 75 percent between 1842 and 1865 and by another 65 percent between 1865 and 1887, before declining slightly in the 1890s. Expansion in the network of lycées accounts for only part of this growth in enrollments: the average size of lycées increased from 371 to 538 students between 1831 and 1887, and the size of the teaching staff increased accordingly. Communal colleges also expanded in enrollments during this period, but with an average of only 153 students in 1887, they remained only one-quarter as large as the average lycée. The expansion of private secondary education was much more impressive, as Catholic educators, in particular, established colleges whose total enrollments surpassed that of the lycées by the 1890s.[41] Many of these private colleges were located in the same towns as public secondary schools, which reinforced the flow of students from smaller localities to the more important administrative and educational centers. The custom of boarding at school facilitated such migratory movement among students, who were counted separately in the censuses of the period if they resided in a lycée or college, as were other people who lived in institutions, such as soldiers, prisoners, and nuns. The presence of a lycée is strongly correlated with the size of this separate population in 1861 and again in 1896.[42] Lycées and private colleges may have also had a direct

[39] On the law of 1895, which founded fifteen provincial universities, see George Weisz, *The Emergence of Modern Universities in France, 1863–1914* (Princeton, 1983), pp. 134–61.

[40] In 1910, communal colleges were located in 14 prefectures, 136 subprefectures, and 51 cantonal seats, as compared with 52 prefectures, 165 subprefectures, and 91 cantonal seats back in 1831. *Almanach royale et nationale* (Paris, 1831); *Almanach national* (Paris, 1910). On changes in the network of secondary schools in nineteenth-century France, see Dominique Julia and Daniel Milo, "Les réseaux scolaires," in Revel, *L'espace français*, pp. 379–406.

[41] Statistics on university enrollments in 1898 are taken from Louis-Henri Parias, ed., *Histoire générale de l'enseignement et de l'éducation en France* 3:561. For statistics on enrollments in lycées, municipal colleges, and private secondary schools between 1842 and 1898, and for the size of the teaching staff in lycées and municipal colleges between 1842 and 1887, see Antoine Prost, *Histoire de l'enseignement en France, 1800–1967* (Paris, 1968), tables on pp. 45, 83.

[42] The correlation coefficient between these two variables is .52 in 1861 and .56 in 1896;

effect on urban growth rates during the Second Empire and the early Third Republic. Towns with lycées by 1861 had an average growth rate of 8.5 per thousand inhabitants between 1836 and 1861, as compared with an average of only 2.9 per thousand for other towns.[43] Similarly, towns with lycées by 1881 had an average growth rate of 9.0 per thousand between 1861 and 1896, as compared with only 1.5 per thousand for other towns.[44] Even towns with communal colleges managed to sustain a modest growth rate of 3.6 per thousand during this latter period, as compared with an average of 0.7 per thousand for towns that did not have any public secondary schools.[45] Regression analysis shows that these correlations remain statistically significant even when the administrative rank of towns is taken into account.[46] Of course, correlation needs to be distinguished from causation. Lycées and colleges were generally located in the larger towns of each department. Lycées, in particular, signified towns that exercised an important cultural influence over a rural hinterland. As the network of lycées expanded, so did the cultural role of a growing number of prefectures and subprefectures in nineteenth-century France.

With respect to military institutions, the revolutionary era influenced urban networks in three ways: by creating a new system of military administration, centered on divisional headquarters; by reclassifying fortified towns as *places de guerre*; and by redistributing troop garrisons in accordance with the administrative hierarchy of prefectures and subprefectures. In comparison with the thirty-nine *gouvernements-généraux* that had been abolished in 1791, the twenty-one towns that served as divisional headquarters in 1820 were more evenly spaced throughout the kingdom. Like appellate courts and seats of faculties, these headquarters were nearly always located in large prefectures. They formed a supradepartmental eche-

the partial correlation between lycées and the size of the separate population in a regression equation that includes variables for department seat, arrondissement seat, and municipal college is .29 in 1861 and .26 in 1896.

[43] Based on 72 towns with lycées and 942 other towns. Analysis of variance: $F = 26.6$, sig. $F = .00$.

[44] Based on 78 towns with lycées and 878 other towns (excludes towns annexed from Savoy in 1861 and those lost to Germany in 1871). Analysis of variance: $F = 58.2$, sig. $F = .00$.

[45] Based on 233 towns with municipal colleges and 645 other towns. Analysis of variance: $F = 21.0$, sig. $F = .00$. During the earlier period, 1836–61, the average growth rate of 249 towns with colleges (3.2 per thousand) did not differ significantly from that of 693 other towns (2.8 per thousand).

[46] Partial correlations for growth rates, 1836–1861: .11 for lycee, as compared with only .01 for college, −.01 for prefecture, and .01 for subprefecture. Multiple $R = .16$, adjusted R square $= .02$.

Partial correlations for growth rates, 1861–1896: .11 for lycée; .08 for college; .07 for prefecture; .06 for subprefecture. Multiple $R = .29$, Adjusted R Square $= .08$.

lon of military capitals that persisted, with minor modifications, throughout the nineteenth century.[47] As for the *places de guerre*, most of them were fortified towns that had been classified before the Revolution as *gouvernements-particuliers*. When the Constituent Assembly abolished the honorific offices of *gouverneurs*, it also took the opportunity of rationalizing the system of fortresses. Those located near the frontiers were preserved, either as *places de guerre* or as *postes*, but nearly all the fortresses that had been directed against Protestants in Languedoc and Dauphiné were suppressed.[48] Many of the remaining fortified towns had fewer than 5,000 inhabitants, and fewer than half of them were prefectures or subprefectures.[49]

By contrast, major garrisons were usually located in administrative towns. Map 11.5 shows that in 1820, after the Restoration Monarchy had reduced the size of the Napoleonic army, nearly all the towns of the interior that had regiments of troops were prefectures. Those in the major river valleys had already been garrisoned before the Revolution, but most of the prefectures in the highlands of the Massif Central now had troop regiments, too. As for subprefectures, those with garrisons in 1820 were usually located near the frontiers or along the Atlantic and Mediterannean coasts. So were the few dozen cantonal seats that also had regiments of troops.[50] Later in the century, the larger subprefectures in the interior obtained troop garrisons, too. After universal military service was established in 1873, every department formed a military subdivision, and by the last decade of the century, seventy-six prefectures and seventy-nine subprefectures, as compared with twenty-three cantonal seats, had at least one regiment of troops.[51]

The presence of a garrison obviously increased the total population of a town. As the size of the army expanded during the Second Empire and the early Third Republic, so did the number of soldiers posted to garrison towns. A full infantry regiment had 1,250 troops, and a cavalry or artillery regiment had around 800 troops and supporting personnel. By the turn of the century, even an army corps with its headquarters as far from the German frontier as Montpellier consisted of 16,000 troops, organized into

[47] Corvisier, "Les circonscriptions militaires," pp. 213–14, 224–27.

[48] For a list of the *places de guerre* and military *postes* preserved by the Constituent Assembly on July 8, 1791, see AP 28:48–49.

[49] Among the 114 *places de guerres* listed in the *Almanach royal* in 1820, only 15 were prefectures and 39 were subprefectures, as compared with 40 cantonal seats and 20 other localities.

[50] This map is based on the *Almanach royal* (Paris, 1820), pp. 540–45, 603–10. Three small garrison towns and 16 other *places de guerre* that were only communes have not been mapped. All were located along the maritime or continental borders of the kingdom.

[51] For troop deployments in the 1890s, I have used the *Annuaire de l'armée français pour 1893* (Paris, 1893).

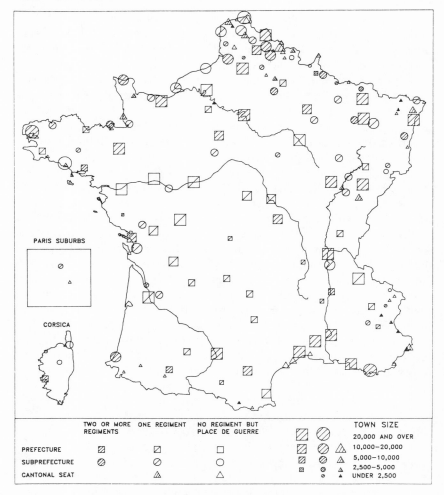

Map 11.5. Garrisons and *Places de Guerre*, by Administrative Rank, 1820

eight infantry regiments, two cavalry regiments, and two artillery regiments, and deployed primarily in prefectures and subprefectures of the region.[52] Not surprisingly, a very strong correlation exists between the number of troop regiments stationed in a town and the size of the population

---

[52] Montpellier had a garrison of 3,000, another five prefectures had a total of 5,975 troops, and five subprefectures housed 6,300 troops, as compared with 1,105 troops stationed in four cantonal seats. See Jules Maurin, *Armée—guerre—société: Soldats Languedociens, 1889–1919* (Paris, 1982), table of troop garrisons before and after 1907, pp. 168–69.

counted separately in the censuses of 1861 and 1896.[53] Towns with smaller garrisons also had a significantly higher proportion of their population counted separately than did towns that had no troops at all.[54]

More interesting is the relationship between the size of garrisons and the growth of the nucleated population of towns, which comprised only civilians. Municipal leaders often believed that the purchasing power of a local garrison would stimulate the local economy.[55] Table 11.6 shows that over the long run, garrison towns grew more rapidly than other towns, suggesting that military expenditures did increase the economic vitality of urban communities. This table distinguishes between the headquarters of military divisions or corps; towns with at least one regiment of infantry, cavalry, or artillery; towns with smaller numbers of troops; and towns that did not have any troops except for gendarmes. As the first set of columns shows, neither military headquarters nor regiments had a significant effect on urban growth rates during the period from 1809 to 1836, when many garrisons were reduced in size. During the middle decades of the century, as fears of urban revolt inspired the concentration of troops in large towns, the average growth rate of divisional headquarters increased dramatically. Other towns with regiments maintained their previous growth rates, but smaller garrison towns and towns without any troops suffered declines in average growth rates. In the last third of the century, when universal military conscription required a larger network of garrison towns, military headquarters continued to grow vigorously, and the nucleated population of other regimental towns tended to increase more rapidly than it had before. Among low-ranking administrative towns, even small garrisons now made a significant difference in average growth rates. Cantonal seats that had fortifications or a garrison with less than a regiment of troops had an average growth rate of 3.9 per thousand between 1861 and 1896, as compared with an average of 0.3 per thousand for nonmilitary towns at this level of the administrative hierarchy.[56] Similarly, subprefectures with fortifications or a modest garrison had an average growth rate during this

[53] This correlation coefficient was .82 in 1861 and .87 in 1896.

[54] Among 133 fortified towns and small garrison towns in 1861, an average of 8 percent of the total population was counted separately, as compared with an average of only 2 percent of the total population in 788 towns that did not have any troops (apart from a few gendarmes) in residence that year. Troop deployments based on *Annuaire militaire de l'Empire français pour l'année 1861* (Paris, 1861).

[55] At Rennes, for example, the municipality welcomed a large garrison during the Empire in order to increase consumption, accelerate the circulation of cash, raise property values, and increase the tax base. See Mun. Delib. Rennes, Jan. 19, 1805, cited by Michel Denis, "Rennes au XIXe siècle: Ville 'parisitaire'?" *Annales de Bretagne* 81 (1974); 409. For examples of small towns in Languedoc that sought garrisons at the end of the nineteenth century in order to boost a stagnant economy, see Maurin, *Armée*, 175–77.

[56] Analysis of variance: $F = 5.00$, sig. $F = .03$.

TABLE 11.6
Annual Rates of Population Change of Towns between 1809 and 1896, by Troop Garrisons

	Average Annual Rates of Change per 1,000 Inhabitants, by Time Period								
	1809–1836			1836–1861			1861–1896		
Troop Garrison	Mean	Standard Deviation	Number of Cases	Mean	Standard Deviation	Number of Cases	Mean	Standard Deviation	Number of Cases
Headquarters	6.2	5.3	20	11.2	8.1	22	10.3	4.1	20
Regiment(s)	4.7	7.5	76	5.3	9.5	72	7.4	7.9	152
Small Garrison	5.4	6.6	127	3.7	8.6	133	4.3	8.7	71
None	6.4	7.5	788	2.9	9.4	788	0.5	8.2	713
	F score = 1.56 Level of significance = .20			F score = 7.1 Level of significance = .00			F score = 39.76 Level of significance = .00		

Sources: Based on the tabulation of companies, batallions, and regiments of infantry, cavalry, and artillery forces, as listed in Annuaire de l'état militaire (Paris, 1836); Annuaire militaire de l'Empire français (Paris, 1861); Annuaire de l'armée français (Paris, 1893). Military headquarters are the divisional seats between 1820 and 1836, during the Second Empire, and between 1873 and 1896, along with the special gouvernements of Paris and Lyon, in the latter period. They are listed in André Corvisier, "Les circonscriptions militaire de la France: Facteurs humains et facteurs techniques," in Actes du 101e Congrès national des sociétés scientifiques (Paris, 1978) 1:224–27. Places de guerre are classified as towns with small garrisons unless they also had regiments. Calculations of growth rates are based on the nucleated population of towns, as published in the Enquête dite 1,000; the Bulletin des lois, Jan.–June 1837, pp. 69–140; Bulletin des lois, 11th ser., first half of 1862, principal part, 19:190–268; and Bulletin des lois, 12th ser., no. 1861 (1897), pp. 1230–1315. All cantonal seats with at least 1,500 nucleated inhabitants in 1836 are included in the analysis, except for those in Nice and Savoy. Towns annexed by Germany in 1871 are not included in the period from 1861 to 1896.

period of 4.6 per thousand, as compared with only 1.2 per thousand for subprefectures that lacked any garrison.[57] As for regiments, they resulted in higher average growth rates for all categories of administrative towns.[58] Regression analysis confirms that the larger the number of regiments, the stronger the effect on growth rates. It also shows that in comparison with the administrative functions of towns in the later nineteenth century, the size of garrisons is slightly more correlated with an expanding urban population.[59]

The commercial institutions of towns also depended to an important degree on the authority of the state, although local merchants and manufacturers had considerable influence over government policy in this area. Even during the old regime, business elites in around seventy-five provincial towns obtained royal permission to elect magistrates to special lawcourts known as *juridictions consulaires*.[60] These lawcourts regulated disputes between local merchants without charging fees. Their example of cheap and voluntary justice impressed legal reformers so much that the National Assembly agreed on August 16, 1790, to establish special *tribunaux de commerce* for merchants who requested them. The new lawcourts were also designed to replace the *amirautés*, or admirality courts, that used to adjudicate maritime disputes in around fifty seaports of the kingdom.[61] Dozens of towns that had never possessed *juridictions consulaires* or *amirautés* also joined the competition for *tribunaux de commerce*, which held out the promise of reducing legal costs and stimulating commerce and industry. Even spokesmen for Aix-en-Provence argued that this former provincial capital could become an important entrepôt and center of industry if it obtained a commercial tribunal.[62] Merchants from small towns that had failed to obtain a district tribunal, such as Montereau, Orbec, and Pertuis, followed suit by portraying the extent of their commerce in glowing

---

[57] Analysis of variance: $F = 8.9$, sig. $F = .00$.

[58] Average growth rates between 1861 and 1893 for cantonal seats (17 cases), subprefectures (79 cases), and prefectures (76 cases) that had at least one regiment of troops in 1893 were 9.4, 6.4, and 8.8, respectively.

[59] Partial correlations in a multiple regression on growth rates between 1861 and 1896: number of regiments = .14; prefecture = .12; subprefecture = .09; small garrison = .08. $R = .30$, adjusted R Square = .09.

[60] See the list of 67 these lawcourts, with their dates of foundation, in Paul Boiteau, *Etat de la France en 1789* (Paris, 1861), pp. 323–24. I have added another seven towns to the list on the basis of petitions to the National Assembly (AN DIV bis). For an example of their organization and jurisdiction, which varied from town to town, see Gresset, *Le monde judiciare*, pp. 78–79.

[61] On the admiralty courts, see Mousnier, *Institutions*, 2:296–99; and Mirot, *Géographie historique de la France* 1:389. On the basis of petitions to the National Assembly (AN DIV bis) as well as these sources, I have located admiralty courts in 57 towns, of which 24 also had *jurisdictions consulaires*.

[62] Letter from the District Directory of Aix, Aug. 16, 1790, AN DIV bis 33:457.

terms. The National Assembly made no effort to restrict *tribunaux de commerce* to important commercial towns, although administrators in a few departments did insist on this policy.[63] Among the 154 towns where the Assembly agreed to establish such tribunals, 35 had not even been mentioned in Gournay's commercial directory, and another 50 had been included with no more than twenty listings. Equally significant is the fact that 30 of the 99 towns that did have over twenty bankers, merchants, and manufacturers listed in Gournay either neglected to request or failed to obtain a commercial tribunal from the Assembly.[64]

This discrepancy between the commercial influence of towns and the location of *tribunaux de commerce* persisted into the Directory and the Empire. Many towns that lost district tribunals in 1795 sought compensation in a commercial lawcourt. Fifty-one former district seats succeeded in this goal, along with ten prefectures that added a *tribunal de commerce* between 1795 and 1812.[65] The most rapid expansion occurred under Napoleon, who appreciated the political benefits of establishing lawcourts, at no cost to the government, wherever merchants wanted them. Napoleon also limited the jurisdiction of these lawcourts to a single arrondissement, which prevented departmental capitals from monopolizing them.[66] By 1812, a total of 211 towns, including 44 cantonal seats, had a *tribunal de commerce*. All businessmen (*commerçants*) who resided for at least five years within the jurisdiction of such a tribunal could participate in annual assemblies to elect their own judges. This democraticization of the former *juridictions consulaires*, which had often been restricted to wealthy merchants, benefited tradesmen and small manufacturers (*fabricants*) in many towns. Naturally, they wanted to preserve the benefits of such lawcourts. Between 1812 and 1861, despite major changes in French commerce and industry, only 10 towns lost *tribunaux de commerce*, and another 16 towns gained them, including 7 cantonal seats. Yet over one-third of the 220 towns with commercial tribunals in 1861 still had a total of fewer than twenty bankers, wholesale merchants, and manufacturers, as measured by the Bottin commercial directory of provincial cities and towns for that year.[67] Not surprisingly, the average growth rate of these commercial backwaters fell to

[63] For examples in the Nord, where departmental administration decided to recommend these lawcourts only to replace the former *jurisdictions consulaires* at Lille, Dunkerque, and Valenciennes, see Zeni, "Urban Networks and the French Revolution in the Nord," pp. 114–19.

[64] Tabulation based on a comparison of the towns with *tribunaux de commerce* by the year III (listed in the *Almanach national* for that year), and towns included in Gournay's *Tableau*.

[65] Tabulation based on the listing of *tribunaux de commerce* in the *Almanach national* (Paris, year III), and the *Almanach impériale* (Paris, 1812).

[66] Godechot, *Institutions*, p. 581.

[67] Didot-Bottin, *Annuaire-Almanach du Commerce*, vol. 2. A total of 79 towns with *tribunaux de commerce* are in this category.

nearly zero between 1836 and 1861, and it stagnated at 2.4 per thousand inhabitants between 1861 and 1896. At best, the location of *tribunaux de commerce* helps to identify a few cantonal seats that had more economic importance than did nearby arrondissement seats.[68] This commercial institution was too widespread to discriminate between dynamic and stagnant towns during the nineteenth century.

Much more significant were official organizations of merchants and industrialists known as chambers of commerce. Organized by Louis XIV in several provincial cities to choose delegates to a royal council of commerce, chambers of commerce had played an important role in the public life of major seaports and commercial towns until the National Assembly abolished them in October 1791.[69] Napoleon restored the institution in 1802 as part of a strategy of cultivating the interests of wealthy merchants. Located during the Empire in only 24 of the largest and most commercial cities, chambers of commerce had important rights and responsibilities.[70] They could submit petitions directly to ministers in Paris, who were obliged to consult them about commercial legislation, and they could levy surtaxes on the commercial license tax paid by all the merchants within their jurisdiction—generally a department or an arrondissement—in order to finance commercial facilities such as ports and stock exchanges.[71] As commerce and industry expanded in nineteenth-century France, business elites in an increasing number of towns requested these useful institutions. Rivalries with existing chambers of commerce and fears of higher taxes to fund new ones sometimes delayed government approval of these requests. Businessmen could always moderate their ambition by asking for a chamber of arts and manufactures, a less important institution founded in several dozen towns by Napoleon to consult with local industrialists. But the chambers of arts and manufactures had very limited powers, and business elites with a serious interest in the economic policies of the government wanted chambers of commerce.[72] The success of such merchants can be

---

[68] In 16 arrondissements, a cantonal seat rather than an arrondissement seat had a *tribunal de commerce*. In only 9 of these cases, however, does the Didot-Bottin directory confirm the economic dominance of a cantonal seat.

[69] On the origins and functions of this institution, see Fr. Olivier-Martin, *L'organisation corporative de la France d'ancien régime* (Paris, 1938), pp. 289–94. For an example of how they represented the interests of merchants in seaports, see John G. Clark, *La Rochelle and the Atlantic Economy during the Eighteenth Century* (Baltimore, 1981), 10–16. Only 12 chambers of commerce had permanent delegates in Paris, but another 21 were consulted by the National Assembly about its policy of creating assignats in 1790. See Michel Marion, "La question du papier-monnaie en 1790: Les premières fautes," *Revue historique* 129 (Sept.–Dec. 1918): 48–51.

[70] Godechot, *Institutions*, pp. 562–63; and *Almanach Impériale* (Paris, 1812).

[71] Pierre Larousse, *Grand dictionnaire universelle du XIXe siècle* (Paris 1867) 3:874.

[72] Ibid., p. 875.

measured by the fact that 37 additional chambers of commerce were established between 1812 and 1861, as compared with 34 additional chambers of arts and manufactures. Another 25 towns obtained chambers of commerce between 1861 and 1881, often by upgrading a chamber of arts and manufactures.[73] Although this institution was not restricted to prefectures, its distribution did vary in accordance with administrative rank. In 1881, 41 of the prefectures had chambers of commerce, as compared with 32 of the subprefectures and only 12 of the cantonal seats.

Striking differences in the numbers of merchants and rates of growth in these two categories of towns confirm the validity of using the distribution of chambers of commerce as an indicator of urban dynamism. In 1861, there were nearly four times as many businessmen in the typical town that had a chamber of commerce.[74] Nearly three-fifths of all the towns with over a total of 100 bankers, wholesale merchants, and *fabricants* listed in the Bottin directory for that year had this institution, including all 8 of the cities with over 500 listings. Only a handful of minor commercial centers, numbering fewer than 50 listings, also possessed a chamber of commerce by 1861, as compared with 55 of the towns that had a chamber of arts and manufactures. Furthermore, 9 of the 15 most important seats of these lesser consultative bodies received a chamber of commerce by 1881. Contrasts in urban growth rates match these differences in the commercial importance of towns: those with a Chamber of Commerce by 1861 had an average growth rate of 11.3 per thousand inhabitants between 1836 and 1861 and 8.5 per thousand between 1861 and 1896, as compared with average rates of 5.7 and 3.8 per thousand during these periods for towns with a chamber of arts and manufactures.[75] Even more impressive is the fact that among the 90 towns in the latter category, the 16 that gained a chamber of commerce by 1881 had an average growth rate of 14.1 per thousand between 1836 and 1861 and 9.9 per thousand between 1861 and 1896. By contrast, the 74 other towns with chambers of arts and manufactures in 1861 had an average growth rate of only 3.9 in the former period and 2.7 per thousand in the latter period.[76] In authorizing the mer-

---

[73] Tabulations based on Felix Ponteil, *Les institutions de la France de 1814 à 1870* (Paris, 1966), p. 78, who mentions that 57 chambers of arts and manufacturers were established in 1802; *Almanach impériale* (Paris, 1812); Joanne, *Dictionnaires des communes*; and *Almanach national pour 1881*, pp. 1184–89.

[74] The median number of bankers, *négociants, marchands en gros, fabricants*, and other businessmen above the level of retail tradesmen was 135 in the 61 towns that had a chamber of commerce in 1861, as compared with a median of 39 in the 91 towns that had a chamber of arts and manufacturers. Calculation based on the listings in Didot-Bottin, *Annuaire-Almanach*, vol. 2.

[75] Analysis of variance in 1836–61: $F = 11.01$, sig. $F = .00$; in 1861–96: $F = 13.6$, sig. $F = .00$.

[76] Analysis of variance in 1836–61: $F = 14.70$, sig. $F = .00$; in 1861–96: $F = 8.0$, sig. $= .01$.

chants and industrialists of a town to elect members to a new chamber of commerce, the government was often acknowledging the rapid economic and demographic development of that town.

With respect to industrial production, which characterized many of the fastest-growing towns in the middle decades of the century, this analysis can be refined by considering the location of special lawcourts known as *conseils de prud'hommes*, established during the First Empire to adjudicate disputes between employers and workers. By 1861, 81 towns, including twenty-three cantonal seats, had this institution.[77] This category of towns had an average growth rate between 1836 and 1861 of 10.8 per thousand inhabitants, as compared with an average of 2.6 for other towns within the administrative network.[78] The growth rates of industrial towns declined in the later nineteenth century, but those with a *conseil de prud'hommes* continued to outpace the average town.[79] Using a government survey of the numbers of workers employed in factories and large workshops in each town, published in 1847, it is possible to estimate more precisely the effect of industry on urban growth rates.[80] This source indicates that the proportion of workers in the urban labor force did not vary significantly in accordance with the administrative rank of towns. The average varied from 5.3 percent for cantonal seats and 5.0 percent for subprefectures to 6.8 percent for prefectures. Yet if we look specifically at towns with a large proportion of workers, we find that cantonal seats predominated.[81] Industrialization had a particularly strong effect on towns at the bottom of the administrative hierarchy. This helps explain why the proportion of workers in the labor force is more strongly correlated than administrative rank with urban growth rates between 1836 and 1861, a period of rapid industrial

---

[77] On this institution, see Godechot, *Institutions*, 575; and Ponteil, *Institutions*, 86, 207, 310–11, 419–20. For its distribution in 1861, see the entries in Joanne, *Dictionnaire des communes*. Most of the important textile towns, along with the largest commercial towns and seaports, had a *conseil de prud'hommes*. Missing are mining and metalworking towns, where large-scale enterprises dominated the labor force.

[78] Analysis of variance: $F = 65.6$, sig. $F = .00$.

[79] Between 1861 and 1896, the 81 towns with this institution by 1861 had an average growth rate of 6.6 per thousand, as compared with 1.7 for 874 other towns ($F = 25.3$, sig. $F = .00$).

[80] *Statistique de la France: Industrie*, 4 vols. (Paris, 1847). The survey, undertaken between 1840 and 1844, is incomplete, and it includes many artisans as well as factory workers. Nonetheless, as a unique attempt to count the number of workers in each town, it is worth using. I have supplemented its data for the region of Lyon by using Yves Lequin, *Les ouvriers de la région lyonnaise, 1848–1914*, vol. 1 (Lyon, 1977). I have also estimated the numbers of textile workers at Elbeuf (overlooked in the census), and I have readjusted the data for a few towns where the work force in the entire canton seems to have been attributed to factories in the cantonal seat.

[81] Among towns above the level of simple communes that had over 20 percent of the population employed in industry in 1841, 62 were cantonal seats, 13 were subprefectures, and only 6 were prefectures.

growth.[82] Yet during the subsequent period, from 1861 to 1896, which spans the depression years of the 1880s, this statistical relationship is reversed. Now administrative institutions are more highly correlated with urban growth rates than are the proportions of workers in towns.[83]

The emergence of a national network of banking institutions confirmed the economic leadership of many departmental capitals in the later nineteenth century.[84] The Bank of France, founded in 1800 by Napoleon and given the exclusive privilege of issuing banknotes in Paris, began extending its operations to the provinces in the 1830s.[85] By the eve of the Revolution of 1848, it had established *comptoirs d'escompte* in 15 provincial cities, including 10 prefectures. Merchants in these cities had urged the directors of the Bank to open local branches, which would reduce the discount rate on commercial paper and facilitate transfers of funds to and from Paris.[86] However, businessmen in 9 of the most important centers of commerce outside Paris, including Lyon and Marseille, continued to prefer "departmental banks," which were authorized by the government to issue their own banknotes. The financial crisis in 1848 jeopardized the solvency of these banks, and the directors of the Bank of France, aided by the new Republican government, seized the opportunity to buy out the local shareholders.[87] This measure fostered a unitary system of credit throughout the nation, as branches of the Bank rediscounted commercial bills at a fixed rate of interest. By the end of the Second Empire, the government had authorized the Bank's management to open a total of 74 branches, operating in 70 different departments. Fifty-six of these branches were located in prefectures, 12 in subprefectures, and 2 in cantonal seats. In 1873, the National Assembly passed a law that obliged the bank to complete the task of financial integration by establishing a branch in every department by 1877. According to one deputy who advocated this law, each new branch

[82] Partial correlations: proportion of workers to total population in 1841 = .24; prefectures = 10; subprefectures = .04. Multiple R = .27, adjusted R square = .07.

[83] Partial correlations: proportion of workers in 1841 = .12; departmental seat in 1861 = .24; subprefecture in 1861 = .13. Unfortunately, an absence of labor force data for small towns after the 1840s reduces the reliability of this regression, but other sources confirm the stagnation of small industrial towns during the later nineteenth century, particularly in southern France. See Raymond Dugrand, *Villes et campagnes en Bas-Languedoc* (Paris, 1963), pp. 445–464; and Lequin, *Les ouvriers de la région lyonnaise* 1:149–52.

[84] On the general development of banking networks in nineteenth-century France, see Louis Bergeron, "Les espaces du capital," in Revel, *L'espace français*, pp. 291–378.

[85] For a concise analysis of the expansion of the Bank of France during this period, see Bertrand Gille, *La banque et le crédit en France de 1815 à 1848* (Paris, 1959), pp. 77–88. For details about the founding of local branches between 1836 and 1871, see Gabriel Ramon, *Histoire de la Banque de France*, 3d ed. (Paris, 1929).

[86] For examples of this pressure from merchants at Reims, Grenoble, Mulhouse, and Strasbourg, see Ramon, *Histoire*, pp. 175–82, 196–98.

[87] Ibid., pp. 228–34.

of the bank would increase monetary circulation, reduce interest rates, and end the plague of usury in "peripheral departments."[88] The Bank nearly always chose prefectures as the seats of these additional branches.[89] As a result, a total of 72 departmental capitals also functioned as banking centers by 1881.

Just as the national banking network went through two basic phases of development, so its effects on urban growth rates changed over time. In the first phase, the Bank of France singled out towns that needed substantial capital for commercial operations. Two-thirds of the branch banks founded by 1860 were also located in cities that had a dominant role within their respective regions. Examples include former provincial capitals such as Grenoble and Toulouse, industrializing cities such as Mulhouse and Saint-Etienne, and seaports such as Bordeaux, Marseille, and Nantes. Such cities were growing rapidly in the boom years of the July Monarchy and the early Second Empire, and they continued to grow at a brisk pace later in the century.[90] In its second phase of expansion, however, the Bank began operations in departments where two or three towns had roughly equal numbers of private bankers and wholesale merchants and where commercial life was either very modest or subordinated to cities in neighboring departments. In such circumstances, whichever town received a branch of the Bank had better prospects of commercial development than did its neighbors; better access to credit might stimulate, in turn, more population growth. This kind of situation existed in 26 departments where the Bank of France established its first branches after 1860.[91] If we compare the 26 towns that obtained these branches with 34 other towns in these departments that had similar numbers of private bankers and wholesalers in 1861, we find no difference at all in average growth rates between 1836 and 1861. Both groups of towns lagged far behind the major commercial cities that received branches of the Bank of France during this period. The situation changed dramatically between 1861 and 1896. Now the average growth rate of towns that acquired a significant role in the

[88] Ibid., p. 383, citing Ducoing, *rapporteur* of the legislative commission that introduced this law to the Assembly.

[89] After 1870, the only exceptions were Aubusson and Meaux.

[90] The 37 cities with branch banks by 1861 and a dominant position within their respective departments, as measured by the listings of private bankers and wholesale merchants in Bottin's commercial directory of that year, had an average growth rate of 12.4 per thousand inhabitants between 1836 and 1861 and 10.2 per thousand inhabitants between 1861 and 1896.

[91] Ain, Basses-Alpes, Hautes-Alpes, Ariège, Aveyron, Cantal, Cher, Corrèze, Côtes-du-Nord, Creuse, Dordogne, Drôme, Eure, Gers, Jura, Landes, Loir-et-Cher, Lot, Lozère, Haute-Marne, Haute-Saône, Seine-et-Marne, Tarn, Vendée, Vosges, Yonne. I have used the Didot-Bottin directory for 1861 to ascertain that no single town in these departments concentrated a disproportionate number of bankers and wholesale merchants.

national banking network during the 1860s or 1870s nearly doubled, from 4.5 per thousand to 8.6 per thousand inhabitants. The other towns, relegated to a subordinate role in commerce, suffered a decline in their average rate of growth, from 4.4 per thousand between 1836 and 1861 to 3.3 per thousand between 1861 and 1896.[92] Nearly all of the successful towns were also prefectures, which signifies the growing interdependency of administrative institutions and commercial activities throughout the nation.

Underpinning the expansion of industry, commerce, and credit were fundamental changes in the transport networks of nineteenth-century France. Here, too, we find that administrative towns, and especially prefectures, benefited disproportionately from government-financed improvements in roads and navigable waterways and from the building of railroad lines. Before the Revolution, a royal corps of civil engineers, known as the Ponts et Chaussées, had undertaken an extensive program of road construction to strengthen communications between Paris and provincial capitals. Favorable terrain, strategic consideratons, and commercial opportunities ensured that towns in northeastern France benefited more from this program than those in the south.[93] Nonetheless, by the eve of the Revolution, all the major administrative towns of the old regime were located on a *route de poste*, with mail delivery from Paris. Most of them had postal roads that converged from three or four directions, following the efforts of intendants to centralize communications within their respective *généralités*.[94] Thus, the road network had both a linear function, linking cities directly to Paris, and a hierarchical function, subordinating smaller towns to the provincial capitals.

When the *généralités* were subdivided into departments at the beginning of the Revolution, the hierarchical pattern of roads no longer corresponded to the administrative system. Unable to finance new road construction or even to maintain the existing roads, the revolutionary governments used the main trunks of the old postal system, along with some secondary roads, to communicate with most of the departmental capitals.[95] The national road system became almost entirely linear during the First Empire, when Napoleon decided that only twenty-six "imperial roads," leading from Paris to the frontiers and Atlantic ports, would receive any

[92] Analysis of variance: $F = 9.69$, sig. $F = .00$.

[93] On the transport system of the old regime and its regional inequalities, see Lepetit, *Chemins de terre et voies d'eau*.

[94] See the map, "Les grandes voies de communication, 1789," which shows all the *routes de poste* as well as other important roads, navigable rivers, and canals, in Bonin, *Atlas de la Révolution française* 1:15.

[95] Ibid., p. 16, map of "Les routes de poste, 1792." On this map, 31 of the former seats of intendancies and only 7 other departmental seats were located on *routes des malles Parisiennes* that provided direct mail service from Paris; 23 were on *routes des malles de province*; 10 were on lesser roads with relay services; and 10 were isolated from the postal roads.

government funds.[96] As Bernard Lepetit has shown, it was the Restoration and July monarchies that restored a hierarchical dimension to the national road system by financing the construction and maintenance of roads that connected prefectures to each other and to nearby subprefectures.[97] By the 1850s, 76 of the prefectures and 117 of the subprefectures were at the junction of at least two national roads, and another 8 prefectures and 127 subprefectures were located on one national road. Only 2 subprefectures and 31 subprefectures still had to depend on locally financed departmental roads. These roads existed primarily to link the cantonal seats to the arrondissement seats in a hierarchical pattern that strengthened the centrality of administrative towns.[98]

The history of the railroad system recapitulated this shift from a linear to a hierarchical organization of space. Although the railroads were financed by private capital, only the first two lines in France, from Lyon to Saint-Etienne and from Paris to Rouen and Le Havre, were actually designed and constructed privately. The engineers of the Ponts et Chaussées insisted on drawing up a national plan for a series of major lines, built according to their technical specifications, that would establish rapid communications between Paris and the most important cities of the provinces.[99] Following the adoption of this plan in 1842, railroad lines were constructed from Paris to Amiens, Lille, and the channel ports in the north; Nancy and Strasbourg in the east; Lyon and Marseille in the south; Limoges and Clermont-Ferrand in the center; Bordeaux in the southwest; and Nantes, Rennes, and Cherbourg in the west. During this first phase of construction, which spanned the decades of the 1840s and 1850s, only one major line—from the Mediterannean port of Cette to the Atlantic port of Bordeaux—did not point toward Paris. However, secondary branches soon began to change the configuration of the system from a star radiating outward from Paris to a web linking provincial cities to each other.[100] Municipal leaders, recognizing the commercial importance of the railroad, urged the government to have lines built through their towns. In this com-

[96] Although the 26 "imperial roads" authorized in 1811 did pass through 53 of the departmental seats, only 2 of them crossed through a provincial city (Lyon). Ibid., p. 19, map of "Le classement routier Napoléonien, 1811."

[97] Lepetit, *Les villes dans la France moderne*, pp. 280–322.

[98] Tabulation based on the road maps of each department, drawn by P. Bineteau and published in *La France illustrée*, ed. Victor A. Malte-Brun (Paris, 1853).

[99] Cecil O. Smith, Jr., "The Longest Run: Public Engineers and Planning in France," *American Historical Review* 95, no. 3 (June 1990): 657–85.

[100] For the railway lines in 1854, see the map in René Rémond, ed., *Atlas historique de la France contemporaine, 1800–1965* (Paris, 1966), p. 76; and for the major and minor lines in 1874, see the map in Fernand Braudel and Ernest Labrousse, eds., *Histoire économique et sociale de la France* (Paris, 1970–82), tome 3, *L'avènement de l'ère industrielle, 1789–années 1880*, 1:297.

petition, departmental seats, which could rely on prefects to defend their interests, were often successful. By 1864, 47 of these administrative towns were on a direct line to Paris and another 26 were on other lines. Nearly half of the subprefectures also had a railroad station by this date.[101] Political pressures for local lines increased dramatically when Republicans came to power in the 1870s.[102] By the end of the century, France had the densest network of railroad lines in Europe.[103] Now all of the prefectures had a railroad station, and so did nearly all of the subprefectures and almost half of the cantonal seats.[104]

As the transport functions of the railroad evolved, the implications of the railroad for urban growth also changed. In the middle decades of the century, the railroad's main task was to move people and goods over considerable distances. It shared this linear function with the system of navigable waterways, which was also expanding during this period. The governments of the July Monarchy and the Second Empire, following the advice of the Ponts et Chaussées, invested heavily in canal-building projects that were designed to complement the new railroads.[105] By linking together separate river basins such as the Saône, the Rhine, and the Seine and by creating canals along rivers that were navigable for only part of the year, these engineering projects improved the accessibility of many towns of the interior. They also encouraged industrial development in regions that had coal and iron deposits. Although some canals never became profitable, the system of navigable waterways played a vital role in the French economy during the July Monarchy and the Second Empire by channeling goods to and from cities that were also located on the new railroad lines. Table 11.7 illustrates this relationship between transport facilities and urban growth between 1836 and 1861. Seaports linked to the national railroad network had the fastest average rate of growth during this period, followed by towns with canal or river ports as well as railroad stations. In comparison with the period from 1809 to 1836, when towns with navigable waterways had not been growing any faster than other towns, the combination of waterways and rail lines produced an acceleration in aver-

[101] Excluding Paris and the newly annexed territories of Nice and Savoy, 86 percent of the prefectures (73/85), 49 percent of the subprefectures (137/278), and only 15 percent of the cantonal seats (358/1958) had train stations. Tabulation based on entries by commune in Joanne, *Dictionnaire des communes*.

[102] Sanford Elwitt, *The Making of the Third Republic: Class and Politics in France, 1868–1884* (Baton Rouge, La. 1975), pp. 103–69.

[103] Smith, "The Longest Run," 683.

[104] Excluding entirely local lines that were built with departmental subsidies, all 86 subprefectures, 262 out of 277 subprefectures, and 1,074 out of 2,303 cantonal seats had a railroad station by the 1890s. Tabulation based on departmental maps of railroad lines published in *La grande encyclopédie* (Paris, 1886–1902).

[105] Smith, "The Longest Run," pp. 661–82.

TABLE 11.7
Annual Rates of Population Change of Towns between 1809 and 1896, by Transport Facilities

Transport Facilities	Average Annual Rates of Change per 1,000 Inhabitants, by Time Period								
	1809–1836			1836–1861			1861–1896		
	Mean	Standard Deviation	Number of Cases	Mean	Standard Deviation	Number of Cases	Mean	Standard Deviation	Number of Cases
Rail and seaport	4.7	8.1	42	9.1	10.0	42	6.1	9.2	69
Rail and canal	6.4	7.1	70	8.2	11.2	70	5.9	7.6	93
Rail and river	4.5	6.5	95	6.6	8.0	95	3.7	8.1	135
Railroad only	6.4	7.7	190	3.9	8.1	190	1.9	7.1	488
Seaport only	7.4	6.0	35	4.5	10.7	35	0.8	3.9	8
Canal port only	4.9	4.7	29	4.4	8.4	29	1.3	7.5	4
River port only	5.7	6.1	58	2.1	7.9	58	-3.9	5.1	9
Road only	6.3	7.6	483	0.9	8.2	483	-3.1	6.0	142
	F score = 1.20 Level of significance = .30			F score = 13.74 Level of significance = .00			F score = 18.56 Level of significance = .00		

Sources: Seaports, navigable rivers, canals, and railroad stations in 1864: Adolphe Joanne, *Dictionnaire des communes de la France* (Paris, 1864); railroad stations in the late-nineteenth century are based on departmental maps in *La grande encyclopédie* (Paris, 1886–1902). Rates of population change are based on the nucleated population of all cantonal seats with at least 1,500 nucleated inhabitants in 1836. Towns in Nice and Savoy have been excluded, and those annexed by Germany in 1871 have been excluded in the period from 1861 to 1896. Population sources and procedures are the same as those cited in table 11.6.

Note: For the periods from 1809 to 1836 and 1836 to 1861, towns are classified on the basis of their transport facilities in 1864; for the period from 1861 to 1896, they are reclassified on the basis of whether they had railroad stations by the late-nineteenth century.

age growth rates.[106] The table also indicates that the railroads had a weaker effect on the growth of towns that did not also have navigable waterways. Indeed, the average growth rate of these towns declined by a third between 1809 and 1836 and 1836 and 1861, from 6.4 per thousand to 3.9 per thousand inhabitants. The average growth rates of towns that had river ports but no railroad stations decelerated even more, from 5.7 per thousand to 2.1 per thousand inhabitants. Bringing up the rear were the many towns that continued to depend on road transport. These towns, which had been growing as fast as the others during the previous thirty years, now approached zero population growth. From these statistics, it seems evident that the transport revolution of the July Monarchy and the Second Empire had a dramatic effect on French cities and towns.

In the second phase of railroad construction, when branch lines proliferated in nearly every department, a new pattern of urban growth emerged. As more and more towns acquired railroad stations, this mode of transportation seemed to have less and less effect on growth rates. Table 11.7 does indicate that towns with canals and seaports, nearly all of which had rail links by the end of the century, continued to grow faster than other towns. It also illustrates the declining fortunes of little towns that remained outside the rail network. Yet the most numerous group of towns—those which depended exclusively on railroads for long-distance transport—also had a feeble growth rate of only 1.9 per thousand inhabitants between 1861 and 1896. During this period, whether towns had a railroad station mattered much less than their location within regional rail networks. Table 11.8 illustrates this by classifying towns into four categories: those at the junction of two-track lines coming from at least four directions; those on a two-track line or single tracks coming from three directions; those on a secondary line that had only a single track; and those without any railroad station at all. The table measures the increasing centrality of towns within a regional network of lines, and it shows that the higher the administrative rank of towns, the more extensive their communications within that network tended to become. Seventy-one percent of the prefectures were in the category of towns with the most rail lines, as compared with only 20 percent of the subprefectures and 5 percent of the cantonal seats.[107] This helps explain why prefectures were growing more vigorously than other admin-

---

[106] This relation between waterways and urban growth may help explain why the geographer D. Pumein has found that before railroad lines were built in the 1840s and 1850s, large towns (over 10,000 inhabitants) were already growing more rapidly than smaller towns. He does not begin calculating urban growth rates until 1831, after some improvements in roads and navigable waterways had been made. D. Pumein, "Chemin de fer et croissance urbaine en France au XIXe siècle," *Annales de géographie* 79 (1982): 529–49.

[107] If all cantonal seats were included in the analysis, then only 1.7 percent (40 out of 2,303) would be located at the junction of two-track lines.

TABLE 11.8

Annual Rates of Population Change of Towns between 1861 and 1896, by Rail Lines and Administrative Rank

Average Annual Rates of Change per 1,000 Inhabitants, by Administrative Rank

Type of Rail Line	Prefectures			Subprefectures		
	Mean	Standard Deviation	Number of Cases	Mean	Standard Deviation	Number of Cases
4 or more tracks	9.0	4.9	59	6.6	7.5	51
2–3 tracks	7.6	5.4	13	3.4	6.2	89
1 track	5.8	4.4	10	1.4	6.4	105
None	—	—	0	1.2	4.9	9
	F score = 2.12 Level of significance = .13			F score = 7.45 Level of significance = .00		

Type of Rail Line	Cantonal Seats			All Towns		
	Mean	Standard Deviation	Number of Cases	Mean	Standard Deviation	Number of Cases
4 or more tracks	10.9	13.6	30	8.5	8.4	140
2–3 tracks	2.4	7.3	168	3.0	7.0	270
1 track	0.6	7.0	260	1.0	6.9	375
None	-2.8	6.0	154	-2.8	6.0	163
	F score = 35.81 Level of significance = .00			F score = 70.6 Level of significance = .00		

Sources: Departmental maps of railroad lines in the late-nineteenth century in *La grande encyclopédie* (Paris, 1886–1902). Population sources and procedures are the same as those cited in table 11.6.

istrative centers during this period. As table 11.8 shows, there is a strong linear relationship between the number of rail lines and variations in urban growth rates. Simply put, the more the lines, the higher the rate of growth.

How do the several components of French urban growth that we have been discussing fit together into a general explanation for the advantages that departmental seats enjoyed in the century after the French Revolution? Using regression analysis, we can confirm that the transportation networks, commercial institutions, and military garrisons fostered by the state had an increasing effect on urban growth rates between 1836 and 1861 and 1861 and 1896. Tables 11.9 and 11.10 present the relevant data in two regression equations. The first equation shows that the transport revolution and economic development of the July Monarchy and Second Empire accounts for 15 percent of the variation in urban growth rates between 1836 and 1861. If we look at the partial correlations for the variables entered in the equation, we see that two characteristics of towns—location on navigable waterways as well as on the new rail lines, and the proportion of workers in the labor force—are especially important. The presence of a chamber of commerce or a branch of the Bank of France significantly affected a town's growth rate, as did, to a lesser extent, either a navigable waterway or a railroad station. Military garrisons are negatively correlated with growth rates after we control for these other variables. During the period from 1861 and 1896, however, military garrisons have a positive effect on growth, and now the location of towns on multiple rail lines accounts for considerably more variation in growth rates than do either location on navigable waterways or the proportion of workers. Commercial and banking institutions continue to have an independent effect on growth rates. This second equation accounts for 21 percent of the variance in growth rates, which reflects the stronger effect of the transport and military variables. As for prefectures and subprefectures, they have no independent effect on growth rates during either period. Yet as we know, departmental seats were considerably more likely than other towns to have large military garrisons, important commercial institutions, and a central location in the railroad network during the later nineteenth century. All of these factors, which depended to an important extent on policies of the central government, help explain why the administrative structure created during the Revolution had an enduring effect on French urban development.

Yet this analysis also confirms that towns did not continue to grow in the later decades of the century simply because they had inherited a subprefecture and a lawcourt from the First Empire. Subprefectures needed the same kinds of transport facilities, commercial opportunities, and military garrisons as the prefectures had in order to prosper and expand. Only two-fifths of them gained such advantages and maintained an average growth rate of 6.0 per thousand inhabitants between 1861 and 1896. The

TABLE 11.9
Multivariate Analysis of Urban Growth Rates, 1836–1861

Variables entered in the equation:

SP36	Subprefecture, 1836
NAVONLY	Seaport, canal, or navigable river, no railroad, 1861
CHBANK61	Chamber of commerce or branch of the Bank of France, 1861
RWORKERS	Rate of workers per 100 inhabitants, 1841
RAILONLY	Railroad station, no navigable waterway, 1861
NAVRAIL	Railroad station and navigable waterway, 1861
DPSEAT36	Departmental seat, 1836
REG1861	Scale for number of regiments, 1861

Multiple *R*   .40
Adjusted *R* square .15

Variable	Correlation	Partial Correlation	T	Significance Level of T
SP36	.02	− .00	− .02	.98
NAVONLY	.00	.10	3.13	.00
CHBANK61	.25	.15	4.81	.00
RWORKERS	.25	.23	7.42	.00
RAILONLY	.04	.11	3.74	.00
NAVRAIL	.25	.21	7.25	.00
DPSEAT36	.11	.01	0.38	.70
REG1861	.09	− .08	− 2.57	.01

Sources: Administrative functions, chambers of commerce, branches of the Bank of France, navigable waterways, and railroad stations are given in Joanne, *Dictionnaire des communes*; the locations of regiments of troops are given in *Annuaire militaire de l'Empire français pour l'année 1861*; estimates of the proportion of workers are based on the *Statistique de la France: Industrie* (Paris, 1847) and "Tableau des Communes," *Bulletin des lois*, 9th ser., pt. 1 (Jan.–June 1843), pp. 59–109. Population sources and procedures are the same as those cited in table 11.6.

Notes: The variable for regiments of troops, REG1861, has been scaled as follows: 0 = none; 0.5 = small garrison; 1 = one or two regiments; 2 = three or more regiments. The analysis is based on 1,006 cantonal seats with a nucleated population of at least 1,500 inhabitants in 1836.

others, including 47 subprefectures that still numbered fewer than 2,500 inhabitants in 1896, stagnated or even declined. In the meantime, industrial towns that had not even existed at the beginning of the century, such as Decazeville and Fourchambault, now had well over 5,000 inhabitants. Another 36 cantonal seats and communes had crossed the threshold of 10,000 inhabitants.[108] Most large cities were prefectures, but even within this administrative category, four towns still had fewer than 5,000 inhabitants and another twelve had between 5,000 and 10,000 inhabitants. By

[108] This tabulation excludes 32 cantonal seats and communes that were in the *banlieu* of Paris and a few other cities.

TABLE 11.10
Multivariate Analysis of Urban Growth Rates, 1861–1896

Variables entered in the equation:

SP61	Subprefecture, 1861
RWORKERS	Rate of workers per 100 inhabitants, 1841
NAVRAIL	Railroad station and navigable waterway, 1900
DPSEAT61	Departmental seat, 1861
RAILRANK	Scale of location on multiple rail lines, around 1900
CHBANK81	Chamber of commerce or branch of the Bank of France, 1881
REG1861	Scale for number of regiments, 1893

Multiple *R*   .47
Adjusted *R* square .21

Variable	Correlation	Partial Correlation	T	Significance Level of T
SP61	.09	−.01	−.40	.69
RWORKERS	.14	.08	2.60	.01
NAVRAIL	.25	.06	1.86	.06
DPSEAT61	.25	.03	−.94	.35
RAILRANK	.42	.24	7.62	.00
CHBANK61	.32	.08	2.74	.01
REG1893	.35	−.11	−3.32	.00

Sources: Sources for administrative functions, navigable waterways, and the proportion of workers are the same as those cited in table 11.9; the locations of regiments of troops are given in *Annuaire de l'armée français pour 1893*; chambers of commerce and branches of the Bank of France are listed in the *Almanach national* (Paris, 1881); towns with railroad stations are shown on the departmental maps in *La grande encyclopédie*. Population sources and procedures are the same as those cited in table 11.6.

Notes: The variable for regiments of troops, REG1893, has been scaled as follows: 0 = none; 0.5 = small garrison; 1 = one or two regiments; 2 = three or more regiments. The variable for railroad lines, *RAILRANK*, has been scaled as follows: 0 = no rail line; 1 = one-track line; 2 = two-track line or junction of one-track lines; 3 = junction of two-track lines. The analysis is based on 948 cantonal seats with a nucleated population of at least 1,500 inhabitants in 1836 (towns annexed to France in 1860 and those annexed to Germany in 1896 have been excluded).

contrast, Paris now had an official population of over 2.5 million, Marseille and Lyon had over 300,000, and another eight cities had over 100,000 inhabitants. Rapidly growing suburbs around these cities pointed toward the urban sprawl of the twentieth century. Against such giants of the French urban system, subprefectures like Ribérac, with a nucleated population of 718 in 1809 and 1,911 in 1896, looked smaller than ever. As for subprefectures like Rocroi, with an agglomeration of 1,480 inhabitants in 1809 and only 808 in 1896, their functionaries and magistrates had obviously failed to stem an irremediable decline.

Against the background of these contrasts between large cities and small towns, we can understand why the governments of the later Third Republic, under severe budgetary pressures, wanted to rationalize the administrative and judicial system inherited from the Revolution and the First Empire. Yet critics disagreed among themselves about whether to regroup the departments into larger regions or consolidate the arrondissements within the existing framework of departments. If the advocates of consolidation triumphed in 1926, this was partly because official institutions, transport networks, and electoral organizations all centered on the departmental capitals, which had played a vital role in French society and politics for over a century. Enough subprefectures were also medium-sized towns, with a central position within economic subregions or historic *pays*, to justify the preservation of this intermediate level of administration and justice, too. As for the small subprefectures, which often suffered from the declining population of the countryside, they continued to fight for their lawcourts throughout the interwar period. In this respect as in so many others, the Third Republic inherited beliefs and institutions from the revolutionary era that had a distinctive resonance for townspeople.

CONCLUSION

THIS BOOK has developed an urban perspective on the territorial reorganization of the French state during the revolutionary era. Its central argument has been that the audacious project of subdividing the kingdom into departments and districts generated intense urban rivalries that deeply influenced the process of institutional reform. These rivalries expressed old beliefs about the economic and cultural dependency of towns on lawcourts and other public establishments. In the context of a political crisis that brought into question the extensive jurisdictions of provincial capitals, urban rivalries also expressed opposition to the concentration of wealth and power in these capitals. The leaders of small and medium-sized towns welcomed egalitarian slogans and populist rhetoric that challenged the "aristocracy" of large towns. Many of them also adopted democratic tactics of political mobilization, involving town meetings and petitioning campaigns, in order to persuade the National Assembly to grant their demands for directories and lawcourts. These petitions greatly complicated the task of the Assembly, whose Constitutional Committee could not possibly satisfy all of the requests that it received for new establishments. Under these circumstances, coalitions of deputies from the various provinces, often representing the interests of particular towns, made the basic decisions about the formation of departments and districts.

Agreement within the Assembly about the average size of departments guaranteed a coherent organization of space at this level, despite continuing rivalries among towns over the departmental capitals. In the absence of similar agreement about the size of districts, the Assembly failed to resolve basic disputes about the new institutional hierarchy of administrative directories and lawcourts. While the Constitutional Committee became convinced that too many districts had been formed, efforts to suppress the smaller districts provoked strong opposition from newly elected officials and their constituents in these districts. Conflicts between large and small towns over intermediate jurisdictions acquired a new dimension during the Terror, when the Convention shifted local responsibility for price controls and grain requisitions from departmental to district directories. In 1795, the Thermidorians restored the authority of departmental directories and abolished all the districts and district tribunals. Partisans of the Constitution of the Year III expressed hostility and contempt for salaried officials in small towns, but their plan for placing unpaid functionaries in thousands of cantonal municipalities ended up saddling the Directory with a costly and ineffectual system of local administration. As for the departmental lawcourts that monopolized civil litigation during the Directory, they became clogged with lawsuits that the former district tribunals would have settled more quickly and at less expense to plaintiffs.

Napoleon's Conseil d'Etat finally created a stable administrative and judicial hierarchy with appellate jurisdictions for a few dozen large towns, prefectures and assize courts for the departmental seats, and subprefectures and civil tribunals for over half of the former district towns, which now became the seats of arrondissements. Even this rational organization of space brought renewed complaints from the leaders of a few hundred towns that suffered territorial losses during the Revolution. Yet a majority of the departmental capitals and a good number of arrondissement seats had expanded their jurisdictions since the collapse of the old regime. Their arguments for institutional stability, when coupled with the efficiency of the prefectoral system and the stringent budgetary policies of Louis XVIII's government, explain why Napoleon's territorial settlement survived the fall of the Empire. From the beginning to the end of the revolutionary era, urban elites remained convinced that the institutions of the state would influence the destiny of towns. As we have seen, the formation of departments did have enduring consequences for urban development, although intermediate jurisdictions, which aroused so much contention during the Revolution, failed to sustain much long-term growth in small towns. The abolition of the old regime aroused many hopes of prosperity that would never be fulfilled, along with many fears of decline that lawcourts alone would be powerless to prevent.

This analysis of urban rivalries and state building has significant implications for the historiography of the French Revolution. In the continuing debate over the meaning of the Revolution, three schools of thought have been especially influential. One group of historians, led by Georges Lefebvre and Albert Soboul, interprets the Revolution as a struggle for power between different social groups or classes. A second group, inspired by Alexis de Tocqueville, interprets the Revolution as an institutional crisis, provoked by the monarchy itself and resulting in a more powerful and centralized state. A third group, led by François Furet, argues that the Revolution invented a new political culture, characterized by revolutionary consciousness, democratic ideology, and Republican symbols, images, and rituals. None of these disputatious groups has written much about the relationship between towns and the state during the Revolution. The social historians have assumed that conflicts within towns were more important than conflicts between towns; most institutional historians have overlooked the extraordinary efforts that townspeople made to gain the new directories and lawcourts; and cultural historians have ignored the fundamental beliefs that these townspeople shared about the economic interests at stake in the reorganization of the kingdom. The subject of urban rivalries over the institutions of the state does not fit easily into any of these interpretative frameworks. Its anomalous position has the advantage of bringing a different angle of vision to bear on contentious issues within the field of revolutionary historiography.

Marxist historians have developed an interpretation of the Revolution as a conflict between a progressive social class, the bourgeoisie, and a reactionary social class, the nobility. Allied with the laboring poor in the towns and with peasants in the countryside, the bourgeoisie triumphed over the nobility, abolished feudalism, and laid the foundations for capitalist development in nineteenth-century France.[1] This interpretation presupposes that nobles and bourgeois had contrary relations to the means of production in eighteenth-century France: the nobles extracted rents and dues from the peasantry, while the bourgeoisie earned profits from commerce and industry. A host of critics have disputed whether nobles and bourgeois did, in fact, belong to separate social classes. Some have argued that nobles, just like the bourgeoisie, were investing in capitalist enterprises. Others have argued that the bourgeoisie was investing in land, just as the nobility was. From the former perspective, the Revolution disrupted the emergence of a unified capitalist elite; from the latter, it split a precapitalist elite into warring factions.[2] In either case, class divisions do not explain political alignments during the Revolution. An alternative critique of the Marxist interpretation of the Revolution has emphasized social divisions within the bourgeoisie. While some bourgeois did engage in commerce, a substantial number entered the legal profession, purchased offices, and shunned trade. According to Alfred Cobban, this bourgeoisie of officeholders was a declining class that led the Revolution, sometimes *against* the merchants.[3] Philip Dawson has shown, however, that *bailliage* court magistrates were not declining in wealth before the Revolution and that few of them became radicals afterward.[4] As for the lawyers, long viewed as the quintessential revolutionaries, many of them opposed the more radical phase of the Revolution, particularly in Paris and other large cities.[5] Historians have been unable to identify any occupational group within the bourgeoisie that consistently supported the Revolution.

---

[1] The classic works within this Marxist tradition are by Georges Lefebvre, *The Coming of the French Revolution*, trans. R. R. Palmer (Princeton, 1947); and Albert Soboul, *A Short History of the French Revolution, 1789–1799*, trans. Geoffrey Symcox (Berkeley, 1977).

[2] For a review of the revisionist literature, see William Doyle, *Origins of the French Revolution*, 2d ed. (Oxford, 1988); for a recent theoretical contribution to the debate, see George Comninel, *Rethinking the French Revolution: Marxism and the Revisionist Challenge* (London, 1987).

[3] Alfred Cobban, *The Social Interpretation of the French Revolution* (Cambridge, 1964), pp. 54–67.

[4] Dawson, *Provincial Magistrates*.

[5] Fitzsimmons, *The Parisian Order of Barristers*; Berlanstein, *The Barristers of Toulouse*. See also Hunt, *Politics, Culture, and Class in the French Revolution*, pp. 149–79. Hunt shows that

Perhaps this problem of the social basis of revolutionary leadership should be redefined. Instead of asking whether the bourgeoisie acted as a class, we need to look more closely at how bourgeois politicians represented communities during the Revolution.[6] This is a task for the social as well as the political historian because it requires careful attention to the kinds of communities that existed in eighteenth-century France. Georges Lefebvre undertook a masterful study of this kind in his great book on the peasantry in the department of the Nord. Other historians have also analyzed rural politics during the Revolution from the vantage point of peasant communities.[7] Much less systematic research has been undertaken on urban communities.[8] Yet as we have seen, townspeople also had interests to defend during the Revolution, and unlike villagers, they often had deputies or special deputies in Paris to represent those interests. Of course, towns varied greatly in their size, economic functions, and institutional traditions. This implies differing interests as well, which need to be examined in the context of fundamental policy issues that confronted the revolutionaries. I have analyzed the conflicts between provincial capitals and smaller towns over the formation of departments and appellate courts, and I have tried to prove that many deputies in the National Assembly took the side of their hometowns in these disputes. I have also emphasized rivalries between administrative and commercial towns, which often originated long before the Revolution. Urban communities that were gaining or losing wealth and institutional power in eighteenth-century France were in a stronger position to make demands on the National Assembly than were rising or falling social classes. This continued to be true later in the Revolution, when many towns faced severe financial and economic problems. Deputies sent on mission by the Convention, often to their home departments, had extraordinary powers to help towns supply their grain markets during the period of the Terror. Lobbyists in Paris could help resolve the crises in municipal finance that plagued many towns throughout the Revolution, too. The representation of urban interests involved practical issues that were often settled in committees and ministerial *bureaux*. This makes

---

while lawyers predominated at the national and departmental level of revolutionary politics, they nearly disappeared from municipal office in several large cities during the radical phase of the Revolution.

[6] I use the word *bourgeois* advisedly, because nobles rarely led the kinds of communities that I have been discussing in this book.

[7] For an excellent work of synthesis that evaluates Lefebvre's work and presents new evidence on rural politics during the Revolution, see Jones, *The Peasantry in the French Revolution*.

[8] The best comparative work on French cities and towns during the Revolution has been done by Lynn Hunt in her book cited above and in her monograph *Revolution and Urban Politics in Provincial France*.

the subject difficult to study, but it is an important aspect of revolutionary politics.

The relationship between towns and the countryside is another aspect of the social history of the Revolution that deserves further research. Spokesmen from small towns often claimed to be representing the interests of nearby rural communities in their demands for districts and lawcourts. The numerous signatures that townspeople collected in the countryside suggest that there was some truth to this claim. So do the petitioning campaigns of district directories in the fall of 1790, when the National Assembly threatened to suppress a large number of districts. Disputes in departmental and district electoral assemblies over the location of capitals also revealed territorial solidarities among delegates from towns and villages. Just as markets, lawcourts, and administrative jurisdictions brought peasants into contact with townspeople during the old regime, so would the directories and tribunals established by the National Assembly. Peasants were not as isolated from townspeople as some historian have suggested. Regional variations in settlement patterns, marketing networks, and the scale of urban development do help explain why peasants in some areas, particularly in western France, opposed revolutionaries in the towns. Yet counterrevolutionary uprisings in the West should not be interpreted as the most characteristic pattern of urban-rural interaction during the Revolution. As Charles Tilly has shown in his pioneering work on the Vendée, even the western department of the Maine-et-Loire had areas of commercialized agriculture where peasants supported revolutionaries in the towns.[9] Social relationships of exchange between townspeople and villagers characterized many areas of France. This helps explain why regional mobilizations in support of the Revolution, such as the Great Fear of 1789 and the federations of national guards in 1790, involved cooperation between urban and rural communities.

Institutional relations between towns and villages are a much-neglected aspect of Tocqueville's history of state building in the old regime. Basically, Tocqueville argues that the monarchy created fiscal privileges for nearly every group in French society except peasants, who were compelled to pay taxes by a bureaucratic hierarchy of intendants and subdelegates. No longer protected by their lords, abandoned by landowners and officeholders in the towns, peasants became isolated, ignorant, and resentful victims of royal centralization. Tocqueville never mentions that royal or seigneurial lawcourts in the towns exercised jurisdiction over rural communities or that peasants had any interest in obtaining legal services from townspeople. Nor does he allude to the importance of lawcourts in the economic life of towns. Tocqueville does emphasize how many officeholders resided in the

[9] Tilly, *The Vendée*, pp. 38–57, 159–98.

towns of the old regime, but he views their petty jealousies and disputes over rank and precedence as one more symptom of the corrupting influence of the monarchy. Only in his discussion of the kind of freedom that existed in the old regime does he praise the lawcourts for preserving customs and procedures that formed "so many obstacles to royal absolutism."[10] Yet in his general interpretation, Tocqueville attributes historical agency exclusively to the monarchy, which increased its power by disrupting the feudal bonds between lords and peasants and by dividing peasants from townspeople and townspeople from each other. The bureaucratic institutions and fiscal policies of the monarchy created a condition of social atomization in which Frenchmen became powerless either to support or to resist the central government. In Tocqueville's words, "Nothing had been left that could obstruct the central government but, by the same token, nothing could shore it up."[11]

This interpretation derives its originality from the premise that state building transforms social structures and mentalities. For Tocqueville, however, the process of centralization was so destructive that no particular social group or community could possibly have benefited from association with the monarchy. I have argued instead that the proliferation of lawcourts in the old regime, which was a deliberate policy of royal ministers to raise revenues through the sale of office, created a social milieu in towns that had a strong interest in preserving its ties to the central government. In the institutional crisis of 1789, the leaders of towns did not greet the decisions of the National Assembly passively. The abolition of seigneurial lawcourts brought immediate requests from dozens of little towns for royal lawcourts. In like manner, word that an entirely new judicial system would be created galvanized declarations of support for the Assembly and plans for new jurisdictions from hundreds of towns. In showering the Assembly with addresses of loyalty and "national gifts," many urban leaders quite consciously hoped to gain a quid pro quo in the new institutional order of the state. The power to suppress and to create lawcourts had been a vital attribute of royal sovereignty in the old regime. As that prerogative passed into the hands of the Assembly, so did the legitimation of this new, centralized authority in the eyes of many townspeople.

Ironically, many leaders of the Revolution shared Tocqueville's underlying premise that political institutions shape the social order. They aspired to reorganize the state in order to regenerate society. Yet Tocqueville himself concluded from the fate of the Revolution that Frenchmen remained powerless to change their habits or their government: "Once central power had passed from the hands of the royal administration into those of irre-

[10] Tocqueville, *The Old Regime and the French Revolution*, p. 117.
[11] Ibid., p. 137.

sponsible sovereign assemblies and a benevolent government had given way to a ruthless one, the latter found nothing to impede it or to hold up its activities even momentarily. The same conditions which had precipitated the fall of the monarchy made for the absolutism of its successor."[12] This disillusioned and paradoxical reflection overlooks the early phase of the Revolution, when political liberty fostered a veritable explosion of civic initiative in provincial towns. Beginning in 1788, townspeople established societies of correspondence to defend the Third Estate, and their municipal committees in 1789 continued to correspond with each other as well as with the National Assembly.[13] Such networks of political communication were then developed on a vast scale by the Jacobin Clubs founded in hundreds of towns to defend the new constitution in 1790–91. As David Kennedy has shown in his multivolume history of these clubs, some of them circulated their views about national issues to dozens of other clubs. Many also lobbied the government on behalf of their local towns, which were still competing for commercial tribunals in 1791. Finally, they paraded in civic festivals, campaigned in local elections, sponsored auxiliary clubs for women, raised money for the poor, defended the constitutional clergy, and recruited volunteers for the army. With a predominantly urban membership that ranged from administrators, lawyers, and merchants to shopkeepers and artisans, the early Jacobin Clubs combined devotion to the nation with an ethos of service to the local community. In both respects, they echoed the civic spirit that appeared in many of the petitions that townspeople sent to the National Assembly in 1789, which mingled requests for new establishments with patriotic sentiments.[14]

Why did the Revolution end in dictatorship? This is the central problem that Tocqueville asked but did not resolve. Theda Skocpol, a historical sociologist who situates state building in an international context of greatpower rivalries and warfare, cites a brilliant passage by Marx that does provide an answer. Commenting on the repressive apparatus of the French state that the Paris Commune tried and failed to overthrow, Marx wrote:

> The centralized state power, with its ubiquitous organs of standing army, police, bureaucracy, clergy, and judicature—organs wrought after the plan of a systematic and hierarchic division of labor—originates from the days of absolute monarchy. . . . Still, its development remained clogged by all manner of medieval

[12] Ibid., p. 206.

[13] For regional examples of how the committees of correspondence operated, see A. Cochin, *Les sociétés de pensée et la Révolution en Bretagne, 1788–1789* (Paris, 1925); and A. Cochin, "La campagne électorale de 1789 en Bourgogne," in *Les sociétés de pensées et la démocratie* (Paris, 1921), pp. 235–82.

[14] Michael L. Kennedy, *The Jacobin Clubs in the French Revolution: The First Years* (Princeton, 1982); and *The Jacobin Clubs in the French Revolution: The Middle Years* (Princeton, 1988).

rubbish, seigneurial rights, local privileges, municipal and guild monopolies, and provincial constitutions. The gigantic broom of the French Revolution swept . . . away all of these relics of bygone times, thus clearing simultaneously the social soil of its last hindrances to the superstructure of the modern State edifice raised under the First Empire, itself the offspring of the coalition wars of old semi-feudal Europe against modern France."[15]

Skocpol gives a concrete focus to this idea of Marx's by contrasting the decentralized system of administration created by the National Assembly with the revolutionary dictatorship of the Committee of Public Safety in 1793–94, the expansion of the central government under the Directory, and the administrative reorganization undertaken by Napoleon. The pressures of foreign and civil war, when coupled with the abolition of earlier obstacles to state power, explain the structural transformation of the French state during the revolutionary era.[16]

In this interpretation, Skocpol rightly calls attention to the importance of administrative institutions for understanding state power. This is one of the most neglected subjects in the history of the Revolution. Only one good monograph has been written, based on evidence from a single department, about fiscal administration during the period of the Constituent and Legislative assemblies.[17] Apart from an essay by Alfred Cobban on local government during the Revolution, little is generally known about this subject, either.[18] As for the departmental and district directories, they have not been examined in any work of synthesis for over a hundred years.[19] On the basis of my research on urban rivalries over these institutions, I would question Skocpol's assumption that townspeople were interested only in municipal autonomy. In relation to other towns as well as to the countryside, urban leaders recognized the importance of administrative jurisdictions at the departmental and the district level. The expeditions of national guardsmen from Marseille to Aix and from Langres to Chaumont in 1792 illustrate how seriously this issue could remain long after the departments had been formed. So do the disputes among small towns over

[15] "The Civil War in France," in Karl Marx and Frederick Engels, *Selected Works in One Volume* (New York, 1968), p. 289.

[16] Theda Skocpol, *States and Social Revolutions: A Comparative Analysis of France, Russia, and China* (Cambridge, 1979), pp. 174–205.

[17] Robert Schnerb, *Les contributions directes à l'époque de la Révolution dans le Puy-de-Dôme* (Paris, 1933). For a more general history of taxation during the Revolution, see Marion, *Histoire financière*, vol 3.

[18] "Local Government during the French Revolution," in Alfred Cobban, *Aspects of the French Revolution* (New York, 1968), pp. 112–30. But see the path-breaking essay by Alison Patrick, "French Revolutionary Local Government."

[19] Baron de Birardot, *Des administrations départementales, électives, et collectives* (Paris, 1857); and E. Monnet, *Histoire de l'administration provinciale, départementale, et communale en France* (Paris, 1885).

control of the district directories during the Terror. Also worth further study from this perspective are the federalist uprisings in the summer of 1793, which often fizzled out because the departmental directories were unable to rally support from officials in the district seats. These political conflicts are usually attributed to the greater wealth and more conservative social views of departmental officials, but they may express deeper antagonisms between townspeople in outlying districts and those in the departmental capitals. By affirming the authority of the Convention, district towns could preserve their independence from departmental capitals, particularly in the area of food supply. As for federalist movements involving towns in neighboring departments, here efforts to recruit manpower and to requisition grain would encounter even more resistance from local populations, as the Lyonnais discovered when they tried to mobilize support at Saint-Etienne for their revolt against the Convention. There is an underlying social logic to the administrative system of the Terror, in which district towns agreed to make sacrifices for Paris and the army but not for other towns within their respective departments.[20]

As for the fiscal problems that none of the revolutionary governments solved, here the administrative reforms of the Constituent Assembly were less to blame than its new tax system. The establishment of departmental and district directories gave the central government a hierarchy of salaried officials to supervise the municipalities. These officials were often familiar with the collegial methods of administration that had characterized the judicial corps of the old regime, and they were armed with considerable legal authority. In fiscal matters, however, they had to rely on municipal officials to draw up tax rolls and have the taxes collected. This delegation of authority actually perpetuated the administrative traditions of the old regime, but it worked much less effectively during the Revolution. For one thing, municipal officials in the towns used to own their offices but were now elected by the taxpayers, which reduced their independence. More important, however, were the complexities of the new tax laws that they were supposed to implement. During the old regime, the land tax had been assessed on communities, which bore a collective responsibility for its payment.[21] The new system of the Constituent Assembly taxed only individuals, whose property could not be assessed at more than one-sixth of its net value. In like manner, taxes on many artisans in the larger towns used to be assessed through the guilds; now these corporations were abolished

---

[20] On the problem of regional and local conflicts over food supply during the Revolution, see Richard Cobb, *The People's Armies* (New Haven, Conn., 1987), pp. 298–312. On similar conflicts during the old regime, see Steven L. Kaplan, *Bread, Politics, and Political Economy in the Reign of Louis XV* (The Hague, 1976) 1:28–42.

[21] On the importance of this point, see Hilton Root, *Peasants and the King in Burgundy* (Berkeley, 1987).

and a commercial license tax imposed on all craftsmen, regardless of where they lived. Fiscal individualism, which was supposed to be more equitable than corporate obligations, threw many municipalities into confusion. To make matters worse, the Assembly tried to increase the overall yield of these direct taxes, following its decision to abolish most of the indirect taxes, which used to account for three-fifths of all the revenues of the royal government. Urban tax revolts against the municipal *octrois* and other taxes on consumer goods in 1789 had undercut this source of revenue, and attempts by the Assembly to restore indirect taxes in 1790 encountered massive resistance in many towns. Under these circumstances, no administrative system, however bureaucratic and coercive in principle, would have been able to cover the growing deficits that the revolutionary governments faced. The Jacobin dictatorship had no more success collecting tax revenues than had either the National Assembly or the Legislative Assembly. Paper money became the policy for coping with the fiscal crisis, but it led to inflation, price controls, terror, and monetary collapse. Only near the end of this inflationary spiral did many landowners who had fallen behind in their tax payments hasten to pay these arrears—in the nearly worthless currency of the Republic.[22]

These fiscal and monetary problems also help explain why towns became increasingly dependent on the central government during the Revolution. The National Assembly, on both theoretical and practical grounds, refused to delegate any of its legislative powers of taxation to administrative directories or municipalities. They could only apportion taxes authorized by the sovereign representatives of the nation. As Gail Bossenga has shown, many towns depended on the *octrois* to service the heavy debts that they had contracted during the old regime. Once these taxes disappeared, they faced a financial crisis that only the National Assembly could resolve. Various expedients were introduced, starting with a system of local surtaxes on national property taxes and culminating with the nationalization of municipal debts and direct subsidies from the central government. At the height of the economic and monetary crisis in 1794–95, when grain markets collapsed in many areas of the nation, subsidies in the form of assignats, grain, or rice became a matter of life and death for some towns. In this competition for government patronage, Paris naturally did best, followed by large provincial cities. Not until the Directory introduced a metallic currency again—the *franc germinal*—did such pleas for help subside. Yet the crisis

---

[22] On the new fiscal system and its failure, see Marion, *Histoire financière*, vol. 2; on the assignats, see Harris, *The Assignats*. For an interesting analysis of the revolutionary consequences of paper money, see Ferenc Fehér, *The Frozen Revolution: An Essay on Jacobinism* (Cambridge, 1987), pp. 30–48.

in municipal finance continued until Napoleon restored the *octrois* and other indirect taxes.[23]

Cultural historians of the Revolution such as François Furet have not paid much attention to these mundane details of administration, taxation, and food supply. Their work highlights instead the rhetorical themes and symbolic practices that characterized revolutionary politics.[24] For Furet, the collapse of the old regime created a unique historical moment in which power ceased to reside in institutions or social classes and became embodied in discourse: "The Revolution replaced the conflict of interests for power with a competition of discourses for the appropriation of legitimacy."[25] Jacobinism, with its legitimizing discourse of popular sovereignty, became the classic form of revolutionary consciousness. Although Furet discusses the historical origins of Jacobin ideals and political practices, his basic argument is that the experience of the Revolution itself brought these ideals and practices together into an explosive mode of new historical consciousness and action. Far from being an expression of social interests, the ideology of Jacobinism thrived on the illusory belief that politics could transform society. From the beginning, terror was an integral part of this revolutionary ideology, which construed all dissent and opposition as an aristocratic conspiracy to thwart the will of the people.

My analysis of the institutional reforms of the National Assembly and the politics of parochialism cannot be reconciled with Furet's extraordinary claim that a terrorist ideology, detached from social interests, emerged as the dominant discourse of the Revolution as soon as royal authority collapsed in 1789. The theoreticians of national unity who used the language of equality and regeneration in the National Assembly, such as Sièyes and Rabaut Saint-Etienne, were strongly committed to institutional reforms. Although the political principles of the Constitutional Committee ruled out any defense of provincial privileges, Sièyes, Rabaut Saint-Etienne,

---

[23] On the urban tax revolts and the crisis in municipal finances, see the important article by Gail Bossenga, "City and State: An Urban Perspective on the Origins of the French Revolution," in Baker, *The French Revolution and the Creation of Modern Political Culture* 1:89–140; on Napoleon's restoration of indirect taxes, see Robert Schnerb, "Les vicissitudes de l'impôt indirect de la Constituante à Napoléon," *Annales: E.S.C.* 2 (Jan.–Mar. 1947), pp. 19–23.

[24] For a theoretical overview of this new interpretation of the Revolution, see Keith Baker, "Introduction," in *The French Revolution and the Creation of Modern Political Culture* 1:xi–xxiv. See also the essays in the three volumes of this work; Baker's collection of essays, *Inventing the French Revolution*; Furet and Ozouf, *A Critical Dictionary of the French Revolution*; Jack R. Censer, "The Coming of a New Interpretation of the French Revolution?" *Journal of Social History* 20 (Winter 1987): 295–309; William H. Sewell, "Ideologies and Social Revolutions: Reflections on the French Case," *Journal of Modern History* 57 (1985): 57–85; and Theda Skocpol, "Cultural Idioms and Political Ideologies in the Revolutionary Reconstruction of State Power: A Rejoinder to Sewell," *Journal of Modern History* 57 (1985): 86–96.

[25] Furet, *Interpreting the French Revolution*, p. 49.

Thouret, and their colleagues on the committee welcomed the participation of deputies from every province in forming the departments and districts. They recognized that the new system of national representation and local administration needed to reconcile the conflicting interests of a great many communities. By delegating authority to provincial and departmental committees of deputies, by making arrangements to rotate directories or share lawcourts, and by referring intractable disputes to electoral assemblies in the departments and districts, the Constitutional Committee presided over an enormous task in a conciliatory spirit. Arguably, the National Assembly functioned as an arena of negotiation and compromise in the manner of modern representative assemblies, whose deputies often are more attentive to the needs of their constituents than to ideological rhetoric.

The parochial conceptions of politics shared by so many townspeople in the first few years of the Revolution are equally inconsistent with the idea that the collapse of the old regime suddenly generated a new revolutionary consciousness that transformed French political culture. Much of the political rhetoric and action that I have been examining in this book can be traced back to the cultural traditions of the old regime: the language of *rapprochement* and *vivification*, which townspeople had used for centuries to justify new lawcourts or to defend old jurisdictions; the belief that the entire community would benefit from lawcourts and other public establishments that attracted visitors from the surrounding area; the strategy of proclaiming loyalty to the central government in order to receive benefits from it; the practice of sending special deputies to Paris. As for revolutionary ideas such as equality and hatred of aristocracy, townspeople appropriated them for their own purposes in their petitions to the National Assembly. Equality became equality among towns; aristocracy became the aristocracy of large towns. As revolutionary language spread from Paris to the provinces, its meaning changed in accordance with older traditions and beliefs.

This raises fascinating issues in the cultural history of the Revolution, which Lynn Hunt has explored in her important book, *Politics, Culture, and Class in the French Revolution*. In a subtle argument about the relationship between social marginality and the integrative ideology of Republicanism, she presents evidence that voters in peripheral regions gave the most consistent support to left-wing deputies and that outsiders and cultural brokers—men who mediated between local communities and the larger world—often became Republican militants. She also emphasizes the profound importance of urban society and culture in revolutionary politics, not only in Paris but in provincial cities and towns.[26] I have found that

---

[26] Hunt, *Politics, Culture, and Class in the French Revolution*, pp. 123–211.

the leaders of small towns responded more enthusiastically to egalitarian rhetoric about institutional reform than did deputies from provincial capitals, who had more to lose from changes in the territorial organization of the French state. Hunt's idea of marginality can be applied to communities as well as to regions and individuals. Small towns were at the bottom of the institutional hierarchies of the old regime. Often their lawcourts were not even royal *bailliages*, their magistrates rarely had noble titles, and their men of law had a reputation for chasing clients wherever they could find them. By promoting a good number of these towns to the rank of district seats, the revolution brought local elites into closer contact with the central government. With respect to institutional structures and career opportunities, outsiders became insiders. Alison Patrick has shown that non-Parisian deputies who supported the Montagnard faction in the Convention often came from relatively small towns.[27] The Montagnards themselves concluded from the federalist uprisings that they had more support among officials in the district seats than in the departmental capitals. Whether the communitarian ideology of Jacobinism also appealed to the artisans and shopkeepers in small towns is an issue worth exploring. It would be consistent with Hunt's finding that relatively traditional towns in central and southwestern France gave more support to left-wing Republicans during the Directory than did commercial cities in the northeast, where social conflicts undermined community cohesion. Republicanism may have synthesized new political ideals with older cultural traditions in such towns.

During the Directory, however, Republicanism at the national level evolved into a machinery of government that lost touch with local populations. The frequent purges of legislative assemblies, the reliance on appointed commissioners rather than on elected officials to supervise tax collection, the hostility to democratic ideals and practices, all foreshadowed the regime of Napoleon. Sièyes, Roederer, and other critics of the Thermidorian constitution concluded that no one entrusted with administrative tasks should be elected by those who would be under his jurisdiction. This abandonment of the elective principle became the hallmark of the Napoleonic state, which relied on functionaries at every level of administration to enforce its will. In principle, the new political class that emerged during the revolutionary era was co-opted by the state. In practice, however, the leaders of many towns continued to assert local interests. Urban rivalries over prefectures, subprefectures, and tribunals of first instance during the Empire and the early Restoration show that municipal officials still viewed themselves as spokesmen for their communities. By incorporating such practices of representation into a democratic ideology, Republicanism would also survive and flourish in the cities and towns of later nineteenth-

---

[27] Patrick, *The Men of the First French Republic.*

century France. Over the long run, only freely elected municipal councils and a representative assembly in Paris could reconcile the interests of townspeople with the administrative hierarchy of the Napoleonic state.

Close attention to the politics of parochialism does confirm in one fundamental respect Alexis de Tocqueville's interpretation of the Revolution: It perpetuated distinctively French attitudes toward the state as a source of institutional power at the local as well as the national level. Historians inspired by the universalistic message and world-historical impact of the Revolution have often overlooked the extent to which the peculiar judicial and administrative institutions of the old regime shaped the social values and political practices of townspeople during the Revolution itself. Of course, those institutions did collapse in 1789, but the rapid territorial reorganization of the state encouraged townspeople to believe that the fate of their communities depended more than ever on institutions created by the central government. In like manner, the egalitarian rhetoric and civic consciousness of Republican political culture remained consistent with an institutional hierarchy that redistributed resources from the government in Paris to local communities. Just as social historians of the Revolution need to look more closely at territorial conflicts over institutions and resources, so cultural historians need to investigate more thoroughly the interplay of Enlightenment ideals and local beliefs and practices. In both respects, the French Revolution was more French and less revolutionary than many of its critics and defenders have acknowledged. But then, where else but in France has revolutionary rhetoric in the modern age so often concealed parochial ambitions behind the enduring framework of a centralized government?

Appendix 1

STATISTICAL PROCEDURES

THIS APPENDIX describes the procedures used to estimate (1) the size of towns; (2) urban growth rates; (3) the scale of jurisdictions before and after the Revolution; and (4) the number of market centers.

THE SIZE OF TOWNS

No comprehensive and reliable source exists for estimating the size of small towns on the eve of the French Revolution. For towns with at least 10,000 inhabitants, Bernard Lepetit has published two estimates, one based on contemporary tabulations of the number of annual births during the period from 1776 to 1789, and the other based on census returns for the year II (1794). Philip Benedict has also compiled estimates for most of the larger towns and for some small ones, based on a variety of sources. He has published some of this data in *Cities and Social Change*, pp. 24–25, and he has kindly sent me a more recent and complete version of his computerized data base. Generally speaking, Benedict's estimates for the largest towns are higher than those of Lepetit, which is consistent with the fact that Lepetit used a uniform multiplier of annual baptisms (28), which probably underestimated the number of unmarried adults who resided in such towns. Lepetit also used four series of baptismal counts that are weighted toward the year 1780, while Benedict uses sources from 1789 or 1790, where possible.

Like Benedict, I have tried to estimate the size of towns that numbered at least 10,000 inhabitants in 1789–90. To do so, I have relied on Benedict's data when it is based on local monographs that use archival sources. For other towns above this size threshold, I have used two contemporary sources, one based on the average number of baptisms for the years 1787–89 ("Population des villes suivant les états envoyés par MM. les Intendants des provinces, années 1787–1789," AN DIV Bis 47), and the other based on a census undertaken by municipalites in 1790 (lists for most district seats in AN DIV bis 48). I have calculated the average of these two sources, where possible. In the few cases where data is missing from both sources, I have relied on Lepetit's estimates (*Les villes dans la France moderne*, pp. 449–50).

For smaller towns, I have followed the same procedure for estimating population size in 1789 in order to calculate growth rates between 1789 and 1809. However, for the purpose of classifying towns of fewer than 10,000 inhabitants into size categories, I have used the *Enquête dite 1,000*, a census of the *nucleated* population of towns and bourgs taken by municipal officials under the supervision of Napoleon's prefects between 1809 and 1812. By distinguishing between the nucleated and the dispersed population of communes, this census gives a more accurate estimate of the size of the urban population in small towns and bourgs whose administrative boundaries included villages, hamlets, and/or farmsteads in the countryside. I have also reclassified a few larger towns that had a substantial number of inhabitants who resided in dispersed settlements: Arles is classified with towns of 10,000–19,999 inhabitants, and Bailleul, Moissac, Tourcoing, and Villeneuve-sur-Lot are classified with towns of 5,000–9,999 inhabitants.

For towns with a nucleated population of at least 2,000 inhabitants, the results of the *Enquête dite 1,000* have been published by René Le Mée in "Population aggomerée, population éparse au début du XIXe siècle," pp. 467–93. For smaller towns and bourgs, I have used the manuscript reports of the prefects, in AN F20:428–29. In several departments, the results of this *enquête* are missing, so I have used an *Enquête dite 2,000*, undertaken in 1809, which included all towns with a nucleated population of at least 2,000 inhabitants. For smaller towns and bourgs in these departments, I have used data compiled by the French Laboratoire de Cartographie Thématique and presented on an unpublished map of settlement patterns during the First Empire. This map gives the approximate size of the nucleated population of communes when it was near the threshold of 1,000 inhabitants (estimates are rounded off so that 1.1 equals approximately 1,100 inhabitants, etc.) I am indebted to M. Mallet, the former director of this laboratory, for providing me with a copy of this map, which I also used to digitize the boundaries of France and the location of towns and bourgs for my computerized mapping program.

In most of the tables of this book, I have used geometrical size intervals to classify towns by the size their nucleated population. This means that the upper limit of each interval is twice as large as the lower interval, for example, 1,250, 2,500, 5,000, and so forth. I chose these particular intervals to be consistent with the work of Lepetit and others who use the thresholds of 5,000 and 10,000 inhabitants. Geometrical intervals have the advantage of facilitating analysis of the extent to which town size increases or decreases in relation to the distribution of another variable, as presented in a cross-tabulation.

URBAN GROWTH RATES

Computations of annual growth rates for towns in the nineteenth century are based on the nucleated population rather than on the total population in 1809, 1836, 1861, and 1896. Sources are the following: for communes with a nucleated population of at least 1,000 inhabitants in 1809, the *Enquête dite 1,000*, as described above; for communes with a nucleated population of at least 1,500 inhabitants in 1836, the *Bulletin des lois* (Jan.–June 1837), pp. 69–140; for all cantonal seats, regardless of size, and all other communes with a nucleated population of at least 2,000 inhabitants in 1861, *Bulletin des lois*, 11th ser., first half of 1862, main part, 19:190–268; and for the same types of communes in 1896, *Bulletin des lois*, 12th ser., no. 1861 (1897): 1230–1315.

To compute annual growth rates, I have used a logarathmic equation for calculating a rate of interest compounded over a specified period of time: the formula divides the population of each town at the end of the period by the population at the beginning of the period, computes the log of that quotient, divides the log by the difference in years between the two periods, and multiplies the resulting rate by 1,000 to express it per 1,000 inhabitants.

To measure the statistical significance of differences in the growth rates of categories of towns, I have used the technique known as analysis of variance. This technique compares the variance *between* the categories with the variance *within* each category, and computes a statistical level of significance, using a T test. If the level of significance is less than .05, the distribution of means between the categories is unlikely to have occurred randomly. For an application of this technique to the analysis of urban growth rates in postrevolutionary France, see Lepetit, *Les villes dans la France moderne*, 224–36.

THE SCALE OF JURISDICTIONS

To measure the scale of administrative jurisdictions in nineteenth-century France, first I tabulated the number of cantons within each department and arrondissement, using Joanne's *Dictionnaire des communes* (1864). Next, I created separate scales for the seats of prefectures and subprefectures; the seats of *directeurs* and *receveurs* of direct taxes (located invariably in the seats of departments and arrondissements); the seats of *directeurs* (always in department seats) and *receveurs-entreposeurs* of indirect taxes (the latter sometimes located in a different town than the subprefecture, as noted in

Joanne, *Dictionnaire des communes*); and the seats of *conservateurs* and *in-specteurs* of the forest administration (whose jurisdictions, although not based on arrondissements, can be expressed in terms of the average number of cantons per *conservateur* or *inspecteur* in each arrondissement). Finally, I aggregated these scales to create a general measure of the administrative jurisdiction of each town, which ranged from 1 in the case of simple cantonal seats to between 15 and 30 in the case of most arrondissement seats and between 60 and 120 in the case of most departmental seats.

I followed a comparable procedure for estimating the jurisdictional scale of intendancies, *receveurs-généraux des finances* (one per intendancy), sub-delegations, and *élections* at the end of the old regime, using the very detailed maps in Guy Arbellot, et al., *Carte des généralités, subdélégations, et élections*. On these maps I located the same cantonal seats that existed in 1864, tabulated the number of those cantonal seats within the jurisdiction of each subdelegation and *élection*, and then aggregated the number of cantonal seats within all the subdelegations of each intendancy.

To estimate the scale of other administrative jurisdictions, I followed two procedures, depending on whether I could locate data on the numbers of parishes within those jurisdictions. Such data was published by Expilly for fiscal subdivisions of the *généralités* and intendancies that did not have *élections* (*Dictionnaire*, 1766). Similarly, Dupaquier has published data on the number of parishes within the jurisdiction of each salt granary in the *généralités* of the Paris basin in 1725 (*La population du Bassin Parisien*). Expilly published some comparable data for the 1760s in his *Dictionnaire*. To estimate the number of cantonal seats within these jurisdictions, I have computed the ratio of parishes per jurisdiction to parishes per intendancy and multiplied it by the number of cantons per intendancy.

For the jurisdiction of the *directeurs* and *receveurs des fermes* and the *receveurs-géneraux* and *recettes particuliers* of the Régie Générale, I divided the number of cantons in each intendancy by the number of these agencies within the same intendancies. Then I aggregated the scales and divided by two in order to have a single measure that would be comparable to the jurisdiction of the nineteenth-century agencies for the collection of indirect taxes. With respect to the *maîtrises des eaux et forêts*, whose main responsibility was restricted to the forested area of jurisdictions that varied greatly in size, I used the number of *maîtrises* located within the area of a single arrondissement in order to compute a cantonal scale for comparison with the nineteenth-century forest administration.

These five scales—the estimated number of cantonal seats within the intendancies and subdelegations; the jurisdictions of *receveurs-généraux*, *élections* and other *recettes* for direct taxation; the *receveurs* and *recettes* for indirect taxes; the salt granaries; and the *maîtrises*—were then aggregated and compared with the aggregate scale of administrative jurisdicition in 1815.

I followed a comparable procedure for estimating the size of judicial *ressorts* before and after the Revolution. Here I relied on Brette's very detailed maps of the royal bailliages and other jurisidictions that were used for elections to the Estates-General in 1789 (*Atlas des Bailliages où juridictions assimilées ayant formé unité électorale en 1789*). To compute the jurisdiction of *parlements* and sovereign courts, I used Dawson's listing of the *bailliages* within the jurisdiction of each *parlement* as well as Brette's maps. Then I aggregated these scales for *bailliages* and sovereign courts, and I compared the totals with an aggregate scale of judicial *ressorts* in 1815, based on the number of cantons within the jurisdiction of the appellate courts, assize courts, and tribunals of first instance located in each town.

MARKET CENTERS

Using the census returns for the year II (in AN ser. F 20), which covered 90 percent of the districts in France, Dominique Margairaz has tabulated a total of 2,446 market centers (*Foires et marchés dans la France préindustrielle*, pp. 48–50). However, the proliferation of markets in rural communities at the beginning of the Revolution, after market privileges were abolished, makes some of these totals seem exaggerated. For example, among the 62 towns, bourgs, and villages that reported holding a weekly market in the Puy-de-Dôme, only 25 had been mentioned in an administrative survey of markets in this area in 1768 (ibid., p. 270), and a total of only 49 communes were still holding markets in this department in 1856, of which all but five were cantonal seats (*Annuaire du département du Puy-de-Dôme*, p. 30). Consequently, I have followed an eclectic procedure for defining market towns: (1) cantonal seats that were still holding markets in the 1850s, according to departmental *annuaires* for that period (2,075 cases); and 216 additional towns and bourgs that competed for lawcourts and district directories in 1789–90 and that either mentioned markets in their petitions or had markets according to the census of the year II (216 cases). This total of 2,291 market centers, although not exhaustive, includes nearly all of the communes of over 1,000 inhabitants that held markets throughout the period from the 1790s to the 1850s.

Appendix 2

POPULATION SIZE ESTIMATES AND INSTITUTIONAL CHARACTERISTICS OF MAJOR TOWNS

RTP1789 - Estimated total population of town, 1788–90
TGOURNAY - Number of listings in Gournay
PARLCT - *Parlement* or other major lawcourts, as follows: (P) *parlement*;
  (CS) *conseil souverain*; (CC) *chambres des comptes*; (CA) *cour des aides*; (p) *présidial*
INT - (I) intendant
BISHOP - (B) bishop (A) archbishop
UNIV - (L) law faculty (M) medical faculty
GOVGEN - (GG) Gouvernement générale

	RTP1789	TGOURNAY	PARLCT		INT	BISHOP	UNIV	GOVGEN
Paris	660,000	974	P,CC,CA	p	I	B	L,M	GG
Lyon	146,000	274		p	I	A	—	GG
Bordeaux	111,000	235	P,	p	I	A	L,M	GG
Marseille	110,000	289	—		—	B	—	—
Rouen	73,000	374	P,CC	p	I	A	—	GG
Nantes	71,300	218	CC	p	I	B	M	—
Lille	62,500	183	—		I	—	—	GG
Toulouse	53,000	134	P	p	—	A	L,M	GG
Versailles	51,000	26	—		—	—	—	—
Nîmes	50,000	86		p	—	B	—	—
Strasbourg	50,000	47	—		I	B	L,M	GG
Orléans	48,500	285		p	I	B	L	GG
Amiens	44,000	87		p	I	B	—	GG
Metz	36,500	93	P,CC,	p	I	B	—	GG
Rennes	35,000	39	P	p	I	B	L	GG
Caen	34,000	33		p	I	—	L,M	—
Montpellier	32,600	86	CC	p	I	B	L,M	—
Besançon	32,000	33	P,CC	p	I	A	L,M	GG
Reims	32,000	130		p	—	A	L,M	—
Troyes	30,600	102		p	—	B	—	GG
Brest	30,000	20	—		—	—	—	—
Angers	29,500	17		p	—	B	L	GG
Nancy	29,500	19	P,CC	p	I	B	L	GG

	RTP1789	TGOURNAY	PARLCT		INT	BISHOP	UNIV	GOVGEN
Aix-en-Provence	28,500	35	P,CC		I	A	L,M	GG
Montauban	28,500	22	CA	p	I	B	—	—
St.-Etienne	28,200	47	—		—	—	—	—
Clermont-Ferrand	28,000	11	CA	p	I	B	—	GG
Toulon	26,000	14	—		—	B	—	—
Avignon	26,000	35	—		—	B	L	—
Dunkerque	26,000	129	—		—	—	—	—
Grenoble	25,000	22	P,CC	p	I	B	—	GG
Limoges	24,000	64		p	I	B	—	GG
Arles	22,000	—	—		—	A	—	—
Dijon	22,000	32	P,CC	p	I	B	L	GG
Tours	22,000	70		p	I	A	—	GG
La Rochelle	21,500	28		p	I	B	—	GG
Poitiers	21,500	16		p	I	B	L,M	GG
Arras	21,200	30	CS		—	B	—	GG
Dieppe	20,100	80	—		—	—	—	—
St.-Omer	20,000	17	—		—	B	—	—
Valenciennes	20,000	33	—		I	—	—	—
Douai	19,900	37	P		I	—	L	—
Rochefort	19,300	8	—		—	—	—	—
Bourges	19,100	20		p	I	A	L,M	GG
Lorient	18,500	48	—		—	—	—	—
Abbeville	18,300	117		p	—	—	—	—
Le Havre	18,000	115	—		—	—	—	GG
Sedan	17,500	94		p	—	—	—	GG
Le Puy	15,700	39		p	—	B	—	—
Cambrai	15,500	15	—		—	A	—	—
Le Mans	15,500	44		p	—	B	—	GG
Béziers	15,300	39		p	—	B	—	—
Moulins	15,200	20		p	I	—	—	GG
Perpignan	14,750	23	CS		I	B	L,S	GG
Thiers	14,400	22	—		—	—	—	—
Carcassonne	14,000	31		p	—	B	—	—
Chartres	13,500	34		p	—	B	—	—
Colmar	13,500	4	CS		—	—	—	—
Castres	13,400	26	—		—	B	—	—
Riom	12,900	8		p	—	—	—	—
Angoulême	12,800	31		p	—	B	—	—
Alençon	12,500	27		p	I	—	—	—
Tarascon	12,400	7	—		—	—	—	—
Châlons-Marne	12,300	26		p	I	B	—	—
Niort	12,300	21	—		—	—	—	—

	RTP1789	TGOURNAY	PARLCT	INT	BISHOP	UNIV	GOVGEN
Verdun-sur-Meuse	12,100	9		P	—	B	—	—
Laval	12,000	66	—	—	—	—	—
Nevers	12,000	13	CC	—	B	—	GG
Beauvais	12,000	45		P	—	B	—	—
St.-Germain-en-Laye	12,000	12	—	—	—	—	—
Vitré	11,700	2	—	—	—	—	—
Vienne	11,500	25	—	—	A	—	—
Lunéville	11,500	5	—	—	—	—	—
Issoudun	11,100	27	—	—	—	—	—
Blois	11,100	39		P	—	B	—	—
Bayonne	11,100	27	—	—	B	—	—
Cherbourg	11,000	18	—	—	—	—	—
Sens	11,000	10		P	—	A	—	—
St.-Malo	10,700	51	—	—	B	—	—
Vannes	10,600	0		P	—	B	—	—
Grasse	10,500	45	—	—	B	—	—
Agen	10,500	34		P	—	B	—	—
Saumur	10,500	10	—	—	—	—	GG
Boulogne-sur-Mer	10,500	24	—	—	B	—	GG
Auxerre	10,500	20		P	—	B	—	—
Alais	10,400	27	—	—	B	—	—
Cahors	10,400	6		P	—	B	—	—
Bar-le-Duc	10,400	10	CC	—	—	—	—
Bayeux	10,300	8	—	—	B	—	—
Lisieux	10,100	0	—	—	B	—	—
Châlon-sur-Saône	10,100	5		P	—	B	—	—
Morlaix	10,000	21	—	—	—	—	—
Narbonne	9,800	0	—	—	A	—	—
Saintes	9,800	42		P	—	B	—	GG
Pau	9,700	0	P,CC	—	—	L	GG
Valence	9,500	0		P	—	B	L,M	—
Albi	9,000	12	—	—	A	—	—
Auch	8,500	0		P	I	A	—	—
Toul	7,800	17		P	—	B	—	GG
Soissons	7,000	6		P	I	B	—	—
Orange	7,000	18	—	—	B	L	—
Guéret	3,500	0		P	—	—	—	GG
Foix	3,400	0	—	—	—	—	GG
Embrun	3,000	0	—	—	A	—	—

BIBLIOGRAPHY

PRIMARY SOURCES

Archives

The fundamental sources for this book are manuscript petitions, *adresses*, letters, and published pamphlets in the archives of the French National Assembly. These documents are filed primarily in the following archival series:

AN DIV bis. Papers of the Constitutional Committee of the National Assembly and of the Comité de Division of the Legislative Assembly and the Convention, classified by department

3–18	Requests for departments and districts, 1789–90
19–32	Requests for district tribunals, 1789–90
33–34	Requests for Tribunaux de Commerce, 1790–91
47	Population estimates, including estimates of the size of towns compiled by the intendants, 1787–89
56–76	Disputes over districts, 1790–95
80–91	Disputes over districts and tribunals, 1792–95
108–10	Scattered requests for tribunals and administrative directories, 1789–90

AN ADXVI

18–81	Printed pamphlets from towns requesting districts and tribunals, 1789–99, classified by town

AN ADVII
  40–41   Requests from towns for bishoprics, 1790

AN ADVIIIC
  3–4   Pamphlets requesting tribunals
  502–6   Pamphlets proposing judicial reform, 1799–1800

AN ADXIX
  23–29   Pamphlets requesting tribunals

AN AF III
  32–50   Scattered requests for tribunals, 1795–99
  107–9   Requests from towns for *ecoles secondaires*, 1795–99

AN BB5   Ministry of Justice
  362–65   Disputes over the suppression of tribunals, 1815–17

AN C   Petitions to Legislative Assemblies
  90–123   *Adresses* by towns requesting lawcourts, 1789–90
  470–95   Scattered petitions for civil tribunals, 1799–1800
  2554   Petitions defending tribunals, 1848

AN DXVII
  1–2   Requests for districts and tribunals, 1789–90

AN FIB 1   Ministry of the Interior
  913   Prefectoral reports about suppression of subprefectures, 1910

AN F2 I   Ministry of the Interior
  496–502 Requests for department seats, 1790–1832
  504–30   Requests for arrondissement seats and tribunals of first instance, year VIII–1840, classified by department

AN F2   Ministry of the Interior
  2000   Plans for suppression of subprefectures, 1926

Documents in a few departmental and municipal archives have also been consulted. These include the municipal archives of Besançon and Rennes, and the departmental archives of the Marne and the Seine-et-Oise.

Books and Pamphlets

Barère, Bertrand. *Mémoires de Barère*. 2 vols. Paris, 1842.

Bergier. *Esquisse d'un nouveau plan de l'ordre judiciare*. Paris, year 8.

Cavoleau, Jean-Alexandre, and A. D. de la Fontennelle de Vaudorée. *Statistique ou description générale du département de la Vendée*. Fontenay-le-Comte, 1844.

Condorcet, le marquis de. *Oeuvres de Condorcet*. Edited by A. Condorcet O'Connor and M. F. Arago. 12 vols. Paris, 1847–49; Stuttgart-Bad Cannstatt: Frommann, 1968.

D'Argenson, le marquis de. *Considerations sur le gouvernement ancien et présent de la France*. Amsterdam, 1764.

De Roussel. *Etat militaire de France pour l'année 1788.* Paris, 1788.

Didot-Bottin. *Annuaire-Almanach du commerce.* Vol. 2, *Départements.* Paris, 1861.

Dupont de Nemours. *Des administrations provinciales: Mémoire présenté au Roi, par feu M. Turgot.* Lausanne, 1788.

————. *Observations sur les principes qui doivent déterminer le nombre des districts et celui des tribunaux dans les départements.* Paris, 1789.

Expilly, J. J. de. *Dictionnaire géographique, historique, et politique des Gaules et de la France.* 6 vols. Paris, 1766; Nendeln: Kraus Reprint, 1978.

Faure, P. J. D. G. *Touche légère sur la Constitution des Onze.* Paris, year III (1795).

Gournay, M. *Tableau général du commerce des marchands, négociants, armateurs, etc., de la France, de l'Europe, et des autres parties du monde, années 1789 et 1790.* Paris, 1789.

La grande encyclopédie. Paris, 1886–1902.

Guyot. *Dictionnaire des postes et du commerce.* Paris, 1787.

Herbin, P. E., et al. *Statistique générale et particulière de la France.* Paris, year XII (1803).

Hesseln, Robert de. *Dictionnaire universel de la France.* Paris, 1771.

Joanne, Adolphe. *Dictionnaire des communes de la France.* Paris, 1864.

Larousse, Pierre. *Grand dictionnaire universelle du XIXe siècle.* 17 vols. Paris, 1865–90.

Le Trosne. *De l'administration provinciale et de la réforme de l'impôt.* Basle, 1779.

Malte-Brun, A., ed. *La France illustrée.* Paris, 1853.

Peuchet, Jacques. *Dictionnaire universel de la géographie commerçante.* 4 vols. Paris, years VII–VIII.

Prudhomme, L. *Dictionnaire géographique et méthodique de la République française en CXX départements.* 2 vols. Paris, year VII.

Rabaut Saint-Etienne, Jean-Paul. *Réflexions sur la nouvelle division du royaume et sur les privilèges et les assemblées des provinces d'etats.* Paris, 1789.

————. *Nouvelles réflexions sur la nouvelle division du royaume.* Paris, 1789.

Roederer, A. M., ed. *Oeuvres de Pierre-Louis Roederer.* 7 vols. Paris, 1853–59.

Saugrain. *Dictionnaire universel de la France.* Paris, 1726.

[Sièyes, Emmanuel Joseph.] *Observations sur le rapport du Comité de Constitution concernant la nouvelle organisation de la France, par un député à l'Assemblée Nationale, au 2 octobre 1789* [Paris, 1789].

————. *Quelques idées de constitution applicable à la ville de Paris en juillet 1789.* Versailles, 1789.

Smollett, Tobias. *Travels through France and Italy.* Edited by Frank Fellenstein. New York: Oxford University Press, 1979.

Statistique de la France: Industrie. 4 vols. Paris: Imprimerie Nationale, 1847–52.

Vasse. *Opinion du représentant du peuple Vasse sur l'administration municipale et judiciare.* Paris, year VIII.

Periodicals

Almanach de la province de Bourgogne . . . , pour l'année 1786. Dijon, 1786.

Almanach historique de la province de Languedoc pour l'année 1788. Toulouse, 1788.

Almanach impérial. Paris, 1812.

Almanach national. Paris, years III–IX, 1881, 1910.

Almanach royal. Paris, 1789–91, 1816, 1820.

Almanach royale et nationale. Paris, 1831.

Annuaire de l'armée français. Paris, 1893.

Annuaire de l'état militaire. Paris, 1836.

Annuaire militaire de l'Empire français. Paris, 1861.

Bulletin des lois. Paris, years VI–VII, 1837, 1843, 1862, 1897.

Calendrier historique de l'Orléanais. Orléans, 1788.

Journal des Etats-Généraux. Paris, 1789–90.

Le point du jour. Paris, 1789–90.

Réimpression de l'ancien Moniteur. 32 vols. Paris: H. Plon, 1858–63. First published as *Le Moniteur Universel*, May 1789–Nov. 1799.

Documentary Collections

Anchel, Robert, et al. *Les papiers des Assemblées du Directoire aux Archives Nationale, Inventaire de la série C.* Paris: Archives Nationales, 1976.

Brette, Armand. *Recueil de documents relatifs à la convocation des Etats Généraux de 1789.* 5 vols. Paris: Imprimerie Nationale, 1894–1915.

Carré, H., and P. Boissonade, eds. *Correspondance inédite du constituant Thibaudeau, 1789–1791.* Paris: Champion, 1898.

Dauban, C. A., ed. *Mémoires inédits de Pétion et mémoires de Buzot et de Barbaroux.* Paris: Plan, 1866.

Debien, G., ed. *Correspondance de Félix Faulcon.* 2 vols. Poitiers: Archives historique du Poitou, 1955.

Delourmel, Louis, and Louis Esquieu. *Brest pendant la Révolution: La correspondance de la municipalité de Brest avec les députés de la sénéchaussée de Brest aux Etats Généraux et à l'Assemblée Constituante, 1789–1791.* Brest, 1909.

Godechot, Jacques, ed. *Les constitutions de la France depuis 1789.* Paris: Garnier-Flammarion, 1970.

Guillaume, M. J., ed. *Procès-verbaux du Comité d'instruction publique de la Convention nationale.* 6 vols. Paris: Imprimerie Nationale, 1891–1907.

Jary, A., ed. *Notice sur le tribunal de Château-Chinon: Documents sur la translation et la rivalité entre Moulins-Englibert et Château-Chinon.* Château-Chinon: E. Blin, 1905.

Jovy, Ernest, ed. *Le spicilège de Vitry.* Vol. 1, letters from Pierre-François Barbié, deputy from Vitry in 1789. Vitry-le-Francois, 1899.

"Lettres de Michel-René Maupetit, député à l'Assemblée nationale constituante, 1789–1791." *Bulletin de la Commission historique et archéologique de la Mayenne,* 2d ser., 19–20 (1903–4).

Ligou, Daniel. *La première année de la Révolution vue par un témoin, 1789–1790: Les 'bulletins' de Poncet-Delpech, député du Quercy aux Etats Généraux de 1789.* Paris: Presses Universitaires de France, 1961.

Lorain, Charles, ed. *Les subsistances en céréales dans le district de Chaumont de 1788 à l'an V.* Chaumont: R. Canaviol, 1911–12.

Madival, M. J., ed. *Archives parlementaires.* 1st ser. 82 vols. Paris, 1875–1913; Nendeln: Kraus-Thomson Reprint, 1969.

Montier, Amand, ed. *Correspondance de Thomas Lindet pendant la Constituante et la Législative, 1789–1792.* Paris: Société d'histoire de la Révolution française, 1899.

"Origines du département des Hautes-Alpes et l'abbé Rolland, deputé à l'Assemblée Constituante." *Annales de Alpes* (July–Aug. 1911): 5–15.

Reuss, Rudolph. *L'Alsace pendant la Révolution française.* Vol. 1, *Correspondance des députés de Strasbourg à l'Assemblée nationale (année 1789).* Paris, 1880.

Ville de Rouen. *Analyses des déliberations de l'assemblée municipale et électorale du 16 juillet 1789 au 4 mars 1790.* Rouen, 1905.

SECONDARY SOURCES

Works on the Formation of Departments

Only works used in this book are listed. For a complete bibliography of local studies, classified by department, see Marie-Vic Ozouf-Marignier, *La formation des départements*, pp. 334–45.

Albitreccia, Antoine. *La formation du département de la Corse de 1801 à 1811.* Paris: Gibert, 1938.

Amans, Patrice. "Les départements français, étude de géographie administrative." *Revue de géographie* 24 (Jan.–June 1889): 401–11; 25 (July–Dec. 1889): 35–43, 108–16.

Appolis, Emile. "La formation du département du Tarn." *Revue du Tarn*, n.s., 13 (1938): 74–84.

———. *La rivalité administrative entre Castres et Albi, 1789–1823.* Albi: Bibliothèque de la Révolution du Tarn, 1938.

Arizzoli, Alexandre. *Le chef-lieu du département des Bouches-du-Rhône.* Aix-en-Provence, 1901.

Arnaud, Gaston. *Histoire de la Révolution dans le département de l'Ariège.* Toulouse, 1904; Marseille: Laffitte Reprints, 1981.

Aulard, Alphonse. "Départements et régionalisme." In *Etudes et leçons sur la Révolution française*, 7th ser. Paris: F. Alcan, 1913.

Baumont, H. "Le département de l'Oise: Sa formation en 1790." *Bulletin de la Société des Etudes Historiques et Scientifiques de l'Oise* 1–5 (1905–10).

Berlet, Charles. *Les provinces au XVIIIe siècle et leur division en départements: Essai sur la formation de l'unité française.* Paris: Bloud et Cie., 1913.

Berthoumeau, L. *La formation du département de Seine-et-Marne.* Dijon: Imprimerie Bourguignonne, 1914.

Blanchard, Marcel. "Contribution à l'étude de la formation du département de l'Isère." *Recueil des travaux de l'Institut de géographie alpine* 2 (1914): 412–13.

Boivin-Champeaux, L. *Création et formation du département de l'Eure, 1789–1790.* Paris: Imprimerie Impériale, 1868.

Bourdon, Jean. "La formation des départements de l'Est en 1790." *Annales de l'Est* (1951): 187–217.

———. "Pinteville de Cernon, ses chiffres de population, et sa critique des départements." *Annales historiques de la Révolution française* (1954): 345–56.

Bournon, Fernand. *La création du département de Paris et son étendue, 1789–1790.* Paris: Champion, 1897.

Bruneau, Marcel. *Les débuts de la Révolution dans le Cher et dans l'Indre*. Paris: Hachette, 1902.

Desgranges, Eugène. *La formation territoriale du département de la Haute-Vienne, 1789–an X*. Paris: Librairie générale du droit et de la jurisprudence, 1942.

Desgraves, Louis. *La formation territoriale du département de Lot-et-Garonne*. Nérac: Couderc, 1956.

Dubois, Eugène. *Histoire de la Révolution dans l'Ain*. 2 vols. Bourg: Borchot, 1930–32.

Dubreuil, Léon. *La Révolution dans le département des Côtes-du-Nord*. Paris: Champion, 1909.

Du Chambon, Pierre. *La formation du département de la Charente*. Ruffec: Dubois, 1934.

Gailly de Taurines, Charles. *La formation territoriale du département des Ardennes en 1789–1790*. Paris: Imprimerie Nationale, 1933.

Girardot, Jean. *Le département de la Haute-Saône pendant la Révolution*. 2 vols. Vesoul: Société d'Agriculture, Lettres, Sciences et Arts de la Haute-Saône, 1973.

Hennequin, René. *La formation du département de l'Aisne en 1790*. Soissons: Nougarède, 1911.

Jouany, Désiré. *La formation du département du Morbihan*. Vannes: Ouvrière Vannetaise, 1920.

Lebaindre, A. *La formation du département de la Manche*. Caen: Poisson, 1911.

L'Hermitte, J. "Proces-verbaux de la formation de l'assemblee administrative du département de la Sarthe et son Directoire, 10–16 Juillet 1790." *La Révolution dans la Sarthe et dans les pays voisins* (1911): 161–224; (1912): 5–22, 49–92.

Mage, Georges. *La division de la France en départements*. Toulouse: Imprimerie Saint-Michel, 1924.

Masson, Jean Louis. *Histoire administrative de la Lorraine: Des provinces au départements et à la région*. Paris: Editions F. Lanore, 1982.

Mater, M. D. "Formation du département du Cher." *Mémoires de la Société historique, littéraire et scientifique du Cher*, 4th ser., 14 (1899): 112–213.

Mège, Francisque. *Formation et organisation du département du Puy-de-Dôme, 1789–1801*. Paris, 1874; Marseille: Laffitte Reprints, 1979.

Merle, Louis. *La formation territoriale du département des Deux-Sèvres: Étude de géographie historique*. Niort: Société Historique et Scientifique des Deux-Sèvres, 1938.

Mettrier, Henri. *La formation du département de la Haute-Marne en 1790*. Chaumont: Andriot-Moissonnier, 1911.

Ozouf-Marignier, Marie-Vic. "De l'universalisme constituant aux intérêts locaux: Le débat sur la formation des départements en France, 1789–1790." *Annales: Economies, Sociétés, Civilisations* 41 (1986): 1193–1213.

———. *La formation des départements: La représentation du territoire français à la fin du 18e siècle*. Paris: Editions de l'Ecole des Hautes Etudes en Sciences Sociales, 1989.

———. "Politique et géographie lors de la création des départements français, 1789–1790." *Hérodote* 40 (1986): 140–60.

———. "Territoire géometrique et centralité urbaine: Le découpage de la France en départements, 1789–1790." *Les annales de la recherche urbaine* 22 (1948): 58–70.

Porée, Charles. *La formation du département de l'Yonne en 1790.* Auxerre: A. Gallot, 1910.

Pothier, Josanne. "Création du département de la Haute-Loire, 1789–1790." *Almanach de Brioude et de son arrondissement* 56 (1976): 101–15.

Rumeau, R. *Formation du district de Grenade.* Toulouse, 1897.

Schultz, Patrick. *La décentralisation administrative dans le département du Nord, 1790–1793.* Lille: Presses Universitaires de Lille, 1982.

Siraud, F. "Etude sur la formation du département de Saône-et-Loire." *Annales de l'Académie de Mâcon,* 2d ser., 11 (1894): 217–42.

Soulas, Jean. "Rivalités urbaines en France, 1789–1790," *L'information historique* 18 (1956): 138–43.

Villepelet, R. *La formation du département de la Dordogne: Étude de géographie politique.* Périgueux: Joucla, 1908.

Zeni, Claire Marie. "Urban Networks and the French Revolution in the Nord." Master's thesis, University of California, Davis, 1983.

Local Histories

Babeau, Albert. *Histoire de Troyes pendant la Revolution.* 2 vols. Paris: Dumoulin, 1873–74.

Biernawski, Louis. *Un département sous la Révolution française: L'Allier de 1789 à l'an III.* Moulins: Grégoire, 1909.

Brelot, Jean, and Gustave Duhem. *Histoire de Lons-le-Saulnier.* Lons-le-Saulnier: Imprimerie Declume, 1957.

Brossard, E. *Histoire du département de la Loire pendant la Révolution française.* 2 vols. Paris: Champion, 1904.

Clark, John G. *La Rochelle and the Atlantic Economy during the Eighteenth Century.* Baltimore: Johns Hopkins University Press, 1981.

Corgne, Eugène. *Pontivy et son district pendant la Révolution, 1789–Germinal an V.* Rennes: Plihon, 1938.

Coron, André. *Essai sur la sénéchaussée de Saint-Etienne dans ses rapports avec le bailliage de Forez.* Lyon: Bosc frères, 1936.

D'Aigrefeuille, Charles. *Histoire de la ville de Montpellier.* 2d ed. 4 vols. Montpellier: C. Coulet, 1875–82.

Delon, Abbé P. J. B. *La Révolution en Lozère.* Mende: Imprimerie Lozèrienne, 1922.

Dériès, Madeleine. *Le district de Saint-Lô pendant la Révolution, 1787–an IV.* Paris: A. Picard, 1922.

Desme de Chavigny, O. *Histoire de Saumur pendant la Révolution.* Vannes: Lavoyle, 1892.

Devic, Claude, and Joseph Vaissette. *Histoire générale de Languedoc.* 2d ed. 15 vols. Toulouse: Privat, 1872–92.

Duboul, Axel. *L'armée révolutionnaire de Toulouse.* Toulouse: F. Tardieu, 1891.

Everat, E. *La sénéchaussée d'Auvergne et siège présidial de Riom au XVIII siècle.* Paris: Thorin, 1886.

Gallier, Anatole de. *La vie de province au 18e siècle*. Paris, 1877.

Gaussen, Ivan. *Considérations sur les foires et les marchés de Sommières en Languedoc depuis leurs origines jusqu'à la Révolution*. Nîmes: Chastanier, 1921.

Giffard, André. *Les justices seigneuriales en Bretagne au XVIIe et XVIIIe siècles*. Paris: A. Rousseau, 1902.

Lameire, G. *Les municipalités de canton dans le département du Rhône sous le Directoire*. Lyon: Bosc frères, 1941.

Lefevre, L. P. *Yvetot pendant la Révolution de 1788 à 1815*. Yvetot: Lachèvre, 1908.

Lemaitre, Nicole. *Un horizon bloqué: Ussel et la montagne limousine aux XVIIe et XVIIIe siècles*. Ussel: Musée du pays d'Ussel, 1978.

Ligou, Daniel, ed. *Histoire de Montauban*. Toulouse: Privat, 1984.

Longy, Albert. *Histoire de la ville d'Issoire*. Clermont-Ferrand, 1890; Marseille: Laffitte Reprints, 1975.

Normand, Charles. *Etude sur les relations de l'état et des communautés aux XVIIe et XVIIIe siècles: Saint-Quentin et la royauté*. Paris: Champion, 1881.

Paquin, Pierre. *Essai sur la profession d'avocat dans les duchés de Lorraine et de Bar au dix-huitième siècle*. Verdun: Imprimerie Fremont, 1967.

Perrin, Maxime. *Saint-Etienne et sa région économique: Un type de la vie industrielle en France*. Tours: Arrault, 1937.

Rabouin, M. *Châteaudun pendant la Révolution*. Châteaudun: Imprimerie de la Société typographique, 1904.

Reinhard, Marcel. *Le département de la Sarthe sous le régime directorial*. Saint-Brieuc: Les presses Bretonnes, 1935.

Schnerb, Robert. *Les contributions directes à l'époque de la Révolution dans le departement du Puy-de-Dôme*. Paris: F. Alcan, 1933.

Sol, Eugène. *La Révolution en Quercy, 1788–1791*. 2d ed. Paris: A. Picard, 1932.

Viguier, Jules. *La convocation des Etats Généraux en Provence*. Paris: Lenoir, 1896.

Biographical Studies

Baker, Keith Michael. *Condorcet: From Natural Philosophy to Social Mathematics*. Chicago: University of Chicago Press, 1975.

Bredin, Jean-Louis. *Sièyes: La clé de la Révolution française*. Paris: Editions de Fallois, 1988.

Brette, Armand. *Les Constituants: Liste des députés et des suppléants élus à l'Assemblée Constituante de 1789*. Paris, 1897; Geneva: Megariotis, 1977.

Forsyth, Murray Greensmith. *Reason and Revolution: The Political Thought of the Abbé Sièyes*. New York: Holmes and Meier, 1987.

Harris, Robert D. *Necker: Reform Statesman of the Ancien Regime*. Berkeley: University of California Press, 1980.

Kuscinski, August. *Les députés à l'Assemblée Législative de 1791*. Paris: Société d'histoire de la Révolution française, 1900.

―――. *Dictionnaire des Conventionnels*. Paris: Société d'histoire de la Révolution française, 1917.

Lebègue, Ernest. *La vie et l'oeuvre d'un Constituant: Thouret, 1746–1794*. Paris: F. Alcan, 1910.

Mège, Francisque. *Gaultier de Biauzat, député du Tiers-Etat aux Etats Généraux de 1789: Sa vie et sa correspondence*. 2 vols. Paris: Lechevalier, 1890.

Mergerison, Kenneth. *Pierre-Louis Roederer: Political Thought and Practice during the French Revolution*. Philadelphia: American Philosophical Society, 1983.

Michon, Georges. *Essai sur l'histoire du parti Feuillant: Adrien Duport, 1789–1792*. Paris: Payot, 1924.

Other Books

Alliès, Paul. *L'invention du territoire*. Grenoble: Presses Universitaires de Grenoble, 1980.

Arbellot, Guy, Jean-Pierre Goubert, Jacques Mallet, and Yvette Palazot. *Carte des généralités, subdélégations, et élections en France à la veille de la Révolution de 1789*. Paris: Editions du Centre National de la Recherche Scientifique, 1986.

Aydalot, P., L. Bergeron, and M. Roncayolo. *L'industrialisation et croissance urbain dans la France du XIXe siècle*. Paris: Université de Paris I, 1981.

Azimi, Vida. *Un modèle administratif de l'ancien régime: Les commis de la ferme générale et de la régie générale des aides*. Paris: Editions du Centre National de la Recherche Scientifique, 1987.

Baker, Keith, ed. *The French Revolution and the Creation of Modern Political Culture*. Vol. 1, *The Political Culture of the Old Regime*. New York: Pergamon Press, 1987.

———. *Inventing the French Revolution: Essays on French Political Culture in the Eighteenth Century*. New York: Cambridge University Press, 1990.

Benedict, Philip, ed. *Cities and Social Change in Early Modern France*. London: Unwin Hyman, 1990.

Berlanstein, Lenard R. *The Barristers of Toulouse in the Eighteenth Century, 1740–1793*. Baltimore: Johns Hopkins University Press, 1975.

Birardot, Baron de. *Des administrations départementales, électives, et collectives*. Paris, 1857.

Boissonnade, P. *Essai sur l'organisation du travail en Poitou depuis le XIe siècle jusqu'à la Révolution*. 2 vols. Paris: Champion, 1900.

Boiteau, Paul. *Etat de la France en 1789*. Paris: Perrotin, 1861.

Bonin, Serge, and Claude Langlois, eds. *Atlas de la Révolution française*. 5 vols. Paris: Editions de l'Ecole des Hautes Etudes en Sciences Sociales, 1986–89. Vol. 1, *Routes et communications*, edited by Guy Arbellot and Bernard Lepetit; vol. 2, *L'enseignement, 1760–1815*, edited by Dominique Julia; vol. 3, *L'armée et la guerre*, edited by Jean-Paul Bertaud and Danile Reichel; vol. 4, *Le territoire: Réalités et représentations*, edited by Daniel Nordman and Marie-Vic Ozouf-Marignier; vol. 5, *Le territoire et les limites administratives*, edited by Daniel Nordman and Marie-Vic Ozouf-Marignier.

Bordes, Maurice. *L'administration provinciale et municipale en France au XVIIIe siècle*. Paris: Société d'édition d'enseignement supérieur, 1972.

Bosher, J. F. *French Finances, 1770–1795: From Business to Bureaucracy*. Cambridge: Cambridge University Press, 1970.

Bourdon, Jean. *La Constitution de l'an VIII*. Rodez: Carrère, 1941.

———. *La réforme judiciare de l'an VIII*. 2 vols. Rodez, 1941.

Braudel, Fernand. *Civilization and Capitalism, Fifteenth–Eighteenth Century*. Vol. 1, *The Structures of Everyday Life: The Limits of the Possible*, translation revised by Siân Reynolds. London: Collins, 1981; vol. 2, *The Wheels of Commerce*, translation by Siân Reynolds. New York: Harper and Row, 1982; vol. 3, *The Perspective of the World*, translation by Siân Reynolds. New York: Harper and Row, 1984.

———. *The Identity of France*. Translated by Siân Reynolds. New York: Harper and Row, 1988–90.

Braudel, Fernand, and Ernest Labrousse, eds. *Histoire économique et sociale de la France*. 4 vols. in 8. Paris: Presses Universitaires de France, 1970–82.

Brette, Armand. *Les limites et les divisions territoriales de la France en 1789*. Paris: E. Cornély, 1907.

Broc, Numa. *La géographie des philosophes: Géographes et voyageurs français au XVIIIe siècle*. Paris: Ophrys, 1975.

Burguière, André, ed., et al. *Histoire de la famille*. 2 vols. Paris: A. Colin, 1986.

Cabourdin, Guy, and Georges Viard. *Lexique historique de la France d'ancien régime*. Paris: A. Colin, 1978.

Carey, John A. *Judicial Reform in France before the Revolution of 1789*. Cambridge: Harvard University Press, 1981.

Carré, Henri. *La fin des parlements, 1788–1790*. Paris: Hachette, 1912.

Chevalier, Bernard. *Les bonnes villes de France du XIVe au XVIe siècle*. Paris: Aubier Montaigne, 1982.

Christaller, Walter. *Central Places in Southern Germany*. Translated by C. W. Baskin. Englewood Cliffs, N.J.: Prentice-Hall, 1966.

Clout, Hugh D. *Themes in the Historical Geography of France*. New York: Academic Press, 1977.

Cobb, Richard. *Les armées révolutionnaires des départements du Midi*. Toulouse: Soubiron, 1955.

———. *The People's Armies*. New Haven: Yale University Press, 1987.

———. *Terreur et subsistances, 1793–1795*. Paris, 1965.

Cobban, Alfred. *Aspects of the French Revolution*. New York: G. Braziller, 1968.

———. *The Social Interpretation of the French Revolution*. Cambridge: Cambridge University Press, 1964.

Cochin, August. *Les sociétés de pensée et la Révolution en Bretagne, 1788–1789*. Paris: Champion, 1925.

Colombet, Albert. *Les parlementaires bourguignons à la fin du XVIIIe siècle*. 2d ed. Dijon: Chez l'auteur, 1937.

Comninel, George. *Rethinking the French Revolution: Marxism and the Revisionist Challenge*. New York: Verso, 1987.

Compère, Marie-Madeleine, and Dominique Julia. *Les collèges français, 16e–18e siècles*. 2 vols. Paris: Editions du Centre National de la Recherche Scientifique, 1984–88.

Dawson, Philip. *Provincial Magistrates and Revolutionary Politics in France, 1789–1795*. Cambridge: Harvard University Press, 1972.

De Vries, Jan. *European Urbanization, 1500–1800*. Cambridge: Harvard University Press, 1984.

Deyon, Pierre. *Amiens, capital provinciale: Étude sur la société urbaine au 17e siècle*. Paris: Mouton, 1967.

Dockès, Pierre. *L'espace dans la pensée économique du XVIe au XVIIIe siècle*. Paris: Flammarion, 1969.

Doyle, William. *Origins of the French Revolution*. 2d ed. Oxford: Oxford University Press, 1988.

———. *The Parlement of Bordeaux and the End of the Old Regime, 1771–1790*. New York: St. Martin's Press, 1974.

Duby, Georges, ed. *Histoire de la France urbaine*. 4 vols. Paris: Seuil, 1980–83.

Dugrand, Raymond. *Villes et campagnes en Bas-Languedoc*. Paris: Presses Universitaires de France, 1963.

Dupaquier, Jacques. *La population du bassin Parisien à l'époque de Louis XIV*. Paris: Editions de l'Ecole des Hautes Etudes en Sciences Sociales, 1979.

Dupuy, Roger. *La Garde Nationale et les débuts de la Révolution en Ille-et-Vilaine, 1789–mars 1793*. Paris: Klincksieck, 1972.

Egret, Jean. *The French Prerevolution, 1787–1788*. Translated by Wesley D. Camp. Chicago: University of Chicago Press, 1977.

———. *Le Parlement de Dauphiné et les affaires publiques dans la deuxième moitié du XVIIIe siècle*. 2 vols. Grenoble: B. Arthaud, 1942.

Elwitt, Sanford. *The Making of the Third Republic: Class and Politics in France, 1868–1884*. Baton Rouge: Louisiana State University Press, 1975.

Fehér, Ferenc, ed. *The French Revolution and the Birth of Modernity*. Berkeley: University of California Press, 1990.

———. *The Frozen Revolution: An Essay on Jacobinism*. Cambridge: Cambridge University Press, 1987.

Fitzsimmons, Michael P. *The Parisian Order of Barristers and the French Revolution*. Cambridge: Harvard University Press, 1987.

Forrest, Alan. *Society and Politics in Revolutionary Bordeaux*. Oxford: Oxford University Press, 1975.

Fox, Edward. *History in Geographic Perspective: The Other France*. New York: Norton, 1971.

Frêche, Georges. *Toulouse et la région Midi-Pyrénées au siècle des lumières, vers 1670–1789*. Toulouse: Editions Cujas, 1974.

Furet, François. *Interpreting the French Revolution*. Translated by Elborg Forster. Cambridge: Cambridge University Press, 1981.

Furet, François, and Mona Ozouf, eds. *A Critical Dictionary of the French Revolution*. Translated by Arthur Goldhammer. Cambridge: Harvard University Press, 1989.

———, eds. *The French Revolution and the Creation of Modern Political Culture*. Vol. 3, *The Transformation of Political Culture, 1789–1848*. New York: Pergamon Press, 1989.

Garden, Maurice. *Lyon et les lyonnais au XVIIIe siècle*. Paris: Flammarion, 1975.

Gascon, Richard. *Grand commerce et vie urbaine au XVIe siècle: Lyon et ses marchands, environs de 1520–environs de 1580*. 2 vols. Paris: S.E.V.P.E.N., 1971.

Gille, Bertrand. *La banque et le crédit en France de 1815 à 1848*. Paris, 1959.

Giraud, Emile. *L'oeuvre d'organisation judiciare de l'Assemblée Nationale Constituante*. Paris: M. Giard and Cie., 1921.

Godechot, Jacques. *Les institutions de la France sous la Révolution et l'Empire*. Paris: Presses Universitaires de France, 1951.

Goubert, Pierre. *Beauvais et le Beauvaisis de 1600 à 1730*. Paris: S.E.V.P.E.N., 1960.

Gresset, Maurice. *Gens de justice à Besançon de la conquête par Louis XIV à la Révolution française, 1674–1789*. Paris: Bibliothèque Nationale, 1978.

Guénée, Bernard. *Tribunaux et gens de justice dans le bailliage de Senlis à la fin du Moyen Age, vers 1380–vers 1550*. Paris: Les Belles Lettres, 1963.

Harris, S. E. *The Assignats*. Cambridge: Harvard Univeristy Press, 1930.

Hirschman, Albert O. *The Passions and the Interests: Political Arguments for Capitalism before Its Triumph*. Princeton: Princeton University Press, 1977.

Hiver de Beauvoir, Alfred. *Histoire critique des institutions judiciares de la France de 1789 à 1848*. Paris: A. Burand, 1851.

Hohenberg, Paul M., and Lynn Hollen Lees. *The Making of Urban Europe, 1000–1950*. Cambridge: Harvard University Press, 1985.

Hufton, Olwen. *Bayeux in the Late Eighteenth Century: A Social Study*. Oxford: Oxford University Press, 1967.

Hunt, Lynn. *Politics, Culture, and Class in the French Revolution*. Berkeley: University of California Press, 1984.

———. *Revolution and Urban Politics in Provincial France: Troyes and Reims, 1786–1790*. Stanford: Stanford University Press, 1978.

Hyslop, Beatrice Fry. *French Nationalism in 1789 according to the General Cahiers*. New York, 1934. New York: Octagon Books, 1968.

Jones, P. M. *The Peasantry in the French Revolution*. Cambridge: Cambridge University Press, 1988.

Julia, Dominique. *Les trois couleurs du tableau noir: La Révolution*. Paris, 1981.

Kaplan, Steven L. *Bread, Politics, and Political Economy in the Reign of Louis XV*. 2 vols. The Hague: Martinus Nijohff, 1976.

———. *Provisioning Paris: Merchants and Millers in the Grain and Flour Trade during the Eighteenth Century*. Ithaca: Cornell University Press, 1984.

Kennedy, Michael L. *The Jacobin Club of Marseille, 1790–1794*. Ithaca: Cornell University Press, 1973.

———. *The Jacobin Clubs in the French Revolution: The First Years*. Princeton: Princeton University Press, 1982.

———. *The Jacobin Clubs in the French Revolution: The Middle Years*. Princeton: Princeton University Press, 1988.

Konvitz, Josef. *Cartography in France, 1660–1848*. Chicago: University of Chicago Press, 1987.

———. *Cities and the Sea: Port City Planning in Early Modern Europe*. Baltimore: Johns Hopkins University Press, 1978.

Langlois, Claude. *Le catholicisme au féminin: Les congrégations françaises à supérieure générale au XIXe siècle*. Paris: Cerf, 1984.

Laurain, Ernest. *Essai sur les Présidiaux*. Paris, 1896.

Lavedan, Pierre. *Histoire de l'urbanisme*. 3 vols. Paris: H. Laurens, 1926–52.

Lavergne, Léonce de. *Les assemblées provinciales sous Louis XVI*. Paris: Michel Lévy frères, 1864.

Lefebvre, Georges. *The Coming of the French Revolution*. Translated by R. R. Palmer. Princeton: Princeton University Press, 1947.

————. *The Great Fear: Rural Panic in Revolutionary France.* Translated by Joan White. New York: Vintage Books, 1973.

————. *The Thermidorians.* Translated by Robert Baldick. London, 1964.

Lepetit, Bernard. *Chemins de terre et voies d'eau: Réseaux de transports, organisation de l'espace.* Paris: Editions de l'Ecole des Hautes Etudes en Sciences Sociales, 1984.

————. *Les villes dans la France moderne, 1740–1840.* Paris: Albin Michel, 1988.

Lequin, Yves. *Les ouvriers de la région lyonnaise, 1848–1914.* 2 vols. Lyon: Presses Universitaires de Lyon, 1977.

Letaconnoux, Joseph. *Les subsistances et le commerce des grains en Bretagne au XVIIIe siècle.* Rennes: Imprimerie Oberthur, 1909.

Lucas, Colin. *The Structure of the Terror: The Example of Javogues and the Loire.* Oxford: Oxford University Press, 1973.

————, ed. *The French Revolution and the Creation of Modern Political Culture.* Vol. 2, *The Political Culture of the French Revolution.* New York: Pergamon Press, 1988.

Lyons, Martin. *France under the Directory.* New York: Cambridge University Press, 1975.

McManners, John. *The French Revolution and the Church.* New York: Harper and Row, 1970.

Major, J. Russell. *Representative Government in Early Modern France.* New Haven: Yale University Press, 1980.

Margairaz, Dominique. *Foires et marchés dans la France pré-industrielle.* Paris: Editions de l'Ecole des Hautes Etudes en Sciences Sociales, 1988.

Marion, Marcel. *Le Garde des Sceaux Lamoignon et la réforme judiciare de 1788.* Paris: Hachette, 1905.

————. *Histoire financière de la France depuis 1715.* 6 vols. Paris: A. Rousseau, 1914–31.

Marx, Karl, and Frederick Engels. *Selected Works in One Volume.* New York: International Publishers, 1968.

Matthews, George T. *The Royal General Farms in Eighteenth-Century France.* New York: Columbia University Press, 1958.

Maurin, Jules. *Armée—guerre—sociéte: Soldats Languedociens, 1889–1919.* Paris: Publications de la Sorbonne, 1982.

Merriman, John. *The Margins of City Life: Explorations on the French Urban Frontier, 1815–1851.* New York: Oxford University Press, 1991.

Meuriot, P. *Pourquoi et comment furent dénommé nos circonscriptions départementales.* Paris: A. Picard, 1917.

————. *Le recensement de l'an II.* Paris: Berger-Levrault, 1918.

Meuvret, Jean. *Etudes d'histoire économique: Recueil d'articles.* Paris: A. Colin, 1971.

Meyer, Jean. *Etudes sur les villes en Europe occidentale.* 2 vols. Paris: Société d'Edition d'Enseignement Supérieur, 1983.

Mirot, Léon. *Manuel de géographie historique de la France.* 2d ed. 2 vols. Paris: A. Picard, 1947–50.

Monnet, E. *Histoire de l'administration provinciale, départementale, et communale en France.* Paris: A. Rousseau, 1885.

Morizé, André. *L'apologie du luxe au XVIIIe siècle et "Le Mondain" de Voltaire*. Paris: H. Didier, 1909.

Mousnier, Roland. *The Institutions of France under the Absolute Monarchy, 1598–1789*. Translated by Brian Pearce. 2 vols. Chicago: University of Chicago Press, 1979–80.

Olivier-Martin, Fr. *L'organisation corporative de la France d'ancien régime*. Paris: Recueil Sirey, 1938.

Pardailhé-Galabran, Annik. *La naissance de l'intime: 3,000 foyers parisiens, XVIIe–XVIIIe siècles*. Paris: Presses Universitaires de France, 1988.

Parias, Louis-Henri, ed. *Histoire générale de l'enseignement et de l'éducation en France*. 4 vols. Paris: Nouvelle Librairie de France, 1981.

Parker, Harold T. *The Bureau of Commerce in 1781 and Its Policies with Respect to French Industry*. Durham, N.C.: Carolina Academic Press, 1979.

Patrick, Alison. *The Men of the First French Republic: Political Alignments and the National Convention of 1792*. Baltimore: Johns Hopkins University Press, 1972.

Perrot, Jean-Claude. *Genèse d'une ville moderne: Caen au XVIIIe siècle*. 2 vols. Paris: Mouton, 1975.

Ponteil, Felix. *Les institutions de la France de 1814 à 1870*. Paris: Presses Universitaires de France, 1966.

Poussou, Jean-Pierre. *Bordeaux et le sud-oeust au XVIIIe siècle: Croissance économique et attraction urbaine*. Paris: Editions de l'Ecole des Hautes Etudes en Sciences Sociales, 1982.

Pouthas, Charles A. *La population française pendant la première moitié du XIXe siècle*. Paris: Presses Universitaires de France, 1956.

Prost, Antoine. *Histoire de l'enseignement en France, 1800–1967*. Paris: A. Colin, 1968.

Ramon, Gabriel. *Histoire de la Banque de France, d'après les sources originales*. 3d ed. Paris: B. Grasset, 1929.

Rémond, René, ed. *Atlas historique de la France contemporaine, 1800–1965*. Paris: A. Colin, 1966.

Renouvin, Pierre. *Les assemblées provinciales de 1787: Origines, développement, résultats*. Paris: A. Picard, 1921.

Revel, Jacques, ed. *L'espace français*. Paris: Seuil, 1989.

Roche, Daniel. *Le siècle des lumières en province: Académies et acadaméciens provinciaux, 1680–1789*. 2 vols. Paris: Mouton, 1978.

Rolland, Henri. *Les institutions judicaires*. 2d ed. Lyon, 1983.

Root, Hilton. *Peasants and the King in Burgundy: Agrarian Foundations of French Absolutism*. Berkeley: University of California Press, 1987.

Rozman, Gilbert. *Urban Networks in Russia, 1750–1800, and Premodern Periodization*. Princeton: Princeton University Press, 1976.

Sahlins, Peter. *Boundaries: The Making of France and Spain in the Pyrenees*. Berkeley: University of California Press, 1989.

Scott, William. *Terror and Repression in Revolutionary Marseille*. New York: Barnes and Noble, 1973.

Sekora, Jean. *Luxury: The Concept in Western Thought, Eden to Smollett*. Baltimore: Johns Hopkins University Press, 1977.

Seligman, Edmond. *La justice en France pendant la Révolution, 1789–1792.* 2 vols. Paris: Plon-Nourrit et Cie., 1901–13.

Sinclair, Stéphane. *Atlas de géographie historique de la France et de la Gaule.* Paris: Société d'Edition de Enseignement Supérieur, 1985.

Skinner, G. William, ed. *The City in Late Imperial China.* Stanford: Stanford University Press, 1977.

Skocpol, Theda. *States and Social Revolutions: A Comparative Analysis of France, Russia, and China.* Cambridge: Cambridge University Press, 1979.

Soboul, Albert. *A Short History of the French Revolution, 1789–1799.* Translated by Geoffrey Symcox. Berkeley: University of California Press, 1977.

Sutherland, D. M. G. *The Chouans: The Social Origins of Popular Counterrevolution in Upper Brittany, 1770–1796.* New York: Oxford University Press, 1982.

———. *France, 1789–1815: Revolution and Counterrevolution.* New York: Oxford University Press, 1986.

Sydenham, M. J. *The First French Republic, 1792–1804.* Berkeley: University of California Press, 1973.

Tackett, Timothy. *Religion, Revolution, and Regional Culture in Eighteenth-Century France: The Ecclesiastical Oath of 1791.* Princeton: Princeton University Press, 1986.

Thomson, J. K. J. *Clermont-de-Lodève, 1633–1789: Fluctuations in the Prosperity of a Languedocian Cloth-Making Town.* New York: Cambridge University Press, 1982.

Tilly, Charles. *Coercion, Capital, and European States, A.D. 990–1990.* Cambridge, Mass.: Basil Blackwell, 1990.

———. *The Vendée: A Sociological Analysis of the Counterrevolution of 1793.* Cambridge: Harvard University Press, 1964.

Tocqueville, Alexis de. *The Old Regime and the French Revolution.* Translated by Stuart Gilbert. New York: Doubleday, 1955.

Usher, Abbott Payson. *The History of the Grain Trade in France, 1400–1710.* Cambridge: Harvard University Press, 1913.

Vidalenc, Jean. *Le département de l'Eure sous la Monarchie constitutionnelle, 1814–1848.* Paris: M. Rivière, 1952.

Walter, Gérard. *Répertoire de l'histoire de la Révolution française, travaux publiés de 1800 à 1940.* 2 vols. Paris: Bibliothèque Nationale, 1951.

Weisz, George. *The Emergence of Modern Universities in France, 1863–1914.* Princeton: Princeton University Press, 1983.

Other Articles

Agulhon, Maurice. "La notion de ville en Basse-Provence vers la fin de l'ancien régime." In *Actes du 90e Congrès National des Sociétés Savantes,* 1:277–301. Paris: Bibliothèque Nationale, 1966.

Arbellot, Guy. "La grande mutation des routes de France au XVIIIe siècle." *Annales: Economies, Sociétés, Civilisations* 28 (1973): 765–91.

Arbellot, Guy, and Jean-Pierre Goubert. "De la cartographie historique à l'histoire de l'espace administratif: Les subdélégations française à la fin du XVIIIe siècle." *Francia: Beiheft* 9 (1980): 405–21.

Benedict, Philip. "French cities from the Sixteenth Century to the Revolution: An Overview." In *Cities and Social Change in Early Modern France*, edited by Philip Benedict, 7–64. London: Unwin Hyman, 1990.

Bergeron, Louis, and Marcel Roncayola. "De la ville pré-industrielle à la ville industrielle: Essai sur l'historiographie française." *Quaderni storici* 24 (1974): 827–76.

Bossenga, Gail. "City and State: An Urban Perspective on the Origins of the French Revolution." In *The French Revolution and the Creation of Modern Political Culture*, edited by Keith Baker, 1:89–140. New York: Pergamon, 1987.

Butel, Paul. "Contribution à l'étude de la circulation de l'argent en Aquitaine au XVIIIe siècle: Le commerce des rescriptions sur les recettes des finances." *Revue d'histoire économique et sociale* 52 (1974): 83–109.

Censer, Jack R. "The Coming of a New Interpretation of the French Revolution?" *Journal of Social History* 20 (Winter 1987): 295–309.

Chartier, Roger. "Culture, lumières, doléances: Les cahiers de 1789." *Revue d'histoire moderne et contemporaine* 29 (Jan.–Mar. 1981): 68–93.

Chassagne, Serge. "Essai d'analyse d'un marché: L'exemple des foires de Poitou au XVIIIe siècle." In *Actes du 97e Congrès National des Sociétés Savantes*, vol. 2, *Les pays de la Loire*, 137–51. Paris: Bibliothèque Nationale, 1977.

Claverie, Jean-Claude. "Les cadres spatiaux de la vie de relation dans le sud-oeust de la France durant la première moitié du XIXe siècle." *Revue géographique de l'Est* 13 (July–Sept. 1973): 335–51.

Cochin, August. "La campagne électorale de 1789 en Bourgogne." In *Les sociétés de pensées et la démocratie*, 235–82. Paris, 1921.

Corvisier, André. "Les circonscriptions militaires de la France: Facteurs humains et facteurs techniques." *Actes du 101e Congrès National des Sociétés Savantes*, vol. 1, *Frontières et limites*, 207–27. Paris: Bibliothèque Nationale, 1978.

Denis, Michel. "Rennes au XIXe siècle: Ville 'parisitaire'?" *Annales de Bretagne* 81 (1974): 403–39.

Dickinson, John A. "L'activité judiciare d'après la procédure civile: Le bailliage de Falaise, 1668–1790." *Revue d'histoire économique et sociale* 54 (1976): 145–68.

Duby, Georges. "L'urbanisation dans l'histoire." *Etudes rurales* 49–50 (1973): 10–13.

Dupaquier, Jacques. "Le réseau urbain du bassin Parisien au XVIIIe et au début du XIXe siècle: Essai de statistique." In *Actes du 100e Congrès National des Sociétés Savantes: Le développement urbain de 1610 à nos jours, questions diverses*, 125–34. Paris: Bibliothèque Nationale, 1977.

Dupeux, Georges. "La croissance urbaine en France au XIXe siècle." *Revue d'histoire économique et sociale* 52 (1974): 173–89.

Dupont-Ferrier, Gustave. "Sur l'emploi du mot 'province,' notamment dans le language administratif de l'ancienne France." *Revue historique* 160 (1929): 241–67; 161 (1929): 278–303.

Edmonds, Bill. " 'Federalism' and Urban Revolt in France in 1793." *Journal of Modern History* 55, no. 1 (Mar. 1983): 22–53.

Favier, René. "Economic Change, Demographic Growth, and the Fate of Dauphiné's Small Towns, 1698–1790." In *Cities and Social Change in Early Modern France*, edited by Philip Benedict, 221–41. London: Unwin Hyman, 1989.

Frêche, Georges. "Etudes statistiques sur le commerce céréalier de la France méridionale au XVIIIe siècle." *Revue d'histoire économique et sociale* 49, nos. 1–2 (1971): 5–43, 180–224.

Higonnet, Patrice. "Cultural Upheaval and Class Formation during the French Revolution." In *The French Revolution and the Birth of Modernity*, edited by Ferenc Fehér, 69–102. Berkeley: University of California Press, 1990.

Hufton, Olwen. "Le paysan et la loi en France au XVIIIe siècle." *Annales: Economies, Sociétés, Civilisations* 38 (1983): 679–701.

Hunt, Lynn. "Committees and Communes: Local Politics and National Revolution in 1789." *Comparative Studies in Society and History* 18 (July 1976): 321–46.

Jeannin, Pierre. "La protoindustrialisation: Développement ou impasse?" *Annales: Economies, Sociétés, Civilisations* 35 (1980): 52–65.

Jones, P. M. "The Rural Bourgeoisie of the Southern Massif Central: A Contribution to the Study of the Social Structure of Ancien Regime France." *Social History* 4 (Jan. 1979): 65–83.

Julia, Dominique, and Paul Pressly. "La population scolaire en 1789: Les extravagances statistiques du ministre Villemain." *Annales: Economies, Sociétés, Civilisations* 30 (1975): 1516–61.

Julliard, Etienne. "L'armature urbaine de la France pré-industrielle." *Bulletin de la Faculté des Lettres de L'Université de Strasbourg* 48 (Mar. 1970).

Kagan, Richard L. "Law Students and Legal Careers in Eighteenth-Century France." *Past and Present* 68 (Aug. 1975): 38–72.

Le Goff, Jacques. "Ordres mendiants et urbanisation dans la France médiévale." *Annales: Economies, Sociétés, Civilisations* 25 (1970): 924–46.

Le Mée, René. "Population agglomérée, population éparse au début du XIXe siècle. *Annales de démographie historique* (1971): 467–93.

Léon, Pierre. "La région lyonnaise dans l'histoire économique et sociale de la France, une esquisse, XVIe–XXe siècles." *Revue historique* 237 (1967): 31–62.

Lepetit, Bernard. "L'évolution de la notion de ville d'après les tableaux et descriptions géographiques de la France, 1650–1850." *Urbi* 2 (1979): 99–107.

———. "Fonction administrative et armature urbaine: Remarques sur la distribution des chefs-lieux de subdélégation en France à la fin de l'ancien régime." *Institut d'histoire économique et sociale de l'Université de Paris I, Recherches et travaux*, bulletin no. 11 (Nov. 1982): 19–34.

Lepetit, Bernard, and Jean-François Royer. "Croissance et taille des villes: Contribution à l'étude de l'urbanisation de la France au début du XIXe siècle." *Annales: Economies, Sociétés, Civilisations* 35 (1980): 987–1010.

Ligou, Daniel. "A propos de la révolution municipale." *Revue d'histoire économique et sociale* 30 (1960): 146–77.

Mackrell, John. "Criticism of Seigniorial Justice in Eighteenth-Century France." In

French Government and Society, 1500–1850: Essays in Memory of Alfred Cobban, edited by J. F. Bosher, 123–44. London, 1973.

Marion, Michel. "La question du papier-monnaie en 1790: Les premières fautes." *Revue historique* 129 (Sept.–Dec. 1918): 22–75.

Meuriot, Paul. "Les districts de 1790, comment ils sont devenus les arrondissements de l'an VIII." *Séances et travaux de l'Académie des Sciences Morales et Politiques*, 81st year, n.s. (Jan.–Feb. 1921): 448–77.

———. "La petite ville française." *Journal de la Société de Statistique de Paris* 49 (1908): 235–40, 245–53.

Murphy, James, and Patrice Higonnet. "Les députés de la noblesse aux Etats Généraux de 1789." *Revue d'histoire moderne et contemporaine* 20 (Apr.–June 1973): 230–47.

Nussbaum, Frederick L. "The Deputies Extraordinary of Commerce and the French Monarchy." *Political Science Quarterly* 48 (Dec. 1933): 534–55.

Palmer, R. R. "The Central Schools of the First French Republic: A Statistical Survey." *Historical Reflections* 7, nos. 12–13 (Summer–Fall 1980): 223–47.

Patrick, Alison. "French Revolutionary Local Government, 1789–1792." In *The French Revolution and the Creation of Modern Political Culture*, edited by Colin Lucas, 2:399–420. New York: Pergamon Press, 1988.

Pumein, D. "Chemin de fer et croissance urbaine en France au XIXe siècle." *Annales de géographie* 79 (1982): 529–49.

Reinhardt, Steven G. "Crime and Royal Justice in Ancien Régime France: Modes of Analysis." *Journal of Interdisciplinary History* 13 (Winter 1983): 437–60.

Ricommard, Julien. "Les subdélégués des intendants aux XVIIe et XVIIIe siècles." *L'information historique* 24 (1962): 139–48.

Rodrigues Ochoa, Patricia. "Les rapports entre l'évolution de la structure administrative et le réseau urbain de la France, 1789–1856." Unpublished *mémoire* for a degree at the Ecole des Hautes Etudes en Sciences Sociales, Paris, 1976.

Schnerb, Robert. "Les vicissitudes de l'impôt indirect de la Constituante à Napoléon." *Annales: Economies, Sociétés, Civilisations* 2 (1947): 19–23.

Sée, Henri. "La rédaction et la valeur historique des cahiers de paroisse pour les Etats-Généraux de 1789." *Revue historique* 102 (1910): 292–306.

Sewell, William H. "Ideologies and Social Revolutions: Reflections on the French Case." *Journal of Modern History* 57 (1985): 57–85.

Skocpol, Theda. "Cultural Idioms and Political Ideologies in the Revolutionary Reconstruction of State Power: A Rejoinder to Sewell." *Journal of Modern History* 57 (1985): 86–96.

Smith, Cecil O., Jr. "The Longest Run: Public Engineers and Planning in France." *American Historical Review* 95, no. 3 (June 1990): 657–85.

Stevelberg, Eugène. "L'influence de la perception et de l'organisation de l'espace sur la réforme administrative: Le cas du Nord et du Pas-de-Calais." In *Actes du 101e Congrès National des Sociétés Savantes*, vol. 2, *La France du Nord de 1610 à nos jours*, 112–22. Paris: Bibliothèque Nationale, 1978.

Tackett, Timothy. "Nobles and Third Estate in the Revolutionary Dynamic of the National Assembly, 1789–1790." *American Historical Review* 94, no. 2 (Apr. 1989): 271–301.

Tilly, Charles. "Rivalités de bourgs et conflits de partis dans les Mauges de 1789 à 1793." *Revue du Bas-Poitou et des Provinces de l'Oeust* 73, no. 4 (1962): 4–15.

————. "State and Counterrevolution in France." In *The French Revolution and the Birth of Modernity*, edited by Ferenc Fehér, 49–68. Berkeley: University of California Press, 1990.

Trénard, Louis. "De la route royale à l'age d'or des diligences." In *Les routes de France depuis les origines jusqu'à nos jours*, 101–13. Paris: L'Association pour la diffusion de la pensée française, 1959.

Viguerie, Jean de. "Quelques remarques sur les universités françaises au dix-huitième siècle." *Revue historique* 262 (1979): 29–49.

Woloch, Isser. "The Fall and Resurrection of the Civil Bar, 1789–1820s." *French Historical Studies* 15, no. 2 (Fall 1987): 241–62.

INDEX OF PLACE NAMES

GENERAL INDEX

abbeys. *See* monasteries

administrative costs, 106, 166–67, 357–58, 366; local responsibility for, 335–37; policy of limiting, 106, 166–67, 272, 283, 338, 340, 370, 381, 388

administrative institutions: changes in hierarchy of, 399–403; under Napoleon, 368–73; in the old regime, 55–64; plans for reform of, 84–88, 394; during the Revolution, 98–100, 106–7, 320–21, 347–50, 358–62, 365–66

administrative rationality: principle of, 257, 273; and size of districts, 288–89

alternats: disputes over, 265–66, 269–72; policy of, 107–8, 259–62, 271–72, 453; suppression of, 272–73; and urban alliances, 189, 193, 249, 253–54, 329

Ambly, Claude-Jean-Antoine, marquis de, 335

amirautés, 61, 425

Angoulême, la duchesse de, 387

Angoulême, Louis Antoine de Bourbon, Duc d', 387

appellate courts: attempts to suppress, 389–90; defense of, 391–93; opposition to, 331–34; reform of, 90–94, 109; restoration of, 363, 368–69, 373; rivalries over, 136, 187, 212, 216, 229, 246; and urban growth, 412–13. *See also* judicial hierarchy

archbishoprics, 32–33, 462–65. *See also* bishoprics

army. *See* garrisons; military institutions

arrondissement councils, 380

arrondissements: debate over, 441; formation of, 366, 368–70, 378, 383–84, 388, 396; requests for, 378–84, 388–89. *See also* subprefectures

arrondissements seats. *See* subprefectures

artisans, 10, 120, 124–25, 134, 209–11, 263, 393

Assembly of Notables, 87

assize courts, 405–7, 412–13, 443

avocats. See lawyers; men of law

bailliages: and districts, 291–92, 294–95;

and elections, 88, 93, 182; functions of, 47, 50; and *grands bailliages*, 91; location of, 51–55; loss of, 83, 319, 405–7, 412; and urban rivalries, 301–3, 306, 311–15, 317. *See also* judicial hierarchy; lawcourts; magistrates

Bank of France, 430–32, 438–40

bankers, 4, 33, 428

Barbié, Pierre-François, 187

Barnave, Antoine Pierre, 91, 106n, 336–37

barristers. *See* lawyers

Basques, 226–27, 247, 266, 303, 305–6

Bengy de Puyvallée, Philippe-Jacques de, 103, 105

Béradier, Denis (abbé), 269

Bergasse, Nicolas, 94

Berlet, Charles, 5

Berlier, Théophile, 361

Billaud-Varenne, Jacques-Nicolas, 350

bishoprics: location of, 65–67, 462–65; suppression of, 83, 123–25, 126; territorial reorganization of, 414–15; and urban growth, 416; and urban prosperity, 122–25; and urban rivalries, 107, 249, 269–70

Boissy d'Anglas, François-Antoine, 359–61

Bonaparte, Lucien, 382

boosterism, 134–40

Bossenga, Gail, 451

Bouche, Charles-François, 164, 258, 344

Boudin, Jacques-Antoine, 360–61

boundaries: of arrondissements, 370–71, 376; of departments, 95–98, 104–5, 107, 143, 186, 189, 192, 220–23, 237, 239, 244–45, 251–55, 275–76; of districts, 292, 308, 352; of electoral constituencies, 93; natural, 6, 95, 98, 105, 151, 227–29; of old regime jurisdictions, 17, 86, 89–90, 99, 221–24, 239, 247, 327; of provinces, 94, 97, 105

Bourdon, Antoine (abbé), 344

bourgeoisie, 4–5, 13, 21, 114, 161–62, 331, 444–46. *See also* urban elites

bourgs, 106, 109, 262; as market centers, 35, 39, 80, 137, 309

Braudel, Fernand, 21–22, 24, 46